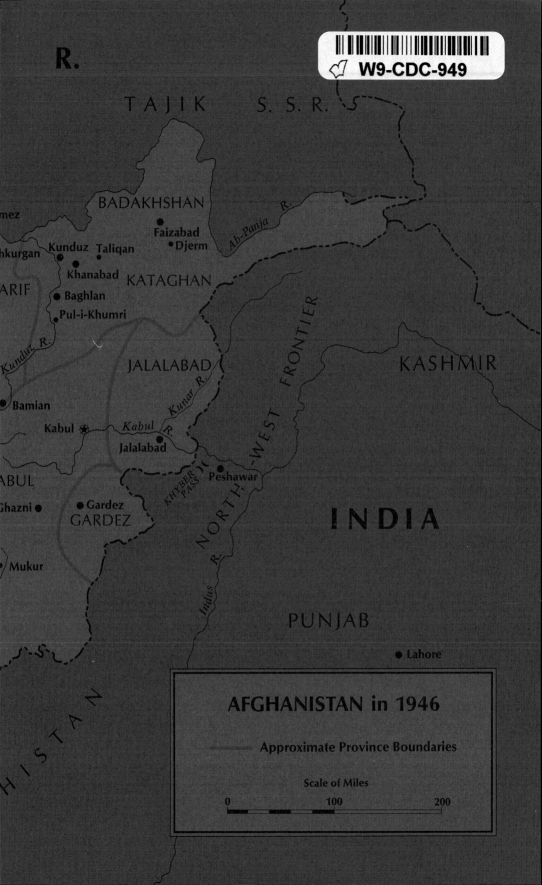

R.

TAJIK   S. S. R.

BADAKHSHAN

•Faizabad
mez   •Djerm
hkurgan Kunduz Taliqan
         Khanabad   KATAGHAN
ARIF   •Baghlan
     •Pul-i-Khumri

Kunduz R.   KASHMIR

•Bamian   JALALABAD

Kabul ⊕   Kabul R.
     Jalalabad

ABUL   •Peshawar

Ghazni • •Gardez   INDIA
        GARDEZ

/Mukur

                    PUNJAB

                              •Lahore

┌───┐
│   │
│   AFGHANISTAN in 1946   │
│   │
│   ──── Approximate Province Boundaries │
│   │
│   Scale of Miles   │
│   0   100   200   │
│   │
└───┘

Ab-Panja R.

NORTH-WEST FRONTIER

Kunar R.

Indus R.

HISTAN

The Emergence of
Modern Afghanistan

The Emergence of
Modern Afghanistan

Politics of Reform and Modernization, 1880–1946

Vartan Gregorian

Stanford University Press, Stanford, California   1969

099529

Stanford University Press
Stanford, California
© 1969 by the Board of Trustees of the
Leland Stanford Junior University
Printed in the United States of America
SBN 8047-0706-5
LC 69-13178

To Antoine Kehyayian, Collège Arménien
  —my teacher and friend

Preface

My research for this study, a modern history of Afghanistan, with special emphasis on its socioeconomic development and the policies that determined it, was carried out over an eight-year period, 1960–68. I here acknowledge my great indebtedness and gratitude to the Ford Foundation for a Foreign Area Training Fellowship that enabled me to pursue my research in England, Afghanistan, India, Pakistan, Iran, and Lebanon in the years 1960–62; and in particular I wish to thank Dorothy Soderlund, administrative assistant of the Foreign Area Fellowship Program. I would like also to thank the authorities and the staffs of the following institutions: the British Museum and the Public Records Office (London); the Bibliothèque Nationale (Paris); the libraries of the University of Saint-Joseph and the American University (Beirut); the library of Majless (Teheran); the libraries of the Liaqat Ali Khan and the Muslim League (Karachi); the Library of Parliament (New Delhi); the New York Public Library; the Library of Congress; the Hoover Institution on War, Revolution and Peace (Stanford, Calif.); and the libraries of Stanford University and the University of California at Berkeley.

For assistance in my research in Afghanistan, I am most grateful to the Délégation Archéologique Française en Afghanistan (DAFA) for the use of its library facilities and resources, and to the staff of the libraries of the Department of Press and the Ministry of Education in Kabul. In England I owe special thanks to Sir Francis Humphreys, one-time British Minister to Afghanistan, who graciously granted me an interview; to the late Sir W. Kerr Fraser-Tytler, author and former British envoy to Afghanistan; to Col. F. M. Bailey and Col. C. H. Ellis; and especially to Col. Geoffrey E. Wheeler, the former director of the Central Asian Research Centre, who provided me much help and a great deal of material on two periods of Afghan history: 1918–19 and 1928–29.

Among the other people who assisted me and to whom I owe much are

Wahé Sethian, of Beirut, for the use of his rich collection of Armenian literature and rare books; Professor Seymour Becker, of Rutgers University, for permission to consult his Ph.D. dissertation, "Russia's Central Asian Protectorates: Bukhara and Khiva, 1865–1917" (which has since been published as a book); Professor John W. Strong, of Carleton University, for allowing me to consult his Ph.D. dissertation, "Russian Relations with Khiva, Bukhara, and Kokand, 1800–1858"; David L. Morison, the director of the Central Asian Research Centre, for his kind permission to reproduce an ethnographic map of Afghanistan; and A. Wala, former cultural attaché of the Afghan embassy in London, and Dr. M. O. Anwari, the present Afghan cultural attaché in Washington, D.C., for their assistance in providing pictures and official publications.

In 1964 portions of this study were presented as a Ph.D. dissertation to the departments of History and Humanities at Stanford University. Most of the chapter on Mahmud Tarzi and *Siraj al-Akhbar* was published in *The Middle East Journal* (Washington, D.C.). I owe thanks to Stanford professors Wayne S. Vucinich, Christina Phelps Harris, and Robert C. North, all of whom read my dissertation and made helpful suggestions and criticisms. I am particularly indebted to Professor Vucinich for his valuable advice, encouragement, and assistance throughout my student career at Stanford and in the preparation of this study. Professor Franz H. Schurmann, of the University of California at Berkeley, and Professor Leonard Binder, of the University of Chicago, both gave me valuable advice in the early stages of my work. I must also thank Professor Arnold Fletcher, of Los Angeles Valley College, whose critique of my manuscript was both enjoyable and helpful.

I am indebted to Gene Tanke for valuable editorial advice and assistance. I am especially grateful to Barbara Mnookin, of Stanford Press, who made a significant contribution in editing my manuscript, a contribution invisible to the reader but known to me and much appreciated. I am greatly indebted to Patricia Green, one of my graduate students at San Francisco State College, for her fine translations of German works; to Mrs. F. G. Hunt, of Pacifica, Calif., for her diligence and patience in typing various drafts of my manuscript; and to Marina Tinkoff-Utechin, the reference librarian for the Slavic collection at the Hoover Institution, for her valuable, expert assistance. Above all, I am grateful to my wife, Clare, for her patience, her help, and her sense of humor in the past eight years.

V.G.

Contents

Eight pages of pictures follow page 196.

Note on Transliteration and Dates

In transliterating Persian, I have followed the method adopted in Amin Banani, *The Modernization of Iran, 1921–1941* (Stanford University Press, 1961), except where words have become familiar in English in a different transliteration. For Arabic, I have generally used the most common transliteration system. For Turkish, I have used modern Turkish romanization. Place-names and words included in unabridged English dictionaries are used in their anglicized forms. In 1935 Persia officially adopted the name Iran; I have used the two names interchangeably.

The first year of the Muslim calendar is A.D. 622, the year of the Hijrat (emigration) of the Prophet Muhammed from Mecca to Medina. There are two standard Muslim chronologies, the Qamari Hijri, or lunar calendar (with a lunar year of 354 days, nine hours), and the Shamsi, or solar calendar (with about 97 solar years equal to 100 lunar years). The Muslim calendars start in March. In the text I have converted to single dates according to the Gregorian calendar (e.g., 1334 Shamsi becomes simply 1955, and 1374 Qamari Hijri simply 1954).

Introduction

The apparent placidity, even stability, of Afghan society during the past 125 years has misled one writer to generalize that conditions there "are very much as they were 100 or 200 years ago" and another to assert that "social and economic factors have had less importance in Afghan history than in other countries, since up until about thirty years ago they were relatively static."[1] In fact, nearly all of the country's socioeconomic and political foundations have undergone important changes: the period has witnessed the emergence of new social groups, institutions, and sociopolitical philosophies, the formation of new loyalties, and the examination and reinterpretation of many traditional tenets. Afghanistan is by no means unique in this respect. The transformation of Afghan society has been an integral, and in many ways original, part of a general process of social change still under way in the Middle East—and in most of the traditional Muslim and non-Muslim societies of the East, as well.

This vast and complex historical development has been described variously as the "response" of the East to the "challenge" of the West;[2] as the impact, transmitted via imperialism, of ideas, techniques, and institutions emerging from many centuries of European history; as "the penetration into Eastern society of a new principle of life, a new conception: the modern Western culture in its essence or, in economic terms, the capitalist system";[3] as a religious "reformation," a "renaissance" accompanied by "national awakenings" brought about by the impact of a Western civilization that is transforming "the whole intellectual and emotional outlook of the Oriental and the conceptions on which he has based them"; as the "impact of modern civilization on the social and economic fabric of the East"; and as a process of technological, linguistic, juridical, and political borrowings designed to achieve "emancipation through imitation."[4]

Although there is universal agreement that Europe and European culture served to stimulate and accelerate social change in the East, there is no unity on a definition of the process involved or on the nature of the change. Many scholars have termed the process Westernization, Europeanization, or industrialization; others have labeled it a continuation of the "idea of progress" in a non-Western context or described it as social mobilization—a "process in which major clusters of old social, economic, and psychological commitments are eroded and broken, and people become available for new patterns of socialization and behavior."[5] Still others have used such terms as secularization, social reconstruction, modernization of men, and more and more in recent years, the familiar term modernization.[6]

The use of these terms and concepts without qualification or reservation can lead to difficulties of a methodological, historical, and sociological nature. For the purpose of this study I have used the terms reform, modernism, and modernization in order to overcome some of the inadequacies of the term Westernization, a term whose use can easily lead to value judgments and which tends to perpetuate parochial attitudes and notions, particularly the notion that the impact of the West represents the sole dynamic element in the development of non-Western countries. Although the West may serve as a prototype, a stimulus, or an accelerator of social change, the term Westernization does not take into consideration the possibility of change or reform along traditional models and forms; it does not convey the complex character of cultural interaction and coexistence, the mutual modification and fusion of new cultural patterns with indigenous ones.[7]

Modernization, on the other hand, denotes more than technological borrowings from the West; it characterizes a complex historical process involving "the systematic, sustained, and purposeful application of human energies to the rational control of man's physical and social environment for various purposes."[8] Although the precise definition of modernization is a matter of debate, basically it involves the process of the integration and industrialization of a country's economy, the expansion of its communications and trade, a marked increase in the geographic and social mobility of its people, improved standards of health and sanitation, the breakdown of communal and hereditary social groupings, and the gradual subordination of old social units (family, village, or tribe) to a national community. Traditional values are to a large extent undermined or modified by a new faith, essentially a belief in progress, a belief that change is not only possible but also beneficial, inevitable, and on balance desirable. A providential view of historic events is replaced by a rational interpretation based on physical and psychological forces. Modernization involves the spread of secular, scientific, and technical education, accompanied by the growth of an extensive network of mass media; it involves an increasing awareness on the part of both old and new social groups of their interests and their claims on each other; it involves changes in both the distribution of political power and the amount of power within a given political system. The process of social change is characterized by the rapid growth of such institutions as government, business, and industry. An old elite based on birth either dies out or becomes assimilated into a new one based on achievement and education. Along with increasing urbanization and urban-centeredness, industrialization, and secularization, there is a tendency toward national political unification and greater international contacts and cooperation. Ideologically, modernization necessitates either establishing a new, more popular basis of legitimacy for the *ancien régime* or providing authority for a new regime; it requires the reformulation of the concepts of nationality, nationhood, and nationalism, and the promotion of the doctrine that citizens are equal before the law to which they individually consent.[9]

The history of Afghan reforms and the study of the development and intellectual genesis of the Afghan modernist movement, as well as of the process of social change in Afghanistan, have not received the attention they merit from American and West European sociologists, anthropologists, political scientists, Islamicists, and historians.[10] As the Afghan historian Mohammed Ali puts it: "No country comparable to Afghanistan in size and no people approaching the Afghans in historical interest and importance have received so little consideration at the hands of modern writers as have Afghanistan and the Afghans."[11] This neglect is understandable. For most of the nineteenth century, Afghanistan remained culturally one of the most isolated and parochial regions of the Muslim world, almost totally cut off from the mainstream of European thought. It did not undergo any direct and intensive experience of European colonial rule; on the contrary, imperialism, while impressing upon the Afghans the necessity of technological borrowing, contributed to Afghan political and cultural isolationism. It was instrumental in the development of a peculiarly Afghan policy of modernism—that of pursuing a limited, eclectic, and guided modernization in developing the country's economy without outside assistance—a policy that was considered the best means of safeguarding both the Afghan monarchy and the territorial integrity and independence of Afghanistan.

The overall political and cultural isolation of the country in the nineteenth century, along with an absence or inadequacy of centers of higher learning, educational facilities, libraries, periodicals and newspapers, and modern roads and communications, has greatly retarded the study of the history and socioeconomic institutions of Afghanistan. The task of the student of Afghan history is made even more difficult by the complexity of the country's ethnic, linguistic, and social divisions. (One of the two principal languages of the country, Pashto, was not studied systematically until the nineteenth century; and inside Afghanistan itself, Pashto remained unstudied until a few decades ago.)

With a few rare exceptions, nineteenth- and early twentieth-century European (predominantly English) historical literature on Afghanistan either deals with the geopolitical importance of the region and its topography or consists of detailed memoirs and treatises on the First and Second Anglo-Afghan wars, the Russian advances in Central Asia, and the position of Afghanistan in the power struggle between two imperial rivals, Great Britain and Czarist Russia. Historical data and information about Afghan socioeconomic institutions and culture of the period are fragmentary, scattered, and negligible.* It is only in recent years that Afghan historians have undertaken the task of consulting, compiling, and translating manuscripts (in the Kabul Museum and in the libraries of the Afghan Department of Press and the Ministry of Education) that provide additional information on the nature of Afghan internal politics and the development of some of the country's institutions during the past two centuries.[12]

Because of the scarcity of source material and the pioneering state of Afghan historiography,[13] the complete history of the region has yet to be told. Even contemporary Afghan historians like Qasim Reshtiya, who has attempted to write the first extensive political history of nineteenth-century Afghanistan, have had to rely on the very few Afghan secondary sources, or, more often, on English ones.[14] To study the Afghan monarchy at the beginning of the nineteenth century, or to look into the origins and characteristics of Afghan feudalism or the organization of the Afghan tribes, one still has to rely heavily on the work of Mountstuart Elphinstone.

A great amount of systematic work has been done in Russian, especially during the Soviet period, on the Pashto language, Afghan literature, and various aspects of the economic history and institutions of Afghanistan.

---

* Faced with the paucity of historical literature, one authority has gone so far as to assert that the Afghans do not have a history, since chaos does not have any (Darmesteter, *Chants populaires*, p. clii). Another writes that we know more about the surface of the moon than we do about the "region we call Afghanistan" (Gowen, p. 167). Complete authors' names, titles, and publication data for works cited in short forms will be found in the Bibliography, pp. 503–69.

Despite the strenuous and often objectionable attempts of the Soviet Afghanists to accommodate their studies to the varying objectives of Soviet historiography, the range, the extent, and often the quality of their work are impressive. Their main emphasis has been on the Durrani empire, the Afghan and Pathan tribes, and the development of feudalism in Afghanistan, but considerable attention has also been paid to the economic development of post–World War II Afghanistan, and to the Tajik and Turkic ethnic groups of the country.[15] However, there are no Soviet monographic, comprehensive studies available tracing the historical development of the Afghan reformist and modernist movement.*

The absence of monographic historical literature on Afghan nationalism and on various phases of the social, economic, and cultural development of modern Afghanistan (especially for the nineteenth-century and pre–World War II era) presents the student of Afghan history with great methodological difficulties.[16] The vastly scattered and fragmentary source material requires a knowledge of a number of languages, including Persian, Pashto, Eastern Turkish, and to some extent, Urdu, as well as English, Russian, and French. In addition, in order to study Afghan political, institutional, economic, and cultural changes, one has to be familiar with the political and social history of the entire region, including the Middle East, Central Asia, and northern India. Ideally, any attempt to write a social and economic history ought to be undertaken by one who combines the qualities of the orientalist with those of the professional historian—a rare amalgam indeed. Any study of the social history of Afghanistan is further complicated by the absence of certain essential studies, specifically the regional, administrative, and economic histories of a number of Middle Eastern countries, the development of the Muslim guild system, the growth and decline of Middle Eastern urban centers, the evolution of feudal-tribal economies and societies, and the history of Muslim interregional trade.[17] The task of the student of Afghan history is not made any easier by the fact that Afghanistan, because of its geographical position, is often excluded from regional studies; for the most part, it is not included in histories of the Middle East or in works on Central Asia.[18]

---

* Summaries and analyses of the works of Soviet Afghanists appear regularly in the *Central Asian Review* and occasionally in the *Royal Central Asian Journal,* both published in London. Soviet experts in turn frequently translate and analyze the contributions of Afghan writers and historians. Unfortunately, accounts or reviews of the works of contemporary Afghan historians are very rare in the West. To the best of the author's knowledge, Massé's "L'Académie afghane et ses publications," Frye's short article "Oriental Studies in Afghanistan," and a few pertinent materials in Dianous's "La littérature afghane" stand out as lone exceptions.

The present study is an attempt to trace the evolution of the modern Afghan state by studying the politics of reform and modernization in Afghanistan between 1880 and 1946. Here, I use the term politics in its broadest sense, the "conceptualization and implementation of plans of action." I agree with Cyril Black that, at least in the case of countries like Afghanistan, the "growth and diffusion of modernity can best be understood in terms of its political aspect," since the political aspect provides a relatively easy framework for analysis, comparison, and periodization.[19]

It is the author's contention that both the course and the politics of Afghan reform and modernism were determined primarily by two major historical factors: one was the Afghan struggle with and subsequent political attitude toward Great Britain and Russia; the other was the Afghan ruling dynasty's dependence on the support of the tribes under its jurisdiction to maintain its rule and to preserve the integrity and independence of Afghanistan. In the first instance, the two Anglo-Afghan wars and the successful resistance of the Afghans, while necessitating some technological borrowings from Europe, reinforced the self-confidence of the Afghans and contributed to the growth of a politico-religious nationalism. The struggle at the same time strengthened the position of the Afghan tribes and increased the monarchy's dependence on their military might. Moreover, it reinforced the position of the Afghan religious establishment, since Islam became a necessary spiritual weapon against foreign, "infidel" aggression, a rallying point for the ethnically heterogeneous groups of Afghanistan, and a source of legitimacy for the Afghan monarchy and kingdom.

The history of reform and modernism in the nineteenth and early twentieth centuries is a history of persistent attempts by the Afghan ruling dynasty to assert and strengthen its rule. The monarchy sought to unify Afghanistan politically and economically and to achieve a degree of economic and military self-sufficiency in order to preserve its authority, threatened from within by the proud and powerful tribes and from without by the Sikhs, Persians, British, and Russians. The Afghan rulers were successful in restoring political and administrative unity to Afghanistan, using technological and institutional borrowings as well as skillful diplomacy to advance their designs. They failed, however, to achieve the economic, social, and cultural integration of the kingdom, in large part because of their dependence on the Afghan tribes, which committed them to a policy of sustaining the tribal-feudal structure of the Afghan kingdom. To implement its limited reform and modernization schemes, the monarchy was forced to rely chiefly on heavy taxation of the economically weak and ethnically non-Afghan urban and sedentary populations, making the prospect of substantial support from that direction doubtful. Inadequate financial resources and a reluctance to "open" Afghanistan to the foreign investment and technical assistance needed for the exploitation of the country's natural resources were primary causes for the monarchy's failure to undertake, or inability to implement, large-scale modernization schemes. The "closed-door" policy of the Afghan rulers was motivated by their fear of European political and economic encroachments and their apprehensions about the reactions of the religious establishment and the Afghan feudal-tribal chieftains.

In the absence of noteworthy learning institutions, a secular intelligentsia, or reformist movements among the Afghan *ulama* (Islamic theologians), the formulation and propagation of the aims of Afghan nationalism and modernism came late. The two causes were not linked until the first two decades of the twentieth century, when a small group of educated Afghans sought to broaden the base of support for political and economic reform by merging the two movements. Under the leadership of King Amanullah (1919–29), these "Young Afghans" made ambitious plans for the modernization of the country; their ultimate failure determined the course and nature of all future reforms and modernization programs in Afghanistan.

For reasons of convenience I have divided the history of the socioeconomic development of modern Afghanistan into seven periods: 1832–39, 1839–80, 1880–1901, 1901–19, 1919–29, 1930–46, and 1946 to the present.

1832–1839. During this period the Afghan monarchy had not yet come into direct conflict with British or Russian power and so was not fully aware of the far-reaching political implications of Anglo-Russian imperial rivalries. In these years, the Afghan monarchy adopted some European military technology and tried to establish a few institutional innovations with the technical assistance of a few Europeans. The limited Afghan reforms and borrowings were not directed against the West at this stage; they were designed to consolidate the position of the monarchy at home and to preserve Afghan rule over northern and western Afghanistan as well as Peshawar, a rule that was being challenged by the Sikhs in the east, the Persians in the west, and the Bukharans in the north.

1839–1880. Anglo-Russian rivalries in the Middle East and Central Asia led to two Anglo-Afghan wars (1839, 1879). The results were a British occupation of eastern Afghanistan, a successful resistance to that occupation, or "presence," on the part of the Afghans, a British withdrawal (though they retained the right to control Afghanistan's foreign relations), and the political and diplomatic isolation of the country. The wars, representing the Afghans' first exposure to Europeans in any significant numbers, gave impetus to Afghan nationalism and xenophobia; the few attempts at reform and the concept of modernization assumed an anti-Western character.

1880–1901. During the reign of Abdur Rahman Khan, which coincides with this period, modest technological borrowings and institutional reforms were successfully used to centralize and stabilize the position of the Afghan monarchy. A policy of limited and indigenous modernization and national self-sufficiency was anchored to a policy of self-imposed isolation and economic underdevelopment on the assumption that these policies best safeguarded the independence of a country caught up in the rivalries of two great imperialist powers.

1901–1919. A number of advances were made during the reign of Habibullah Khan. Chief among them were the establishment of the first schools with modern curricula, including the country's first secular secondary school, and the successful publication of the first Afghan periodical, which served as the voice of the proponents of Afghan nationalism and modernism.

1919–1929. During this period, Afghanistan fought against British India and achieved its total independence, casting off British control over its external affairs. The Afghans established extensive contacts with Europe, the Soviet Union, and various independent and emerging countries of the East. King Amanullah and his supporters initiated the first comprehensive and large-scale modernization programs in an attempt to transform the entire socioeconomic structure of Afghanistan, but the attempt ended in the midst of a bloody revolt and the period of anarchy that followed it.

1930–1946. Order was restored in these years under a new royal dynasty, which pursued a gradualist policy of modernization, carefully picking and choosing the reforms and foreign assistance it would accept. However, Afghan efforts at modernization were seriously impeded by World War II.

1946 to the present. Post–World War II conditions, specifically the Cold War and Afghanistan's strategic position and traditional foreign policy of "positive neutralism" in it, the collapse of colonialism, accompanied by a growing Asian and Muslim self-assertiveness, and great socioeconomic and political changes and intellectual ferment, have combined to accelerate the process of modernization in Afghanistan. In recent years, the country has embarked upon a program aimed at major economic growth and large-scale modernization schemes, and Muslim reformist-revivalist movements and the Cold War have been effectively used to emphasize the need for fundamental reform and industrialization. Foreign aid, both from the Soviet Union and the Eastern bloc and from the United States and West Europe, as well as United Nations technical assistance, has helped Afghanistan make great advances, particularly in the areas of economic growth, public health, communications, education, and the political integration of Afghan society.

In the years since World War II, Afghanistan has been preoccupied with the new state of Pakistan and the incorporation of Pathan tribal territories within it. Afghan policies and Afghan nationalism have championed the right of the Pathans to self-determination and to form a separate state, a position that has often led to strained Pakistan-Afghanistan relations. Otherwise, Afghanistan has attempted to become a "model neutral state," keeping clear of Cold War entanglements. The present work, however, deals only with the period up to 1946. Political trends, socioeconomic reforms, and ideological developments in postwar Afghanistan are subjects for future study.

Chapter One

The Difficult Legacy

Afghanistan as we know it today emerged as an independent political entity in the middle of the eighteenth century, when the Afghans finally imposed their rule upon territories extending from the Punjab to Baluchistan, an area containing populations that lacked ethnic, linguistic, and political unity. The present frontiers of Afghanistan, however, were not established until the beginning of the twentieth century. The frontier with the Indian subcontinent was determined in 1893 by the Durand Line; the frontier with Russia was settled in 1896 (with minor adjustments in the 1920's, the 1930's, and 1948); and the final corrections along the Irano-Afghan frontier, originally defined in 1903–5, were made in 1935. The border with China was demarcated in 1964. No systematic area survey or population census of Afghanistan has yet been prepared.* Consequently, all statistical data must be used with caution, since writers on Afghanistan either have accepted previously published estimates or have made up their own, with the result that estimates of the area of modern Afghanistan range between 245,000 and 270,000 square miles and those of the country's population between eight and 15 million.[1]

Afghanistan has justly been described as a "highway of conquest" for migratory peoples and expanding empires, a crossroads of civilizations and religions, and a "roundabout" for various trade routes linking Europe with the Far East and the Indian subcontinent. Her geographic position has made Afghanistan vulnerable to invasions from both Central Asia and the West. The sharp racial, ethnic, and linguistic differences throughout the country reflect its particular historical geopolitical position. Similarly,

* In 1957–60 Fairchild Aerial Surveys Inc. undertook to make the first topographic map of the country. The survey covered the entire kingdom, with the exception of the Soviet and Afghan frontier region, which was being mapped for the Afghan government by a team from the Soviet Union. See "Making a Map of Afghanistan. Prepared by Fairchild Aerial Surveys Inc. for the American Society of Photogrammetry," *Afghanistan*, July-August-September 1960, pp. 1–10.

the country's economy was constantly affected by political developments in the Middle East, which frequently resulted in the disruption, cessation, or obstruction of trade along the major overland routes crossing the Afghan territories. Most of the important urban centers of Afghanistan—Kandahar, Herat, Ghazni, Mazar-i-Sharif—were located in fertile valleys and at the junctions of trade routes, where they were difficult to defend against attack. The proximity of these urban centers to Afghanistan's borders led to their capture by various invaders and the consequent paralysis of Afghanistan's urban economy. Kabul and Kandahar, as strategic "Gates of India," were coveted by contending empires, who used them for the defense of India or as springboards for the invasion of that subcontinent. The important geographic position of Afghanistan has also influenced the delimitation of the country's frontiers, which are more political and strategic than ethnic or economic in origin. Because it is landlocked, the country continues to depend on its neighbors for the bulk of its import and export trade, with predictable effects on the course and character of its foreign and economic policies.[2]

Afghanistan's most prominent topographic feature is a mountain range (variously known on its 700-mile course as the Hindu Kush, Kuh-i-Baba, and Siyah Bubuk) that runs east to west with normal elevations of 13,000 to 20,000 feet and peaks up to 25,000 feet. The range divides the country's northern regions (Afghan Turkestan) from the major provinces of Kabul, Kandahar, and Herat. Ranges radiating southwest from the Pamirs include Safid Kuh (Koh), with peaks to 15,600 feet, the Suleiman Mountains, reaching 11,500 feet, and the Kirthar ranges which swing across Baluchistan.

The Hindu Kush served as an ethnic breakwater by diverting westward the flood of major Central Asian migrations. Later, however, the mountain range proved to be a barrier to the political and economic integration of northern and southern Afghanistan. Until 1933, for example, there was no adequate direct road linking the Kabul and Kandahar provinces with northern Afghanistan. The existing routes through the Hindu Kush traversed such hazardous passes as Khawak (11,640 feet), Ak-Robat (12,560 feet), and Qipchak (13,900 feet), which were impassable for at least six months of the year. These conditions often forced both commercial and military expeditions to take the long and circuitous route from Herat to Kandahar and Kabul.

Although snow and rain, originating largely in the high, precipitous ranges of central Afghanistan, provide adequate water resources, most of the water is wasted rather than retained and used for cultivation. Of

Afghanistan's four river systems—the Helmand, Amu Darya (Oxus), Hari Rud (Arius), and Kabul—only one has sufficient water to flow to the sea, and then only as a tributary of the Indus. Consequently, the agricultural economy of a dry Afghanistan, where the average annual rainfall is only ten inches, has had to rely on man-made systems of irrigation. The demand for water was met by wells (*kariz*) or by the *qanat* system (underground channels directing water to the surface). The country's heavy dependence on man-made irrigation persists today.* According to Wilber, in 1950–60 some 47 per cent of the cultivated land still depended on kariz water, 10 per cent on source water from the qanat, and only 13 per cent on river water.

The climate has been a major obstacle to the economic development of the region. Cut off from the monsoon system of the Arabian Sea, Afghanistan has a climate that ranges from alpine and subarctic in the northeast to absolute desert along the Amu Darya and Helmand rivers. The severity of the climate, marked also by strong seasonal winds (May to September), has limited the variety of agricultural products, hindered the development of communications, and encouraged indiscriminate deforestation to meet the need for fuel.

Constant political and socioeconomic upheavals, which often led to the collapse of regional authority and the neglect or destruction of irrigation networks, discouraged the economic development of Afghanistan and encouraged sedentary populations to return to a nomadic way of life.[3] The sedentary and urban sectors of the Afghan population were also prey to tribesmen of the border hills, whose homelands were almost devoid of economic potential. To sustain themselves, these tribesmen were driven to raiding the fertile lowlands and passing commercial caravans. As late as 1929 only about 2 to 3 per cent of the country was under cultivation, and people living in towns and cities of more than 10,000 comprised only

* Karl Marx advanced an interesting theory linking the economic stagnation of Asia to its irrigation systems: "The prime necessity of an economical and common use of water, which in the Occident drove private enterprise to voluntary association, as in Flanders and Italy, necessitated the interference of the centralizing power of government in the Orient, where civilization was too low and the territorial extent too vast to call into life voluntary association. Hence an economic function developed upon all Asiatic governments the function of providing public works. This artificial fertilization of the soil, dependent on a central government and immediately decaying with the neglect of irrigation and drainage, explains the otherwise strange fact that we now find whole territories barren and desert that were once brilliantly cultivated. . . . It also explains how a single war of devastation has been able to depopulate a country for centuries and to strip it of all civilization." (Karl Marx and Friedrich Engels, *The First Indian War of Independence: 1857–1859*, Moscow, 1959, pp. 16–17.) For a development of the above theme, with a non-Marxian interpretation and conclusions, see Wittfogel, *Oriental Despotism.*

3 to 8 per cent of the total population.[4] Current statistics indicate that 85 per cent of the people are engaged in agriculture, but that only about 3 per cent of the land is cultivated. (Out of an estimated 14 million hectares of cultivable land, reportedly only 7.8 million hectares are being cultivated.)[5]

HISTORICAL BACKGROUND

During the pre-Islamic era, certain invading empires contributed greatly to the trade, economy, administrative organization, and culture of Afghanistan; this was true of the Persian Achaemenid Empire (sixth to fourth centuries B.C.), the Graeco-Bactrian Kingdom (fourth to second centuries B.C.), and the Kushan Empire (first century B.C. to third century A.D.). The Kushan Empire was especially significant in the cultural and political development of the country. Under Kushan rule, there was a fusion of Hellenistic and Buddhist cultures that gave birth to a new form of art and civilization known as the Graeco-Buddhist or Gandharan.[6] Other invaders, however, notably the Hephtalite Huns and certain Turkic groups, wrought wholesale destruction and caused major social dislocations in Afghanistan. In some cases, massacres were so widespread and thorough that cities remained depopulated for centuries.

Despite Afghanistan's brilliant and varied pre-Islamic cultural heritage, she lacked ethnic homogeneity, a unified economic and administrative system, religious unity, and political stablity. The continuous migrations of nomadic peoples prevented the full integration of their pastoral economies with the region's rural and urban economies.

Islam, which displaced the remnants of the Graeco-Buddhist civilization, brought about an abrupt change in the social, cultural, and historical development of Afghanistan, though from a historical point of view it was not detrimental to the future growth of urban civilization there.* To an ethnically heterogeneous, politically divided region it brought a cosmopolitanism and lack of racial consciousness that forged new religious and

* Afghan historians, apologists of Islam, hold that although the Arabs were diligent in their destruction of the pre-Islamic heritage of Afghanistan, the advent of Islam was not a catastrophe but rather a great revolution. See, for example, Ghubar, "Adabiyat," p. 14; and Pazhwak, *Afghanistan*, p. 18. Ghubar goes so far as to suggest that for the Afghans Islam was a "national religion" that served as a vehicle for their liberation from the Chinese, the Turks, and the Persians. See also Ghubar's contribution in Latifi, p. 21. Soviet historians, on the other hand, contend that the Arab invasion and Islam were retrogressive factors that greatly contributed to the eventual cultural and socioeconomic backwardness of the region. Islam as a religion is generally regarded as primitive, fanatical, conservative, and regressive, and as having served, since its inception, as an instrument for exploitation and expansion, first for the Arab aristocracy and "feudal merchant" class, and later for foreign

cultural bonds—bonds that to a certain extent overrode the prevalent ethnic diversities.[7] Islam brought a concept of community (*ummah*) that was based on law as well as religion. Islamic universalism and missionary zeal exposed many migratory groups to a monotheistic religion, and by absorbing them into a larger and superior cultural realm, counteracted the disruptive effect of such groups.[8] The Muslim conquest brought Afghanistan within a greater political entity, stimulated trade in the region, and preserved the country's geographic importance as a crossroads between India, Central Asia, and the Mediterranean world. During the early centuries, Islam contributed to the achievement of a "bourgeois revolution" in certain regions of Afghanistan: in a society with a small or negligible bourgeois class, a society in which aristocrats and members of the bureaucracy showed contempt for merchants, Islam brought social status and religious sanction to the merchant class.[9]

Culturally, Islam did not and could not destroy all of the existing cultural legacies; instead, elements of the indigenous civilization were incorporated into its main body. It served as a molder of various cultural traditions, bringing together a vast repository of Greek, Syriac, Persian, and Indian scientific and philosophical thought, thus promoting the universality of learning and knowledge.[10] Although Islam impeded the overall development of the visual arts (especially the art of human representation), it contributed to a renaissance in various other arts and sciences. Under the aegis of such local ruling dynasties as the Tahirids (820–70), the Saffarids (870–90), and especially the Samanids (874–999), a fertile and flourishing cultural era was inaugurated that has had lasting effect on Iran, Afghanistan, and portions of Soviet Central Asia.[11] The cities of Merv, Balkh, Nishapur, and Bukhara emerged as great centers of learning. Intellectual life was enriched by such famous men as the poets Rudaki and Dakiki; Balami, the founder of Muslim Persian historiography; the geographer Abu-Sayid al Balkhi; and the philosopher-physician Abu Ali Ibn Sina (Avicenna). According to Bosworth, "The age of the Samanids saw the forging in Khurasan and Transoxiana of New Persian (Farsi) as a fine instrument for literary expression." The spread of Farsi in Afghanistan continued under the Ghaznawids (999–1186). The Ghaznawid Empire, notes Bosworth, "gradually became integrated with Khurasan and the eastern Iranian world in general. Once this seed was implanted, Ghazna and eastern Afghanistan began to develop a Persian culture of

---

invaders as well. (See, for example, Tolstov, pp. 221–22; Gafurov, I, Chap. 9; *BSE*, 2d ed., XXVIII, 537, and XLI, 473. For a comprehensive survey of the Soviet literature on the topic, see Bennigsen, "Muslim Peoples.")

their own, a culture which survived the Ghurid takeover of the Ghaznawid Empire, and endured right down to the Mongol invasion."[12]

Despite its many contributions in the cultural, social, and economic realms, the Muslim Empire at the time of its breakup left eastern Afghanistan a militarized borderland of Islam. Under the rule of the Ghaznawids and later that of the Seljuks and the Ghurids, political developments and strategic considerations encouraged the militarization of Afghanistan. The Afghan tribes of the Suleiman Range were used by the Ghaznawids in their periodic incursions into India as an advance guard and a reservoir of recruits to extend the frontiers of Dar-ul-Islam (the Muslim world). Ghaznawid conquests brought incalculable wealth; the flow of money and goods into Afghanistan, the political center of the Ghaznawids, stimulated the economy and commerce of the region and linked the Afghan economy to the Punjab, Sind, and northern India; but though the Ghaznawids protected and encouraged commerce, their empire retained a military character.[13] Their rule contributed to the emergence of Afghan military feudalism and opened the Indian subcontinent to economic exploitation and political expansionism by the Afghan frontier tribes.

With the collapse of the Ghaznawids and the rise of the Seljuks (1038–1157), central authority gave way to feudalism and regionalism. The Seljuks systematized the legal framework of a feudal system with *iqta,* or military fiefs, as its socioeconomic basis.[14] The power of feudal lords grew appreciably when the holders of military fiefs and land grants became entitled to the greatest portion of the royal revenues, rather than simply a commission on taxes collected in their domain, a practice that had prevailed in earlier times.[15] Some of the Afghan tribal chieftains benefited greatly by this change because of their military strength and strategic geographical position. The policies and exactions of the Seljuks, following on the footsteps of Ghaznawid exactions, caused disruption of trade and agriculture. Land values plummeted, with ruinous effect on the *dihqān* (peasant) and small landowner classes.[16] The growth of regionalism and feudalism under the Seljuks marked a clear transition from a money economy to a natural one.

Under the Ghurids (1150–1217)—in the opinion of some, the first Afghan dynasty*—the dependence upon tribal military power for the

---

* "Afghanistan," in *EI*, 2d ed., Vol. I. Afghan historians disagree. They regard the majority of the inhabitants who have lived in the region since the coming of the Aryans as Afghan. The line of dynasties is viewed, therefore, as a continuum from the first Aryan kingdom to the present day. Among Western authorities, Caroe, in his study *The Pathans,* rejects the view that the Ghurids were of Afghan origin.

protection and extension of the political realm (which included major portions of present-day Afghanistan and extended to Bengal and the basin of the Ganges) was accentuated. The practice of granting lands to Afghan chieftains as military fiefs continued, and Afghan political power rose accordingly. Ghurid rule in a sense retarded the development of Afghanistan: India became accessible to the Afghans, who went there as mercenaries or as conquerors (some eventually to found dynasties, e.g., the Lodi, 1451–1526, and the Suri, 1540–55). Thus, the Ghurids enabled the Afghans to perpetuate and strengthen their feudal society at home. Though their economy had an artificial and ephemeral prosperity, Afghan energies were almost completely dissipated in the vast plains of India.[17] The consequent neglect of the Afghan homeland, which came to be regarded mainly as a reservoir for recruits, retarded the development of a national consciousness and a sense of unity among the Afghans.

Culturally, the Ghaznawid, Seljuk, and Ghurid eras were of great significance for Afghanistan, as well as for adjacent Muslim regions. The cultural renaissance during the two-century rule of the Samanid dynasty did not have an opportunity to develop fully. The creeping "disease of orthodoxy" spread under the Ghaznawid rule and resulted in the persecution of "Shi'ah heretics," the crucifixion of Isma'ilis, the exiling of Mu'tazilites, and the burning of philosophical, scientific, and "heretical" books.[18] These policies were continued under the Seljuks, who, in their attempt to stamp out "irreligion, heresy, schism, philosophy and metaphysics," identified Sunni orthodoxy with the legal and political stability of the state.[19] Sciences that had been tolerated or encouraged in the twelfth century were denigrated for fostering a "loss of belief in the origin of the world and in the Creator." The victory of theological orthodoxy was facilitated by the need to establish a united front to combat a new series of nomadic invasions, which broke over the Muslim world from the eleventh century on, and the excesses perpetrated by the Isma'ilis.

The pressures of Muslim orthodoxy produced a sense of resignation and submissiveness among the majority of Muslim theologians and thinkers. Faith became "the official credo of constituted state and society. ... Conformity, however perfunctory, was the token pledge of loyalty. Orthodoxy meant the acceptance of the existing order, heresy or apostasy its criticism and rejection."[20] The success of Muslim rulers and states in manipulating religion for political purposes brought about a cleavage between Muslim scholars and jurists on the one hand and the masses on the other.[21] The result was a rigid intellectual system that created a gulf between the ideal and the actual and that led to many intellectual compromises or capitulations by Muslim institutions and ulama.[22] Theological systems became more and more divorced from personal religious experience, and the identification of the interests of the religious institutions with those of the Seljuk sultanate made the institutions of higher learning (*madrassas*) centers for the enforcement of orthodox conformity.

The triumph of theological orthodoxy, accompanied by the closing of the "gate" of interpretation to Muslim jurists, reinforced the power of Quranic legislation and gave strong support to the contention that Islamic law was of divine inspiration and guidance. In the words of one scholar, "Not unlike the idea of natural law in medieval Christendom, Islamic law was regarded as transcendental and perfect . . . designed for all time and characterized by its universal application to all men. . . . In theory the divine law preceded the state and was independent of man's own existence."[23] The function of the state was to enforce the eternal law as the basis of social cohesion. This concept of unity became so deeply embedded in the Islamic tradition that even the noted medieval Arab historian Ibn Khaldūn, despite his ideas concerning the principle of ordered social change, spoke with great caution and reservation about the use of reason in politics. He rejected the study of philosophy and physics as of no importance to a Muslim's religious and practical life, proclaiming that the only subjects worthy of study were those that promoted a Muslim's spiritual and moral welfare, those subjects that did not jeopardize his faith.[24] In such circumstances, Islamic law became increasingly divorced from the practical needs of individual Muslims and increasingly preoccupied with the abstract ethical and religious ideals of Islam.

THE MONGOL INVASION

The Mongol invasion, which began in 1220 with the conquests of Genghis Khan and culminated in the sack of Baghdad (1258), had a disastrous effect on Afghanistan as well as on Central Asia, Iran, and Mesopotamia. "In its suddenness, devastating destruction, appalling ferocity, passionless and purposeless cruelty, it resembled more to some brute cataclysm of the blind forces of nature than a phenomenon of human history."[25] The destruction wrought by the Mongols brought economic disaster to the region, disrupted the political power of Islam, and dealt the Muslim world a great psychological blow by placing its urban societies and civilization under a pagan nomadic yoke.

For a few decades the Mongol invaders failed to recognize or utilize the benefits of an urban and agricultural civilization. They set out to protect their empire and ensure their military control by laying waste land to create artificial boundaries, destroying urban centers and irrigation systems, and carrying out mass executions of indigenous populations. The population of Balkh, one of the richest and largest cities of the region, was massacred. Other Afghan cities, notably Gurzivan, Taligan, and Bamian, were razed. The entire population of Ghazni, with the exception of a few artisans, was exterminated, and the city destroyed.[26] The devastation in the Khorassan region was so thorough, and the massacres so overwhelming, that, according to Juvainī, "even though there be generation and increase until the Resurrection, the population will not attain to a tenth part of what it was before."[27] The wholesale massacres of local populations, the razing of cities and towns, the practice of filling the moats of one besieged city with the bodies of prisoners from another, the use of thousands of people as human shields against besieged garrisons, the destruction of all stored grain, and the obliteration of irrigation systems, libraries, and centers of learning paralyzed the Muslim world.

Some historians have argued that the Mongol invasions had positive as well as negative effects on the historical development of Central Asia, Iran, and Afghanistan.* Ba'hadour Khan, for one, has pointed to the reign of peace and widespread security—a kind of Pax Mongolica—that followed the initial phase of invasions and devastation.[28] The renewing of cultural and commercial contacts between Europe and Asia and the religious tolerance of the Mongols are also cited among the historically beneficial developments.[29] In the words of H. A. R. Gibb, "This event [the Mongol invasion], the shock of which seemed to the Muslim peoples like the last Judgement of the wrath of God, proved in the end a blessing in disguise. Once again the eastern provinces enjoyed a period of firm and relatively undisturbed government, under which trade and agriculture took heart and began to re-create a prosperity that seemed to have vanished forever."[30] Advocates of this interpretation emphasize that under the impact of Arabo-Iranian civilization and after accepting Islam and a sedentary life, the Mongols came to attach considerable importance to the development of the natural sciences and the study of history, and extended

* Sayyid Ameer Ali, the famous Indian Muslim scholar (*Spirit of Islam*, pp. 399–402), attributed the stagnation of the entire Muslim world, including Afghanistan, primarily to Mongol and later nomadic invasions. Modern Afghan historiography places similar emphasis on the role played by these invasions in retarding the socioeconomic development of Afghanistan. See, for example, Mohammed Ali, *Manners and Customs*, pp. 3–4, and *National Awakening*, pp. iii–iv. Soviet historians reject the notion of any positive factors in the Mongol rule. (See, for example, Belenitskii, "Les Mongols," pp. 606–20; and Grekov and Yakubovskii.)

their protection to scholars and poets. Those holding this view argue that cities like Bukhara and Urgendj (Ourganch), as well as other Central Asian regions like Khwarezm, achieved unparalleled prosperity under the successors of Genghis Khan.[31]

Agriculture, however, never reached its pre-Mongol level. By destroying most of the sedentary populations and turning the bulk of arable land into barren stubble or untended pasturage, the Mongols created a strategic, artificial steppe, a no-man's-land that served to protect their empire. Mongol rule also seriously hindered the development of trades and crafts; the Mongol feudal system and the continuous exorbitant extractions of money from the city-dwellers acted as brakes on urban development. By 1253, many small towns had disappeared, and their sites had become pasture land.[32] Nor did all of the large cities enjoy peace, protection, and prosperity under the so-called Pax Mongolica. Some of them were destroyed a second time, as was Bukhara in 1273, or were plundered, as was Ghazni in 1326.[33] When Ibn Battuta visited Afghanistan a century after the invasion of Genghis Khan, he found the city of Balkh in an utterly desolate condition, the Panjshir region uninhabitable, Kabul a mere village, and little left of Ghazni.[34]

THE TURKIC INVADERS AND THE IMPACT OF SHI'AH PERSIA

One hundred sixty years after the Mongol invasion, Afghanistan was overrun by the armies of a Turko-Mongol invader, Timur-i-Leng (Tamerlane, 1336–1405). Although Timur was a Muslim, his atrocities against his coreligionists in Afghanistan equaled those of Genghis Khan. The inhabitants of the province of Sistan and the Afghans of the Suleiman Range bore the brunt of the invader's blows. Attempts at resistance or rebellion on the part of local populations were brutally crushed; thousands were slaughtered and their skulls stacked into pyramids. The destruction of the irrigation system of the Helmand valley turned nearly all of Sistan Province into a desert.[35] The major libraries of the conquered lands, as well as most of the scholars, artisans, and craftsmen, were removed to Samarkand, Timur's metropolis.

A great rebirth of the Persian and East Turkic cultures took place under Shahrukh (1407–47) and the other successors of Timur, even though their empire was in a state of political disintegration at the time. The city of Herat became the focal point of this cultural renaissance. As patrons of poetry and the sciences, the Timurids attracted scholars and artists to Herat, opened madrassas, and even built an observatory (in Samarkand).[36] Learning and the arts flourished again in Persia and Afghanistan. This period, which is commonly referred to as the "Timurid Renaissance," has been compared by some historians to the Renaissance of Western Europe,[37] but the comparison seems clearly excessive. Although the Timurid Renaissance revived interest in learning and gave impetus to artistic endeavor, it did not usher in revolutionary change. Any movements similar to those characterizing the European Renaissance were short-lived and were always followed by periods of "medievalism."[38] Centered around the courts of the rulers and lesser princes, the Timurid Renaissance was confined to a narrow layer of urban society. It failed to dig deep roots or disengage itself totally from scholasticism and formalism. The era of cultural rebirth inaugurated by the Timurids did not last long enough to exert profound influence on subsequent generations. (The observatory, for example, was closed after the death of its founder, Ulugh Beg.)[39]

In the sixteenth century, Transoxiana, Khorassan, Herat, and the northern regions of Afghanistan were invaded by the Uzbek Shaybanid (Shibanid) rulers. These invaders drove Zahiruddin Muhammed Babur, the last representative of the Timurids of Transoxiana, into Kabul and thence to India, where in 1526 he founded the dynasty of the Great Moghuls. Eastern Afghanistan became incorporated into his Moghul Empire, resulting in repeated expeditions against such ethnic groups as the Kafirs and the Ghilzais, and the sacking of Kandahar and other urban centers of the area.[40]

The emergence and political predominance of the culturally and economically retarded Uzbeks in Central Asia and their control of northern Afghanistan inhibited the growth of international trade in both areas. Commerce was greatly hampered by the absence of central authority and uniform and regular customs dues. Culturally, the intransigent religious fanaticism of the Uzbeks and their opposition to all foreign innovations led to an intolerance of all deviationists; absolute conformity to Sunni orthodoxy was required. Medieval philosophy and science were replaced by a rigid scholasticism.[41]

The advent of the Uzbeks climaxed centuries of invasions by Turkic nomads, invasions that frequently interrupted the growth of Islamic civilization in the region, destroyed irrigation systems, and undermined the economic position of urban centers, whose populations suffered most from the low level of cultural and socioeconomic development of these nomads. In addition, the four centuries of Turko-Mongol invasions helped to "harden the division of the Muslim lands into separate Arabic, Persian, and Turkish linguistic regions between which literary communication was confined to the restricted circles of the educated."[42]

The coming of the Uzbeks coincided with the triumph of the Muslim

Shi'is of Persia, whose Safawid Empire brought western Afghanistan under its political control. Thus, in the sixteenth century, Afghanistan was part of three political realms: the northern regions were under Uzbek domination, and the remainder was divided between Moghul India and Safawid Persia. In their "re-creation of the Persian nationality" and their proclamation of Shi'ah Islam as the official religion, the Safawids played an extremely important historical role. They formalized, intensified, and politicized the Sunni-Shi'ah doctrinal and regional schism within the Islamic world. The growth and consolidation of the Shi'ah Empire halted the Ottoman drive in Europe by turning the Ottomans' attention east-ward. It also contributed to the establishment of wider contacts between Persia and Europe. However, the rise of Shi'ah Persia adversely affected the intellectual and cultural development of predominantly Sunni Central Asia and Afghanistan, cutting them off from extensive intercourse with the Muslim Mediterranean world. As Vambery has observed, "Whilst great political changes, as well as constant intercourse with Christian Europe, combined to bring the Western Sunnites under the influence of foreign social relations, the Eastern Sunnites, left entirely to themselves, had no opportunity offered them of introducing either changes or reforms. They looked with quite as much abhorrence at the Chinese and Hindoos as upon heretical Persia, the only country which offered them the means of communication with the West."[43]

Afghanistan, as an object of the political ambitions of the Uzbeks, the Persians, and the Moghuls, was particularly affected by the Sunni-Shi'ah religious strife. Persecutions were common, for, in the ensuing politico-religious struggle, each religious group under the political jurisdiction of an opposing power was treated as an actual or potential enemy.[44] The city of Herat, for instance, suffered greatly in the Uzbek-Persian wars, and Kandahar was ravaged by wars between Moghul India and Safawid Persia, with political control of the city passing from one rival empire to the other.[45] Shi'ah Persia's wars against the Uzbeks, the Moghuls, and the Ottoman Empire also restricted the flow of pilgrims to Mecca and Medina, limiting the petty commerce and interchange of ideas that had taken place at the pilgrim centers.[46]

CHANGES IN THE TRADE ROUTES

The cultural and economic isolation of Afghanistan was aggravated by the discovery of maritime routes between Europe and the East. The open-ing of these routes, which were safer, cheaper, and in many respects faster, greatly undermined the monopolistic position of Central Asia and Afghanistan as transit trade centers. The use of the new routes, coinciding with the politico-religious strife within the region, slowed the pace and decreased the volume of trade that flowed through the overland routes crossing Afghanistan; the region was soon reduced to a secondary position in world trade. The prosperity of many urban centers in Afghanistan was permanently threatened and the cause of feudalism strengthened by the consequent weakening of the merchant class. In many regions of Central Asia and Afghanistan, the economic decline marked a regression from a money economy to a natural economy and resulted in the transfer of political power from thriving urban centers to a landed aristocracy. "As commerce declined, the merchant element sank to the level of the artisans and craftsmen, and society returned [to] its old simple structure of landlords, officials, and peasants."[47]

Use of the overland trade routes also decreased because of the establishment of Portuguese colonies in India. In an attempt to monopolize Indo-European trade, the Portuguese undertook a naval blockade of both the Red Sea and the Persian Gulf in order to intercept and control Muslim sea trade. They succeeded in gaining control of the Indian Ocean and put a tight rein on both Muslim-controlled commerce and the flow of pilgrims from India to the Arabian Peninsula. Neither Persia nor Moghul India had sea power capable of containing the Portuguese, and attempts by the Ottoman Empire and Venice to drive them from the Indian Ocean were unsuccessful. In the meantime, in the north the Russians, under Ivan the Terrible, occupied Kazan and Astrakhan, thus driving a wedge in the Central Asian trade route north of the Caspian.

European naval supremacy and control of maritime trade were reinforced by the emergence of joint-stock companies, with their separate functions of saving, risk-taking, and management. Such enterprises as the Muscovy Company, the Levant Company, and the English, French, and Dutch East India companies gradually gained control of both the flow and the substance of the Eastern trade. The position of Afghanistan and Central Asia as trade centers suffered further when Russian expansion into Siberia led to the opening of a new route between Europe and the Far East. The subsequent Russian capture of the Caspian sea trade killed Muslim hopes of playing a major independent role in world commerce.

The Muslim merchants, who had traditionally traded as individuals or in private partnership, were gradually supplanted, especially in the late seventeenth and eighteenth centuries, by their powerful European competitors. Local merchants had a number of handicaps, among them the lack of organized banking facilities and credit systems, the lack of govern-

mental support or subsidy, and the lack of commercial agencies and permanent diplomatic missions in non-Muslim countries.[48] Moreover, they were
unable to adopt long-range economic policies, since monarchs and petty
rulers in Central Asia, the Moghul Empire, and Safawid Persia were inclined to claim a royal monopoly over profitable items of foreign trade.
The development of internal trade was also impeded; the communications
and transport systems were antiquated, and travelers and tradesmen were
prey to the raids of highwaymen, a situation that had been endemic since
the early seventeenth century.* The condition of the roads deteriorated as
the trade routes shifted and the political authority of the Safawid and
Moghul empires declined in Afghanistan. Most goods were still carried by
pack animals; wagons were virtually unknown.[49] The insecurity of the
trade routes and the absence of effective central power forced merchants
to wait until they could join large caravans (*kafila*) that could defend
themselves.† The collapse of a more or less uniform customs system for
both foreign and interregional trade compounded all the other difficulties
of the merchants.

Despite these adverse conditions, at the beginning of the seventeenth

* See the 1602 account of the Jesuit Father Goëz, who traveled from Khyber to Badakhshan. Attacked frequently by the Pathan tribesmen, his caravan reached Kabul only
after suffering great material losses. The caravan experienced a similar fate at the
hands of brigands in Badakhshan, in northeastern Afghanistan (see Goëz, pp. 579ff;
Yule, II, 527–91; and Barthold, *La découverte*, pp. 113–14). William Finch, an agent
of the East India Company, reported in 1611 that communications between Peshawar
and Kabul were insecure and dangerous because of rebels in the area, who numbered
ten to twelve thousand men (see Purchas, IV, 1–77). In the same period, Thomas
Best, another agent, spoke of "insolent Afghans" and of fortresses built near Kandahar
for the protection of communications against their incursions (Purchas, IV, 119–47,
especially p. 124). Some two decades later, Fray Sebastien Manrique (II, 956–57)
reported the presence of many Moghul garrisons in the region, deployed for the protection and security of roads and trade against the Afghans, "folk who inhabit those
rough mountains and inhospitable ranges and sally forth thence like wild intractable
animals to attack the defenceless travellers who pass these wilds."

† The slow pace of trade and the conditions of transportation from the seventeenth
to the nineteenth centuries were reported by many travelers. Goëz, for instance, wrote
that it took him 45 days to travel from Peshawar to Kabul in 1602 (see also Yule, II,
527–91). Steel and Crouther of the East India Company took 47 days traveling from
Multan to Kandahar. Crouther, on his return to India in 1617, spent seven days in
Farah because of rain, 30 days in Kandahar waiting for a major caravan to pass the
mountains, and some 12 or 14 days at Multan waiting for companions in order to be
able to travel safely (see Crouther to East India Company, March 1, 1616, in Foster,
Letters Received, p. v). In the early nineteenth century, Burnes and Wood spent 19
days traveling the road from Peshawar to Kabul (see Burnes, *Travels*, II, 97ff; and
Burnes, Leech, *et al.*). Burnes and Gerard, who left Peshawar on March 15, 1832,
reached Balkh on June 10, after making some 26 marches (see Gerard, "Peshawar
to Bokhara," p. 1).

century the volume of merchandise passing from India to Persia and Central Asia through Afghanistan was stilll considerable: an estimated 14,000 camel-loads per year.[50] The foundations of this trade were weak, however, and were further shaken by the political ascendancy of the Afghan frontier tribes, which controlled the economic lifeline of the major urban centers of eastern Afghanistan—Kabul, Kandahar, Jalalabad, and Ghazni. So powerful were these tribes that even the famous eighteenth-century conquerors Nadir Shah, of Persia, and Ahmad Shah Durrani, the founder of Afghan statehood, were forced to pay tribute to the tribes of the Khyber Pass—a region known as Yaghistan, or land of rebels—to obtain passage to India.[51] Individual Afghan tribes continued to collect private head taxes on merchants and travelers well into the nineteenth century.

Thus, from the seventeenth century on, the booming maritime trade, the insecurity of the Lahore-Kandahar and Peshawar-Kabul roads, and the Persian-Ottoman and Moghul-Persian wars cut down the great flow of overland trade across Afghanistan. Much of the trade sent overland was routed by way of Central Asia (Bukhara), and major commodities of Indo-Persian trade like sugar and tea, which previously had been supplied through the Afghan territory, began to be transported mainly via the Persian Gulf.[52]

The collapse of effective central power and the decline of overland trade undermined the development of Afghanistan's urban economy and hardened the framework of feudal society, increasing the power of the feudal lords and the tribal chieftains. The urban centers and the merchant class were subjected to arbitrary fiscal, judicial, and administrative measures. Nor were the Muslim guilds strong enough to resist the political and fiscal encroachments of the feudal lords and local authorities; the position of the guilds was especially weak because they had no legal foundation in Islamic law. Religious opposition to banking and usury limited membership in certain guilds—notably those that practiced banking—to Jews, Christians, and Hindus, who were not subject to the Islamic strictures. Moreover, the institution of polygamy and the Islamic laws of inheritance tended to stifle economic development and prevent any concentration of private property, since they fostered constant fragmentation.[53] As the urban economy grew weak, artisans, skilled craftsmen, and guilds declined in number and in political importance. The artisans as a class became increasingly dependent on feudal patronage. The growing power of the feudal lords was a formidable obstacle to urban attempts at self-regulation and self-government, and a serious impediment to the socioeconomic development of Afghanistan.

Chapter Two

Divisive Forces: Ethnic Diversity, Sectarianism, and Social Organization

Nowhere is the difficult legacy of Afghanistan more sharply revealed than in her ethnic mosaic and socioeconomic structure. Linguistic, racial, cultural, and religious diversities, coupled with the country's predominantly semifeudal, tribal, and nomadic social organization, presented great obstacles to the development of a modern state. A history of political instability and a primitive communications system impeded the development of a homogeneous culture and a unified economy, sustaining and prolonging the parochialism that discouraged national and social integration.

THE AFGHANS

The Afghans are the principal ethnic group in the country, comprising an estimated 50 to 55 per cent of the population.[1] The rest are of Tajik-Iranian, Turko-Mongol, or other stock.* According to Schurmann:

All of southern Afghanistan, with the exception of small Tajik and Hazara settlements, is populated by Afghans. . . . Though Pashto [an Iranian tongue] is the principal language of the south, the Kabuli and Herati Afghans, as well as most of the Afghans north of the Hindu Kush, speak Persian. In the colloquial speech, the ethnic term Pashtun is rarely used: an Afghan is called an Afghan, differentiating him from Tajiks, Hazaras, Uzbeks, etc. The Afghans are ethnically and linguistically allied with the Pathans of Pakistan, who inhabit the region of the North-West Frontier Province and eastern Baluchistan.[2]

---

* Bellew (*Afghanistan*, p. 209) notes that "the people of Afghanistan, in fact, are not a mixed race in the sense of miscegenation; on the contrary, they are a conglomeration of several distinct nationalities . . . more or less completely distinct from the others. The Afghan is merely the dominant race among them." Percy Sykes (*Afghanistan*, I, 13) also states that "considerable intermixture has taken place," but adds that each race possesses "outstanding features." See also Caroe, *Pathans*, pp. 160, 363. Whereas these writers follow a racial and ethnic line of division, Wilber (*Afghanistan,* 1st ed., p. 65), Humlum (p. 95), and Morgenstierne ("Afghanistan") follow a much safer linguistic division, separating the people of Afghanistan into four basic groups: Ira-

The term Pathan (the Indianized form of Pushtun) is generally used more broadly to include the Pashto-speaking peoples* of both Afghanistan and Pakistan.[3] The term Afghan was not used by the Afghans themselves until comparatively recent times; they called themselves Pushtuneh or Pukhtuneh. Because of the difficulty of drawing clear ethnic and linguistic lines, the terms Pathan and Afghan are often used synonymously. Caroe has attempted to delimit the terms on the basis of geographical, linguistic, cultural, and historical factors. According to him,

A clear distinction can be drawn between those who inhabit plains and open plateaux on the one hand and the highlanders on the other. The former have always been regarded as the senior branch of the race and peculiarly entitled to the Afghan name. They again can be broadly divided into (i) the Western Afghans, of whom the most important are the Abdalis (now known as the Durranis) and the ... Ghilzais, and (ii) the Eastern Afghans, namely the Yusufzais and other kindred tribes of the Peshawar plain and the valleys to the north of it.
The Western Afghans have been subject in history to certain Persian influences which have affected the Durranis even to their language. Their contacts and development lay with the Safawi Empire of Persia, and Herat and Kandahar were their cultural centers. The Eastern Afghans, whom Elphinstone and other early writers called "Berdooraunees," are less amenable to the Persian tradition, partly because their contacts lay with the Mughal Empire which ruled from Delhi. [Their cultural centers were Peshawar and Kabul.] ... Both Eastern and Western are equally entitled to the Afghan name, which has a connotation far wider than that of a subject of the modern Afghan state, founded only in 1747.
In between the Eastern and the Western Afghans, and to some extent keeping them apart, are interposed the highlanders. These include most of the famous names of the North-West Frontier: Afridi, Khatak, Orakzai, Bangash, Wazir, Mahsud, Turi.... The dialects of these tribes have something in common, and all are presented in genealogical legend as descended from a foundling common ancestor named Karlanri, not in the true Afghan line. These are preeminently the Pakhtuns, or Pashtuns.[4]

---

nian, 86 per cent, Turkic, 13 per cent, Dardic, one-half of 1 per cent, and others, one-half of 1 per cent. Such a classification overcomes Afghan objections that foreign authors tend to represent Afghanistan as a multinational political entity.
* There are two main variants of the language of the Pathans and the Afghans: Pukhtu, spoken predominantly by the northeastern tribes, and Pashto, the language of those to the southwest. According to Penzl, the forms Pukhtu, Pushtu, and Pushtun are suggestive of a Peshawar pronunciation of a type not found in Afghanistan, where the usual forms are Pashto or Pashtun (see Penzl's review of Wilber, *Afghanistan,* 2d ed., in the *Journal of American Oriental Society,* April–June 1963, p. 264). Bellew (*Afghanistan,* pp. 216–18) identifies the term Pathan with the Pactea of Herodotus (the thirteenth political division of Darius the Great's empire). He and Raverty give the most plausible etymological explanation of its origin: they derive it from the Tajik word *pasht* (the back of a mountain range), with the derivative form Pashtun and the Indianized form Pathan signifying highlanders (see Bellew, *Races,* pp. 24–25; Raverty, *Notes,* p. 467; see also Field, p. 3; Furon, *L'Iran,* p. 200; Fraser-Tytler, *Afghanistan,* p. 49; and Caroe, *Pathans,* pp. 35–36). The identification of Pactea with Pathan is rejected on linguistic grounds by Morgenstierne ("Afghān," p. 223).

For political reasons such delimitations are unacceptable in both Pakistan and Afghanistan: in Pakistan, because they are thought to lend weight to Afghan irredentism; in Afghanistan, because they provide divisions for the Pathans that rationalize the Durand Agreement of 1893 and justify what the Afghans consider artificial political divisions and boundaries imposed on the region by British imperialism.

The ethnic origin of the Afghans has not been satisfactorily established. In the past, most Afghan authors, in line with popular tradition and tribal genealogies, ascribed a Jewish origin to their people.* According to this tradition, the Afghans were the descendents of the Beni-Israel, who were deported by Buktanasar (Nebuchadnezzar) to Hazara or Hazarajat, believed to be the Arzareth of the Bible.[5] The Western writers who have accepted the theory of the Jewish origin of the Afghans have tried to substantiate it by invoking several factors: Pathan legends and genealogies; common Afghan-Hebraic nomenclature (e.g., Suleiman, Yusuf, and Daoud for Solomon, Joseph, and David); physical resemblances between Afghans and Jews; reported traces of Levitical ritual in the observances of Pathan tribes; certain tribal customs similar to those ordained by the Mosaic code; and the occurrence of the name Kabul in the Old Testament (1 Kings ix.13). As part of their "proof" these authors have questioned why the Afghans, "as ethnically arrogant as any people on earth" and "prejudiced against the Jews," would willingly choose Jews as ancestors.[6]

There is no convincing evidence substantiating the theory of the Jewish origin of the Afghans. There is certainly no relationship between the Pashto and Hebrew languages; nor can reliance be placed on Afghan tribal genealogies, in which facts and chronology are often neglected in favor of legend. A plausible explanation of the origin of the Afghan tradition has been advanced by some modern writers, who hold that the Afghans may have desired to provide a common cultural and ethnic bond between themselves and other Pathan tribes in order to promote unity and to inculcate pride in their alleged pre-Islamic monotheism—goals that could be achieved by accepting a common Biblical ancestry and grafting tribal genealogies onto the Islamic and Biblical traditions.[7]

Modern scholars trace the Afghans to the Irano-Afghan branch of the

---

* See Vansittart (pp. 70–71) for a very interesting article summarizing Maulavi Khairuddin's *Asrarul Afghaniha* (The Secrets of the Afghans), in which the tradition that Afghans are descendants of Melik Talut (King Saul) is elaborated in some detail. According to this tradition, Melik had a grandson named Afghan. He was "distinguished by his corporal strength, which struck terror into demons and genii ... and used frequently to make excursions to the mountains, where his progeny after his death established themselves, lived in a state of independence, built forts, and exterminated the infidels."

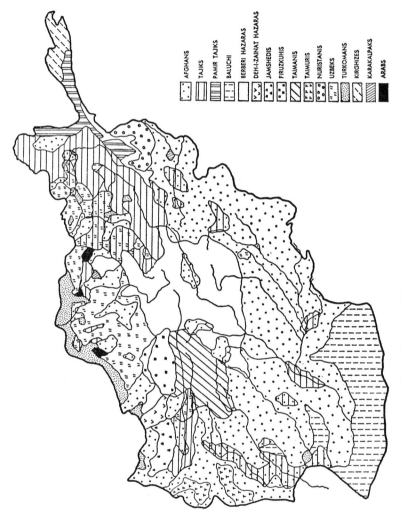

Distribution of Ethnic Groups in Afghanistan

AFGHANS
TAJIKS
PAMIR TAJIKS
BALUCHI
BERBERI HAZARAS
DEH-I-ZAINAT HAZARAS
JAMSHEDIS
FIRUZKUHIS
TAIMANIS
TAIMURIS
NURISTANIS
UZBEKS
TURKOMANS
KIRGHIZES
KARAKALPAKS
ARABS

Indo-European or Aryan peoples, with some admixture of Turkic, Mongol, and other groups. The first mention of a people suggestive of Afghans* dates from the sixth century, when the Indian astrologer Varaha Mihira referred in his *Brhat Samhita* to "Avagana," presumably Afghans, living within the territory of what is now eastern Afghanistan.[8] In the seventh century, the Chinese pilgrim Hsuan Tsang spoke of "A-p'o'kien," a people suggestive of Afghans, and located them more precisely in the area of the Suleiman Range. He reported: "They are hard and fierce by nature.... Their manners are rough, but they are superior to their neighbors in the candour of their faith."[9]

The earliest mention of Afghans in Muslim sources is to be found in the work of the Arab chronicler Ibn'l Athir (976)[10] and in the anonymous Persian geography *Hūdūd al-'Alam* (982). In the Persian work the Afghans are described as a small population inhabiting the region of the Suleiman Range. Al-Utbī, the secretary of King Mahmud of Ghazni, reported in his eleventh-century work *Tarikh-i-Yamini* that the Afghans formed a contingent in the Ghaznawid monarch's army. Much later, al-Bīrūnī identified various Afghan tribes located along the frontier of western India. In *Tabakat-i-Nasiri*, Juzjānī mentioned that Afghans were among the mercenaries of Ulugh Khan who participated in the invasion of India around 1260. In an early-fourteenth-century work, *Tarikhnama-i-Herat*, written by al-Harāwī, Afghanistan is designated as the region lying between Sistan (west), Ghur-Zamindawar-Zabulistan (north), Makran (south), and Sind-Hindustan (east), and centered around Mastung (Quetta). Ibn Battuta, who passed through Kabul in 1333, claimed that he met "a tribe of Persians called Afghans" who lived in the Suleiman Range, "possessed considerable strength, and were mostly highwaymen."

---

* The etymology of the name Afghan is uncertain. Amir Abdur Rahman Khan, using a Pushtu history, *Tazkirat ul-Muluk*, as the basis of his information, stated that the Afghans took their name from Afghana, the commander-in-chief of King Solomon, and that some Afghans were descended from Afghana and others from Jeremiah, the son of Saul (see Curzon, *Tales of Travel*, pp. 72–73). According to Malcolm (II, 596), some held that the name Afghan meant "lamentation" and was given to the descendants of the Beni-Israel because they never ceased lamenting the deportation of their ancestors "from their ancient home in Syria." Caroe (*Pathans*, pp. 79–80) writes that he is "tempted to see the earliest mention of Afghans in two Sassanian designations of the word 'abgan' (by Shapur II and Shapur III)." However, we should not be misled by phonetic similarities: the words Abgan and Apakan were used to designate the ancient inhabitants of what is now Soviet Azerbaijan; both words appear constantly in that context in fifth-century Armenian literature (see Dashxurançi). Vivien de Saint-Martin in *Année géographique* (1863) states that the word derives from the Sanskrit *acvaka*, or *asaka*, meaning horsemen (cited in Reclus, p. 59). According to a legend current in nineteenth-century Afghanistan, Afghan meant free (Bellew, *Journal*, pp. 56–57).

Qāzwinī, in a work entitled *Tarikh-i-Guzida*, complained that the Afghans caused much trouble in southern Persia in the middle of the fourteenth century.[11] According to Schurmann, "In Babur's time, the term Afghanistan was still used in a restricted sense to describe the country south of Ghazni which was inhabited by Afghans. However, from the end of the thirteenth century on, Afghans are mentioned in the Kirman-Yazd-Fars regions of Persia, fighting as mercenaries of the Kurt rulers of Herat, and plundering caravans going between Persia and India."[12] For the most part, the expansion of the Afghans from the area of the Suleiman Range between the eleventh and eighteenth centuries and the nature of early Afghan society remain unstudied.[13]

The largest and most important Afghan tribe is the Abdali or Durrani tribe. The name Durrani probably derives from Duri-i-Duran (Pearl of Pearls), a title adopted by Ahmad Shah Abdali, the founder of the modern Afghan state.* The present ruling dynasty of Afghanistan and a number of the most prominent families in the country are members of this tribe. There are between one and two million Durranis, living primarily in the regions west and southeast of Kandahar and in Chaman.[14] They are divided into seven subtribes: the Popalzai, Barakzai, Alizai, Nurzai, Ishakzai, Achakzai, and Alikozai.[15] The Sadozai clan (an offshoot of the Popalzai subtribe) and the Muhammedzai clan (an offshoot of the Barakzai) are the two Afghan royal clans; with some brief interruptions, they have alternated on the throne of Afghanistan for the last two centuries. The present Afghan royal family belongs to the Muhammedzai clan. The Durranis not only dominate the Afghan political scene but also represent the strongest economic segment among the Afghans, possessing large flocks and vast lands (arable as well as pasture) between Herat and Kandahar.

* The name might have an earlier origin than suggested. A Persian manuscript indicates that the Afghans in the region of Herat were known as Durranis long before Ahmad Khan ascended the Afghan throne (see C. Hamilton, p. 75). Malcolm (II, 599), Elphinstone (Appendix A), Dubeux and Valmont (p. 23), and J. Fraser (*Historical and Descriptive Account*, pp. 319–20), all attribute the origin of the name Durrani to superstition. They claim that Ahmad Khan, acting on the advice of a holy man (which was based on a dream), assumed the title Dur-i-Duran, meaning "Age of Fortune," and changed the name of his tribe accordingly. Boulger (*Central Asian Questions*, p. 50) suggests the meaning "Pearl of Age," whereas P. Sykes (*Persia*, II, 311, and *Afghanistan*, I, 353) and Fraser-Tytler (*Afghanistan*, p. 62) give the translation "Pearl of Pearls." Caroe (*Pathans*, p. 256) agrees with the translation "Pearl of Pearls," attributing its background to Ahmad Khan's habit of wearing a pearl earring. A similar explanation was given in the nineteenth century by Atkinson (p. 10). The Afghan historian Kohzad (*Men and Events*, p. 2) uses the title "Duray Duran," which he translates as "Pear of Lusture" (sic).

The second-largest Afghan tribe appears to be the Ghilzai. (Some authorities claim the tribe is larger than the Durrani.) Scholars do not all agree that the Ghilzais are ethnically related to the Afghan tribal family; some trace their origin to the Khilich (Khilij or Khalji) Turks, who at one time lived along the upper course of the Jaxartes River.[16] For many years the Durranis and the Ghilzais fought each other for supremacy. In the early eighteenth century the Ghilzais gained ascendancy, occupying Kandahar and for a brief period (1721–29) extending their rule over the Persian kingdom, but their power was broken by Nadir Shah, the famous ruler of Persia; eventually they were completely subdued by Ahmad Shah (1747).

The Ghilzais live in the region between Kandahar and Ghazni. During their ascendancy in the eighteenth century, the Hotak subtribe was dominant among them. At present the Suleiman Khel is apparently the largest and most important subtribe; others are the Tokhi, Andar, Ali Khel, Nassar, and Tarakhi. The Ghilzais have been estimated to number anywhere from 100,000 families, comprising between 600,000 and something over one million people, to "the most numerous of all Afghan tribes."[17]

The other important tribes are the Waziris, the Khattaks, the Afridis, the Mohmands, the Yusufzais, and the Shinwaris; along with such smaller tribes as the Jadrans, the Khugianis, and the Safis, they comprise most of the remaining Pashto-speaking people of Afghanistan.[18] The Waziris live on both sides of the Afghan-Pakistan border. There are more than a quarter of a million of them, the majority in Pakistan. Their two main branches are the Ahmedzais and the Utmanzais.[19] The Mahsud tribe, whose members are related to the Waziris, is made up of the Alizai, Balozai, and Shaman subtribes, which are divided into many clans. There are an estimated 50,000–100,000 Mahsuds.

The Khattaks, who have been described by one English authority as "the most favorable specimens of Pathan on the whole frontier," live in the vicinity of Kohat, Peshawar, and Mardan. The tribe is divided into the Teri, Taraki, and Bolak subtribes; its structure is the most complex among the Afghan tribes.[20] The Khattaks number between 100,000 and 160,000.

The Afridis, who are divided into eight subtribes (Adam, Aka, Kambar, Kamar, Kuki, Zakka, Malikdin, and Sipah), live in the range of hills between Jalalabad and Peshawar and number about 250,000. As guardians of the Khyber Pass and a constant source of trouble, the Afridis at one time received subsidies from the Moghul, British, and Afghan governments to guarantee the safety of merchants and travelers. Moreover, the Afghan monarchy and later the British in India were forced to abandon their efforts to collect taxes from the tribe.*

Among the other frontier tribes, the Mohmands are of particular importance. Divided into some 12 subtribes and major clans (the Alamzai, Tarakzai, Dawezai, Baizai, Musazai, Sapi, Kayakzai, Shilmani, Khwaezai, Mandi, Matanni, and Sirganni), with perhaps 200,000 members altogether, the Mohmands live on both sides of the Durand Line in an area extending north of the Kabul River to the border of Bajaur and in the district of Peshawar. During the nineteenth century, their strategic location, military strength, and reputation as fighters allowed them to tax passing merchants and travelers at will.†

Two tribes live near the Mohmands. To the east are the Yusufzais and their related tribes, who occupy part of the range of hills between Jalalabad and Peshawar; to the north are the Shinwaris, who number some 80,000. In the past the Shinwaris were mule breeders and freight handlers. Because of their commercial interests, they were extremely jealous of their independence (as were most of the eastern Afghan tribes) and were a constant source of trouble for the Afghan government. In the late nineteenth century, the Shinwaris were effectively subdued for the first time in modern Afghan history by Abdur Rahman Khan. In 1928, they rebelled, precipitating the fall of the reformer-monarch Amanullah.

The tribal belt along the Afghanistan-Pakistan border also is the home of some other tribes, including the Bajauri (125,000), the Bangash (10,000–25,000), the Orakzai (80,000), the Daur or Dawar (20,000–50,000), the Jaji (40,000), and the Turi (20,000–25,000).[21]

THE TAJIKS

The Tajiks are the second-largest ethnic group in Afghanistan. They speak Persian, live a sedentary life, and are the most probable aboriginal

* In the sixteenth century, the Afridis collected 125,000 rupees a year from the Moghul Empire in addition to levies on individual travelers. Afghan rulers continued paying them tribute throughout the nineteenth century (see Spain, *Pathan Borderland,* p. 46n); in exchange, the Afridis agreed to keep the Khyber Pass open Mondays and Thursdays (see Burnes, *Travels,* II, 97; Dubeux and Valmont, p. 19; Muhammed Abdul Kerim Munshi, in Schérzer and Léger, pp. 361–62; J. Gray, p. 5; see also Spain, *People of Khyber,* Chap. 6). According to Toynbee (*Oxus and Jumna,* pp. 16–17), this "ancient tribute" has dwindled to mere bus fare, since the Khyber bus service is handled largely by Afridis. See also Spain, *Pathan Borderland,* p. 47.
† Burnes wrote that "they demanded half a rupee of every Mahommedan, and double of the sum of a Hindu, but much less satisfied them, though they quarrelled about its distribution" (*Travels,* II, 98).

inhabitants of the country.* They live chiefly around Kohistan and Kabul, and in the valleys of the Panjshir River and the Upper Oxus. Despite heavy losses suffered at the hands of foreign and nomadic invaders, the Tajiks remained the most important element of the sedentary population, representing until two or three decades ago the bulk of the urban population and of the merchant and artisan class of Afghanistan. Afghan sources estimate that they constitute 30 per cent of the population.[22]

According to Schurmann, the name Tajik covers a number of other distinct ethnic groups, among them the Persian-speaking inhabitants of the Herat oasis and adjacent oases in western Afghanistan, who are alternately known as Tajiks or Heratis; the Persian-speaking inhabitants of Afghan Turkestan; the so-called Tajik semi-nomads, who live in the Dara-i-Shikari Valley; and the Mountain Tajiks, who live in the area between the western Paropamisus Mountains and the Soviet-Chinese Pamirs. Though in general the Tajiks, like the Hazaras, have Mongoloid features, many of the Mountain Tajiks have Dinaric features.[23]

THE HAZARAS

The Hazaras, the third-largest ethnic group in Afghanistan, are estimated to number between 400,000 and one million.[24] In the past, historians believed they were the descendants of the soldiers of the Mongol-Tatar regiments (*mings*) who came to Afghanistan as garrison troops during the Mongol campaigns of the thirteenth century.† Modern scholars, especially Bacon, Shinobu, and Schurmann, reject such an oversimplified identification. According to Schurmann, the Hazaras represent a mixed popu-

---

* There are many conflicting theories about the origin of the Tajiks. Soviet historians reject the theory that they are of Aryan origin, contending that they were not latecomers but rather were formed of the most ancient ethnic groups of the region (see, for example, Gafurov, I, v). Some Western historians believe the Tajiks are the descendants of the ancient Bactrians, who were called Ta-hia by the Chinese traveler Chian-K'ien in 128 B.C. (see Fraser-Tytler, *Afghanistan*, pp. 54–55; Wilber, *Afghanistan*, 1st ed., p. 45; and Grousset, Auboyer, and Buhot, p. 66). Others have claimed that the term tajik (Arabic *taz*) was used to denote "anything of Arab origin produced or reared out of Arabia, especially in Persia" (Bellew, *Afghanistan*, pp. 223–24), or that it applied to ethnic groups in Central Asia who had retained the Persian language (Barthold, *Four Studies*, I, 63–64). This interpretation agrees with that of Elphinstone, who wrote (p. 99) that the term "Taujik applied to all people of Afghanistan whose vernacular language is Persian."

† In Persian the word *hazar* means one thousand; its application in this case is the equivalent of *min* or *ming*, meaning a camp or military division by thousands (Bellew, *Afghanistan*, pp. 204–5). According to Vigne (p. 168), the Hazaras were so called because of "the innumerable *taifa*, or tribes, into which they are divided."

lation made up of "an Iranian substratum with a heavy Mongolian over-
lay." He states:

There is no link between Mongols and Hazaras at the present time. However,
that fact does not exclude an earlier link. The large Mongolian element in the
Hazara dialect alone suggests some fundamental culture contact with Mongols
in the past, or a possible partial Mongol origin for the Hazaras themselves....
Direct linguistic connections between Hazaras and Mongols are difficult
to establish. The Mongol vocabulary of the Hazaras shows characteristics
which are foreign to those of Mogholi.[25]

The main body of the Hazaras, divided into three principal groups—
the Dai-Kundi, Dai-Zengi (Sengi), and Bahsud (Besud)—inhabit the
central mountainous part of the country known as Hazarajat. They are
primarily engaged in agriculture and animal husbandry. Until the second
half of the nineteenth century, a money economy was reportedly unknown
to them.[26] In addition to the Hazarajat Hazaras, Schurmann identifies
six other groups as Hazaras: the Koh-i-Baba, Shaikh Ali (who live near
Bamian and northward past Doab), Badakhshan, Aimaq, and Taimani
Hazaras, and the Berberis (who live around Turbat-i-Jam, southeast of
Meshed in Iran). Most of these groups, too, are sedentary and engage
either in agriculture or in herding; in a few cases they have a mixed
agricultural-pastoral economy. The language of the Hazaras is Persian,
but includes many Turkic and Mongol words. Most of the Hazaras are
Shi'ah Muslims; however, Ismailism is widespread among the Shaikh
Ali Hazaras, and the Aimaq and Taimani Hazaras are Sunni Muslims.[27]

The Hazaras were traditionally treated as a nonconformist, hostile, and
heretical element.* In the early nineteenth century, the Sunni Uzbeks
fought the Shi'ah Hazaras more than once in the name of religious unity

---

* In the middle of the nineteenth century, certain Hazara tribes were persecuted as
Shi'ah Muslims by the Uzbek ruler of Kunduz, Murad Beg—this in spite of the fact
that they were under Afghan sovereignty (see Dianous, "Hazaras," Part 1, p. 85).
John Wood (pp. 133–34), writing about a slave party of Hazaras owned by Kabulis,
reported that the Afghans in general thought the practice of slavery fitting only for
Uzbeks. According to Burnes ("Description of Bokhara," p. 232), the Uzbeks were
the chief traffickers in slavery. In the 1860's, Vambery (*Sketches,* pp. 212–13) spoke
of Persian, Jamshidi, and Hazara slaves, all of them Shi'ah Muslims. John Gray
(pp. 211–12), the private physician of Amir Abdur Rahman Khan, wrote in the 1890's
that "in Kabul a short time ago, a Hazara baby was bought for half a crown, and
the purchaser got the mother for fifteen shillings." One source, noting that the Shi'ah
Hazaras were at times traded between Taimanis and Uzbeks for guns, ammunition,
and horses, reported that "nearly every well-to-do establishment in Afghan Turkestan
has one or two Hazara slaves" (Holdich, *Gates of India,* p. 253). Another stated that
the Hazaras furnished a large quota of slaves, "frequently in lieu of arrears of revenue
or when there was difficulty in realizing government assignments against different
villages" (Angus Hamilton, *Afghanistan,* pp. 168–69).

and purity, but religion often served merely as a pretext for subjugating them, seizing their land, taxing them heavily, or enslaving them.[28] The Hazaras of Hazarajat fought off incursions and managed to remain autonomous, paying only nominal allegiance to the Afghan government until the 1880's, when they were completely subjugated by Abdur Rahman Khan after a bitter struggle. According to many Western scholars, most of the Hazara lands were taken over by the Afghans. Slavery was officially abolished in Afghanistan in 1895, but the Hazaras continued to have little economic or social status.

As a result of political upheavals or because of their own depressed position within Afghanistan, many Hazaras were forced to leave their traditional homeland in central Afghanistan. Some moved to Quetta in Baluchistan, others to Meshed or to other foreign cities, still others to Kabul, and some (notably the Berberis) to the area around the Iranian frontier. Some Hazaras enlisted in the Pioneer regiments of the Indian army, were organized as a battalion in 1903, and served in France and Mesopotamia during World War I. At the beginning of the twentieth century, Habibullah Khan granted amnesty to the Hazara political refugees who had been banished from the country by his father; as a result several thousand reportedly returned to Afghanistan and settled in Afghan Turkestan.

TURKIC MINORITIES: THE UZBEKS, TURKOMANS, AND QIZIL-BASH

The Uzbeks, the largest Turkic-speaking group in Afghanistan, are estimated to number 1–1.5 million.[29] They live mainly in the northern part of the country. Until the end of the nineteenth century, they formed ten semi-independent petty khanates and were predominantly nomadic. Today the majority have settled near the major towns of northern Afghanistan—Mazar-i-Sharif, Maimana, Khanabad, and Kunduz—or in the provinces of Kataghan and Badakhshan. Most Uzbeks are farmers, merchants, or craftsmen; some breed horses and karakul sheep, which provide the familiar Persian lamb, the country's most valuable export item.[30]

The Turkomans (Turkomen) are another substantial Turkic group within the country. Divided into seven tribes, they live chiefly along the southern bank of the Oxus and in the towns of Bala Murghab, Daulatabad, and Aktcha. They are predominantly nomadic or semi-nomadic, and in the past often moved freely across the Persian and Russian borders.[31] Mostly stockbreeders, they too breed karakul sheep. Most of the Turkomans are in two main tribes, the Salor and the Ersari. In 1880, the Ersaris furnished substantial military help to Abdur Rahman Khan in his effort to assume full power, and many Turkomans were later recruited into his cavalry.[32] The total Turkoman population may be as high as 380,000, though most recent estimates have been nearer 200,000.[33] Apart from the difficulty of obtaining accurate population figures, political developments in Central Asia (e.g., Russian advances in the region, the first demarcation of the Russo-Afghan boundary in 1887, the October Revolution in 1917) have caused considerable fluctuation in the size of the Turkoman population of Afghanistan.

The Qizil-Bash, who settled in Kabul in the early eighteenth century as garrison troops of Nadir Shah, are also of Turkic origin. Estimated to number from 50,000 to 100,000, they profess the Shi'ah form of Islam.[34] The Qizil-Bash were an important fighting force in the Afghan civil wars of the eighteenth and nineteenth centuries. They later drifted into trades and crafts, as well as the armed forces and other government services. Some of them migrated from Kabul to the Punjab in 1842. Small numbers of Qizil-Bash apparently live today in isolated areas in the high valley of Foladi.[35]

OTHER MINORITIES

Several other minority ethnic groups in Afghanistan deserve notice. The Chahar Aimak (Aimaq), or Four Tribes, are an Iranian-speaking group made up of several tribes: the Jamshidis, Firuzkuhis, Taimanis, Timuris, and Hazara-i-Qala'-i Nau.* They seem to be a mixture of Turkic, Mongol, and Tajik elements, and their language resembles modern Persian, although it includes a large number of Turkic words. Except for the Taimuri tribe, they are mostly Shi'ah Muslims. Data on the history of the Chahar Aimak are scanty. At one time they lived a semi-nomadic life. In 1815, their number was estimated at half a million, a figure that seems grossly exaggerated; current estimates range between 200,000 and 300,000.[36]

---

* According to A. C. Yate (*England and Russia*, p. 230), the name Aimak designates a semipastoral, semiagricultural tribe "generally of Persian origin and speaking Persian." C. E. Stewart (pp. 369–70) wrote that Chahar Aimak meant four nomads, and that the word *aimak* was used in Herat to denote a nomad. According to him, the Timuris had their headquarters at Khaf in Iran, but most of them lived in Afghanistan, near Sabzawar; the Jamshidis lived near Kushk and claimed to have come from Sistan; and the Firuzkuhis and the Hazara-i-Qala'-i Nau also claimed to have been brought to Afghanistan from Persia. Schurmann (pp. 50, 53), who does not classify the Timuris as Chahar Aimak, suggests that the Chahar Aimak might have established themselves as an ethnic group during the reign of Babur, in the early sixteenth century.

The Nuris, or Kafirs, one of the Indo-Aryan peoples of the Hindu Kush, are another ethnic group whose history is obscure. Some think that they are the descendants of the aborigines of central Afghanistan; others believe them to be of Greek extraction. Their physical features are suggestive of Oriental, Dinaric, and Nordic elements, but of the five main Kafir languages—Kati, Ashkun, Waigal, Paruni, and Wamai—four are Dardic. The Nuris, who number between 40,000 and 100,000,[37] were at one time divided into two groups, the Siahpush (clothed in black) and the Sefidpush (clothed in white). The first group consisted of five tribes and the second of three.

Before the Nuris accepted Islam, they were referred to as Kafirs (infidels) by the Muslims. The only major pagan group inside Afghanistan, they professed a polytheistic religion that combined elements of animism, fire worship, and ancestor worship.[38] Torn by intratribal and blood feuds, Kafir society at the end of the nineteenth century presented a peculiar socioeconomic system that included Shaikhs (Kafirs converted to Islam), a slave community, a distinct class structure, an economy based on barter, and common family ownership of property.*

The Kafirs were often the targets of Muslim *jihads* (holy wars). Islam had made some inroads in Kafiristan in the nineteenth century, but it was only in 1895–96 that the Kafirs were forcibly converted to Islam by Abdur Rahman Khan; their Islamization was completed during the rule of Habibullah Khan. To mark the triumph of Islam, the country of the Kafirs was given the name Nuristan (Country of Light, i.e., illuminated by Islam). The people were dubbed Nuris, or Jadids, since they had come to belong to the land of Jadid-ul-Islam or New Islam.[39]

The Baluchis, numbering between 20,000 and 40,000, live along the southern and southwestern frontiers of Afghanistan. Most of them speak Baluchi, an Iranian tongue; a smaller number speak Brahui, a Dravidian language. It is believed that they are the survivors of one of the last of the Indo-European migrations from Central Asia that occurred during the early centuries of the Christian era. Predominantly pastoral nomads, the Baluchis until recently lived an isolated life. In the nineteenth century,

---

* Burnes (*Travels*, II, 142), Lal ("Siah Posh Tribe," pp. 76–77), and Dubeux and Valmont (pp. 105–6) give only secondhand reports about Kafir society and institutions. According to Burnes, the Kafirs lived in an almost barbaric state, "eating bears and monkey." He asserted that "women have no place in Kafir society save as beasts of burden and bearers of children," and that the Kafirs were "highly immoral and repulsively dirty." The only firsthand and authoritative account of Kafir society and its structure is that of Sir George Robertson, who spent the year 1890–91 in Kafiristan. See his *Kafirs*, particularly pp. 72–75, 84–87, 100–110, 181–90, 434–38, 474–77, 561 ff. See also Raverty, "Notes on Kaffiristan."

Baluchi tribal elements disrupted commercial relations between Iran and Afghanistan with constant raids in the province of Sistan.[40]

In addition to the groups discussed above, there are some 30,000 to 45,000 people in Afghanistan who speak other languages, including Lahunda (an Indian language), Parachi, Urmuri, and Pashai (Indo-Iranian languages), Mongolian, and Arabic. There is also a small group that speaks an Iranian tongue, Pamiri; this group has several villages in the Wakhan region, which borders on China, Pakistan, and the USSR, and is believed to number between 45,000 and 75,000, only a smaller number of whom live in Afghanistan.[41]

RELIGIOUS DIVERSITY

Though 99 per cent of the Afghans profess Islam, the country is divided religiously. Most Afghans are Sunnis of the Hanafi school; most of the rest are Shi'ah Muslims. There are no precise figures on the ratio of Sunni to Shi'ah Muslims. Official Afghan sources state that "more than 90 per cent of the Afghan Muslims are Sunni," but there are indications that the Sunni majority probably does not exceed 75–80 per cent of the total population. The Shi'ah form of Islam is professed by the Hazaras, some Tajiks, and several groups scattered throughout the country, including the Qizil-Bash, a majority of the Chahar Aimak, and the Kayanis of Sistan and Herat. There are also adherents of Shi'ah Islam among the frontier Pathan tribes, notably the Turis. In the mountainous regions of Badakhshan and Wakhan there is a large community of Isma'ilis (extreme Shi'ahs) who are known as Mulla'is; a rough estimate sets their number at 300,000. Certain frontier subtribes, among them the Muhammed Khel of the Orakzai tribes, are classified by some as Shi'ah Muslims and by others as Roshanis, or followers of the religious reformer Bayazid Ansari. There are also reports of a scattered number of followers of the Ahmadiya sect in the region of Khost.[42]

There are two numerically insignificant non-Muslim religious communities in Afghanistan: the Hindus and the Jews. Their small numbers, however, belie their historical importance. They played a major role in the trade of Afghanistan as merchants, moneylenders, grain sellers, scribes, and even officers of the Afghan treasury. There are no Christians among the Afghans; there are a few foreign women married to Afghans, but they are considered Muslim in the eyes of the state. There was once a small Christian community of Armenians; established as a colony by Nadir Shah, it had dwindled to only a few families before its expulsion in 1896.

The differences between the Sunni and Shi'ah Muslim communities were a major problem for those who wanted to build a modern Afghan state. Neither group represented a homogeneous social force, and neither had developed uniform and centralized institutions. Different stages of socioeconomic development were reflected in the two communities' religious institutions. Among the nomad Sunnis, for instance, institutional developments were less advanced than among the sedentary groups. As for the Afghan tribes, both Sunni Islam and the Shar'ia (religious) law had to coexist with local practices and with the Pushtunwali, or Afghan tribal code. Moreover, Muslim sectarianism often divided the Sunnis and the Shi'ahs themselves, witness the Roshani movement in eastern Afghanistan, Sufism in western Afghanistan (Khorassan), the Nakshibandi dervish order in the northern regions.[43]

In the past, social organization, ethnic and linguistic ties, and regional economic interests sometimes transcended the importance of religious affinity; for instance, in the seventeenth century, Shi'ah and Sunni communities alike suffered in the three-way wars between the Shi'ah Persians, the Sunni Uzbeks, and the Sunni Moghuls. However, in general Shi'ah Muslims were traditionally subjected to a variety of exactions, and religious affinity was often regarded as an excuse for economic and political demands or for the extension of political control. In the nineteenth century, after the collapse of centralized political power in the Afghan kingdom, the Shi'ahs of northern and central Afghanistan were subject to Uzbek raids and heavily taxed, and many of them were enslaved.[44]

The builders of the modern Afghan state and the ideologues of Afghan nationalism, faced with social tensions arising from religious animosity and historical antagonism, had to rely on the Sunni Afghans as the dominant political force in order to promote cohesion within the country; at the same time, they had to emphasize tenets of Islam that would be acceptable to both sects. The ultimate aim of both the Afghan monarchy and the Afghan nationalists was to make Islam an important element of Afghan nationalism and a major force in the unification of the country.

AFGHAN TRIBALISM

The first Afghan rulers, faced with ethnic and religious divisions within the country and threats of foreign encroachments without, were forced to rely on the military power of the Afghan and Pathan tribes to preserve the position of the monarchy, the preeminence of the Afghan ethnic element, and the integrity of the Afghan kingdom. Despite the attempts of the Afghan monarchs to broaden their political base and to pursue a policy of centralization, their dependence on the strength of the Afghan tribes committed them to defending the feudal tribal social structure.

Though individual tribes had varying traditions, theoretically each tribe was composed of agnatic kin groups claiming a common ancestor, real or legendary. The main core of each tribe (*kaum* or *qaum*) was surrounded by various subtribes or large clans, which were designated by the word khel or the suffix -zai (zay) or -i. (Thus, for example, Suleiman Khel, Muhammedzai, Hotaki.)* The subtribes were divided into extended family units or clans, which were also often designated as khels; certain smaller units were called kors or kahols. The clans generally lived in an ancestral territory and often held land in common.

Within a tribe, the families of a khel chose an elder or chief, the *malik*. The maliks in turn elected a khan, who was the leader of the tribe. As certain tribes developed feudal ties with the Safawid and Moghul emperors, and later with the Afghan ruling dynasties, the choice of the tribal chieftains had to be sanctioned by their feudal lords. Other considerations in the choice of leaders were primogeniture, age, experience, and character. Among the tribes whose feudal relations were highly developed, the eldest son customarily succeeded his father in time of peace, but there was no rigid law of succession. During hard times or in period of war, leadership often went to the ablest member of a family; sometimes it was even acquired by a non-member of a family in which the office had become hereditary. Often in time of war a *toelwashtu* (magistrate or leader) was elected by the leaders of the clans. He was given broad powers, which were to be relinquished when his period of office expired or when the emergency ended. The flexibility of the law of succession encouraged the development of tribal disputes and intrigues; existing alliances lapsed, and new ones were formed between factions and clans bidding for the leadership of a tribe. The lack of a firm succession law affected the Afghan ruling dynasty itself and hindered the development of the monarchy as an institution.

In dealing with the Afghan tribes, the Afghan monarchs were subject to the same limitation of authority as the tribal chieftains. Their actions had to conform to Shar'ia law, to the Pushtunwali, and especially to the decisions of the *jirgas,* or tribal councils. The jirga was based on the con-

---

* The suffix -*zai,* which is added to the name of most of the Afghan clans, does not necessarily indicate simply common descent. It has also been used to indicate a common cause, grouping, or even political affiliation. For instance, during the Second Anglo-Afghan War, one segment of the Kabuli population was termed Cavagnarizai (pro-British) and another Yakubzai (pro-Afghan). See Bellew, *Races,* p. 111.

cept of communal authority; theoretically, every tribesman was both soldier and lawmaker and could aspire to leadership. As an institution, the jirga reflected the distinctive features of an Afghan tribalism in which the attachment of the individual was to the tribal community rather than to the chief; rarely could a chief induce a tribe to take any major action that was not consistent with the interests or honor of the tribe. In cases involving internal disputes or temporary tribal alliances, the jirgas were all-powerful. Frequently, they amended or repudiated the decisions of the maliks or khans. With its democratic spirit and tenets, the jirga defied political centralization, and its constant accommodation of regional interests made it a particularly divisive force in the drive to form a modern and unified state.

Another institution that defied centralization of political power and legal and economic encroachment was the Pushtunwali, or Pathan tribal code, which set the limits of acceptable behavior within the community and governed the relations between tribes. In theory, the system of tribal law was complete; in cases of doubt, it allowed only interpretation. A few of its positive injunctions—for instance, *nanawatai, melmastia,* and *badragga* (respectively, the laws of asylum and intercession, hospitality and protection for all guests, and safe conduct)—were moral restraints that checked lawlessness. Other features, however, particularly the concept of *nang-i-Pukhtun* or *nang-i-Pukhtana* (Pathan honor), which embodied the principles of equity and *badal,* or revenge at all costs, seriously impeded the development of a secular legal system. As one authority notes: "In appealing to the customary law the injured person is actuated by a desire for redress or revenge. It would afford him little satisfaction to see the man who had robbed him punished, unless he were indemnified for his loss.... There is no conception of a criminal act as an outrage against the peace of the community. There is no state whose peace could be violated, and only a rudimentary conception of a commonwealth. Hence every offense is merely a tort which entitles or requires the person injured to seek redress and obtain it if he can."[45]

Rawaj or *ravaj-i-am* (customary law) was another institution that resisted the process of social, political, and economic integration. The rawaj varied from tribe to tribe and from region to region; in general, it institutionalized local socioeconomic interests. It often not only circumvented the laws of the kingdom but also modified certain tenets of Islamic law, especially in matters of marriage, inheritance, and women's rights. For instance, though Islamic law prescribed that all sons were to inherit equally and that daughters and widows had the right to inherit, some tribes by custom favored the eldest son and denied inheritance rights to women, and others divided the inheritance into as many equal parts as there were wives who had borne sons, and then divided it among the sons on this basis.

Political and economic interests, disputes over water rights, the exigencies of tribal honor, and traditional feuds kept a wide range of rivalries and vendettas alive among the Afghan tribes; the result was constant tribal warfare. (In 1809, Elphinstone reported that there was no tribe in eastern Afghanistan that was not "in a state of actual war or suspended hostilities.")[46] Most of the disputes, if not solved by the bullet, were mediated. Within a tribe the community sometimes interceded in the form of a jirga; the disputants were compelled to accept the decision of the jirga or leave the tribe. Often a third clan or tribe was chosen to settle the differences between two groups. Occasionally, a tribal *lashkar* (a conscripted force) was called upon to enforce the decisions of a tribe. However, this procedure was rare, difficult, and complicated; it seldom stopped feuds and sometimes provoked further outbursts.

The tribes vigorously resisted any regulation that threatened their traditional privileges, especially their property rights. Land was usually held according to tribal or sectional shares.* Land taken by force was generally divided within the tribe on the basis of these shares, and many tribes jealously guarded the privilege of keeping and distributing lands acquired through migration or conquest. Some tribes practiced *wesh* (*vesh*), a periodic redistribution of tribal lands intended to promote tribal cohesion and prevent the growth of economic inequality. Often, however, regional economic interests overrode ethnic and tribal considerations and brought tribesmen into open conflict with their kinsmen. There were, for instance, occasions when the Ghilzais and Tajiks of Logar were allied against the Ghilzais and Tajiks of the Laghman region.[47]

Feudalism developed at an uneven rate among the tribes. Reysner, in his study of the development of feudalism in Afghanistan, distinguishes three degrees of socioeconomic development of the tribes. In one category he includes those tribes having the largest number of feudal ties and the most advanced disintegration of the patrimonial commune system (e.g., the Durranis, the Khattaks); in the second he includes those having a

---

* Traditionally, about half of a tribe's land was set aside for common grazing use. This land was known as the *shamilat*, and the individual's share in it as an *inam*. For the remaining half, a small portion was set aside for other common purposes, including an allotment (*tserai* or *seri*) for the mosque, the mullahs, and other religious luminaries. The rest was divided into roughly equal shares among the major groups of the tribe, who then allotted shares to various subgroups and families. Each adult male in a family was allocated a plot (*bukhra*); the bukhra and the inam together represented the individual tribesman's *daftar*. Abandoned land could be used by anyone, but the original owner or his descendants could claim it and all improvements on it at any time. For details, see Spain, *Pathan Borderland*, pp. 75–84; Caroe, *Pathans*, pp. 182ff.

fairly large number of feudal ties, interwoven, however, with patrimonial ties (e.g., the Yusufzais) ; and in the third he includes those having the fewest feudal ties (e.g., the Waziris, the Afridis).[48] Within the Durrani and Khattak tribes, the commune system was gradually replaced by a patrimonial aristocracy. The leadership became hereditary in one family or clan (khan khel), with a corresponding reduction of the power of the jirga. Within such tribes as the Waziris and the Afridis, which had few feudal ties, the communal system of government prevailed, and the most important matters continued to be decided by jirgas. However, even in cases where the leaders had not acquired full authority, by the early nineteenth century they had gained complete power over the *hamsaya,* the dependent "client" populations who enjoyed the protection of a tribe and were settled on its lands. In tribes like the Yusufzai, which had a fairly large hamsaya population, this authority provided an important basis for the development of a tribal aristocracy.

EARLY ATTEMPTS TO FORM AN AFGHAN STATE

The earliest manifestations of Afghan nationalism can be found in the religious sectarian Roshania (enlightened, illuminated) movement of the sixteenth and seventeenth centuries. Under the leadership of Bayazid Ansari (1525–81) and his successors, whose aim, among other things, was to establish a national religion, the movement encouraged the Afghans in the tribal belt to struggle against Moghul rule. The Roshania movement thus promoted the first political formulation of the concept of Afghan nationality.[49] Khushhal Khan Khattak (1613–89), a celebrated Afghan poet and tribal chieftain, endeavored to inspire the tribes to defend their independence against Moghul encroachments and to strive toward political unity.* Full of pride in Afghan *nang* (honor), he lamented his

---

* In a celebrated poem (in Biddulph, "Afghan Poetry," pp. 109, 113, 114), Khushhal Khan wrote:

> More skilled in the swords are the Pathans than the Moghals,
> Would only more intelligence was theirs.
> Were the tribes but of agreement amongst themselves,
> Emperors would prefer to bow before them.
> . . .
> Devoid are the Pathans of reason and understanding.
> As the dogs in the courtyards of the butchers are they:
> They sold their sovereignty to the Moghals for gold.
> For the titles of the Moghals is all their desire.
> With gold and fair promises have they beguiled the Pathan.
> . . .
> Every deed of the Pathan is better than that of the Moghals.
> Concord is what they lack—the pity of it.

countrymen's lack of discipline, disinclination to close ranks, and religious intolerance or fanaticism, charging them with never looking beyond tribal and personal self-interest. He wrote: "We talk the same language, we both talk Pashto, but we understand not in the least what we say to one another."[50]

Although Khushhal Khan was once chief of the Khattak tribe, he constantly emphasized that he was first of all an Afghan. In his poems he attacked those tribes who remained neutral or indifferent to the national liberation of the Afghans from Moghul rule, and appealed to their honor, love of freedom, longing for independence, and memories of the days when Afghans ruled large parts of India. Death, he wrote, was better than life without honor. The best safeguard for Afghan honor was liberty and independence, which could be achieved and preserved only through unity and concord among the Afghans. Once the Afghans achieved unity, they could not only liberate themselves but establish a political force that would make kings prostrate themselves before them.[51]

Because of the sporadic uprisings of Pathan tribes in the sixteenth and seventeenth centuries, the Moghul emperors were forced to undertake frequent military expeditions, station garrisons, or pay huge subsidies to various tribal chieftains in order to reassert their sovereignty and keep the Peshawar-Kabul road open. Since military measures were costly and more often than not ineffectual or inconclusive, the Moghul authorities in Kabul pursued a delicate policy of divide and rule, hoping that the Afghans would dissipate their energies in tribal warfare.

The Persian Safawids devised a more successful method of coping with the Afghan tribes: they channeled their military forces into the Persian armies and banished or appeased those chieftains who became too powerful or troublesome. At times, they even transplanted whole clans or tribes to various regions of western Afghanistan. Thus, Shah Abbas the Great (1588–1624), in an attempt to break the power of the strong Abdali tribe, transferred large numbers of Abdalis from Kandahar to Herat. However, such measures merely represented a policy of containment; they did not solve the problem presented by the Afghan tribes. By the end of the seventeenth century, only a few tribes had firm feudal relationships with the Persian and Moghul empires; the majority maintained an independent or semi-independent status in their strongholds along the Indian frontier. Persian and Moghul control over the Afghan tribes was tenuous at best, especially in the case of Persia, whose dedication to Shi'ah Islam jeopardized its relations with the predominantly Sunni Afghan tribes.

The first successful attempt to establish an autonomous Afghan state was made in 1709. In that year, following a period of intrigue and conspiracy, Mir Wais (Mir Ways), a prominent Ghilzai chieftain of the Hotak clan, rallied his tribe in a successful revolt against the Persian Empire and assumed power in the city and province of Kandahar, thus providing a base for the nucleus of an Afghan state. The political concepts of the Ghilzais were exceedingly parochial, however; they organized their state on regional rather than national lines and did not aspire to unify all of the Afghan tribes. The successful Ghilzai revolt and the inability of Persia to reassert her sovereignty encouraged separatist movements among other Afghan tribes. In 1716, the Abdali tribe revolted, defeated the Persian forces, took the city and province of Herat, and declared its independence.

Ghilzai power reached its zenith in 1722, when Ghilzai forces inflicted a disastrous defeat on the Persian armies and seized Isfahan, the Safawid capital. The Ghilzai rule was precarious, short, and bloody: as rulers, the Ghilzais were an outnumbered minority; as members of a tribal nomadic society, they were unable to extend or secure their rule over a sedentary urban population with a highly developed culture; as Sunni Muslims, they were isolated from their Shi'ah subjects. In addition, the Ghilzai rulers of Persia and Kandahar feuded among themselves, thereby weakening their military strength. These factors, together with a strenuous Ghilzai rivalry with the Abdali tribe, made the emergence of a secure Afghan state under the aegis of the Ghilzais virtually impossible. The Ghilzai conquest of Persia turned out to be a very costly adventure. It sapped the political and military power of the tribe, it resulted in the neglect of the Ghilzai homelands, and it hampered the institutional development of Ghilzai power in Kandahar.[52]

In 1729, Persian forces led by Tahmasp Quli Khan (1688–1747), later known as Nadir Shah Afshar, expelled the Ghilzais from Persia, wrested political control from the Abdalis in Herat, and reasserted Persian feudal authority over both tribes. After two futile Abdali rebellions, Nadir Shah adopted the traditional Safawid policy toward the Afghan tribes, exiling thousands of Abdalis to Meshed, Nishapur, Damghan, and other Persian cities, and recruiting many Abdali chieftains into his army. Later, to eliminate the threat of Abdali military action in the strategically located and rich province of Khorassan and to use the Abdali forces against the Ghilzais, Nadir Shah transplanted the bulk of that tribe from Herat to the Kandahar region, the Abdalis' former habitat. In 1737, the Abdalis supported Nadir Shah during his final assault on Kandahar, receiving as a reward the lands of the Hotakis, the princely clan of the Ghilzais.[53]

THE DURRANI KINGDOM

The elimination of Ghilzai power by Nadir Shah was historically important for several reasons: it made possible the eventual ascendancy of the Abdali tribe in Kandahar and the subsequent emergence of an Afghan kingdom; it resulted in the unification of eastern, northern, and western Afghanistan for the first time in modern history (1739); and it promoted the development of a unified administration in Afghanistan by reestablishing and extending the feudal relationships between the Persian monarchy and the Afghan tribes.

Nadir was assassinated in 1747. In the ensuing political turmoil in the Persian Empire, the Abdalis, who formed the *corps d'élite* of his army, seized some of his treasures and returned to Kandahar, under the leadership of Ahmad Khan Abdali.* There the Abdali leaders decided to terminate their feudal ties with Persia and to declare the independence of Afghanistan. Ahmad Khan was crowned king (shah) of the Afghans. Though his selection as king was undoubtedly a tribute to his personal valor and political acumen, it helped that he was a member of the comparatively weak Sadozai clan of the Popalzai subtribe of the Durranis. The Afghan chieftains presumably believed that they could remove him from power if he did not act in their interests.[54]

Thus from the outset the Afghan monarchy and the budding Afghan state had to contend with tribal chieftains and feudal lords bent on preserving their privileged positions, a situation that made the task of Ahmad Shah and his successors both difficult and complex. By definition, the Afghan king was the hereditary chief and military commander of the Durrani tribe; nevertheless, he was bound by the will of the Durrani *sardars,* since his rule depended on their good will and military strength. (The heads of the Durrani clans held the military title sardar or sirdar, meaning leader, general, or prince; today, the title is reserved for male members of the royal family.) In such circumstances, the Afghan mon-

---

* According to a Persian manuscript, Ahmad Khan Abdali, as Nadir's treasurer during the conqueror's last expedition to India, "[took] advantage of the universal confusion which succeeded the murder of the tyrant [and] found means to carry off a great part of his wealth, with the care of which he was entrusted by the nature of his employment, into some strong recesses in the hills near Ghôrebund in Zabulistan, which had been the residence of his ancestors. Here he was joined by such of his tribe as had served in Nadir Shah's army and having collected together a body of thirty thousand Durannees ... issued forth into the neighbouring country, which being at present without any acknowledged head, was easily subjected to his authority." See C. Hamilton, p. 75.

arch's first task was to satisfy the interests of his own clansmen, the Popalzais, as well as those of the six other Durrani subtribes, especially the Barakzais, who ranked first in numerical, economic, and political strength.

In order to strengthen his rule over the Durrani clans, Ahmad Shah confirmed their landholdings and bestowed most of the important state offices upon various Durrani chiefs, making these offices either explicitly or implicitly hereditary within specific clans. The office of *ashraf-ul-vuzara* (equivalent to prime minister, or grand vizir) was given to the Bamizai clan; that of *ishikaghassi bashi* (lord chamberlain) to the Popalzais; that of *mir akhor* (master of the horse or royal stables) to the Ishakzais; and that of *arzbegi* (chief petitioner of the court) to the family of Akram Khan, one of the king's adjutants.[55]

In return for contingents of soldiers for his army, Ahmad Shah granted vast *jagirs* (land allotments) in the Kandahar region to the Durrani subtribes. Some subtribes fared better than others; according to Reysner, the Alikozai subtribe received almost one-fourth more land than the Nurzai clan, but provided fewer soldiers. By contrast, the non-Durrani tribes received an insignificant amount of land, but had to provide 50 to 60 per cent more soldiers than the Durranis. Ahmad Shah's land taxation policies also favored the Durrani subtribes. In the province of Kandahar and its adjacent regions, for example, the tax on arid lands was lowered considerably for the Durranis, whereas it was increased for the non-Afghan, mainly Tajik, peasants, who had to pay one-tenth of their gross harvest to the Afghan state. In addition, the collection of taxes from the non-Afghan peasantry was in the hands of various Durrani khans, an arrangement that further enhanced the political and economic position of the Durrani subtribes and contributed to their gradual takeover of the arable lands of the non-Afghan peasants of Kandahar province. Finally, the Durranis, unlike the other subjects of the Afghan kingdom, were not required to pay a capitation tax or taxes on cattle, land, fruit trees, and grapevines.[56]

The new Afghan government, though formally an admixture of the Persian and Moghul administrative systems, was in practice dominated by the Afghan tribal-feudal socioeconomic framework. The monarch's freedom of action was limited by a council of nine Afghan chieftains, whose consultation and advice were mandatory for the adoption of important measures.[57] Although the crown was hereditary, there was no established law of succession. Upon the death of the king, the sardars chose one of his sons to succeed him, giving due consideration to the will of the father, the age and character of the candidate, and above all their own interests. The king controlled the disbursement of revenue, but valuation on land for revenue was far from uniform, and he had no power to increase the land tax, the principal source of income of his kingdom. Some Afghan tribes, jealous of their privileges and autonomy, defied all attempts to collect taxes through a centralized government agency, insisting that collections be left to the malik of each village or clan and that the government be paid through the tribal chieftains. Some Afghan tribes were not subject to any kind of tax assessment, but instead paid an annual fixed sum as a token of their allegiance to the crown. In addition to receiving jagirs, the Durrani clans enjoyed rent-free lands in exchange for their military services. They were also allowed to retain their tribal subdivisions within the army, with the head of each clan commanding the contingent it furnished to the king.

Although the king had the right to wage war, conclude peace, and make treaties, he could not cede any part of the territories occupied by the Afghan tribes without jeopardizing his position.[58] The king's power was further circumscribed by the Muslim religious establishment, which enjoyed economic self-sufficiency and was in charge of learning, education, the interpretation of Shar'ia law, the administration of justice, and the supervision of public morality through the office of the *muhtasib* (a court attendant who checked upon religious observances). Muslim clerics often acted as intermediaries or served as peacemakers for feuding tribes, a role that gave them considerable social and political power.[59]

Thus the Durrani kingdom more closely resembled a confederation of tribes and khanates than a centralized monarchy. In effect, the kingdom was administered by various Afghan and non-Afghan tribal chieftains, the monarchy exercising only a loose suzerainty over them. The resulting de facto commitment to the status quo created a precarious coexistence between two radically different economic systems: a tribal-pastoral-nomadic economy on the one hand, and a declining urban economy on the other.

Ahmad Shah took a number of steps designed to unify his new kingdom politically and economically. To broaden the basis of his support, he appealed to the Afghans' religious ties, common nationality, patriotism, and national honor. He also attempted to strengthen his position with various Afghan tribes by taking wives for himself and his sons from them. In an effort to achieve economic unity, he struck his own coins and attempted to collect taxes and revenues, if not directly, at least on a uniform basis and at regular intervals. His main endeavor was to create a standing army, which would at the same time make the monarchy largely independent of tribal support, bind his vassals and Afghan soldiers to him in personal loyalty, and give the tribes a more suitable outlet for their energies than intertribal feuds. To this end, he adopted a policy of expansionism. He led eight Afghan expeditions into India, and ultimately incorporated the Punjab, Kashmir, and Multan into his empire. His successes not only increased the prestige of the monarchy among the tribes, but strengthened the concept of Afghan nationality by bringing together numerous Pashto-speaking tribes for the first time as allies against a common enemy. Finally, he established new and firmer relationships between the monarchy and various Afghan and non-Afghan tribes by the judicious distribution of the newly acquired lands.[60]

Despite these successes, however, Ahmad Shah was unable in the end to build a comprehensive and systematic feudal structure around the monarchy or to establish a lasting framework of loyalties and obligations, largely because of his inability to create a strong urban economy independent of the tribes. He did his best—among his noteworthy undertakings were the founding of modern Kandahar, the reconstruction of the city of Kabul, the building of Tashkurgan in northern Afghanistan, the patronage of masons and wood carvers, the support of Pashto letters, and the active encouragement of the immigration of artisans from India[61]— but his best was not enough. Ahmad Shah was caught in a difficult dilemma, one that was to face his successors for many years to come. To maintain his rule and consolidate the position of the monarchy he was dependent on the important Afghan tribes; at the same time, the country's long-term interests called for a centralized monarchy on the Persian model, one that would not only be independent of the tribes, but assert its authority over them.

Timur Shah (1773–93), Ahmad Shah's son and successor, was compelled to pursue many of the same policies as his father. He maintained a close alliance with the Barakzais, the most powerful of the Durrani clans, while at the same time making marriage alliances with various influential Afghan and non-Afghan tribes. He retained his father's system of hereditary offices, but established new ones as well for men owing their loyalty directly to him, hoping by this means to minimize the importance of the hereditary offices and retain some freedom of action. For the same reason, he transferred the capital of Afghanistan from Kandahar, which was under the sway of the Durranis, to Kabul, which was inhabited mainly by Tajiks. Timur also continued his father's efforts to create a strong standing army. He raised a 12,000-man cavalry division among the ethnically non-Afghan and religiously Shi'ah Qizil-Bash of Kabul,* and formed a *corps d'élite* composed mainly of Persians and Tajiks, known as *ghulamshahs,* or "slaves" of the king. To gain a firmer control over the rich city of Peshawar and to ensure the steady flow of its revenues, he made it his winter capital. He even attempted to restrict the power of the Afghan mullahs. He used Persian scribes (*munshis*), tried to make the royal court an intellectual and artistic center through his patronage of scholars and artists, and regularly held *Majles-e Ulama* (Assemblies or Councils of the Learned).[62]

In the end, however, Timur succeeded no better than his father in diminishing the political and military power of the tribes. Indeed, certain Durrani clans, whose privileged position was threatened by Timur's policies, openly allied themselves with the powerful Ghilzai tribe, thus weakening the monarchy's position. Like his father, Timur was unable to increase land taxes or to revoke the many economic privileges enjoyed by the powerful tribes, especially since the rising Sikh power in India made him more dependent on military levies than ever. As a result, the non-Afghan ethnic groups and the urban sectors of the country had to bear the main burden of taxation, an unfortunate situation that led to the alienation and weakening of the very forces whose prosperity and collaboration were essential to the effective centralization of Afghanistan.

Ironically, Timur's numerous marital alliances, undertaken to strengthen the position of the monarchy among the Afghan tribes, were instrumental in weakening it further after his death. He left a great many sons— some authorities say 24, others as many as 50 or 60[63]—a number of whom he appointed provincial governors. The unsettled law of succession and the desire of various disgruntled Afghan tribes to preserve or reassert their traditional privileges led to the creation of alliances between tribal chieftains and the various contenders to the throne, inaugurating an era of palace revolutions, protracted civil strife, and anarchy. Zaman Shah, Timur's fifth son, eventually ascended to the throne with the support of the Barakzai clan and the Qizil-Bash of Kabul. Like his father, he attempted to centralize political authority in the hands of the ruling Sadozai clan. He gradually abolished some hereditary offices and in other ways challenged the power of the tribal chiefs.[64]

---

* In the opinion of Fraser-Tytler, the recruitment of a non-Afghan force was a major error on the part of Timur Shah, since it was likely to breed suspicion among the ranks of his Afghan subjects (*Afghanistan,* p. 66). This measure did not originate with Timur, however; Ahmad Shah had also raised a 3,000-man Qizil-Bash corps (see P. Sykes, *Afghanistan,* I, 354; see also Gupta, "Timur Shah's Army," pp. 100–104).

In time Zaman Shah's policies brought about a rupture in the alliance between the Barakzai subtribes and the royal Sadozai clan, a rupture that resulted in the execution of Payanda Khan, leader of the Barakzais. The political struggle between the two Durrani clans was transformed into a protracted blood feud, which was aggravated by the rivalries and ambitions of the king's brothers and their tribal allies. In these circumstances, Zaman Shah asserted the authority of the throne by making an alliance with the Ghilzais and by securing the cooperation of the Qizil-Bash. He also attempted to follow in the footsteps of Ahmad Shah and invaded India as the champion of Islam; internal questions apart, his campaigns of 1797–99 were intended to check the expansion of Sikh power and secure his hold over the rich Punjab. In pursuit of his political aims, he tried to win the support of the Muslim religious establishment by embracing the cause of Muslim orthodoxy; he went so far as to issue a proclamation that forbade the study of logic as dangerous to the Muslim faith.

Zaman Shah, like his father and grandfather, failed to achieve his aims. Not only were his efforts at centralization and consolidation rejected by the tribes, but his Indian campaigns proved disastrous.[65] Indeed, external threats to the Afghan monarchy were greater than ever before. Persia was pressing for the reestablishment of its sovereignty over the province of Herat in western Afghanistan, the Sikhs were expanding their power in the Punjab, and the Khan of Kalat was attempting to throw off Afghan rule. Moreover, new difficulties faced the king in the form of two Western imperialist rivals, France and Britain. The French sought to use Afghanistan, as well as Persia, in their power struggle with the British; at the same time, the threat of a consolidation of Afghan rule in India capable of displacing British rule there led the East India Company and the British government to attempt to contain or undermine Zaman Shah.

Afghanistan thus entered the nineteenth century a politically disunited, ethnically and religiously heterogeneous, tribal-feudal state. As an institution the Afghan monarchy had failed to check the disintegration of the Durrani empire, had failed to solve the problems of the succession to the throne, and had failed to bring about the economic and cultural integration of Afghanistan.

Chapter Three

Afghanistan in Decline: The Reforms of Dost Muhammed and Sher Ali

From the late eighteenth century on, the development of urban Afganistan was impeded by the decline of overland trade, the growing economic isolation of the region, the political ascendancy of the Afghan tribes, and the growth of semifeudal, semipastoral tribal communities, with parochial notions of economic self-sufficiency and a tendency to lapse into a natural economy. The disintegration of central power, protracted civil wars, and hazards of travel in Afghanistan contributed to the political fragmentation of the region and the decline of the urban population and economy.

Trade regulations depended on the whims of various petty rulers and chieftains. Towns and countryside alike were at the mercy of various rivals for the Afghan throne and subject to pillaging by their armies. The ruinous internal struggles, usually followed by the imposition of heavy taxes on the artisans and merchants, as well as on the non-Afghan ethnic groups, caused an emigration of these merchants and artisans from Afghanistan to neighboring countries.[1] In 1817, Baron Meyendorf reported from Bukhara that "the number of Afghans has very much increased owing to the quantity of emigrants from Kabul, who on account of disturbances in their country have sought refuge here; at present they number about two thousand."[2] The trade situation was further complicated by the growing hazards and costs of the overland route through Kandahar-Herat. An increasing percentage of the Indian trade began to travel by the maritime route of Bombay-Bushire. Afghan nomad tribes traditionally engaged in the overland transit trade lost a substantial part of their income, and the country's major commercial and administrative centers suffered a serious decline. Some of the urban centers were further weakened by an influx of tribal elements, who extended their feudal privileges and influence over the urban centers and turned them into "service stations," catering to the limited economic needs of the tribesmen.

The city of Herat, once a major entrepôt of international trade, began to deteriorate in the early nineteenth century; however, it still had some 4,000–6,000 houses, 1,200 shops, at least seven caravanserais, 20 public baths, four bazaars, six madrassas, and a large cistern filled by an underground aqueduct, and continued to produce some goods, including worsted woolens, carpets, and silk.³ The annual revenue of the city and its surrounding areas was an estimated 1–1.3 million rupees in the early nineteenth century,* but this was not considered sufficient to cover Herat's military and administrative expenses at that time, and it sharply declined thereafter.⁴ Civil strife, the Persian-Afghan War, which resulted in a long siege of the city, and the First Anglo-Afghan War (1839–42) completely disrupted Herat's economy.⁵ Trade with Bukhara, Kandahar, Kabul, Meshed, and Yezd declined.† The population dropped from about 100,000 in 1810 to 40,000 in 1826 and 20,000 in 1845.⁶ Merchants and artisans were subjected to heavy taxes, including an exorbitant war tax, the *harbieh*. Near the city, the Aimak tribes assumed an independent or semi-independent status. The frequent highway robberies made the Herat-Kandahar trade route insecure, while Turkoman and Baluchi raids jeopardized the commercial and pilgrim traffic to Meshed and the Sistan province.‡ A French observer noted in 1826 that the road between Herat and Yezd (a major route between Afghanistan and Persia) had been reduced to a mere "footpath," and that most of the wells along the way were filled up. One of the towns of the province of Herat, Farah, an important junction of Indo-Persian trade during the seventeenth century and still a major town as late as 1809, gradually declined. On the eve of the Afghan-Persian war of 1838, most of its 6,000 inhabitants were moved to Kandahar, and the city was reduced to a heap of mud houses by the second half of the nineteenth century. Other once important urban centers, such

---

* See Appendix A for information on the approximate value of Afghan, Indian, and Persian money in the nineteenth century.

† Lal ("Description of Herat," p. 10) reported that "since Kamran's dynasty, the commerce of Herat has fallen to nothing. The caravans are plundered, as we ourselves were witnesses of. The resident merchants are fined a large sum of money upon any foolish pretext of the Government." He also noted that "from Herat to Bokhara, the caravans had to pay duties in four locations." See also A. Conolly, II, 10–11, 48. C. Masson (*Narrative*, I, 205) reported that in the city of Herat there was "no protection for life, liberty or property."

‡ According to one report, 100 pilgrims were killed during such raids in 1823 alone. See "Itinerary from Yezd to Herat," pp. 3–7. This situation continued well into the 1870's, when there were reports of Turkomans raiding caravans between Meshed and Herat. See Marsh, p. 69. In 1845, Ferrier (*Caravan Journeys*, pp. 280–81) reported that the Baluchi raids into the valley of Helmand had brought "desolation and depopulation of the plain" and posed a great threat to caravans.

as Ghorian and Sabzawar, were in ruins. The agriculture of the province, despite two annual crops, barely met local needs.[7]

Kandahar, a major transit center for overland trade, which in 1809 had a population of about 100,000, four bazaars, and numerous caravanserais and mosques, was only one-third or one-fourth this size by 1826–36.* The only major city in the country with a predominantly Afghan population, its socioeconomic structure became increasingly semifeudal and semitribal in character. As the main center for the Durrani clans, Kandahar was often crippled by tribal wars, resulting in the neglect of the city's water canals, the exploitation of the residents, and a general deterioration. Arbitrary transit duties, including a 5 per cent tax on foreign currency, discouraged foreign trade. In spite of a reported annual revenue of 1.2 million rupees in the late 1820's, Kandahar, maladministered and economically depressed, had only one major caravanserai, and that little used. Cotton and silk, formerly exportable items, were barely sufficient for home consumption. In sharp contrast to the city's varied and voluminous agricultural exports to India in the seventeenth and eighteenth centuries, there were only two major exports by the 1820's—madder tobacco and dried fruits.[8]

Economic conditions in Kandahar deteriorated further after the First Anglo-Afghan War. Manufactured products were confined to coarse cotton cloth, turbans, felts, and sheepskin coats; only the last two were exported. Provincial governors and powerful tribes in the area succeeded in monopolizing two profitable items of interregional trade, gunpowder and assafoetida. A depreciation of the copper currency, combined with a famine in the 1850's, completely crippled the city's economy.[9]

Within the province of Kandahar, the Durrani rulers were forced to cater to the interests of various Durrani clans. Moreover, for some decades they had been unable to cope with the powerful Ghilzai clans who occupied most of the country between Kandahar and Ghazni. The Ghilzais had become virtually independent and, in the 1820's, levied transit fees on the trade caravans from Kabul and Kandahar, collecting as a rule a duty of four rupees per camel, two per horse, and one per donkey. Wrote a con-

---

* Wrote Masson: "Of the area included within the city walls so much is spread over with ruinous and deserted houses, extensive courts, gardens and ranges of stabling, that it is probable there are not above five thousand inhabited houses, by which estimate the population would be from 25–30,000 souls" (*Narrative*, I, 280). On the eve of the First Anglo-Afghan War, the city, with the exception of its noteworthy Chahar Sou bazaar, was described as "a mere collection of mud-hovels, very generally, nay almost entirely, only one story high." Its population was estimated then to be 30,000. Many parts of the city were reported to be uninhabited. See Kennedy, I, 250–52; and I. N. Allen, pp. 180–86.

temporary: "The collection was made in a summary way by counting the animals, as the Ghilzis, to avoid discussion and the frauds of the merchants, levy on the beasts of burden, not on the merchandise; and to incur no chance of being duped as to them, levy on all indiscriminately, whether laden or not. Any attempt to impose upon them brought a free application of the horsewhip."[10] In addition to these transit fees, the Ghilzais also collected 40 rupees per caravan as an entertainment or hospitality fee.

By the 1820's the famous city of Ghazni had shrunk to a town of 1,000–1,500 houses, and by 1838, there were only 900 to 1,000 families in the city, which consisted of "a few narrow, straggling streets."[11] The revenue of Ghazni and its districts was only about 400,000 rupees; land taxes were paid mostly in kind. Caravans engaged in trade with Ghazni had to pay special duties to the Suleiman Khel, the powerful Ghilzai clan, which was located east of the city. When Abdul Kerim Munshi visited Ghazni in 1847, its population had dwindled to some 2,000–3,000 Afghans and Tajiks; he reported that a heavy snowfall had almost totally destroyed the town. Ten years later, it was hardly more than a large village; its one noteworthy industry was the small-scale production of sheepskin coats.[12]

Kabul, the capital of Afghanistan, appeared to be the only healthy major urban center in the country in this period. It had about 80 mosques, 14 or 15 caravanserais, well-stocked bazaars, and an annual revenue of 1.2–1.4 million rupees. Kabul was less affected by the decline of the Indo-Persian overland trade than Kandahar and Herat and retained a degree of importance in the trade between India and Central Asia. Chahar Sou, the city's great covered bazaar, still ranked among the richest in the Muslim East and included a variety of Russian, English, and Indian articles. There was some local manufacturing, primarily of articles of war—muskets, pistols, blunderbusses, swords, daggers, matchlocks, and steel armor. The inhabitants of the city, mostly Tajiks, Afghans, Qizil-Bash, and Hazaras, numbered some 60,000, making Kabul the largest urban center in Afghanistan.[13] Its apparently strong economic position was jeopardized, however, by the same conditions that led to the decline of the other Afghan urban centers, especially the increasing number of raids by the tribes of the Khyber Pass. The Afghan monarchy had not only given up the idea of collecting taxes in the Khyber Valley, but had been forced to ensure the free flow of commercial traffic by paying a fixed and regular tribute to the Afridi tribe.* Other Afghan tribes, notably the Mohmands, Waziris, Shin-

* As early as 1809, some merchants traveled via the Multan road between Peshawar and Kabul, considerably prolonging their journey (nine weeks) rather than go through the Khyber Pass (11 days). See Cotton, p. 68. In 1833, Honigberger left Dara Bend on

waris, and Suleiman Khel, also imposed head taxes and duties on travelers and merchants, as at times did the Achikzai and Nurzai Durrani clans.[14] In 1836, John Wood reported that the maliks of the Khyber Pass assembled to receive a reward from Captain Burnes for "their praiseworthy forbearance towards us whilst we were among their mountains."[15] The hazardous traveling conditions continued after the First Anglo-Afghan War.*

By the second quarter of the century, Kabul was showing signs of decline. There was only one bridge across the river that flowed through the city, the others having been damaged through age and neglect. The city's architecture (in part because of a lack of timber) was undistinguished in comparison to the rest of the Muslim East; most of the houses were built of mud and unfired bricks. The manufactures of Kabul had become mediocre and suitable only for "the consumption of the lower and less wealthy classes," wrote Masson, noting that "there was not an article made or wrought in Kabul which [was] not surpassed by specimens from other countries."[16]

The deterioration of the Afghan urban centers is best illustrated by the condition of Jalalabad, which by 1812, according to one visitor, could not even be called a town. At that time Jalalabad had only one brick building, that of the governor; many of the other buildings were in ruins. The city's annual revenue was estimated at the time at 70,000 rupees; in 1826, Masson estimated the revenue of the entire district to be 300,000 rupees.[17] (The official estimated revenue of the province—1.2 million rupees—was clearly exaggerated, especially in light of the fact that the provincial gov-

---

May 18 and reached Kabul on June 28. During his journey, he reported, his party was "in constant alarm of Weziris. Notwithstanding the vigilance of the armed men of our party, . . . the Weziris succeeded in carrying off several camels." He also noted that the "Suleiman Khel resemble the Weziris in their predatory habits and like them have the virtue not to take the life of their victims" (pp. 175–76). There are numerous other reports of a similar nature, some as late as the 1870's. See, for example, Gerard, "Peshawar to Bokhara," p. 1; A. Conolly, II, 198; Todd, "Report: 1844," p. 357; and Burnaby, pp. 446–47.

* The insecurity of Indo-Afghan trade is best reflected in the inflated price of Indian products in the Kabul markets, especially such items as spices, sugar candy, and indigo. In the early nineteenth century the price of these items was 200 per cent higher in Kabul than in India. The price of British piece goods yielded between 100 and 110 per cent profit in Afghanistan and 150 per cent in Bukhara over the prime cost in Bombay. Another indication of the insecurity of the trade routes can be seen in the great fluctuations that took place in the price of agricultural commodities, particularly grain, in the Kabul markets; the regular fluctuations also indicate that grain had become an article of import. See C. Masson, *Narrative*, II, 270; A. Conolly, II, 271–72; Hyder Khan, Part 2, p. 100.

ernor's authority was recognized only in the city.) The town, which Burnes described as "one of the filthiest places I have seen in the East," had a bazaar of 50 shops and a population of approximately 2,000 in the 1830's. However, the population increased tenfold in the winter, when tribesmen flocked to the city from the surrounding hills. Throughout the province decline and decadence were widespread; forts were in ruins, kariz drying up, arable land uncultivated. The acreage devoted to the cultivation of sugarcane, one of the staples of Jalalabad's agriculture, was decreasing. The trade routes between Peshawar and the Jalalabad valley were subject to the same lawless and predatory tribes that plagued travelers and merchants to and from Kabul, Kandahar, and Ghazni. In addition, the city was sacked during the internecine struggles of the 1830's and was hit by an earthquake in 1842. Because of these conditions and occasional droughts, some tribesmen gave up agriculture and returned to a pastoral economy.[18]

Similar conditions prevailed in central Afghanistan, where the Hazaras had established virtual independence and were engaged in a constant struggle against the Sunni Afghans and Uzbeks. In Hazarajat and other districts, a money economy had lapsed into a natural economy. Burnes and Broadfoot noted: "These people [the Hazaras] have no money and are almost ignorant of its value; we got everything from them by barter." In an effort to create a self-sufficient economy with only a few rudimentary manufactures, the Ghilzais and the Hazaras, as well as other groups, had almost completely freed themselves of economic and political dependence on the urban centers and the monarchy.[19]

Afghan influence and control over the region of Balkh, tenuous at best, all but disappeared during the first decade of the nineteenth century, when Killich Ali Beg, taking advantage of internal warfare among the Durranis, in effect made the region independent. After his death, Balkh became a dependency of Bukhara, and the population of the city declined rapidly; by the late 1830's it was less than 2,000. Subject to frequent attacks, pillaging, and exactions by the Uzbeks, Balkh became a tributary to Murad Beg, the Khan of Kunduz, a region between Kabul and Bukhara. Many of the inhabitants either migrated to Kunduz and other regions or abandoned the town for agriculture. The formerly great urban center became a minor town, devoid of industries and manufactures; its chief item of trade was fruit. The ruined city served as a source of bricks and other building materials. Its canals, neglected and in disrepair, were abandoned.[20]

The situation was not much different in Afghan Turkestan, where there was constant strife and a decline in the urban population.* The Uzbeks of Kataghan had ravaged the region in the early part of the century. Their frequent raids were climaxed in 1829 by the invasion of Murad Beg, who overran the province of Badakhshan and "swept away a large part of the inhabitants whom he sold into slavery, or set down to perish in the swampy plains of Kunduz."[21] In 1836 Murad Beg led a successful marauding excursion into Bamian, a region reputed for its own lawlessness, and carried off several hundred people.[22]

In the 1830's Kunduz proper probably had between 500 and 1,500 houses. The revenues of the khanate were collected chiefly in grain. Despite relative security within the region and encouragement of trade by the despotic Khan, the circulation of hard currency, which consisted in large part of old coins struck in Delhi, was limited. Tashkurgan, situated between Balkh and Kunduz, was the largest city of the region, with approximately 10,000 inhabitants, mostly Tajiks from Kabul. There were also a small number of Uzbeks. The economy of Tashkurgan was based mainly on trade in horses, mules, donkeys, cattle, dried fruit, spices, and cottonades. The town was a kind of regional clearing house for trade between Central Asia and India, Kabul, Kandahar, and Yarkend, but there are some indications that even this trade was conducted on a barter basis. Other cities in the khanate included Taligan, also a trade center, which had some 400 mud houses; Khanabad, which consisted of a fort and some 600 mud houses; and Mazar-i-Sharif, a great pilgrim center, which had about 500 houses. Faizabad, the ancient capital of Badakhshan province, was completely destroyed in the 1830's by Murad Beg. A large proportion of its population was transferred to Kunduz, where the majority perished from climatic conditions. Djerm (Jurm), the new capital, was only a collection of villages defended by a fort, with a population that did not exceed 1,500.[23]

THE TRADE AND EXTERNAL CONTACTS OF AFGHANISTAN

The collapse of effective central power and the rising power of feudal lords and tribal chieftains resulted in arbitrary fiscal, judicial, and political measures that further weakened the already faltering urban economy of

* Wrote Ferrier (*Caravan Journeys*, p. 204): "The amount of rivalry and intrigue that exist amongst the petty Khans of Turkistan is perfectly incredible to anyone who has not been in the country, and instead of trying to decrease or modify either, they exert their intelligence to the utmost to complicate and carry out their paltry schemes. The certain consequence is a permanent state of warfare, in which it is impossible for the

Afghanistan. The country lost its focal economic position in the transit trade of India and Central Asia to Bukhara. The Bukharan monetary unit (the *tilla* gold) replaced the Afghan Zaman Shahi rupee, even in Afghanistan itself, as the dominant currency. International transit trade had decreased to the point where many European currencies were limited exclusively to the Central Asian bullion trade.[24]

There are no figures on the volume of Indian-Bukharan trade that traversed Afghanistan in the early nineteenth century. An estimated eight or nine trade caravans left Kabul annually for Central Asia, mostly for Bukhara. They carried chintz, *loongees* (cloth used as a wrap), cottonades, Cashmere shawls, and European broadcloths, as well as sugar candy, spices, and indigo. From Bukhara, they brought back horses, cochineal, gold thread, raw silk, and other goods.[25] European or Russian goods that reached Afghanistan from Bukhara included cast-iron pots, cutlery, hardware, copper, steel, iron, tin, leather, needles, mirrors, spectacles, and lace paper.[26] Afghan imports from India consisted mainly of indigo, muslins, British and Indian chintzes, gold cloth, mixed silks, cotton goods, sugar, spices, salt, medicines, gunlocks, and some utensils. These imports were exchanged for Afghan horses and wool, and especially for fruit.[27] The Afghan-Persian trade dealt primarily with clothing, sugar and some spices, Herat sword blades, and bullion.[28] Trade with Chinese Turkestan was in woolens, Chinese silk and satin, chinaware, porcelain, raw silk, and gold ingots.[29] By the 1830's, however, the number and variety of transactions had declined greatly. Exports to India, for example, were reduced to two major items—fruit and horses.[30]

Trade with Bukhara was hampered by rising transportation costs, Afghan-Bukharan conflicts, and the chaotic customs system. Bukharan caravans en route to India through Afghanistan were stopped and taxed eight to ten times before they even reached Kabul and Ghazni, where additional heavy taxes were imposed. Caravans from India to Afghanistan and Bukhara were also subject to exorbitant taxation. In the 1830's travelers and merchants visiting Afghanistan had to pay a 5 per cent duty on their merchandise at Multan, six annas (about nine pence) per load at Larga for the Sikh ruler, and still another six annas per load to the governor of Dera Ismail Khan. Once in Afghanistan, they had to pay 50 rupees

---

people to attempt the development of the resources of the country, or undertake any enterprise with a view to its future improvement. They [the Khans] recognize the suzerainty of the princes of Herat, Bokhara, or Khulm, only because they have not sufficient power to throw it off, or that occasionally it happens to be to their interest to acknowledge it."

at Ghazni as custom dues on such personal effects as caps, cloaks—even teacups.* Caravans crossing dependencies of the Khan of Kalat (Baluchistan) had to pay three Karim Khani rupees on every load of merchandise. As a result, the already small volume of Afghan-Baluch trade was further reduced.† Meanwhile, conflicting political and economic aims were also undermining Afghan-Persian trade. The importation of such items as rugs, silk, and carpets from Afghanistan was sometimes discouraged or obstructed by the Persian authorities in order to protect Persian industries[31] or as a means of political reprisal.

The chaotic taxation and customs systems resulted in a strengthening of the trend toward regionalism, economic parochialism, and natural economy. Barter was widely practiced by the 1820's and even as late as the 1890's was used in Afghan transactions with the Kafirs, who, in exchange for salt, earthen jars, coarse cloth, knives, needles, firearms, and gunpowder, traded dried fruits, honey, vinegar, and wine.[32] European goods became expensive and scarce in Afghanistan. The price of English or Indian manufactured goods imported from Bombay doubled by the time they reached Kandahar.[33] Great value was placed on foreign manufactured goods, as is exemplified by the fact that Russian manufactured goods were among the coronation presents sent from the rulers of Turkestan to the Afghan monarch Shah Shuja.[34]

In such circumstances the loss of Kashmir and the extension of Sikh power to Peshawar during the first quarter of the nineteenth century dealt a severe blow to the Afghan urban economy and the royal treasury.[35] The monarchy, which also gradually lost its tenuous hold over Baluchistan and the tribal trade-fair centers of Dera Ghazi Khan, Dera Ismail Khan, and Daraband,[36] was left with few hopes of freeing itself of its dependence on the Afghan tribes or of achieving the political and economic integration of the country.

---

* There was also a tax on the money that travelers or merchants had with them. In the 1830's, the authorities of the town of Balkh required Armenians to pay one-tenth of the money they carried as tax, Hindus one-twentieth, and Muslims one-fortieth. See Gerard, "Peshawar to Bokhara," p. 14. According to Ferrier (*Caravan Journeys*, p. 275), the situation was much the same in the 1840's.

† Baluchistan, too, was in a state of decline. The export trade of Kalat, for instance, a city that was "once the great channel of merchandise from Khorassan, Kandahar, and Kabul to India," was unimportant in the export trade by the 1820's. See W. Hamilton, II, 528; and C. Masson, *Narrative*, II, 122–23. Boukhary (p. 7) estimates the entire income of Baluchistan and its dependencies in 1810 at no more than 200,000 rupees; in 1877, Thomas Thornton (p. 64) reported that the total annual revenue of the ruler of Kalat was only 25,000–30,000 pounds sterling, derived mainly from his share of the agricultural produce of Baluchistan.

THE COSMOPOLITAN MINORITIES

Afghanistan's contacts with Europe and the Muslim Mediterranean world between the sixteenth century and the early nineteenth century were extremely limited in scope and impact. Essentially, they were maintained first through Safawid Persia, Moghul India, and Central Asia, and later through the trade routes linking India, Central Asia, and the Iranian plateau. The continuing decline of overland trade thus not only jeopardized the country's economic position but also further reduced its external contacts.

Unlike Persia, the Ottoman Empire, the Central Asian khanates, and Moghul India, Afghanistan did not experience any significant European penetration during most of the first century of its independent existence (1747–1838). It had no major capitulatory treaties with European states, and there were no permanent European trading agencies or missionary activities inside its borders. A few European manufactured goods were introduced into Afghanistan via Persia, the Central Asian khanates (notably Bukhara and Khiva), and especially India, and a few European military technological innovations had been borrowed by Ahmad Shah and his successors. However, these contacts did not provide any intellectual stimulus or challenge Afghan traditions, nor did the travels of a handful of Europeans in the country in the early decades of the nineteenth century have noticeable effect.[37]

Afghanistan's limited external contacts were carried on chiefly by the three cosmopolitan minorities of the country, the Hindus, the Jews, and the Armenians. Members of these groups, which were widely dispersed throughout the Middle East, Central Asia, and India, served as middlemen between Afghanistan and Europe and handled most of the country's transactions with Central Asia and India. Their role may be properly compared to that played by the Chinese in the commerce of Southeast Asia. However, these groups did not enjoy social equality in Afghanistan; consequently they were unable to perform the role of a middle class and serve as vehicles of modernization and "Westernization." On the contrary, as social outcasts, they avoided identification with any alien force or ideology that might have endangered their economic position or made their loyalty questionable. Their position within Afghanistan and throughout the Middle East (and in Central Asia until its incorporation into the Russian Empire) was primarily that of a middle or lower caste with specific economic functions.[38]

Sources dealing with the social history of the Hindus, Jews, and Armenians of the region indicate the great problems they faced in the wake of the decline of the overland trade routes, the stiff competition they had to wage with each other and against the well-organized European joint-stock companies, and the difficulties they encountered from Moghul, Persian, and Afghan authorities. From the seventeenth century on, their contacts with Europe declined. Their relations were gradually limited to European companies and individuals in Asia, and, as the overland trade routes declined, they lost their control over the great bulk of the Indian and Persian trade. Furthermore, the Jews and the Armenians, unlike their sister communities in the Ottoman Empire and Persia, had become isolated and in many respects culturally rigid, unable to sustain, enrich, or transform the social and structural makeup of their own communities. This was perhaps the clearest indication of the degree to which Afghanistan had become economically and culturally isolated.

Of the three groups, the Hindus played the most significant role in the economy of Afghanistan. Hindu merchants were well established in the seventeenth and eighteenth centuries in the important cities of Persia (Isfahan, Bandar Abbas, Shiraz, and Meshed), in Persian Afghanistan (Herat and Kandahar), and in Kabul province (Jalalabad, Ghazni, and Kabul, which were then part of Moghul India); by the nineteenth century, they had extended their activities to the Persian Gulf (mainly Basra and Muscat), the Arab Middle East, Central Asia, and even Astrakhan.[39]

Under the Durrani empire and throughout the nineteenth century, the Hindus were economically active in a number of fields, especially trade, banking, goldsmithing, and horticulture. Many owned drug or dye shops. Within the royal administration, they often served as scribes, secretaries, treasurers, and bookkeepers. Most of the shopkeepers of eastern Afghanistan during the first decades of the century were Hindus, and there was not an important Afghan town that did not have at least one or two Hindu families engaged in industry and commerce. In the 1830's there were between 50 and 100 Hindu merchants in Kandahar and some 500 to 1,000 Hindus living in Herat.[40] Because of the Quranic sanctions against money-lending, the banking business gradually was concentrated in the hands of non-Muslims, primarily the Hindus; in almost all of the major towns of Central Asia credit could be obtained and financial transactions made through the Hindu merchants. The Hindus also controlled a large portion of the trade of Afghanistan and India with Central Asia, and most of the export trade of Afghanistan and Baluchistan.

In the second half of the nineteenth century, as Afghanistan became increasingly isolated and the British assumed control of the country's external relations, the Hindu merchant class emerged as the chief economic force in the foreign trade of Afghanistan, which was mainly transacted with India. However, the Hindu merchants continued to maintain trading agencies in Khorassan near the Perso-Afghan border, and some even extended their activities to the Caucasus and Nizhnii Novgorod.[41] In 1880, Sir Bartle Frere wrote, "The trade of Candahar and Herat is almost entirely in the hands of Hindu merchants ... generally British Indian subjects ... who with few exceptions take care to keep their spare capital and principal houses of business in British territory."[42] In the early twentieth century, the Hindus were reportedly the most numerous and wealthiest merchant class in Herat (with some 700 Hindus), Kabul, and Kandahar. They retained their commercial position in Peshawar and in Baluchistan and continued to maintain trading colonies in Balkh, Kabul, Kandahar, Ghazni, Sabzawar, Tashkurgan, and Maimana, controlling most of the export trade.[43]

According to some sources, the Afghan rulers valued their Hindu subjects highly because of their contributions to the economic life of the country.[44] However, many other sources speak of the social discrimination, indignities, financial exactions, and other forms of punishment they suffered. In Kabul they had to pay a poll tax and wear a yellow or red turban; in Ghazni, too, they had to pay a poll tax and were required to wear tight trousers and a black cap; in Kandahar, public exactions of great sums of money by the ruling princes of the province had become routine by the early nineteenth century.[45]

The history of the Jewish community in Afghanistan is similar to that of the Hindus. The community, whose roots in Afghanistan were very old, was constantly rejuvenated by immigrations from Bukhara, Persia, and Georgia. A large number of Jews were resettled in Afghanistan in 1736 by Nadir Shah, who sought thereby to encourage Indo-Persian trade.[46] The Jews maintained widespread commercial relations throughout the entire Middle East, Central Asia, India, and Russia. In the eighteenth century, according to one authority, they controlled most of the trade of the Levant: "They farmed the taxes for the Turks, especially the customs, they were the bankers to whom the Franks had recourse when they had to borrow to pay an *avania* [an excessive or extortionate tax], and it was with the Jewish middlemen, not with the Turkish customer, that the English merchant usually conducted his trade."[47] The Jewish merchants received a brokerage fee of 1 per cent on all goods and one-quarter of 1 per cent on all money they handled. At the end of the eighteenth century, half of the Venetian cargoes were handled by Jewish firms at Alexandria and Cairo. Tuscan trade with the East, too, was chiefly carried on by the Jewish merchants of Leghorn, "who acted as agents of European exporters of all nationalities and were in correspondence with Christian merchants at Damascus and Aleppo."[48]

From the sixteenth century on, Jewish merchants played a prominent role in Persia's commercial transactions. The Jewish merchants of Afghanistan had contacts in such major Persian cities as Isfahan and Shiraz, in the ports and adjacent regions of the Persian Gulf, including Basra, Mosul, Bandar Abbas, and Muscat, and in Aden and Egypt.[49] They also had contact with the Jews of India, who enjoyed certain trade privileges after the rise of the East India Company.[50] They may have maintained some contact with Russia and Europe through their sister communities in Khiva, Bukhara, Tashkent, and Samarkand, which had ties in the nineteenth century in such distant regions as Lithuania, Nizhnii Novgorod, and Irkutsk.* Some Jewish community leaders (*kaluntars*) in Central Asia visited Europe, and often rabbis were brought to the area from as far away as Algiers and Russia. Religious publications and educational materials were imported from Baghdad, Constantinople, Tehran, and Muscat.[51] To maintain communication, the Jewish merchants of Central Asia and Afghanistan often used Muslim pilgrims visiting the holy lands of Islam.[52]

For a time, the Jews held an important economic position in Afghanistan and, along with the Hindus, served as a major channel of contact between that country and Europe. According to Brauer, "Afghan Jews had settled in London and Leipzig as well as in chief cities of Russia and India.... Their purchases of wool and hides were especially large.... They exported carpets to England, Russia, and India and imported textiles for the most part."[53] However, as a result of the deterioration of economic and social conditions in Afghanistan and the incorporation of Central Asia into the Russian Empire (which introduced new competitive elements into the Central Asian trade), and especially as a result of increasingly discriminatory policies, their economic role declined. Many Jews were forced to leave Afghanistan secretly between 1860 and 1866 and established homes in the Ottoman Empire and Persia.[54] The activities of the Jews of Afghanistan became increasingly localized. The focus of their activities shifted away from commerce. The fiercely competitive Hindu merchants gradually

---

* In the khanate of Bukhara there was a community of Marranos, or Chalas, who were of Jewish origin. Estimated to number 1,000, they were forcibly converted to Islam in the nineteenth century, but retained an identity separate from both the Jews and the Muslims. See Löewenthal, *Judeo-Muslim Marranos*.

ousted the Jews from money-changing and the wholesale trade in drugs, forcing them into new occupations. Some became shopkeepers; others doctors, druggists, distillers, or traders in lambskin.[55]

During the late nineteenth century, the Jewish population in Afghanistan dwindled. Their fortunes continued to wane in the twentieth century. The Russian Revolution wiped out most of their investments in Central Asia. By 1930 there were only an estimated 5,000 Jews in the country and by 1937 only 3,000. Following their forced removal from northern Afghanistan in the 1930's and the restrictive government economic policies thereafter, most Afghan Jews emigrated to Israel.[56]

The Armenians, the only Christian community in Afghanistan, played a limited role in the country's economic history, acting primarily as middlemen in the seventeenth and eighteenth centuries. Their well-entrenched economic position in Safawid Persia, Moghul India, and the Ottoman Empire, and their familiarity with the respective languages and cultures, put them in a good position to establish economic relations with Afghanistan and carry on their overland trade through it. The Armenians had trading centers in all the major cities of Persia, Russia, and Europe, and handled a major portion of Persia's trade with India and Europe during these centuries. They controlled the wool and silk supplies of the Persian Empire and dealt extensively in the spice and European clothing traffic.[57] After an initial phase of fierce competition with the East India Company, they obtained various trading privileges from the company.[58]

Armenian merchants established themselves in the important transit trade centers of Kabul, Herat, Jalalabad, and Kandahar in the seventeenth and eighteenth centuries.[59] That the Armenian merchant was a familiar figure to inhabitants of the region is well illustrated by the fact that many European visitors of the period pretended to be Armenian merchants and took fictitious Armenian names.* The Armenian merchant colony of Kabul was thriving by 1670; by 1707, it had managed to obtain special privileges from the Moghul authorities of Kabul, including complete freedom of movement, freedom from restrictions on dress, and reductions of various taxes.[60] The community was strengthened in 1737, when Nadir Shah settled 200–300 Armenian families there in order to encourage Indo-

---

* The Jesuit priest Goëz was one of those who posed as an Armenian, as did Burnes, who traveled about in Balkh, Kunduz, and Bukhara as an impoverished Armenian watchmaker. (See Goëz, p. 579; Yule, III, 552–53; Bernier, "Voyages," p. 60; Forster, "Extracts," p. 284; "Extracts of a Letter," p. 418; Burnes, "Description of Bokhara," p. 228; and Gerard, "Peshawar to Bokhara," p. 14.) Colonel Stewart, too, impersonated an Armenian merchant while traveling in Afghanistan. (See C. E. Stewart, p. 264.)

Persian overland trade. It was during this period that the Armenians built the first (and only) Christian church in modern Afghanistan.[61] However, attempts of the Armenian Apostolic and the Armenian Catholic Church between 1762 and 1812 to provide the Armenians of Afghanistan with some kind of religious leadership and to reestablish close contacts between them and the Armenian communities of Persia and the Ottoman Empire failed.*

Letters from Armenian merchants in Afghanistan indicate that in 1799 they were carrying on trade with Transcaucasia (especially Tiflis) and the Ottoman Empire (Istanbul). Later accounts (1812, 1826, 1848) show that the range of their activities extended beyond the Central Asian khanates to such frontier tribal trading centers as Dera Ismail Khan, that they served among other things as bankers in Kabul (where they had special quarters and a cemetery), and that they had colonies in Ghazni. During the First Anglo-Afghan War, two Armenian merchants were instrumental in procuring provisions for the Anglo-Indian forces in Kabul.[62]

In the nineteenth century, the number of Armenians in Afghanistan and their importance declined sharply. They were drawn for a while into such occupations as artisans, administrators, treasurers, interpreters, doctors, and vintners,[63] but even in these fields, their contributions were minimal; they were no longer numerically strong, and although as Christians they were tolerated and respected,[64] they were still socially unequal and so cut off from the outside world as to be unable to serve as agents of social change. Under such circumstances, some Armenians were assimilated and others left for Persia and India; their church was destroyed during the Second Anglo-Afghan War.[65] By the 1890's there were only about 20 Armenians in Kabul; they were expelled in 1897 by order of Abdur Rahman Khan.[66] Despite the incorporation of Central Asia into the Russian Empire and the subsequent influx of many Armenian merchants into the Russo-Afghan borderlands, as well as the presence of Armenians in the Persian-Afghan frontier regions, Armenians played no further role in Afghanistan after the first half of the nineteenth century.

It is impossible to assess the role Georgian troops and merchants may have played in Afghanistan. From the fragmentary sources available, it is safe to assume that any Georgian influence was confined to the seventeenth and eighteenth centuries, when there was a large Georgian cavalry force

* Chaplains of the invading British-Indian Army (1839, 1842) administered baptismal rites. In 1842, I. N. Allen wrote of the joy of the isolated Armenians of Kabul at meeting a Christian priest. They had not had a priest for 13 years; one "had come from Hindoostan, and got as far as Peshawar, but was afraid to venture farther."

in the country and when a Georgian prince, Gurgin Khan, was the governor of the province of Kandahar. The few Georgian merchants in the country in that period were undoubtedly involved in trade within the Persian Empire; some were settled in Kabul as a colony by Nadir Shah and must have been involved in Persian-Afghan trade. However, even this limited role must have ended by the 1820's, for (except for one secondary source) there is no mention of Georgians living in Afghanistan in the works of European travelers and explorers of the time.[67]

EUROPEAN TRAVELERS AND MISSIONARIES

In the early nineteenth century, various official and non-official British missions, intelligence expeditions, and individual travelers visited Afghanistan. Most of these visits were undertaken under the auspices of the British government and the East India Company as part of an extensive study of the regions adjacent to British India. Their chief purpose was to extend and secure British economic interests and to neutralize foreign influences, particularly European ones, that might injure British interests in India and the Middle East. The accounts of these travelers contributed much to a knowledge of the topography, geography, political developments, and history of Afghanistan. One of the most important accounts is that of Mountstuart Elphinstone, whose diplomatic mission in 1808–9 brought the Afghans their first significant direct contact with a European power and whose book represents the first comprehensive description of the kingdom of Kabul and the Afghan tribes.[68] Other works included those of Capt. Charles Christie, Lt. Henry Pottinger, Izzet Ullah, and William Moorcroft and his companions Trebeck and Guthrie, all of whom were English agents sent to Afghanistan between 1810 and 1823.[69] Still others were those of Charles Masson,* whose travel journals of the 1820's are

* Masson's nationality has been the subject of debate. The first report about him was made in the 1820's by the British Resident in Bushir, who stated that Masson was a Kentuckian. Forrest, who included Masson's "Journal" in his *Selections from the Travels and Journals Preserved in the Bombay Secretariat*, and Holdich, in his *Gates of India*, did not dispute that report. Honigberger, however, wrote that Masson was a European (p. 178). More recently, Spain (*Pathan Borderland*, p. 101) has asserted that Masson's real name was James Lewis, that he was a deserter from the East India Company's army, that he fell in with Josiah Harlan, an American adventurer, and that, in order to avoid arrest as a deserter, he changed his name and posed as an American. According to Spain, Harlan eventually informed the British authorities of Masson's identity, and Masson escaped imprisonment only by agreeing to supply the East India Company secret intelligence. Caroe (p. 452n) describes him as a "British news writer in Kabul." Fletcher (*Afghanistan*, p. 81) contends that the fact that Lord Auck-

an important source of information on the socioeconomic history of nine-teenth-century Afghanistan;[70] James Fraser, who also visited the area in the 1820's; an anonymous French officer, whose chronicle of a journey from Persia to Herat, Kabul, and Kandahar in 1826 provides a good account of urban Afghanistan;[71] Arthur Conolly of the Bengal Cavalry, who traveled to the country in 1830; Alexander Burnes of the Bombay Infantry and James Gerard, whose reports of their famous missions in 1832 shed further light on economic and political conditions in the region; and Munshi Mohan Lal (the Indian traveling companion of Burnes), who wrote a detailed description of Afghan political and social developments.[72]

Between 1836 and 1839 further British explorations were carried out. During a second mission, Burnes, accompanied by John Wood and Dr. Percival Lord, explored the Kabul and Oxus rivers, providing valuable data on the Kirghiz nomads and setting up an intelligence service between the Oxus and the Afghan frontier.[73] During and after the Persian siege of Herat (1837–38), the city was visited by John Court and Maj. D'Arcy Todd, whose report gave data on the economy and politics of Herat province.* Eldred Pottinger, a British officer, participated in planning the defense of the besieged city. In 1839, Lieutenant Irwin, who had been a member of Elphinstone's mission, published a comprehensive and valuable survey of the economy of the Afghan kingdom. Joseph Ferrier, a French officer, visited Afghanistan in 1845. His work *Caravan Journeys* has also added much to our knowledge of Herat and southern Afghanistan in this period.

Christian missionaries made various attempts to establish a foothold in Afghanistan. In 1811, Dr. Leyden, of the College of Fort Williams in Calcutta, began translating the Bible into Pashto. His work was completed in 1818 by Baptist missionaries at Serampore, led by William Carey. One thousand copies of the translation of the New Testament were printed.

---

land knew Masson was a deserter explains why the viceroy did not heed Masson's advice on the eve of the First Anglo-Afghan War. The theory that Masson was a deserter has many loopholes: his education and erudition, as well as his financial re-sources, raise the question of whether he was not in fact a British political agent all along, assigned to intelligence work first in northern Persia and the Caucasus, and later in Afghanistan.

* In 1839, Todd was named the British Resident at the court of Shah Kamran, the ruler of Herat, and put in charge of a political and military mission. Members of this group, some of whom had been in Herat since 1838, helped restore the city's fortifications, surveyed the topography of the area, and reported on conditions in northern Afghani-stan in general. Some led perilous missions to Bukhara. See Ferrier, *Caravan Journeys*, pp. 171n, 526–27n.

Apparently a few copies reached Afghanistan via Indian (Lohani) merchants, but most of the books remained in a depository.[74] Missionary
activities were generally discouraged by the East India Company, especially under the administration of the Marquis of Wellesley.[75] Direct missionary contacts with Afghanistan were rare, and visits from missionaries,
like that of the Rev. Joseph Wolff, even rarer. Wolff, the son of a rabbi,
had been converted first to Catholicism and then to Anglicanism. On a
visit to Bukhara, Kabul, and Peshawar in 1837–38 in search of the Ten
Lost Tribes of Israel, he engaged in theological discussions with various
mullahs.[76]

English missionaries attempted to penetrate Turkestan through Russian
colonial outposts and to push their activities into northern Afghanistan,
but they were prevented from doing so by an official Russian ban.[77] American Presbyterian missionaries made a pioneering attempt to establish
direct contact with the Afghans. They established a mission at Ludiana,
a location that was well suited for the purpose: it was the northwestern
station of the East India Company, the headquarters of the British political
agent, the site of an army camp, and the temporary home of several prominent Afghan political refugees, including the blind ex-Amir Zaman Shah
and Shah Shuja, the pretender to the Afghan throne.[78] However, the
missionaries had little or no success among the exiled Afghan leaders or
their retinues.

The early contacts between the English and the Afghans had greater
significance for the British than for the Afghans. The British studies and
intelligence reports brought a knowledge of Afghanistan and its people to
the West; they did not, however, promote an Afghan interest in Europe.
Though an Anglo-Afghan treaty was concluded in 1809, it was directed
almost wholly against an already abandoned Franco-Persian plan for the
invasion of India and did not further political and cultural contacts between
Afghanistan and the West.

THE STATE OF CULTURE AND LEARNING

Afghanistan, like all of Central Asia in the early nineteenth century,
was in a state of cultural decay.[79] Its educational institutions were medieval
and parochial, devoted chiefly to religious instruction and reaching only a
small segment of the population. Theoretically, each large community had
one or more *maktabs,* schools maintained by the mosques and conducted
by mullahs. In the rural area, the mullahs drew their maintenance from
small land holdings allotted to them by the village; in the urban centers

they received *waqfs* (religious endowments). In both the rural and city areas, they also collected small contributions from their students. Often, the well-to-do hired a mullah to tutor their children privately. There were no curriculum standards or state control in the maktabs. Instruction usually consisted of lessons in the Persian language, the study of Persian classics, notably the works of Saadi and Hafez, and an introduction to Arabic grammar. Some students, after a few years of maktab education, advanced to madrassas, which were few, accessible only to a select group, and concerned with the instruction of theology.[80] In general, rigid scholasticism characterized all education, whose purpose was the strict observance of Islamic law and traditions. To this end, instruction was limited to reiterations of theological dogma and was marked by zealous orthodoxy, conformity, and anti-intellectualism.[81]

Some religious teachers and leaders, as well as scribes and poets, furthered their education by attaching themselves to renowned teachers or studied in the madrassas of Peshawar, Hushtnuggur (India), or Bukhara.[82] A few went to Lahore, Mesopotamia, or Arabia to study. Many of Afghanistan's eighteenth- and nineteenth-century writers, we can safely assume, had visited Mecca and Medina or studied in Bukhara and Lahore. Lamentably, until the last half of the nineteenth century, everything they learned, whether in the Afghan madrassas or those of India and Bukhara, was essentially the same; their studies of the Quran, Islamic law, logic, theology, and metaphysics were all based on Muslim scholastic sources of the Middle Ages.[83] The lack of scientific knowledge was almost total. The Copernican system, mentioned for the first time in Muslim literature in the Turkish translation of Blau's *Atlas Majeur* (1685), was not introduced into Afghanistan until Elphinstone's mission in 1809.[84] Even then, it does not seem to have generated any extensive speculation or controversy. As late as the second half of the nineteenth century, the overwhelming majority of the people of Afghanistan still had a geocentric view of the universe[85]—a view held throughout Central Asia in general. Geographical knowledge of Asia and Europe was also very scant.[86] The declining state of education is illustrated by the fact that, whereas in 1812 there were three madrassas in Kabul, with instructors who taught Arabic, Persian, Turkish, and perhaps some scholastic science, in the 1830's there was reportedly only one, and it had neither endowment nor scholars.[87]

The consequences of the prolonged and unchallenged rule of scholasticism were grave. The madrassas of Central Asia, India, and the Middle East succumbed to theological dogma and intuitionism. According to H. A. R. Gibb, "The orthodox presentation of Islamic history was invested with religious sanctions, so that to question it came to be regarded as heresy."[88] Not only Quranic injunctions but all Islamic law was regarded as of divine inspiration and guidance.[89] Free and speculative inquiry had been gradually replaced by the repetitious writings of epigones: "It was felt that all truths had already been discovered; to guide one's life one had to search for some proper authority in the past. The patterns of life that were handed down from generation to generation received the stamp of divinely ordained dispensations. All free juristic activity ceased except the quarrel of commentators about inessential details."[90] Muslim scholasticism also preserved and transmitted the sense of superiority that Islam had developed toward Europe during the Middle Ages, an attitude that had been reinforced by the fall of Constantinople (1453) and the crushing victories of the Ottoman Empire.[91] Romanticization of past Muslim achievements, coupled with intellectual stagnation and the absence of historical rationalism, perpetuated the illusion of invincibility, which served both as a handy refuge and as a moral compensation for the technological inferiority of the Muslims of the region to their Western or "Westernizing" adversaries.[92]

Throughout the eighteenth and most of the nineteenth centuries, the various intellectual currents in Europe—the scientific discoveries and theories of Copernicus, Galileo, Newton, Bacon, Leibnitz, and Descartes, the ideas of the Enlightenment and the French Revolution, Romanticism— had no impact on Afghanistan. Afghan literature of the period, which was written in both Persian and Pashto and cultivated in such centers as Herat, Kabul, Kandahar, and the regions of Badakhshan and Panjshir, dealt mainly with personal rather than social themes. Lyric poetry, with themes of love and nostalgia, or with didactic moral lessons, dominated the literary *divans* (collections of poetry) of the time. There were very few Afghans with the background of the eighteenth-century writer Seyed Abul Hassan, who had been educated in Badakhshan, Mecca, Medina, and Egypt, had visited Constantinople, the Caucasus, and Bukhara, and had become aware of the general conditions of the Islamic world. The few writers who lamented the vanishing glories of the Muslim world attributed the deterioration to a lack of genuine adherence to the precepts of the Quran or blamed it on the inequities and cruelties of the Charkh-e Falak (Wheel of Destiny).[93] The general absence of discussion in Afghanistan on the decadence of Muslim institutions can be attributed in part to the fact that until the First Anglo-Afghan War the Afghans had not been exposed to the massive technological power and military strength of any European power. Moreover, from a psychological point of view, the Afghans enjoyed a greater sense of security than other Muslims, since they had only recently developed a society forceful enough to undertake foreign adventures or create an empire.[94]

The position of writers and scholars in Afghanistan was weak. They were economically and socially bound to the established order. Some were under the patronage of the Afghan rulers or the rulers of Herat and Badakhshan;[95] many were ulama or mullahs, attached to the mosques; a few held multiple posts, for instance as court poet, physician, secretary, and tutor, within the royal entourage. In all instances they were heavily committed to sustaining the established intellectual and theological order. Among the learned of Afghanistan there were only a handful of scholars who were interested in the sciences, medicine, geometry, or chemistry. In this realm, the interests of even such eminent learned men as Mir Zhur ad-Din Ahmad "Zhur" did not go beyond the Muslim scientific achievements of the Middle Ages.[96] The few scholars who customarily traveled from Afghanistan to Bukhara, India, the Ottoman Empire, or Arabia did so mainly as pilgrims or to study such subjects as Arabic and Muslim jurisprudence. By the second half of the nineteenth century, the number of journeys for the sake of scholarship had sharply declined. At the same time, the economic and political dislocation of the region resulted in a decrease in the practice and extent of patronage of scholars.

The works of the writers, chroniclers, and poets of the period had little impact on Afghan society. Apart from perpetuating Islamic traditions and upholding orthodoxy, the main function of the literati was to contribute to *adab* (polite education), which involved a familiarity with the literary, aesthetic, and philosophic treatises and commentaries of the past and was confined to a very narrow layer of society. The lack of printing facilities and public libraries prevented the circulation of literary divans and other writings of the period; the few works that appeared in print were published either in Lahore or in Karachi (as were those of Qazi Mir Hussein and Ghulam Muhammed Khan Tarzi).[97] Many manuscripts were either lost or survived only in a few handwritten copies. Lichtenstadter's characterization of the Islamic society of the Middle East in the fifteenth and sixteenth centuries applies to early-nineteenth-century Afghanistan as well: "Side by side with the erudite scholar, the sophisticated courtier and rich lover of books and the arts stood the illiterate proletarian and peasant. . . . Even the highly trained craftsman and the artisan of the East was illiterate then as he still frequently is."[98]

Afghan historiography of the period added little to the intellectual atmosphere. A survey of the available manuscript literature dealing with the history of the time (collected at present in the Kabul Museum and the libraries of the Afghan Ministry of Education and Press Department) indicates that the historical works consisted mainly of narratives and legends.[99] Historiography lacked the spirit of rational and sociological analysis in the tradition of Ibn Khaldún.

The general decline in the political, economic, and cultural domains threatened the position of the Afghan monarchy, as well as the existence of the Afghan state. The need for general or partial reform became mandatory, particularly as a defensive measure against bordering states. The Sikh kingdom, Persia, and the Central Asian khanates of Bukhara and Khiva had all embarked upon a limited program of military reorganization and technological borrowings during the first decades of the century, and all had claims on or designs against certain regions of Afghanistan. The Sikhs under Maharaja Runjit Singh had built an army on the European pattern. French, Italian, American, and English adventurers and ex-officers, as well as Hindustani deserters from the East India Company's army, had trained the Sikh army, provided it with a powerful artillery, and assumed positions of command in it.[100] The Persian monarchy, confronted with Russian expansionism in Transcaucasia, was also eager to raise a modern army. To do so, the Persians were ready to seek military aid in the form of financial loans, armaments, and advisers—first from France, then England, and later even Russia itself. The most notable attempt at military modernization was made by Prince Abbas Mirza, whose army reportedly included some 300 Afghans.[101] Persian plans of military modernization continued into the 1860's, when the monarchy recruited Austrian and Russian officers to train its army. From 1806 on, the rulers of Khiva and Bukhara introduced various minor reforms in their countries. These included the creation of councils, improvements in irrigation and customs procedures, and the encouragement of trade. By the 1870's the Bukharans were asking for and receiving Russian military aid in the form of arms, technical aid, and instruction.[102]

THE ASCENDANCY OF DOST MUHAMMED

Afghan political life was dominated throughout the first quarter of the nineteenth century by a fierce struggle between the princely Sadozai and Muhammedzai clans of the Durrani tribe. The Sadozais were supported by the Popalzais, and the Muhammedzais by the Barakzais. The struggle, sparked by the attempts of the Sadozai dynasty to consolidate political authority in its hands by curbing the power of the Barakzais and the other Durrani subtribes, was compounded by the blood feud that had grown out of the killing of the Muhammedzai leaders Payanda Khan and Fateh Khan. That act had not only alienated the Muhammedzai and the Sadozai clans but also pitted their respective subtribes, the Barakzais and Popalzais, against each other. After an initially successful resistance by the Sadozai rulers Shah Mahmud and Shah Shuja, the kinsmen of Payanda Khan and Fateh Khan forced Shah Shuja into exile in India (1813); Shah Mahmud was driven to Herat (1818), where he founded a Sadozai principality. The rest of Afghanistan came under either nominal or effective control of the Barakzais. The brothers of the slain Fateh Khan ruled the region of Peshawar (Sultan Muhammed Khan), the province of Kashmir (Nawab Jabbar Khan), Kandahar province (Kohendil Khan, Rahimdil Khan, Poordil Khan), and Kabul (Muhammed Azim Khan). The intertribal and intrafamily strife between 1818 and 1834 not only dismembered and weakened the Afghan empire but also resulted in the loss of Kashmir, Multan, Peshawar, and Baluchistan. The Uzbek chieftains of northern Afghanistan, nominally tributaries of the Emir of Bukhara, dominated that region of the Afghan empire.[103]

Dost Muhammed Khan (1826–38, 1842–63) had the difficult task of reuniting and building onto what was left of the Afghan empire while resisting the further encroachments of the Sikhs, Uzbeks, and rival Sadozais. Upon the death of Muhammed Azim Khan in 1826, Dost Muhammed, who was the youngest of the Barakzai brothers and then governor of Ghazni, became the ruler of Kabul. His domain included only Kabul, Ghazni, Jalalabad, and Charikar. In an attempt to assert his authority over all of Afghanistan, he embarked upon a policy of curtailing the power of the other Durrani subtribes by concentrating political and administrative control in the hands of the Barakzai clans, especially his kinsmen, thereby creating a Barakzai political confederacy. He also attempted to place his sons on the thrones held by his brothers.[104]

According to Masson, "Dost Muhammed Khan exercised all his ability, gaining his ends by strategem or by force, but never employing the latter when the former was sufficient. Some of the obnoxious chiefs he inveighed by Korans and false oaths; others by intermarriage—a mean not unfrequently resorted to by Durranis in order to get their enemies into their power when other wiles have failed."[105] A list of Dost Muhammed's wives bears testimony to his judicious use of the institution of marriage to advance his political designs: he selected wives from the families of important religious leaders, wealthy merchants, and tribal chieftains (notably of the Ghilzai, Turi, and Bangash tribes), and from those of the dignitaries of various turbulent regions, for instance Kohistan.[106]

Dost Muhammed was the first Afghan ruler to obtain advice from Europeans on military technology. He was greatly interested in the European method of raising armies by conscription and queried Alexander Burnes closely on the subject. He also showed keen interest in European machinery, steam engines, and other technical innovations. In order to modernize his army, he was ready to hire Burnes, or an Englishman of comparable rank, as a general with full command of certain Afghan army units.[107] His hope was that with a modernized army he could consolidate his position and check the encroachments of his "Westernizing" neighbors.

Unfortunately, instead of hiring qualified European experts, the Afghan Amir came to rely on the services of a handful of American, English, Persian, and French adventurers. Among them, the name of Josiah Harlan figures prominently. Harlan, who came from Newlin Township, in Pennsylvania, was the first American known to have visited and resided in Afghanistan. He has been described by Kaye as "an American adventurer, now a doctor and now a general, who was ready to take any kind of service, with any one disposed to pay him and to do any kind of work at the instance of his master." Labeled "clever" and "unscrupulous," Harlan had enlisted in the Bengal Artillery Corps as a surgeon, later offering his services to Runjit Singh. In the service of the Sikh ruler, Harlan was assigned the task of sowing discord among the ruling Afghan princes; in 1835, however, he broke with the Sikhs and offered his services to Dost Muhammed. In Kabul, Harlan instructed Afghan troops in European military tactics, subsequently becoming an officer and aide-de-camp to Dost Muhammed, who later appointed him a general. Although Harlan claimed that he rose to the position of commander-in-chief of the Afghan armed forces, this seems very unlikely.[108]

Another of Dost Muhammed's advisers was a Lieutenant Campbell, a British officer. Formerly in the service of Shah Shuja, Campbell was wounded on the battlefield and captured by Dost Muhammed, who engaged him as a military adviser, an instructor of artillery, and a general in the Afghan army.[109] According to some sources, Campbell became a Muslim and assumed the name Shir Muhammed Khan; he was named commander-in-chief of the Afghan forces in Balkh.[110] Among the other Europeans in Dost Muhammed's employ were Colonel Leslie (alias Rattray) and a Frenchman, Argoo, who left a post with the Sikhs in 1836. The Afghans, while "regretting [Argoo's] attachment to the bottle," reportedly gave him command of a regiment.[111] There were one or two other Europeans who became converts to Islam and were hired by the ruler of Kabul.[112]

Dost Muhammed did not confine his recruitment efforts to European fortune-seekers; he also employed various British-trained Persian or Muslim Indian adventurers and deserters to help in the task of remodeling his army. Vigne reported in 1835 that the royal army was composed of "Patans, Hindus, Kuzzelbashes, and a few deserters from the Sikh army, whose services were valuable, as they had been regularly drilled. I found one of Mr. Moorcroft's servants here in the artillery."[113] Among the non-Europeans in the Afghan service, Abdul Samad Khan Hindi and Saleh Muhammed were the most important. Abdul Samad, a Persian, was described by Masson as "a profilgate [sic] adventurer, originally of Tabriz, [who] had flagrantly signalised himself in every country he had visited, as well as in his own, which he was compelled to fly." Named a general in Dost Muhammed's army, Abdul Samad distinguished himself in his attempts to reorganize the Afghan artillery.[114] Saleh Muhammed, who had been a *subadar* (equivalent to captain) in the Indian army, had deserted with his men and joined the camp of the Afghan Amir. He became a military instructor and later a commander in the Afghan army.[115]

The task of these soldiers of fortune was immense, their handicaps great, their achievements limited. They faced cultural and language barriers, were often under suspicion, and were frequently regarded with contempt. Argoo, for instance, was removed from his post because of his ignorance of the Persian language, which provided ample opportunities for interpreters to plot against him. Rattray, who became a Muslim and assumed the name Fida Muhammed Khan, was regarded by Dost Muhammed as an opportunist—"a disgrace to any creed," a man who had changed his religion, and would again, to improve his fortune.[116] The few contributions the foreigners made were confined to the army, which was, of course, the main preoccupation of the Afghan Amir.

Among the military innovations Abdul Samad, Campbell, and Harlan introduced were the adoption of uniforms and the formation of a European-style infantry regiment; they also reorganized the tribal levies to some extent.[117] The remodeled army included a cavalry of about 12,000 men divided into two brigades: *khud aspah* (those who had their own horses) and *amlah sarkari* (those who used government horses). The Amir's sons were in command of the cavalry units. The army also included a specially trained infantry unit of some 2,000 men, armed with large muskets. It was composed of the most trustworthy non-Durrani Afghans, probably in order to give the Amir some measure of independence of the Durrani khans. The Afghan artillery consisted of some 50 to 60 serviceable guns of different caliber, 40 of them in Kabul. Dost Muhammed attempted to establish a regular salary system for the troops and to end the anachronistic practice of paying them mainly in goods or requisition orders drawn on certain villages. Under the new system, the soldiers were paid annually in cash, as well as in grain, grass, sheep, blankets, and butter. They received the cash from local tax collectors; the provisions were gathered by the headmen of the villages under orders from the paymaster. Theoretically, the annual general pay of a cavalryman, which had to be used for his living expenses and those of his family, was 120 Kabuli Kham rupees (ten pounds), that of an infantryman 84 rupees. In practice, however, the majority of soldiers were paid only about six pounds a year.

There were serious weaknesses in Dost Muhammed's reorganized army. For one thing, the reforms were confined to the regions of Kabul and Balkh, and did not affect the entire machinery of the Afghan fighting forces, whose character remained predominantly feudal-tribal. For another, the Amir's circumscribed funds and resources prevented regular payment to his troops. Pay and rank in the army depended upon influence and patronage rather than upon merit. The army also suffered a general lack of trained officers and a shortage of equipment.[118]

CONSOLIDATION OF DOST MUHAMMED'S AUTHORITY

Dost Muhammed took drastic measures to establish tranquility within his realm. He eliminated the bands of desperadoes that had devastated the districts of Kabul and disrupted the city's trade. In some cases he granted them amnesty on the promise of good behavior; in others, he hired them himself or subjected them to exemplary deaths. (They were blown from guns.) He gradually disposed of or circumvented various rebellious chieftains of the Kohistan region and executed a few chiefs of Charikar. Through a judicious exploitation of Shi'ah-Sunni differences, he followed a divide-and-rule policy aimed chiefly at preventing an alliance between the politically and economically influential Qizil-Bash of Kabul and the Hazaras of Hazarajat, the two major Shi'ah communities of his realm. The Amir cultivated the friendship of the Qizil-Bash by publicizing the purported Qizil-Bash background of his mother and by intervening to settle conflicts between the Qizil-Bash and the Sunni Muslims in Kabul; at the same time he increased the Sunni Muslims' animosities toward the Hazaras by giving a tacit politico-religious character to his conquest of Hazarajat.

Dost Muhammed also played upon the religious theme in his struggle against the growing Sikh power. In 1834 he assumed the title Amir al-muminin (The Commander of the Faithful), hoping thereby to enlist the military support of the semi-independent Afghan frontier tribes for the defense of Afghanistan, and to procure financial contributions from the faithful Muslims.[119] The declaration of a jihad against the "infidel Sikhs" brought thousands of Muslims to his banner.* With these troops at his side, the Amir was successful in consolidating his authority within the principality of Kabul. He was also able to extend his moral leadership over various regions or tribes by gaining either their active cooperation or at least their neutrality.

Within the principality of Kabul, the Amir attempted to centralize the administration of justice. The police, under the direction of a *kotwal*, and a Shar'ia court, presided over by a *kazi*, adjudicated disputes. However, the settlement of all serious matters had to be referred to the Amir, who thus assumed personal control of the dispensation of justice by preserving his prerogative to circumvent the religious courts. He also attempted to limit the political power of the religious establishment by the judicious manipulation of the allowances that had been granted to the mullahs by his predecessors. Kaye has described the Amir's paternalistic manner of handling justice:

Ever ready to listen to [the people's] complaints and to redress their grievances, he seldom rode abroad without being accosted in the public streets or highways by citizen or by peasant waiting to lay before the *Sirdar* a history of his grievances or his sufferings and to ask for assistance or redress.... [The Amir gives] directions to his attendants to take the necessary steps to render justice to the injured or to alleviate the sufferings of the distressed. Such was his love of equity, indeed, that people asked: "Is Dost Muhammed dead that there is no justice?"[120]

The Amir encouraged interregional and foreign trade, and minted gold, silver, and copper coins in an effort to promote the predominance of Kabul and his dynasty in Afghanistan; all government and mercantile accounts were handled in Kabuli Kham rupees. He also attempted to regularize the country's chaotic customs system, seeking thereby to weaken the power of various chieftains over the customs revenues of his principality. With this in mind, the Amir established new duties on exports, imports, and goods in transit. The collection of the duties, which were designed to ensure a steady income from the traffic of the India–Kabul–Central Asia trade, was supervised by the Amir's administrators.[121]

Dost Muhammed forcibly collected back taxes from the non-Durrani

* "From the Kohistan, from the hills beyond, from the regions of the Hindu Kush, from the remoter fastnesses of Turkestan, multitudes of various denominations, moved by various impulses, but all noisily boasting their true Muhammedan zeal, came flocking in to the Amir's standard. Ghilzais and Kohistanis, sleek Qizilbashes and rugged Uzbeks, horsemen and footmen—all who could wield a sword or lift a matchlock, obeyed the call in the name of the Prophet" (Kaye, *History of the War*, I, 129–30).

tribes that had stopped paying them. The Turi, Jaji, Suleiman Khel, Safi, and Hazara tribes were all gradually coerced into paying their assessed taxes. The fortifications of the Suleiman Khel were destroyed, and they were forced to pay the Amir a tribute of one camel for every 40 men.[122] Meanwhile, the Amir attempted to establish a *modus vivendi* with the powerful and independent frontier tribes over which he had no administrative control, cultivating the friendship of the important Mohmand and Yusufzai chieftains.[123] In this he seems to have been motivated by two considerations: the interdependence of the defenses of the frontier tribes and those of Afghanistan, and a desire to discourage the possibility of an anti-Barakzai political coalition with or among the trans-frontier tribes. He did not venture to attack the Durranis' time-honored privilege of supplying horsemen for service to the state in lieu of land taxes, a feudal obligation that in any case had been allowed to lapse; however, he cautiously began to assert his authority over the Durranis by taxing their hamsaya. By using this and other indirect taxation devices, the Amir apparently hoped to make conditions so difficult that the Durrani chiefs themselves would seek a regular and direct tax assessment system.[124]

The Amir wished to set up a uniform system of taxation in order to halt the increasing irregularities and abuses involved in the collection of taxes.* His plan was to collect one-third of the produce of all lands under cultivation and to impose regular and standard taxes on the merchants and artisans. Some of his other attempted reforms were more specific in scope and more limited in application: he prohibited drinking, the sale of wine, the introduction of any intoxicating drug into Kabul, the performances of dancing girls, and the playing of dice. He ordered all "women of bad character to marry or to leave Kabul." In his determination to eliminate corruption, he even threatened to "grill some of the bakers in their own ovens" for short-weighting the people of Kabul.[125] He did not, however, have an all-encompassing plan for reform and action. His limited reforms were by necessity confined to the province of Kabul. Moreover, he was constantly faced with the problem of procuring steady financing and enough cash to carry out the political and economic integration of his kingdom. The loss of the Peshawar Valley and Kashmir, on which the Afghan

---

* Vigne detailed the taxes required in the purchase of a single sheep, for which the merchants paid one penny apiece initially, one sheep in every 40 becoming the property of the Amir. He wrote: "An officer acting as a broker again taxed them in the market [and] another duty was paid for the mark which showed that the broker's tax had been paid. The *postin* or leathern jacket maker, or currier, paid half a *shahi*—about three farthings—in the rupee, according to the value of the *postin*, so that the purchaser of the sheep in the market had to pay two or three rupees [of tax] for it" (p. 377).

rulers had been dependent for a steady income, was a great blow to his plans for reform. Most of the major Afghan tribes enjoyed tax exemptions, and in some regions of Kabul itself a barter economy prevailed. An increase in indirect taxes, which were mainly in kind, prevented extensive circulation of his new currency and hindered the growth of capital.

The Amir's total annual revenue from the principality of Kabul and its northern dependencies was somewhere between 1.4–2.4 million Kabuli rupees (160,000–220,000 pounds), an amount that was hardly sufficient for any major undertaking or for the modernization of a large standing army. This revenue was derived from land, customs, and the urban centers; over 50 per cent was collected from the urban centers, some 13 per cent from customs. Revenues from the royal lands amounted to no more than 6 per cent of the total income, and those from the tribal landholdings apparently did not exceed 20 per cent.[126] Instead of openly attacking the basic feudal structure of the kingdom in order to obtain additional revenues (a move that would have turned the powerful tribes against the throne), Dost Muhammed merely imposed greater taxes on the merchant class, especially the Hindus. His arbitrary measures included requiring the Hindu merchants to contribute 300,000 rupees to his war effort; levying two years' advance *jezia* (head tax) from the Hindus and other non-Muslims; confiscating the property of politically suspect but undoubtedly opulent merchants; extracting five to ten rupees from every shop in the bazaar; and forcing the merchants to "lend" him large sums of money in emergencies.[127] The predominantly urban and sedentary Tajiks and Hazaras were particularly hard hit: they paid heavy taxes to local tribal chieftains as well as to Dost Muhammed.[128] Though the Amir thought he was establishing stability and law and order, and encouraging the expansion of trade, he was thus actually preventing any lasting beneficial effects by taxing the meager resources of his few urban centers.

The First Anglo-Afghan War brought these modest reform efforts to a halt and disrupted the already strained economy of Afghanistan, especially in the Kabul-Ghazni-Kandahar region. Dost Muhammed lost his throne and was exiled to India, where he remained until 1842. However, in the aftermath of this disastrous war he regained his throne and was in a stronger position to work for the political unity of Afghanistan than before. Afghan historians have wondered why, after his return from India, where he gained firsthand knowledge of various European-type institutions and technological adaptations,[129] he did not propose any extensive reforms or at least strengthen those he had started. Reshtiya, for instance, holds that the Amir's 20-year rule, political control of all of Afghanistan, and great national prestige after the First Anglo-Afghan War gave Dost Muhammed a firm political and psychological grip over the nation; yet he was either unable or unwilling to exploit these advantages and initiate major reforms.[130]

The fact is that there is no evidence that Dost Muhammed ever had any plans for fundamental reforms. His achievements during his second reign (1842–63) did not go beyond the political unification of Afghanistan, the establishment of relative internal stability, and the maintenance of a standing army.* He did next to nothing to improve the health standards of the country. There were no public dispensaries in Afghanistan until 1895; there were no trained doctors, nor was the country visited by physicians from neighboring countries. Mullahs and *hakims* (local physicians) were mostly ignorant and bigoted; their knowledge of medicine had not advanced much beyond that of the Middle Ages. Charms, bleeding, herbs, astrology—and the Quran—were prescribed for all types of diseases. Mixed plasters of mud and salt were used for wounds.[131] Fatalism, fear of the "evil eye," and belief in spirits or genies prevailed; among the Hazaras, for example, when a birth took place, food was placed in a chamber for the genies in order to win their favors. Contact with modern medicine was accessible only to the well-to-do, who went to India for treatment, and to a few desperate hakims, who engaged in the indiscriminate use of modern drugs imported from Europe or India,† often with tragic results.[132]

Under Dost Muhammed's rule, no educational or cultural achievements

---

* J. A. Norris, in discussing the impact the Indian exile had on Dost Muhammed, writes (pp. 4–5): "He now appreciated the full extent of British power in the world: he had come to understand that his 'hosts' were for the time being the most powerful nation on the face of the earth, that the Russians might have more men and a greater expanse of national territory, but that the British more than any other people had engines and engineers, innumerable ships and guns, and an unlimited self-confidence.... Now Dost Muhammed was re-entering his own country. He must reign and he must rule in a land where the British and their sepoys had killed and been killed. On the journey from Jalalabad to Kabul he could see the rotting corpses of one battle and the bleaching bones of another, freshly exposed by the melting of the snow.... Dost Muhammed, on his return, saw how heavily his people had paid, and we need not wonder why he held his country aloof from British India for so long thereafter."

† Wrote Ferrier: "[Some Afghan hakims] brought with them some of their drugs, in order that I might give them some notion of the manner in which certain chemical preparations which they had received from British India should be employed, as they were ignorant of their effects. They had, they said, up to that time given these medicines in progressive doses, until they ascertained the cases in which they were applicable. How many of their unfortunate patients had been killed by this system I dared not ask; but [one of them] filled up the blank by pulling from his pocket a bottle of the cyanate of mercury, requesting to know what devil of a salt it could be? 'It has been of no use to me,' he added, 'for of one hundred patients that I have given it to, only one was cured—all the rest died'" (*Caravan Journeys*, p. 149).

are recorded. His court, which unlike Timur Shah's did not pretend to be a cultural center, underwent no significant structural changes; it continued to resemble a tribal jirga. Although the Amir taught himself to read and write, most of the leaders of the ruling elite were illiterate.[133] The Amir did nothing to alter the rigid Afghan guild system, which was divided into 32 sections, each led by a *katkhuda*; the guilds strenuously resisted innovation.[134] Nor did the Amir introduce new industries or agricultural methods. (The single exception was his encouragement of the cultivation of potatoes, which had reportedly been sent into the country by Wade, the East India Company's political agent at Ludiana, and had been grown in Kabul since the 1820's.)[135]

The political reunification of Afghanistan and the consolidation of his dynastic rule remained the Amir's two major objectives during his second reign. He conquered Balkh in 1850 and Khulm, Kunduz, and Badakhshan five years later, ending the political life of the semi-independent or autonomous khanates of northern Afghanistan. In 1855, Kohendil Khan, the chief of the Kandahar sardars, died. Under his rule, the province of Kandahar had been virtually autonomous. His death precipitated a sharp conflict among his brothers and heirs, and the Amir took this opportunity to consolidate his authority over the province (1856). Unable or perhaps unwilling to conciliate his brothers and nephews, he drove most of them into exile and in some cases confiscated their property. In the last year of his reign, Dost Muhammed conquered Herat. Thus, by 1863, all of Afghanistan had come under Barakzai rule; Dost Muhammed and his sons were masters of the cities of Afghanistan. Even before the conquest of Herat, Sir Harry Lumsden reported from Afghanistan that the Amir "appears to have a much firmer hold of his people than we have hitherto given him credit for, and certainly the general safety of the roads has completely taken me by surprise. People go about their ordinary avocations unarmed, while travelers pass up or down, by day or night, in the most perfect confidence. His system appears to be to divide the country among his sons, allowing each to govern his district in his own fashion, but holding him responsible for its tranquility."[136]

The Amir's drive for political unity in the kingdom was challenged many times. In 1854, there was a serious insurrection in Balkh, which was stirred up by the Emir of Bukhara. Dost Muhammed's disgruntled brothers courted Persia and the British authorities in India, in an attempt to regain their lost position in the province of Kandahar. Yar Muhammed Khan, who had slain the Sadozai ruler of Herat in 1842, attempted to institutionalize and legitimize his rule and the independence of Herat with

British, and at times, Persian support. In this connection, the British authorities vacillated, unable to decide whether Herat should be independent, ceded to Persia, or turned over to Afghanistan. Afghan reunification was also threatened by serious differences both among the Amir's many sons and between some of them and the Amir. For instance, Muhammed Akbar Khan, the Amir's oldest son and heir apparent (who led the successful Afghan resistance against the forces of Shah Shuja and the British during the First Anglo-Afghan War), disagreed with the Amir on the question of forming a Western-style army and on other reforms. Unlike the Amir, he had no faith in a standing army, preferring loose military formations and tribal levies.

Dost Muhammed's efforts to ensure his dynasty's continued rule through an uncontested law of succession were frustrated by the deaths of first his oldest son, Muhammed Akbar Khan, and then his next-named successor, Ghulam Haydar Khan. The Amir had been careful to vest power in the hands of his heirs and to build up a safe political base of operations for them by placing the rich provinces of the kingdom in their hands. Their deaths thus had an unsettling effect.

These difficulties were not the only ones facing the Amir. Many of the Afghan tribes continued their attempts to safeguard their privileges and vested interests. The Amir was both reluctant and powerless to take on the powerful non-Barakzai Durranis. However, he and his sons waged a number of battles with the non-Durrani tribes, especially the Ghilzai tribe. Sher Ali Khan, the governor of the province of Ghazni and heir apparent after the deaths of his two brothers, fought the Ghilzais six times before he was able to subdue them and force one of their principal leaders to "pay revenue into the Amir's treasury."[137]

In the 1850's, the Afghan religious establishment, which had cooperated with Dost Muhammed during his struggle against the Sikhs, Shah Shuja, and the British, showed increasing signs of uneasiness and even at times open hostility over the Anglo-Afghan rapprochement and understandings of 1855 and 1857. During the Indian Mutiny of 1857, the religious leaders exerted great pressure on the Amir to abandon a policy of non-interference and lead a holy war against the British, thereby liberating the Muslims of India and recovering Peshawar. Sir Harry Lumsden, who was in Kandahar at the time, reported that the news of the Mutiny was received with great joy by the people of eastern Afghanistan:

Excitement ran wild among the Afghans. Mullahs in the mosques added fuel to the fire, and preached jihad. . . . Exaggerated reports of events in India continued to excite the minds of the people of Candahar. A deputation of the priesthood waited on the Sirdar and requested to be informed whether the Amir intended to avail himself of the present crisis and to strike a blow for the benefit of Islam.... In the early part of September (1857) Hafiz Ji (High Priest), supported by a gang of fanatical mullahs, instigated in their turn by Sirdars Sultan Muhammed and Pir Muhammed [brothers of the Amir], pressed upon Dost Muhammed the necessity of undertaking a religious war against the British. The moment was a critical one: the fate of Delhi was uncertain, the resolution of the aged ruler seemed for an instant to stagger.[138]

The Amir's second son, Azam Khan, was able to convince the Amir that the British were too powerful. Reminding his father that failure might once again cost him his kingdom, he suggested that self-interest was the only motive his uncles had in urging a holy war against the British. According to Lumsden, the Amir confessed that as a Muslim ruler, he would, if he could, sweep unbelievers from the face of the earth. Since he did not have that power, the Amir said: "I must cling to the British to save me from the cursed Kujjur [the ruling dynasty of Persia], and having made an alliance with the British Government, happens what may, I will keep it faithfully till death."[139]

Though the Amir resisted the temptation to plunge Afghanistan into a second Anglo-Afghan war, he nevertheless carried on a diplomatic war with the British. At issue was the return of Peshawar and the extension and recognition of the Amir's sovereignty over the Pathan tribes of the borderland. Dost Muhammed pressed the British not to deal with "these subjects," except through the intermediary of the Amir of Afghanistan.[140]

In the face of the uneasy political situation, the only modernization schemes the Amir attempted during his second reign were limited military reforms. The regular army continued to use English-type uniforms, some modern weaponry (mainly guns), a European-style drill, and terminology adapted from English, e.g., *komidan* (commandant), *mejir* (major), *kornel* or *djornel* (colonel).[141] In 1857, the Amir accepted the help of a British military mission led by Maj. H. B. Lumsden. Lumsden had some success in modernizing the Afghan army. According to Sir Bartle Frere, some Afghan troops were "quite equal in armament, skill, and drill to any corps in our service." Frere concluded that "against such men our troops must be armed with something better than an old-pattern musket."[142]

However, despite these improvements, the number of regularly trained units and men remained limited: the regular infantry consisted of some 16 regiments of (nominally) 800 men, the regular cavalry had only three regiments of 300 men. The artillery had 80 field-pieces and a few heavy guns. Recruitment for the model army "depended neither on conscriptive nor voluntary enlistment, but on forcible seizure of able-bodied men, from each district, who had no choice but to serve. Failure to do so entailed their personal imprisonment, and the utter ruin of their families."[143] The pay of a foot soldier was supposed to be five rupees a month; two months' pay was deducted annually for clothing and other services. Even this small amount was reported to be paid very irregularly; much of it was paid in kind, in some instances by remitting part of the taxes owed by the families of men in the regular forces. Military discipline was extremely severe. Soldiers were hanged for selling a government musket, and the families of deserters were seized. Other punishments included forfeiture of pay for months at a time or beatings. The lack of a trained officer corps was a great handicap. Though merit was recognized, it did not overcome the traditional ethnic or tribal vested interests. The power of tribal chiefs or Durrani notables superseded that of the generals.*

In addition to the regular army, the Amir had militiamen or *jezailchis* (so called because of their use of a *jezail*, a heavy rifle resting on a forked iron prong). Some of these militiamen were armed by the state and received the same pay as the foot soldiers in the regular army, but often they were tribesmen, whose services were provided by the tribal chieftains in return for tax-free land grants.

In general, the Afghan armed forces retained their feudal characteristics. Once the country was brought under Barakzai rule, the Afghan ruler could theoretically count on the services of some 75,000 cavalrymen and 62,000 infantrymen in case of war. As *daftaris* (registered recipients of land, of pay in the form of indemnities, allowances, pensions, or grain, of tax remissions, or of water rights), these men were required to provide military assistance to the ruler.[144]

SHER ALI AND THE BEGINNINGS OF A NEW AFGHANISTAN

The political unity achieved by Dost Muhammed was shattered after his death. An interregnum marked by civil wars among the rival heirs to the throne lasted for five years (1864–69),† ending with the triumph of Sher Ali (1869–79), who gradually asserted his authority over all Afghan-

---

* Lumsden and Elsmie (pp. 166–67) report the case of Gen. Firamosh Khan, a native of Kafiristan, who commanded the heir-apparent's contingent of troops. Instructed in military science by Campbell, the general continued his education on his own, ordering or obtaining Persian translations of most of the manuals of the Anglo-Indian army. According to Lumsden, although Firamosh Khan had become the most outstanding soldier in Afghanistan, he had no voice in military strategy and every petty chief superseded him, "who is but a *ghulam* [slave, servant]."

† Dost Muhammed left 16 sons. After his death in 1863, most of them refused to accept Sher Ali as their sovereign, whereupon the Amir-designate resorted to military action. He defeated the forces of one brother, Azam Khan, and arranged a truce with another,

istan.[145] Before his accession, however, one of his brothers, Azam Khan, who ruled for a short period (1867–68), attempted to transform the sociopolitical life of Afghanistan. Azam reportedly used the services of the famous Muslim modernist Seyed Jamal ad-Din al-Afghānī, who in his official capacity as adviser is believed to have drawn up a plan for the national recovery and cultural resurrection of Afghanistan. Among the measures he proposed were a network of schools, the publication of a newspaper, and a new form of centralized government with a well-regulated communications system—even the issuance of postage stamps.[146] (A newspaper called *Kabul*, reportedly published by al-Afghānī, was instituted, but it was short-lived.)[147]

The Afghan historian Reshtiya, who considers Sher Ali the founder of a new civilization in Afghanistan, contends that Sher Ali adopted al-Afghānī's reform plans, even though al-Afghānī himself was forced to leave the country because of his close political association with Azam Khan.[148] Whatever the basis, al-Afghānī's plans or his own initiative, Sher Ali made a number of changes in Afghanistan.* He undertook to expand the production of guns and artillery, a program that had been initiated earlier, in 1867, on a small scale by one of the rivals for the throne, Afzal Khan; his new workshops had some success in the manufacture of Armstrong guns.[149] He also encouraged the development of handicrafts and the establishment of small-scale home industries. In an attempt to improve the country's communications, he instituted road-building and bridge-repairing projects, and inaugurated the first regular postal service between Kabul and Peshawar. The first Afghan postage stamps were put into circulation in 1870. Lithography was introduced, and another periodical,

---

Afzal Khan. But he later captured Afzal by a ruse and imprisoned him. Managing to escape, Afzal's son Abdur Rahman continued his father's struggle. In 1865, Sher Ali met still another brother, Amin Khan, in battle, and again was successful. Though a number of reverses followed (including the capture of Kabul and Ghazni by Abdur Rahman's forces in 1866), in January 1869 Sher Ali entered Kabul and was acknowledged as the Amir of Afghanistan, both by his brothers and by the British government in India. See White-King, pp. 294–99, 302–4; and Wyllie, *Essays,* pp. 24–25n.

* In a very interesting article on al-Afghānī (in *Siraj al-Akhbar,* 6th year, No. 5) Mahmud Tarzi reveals that in Afghanistan al-Afghānī was known as Jamal ad-Din al-Rumi and was thought to be from the Ottoman Empire. Two Western scholars also doubt al-Afghānī's Afghan origin; they support the claim of Iranian historians that he was born in Persia. (See Keddie, "Afghani in Afghanistan" and "Biographical Review," p. 519; and Keddourie, "Nouvelle lumière" and *Afghānī and 'Abduh.* Al-Afghānī's importance, however, does not lie in his Afghan origin, but rather in the fact that he took great pride in Afghanistan and its successful resistance against British imperialism (see his *Tarikh al-Afghan*). His ideological and political writings became a source of inspiration for Afghan reformers and nationalists.

Shams-ul-Nahar, appeared in 1875, but it, like *Kabul*, was short-lived, ceasing publication in 1879.[150]

One of Sher Ali's concerns was education. Prior to his reign, there were no public schools in Afghanistan; education was acquired either at home or at a maktab. No European languages were taught, and only a handful of Afghans received the limited, European-style education that was offered by missionaries. (Abdul Ghias Khan, a nephew of Dost Muhammed, received such an education in a school conducted by the American missionaries at Ludiana.)* For the most part, the religious character of the mission schools and their "enforced observance of Christian religious exercises" kept Muslims and Hindus from enrolling their children.[151] Sher Ali founded the first public school in the land at Bala Hissar, in Kabul. It had two divisions, military and civilian, and offered courses in the English language, which were taught by Indians.[152]

Another of the Amir's major concerns was the modernizing of his army. During his reign, European military manuals were translated into Pashto and Persian. The army, already outfitted with relatively modern equipment and European-style uniforms, now adopted European hats as a symbol of modernity. Though some of the troops were equipped with "the discarded flint muskets, swords, belts, and bayonets of the British forces in India" and often wore uniforms that represented the obsolete stores of frontier posts, the fact that Kabul workshops were able and eager to duplicate the new weapons and equipment was in itself a major development. The Amir instituted regular cash payments in full for the troops, thus eliminating a major irritant to the villages that had been forced to fill requisition orders. He secured some British assistance in reorganizing his army. In 1869 the British government in India gave him 1.2 million rupees (about 100,000 pounds), some 12,000 guns, and 12 artillery pieces, and in 1875, some 5,000 Snider rifles. In order to bolster the country's defenses, Sher Ali attempted to set up regular production of military items in the government workshops and had some success in stockpiling large quantities of arms and provisions: when the forces of Lord Roberts captured

---

* Sekunder (Iskandar) Khan, a soldier of fortune and a nephew of Sher Ali, was another of the few Afghans who received a European-type education. According to Burnaby (pp. 386–87), Iskandar Khan and a force of 286 Afghans were sent by the ruler of Balkh to aid the Emir of Bukhara. However, the Bukharan ruler was unable to pay these troops on a regular basis, whereupon the Afghans attached themselves to Gen. K. P. von Kaufman, the Russian governor-general of Turkestan. Iskandar Khan later became a lieutenant-colonel in the tsarist army and was involved in a number of colorful incidents. He finally resigned his commission and went into retirement in England, where he was assigned "a liberal pension."

Kabul during the Second Anglo-Afghan War, they found 85 mortars and howitzers, millions of Enfield and Snider rifle cartridges, 250 tons of gunpowder, a large quantity of small arms and military equipment, stocks of lead, copper and tin, and even European musical instruments in Bala Hissar, the city's chief fortification.[153] An armory and gunshop were also built in Herat, where the Amir's son Yakub Khan raised and trained a modern army.*

Sher Ali also paid special attention to the establishment of close diplomatic links between Afghanistan and its neighbors, especially the Central Asian khanates. During the period 1871–79, various embassies were exchanged between Kabul and Bukhara.[154] His ultimate intention seems to have been to establish permanent diplomatic missions in all the neighboring countries.

Sher Ali was the first Afghan ruler to introduce a cabinet form of government, however rudimentary. He instituted the office of prime minister and established ministries for foreign and internal affairs, as well as war and treasury departments.[155] He also established a 13-member advisory council to participate in administrative decisions and help secure the cooperation of the Afghan tribes. In the economic field, he encouraged interregional and foreign trade. He also tried to expand the government's control of the country's finances by taking the lucrative task of tax collection away from the provincial governors. A new taxation system was introduced that in principle terminated the old complicated system whereby half of the country's revenues were paid in kind; all taxes were to be paid in cash.[156] In order to simplify the country's monetary system, the Amir tried to institute a new currency unit, the afghani, which was to be equal to one rupee and to be divided into 100 *pools*; eventually the new unit was supposed to replace the Kabuli rupee.[157]

Like Dost Muhammed, Sher Ali pursued a policy of friendship toward the frontier tribes in an effort to reassert the moral authority of the Afghan monarchy in the tribal belt. In an appeal issued on the occasion of the designation of Sardar Abdullah Jan as heir to the throne, Sher Ali emphasized Afghan patriotism. He reassured the frontier tribes about his intentions, declaring that he did not contemplate conquering their domains; on

---

* Marsh reported (p. 86) that the Herat workshops and foundry were producing good quality guns and rifles, though they were "roughly made." Yakub Khan, who was the governor of Herat, had raised some six regiments (each having about 1,000 men). Sher Ali's regular troops were estimated to number some 37,000 infantrymen and 6,400 cavalrymen; he also had a force of irregulars, including 3,500 infantrymen and 8,000 cavalrymen. His army was thus treble the strength of Dost Muhammed's. See White-King, p. 298.

the contrary, he would demonstrate that the Afghan court was impartial and dedicated to the welfare of all Afghans: "This Kingdom comprises all of Afghanistan. . . . Being your King I recognize all of you as my subjects, as citizens of my Kingdom, and I act according to the Commandments of God and the Prophet." In the same appeal, he called on the Afghan tribesmen to abandon brigandage and theft, and to cease fighting among themselves—all actions that were forbidden by Islam. Afghans, freed from the exigencies of foreign hostilities, should dedicate themselves to good deeds. He implored the Afghans to concern themselves with progress and science, because all "the kingdoms of the world had progressed except the Afghan one, and this due to their indifference to public good."[158]

Most of Sher Ali's projects either did not materialize or, if they did not fail in their embryonic stage, were unsuccessful. His advisory council, for example, was torn apart by tribal and regional interests. In his attempts to increase and regularize the kingdom's revenues he encountered great difficulties, but he could not increase the land taxes without incurring the wrath of the privileged tribes and feudal lords. The wars of Dost Muhammed and the five-year war of succession had drained the economy; the Afghan exchequer was empty. The annual income of the Afghan rulers had seldom fallen below one million pounds in the first decade of the nineteenth century; during Sher Ali's reign it was 700,000 pounds.[159] Under the circumstances, the Amir could scarcely support his army, let alone finance large-scale modernization schemes or renovate the educational system. He succeeded in reestablishing political unity, but he failed to achieve economic unity within the country. Moreover, the political future of his dynasty was uncertain. During a state visit to India in 1869, he was unable to obtain British *de jure* recognition or a guarantee of the rights of his heirs. Nor was he able to obtain a guarantee of British assistance in the event of foreign aggression against Afghanistan.[160] In such circumstances, he remained dependent upon the major Afghan tribes and was both unable and unwilling to make a frontal assault on the feudal-tribal institutions of his realm.

The halfhearted, hesitant, or simply haphazard reform plans of Dost Muhammed and Sher Ali remained limited and superficial. The tasks of both rulers were made more difficult by the strains and stresses of two Anglo-Afghan wars, which seriously dislocated the Afghan economy, upset the country's tenuous political unity, and increased the monarchy's dependence on the Afghan tribes. More important, because of those wars and the constant Anglo-Russian rivalry in Central Asia and the Middle East, the Afghan rulers adopted a policy of national isolationalism and of minimum Westernization, which was largely confined to the army. The fears and struggles of the Afghans between 1838 and 1880 led to a xenophobic attitude toward Europeans, particularly the British and the Russians, and played a large role in determining the course of the politics of reform and modernization in Afghanistan.

Chapter Four

European Imperialism and the Anglo-Afghan Wars

With Napoleon's invasion of Egypt in 1798, a new chapter in Afghan history opened. For more than a century thereafter, Afghanistan was caught up in a web of economic and political rivalries between the great European powers. The Napoleonic expedition to Egypt had three major objectives: to cut a canal through the isthmus of Suez; "to ensure to the French Republic the free and exclusive possession of the Red Sea"; and, by reopening the Mediterranean–Red Sea route to India, "to combat the satellites of the English government there . . . [and] drive the English from all their Oriental possessions."[1] These objectives were not new; Leibnitz had drawn the attention of Louis XIV to the importance of Egypt and the benefits to be derived from a reopening of the Red Sea trade route to India.[2] There had even been suggestions of a joint Franco-Russian expedition to India. Peter the Great had reportedly proposed in 1717 that the two powers cooperate in establishing a continental route to India through Central Asia and Afghanistan.[3] During the course of the century, other plans had been advanced both in Russia and in France for bilateral or unilateral expeditions to India via Bukhara and Afghanistan or Mesopotamia, or via the Persian Gulf. In all these plans a major role was envisaged for Persia, in anticipation of her acquiescence.[4]

Napoleon contemplated several plans for a military expedition to India, one of the more fanciful of which required the cooperation of Paul I of Russia for an invasion of India through Afghanistan. The plan was abandoned when Paul died; Alexander I, his successor, refused to consider the venture.[5] Napoleon then contemplated a unilateral invasion of India. His thought was to use the French outposts in India, to secure the alliance of local rulers there, and to send a maritime expedition around the Cape. This plan, too, came to naught.[6]

The British government and the East India Company reacted to the French designs on India and the Indian-Mediterranean trade in two ways:

they began making detailed studies of the regions neighboring India, including Persia, Afghanistan, and Central Asia, which had been ignored until then ;* and they formulated a long-range policy designed to contain any threat to their interests in the area. This policy called for an accelerated consolidation of British power in India and an extension of British political influence in nearby countries.†

The British governor-general in India, Lord Mornington (later Marquis Wellesley), with the cooperation of the East India Company, undertook to neutralize the French in India. He unseated Tipu Sultan, the pro-French ruler of Mysore, and attempted to check the establishment of French influence in the Persian Gulf. In this connection, the British East India Company gained control of the conduct of foreign relations in Muscat, in the Arabian peninsula.[7] Wellesley also sought to forestall an invasion of India by Zaman Shah, the Afghan ruler. In particular, the British feared that Afghan incursions into politically weak India might stir up the Indian Muslims and lead to a revival of Moghul power or the reestablishment of Afghan rule in the strategic Punjab, which might then become a base for French activity in India.[8] Distance and a lack of knowledge concerning the strength of the Durrani empire, combined with the French presence in Egypt and diplomatic activities in the Ottoman Empire, Persia, and India, magnified British fears of an Afghan invasion of India. Wellesley wrote that Zaman Shah's heralded invasion had "created the liveliest sensation throughout India," adding that "every Mahomedan, even in the remotest region of the Deccan, waited with anxious expectation for the advance of the champion of Islam."[9] Fears were expressed by various India experts, who (despite grave doubts voiced in England about the

* In 1774, an envoy of the East India Company in Bengal and Tibet reported that he had declined the offer of a map of Tibet, explaining that he "considered the Company could have no interest in this country but that of commerce ... and that to know a number of outlandish names ... to be correct [or] the geography of Tibet ... was of no use to my constituents or indeed to mankind in general" (as quoted by H. W. C. Davis, p. 228). See also Holdich, *Gates of India*, pp. 328–29.
† The ultimate extension of British hegemony "over all the continent of India" was regarded as not only a necessity but a certain, natural, and beneficial development. Sir John Malcolm saw British expansionism as a force that "operated by causes which we have not the power to control. It is in fact the natural progressive growth of civilization." Said Wellesley : "I can declare my conscientious conviction that no greater blessing can be conferred on the native inhabitants of India than the extension of British authority." Even the philosophical radicalist James Mill, who was employed by the East India Company, expressed an eager wish that "every inch of India were subject to our sway." See P. E. Roberts, *India Under Wellesley* (London, 1929), pp. 109, 136, 206.

feasibility of such Alexandrian schemes) foresaw disastrous consequences for British interests in any combination of alliances that linked the Ottoman Empire, Persia, or Afghanistan with France and Russia.[10]

In order to prevent an Afghan invasion of India and overcome the hazards "to which the British interests would be exposed by a connection between the Court of Persia and those European powers whose views have long been directed to this quarter of the British dominion," Wellesley pursued a dual policy: he fostered discord within Afghanistan and, at the same time, encouraged the Persians to attempt to reestablish their sovereignty over the province of Khorassan.* Both moves were successful. Renewed civil strife in Afghanistan and the threat of a full-scale war with Persia placed the Afghan ruler in a critical position and undermined his Indian plans.[11] Through diplomatic activities at the Persian court, notably the mission of Capt. John Malcolm in 1800–1801, the British managed to consolidate their position in Persia. They secured an anti-Afghan, anti-French treaty, which provided that "should an army of the French nation ...attempt to settle, with a view of establishing themselves on any of the islands or shores of Persia, a conjoint force shall be appointed by the two high contracting parties to act in co-operation for their expulsion and extirpation and to destroy and put an end to the foundation of their treason." In a firman the Shah exhorted his provincial governors to "expel and extirpate the French and never allow them to obtain a footing in any place," to which he added: "You are at full liberty to disgrace and slay the intruders."[12] (The treaty was never ratified, because the French were forced out of Egypt first.)

Persia's fears of Russia and the Ottoman Empire, and France's interests in the Middle East, led to a Franco-Persian rapprochement in 1806–7. Napoleon's hopes for an invasion of India were revived with the possibility of a safe passage for a French army through Persia. By the Treaty of Finkenstein, which was concluded in 1807, Napoleon guaranteed the territorial integrity of Persia and recognized her rights in Georgia. He

---

* H. W. C. Davis states (p. 320) that Mehdi Ali Khan, the East India Company's agent in Persia, was assigned the tasks of fomenting a quarrel between the Persian Court and Zaman Shah and stirring up a civil war in Afghanistan. This is corroborated both by the Wellesley papers and those of the East India Company, which reveal that the Shah of Persia, urged on by Mehdi Ali Khan, persuaded Zaman Shah's "treacherous brother" to lead another insurrection against the Afghan ruler (see M. Martin, I, 428, 433; and C. H. Phillips, II, 375). In the wake of Mehdi Ali Khan's successful intrigues, John Malcolm, the British emissary in Tehran, wrote in 1800: "By the blessing of God, he [Zaman Shah] will for some years to come be too much engaged in this quarter to think of any other [move]" (as quoted in Kaye, *History of the War*, I, 6).

also undertook to provide French officers, guns, and artillery for the Persian army. In return, the Shah of Persia agreed to break diplomatic relations with England, to expel all Englishmen from the Persian Empire, and to use his influence to obtain the assistance of the Afghan monarch and tribal chieftains for a French invasion of India. He further agreed to provide military assistance to the French army and port facilities to the navy. A French military mission headed by General Gardane was sent to Persia to prepare the ground for a French expedition to India.[13]

The French scheme was ill-conceived from the beginning. Napoleon's initial goal was a triple alliance between France, the Ottoman Empire, and Persia directed against Russia, but he was unable to reconcile Ottoman-Persian differences, and later Persian-Russian differences, with France's commitments. The Franco-Russian peace treaty—the Treaty of Tilsit (1807)—in effect cancelled the Treaty of Finkenstein, dashing Persia's hope for French assistance against Russia and, along with it, France's hope for a Persian alliance and Afghan assistance against the British in India. The French military mission was forced to leave Persia.[14]

After the failure of the Napoleonic policies in Persia, the British succeeded in reestablishing political influence there. A preliminary treaty was negotiated by Sir Harford Jones in 1809, in which the Persian monarch agreed "not to permit any European force whatever to pass through Persia either towards India, or towards the ports of that country." In the event that British dominions were attacked or invaded by Afghanistan or any other country, Persia agreed "to afford a force for the protection of the said dominions." The British government, for its part, agreed to "afford to the Shah a force, or, in lieu of it, a subsidy, with warlike ammunition, such as guns, muskets, etc., and officers, to the amount that might be to the advantage of both parties," in case of an invasion of Persia by a European power.[15] Another treaty, the Treaty of Tehran, was concluded in 1814; it specifically provided for a Persian attack against Afghanistan in the event the Afghans invaded India.[16]

Meanwhile, the British made diplomatic overtures to the Afghans, the Amirs of Sind, and the Sikhs. Their intention was to use Afghanistan and Sind as buffers against Persian encroachments and the Sikhs as a buffer against the Afghans and the Sindhis. In 1809, Elphinstone secured an agreement from Shah Shuja (the first Afghan pact with a European power) that stipulated joint action in case of Franco-Persian aggression against Afghan or British dominions. The two governments pledged eternal friendship and agreed "in no manner to interfere in each other's country."[17]

THE OPENING OF A NEW ERA OF CONFLICT

The Anglo-Persian treaties of 1809 and 1814, which represented a *de facto* nullification of the Anglo-Afghan treaty, were not directed against France alone. They pledged mutual defense against *any* European power and were, in fact, also directed against Russia, whose expansionist policies were regarded as a threat to British interests in Persia and the Ottoman Empire.[18] By 1814 the British government had adopted Wellesley's policy of treating Persia as "the first line of defense against an invasion of India"; the assumption was that as long as Persia remained an ally there was nothing to be feared from European intrigues in Central Asia.[19]

Within the next 14 years, however, military successes brought Russia substantial diplomatic, political, and economic gains in both the Ottoman Empire and Persia. Two treaties—the Treaty of Turkmanchai (with Persia, 1828) and the Treaty of Adrianople (with the Ottoman Empire, 1829) —legitimized these gains and opened a new era of conflict in the Middle East. The Treaty of Turkmanchai was especially important in its consequences: it led to a shift in British policy toward Persia and Afghanistan. Persia surrendered all territories west of the Caspian Sea, agreed to pay an indemnity of about three million pounds, limited the duty on Russian imports to 5 per cent, and granted extraterritoriality to Russian subjects.[20] Earlier, in the Treaty of Tehran, England had undertaken to remain neutral in the event of a Persian-Afghan conflict. Now she had to alter her position and to regard any Persian encroachment or gain at the expense of Afghanistan as tantamount to an extension of Russia's political and economic gains to the doorstep of India.[21]

Lord Ellenborough, the president of the India Board, was convinced that a Russian army could advance southward to Kabul and into India, though he felt that the initial Russian threat would be economic and political, rather than military: "Russian commerce would be utilized to prepare the way for Russian armies" in Afghanistan.[22] Such worries in official circles were popularized in England by a number of anti-Russian journalists, who not only denounced Russia as a threat to the Ottoman Empire but also stressed the dangers of Russian influence in the borderlands of India. Pamphleteers like Lt. Col. DeLacy Evans and John McNeill (who later became the British minister to Persia) held that, aside from the political threat Russia represented, she might well challenge Britain's predominance in the commerce of Central Asia and Persia and thus reduce Britain's Indian revenues. McNeill, like Wellesley, argued that Persia must be considered the forward line of defense for British interests on the Indian subcontinent.[23]

McNeill's views were shared by Palmerston, the British foreign secretary. Apprehensive of Russian advances, Palmerston adopted a policy, commonly known as the "forward line" policy, aimed at securing British hegemony in Persia and Afghanistan: Afghanistan was henceforth to be considered the "frontier" of India; no European nation would be permitted to carry on commercial or political activities there or interfere, directly or indirectly, in Afghan affairs. Palmerston also tried to neutralize Russian influence in Persia against the eventuality of an Afghan defeat at Persian hands. In his view, the independence of Persia was as essential as the territorial integrity of Afghanistan; both were necessary to ensure peace in Asia and Europe. To this end, Palmerston was ready to grant a British subsidy for the modernization of the Persian army, provided an agreement could be reached with Persia that would secure British economic interests, contain Russia, and safeguard Afghan independence.[24]

Many British political and military experts disagreed with Palmerston on the advisability of meeting a Russian military threat against India in Persia and Afghanistan. Sir Charles Metcalfe and others instead advocated a "stationary" policy, a consolidation on the northwestern frontier of India along the Sutlej River. They argued that this would assure Britain an effective government in India, promote trade, and provide greater security, thus ensuring a better and more economical hold over India.[25] They held it was unwise to ignore natural barriers that would confront a Russian army marching through the steppes of Central Asia or through rugged Afghanistan, and, therefore, "a forcible or even an amicable occupation of any post or tract beyond the trans-Indus foothills was opposed on the grounds that instead of strengthing the power of England either for attack or defense, it would only mean a heavy expenditure and burdensome taxation on the Indian population, apart from fresh military and administrative commitments."[26]

The British had to somehow reconcile these two opposing views and to formulate a delicate Afghan policy. Since the fate of both Persia and Afghanistan was deemed essential to British interests, such a policy had to normalize relations between those two countries, which presented the British with the difficult task of wooing two antagonistic Muslim states without alienating either. Their task was made more difficult by the unresolved question of whether or not a strong Afghanistan was desirable. If the British promoted or at least did not oppose the reemergence of a politically and militarily viable Afghan state to check potential Russo-

Persian aggression, how would they be able to stop an Afghan threat against India? Strengthening the Afghans would alienate not only the Persians but the powerful Sikhs as well, and the neutralization or defeat of the Sikhs meant eliminating an effective force against the Afghans and the Amirs of Sind.

To resolve this dilemma, the British authorities in India decided to continue to seek a balance of power in the area. They would tolerate an Afghanistan strong enough to resist Persian attempts to seize Herat but not strong enough to reduce Sikh power.[27] It was in pursuit of this policy, according to H. W. C. Davis, that the British government in India adopted measures "destined to keep the Afghans weak and divided."[28]

In the meantime, Palmerston had embarked on a diplomatic offensive in an attempt to counterbalance Russian gains in Persia and nullify the Treaty of Unkiar Skelessi (1833), which had given Russia a foothold in the Ottoman Empire. He attempted to place the Ottoman Empire under some sort of collective European guarantee and exerted diplomatic pressure on Persia to grant Great Britain a commercial treaty similar to the one enjoyed by the Russians since 1828. Palmerston wanted a treaty that not only allowed the British to establish consulates but in effect granted them most-favored-nation treatment by eliminating Persia's right to prohibit British exports and imports.[29] Aware of the possibility of the Russians putting pressure on Britain through Persia and Afghanistan, he devised a counter policy of "putting pressure on Russia through the same region." His thought was that "a pro-British power in Afghanistan could influence affairs in Persia, in which Russia was deeply interested."[30] Moreover, economic and political concessions in Persia and Afghanistan would also serve as a means of securing British preponderance in the borderlands of India.

On June 25, 1836, secret instructions were issued by the Committee of the Directors of the East India Company to Lord Auckland, the British governor-general in India, instructing him to conclude political or commercial agreements with Dost Muhammed, the Afghan ruler. The time had arrived, Lord Auckland was told, when it would be "right for you to interfere decidedly in the affairs of Afghanistan. Such an interference would doubtless be requisite either to prevent the extension of Persian dominion in that quarter or to raise a timely barrier against impending encroachments of Russian influence."[31]

As a first step, Auckland sent Capt. Alexander Burnes to Kabul in November 1836. Burnes was to attempt to obtain commercial concessions and, if possible, arrange a political rapprochement with the Afghan ruler.

The British hoped to secure these advantages without making any political commitment that would upset the delicate balance of power between the Afghans and the Sikhs or renew the Afghan hopes of recovering the Peshawar valley. The Afghans, however, were adamant in their demands: they insisted that an Anglo-Afghan commercial treaty delimit their territories, and that the British lend them material and political help in rebuilding and preserving a unified Afghan kingdom. Thus, among other things, the future relationship between Dost Muhammed and the British government in India depended on a settlement of the Peshawar dispute between the Afghan monarchy and the Sikhs.[32] The Amir declared that if the British would mediate that dispute and help the Afghans regain Peshawar, he would even accept a provision making the city a tributary to Runjit Singh, the Sikh ruler. Despite Burnes' report that the Amir had avowed "he prefers the sympathy and friendly offices of the British" to all the alluring offers that might come from Persia or the emperor of Russia,[33] he was unable to obtain any economic concessions from Dost Muhammed.* The authorities in India "were not ready to desert a profitable Sikh alliance for a doubtful Afghan one."[34] As for the question of the political unification of Afghanistan, there were serious disagreements on policy between McNeill, now the British minister in Persia, and the government in India. In McNeill's opinion, British interests in Persia and India dictated a policy of assisting Dost Muhammed to unify his kingdom, provided he agreed to transact all business with foreign powers through a British representative in Kabul. Most India experts opposed this view, agreeing with Capt. Claude Wade that

our policy ought not to be to destroy, but to use our endeavours to preserve and strengthen the different governments of Afghanistan as they at present stand; to promote among themselves a social compact, and to conduce, by our influence, to the establishment of that peace with their neighbours, which we are now endeavouring to produce between them and the Sikhs on one side, and the Sikhs and Sindhians on the other. Whilst distributed into several states, the Afghans are, in my opinion, more likely to subserve the views and interests of the British government than if we attempted to impose on them the yoke of a ruler to whose authority they can never be expected to yield a passive obedience.[35]

---

* Kapadia (pp. 94ff) describes Burnes as "vain, immoral, a bad diplomat, neither judicious nor cautious, in short no match to Dost Muhammed in diplomacy." It is not correct, however, to attribute the failure of the mission to Burnes' personality. The fact is that he was powerless to conclude any agreement that might lead to the reduction of Sikh power, the strengthening of Afghanistan, or the satisfaction of Afghan demands regarding Peshawar. See Kateb, I, 125; Lal, *Amir Dost Mohammed*, I, 260; *Parliamentary Papers*, XXV (1859), 99; Kaye, *History of the War*, I, 260.

THE FIRST ANGLO-AFGHAN WAR

Only one of McNeill's proposals concerning the consolidation of the Afghan empire found favor among the British statesmen in India. That was a plan to promote friendly relations between the rulers of Kandahar and Herat. Political control of Herat was an avowed objective of Persia, but the British were completely opposed to such a move, especially after the conclusion of the Russo-Persian treaties of Gulistan (1813) and Turkmanchai, when Persian "expansionism" came to be viewed as a dangerous extension of Russian commercial and political influence. Moreover, Persian incorporation of Herat would have great impact upon the trade of Bukhara, Balkh, and Kandahar, thereby affecting the political alignment of the Afghan rulers. From a strategic point of view, the British feared that a Perso-Russian entente over Herat would constitute a threat to Kandahar and thus to British defenses in India. Ellis, a British envoy to Persia, summarized his government's apprehensions:[36]

I feel quite assured that the British government cannot permit the extension of the Persian monarchy in the direction of Afghanistan, with a due regard to the internal tranquility of India, for the extension will at once bring Russian influence to the very threshold of our empire.... The success of the Shah in this undertaking is anxiously wished for by Russia, and her Minister here does not fail to press it on to early execution. The motive cannot be mistaken. Herat once annexed to Persia may become, according to the commercial treaty, the residence of a Russian consular agent, who would from thence push its researches and communications, avowed and secret, throughout Afghanistan.*

In this area, British diplomacy failed badly. The British failed to normalize Perso-Afghan relations and to dissuade the Persians from attacking Herat, they failed to obtain a commercial treaty from Persia, and they failed to gain concessions from Afghanistan. All of these failures they

---

* Sir Henry Durand was one of the few British officials who disagreed with the importance attached to Herat and the possible extension of Russian influence there. He later expressed himself in the following sharp terms: "The exaggerated fears of Russian power and intrigue entertained by Ellis, McNeill, Burnes, and Wade, the flame of which was communicated by them to the British and Indian governments, invested Herat with a fictitious importance wholly incommensurate with the strength of the place and its position in regard to Candahar and the Indus. To speak of the integrity of the place as of vital importance to British India was a hyperbole so insulting to common sense as scarcely to need refutation, and which ignorance of the countries West of Indus, and inexperience of military operations in the East could alone palliate. An excursive imagination might deem it of possible importance at some remote future, but it required the hallucination of chimerical alarm to render it an object of solicitude" (Henry Marion Durand, pp. 62–63).

attributed to Russian diplomatic activities.[37] Unable to forestall a Persian attack on Herat (1837) and to obtain an exclusive foothold in Afghanistan, British diplomacy gave way to British military might. Persia was forced to halt its siege on Herat (1838) and to accept a hands-off policy in regard to Afghanistan.[38]

The British took other diplomatic steps at the same time. They made strong representations in St. Petersburg—this despite Russian assurances and disclaimers of any designs against British rule in India[39]—and they concluded a treaty with Shah Kamran, the ruler of Herat (August 1839), making Herat an exclusive British sphere of influence.[40] They also embarked on a long-range program for Afghanistan. Their goal was to establish a firmly committed pro-British regime in the rest of the country, in order to achieve a *modus vivendi* between the Afghans and the Sikhs. This would stabilize the Indian frontier and at the same time safeguard British economic interests in the region. As part of this long-range policy, the British authorities in India negotiated a treaty with the Amirs of Sind (March 1839) that exempted British commerce from duties. According to the East India Company, the treaty was the first step toward extending "the general benefits of commerce throughout Afghanistan, which forms the great end of our designs."[41] The authorities in India hoped to establish a friendlier government in Afghanistan by restoring Shah Shuja to the Afghan throne. The deposed and exiled Sadozai ruler, who was engaged in a bitter struggle to recover his throne from the Barakzais, had heretofore been unable to obtain British assistance; his last major military effort had ended in failure in 1834.* Now, seeing an opportunity to achieve his goal, Shah Shuja was ready to make important political and economic concessions to the British. He was even willing to conclude a disadvantageous agreement with the Sikhs that prohibited him from negotiating with any foreign state without the consent of the British and Sikh governments.[42]

While the British overtures to Shah Shuja were in progress, the Persians retreated from Herat, thereby eliminating the avowed reason for British intervention in Afghanistan. Nevertheless, the British authorities in India went ahead with their plan to reinstate Shah Shuja. (The government in London, under Lord Melbourne, had arrived at a similar decision earlier.) A *casus belli* was found: in a manifesto issued in 1838,

---

* In 1834, Lord William Bentinck, the governor-general of India, refused to assist Shah Shuja in his bid to recapture his throne, writing him as follows: "My friend, I deem it my duty to apprise you distinctly that the British government religiously abstains from intermeddling with the affairs of its neighbours when this can be avoided" (see Kaye, *History of the War,* I, 125).

Auckland charged that Dost Muhammed was guilty of "unprovoked aggression" against the Sikhs, the "ancient ally" of the British, and accused the Amir of unreasonable pretensions, open schemes of aggrandizement, and ambitions injurious to the security and peace of the frontiers of India. Auckland further alleged that Dost Muhammed and his brothers in Kandahar had collaborated with the Persians, and that the Amir was responsible for the failure of the Burnes mission.[43] The government in London, for its part, published a dishonest and garbled *Blue Book*, in order to justify the intervention of Anglo-Indian forces in Afghanistan and the deposing of Dost Muhammed.

The First Anglo-Afghan War itself has been thoroughly studied, and is outside the scope of my subject. Its importance here is that it galvanized the Afghans into a fierce revolt, which resulted in the annihilation of a British force of 4,500 men and 12,000 camp followers (only one Englishman, a Dr. Brydon, survived), the murder of Shah Shuja, and the Indian government's expenditure of some eight million pounds.[44] The British launched a second invasion to punish the Afghans and reestablish British military prestige,* but in the end, their blundering policy led to the reinstatement of Dost Muhammed (1842) and the British evacuation of Afghanistan.[45] The idea of placing part of the Afghan kingdom under Sikh control was also dropped.†

THE RUSSIAN OBJECTIVES

As the British invaded eastern Afghanistan, the Russians launched an attack on Khiva, intending both to fill the political vacuum in the region and to check any extension of British influence from Afghanistan to Cen-

---

* In assessing the impact of the war, Roberts wrote (p. 24) : "Belief in the invincibility of the British soldier ... was seriously weakened by the lamentable occurrences at Kabul during the First Afghan War, terminating in the disastrous retreat in the winter of 1841–1842." The Duke of Wellington noted that Britain's moral force, political power, and influence had received a blow "from the effects of which we shall not recover for some time. . . . There is not a Moslem heart from Pekin to Constantinople which will not vibrate. . . . It is impossible that that fact should not produce a moral effect injurious to British influence and power throughout the whole extent of Asia" (as quoted by Norris, p. 396).

† The Duke of Wellington (and other public figures in England and India) suggested the eventual permanent occupation of Peshawar, the Khyber Pass, Jalalabad, and the "passes between that post and Kabul." Lord Ellenborough, on the other hand, considered the possibility of placing Jalalabad under Sikh control. In such a case, he wrote, "We shall have placed an irreconcilable enemy to the Afghans between them and us." See Ganda Singh, ed., *Private Correspondence Relating to the Anglo-Sikh Wars* (Amritsar, 1955), p. 48.

tral Asia, where Russia had important commercial interests. Russian colonialism had advanced in this region throughout the late eighteenth century and continued to do so well into the nineteenth. Economic expansion was accompanied by military outposts and alliances; political annexation followed. Between 1758 and 1853, the value of Russia's exports to Central Asia increased 12.5 times and the value of imports 16 times. Between 1840 and 1860 alone the value of Russian-Bukharan trade doubled.[46] The Russians considered a pro-British or English-dominated Afghanistan a serious threat to their interests in the area.[47] Moreover, a revitalized Sunni Muslim power in the neighborhood of the weak Central Asian khanates was also considered a threat: if Muslim polities were to become centers of Pan-Islamic uprisings, Russia's economic advantages in the area might be undermined and her chances for future expansion restricted.[48] The Russians were especially alarmed by the British espousal of a tentative (though unrealistic) plan for a Central Asian confederation.[49] The plan's sponsors held that such a confederation would serve as a check against further Russian expansion, but the Russians construed it as a plot to exclude them from the area altogether to the benefit of British political and economic interests in Central Asia as well as in Afghanistan and Persia.[50]

British apprehensions of Russia's long-range political and economic aims in Central Asia matched the Russian fears. Despite Russian assurances that activities in Afghanistan would be limited to the pursuit of commercial aims,[51] the British authorities in India were suspicious of this apparent political self-abnegation.* Russia's favorable position in Persia, her support of Persia's objectives in western Afghanistan, her slow but steady advance in Central Asia, her alleged diplomatic moves in Kabul (which the British insisted contributed to the failure of the Burnes mission)—all had increased British distrust. Under such circumstances, the Russian expedition against Khiva brought stern warnings from Palmerston. He

* Britain's distrust of Russia was manifest in this statement by Palmerston: "The policy and practice of the Russian government has always been to push forward its encroachments as fast and as far as the apathy or want of firmness of other governments would allow it to go; but always to stop and retire when it was met with decided resistance, and then to wait for the next favorable opportunity to make another spring on its intended victim" (letter to Clarendon, July 1853, in Ashley, II, 25; also quoted by Krausse, pp. 29–30). Palmerston held "that the Insolence of Tone and menacing attitude of Russia were founded upon a belief that England was powerless and incapable of effort, and that as this Delusion gradually dispelled, the language and conduct of the Russian government would become more civil and pacific" (as quoted by Norris, pp. 67–68).

threatened to extend the British forward line to Central Asia proper—to capture the upper course of the Oxus River as a measure of "precaution and defense"—if Khivan independence was jeopardized.[52]

The Russian military expedition ended in disaster, and that failure, together with the British inability and unwillingness to maintain prolonged military control over Afghanistan, halted the threat of a major confrontation between the two colonial rivals. The Russian debacle at Khiva and the Straits Convention of 1841 (between Britain, Russia, Austria, Prussia, and France), which destroyed the privileged position Russia had held in the Ottoman Empire since the Treaty of Unkiar Skelessi, temporarily allayed the fears of the British Russophobes and those who feared an imminent Russian invasion of India.[53] The easing of tension, coupled with the British blunders and costly operations in Afghanistan, strengthened the hand of the advocates of the stationary policy. Some of them, notably Sir James Outram and Gen. John Jacob, urged the British government to subsidize the Afghan rulers in order to cultivate their friendship. General Jacob stated his belief that if the British could win the trust of the Afghans, "the whole country would aid us heart and hand, and an invasion of India would be impossible."[54] The proponents of the stationary policy argued that the establishment of amicable relations with the Afghans would decrease the friction between the Anglo-Indian forces and the Pathan tribes along the northwest frontier. They insisted that theirs was an "expedient" policy, especially at a time when the prospect of a war between Russia and the Ottoman Empire loomed in Europe.* In the end, their view prevailed. The British signed an agreement with the Afghans in 1855, and an Anglo-Afghan treaty followed in 1857. Great Britain agreed to "respect the Amir's possessions in Afghanistan and never interfere with them, while the Amir engaged similarly to respect British territory and to be a friend of our [British] friends and enemy to our ene-

---

* After the outbreak of the Crimean War (March 1854), Afghanistan was considered, in the words of Standish (pp. 21–22), "the most effectual barrier against Russian encroachment in whatever direction the Russians might attempt to advance on India. . . . It cannot but be important for our interest in India that the barrier against any attempt at aggression on the part of Russia should be as far as possible from our frontier." To this end, according to Standish, the Secret Committee recommended to Dalhousie, the governor-general, that friendly relations be reestablished with Dost Muhammed, "though such relations should be of purely defensive character." Lord Canning agreed that this step was essential. Otherwise, he noted, a British force could not march through Afghanistan without bringing about a rupture with the Afghans and awakening their hatred and resistance. See *Parliamentary Papers*, LVI (1878–79) : The Minute of Lord Canning, February 5, 1857.

mies."[55] The Amir also was to receive one hundred thousand rupees a month for the duration of the Anglo-Persian war.[56]

The outbreak of the Indian Mutiny in 1857 made the Afghan treaty invaluable to the British; it strengthened their shaky position in the Punjab. According to Lord Roberts, "Had Dost Muhammed turned against the British, I do not see how any part of the country north of Bengal could have been saved."[57] The Afghans not only refrained from hostile action but also "brought in as prisoners all Hindustanis who had deserted, whether with or without arms. Thirty rupees each were paid for all unarmed deserters, and fifty rupees each for all armed men. Many recruits poured down from the Afghan hills to the new Punjab regiments which were being raised to replace the mutinous Hindustanis."[58] The British position was so precarious that serious consideration was given to a proposal to cede Peshawar to the Afghans in order to secure their good will and protect the British posts in the Punjab. However, the proposal generated such heat and opposition, both in India and in Great Britain, that the government ruled out surrendering Peshawar to the Afghans—under any circumstances.[59]

The Anglo-Afghan agreements had both positive and negative implications for the Afghan rulers. On the positive side, the agreements guaranteed the political integrity of Afghanistan against Persian, Russian, or Bukharan encroachments. Moreover, in the Anglo-Persian Treaty of Paris (1857), Persia was forced to relinquish her claims on Herat and to foreswear aggression against Afghanistan.[60] With the threat of foreign intervention removed, Dost Muhammed was able to reunite and centralize the Afghan provinces in the north, west, and south, with British assistance in the form of subsidies and guns. On the negative side, the Anglo-Afghan agreements did not acknowledge a dynastic tie in Afghanistan; they neither guaranteed nor recognized in principle the future status of the Amir's family. Nor were Afghan claims to Peshawar and to authority over the tribal belt recognized. Furthermore the treaty isolated Afghanistan politically and alienated her from Persia and Bukhara. The Bukharans, fearing a strong, British-supported Afghan state, accused the Afghan ruler of apostasy from Islam because of his alliance with Great Britain. As a result, relations between the two realms were further strained and trade declined.[61] Dost Muhammed's reluctance to embark upon a policy of rapid Westernization or to widen the scope of his reforms by securing the services of Europeans can probably be attributed in some part to the effective religious campaign of the Emir of Bukhara.

THE BRITISH NON-INTERVENTION POLICY

Between 1855 and 1874, years in which Lord Dalhousie, Lord Canning, Lord Lawrence, Lord Mayo, and Lord Northbrook were the rulers of India, Britain pursued a policy of non-intervention in the internal affairs of Afghanistan. Lord Lawrence, one of the major architects of this policy, was a spokesman for the stationary school; he not only opposed any British presence or interference in Afghanistan, but in fact opposed the "forcible or amicable" occupation of any territory beyond the Indian frontiers. He argued that intervention in Afghanistan would engender "irritation, defiance, and hatred in the minds of the Afghans, without in the least strengthening our power either for attack or defense. We think it impolitic and unwise to decrease any of the difficulties which would be entailed on Russia, if that power seriously thought of invading India, as we should certainly decrease them if we left our own frontier and met her half-way in a difficult country, and possibly, in the midst of a hostile or exasperated population."[62] Lord Mayo shared this view and suggested that a policy of non-intervention ought to be accompanied by a policy aimed at cultivating the friendship of the Afghans: "By assuring them that the days of annexation are passed ... [we should] make them know that they have everything to gain and nothing to lose by endeavoring to deserve our favor and support. ... We should make them feel that although we are all powerful, we desire to support their nationality."[63]

The policy of non-intervention came under attack following the death of Dost Muhammed in 1863, when internal dissension and anarchy prevailed in Afghanistan. In the face of Afghan political instability, British politicians and India experts became sharply divided. The Conservatives and the Russophobes castigated non-intervention as a policy of "masterly inactivity" and political myopia, and urged that it be replaced by a forward policy. Despite these rumblings, the British continued to follow a policy of consolidation in India and non-intervention in Afghanistan. As part of this policy, they adopted a strategy of divide and rule in the tribal belt.*

---

* In addition to physical force, the British used several approaches in dealing with the tribes: they paid subsidies, they played off one tribe or clan against another, and they took hostages against future good behavior. During this period, the commissioner of Peshawar relied on a policy of sowing discord among the Afghan tribes. See C. E. Stewart, p. 72; and Lambrick, pp. 366–70. Herbert Edwardes devised still another policy. In instances where a group or a clan of a tribe had offended the British, he barred the entire tribe from the Peshawar market, seeking through economic pressure

Their goal was to "avoid as far as possible recognizing any authority of the Amir of Cabul over the frontier tribes" and to keep the tribes as buffers between the Afghan ruler's domain and the British possessions in India. The British-Indian troops, however, were "on no account" to cross the frontier without express instructions from the government and were not to concern themselves with the activities of the tribes as long as they did not cross the frontier. The policy of consolidation was accompanied by a successful economic policy aimed at establishing a direct or indirect hold over the interregional trade between Afghanistan, India, Persia, and Central Asia. To this end, plans were made to hold annual fairs at Karachi from 1852 on.[64]

As another step toward consolidation in India, the British signed a treaty with the Khan of Kalat in 1854, which gave them political control over the khanate. The Khan was to have an annual subsidy of 50,000 rupees. In return, he agreed not to enter into negotiations with other states without the consent of the British government. He further agreed to extradite robbers who might take refuge in his territory, to limit the duty on transit trade to six rupees per camel load, and to "permit British troops to occupy such portions in his territory as they might find advisable."[65]

Between 1869 and 1872, the British and the Afghans established closer relations. The Amir paid an official visit to India and, within that period, secured Russian recognition of the Oxus as the northern frontier of Afghanistan through British mediation. Nevertheless, the Anglo-Afghan agreements had a number of inherent weaknesses. In 1855 and again in 1869, the Afghans tried and failed to obtain a British commitment for future assistance, official recognition of the dynastic rights of the Amir's family, and an unequivocal guarantee of support in the event of any aggression. The British were just as unsuccessful in their efforts to obtain concessions from the Afghans, notably the right to post a permanent English envoy in Kabul and the right to inspect the northern frontiers of Afghanistan. An Anglo-Afghan agreement was concluded in 1869, but it merely reaffirmed the provisions of the treaty of 1855: the British declared they would not interfere in Afghan internal affairs, agreed not to force an English envoy on the Amir, and undertook to support Afghanistan's independence.[66]

---

to force the tribes to take an active interest in the maintenance of "law and order." See H. B. Edwardes, *Memorials*, I, 222–23. For a general review of the British tribal policies of the time, see Davies, *Problem of the NW Frontier*, pp. 24–25; and Spain, *Pathan Borderland*, pp. 108–11.

Meanwhile, the divisions among British foreign policy experts had grown sharper as a result of further Russian advances in Central Asia. Russia made political and economic gains in Khiva and Khokand in 1864, captured Tashkent in 1865, and annexed Samarkand in 1869; Bukhara was transformed into a "subsidiary ally." These advances went hand in hand with a general revision of tsarist foreign policy after the Crimean War that ended both an emphasis on maintenance of the status quo and a tendency to concentrate on Russian interests in Europe.[67] Under these circumstances and in light of the uneasy relationship between the British and the Pathan tribes, the views of Sir Henry Rawlinson and Sir Bartle Frere began to gain ground in England. It was their belief that the British should take a position beyond the Indian frontier by occupying Herat; they insisted that this was both the cheapest possible insurance against a Russian advance and the best means of safeguarding British interests in India. In their view Afghanistan had to be made into a British-supervised barrier against further Russian advances in Central Asia. To this end, they argued for the establishment of a permanent diplomatic mission in the Afghan kingdom to take control of the country's foreign policy and make clear to all interested parties that a pro-British, peaceful Afghanistan was of paramount importance to Britain's interests in India and the East.[68]

Frere felt that the forward policies of Russia and Great Britain could be reconciled, if each recognized the legitimate limits of the other's claims. "I do not look on the Russian advance into Central Asia as any evil," he declared, "and I know a time must come when the limit of our legitimate influence will touch the limit of theirs. This may be done in peace, and I think the sooner the better. But I should like it to be, if possible, far from our own frontier, and that we should meantime, by extending our common and honourable influence, unite our neighbours as closely as possible to us in interest and feeling."[69]

Such views were opposed by the non-interventionists on the ground that the Afghan rulers would be unreliable allies. In Lord Lawrence's words, "They would not be really friendly towards us ... [and] they would in the event of temptation, fall away from us, whatever might be their engagements to the contrary." He declared: "I do not myself see how a truly friendly feeling can be established between the Afghans and the English government in India, when we bear in mind the character of these people and the history of our connection with them during the last thirty years. So long also as we keep them out of Cashmeer and Peshawur, they will be ready to join any combination against us which may give promise of success." Another of the non-interventionists, Sir Charles Wood, cited "the fickleness and faithlessness of most orientals" as a reason why the British could not expect to maintain durable friendly relations with the Afghans.[70] The advocates of non-intervention held that questions of conflicting Anglo-Russian interests should be settled in St. Petersburg and London, and that Russian assurances of non-intervention in Afghanistan should be reaffirmed.

The views of the stationary school prevailed for a time, after English and Russian diplomats tentatively agreed on the creation of an intermediary zone between the British and Russian dominions. The British government was to guarantee the independence of Kalat, Afghanistan, and Yarkend, Russia that of Khiva, Khokand, and Bukhara.* After protracted negotiations (1869–73), a final agreement was reached, by which Russia recognized the northern and northwestern frontiers of Afghanistan and agreed to consider the country outside her sphere of influence.[71] However, Russia occupied Khiva in 1873 and Khokand in 1875, and by 1876 the agreement on the buffer zone was dead. The Russians considered the plan impractical.[72] Reassessing their interests in Central Asia, they proposed instead that the two empires, "while retaining entire freedom of action, should be guided by a mutual desire to pay due regard to their respective interests and necessities, by avoiding as far as possible any immediate contact with each other and collisions between the Asiatic states, placed within the circle of their influence."[73] Here, the Russians had Bukhara and Afghanistan in mind. Russia had economic and political concessions in Bukhara, rights that England did not have in Afghanistan. On the other hand, since 1839 Russia had given England repeated, if reserved, assurances that Afghanistan was outside the Russian sphere of influence, assurances that had not been matched by England with respect to Central Asia as a whole.

THE REVIVAL OF MILITANT ANGLO-RUSSIAN RIVALRY

As tensions mounted between Russia and England, the Conservatives came to power in England (1874–80). Under the leadership of Disraeli and Salisbury, the government adopted a forward policy. Earlier, a mili-

---

* While the discussions between England and Russia about the establishment of a neutral zone were in progress, Russia refused a request of the Bukharan ruler for military help. The Russian authorities cautioned him against an open break with Afghanistan and asked him to limit his territories to the right bank of the Amu-Darya. See Terentiev, *Istoriia zavoevaniia*, I, 485–86.

tarist group, headed by Gen. D. A. Miliutin, had become increasingly powerful in Russia. It, too, advocated an aggressive forward policy in Central Asia. The Russian militarists argued that eventually England would endanger the Russian position in Central Asia through her hostile policies in the Ottoman Empire, her destruction of Afghan independence, and her attempts to establish closer relations with Persia and the Turkomans. They were particularly concerned about the fate of the Caspian region and about Herat, where British preponderance was seen as a major threat.[74]

In both Russia and England, the concerns of the forward policy groups went beyond their countries' immediate interests in Central Asia. Disraeli viewed the problem of Afghanistan in the larger context of the Eastern Question: Russia's plans in the Balkans and the Ottoman Empire were what worried him. In June 1877, he wrote a letter to Queen Victoria in which he asserted that in case of an armed conflict with Russia over Constantinople, "Russia must be attacked from Asia." His recommendation: "Troops should be sent to the Persian Gulf ... [and] the Empress of India should order her armies to clear Central Asia of the Muscovites and drive them into the Caspian."[75] Russian strategists and journalists were voicing equally militant views. Some suggested that Herat should be handed over to Persia, and that the Hindu Kush, not the Oxus, should mark the frontier between the British and Russian empires; they proposed that northern Afghanistan be annexed on the ground that it was a natural and necessary frontier for Russian Central Asia.[76] General Miliutin was one of those who justified further advances in the region for the sake of a unified frontier, but he also saw a strong Russian position in Central Asia as a valuable diplomatic lever against Great Britain: in the event of a European conflict involving England and Russia, Russia would have access to India and could pose a persistent threat to Britain's East Indian possessions.[77]

The Russian militarists also believed that Russia ought to take full advantage of her economic concessions and privileges in Persia and Kashgar.[78] Some of them even proposed that in case of an Anglo-Russian war in Europe, Russia should force a showdown in Afghanistan: she should conclude an alliance with the Afghan Amir and then advance on India. If such an alliance could not be obtained, Russia should then seek to revive the Persian-Afghan conflict over Herat and at the same time support rival claimants to the Afghan throne in order to stir up internal unrest. The more extreme members of the Russian military groups proposed that the Transcaspian railway be extended to Herat and Kandahar. They argued that this threat to India would paralyze British anti-Russian policies in Europe and might induce Great Britain to conclude a broad and mutually advantageous agreement with Russia.[79]

Many Russian statesmen and military men, including those who considered any plan to invade India pure adventurism, sought to publicize such schemes for diplomatic purposes. In general, they agreed with the axiom of Gen. I. N. Skobelev (if not with his plans for India) that the stronger Russia was in Central Asia, the weaker England would be in India, and the weaker England was in India, the more accommodating she would be in Europe.[80] A number of plans, both serious and hypothetical, for a Russian invasion of India were widely publicized.[81] They had great impact in England, where they were viewed against a background of steady Russian advances in Central Asia, the so-called Eastern Crisis of 1875–78, and the Russo-Turkish war of 1877. The position of those in England and India who urged the adoption of a vigorous forward policy was strengthened, and their views found a ready audience among their countrymen, for there was great apprehension in England over the country's limitations as a land power, as well as a tendency to magnify out of proportion any development that could be construed as a threat to India.[82] An important segment of the political leadership in England took the pronouncements of the militarist clique in Russia all the more seriously because Russian foreign policy was not subject to the limitations imposed by a representative form of government. They were convinced that the Russian autocracy could be easily persuaded to undertake any plan, no matter how costly or fantastic.[83]

An extension of the Russian railway system into Central Asia, with all its attendant economic advantages and military implications, heightened the nervousness of British officials in India. Curzon considered it "a sword of Damocles." Fears were raised that the Russians, taking advantage of their political and economic position in the region, might try to stir up the non-Afghan population of northern Afghanistan in an effort to detach the region from Afghan control.[84] The Russian push in Central Asia placed the British in an awkward position: they were committed to defend Afghanistan against Russian aggression, direct or indirect, but they had also agreed not to intervene in Afghan internal affairs, including problems related to the country's northern borders. Their position was even more difficult because of the uncertain delimitation of those borders, Afghanistan's weak defensive capabilities, and the possibility of a border incident escalating into a full-scale war between Russia or her allies and Afghanistan.

THE TRIUMPH OF THE FORWARD POLICY IN ENGLAND

The objectives of the forward policy were to preclude Russian gains in Central Asia, to provide India with a "scientific frontier," and to bring Afghanistan under tighter British supervision and control. Frere, one of the policy's chief exponents, declared in a famous memorandum written in 1874:

Our policy hitherto has been not only stationary and nominally—though I think very imperfectly—defensive; it has also been purely negative. We are ready enough to say what we will not do, but all efforts by any of the other Asiatic powers concerned have hitherto failed to elicit from the Government . . . any declaration of what it will do under any given or conceivable combination of circumstances. This peculiarity in our policy will at once explain to anyone who knows Orientals, or, in fact, to anyone who knows mankind in general, the inherent weakness of our policy, as compared with that of the Russians. . . . Orientals generally misunderstand our present inaction. They suspect some deep design, some secret understanding with Russia. If it is once understood that nothing will move us till the Russians appear on our frontier we shall certainly hasten that event by a great many years. . . . Nothing, I believe, will be effectual to resist Russian progress towards India till we have British officers stationed on the Indian side of a well-defined frontier exercising an effective control over the politics of the semi-civilized races on our side of such a border, and in constant frank diplomatic communication with Russian officers on the other side.

To achieve these objectives, Frere proposed that the Afghan ruler be notified of British intentions to stop all occasion for Russian advance in Afghanistan; that they intended to place the forward post of the British frontier army at Quetta (in Baluchistan) as an excellent strategic point overlooking southern Afghanistan, to extend the railway system to the foot of the Khyber Pass, and to station carefully selected English agents at Kabul, Herat, and Kandahar.[85]

In 1876, upon the request of Lord Salisbury, Frere elaborated his Afghan policy for the consideration of the Conservative government and Lord Lytton, the new viceroy of India. He suggested that the British establish permanent diplomatic representation and the closest possible relations with the Afghans, in order to create a buffer between the British possessions in India and the Russian frontier. The Amir had to be made to see, he said, that

an independent Afghanistan, friendly to us, would be infinitely more valuable in every way than a dependent or conquered Afghanistan. . . . [The Afghan ruler must] clearly realize our view of his position as a weak power between two enormously strong ones—an earthen vessel between two iron ones; that for our own sakes we should infinitely prefer an independent and voluntary alliance to any share of his Kingdom; that rightly or wrongly, we do not believe in the possibility of improving our frontier by advancing it; that nothing would make us desire to advance but a conviction of his unfriendship; but that, if we desired it, he would find no foreign support of any avail in a contest to which we should be driven by our instinct of self-preservation, but which once entered on, we should conduct with all the energy of a struggle for existence and empire, for supremacy in India and rank among the great nations of Europe. For all these reasons we cannot afford to occupy any secondary or doubtful position among his neighbours and allies; that the present state of things could not continue, and that it was for him to indicate what he would like substituted for it.[86]

Lord Lytton agreed with Frere, declaring: "There is something positively startling in the almost exact coincidence of the opinions recorded in your letter . . . to Lord Salisbury with those which . . . I put on paper, confidentially for examination by Lord Salisbury and Mr. Disraeli, who entirely concurred in them. . . . We seem, therefore, to have worked the problem by different formulas, and yet with the same result."[87] Echoing Frere, Lytton wrote: "Afghanistan is a state far too weak and barbarous to remain isolated and wholly uninfluenced between two great military empires. . . . We cannot allow [Sher Ali] to fall under the influence of any power whose interests are antagonistic to our own."[88]

A permanent diplomatic mission, either accepted by the Afghans or imposed upon them, was thus one of the focal points of the Conservative government's India policy. The assumption was that the British would gain control of Afghanistan's foreign relations, removing once and for all any possibility of the establishment of a Russian diplomatic mission or influence in Afghanistan and ending the threat of Russo-Afghan intrigues against India.[89] To achieve this goal, the British at first tried negotiation and persuasion. In this connection, they even attempted to use the good offices of the Ottoman Sultan, the prestigious Caliph of the Sunni Muslim world. A Turkish mission was sent to Afghanistan, during the Russo-Turkish war of 1877–78. The emissaries expressed the Sultan's readiness to help the Afghans maintain cordial relations with England and sought the help of Afghanistan, as well as other Muslim principalities in Asia, against Russia.* Though such joint action would have been advantageous to both the Muslims and Great Britain,[90] Lord Salisbury was not enthusi-

---

* The idea of forming a Muslim league in defense of Islam against Russia, and with the possible blessing of Britain, was a pet project of the Ottoman Sultans. A similar plan, put forward in 1873, proposed to bring about closer relations between Kashgar (western China) and Afghanistan, as well as to cultivate British friendship. To that end, Turkish officers were sent to Kashgar to train the troops. Simultaneously, the British attempted to make use of the power of Yakub Beg (the ruler of Kashgar) in establishing a pro-British and anti-Russian Muslim entente in the region. For details see Frechtling, pp. 479ff; Lee, "Pan-Islamism"; T. E. Gordon, pp. 97–100, 108f, 144; Wyllie, *Essays*, pp. 230–44; Hsu, "British Mediation of China's War with Yakub Beg," pp. 142–49; Demetrius Boulger, *The Life of Yakoob Beg, Ameer of Kashgar* (London, 1878), pp. 196–97, 320–21; Terentiev, *Russia and England*, I, 286–88; and Alder, pp. 49–51.

astic about the idea : if the Afghans were allied with the Ottoman Empire, and the Turks should be defeated by Russia, Great Britain would be compelled to participate in a major and protracted conflict.[91] Sher Ali responded to the Sultan's offer with a complaint about Britain's interference in Afghanistan's internal affairs, despite her treaty obligations. He was upset because the British had sent presents and an envoy to the chief of Vakhan, one of his vassals. Further, wrote the Amir, the Afghans were unhappy about British arbitration of a Perso-Afghan dispute over Sistan. As for the benefits of British friendship, Sher Ali expressed his surprise that the Sultan would attempt to impress upon him the value of a friendship that was so inactive, neutral, or compromising in the face of the struggle of the hard-pressed Ottoman Empire itself. This seeming indifference, he declared, substantiated his distrust of British promises and undertakings. That British friendship had proved to be nothing but "a word written on ice" only justified his previous opinion: "The English look to nothing but their own interests and bide their time. Whosoever's side they see strongest for the time they turn to him as their friend. I will not waste precious life in entertaining false hopes from the English and will enter into friendships with other governments."[92]

In the British view, the Russo-Turkish war, the chance of an Anglo-Russian war in Europe, and the well-publicized Russian plans of action in India and Afghanistan added a note of urgency to the need to settle affairs with Afghanistan. A protracted correspondence between the Afghan ruler and the Russian governor-general of Turkestan increased the anxieties of the British authorities; Lord Lytton's threat to conclude an agreement with Russia at the expense of Afghanistan, if the Afghans refused to come to a speedy understanding with England, became all but meaningless under the circumstances.[93] Lord Lytton saw only two alternatives: to secure a forcible or negotiated diplomatic settlement with the Afghan Amir that would permanently assure British influence in Afghanistan, or, failing that, to break up the Afghan kingdom and conquer as much Afghan territory as was necessary to secure the Indian frontier.[94]

In the end, the British were unable to negotiate or wrest a settlement from the Amir. That failure of diplomacy, coupled with the arrival of a Russian mission in Kabul seeking to conclude a mutual assistance treaty,[95] precipitated a major crisis.* The result was a second Anglo-Afghan war

---

* The dispatch of a Russian mission to Kabul was a diplomatic response to the actions the British were taking in Europe, in their effort to force Russia to relinquish most of the acquisitions she had gained in the Russo-Turkish war of 1877–78. Sher Ali, who viewed the approach of the mission "with alarm and displeasure," asked Gen. K. P. von Kaufman, the governor-general of Russian Turkestan, to postpone the mission. Kauf-

and a British occupation of eastern Afghanistan, an action that was denounced by the non-interventionists. Lord Lawrence asked : "What are we to gain by going to war with the Amir? Can we dethrone him without turning the mass of his countrymen against us? Can we follow the policy of 1838–1839 without, in all probability, incurring similar results?... Are not moral considerations also very strong against such war? Have not the Afghans a right to resist our forcing a Mission on them, bearing in mind to what such missions often lead, and what Burnes' mission in 1836 did actually bring upon them?"*

The Second Anglo-Afghan War resulted in the dethronement and flight of Sher Ali. The Russians, who were diplomatically isolated during the Congress of Berlin (1878), did not intervene in his behalf.† His son Yakub Khan ascended the throne and, in the Treaty of Gandamak signed in May 1879, was forced to cede the strategic districts of Kurram Pass, Pishin, and Sibi. He also accepted a permanent English representative and agreed

---

man replied that it was impossible to comply with such a request, and that the "Amir would be held responsible, not only for [the envoy's] safety, but his honorable reception within Afghan territory." The Russian mission arrived in Kabul on July 28, 1878. Meanwhile, the possibility of war in Europe had been averted at the Congress of Berlin, and the envoy was recalled ; he left Kabul on August 24, 1878. It seemed that with the departure of the Russian mission, the immediate cause of an Anglo-Afghan confrontation was removed. However, the British did not abandon their plan to send a mission to Kabul, even if it had to be imposed on the Amir. A mission was sent in September 1878, but it was refused entry into Afghanistan. On November 2, the British government in India issued an ultimatum to Sher Ali to accept the mission by November 20 ; the receipt of a negative answer or no answer at all was to be construed as an act of enmity. See Lady Balfour, pp. 248, 259ff.

* See Lord Lawrence's letter to *The Times*, September 1878, as quoted by Dutt, p. 430. The opposition also attacked the government's policies as contradictory to the letter and the spirit of international law. Some critics accused the advocates of a "scientific frontier" and a forward policy of maintaining that the rules of international law were not applicable to an Asiatic ruler like Sher Ali. Said one: "He [Sher Ali] was the lawful ruler of Afghanistan, but a scientific Frontier was required, and we proclaimed that Sher Ali's Kingdom might be devastated because he was only an Asiatic Ruler, and we, a civilized and Christian nation" (see Daniel, p. 375).

† On the eve of his abdication and flight, Sher Ali addressed the following letter to the British authorities: "And since you have begun the quarrel and hostilities and have advanced on the Afghan territory, this suppliant before God, with the unanimous consent and advice of all the nobles, grandees, and of the army in Afghanistan, having abandoned his troops, his realm, and all the possessions of his crown, has departed with expedition, accompanied by a few attendants, to St. Petersburg, the capital of the Tsar of Russia, where, before a Congress, the whole history of the transactions between myself and yourselves will be submitted to all the Powers [of Europe]." The Amir, however, did not reach St. Petersburg. In Mazar-i-Sharif he received a letter from the governor-general of Russian Turkestan, advising him to return home and make terms with the British government. He died there on February 21, 1879. See Sir George Forrest, *The Life of Lord Roberts* (London, 1914), pp. 79–80.

to follow the advice of the British viceroy of India in the conduct of foreign relations. Support of the Afghans in case of foreign aggression was left to the discretion of the British government, but Lord Lytton instructed General Roberts to make it clear to the Afghans that "we shall never again altogether withdraw from Afghanistan."[96]

By 1879, Disraeli had succeeded in turning Baluchistan into a protectorate, bringing Afghanistan under "forcible surveillance," and giving India a "scientific frontier."[97] Unfortunately for the proponents of the forward policy, however, the predictions of Lord Lawrence and other non-interventionists were borne out. The new Afghan ruler lacked a hold over his people and could not prevent the outbreak of a general uprising against the British, during which the members of the British political mission were killed. British-Indian troops were again sent into Afghanistan. The chances of a solution of the Afghan problem appeared remote, and a protracted and costly war, possibly including a general uprising along the Indian frontier, seemed imminent.

REEXAMINATION OF BRITISH POLICY

These new developments forced the British to reappraise their Afghan policies. One alternative was to partition Afghanistan into various principalities and make Persia, rather than Afghanistan, the main bulwark in the defense of India.[98] At this point, the disintegration of Afghanistan was considered inevitable. Disraeli asserted that, under the circumstances, the British should retain "what was necessary" for the empire "and dispose of the rest in that manner which would be most conducive to its permanent interests."[99]

Several proposals were put forward. Some experts called for the military occupation and even the annexation of Kandahar, arguing that this would increase Indian trade with Persia and Central Asia, and give British India a strategic hold over Afghanistan.[100] Others proposed the creation of a new, non-Afghan state to include Maimana, Merv, Balkh, and Herat.[101] Still others suggested giving the province of Herat to Persia. Lord Salisbury, for one, declared that if it was not "possible to unite all Afghanistan securely under one head, . . . it may be more prudent to entrust Herat to Persia, under conditions, than to leave it to the chance of guardianship of some petty chief who may be accessible to Russian bribes. We have more control over Persia than we should have over such a chief."[102] A few defended the thesis that British control in Baluchistan was a sufficient check on the Afghans.

The British began a series of negotiations with the Persians. The result was a tentative agreement on a Persian occupation of Herat. However, that occupation was conditional on the continued good will of the British government: Britain retained the right to occupy Herat in case of danger, the right to determine the character and strength of the Persian garrison in Herat, and the right to station British officers there. Persia undertook to bar non-English travelers or residents from Herat, to take appropriate measures to prevent a Russian advance to Merv, and to conclude a commercial treaty with England.[103] Britain also proposed to construct a railway to Kandahar and Herat, a move that would place both Afghanistan and Persia within easy reach of her forces and give her great offensive and defensive flexibility vis-à-vis the Russian positions in Central Asia and Persia.[104]

For a number of reasons the plan to partition Afghanistan was shelved. Among them were the overall success of the British military operations in Afghanistan, the divergent views of the British government and the authorities in India, and the insistence of Persia on an unequivocal British guarantee against any Russian aggression.[105] Most important of all, however, was the return of the Liberals to power in England. The partition of Afghanistan came to be regarded as a highly questionable and unrealistic course of action that would simply hurt the Afghans, annoy the Russians, and do nothing to strengthen the Persians. The arguments against partition and a British presence in Afghanistan have been well summed up by Vincent Smith. He points out that the proponents of the forward policy ignored too many fundamental factors:

The country was too arid to support an army and too hostile to dispense with one. The distances which precluded large Russian concentrations in Afghanistan equally forbade large British movements beyond the Hindu Kush. Above all it went against the known Afghan passion for independence which made the position of every force and the life of every envoy precarious. British control of Afghanistan would have meant Russian concentration on the Oxus, followed by the building up of British armies at Kabul and Herat. The policy would have been financially ruinous in any case; it was fortunate for India that the Afghans' rising demonstrated its unsoundness, before it exacted the penalty of bankruptcy.[106]

One more argument can be added: the partition of Afghanistan would have resulted in the permanent alienation of the Afghans, thus endangering the security of the Indian frontier.[107] Not only would the defenses of India have been weakened, but the British presence in the Punjab might have been threatened.

Influenced by these considerations, the Liberals in England and a new

British administration in India under Lord Ripon took a bold step to achieve a political settlement of the Afghan question: they recognized the candidacy of Abdur Rahman Khan to the throne of Kabul. This was a particularly daring move, since Abdur Rahman had spent some 11 years of exile in Russia and had presumably returned to Afghanistan with the approval of the tsarist government, perhaps even with its financial assistance.[108] Although the new British administration in India was not disposed to relinquish the "scientific frontier" of India or Britain's right to conduct Afghanistan's foreign relations, it was opposed to rigorous control of the Amir or meddling in the country's internal affairs. It was opposed as well to the fragmentation of Afghanistan and British retention or control of Kandahar.[109] The Liberals forged a new Afghan policy whose goals were a well-defended Indian frontier and an independent Afghanistan under British political control. Afghanistan thus became a unique client state. The Afghan monarch had full sovereignty over the internal affairs of Afghanistan. Material assistance from Britain was made conditional on the Amir's acceptance of British advice, the implication being that he could reject such assistance. Britain recognized the independence of a tribal belt between the frontiers of India and Afghanistan, and paid subsidies to the Afridi tribe for safe passage through the Khyber Pass.[110] Further understandings and agreements were made with Abdur Rahman in the years 1880–82, but in general they all strengthened the important provisions of the Treaty of Gandamak: Britain retained full control over the foreign relations of Afghanistan.

During the following years Afghanistan continued to be a major preoccupation of British diplomacy. In the years between 1880 and 1907, the British tried to arrive at a *modus vivendi* with Russia with respect to Afghanistan. They insisted that any understanding had to be based on a reiteration of Russia's guarantee of non-intervention in Afghanistan and on a settlement of Afghanistan's northern frontier. One of Britain's chief aims was to prevent the Russians from attempting to manipulate the non-Afghan ethnic groups of northern Afghanistan to procure a foothold in the country.[111] Anglo-Russian relations were marred by continued Russian incursions into Central Asia (1880–92), conflicting interests in Persia, and Russo-Afghan conflicts, one of which, the Panjdeh crisis (1885), threatened to turn into a major Anglo-Russian military confrontation in Central Asia.[112]

Despite a successful delimitation of Afghanistan's northern borders and repeated Russian assurances (1838, 1869, 1876–77, 1878, 1882, 1883, 1884, 1885) of disinterest in Afghanistan, the Anglo-Russian "peaceful conflict" over Afghanistan remained an active issue. In 1900 the Russians reopened the "Afghan question" by seeking to establish diplomatic relations and close economic links with Afghanistan. This move was accompanied by Russian troop concentrations and maneuvers along the Afghan borders.[113] In response, Great Britain expressed her determination to keep Afghanistan free from the influence or interference of any foreign power, and reasserted her right to control Afghanistan's foreign relations. Nevertheless, it was not until the conclusion of the Anglo-Russian Convention of 1907 that Russia acceded to Britain's claims in Afghanistan. In return, the Russians were promised British cooperation in securing an equal opportunity for trade in Afghanistan, and were given the right to deal directly with the Afghans on non-political problems.[114] The Afghan ruler refused to approve the Anglo-Russian Convention, but as far as the Russians and the British were concerned, the agreement became operative with or without his approval.[115] In the eyes of Russia and Great Britain, Afghanistan now became a genuine buffer state.* During the World War I period, the exigencies of the Anglo-Russian alliance led to new agreements and concessions. Between 1912 and 1916 Anglo-Russian understandings were reached concerning Afghanistan, as well as Tibet, the Ottoman Empire, and Persia. By early 1917 both parties had agreed to partition Afghanistan into new spheres of influence, with Russia receiving commercial privileges in northern Afghanistan.[116] However, the Russian Revolution put an end to these agreements.

THE AFGHAN IMAGE OF EUROPE

Until the First Anglo-Afghan War, the Afghan attitude toward Europe was not an antagonistic one. Though the Afghans' contacts with Europeans were limited and the country's educational establishment was governed by rigid scholasticism and formalism, there seems to have been no official policy, religious or secular, of hostility to Europeans. In 1809, when fear and mistrust of Europeans had not yet taken root, when the "Afghans had little fear of an English invasion," Mountstuart Elphinstone and his retinue

---

* At the time, some Russian circles, eager to promote an Anglo-Russian entente, not only accepted neutralization of Afghanistan (and China) as necessary for universal peace and a demonstration of Russia's disinterest in India, but went so far as to propose that Persia be revived as a major political and military power, with European assistance. They held that this would lessen British anxieties about Russian designs on India and at the same time prevent Pan-Islamic unity by interposing Shi'ah Persia between the Sunni Arabs, Turks, and Afghans. See Notovitch, pp. 313–16.

of some 400 Anglo-Indian soldiers were well received by the Afghans. Similarly, in 1810 Christie and Pottinger found no hostility toward English policies "bred by fanaticism or suspicion." In two separate accounts, in 1815 and 1826, the Sunni Afghans were reported to be tolerant toward Christians.[117] Charles Masson, although robbed by Baluchis, was well treated by Muslim religious men and Afghan tribesmen. Of his stay in Kabul in 1832, he reported: "It is a matter of agreeable surprise to any one acquainted with Mahomedans of India, Persia, and Turkey, and with their religious prejudices and antipathies, to find that the people of Kabul are entirely [devoid of] them. In most countries few Mahomedans will eat with a Christian; to salute him, even in error, is deemed unfortunate, and he is looked upon as unclean. Here none of these difficulties or feelings exist. The Christian is respectfully called a 'Kitabi' or 'one of the Book.' "[118] Burnes, too, noted the apparent absence of anti-Christian feeling. In a letter to his mother (May 1832) he wrote: "The people of this country are kind-hearted and hospitable. They have no prejudice against a Christian and none against our nation."[119] The readiness of Dost Muhammed and other Afghan princes to employ Masson, Burnes, and other aliens in their armies clearly indicates that the Afghans were not hostile to foreigners. In general, until the third decade of the nineteenth century, the Afghans tended to associate Europeans with medicine or artillery rather than with politics.[120] After the First Anglo-Afghan War, however, the Afghan attitude changed drastically. All Europeans were distrusted; Englishmen and later Russians were considered not only infidels but also enemies who threatened Afghan independence. The Second Anglo-Afghan War deepened this religio-political antagonism; the off-and-on conflicts between the frontier tribes and the British authorities in India, and the general political conditions following the war, sustained it.

According to most British historians and chroniclers, the First Afghan War was a blunder as well as an "unprovoked injustice."[121] Other political and administrative blunders were made during the temporary Anglo-Indian military occupation of eastern Afghanistan. The British misjudged both the character and the temper of the Afghan people,[122] and failed in their attempts to reorganize the Afghan economy and strengthen the Afghan monarchy. In part their failure can be attributed to the fact that the Afghan ruler, Shah Shuja, had little popular support* and had to rely on

---

* Kennedy, writing of Shah Shuja's reception in the Afghan capital, declared that the "Kaboolis did not fling him either a crust or a nosegay, nor shouted a single welcome that reached my hearing," and termed this "a sullen, surly submission to what could not be helped" (Kennedy, II, 83).

British financial, material, and military assistance to maintain his rule.[123] In Kaye's view, British assistance only weakened Shah Shuja's position:

Shah Shuja himself said that there would be little chance of his becoming popular in Afghanistan, if he returned to the country openly and avowedly supported, not by his own troops, but by those of the Feringhees [Europeans]. Even the less overt assistance of an infidel government was likely to cast discredit upon the undertaking in the eyes of true believers. . . . He informed [Captain Wade] that some Mahomedans of Delhi had been writing to him, to inquire how he could reconcile it to his conscience, as a true believer in the Koran, to accept the assistance of a Christian people to recover his Kingdom.[124]

Under the circumstances, the Afghans regarded British administrative measures as subversive to Afghan independence rather than as helpful to the country's political and economic unity. Limits on tribal privileges were seen as part of a British plot to control Afghanistan through a puppet monarch. Moreover, once the British extended their activities to all phases of Afghan life, the base of anti-British opposition was broadened. The arrival of the families of British political and military personnel, as well as those of the Gurkha soldiers, the building and furnishing of residences, the laying out of gardens—all indicated to the Afghans that the British had no intention of making an early departure from Afghanistan.

If the British were to consolidate the rule of Shah Shuja, they needed the support or at least the neutrality of the major Afghan tribes. This could be achieved either by "courting, conciliating and managing the chiefs, as [Shah Shuja's] predecessors had done, or by destroying their power and influence. To attempt the latter demanded the permanent occupation of the country in great strength by the British troops," which held out the prospect of a long struggle in a country with rugged terrain and "a bold people attached to their chiefs."[125] A British attempt to create a strong and centralized standing army in support of the Afghan throne was rightly construed by the Afghan aristocracy and feudal lords as an attempt to undermine their power. The measure succeeded only in alienating many powerful tribal chieftains; the army did not elicit the kind of devotion to the Amir and military discipline the British anticipated.[126] British efforts to put Shah Shuja's finances in order were equally unsuccessful. In many regions of the country no taxes had been collected for several years, and the new monarch, in a bid to gain popularity, had exempted various domains of his kingdom from taxation. British political agents undertook the sorry task of gathering revenues on his behalf. Wrote Kaye: "The chiefs . . . began to feel the evils of the new revenue system, or rather the manner of its administration, which rendered the tax-gathering something more than a name. Supported by British power, the executive officers of the Shah no longer stood in awe of the petty chieftains, who soon began to murmur against the change of government and to lay all their grievances at the door of the Feringhees."[127] As Kaye points out, abuses and excesses by native tax collectors went unchecked:

The political agents were, however well-intentioned, unable to cope with the interested duplicity of their subordinates; and the latter knew that the strong arm of the British force was ever at hand to strike down rebellion and enforce the payments of revenue. The system was the more severe from the practice of paying the Shah's levies by assignments on the revenues of particular districts. These levies were larger and of a more permanent character than those heretofore entertained, and the collectors quartered themselves on the assigned districts, living at the cost of the inhabitants until the latter liquidated the prescribed contribution.[128]

Tribal chieftains gradually came to the conclusion that the British-imposed change of rulers was inimical to their interests and power; they had been given a master who was able, with foreign assistance, to compel obedience, instead of a ruler who was obliged to overlook their excesses in exchange for their support.*

The British attempted to "pacify" by "gold or bayonets" those tribes that were hostile to Shah Shuja. Whenever "it was found necessary to coerce the disobedient or to punish the rebellious, then it was British authority that drew the sword out of the scabbard, and hunted down offenders to death." Often called on to enforce unpopular and perhaps unjust measures, the British thus "brought down upon themselves opprobrium which was not always their due."[129] The strategy of divide and rule eventually backfired; the influential leaders of both the Durrani and the Ghilzai tribes were alienated. Durrani chieftains resented British encroachments on their time-honored privileges and the taking of hostages to ensure clan fidelity. The tribal chiefs resented the use of an Anglo-Indian military force, which collected taxes and put down tribal rebellions, and in so doing, leveled forts and destroyed villages; most of all, they resented the use of the Anglo-Indian troops to depose tribal chiefs and name new khans.[130] Some English observers, among them Rawlinson, were aware of the increasingly strong and dangerous national feeling against the British. However, Macnaghten, the British envoy, persisted in seeing Afghanistan as a country "split into rival sects." "And," he asserted, "we all know that of all antipathies the sectarian is the most virulent. We have

---

* The leaders of the Ghilzai tribe, for instance, demanded from Shah Shuja that "he should bind himself by an oath, to be recorded on the fly-leaf of the sacred book, to respect their independence and privileges, and that his future government should not be under the dictation of the infidels." See Kennedy, II, 3.

Hazaras, Ghilzais, Durranis, and Kizilbashes, all at daggers drawn with each other, and in every family there are rivals and enemies."[131] The British hoped to exploit these divisions, but they were unable to win the support of major non-Afghan ethnic groups, or even retain the support they had. Their handling of the Hazaras is significant in this respect. When certain Hazara villages refused to sell fodder to the British army on the grounds that they had only enough for their own needs, the British attacked them and burned their fields.[132]

Anti-British sentiment was prevalent among the urban segment of the population. The carousing of the British forces in Kabul caused great public indignation at what was construed to be a deliberate disregard of traditional social values. The Afghans not only considered the behavior of the British immoral, but also regarded it as both an infringement by infidel foreign intruders upon Muslim religious tenets and a reflection upon the honor of Afghan women.[133] In addition, the urban population was hit by inflation and a scarcity of basic commodities. With large numbers of troops in the country, the cities, especially Kabul and Kandahar, suffered serious shortages, and prices were driven up by the British army's "Commissariat Department, with a mighty treasury at its command buying up all the commodities of Kabul, and not only paying preposterous sums for everything they purchased, but holding out the strongest inducement to purveyors to keep back their supplies, in order to force a higher range of prices."[134] There were many popular Pashto and Persian songs deploring the evils and abuses of the "Commissariat." As Mohan Lal described the situation: "Grass for cattle, meat and vegetables, and in short all the necessaries of life rose to a considerable price, and the cry of starvation was universal, and there were very many hardly able to procure a piece of bread even by begging in the street, while everything would have been in abundance but for our purchase."[135] The Afghan government was placed in the difficult position of imposing severe punishment on speculators and profiteers when it could itself neither fill the needs of the British nor prevent them from purchasing whatever they needed at high prices. Even so, the situation of the Indian troops was desperate, causing them to riot and loot on a few occasions.[136] Disputes between landlords and British officers over the alleged non-payment of rent were also a source of friction. This situation developed when the houses of Afghan tribal chiefs who had withdrawn from Kabul were treated as confiscated property and given or rented to British officers.[137] The result of all this was widespread resentment against the British. The dualism of executive power in Afghanistan made administrative problems even more difficult and contributed to strained relations between Shah Shuja and the British. Commented Lal: "Inwardly or secretly we interfered in all transactions, contrary to the terms of our own engagement with the Shah; and outwardly we wore the mask of neutrality. In this manner we gave annoyance to the King upon the one hand and disappointment to the people upon the other."[188]

In the end, the Shah and the British were unsuccessful in their attempts to achieve the political and economic unification and the pacification of the kingdom of Kabul. In 1841, an upsurge of a truly national and religious anti-British movement ended the rule of Shah Shuja; owing to the incompetence of British military leaders and the shortsightedness of the British envoy, the uprising resulted in the annihilation of the Anglo-Indian army of the province of Kabul.[139] Though the British authorities in India were aware that there was "a universal hostility on the part of the entire people of Afghanistan, united in a war which has assumed a religious as well as national character,"[140] they nevertheless felt compelled to avenge their immense losses and reestablish the prestige of the British army. The severe retaliatory measures they took only widened the gulf between the Afghans and the British, and strengthened Afghan nationalism and xenophobia. One act of retribution was the destruction of the great bazaar of Kabul; the British plundered the market as well as many houses, setting fires that swept over a great area of the city.[141] Another was the removal of the gates from the venerated tomb of Mahmud of Ghazni for trophies, a desecration that only heightened the religious fervor and national sentiments of the Afghans.[142]

The situation deteriorated badly. The British forced most of the Afghan population to leave Kandahar, Jalalabad, and Ghazni during the winter; this move guaranteed British defenses, but further alienated the local populations.[143] There were cases of whole villages being set afire and their orchards destroyed, of the massacre of the entire population in response to a few shots from a village. Fearsome revenge was exacted by the Anglo-Indian army during the battles of Argandab and Ghazni, including in some instances the annihilation of all the inhabitants of villages. Charikar and Istalif were destroyed by the British, as were the fortifications and other areas of Jalalabad and Ghazni. All of these acts only increased the Afghans' bitterness and hatred.[144] Kaye summarized the impact of the war on Anglo-Afghan relations in this way: "The Afghans are an unforgiving race, and everywhere from Kandahar to Kabul, and from Kabul to Peshawar are traces of the injuries we have inflicted upon the tribes. There is scarcely a family in the country which has not the blood of kindred to revenge upon the accursed Feringhis. The door of reconciliation is closed against us; and if the hostility of the Afghans be an element of weakness, it is certain that we have contrived to secure it."[145]

Even after the British withdrew from Afghanistan and avowedly adopted a policy of non-intervention, their punitive and devastating military expeditions against various frontier tribes contrived to keep the memories of the Anglo-Afghan war and the sparks of Afghan nationalism alive. Frere drew the attention of the British authorities to the potentially harmful effects of such military undertakings, and asked: "What can these people think of us? Bad as they may be themselves do we give them any cause for thinking better of us, or for believing that we war in a more generous or chivalrous fashion? Is it to be wondered at, that when offered the privilege of taking away their slain, they did not trust us? I do not find mention of a single prisoner throughout these proceedings. Surely some must have been taken among the wounded?"[146] The struggle of the independent frontier tribes with the British in India thus indirectly gave sustenance to Afghan nationalism.

The outbreak of a second Anglo-Afghan war 38 years after the first intensified the already widespread anti-British sentiment in Afghanistan. The war resulted in another British occupation of eastern Afghanistan, the flight of Sher Ali to northern Afghanistan, and the imposition of a British envoy on the Afghan court. Events followed a familiar pattern: the new Amir, Yakub Khan, was incapable of mustering national support; the British envoy intervened actively in Afghan internal affairs; the British failed once more in their attempt to use financial and material aid to centralize power and stabilize the country under a British-controlled ruler. The British envoy was assassinated, and once again the British felt compelled to retaliate, this time destroying Bala Hissar, the major fortification of Kabul, in revenge.[147]

THE EFFECTS OF EUROPEAN IMPERIALISM

From an historical point of view it is difficult to assess the overall impact of European imperialism on the socioeconomic development of Afghanistan. Afghan historians and statesmen attribute their country's backwardness to imperialism and capitalism. For instance, in 1959 former Prime Minister Daud declared: "After a long struggle against capitalism, a struggle to attain and preserve national independence, the Afghan people have only in the past few years acquired an opportunity of making efforts to liquidate our backwardness and to concentrate attention on moral and material progress as well as on the development of our country."[148] In general, Comintern spokesmen and Soviet historians (the Pokrovskii school) also contend that Anglo-Russian imperialism greatly impeded the cultural and economic development of the region.[149] The majority of nineteenth-century Western writers, on the other hand, either ignored altogether or minimized the harmful effects of the Anglo-Afghan wars and the diplomatic duels of England and Russia. In fact, some English writers placed great emphasis upon the so-called endemic Afghan national traditions of "misrule, pillage, and destruction," and proposed the extension of a redemptive British imperialism as the answer to the socioeconomic plight of Afghanistan.[150] Others, however, have argued, with some justification, that Anglo-Russian rivalry contributed to the maintenance of Afghanistan as an independent buffer state, and that the threat of foreign interference and invasion encouraged the Afghans to achieve national unity.[151]

There is no debating the fact that Afghanistan's political structure and social order were profoundly affected by the diplomacy of imperialism. Because of colonial rivalries, Afghanistan was subjected to two major wars and foreign occupation; its economy was dislocated and some of its territories annexed. On the positive side, the Anglo-Russian rivalry helped sustain Afghan rule over northern Afghanistan and the province of Herat. Moreover, the Anglo-Afghan wars unleashed a potent force in Afghan nationalism, which inculcated an ardent love of fatherland and national pride among the Afghans. Finally, the exposure to European military technology generated change and made a sociopolitical reorganization of the country, and especially a reorganization of the armed forces, necessary. At the same time, the colonial rivalries led to xenophobia and isolationism and consolidated the position of both the Afghan tribes and the Afghan religious establishment, thereby greatly influencing the course and character of Afghan reforms and modernization.

From the middle of the nineteenth century until the early twentieth century, Afghanistan was a country turned in on itself. Its sole political link was with the British government in India, and even then, except for two brief periods—1839–42 and 1879–80—there were no English resident envoys at the Afghan court; until 1919, a Muslim national of India represented the British government at Kabul. After 1879 Great Britain succeeded in obtaining and maintaining the diplomatic isolation of Afghanistan. Even the Ottoman Sultan, the Caliph of the Sunni Muslims (and politically close to the British at the time) had to obtain British permission to send an emissary to Afghanistan. The Afghans, for their part, adopted isolationism as a national policy, seeing in it the surest guarantee of their independence—a defense against the threat of an occupation or fragmentation of their country by the British or the Russians or both. Their hope was that Afghanistan's natural barriers and primitive communications, underdeveloped economy and political isolation, would be assets in preserving their independence.[152] Inaccessibility, for instance, would permit the most effective use of the Afghan fighting forces and traditional tactics of warfare; difficult communications would make the operation of foreign armies in Afghanistan both costly and precarious; economic underdevelopment might deter the "greedy temptations" of British India and Russia. The Afghan rulers believed that barring foreign residents and foreign investments was the most effective way to control an anti-European, anti-foreign national sentiment that could easily endanger their own lives as well as those of foreigners. They feared that the introduction of capitulations and European-sponsored technological and economic improvements would impose an "open door" policy on Afghanistan, bringing in its wake extraterritoriality and most-favored-nation agreements with various European powers, especially England and Russia; these privileges might then provide the foreign powers ready pretexts for intervention.

The two Afghan wars seriously damaged the country's meager economy, especially the urban economy. The population and the economy of Kabul and of the Kandahar region declined sharply; the province of Herat also suffered enormous material losses.[153] The modest achievements of the Amirs Dost Muhammed and Sher Ali were undone. The sad state of Afghanistan is perhaps best illustrated by the mournful words of Yakub Khan. In a letter to the British authorities dated September 4, 1879, he wrote: "Afghanistan is ruined; the troops, the city [Kabul] and surrounding country have thrown off their yoke of allegiance. The workshops and magazines are totally gutted. . . . In fact my Kingdom is ruined."[154]

The fact that it was the urban centers of eastern Afghanistan rather than the Afghan tribes that were most severely damaged by these wars is of great historical significance. Because of the weakened position of the urban sectors, the nationalist, anti-British struggle was led primarily by the Afghan tribes and the religious establishment, and became a religious war as well as a nationalist one. Islam became a potent national force, a unifying force that overrode, to a great extent, ethnic, racial, and linguistic divisions, a force used by the Afghan rulers to mobilize popular opinion and enlist the support of the masses in their struggle against the Sikhs and against British imperialism.[155] Though in this sense the religious character of the Afghan wars had positive effects, contributing greatly to Afghan nationalism and political consciousness and bolstering the Afghans' will to defend their country, the transformation of the struggle into a religious war also had negative effects: it resulted in a strengthening of the social position of the traditionalist ulama and promoted Afghan xenophobia and cultural isolationism. Many of the religious leaders resisted the introduction and adoption of major socioeconomic and cultural innovations, despising them as alien to the spirit and tenets of Afghan traditions. Most of them associated such innovations with the Christian enemy; to reject European civilization was to reject European imperialism.

The Anglo-Afghan wars also contributed to the consolidation of Afghan feudalism and tribalism. The loss of Peshawar and the Punjab to the Sikhs on the eve of the First Afghan War deprived the Afghan monarchy of an important economic asset. That loss, together with the weakness of the urban sectors and the feudal character of the monarchy itself, forced the Afghan rulers to become increasingly dependent on the Durrani clans and the other tribes for the defense of the country and the maintenance of the dynasty. The military importance of the independent frontier tribes also strengthened the position of the tribes within Afghanistan: through blood ties or political alliances they could obtain needed support. Tribalism was thus preserved at the expense of the Afghan monarchy and the growth of national institutions.

Wars and foreign occupation introduced the Afghans to a wide array of European institutions and technology. For the first time, they were exposed to modern armies, an advanced military technology, Western mores, and European diplomacy. These experiences could not help but create a certain amount of social ferment. Despite the resistance of traditionalists, some members of the Afghan ruling elite favored the introduction of limited reforms and elements of European military technology. European and American adventurers, deserters from the British army in India, and Pathan tribesmen who had served with the British troops introduced new military techniques, and the warlike Afghan tribesmen borrowed from or copied captured European weaponry.[156] The greatest impact of the Anglo-Afghan military conflict, however, was on the Afghan monarchy itself. The Afghan rulers saw in limited modernization an instrument to strengthen their own position as well as the defenses of Afghanistan. They became aware of the need for a government-sponsored program of arms production, of the importance of heavy batteries, and of the necessity of a strong standing army. The modest attempts at reform of Azam Khan and Sher Ali can be viewed as reactions to the impact of the First Afghan War and European imperialism. Sher Ali's official visit to India in 1869, in defiance of the xenophobic traditionalists, aroused his interest in European history, politics, and modern technology, and led him to institute a number of reforms, largely of a military nature.

Despite the opposition of die-hard traditionalists[157] and the fact that the Second Anglo-Afghan War destroyed much, if not all, of Sher Ali's work, the Afghan monarchs continued to pursue a policy of centralization and limited modernization. Their goals remained the same: a modern army, some government-controlled industry, a politically and economically united country. The difficulties they faced in implementing their policies were enormous, for they wanted to develop Afghanistan only enough to secure its defenses without opening it to extensive foreign influences or inviting English or Russian intervention. They therefore tried to combine a policy of secluded independence with one of indigenous, self-sufficient modernization and limited reform. Their distrust of European imperialist countries and Europeans in general led them to cut themselves off from needed capital and expertise. (One French observer noted that to the Afghans an explorer was always an enemy: "They will take him for an Englishman or Russian who has come to survey their country to prepare ground for armies.")[158]

The Afghan rulers faced other problems in implementing reforms. One was the country's landlocked position, the result of the definitive loss of the khanate of Kalat. Another was the need to accommodate the important Afghan tribes, which kept the army feudal in character, dependent on tribal and feudal levies. Still another was the great self-confidence and self-reliance of the Afghans themselves. To use the language of Toynbee, the Anglo-Afghan wars resulted in a relatively successful Afghan "response" to the Anglo-Indian "challenge." The traditional methods of Afghan warfare were not altogether discredited: the Afghans preserved their independence and forced the British out of Afghanistan. They thus believed that their fighting spirit and will to resist, together with their country's rugged terrain, more than made up for their technological inferiority. This self-acclaimed success boosted the Afghans' national confidence, but it did little to encourage popular acceptance of the necessity of fundamental socioeconomic reform and modernization.

Chapter Five

Abdur Rahman Khan: From Anarchy to Absolute Monarchy

The first major and concerted effort to reform Afghanistan began after 1880, when Abdur Rahman Khan, "the Iron Amir," ascended the Afghan throne. The new Amir inherited a country weakened by wars and foreign occupation, and torn by internecine strife. The urban economy was debilitated, and the trade routes and rural economy were continuously threatened by the encroachments and murderous raids of various tribes. Feudal landlords and tribal chieftains had usurped the already limited powers of the Afghan central government, and the religious establishment had assumed an increasingly important role in Afghan society.[1] The Amir himself best described the situation: "Every priest, mullah and chief of every tribe and village considered himself an independent King, and for about 200 years past, the freedom and independence of many of these priests were never broken by their sovereigns. The Mirs of Turkestan, the Mirs of Hazara, the chiefs of Ghilzai were all stronger than their Amirs."*

From the outset, the Amir ascribed a divine sanction as well as a divine purpose to his rule: "As God wished to relieve Afghanistan from foreign aggression and internal disturbances, He honoured this, His humble servant, by placing him in this responsible position, and He caused him to

---

* Munshi, *Life of Abdur Rahman,* I, 217. The complete authenticity of this work is currently being questioned by some Afghan writers, especially those portions that deal with the Durand mission. According to Munshi, some parts of the book were written by the Amir himself, and the rest he dictated (see I, vii–viii). The original copy is in the British Museum. The work is accepted as authentic by Mohammed Ali (*The Mohammedzai Period,* pp. 141–43), and it was not questioned by H. Mortimer Durand ("The Amir," p. 5), Lord Curzon (see Singhal, p. 176n), or Mahmud Tarzi (see *SA,* 2d year, No. 13, p. 4). Apparently the Amir wanted Dr. Griesbach, an English official in his service, to edit the portion that covered the years up to 1886, but "the Government of India found it inconvenient to have that valuable contribution to history published by one of its officials" (see A. C. Yate, "Visit to India," p. 36).

become absorbed in thoughts of the welfare of the nation and inspired him to be devoted to the progress of this people . . . for the welfare and true faith of the Holy Prophet Mahomed."[2] In a sharp departure from the previously held notion that the power of the monarch derived from the Afghan tribal jirga, Abdur Rahman formulated a religious justification for the monarchy, becoming in effect the first Afghan ruler to invoke the concept of the divine right of kings. Although he conceded that the Afghan people had the right to choose their monarch, he insisted that only divine guidance could assure them the choice of a true and legitimate ruler. The strength, the authority, and the legitimacy of the monarch emanated from God alone. The throne was "the property of the Almighty King of Kings, our Creator," who appointed kings "as shepherds to guard His flock" and confided into their care "the Creatures of His hands." Kings were "vice-regents of God," who derived great duties and equally great responsibilities from the will of God. Various Eastern kingdoms were backward and in decline because their rulers, either out of carelessness or through laziness or ignorance, failed to fulfill the mandate of God, thus alienating their people and causing both their own downfall and the downfall of their countries.[3]

Proclaiming himself the champion of Islam and liberator of the Afghan lands from "infidel and foreign" domination, the Amir effectively used the theme of imminent external aggression and the need for national unity in a religious context.[4] In a royal proclamation issued in 1887, he appealed to the Afghans' sense of honor, national dignity, religious sentiment, patriotism, and xenophobia, drawing their attention to the Anglo-Russian threat and their own disunity. Disgust and contempt sharpened the edge of his words:

The country of Afghanistan is a mere spot under the compass of two Infidels. . . . It is closely besieged; yet although imprisoned men are always thinking of their release, you are indifferent to your bonds. . . . You leave all to luck in a matter of life and death. . . . The name of Afghan should not have been given you by the giver of names, as you do not deserve it.

He pointed out that England and Russia, though ostensibly rivals, were united in the task of destroying Afghanistan and its Muslim heritage. In the face of this threat, the Afghans had not united and consolidated the state and the monarchy, the guardians of Afghan freedom and faith, but instead were engaged either in massacring each other or in irrelevant and futile debates.[5]

Even as Abdur Rahman invoked anti-foreign sentiment at home, he successfully negotiated with the British government in India for assistance, securing help in the form of arms, ammunition, and money. In 1880–81 alone, he received 3,615,009 Indian rupees.* The British also undertook to give him an annual subsidy of 1,200,000 rupees, with which he was to pay his troops and strengthen the defenses of Afghanistan's northwest frontier. By 1889, the Indian government had given him 74 guns, 25,000 breech-loading rifles, 11,500 muzzle-loading rifles, and several million rounds of ammunition.[6]

As a device to stimulate patriotism and legitimize his own absolutism, Abdur Rahman issued a map (which was printed on canvas and measured five by four-and-a-half feet). It was reportedly posted in every village and bore a royal proclamation, a public lecture of a sort, which was read out in the bazaars and mosques of all the principal towns. Passages from that unique document read as follows:

I have now prepared for you a kind of map, which shows the condition of Afghanistan as compared with that of its surrounding countries. This I have done in order to enable you to study the matter attentively and to make out a path for yourselves in such a way that good may accrue both to your country and to your religion. I am hopeful that a careful study of this map will suffice for your prosperity and happiness both in this world and the next.

In entering into the details of this map, I hereby declare that whatever has been predestined by the Almighty for each one of you, the same has been put into the heart of your King, and he is thus enabled to find suitable appointments for all. Some of you have attained to the rank of Commander-in-Chief, while others are still in the position of sepoy. It is, however, fitting for you all to offer thanks to God and to your King, and to be contented with your lot. . . .

Take care and listen to me, who am your King, with all your heart, and weigh well what I say, for it is of no use to make lamentations for that which has past and gone. This advice is for all, from the Commander-in-Chief down to the sepoy, and also for the subjects, who are inferior to all, and for those who carry guns on their shoulders. A sepoy should look upon the subjects, who are inferior to him, as members of his own society, for it is with the help of God and by the kindness of the King that he has obtained his rank. You should sympathise with the subjects, who are your own tribesmen and who are continually employed in cultivating their lands, in cutting their crops, in thrashing their corn, in gathering in the harvests, and in winnowing the wheat from the chaff. They are also occupied in trade and undergo hardships and troubles by night and by day, and only enjoy a portion of the produce themselves after they have paid in the taxes which are necessary for the expenses of the State. I, who am your King, spend all this money on the army. It therefore behooves you all, whether you are men in high places or sepoys or subjects, to be grateful, because all that you pay is given back to your brothers, sons, and tribesmen. By this God is pleased, religion flourishes, and honour is preserved. In a like manner, the subjects should also be grateful, so that God's blessing may increase day by day, for it is written, that on him who is grateful He increases his boun-

---

* According to Singhal (pp. 72, 149n), the British gave the Amir a gift of 1,500,000 rupees at the time they recognized him as the Afghan ruler, as well as 950,000 rupees left in the treasury by Yakub Khan and some guns.

ties. It is therefore incumbent on you to be grateful both to God and to your King.

The real object of my teaching is that the kindness and compassion of the King towards his subjects resemble the feelings of a father towards his son; and as it is natural that a father should be kind to his son, so it is also natural that the King should be kind to his subjects. These are also the orders of God to the King. But when the father sees the errors of his son, he admonishes and punishes him. Now this punishment is not due to ill-feeling, but rather to the excessive love which the father bears towards his son, so that he cannot even bear the sight of any wrongdoings on the part of the son; in the same way the King has the same feelings towards his subjects as a father has towards his son. The King only wishes to spread the blessings of tranquillity and peace among his subjects and to gain a good name thereby. When a boy is young and ignorant, he hates and despises the advice of his father, but when he becomes of age and becomes endued with wisdom and intellect, he considers that there is none so kind and affectionate as his father, and it is the whole purport and desire of his life to obey the orders of his father. In the same way, I, the ruler of you Afghans, have the same desire of being kind and generous to you, even as a father is kind and generous to his son. If you are wise enough to understand and benefit by my advice, I am confident that you will see that your religion will flourish and that your country will be prosperous. May it so please God.[7]

BREAKING TRIBAL RESISTANCE

But the Amir went beyond sheer sentimental appeals and the exploitation of the Anglo-Russian colonial rivalries to further his political objectives. Force, bloody reprisals, matrimonial alliances, bribes, and intrigues were all used in his battle to overcome tribal resistance to his authority. With a newly formed and quickly growing army, he fought, one by one, numerous independent and semi-independent Afghan tribes. His victories did not come easily; it took, for instance, some 12,000 men and 26 days to subdue the Shinwari tribe.[8] The Afghan monarch used his own marriages and those of his sons to tighten his ties with tribal chieftains, religious leaders, and important members of non-Afghan ethnic groups.[9] He also followed the principle of *divide et impera,* exploiting the traditional rivalry of the Durranis and the Ghilzais to suppress a Ghilzai rebellion and force the rebels to pay him regular taxes.[10] Religious injunctions were used against the Ghilzais—and, in fact, against all the feudal lords and tribal chieftains who revolted against the monarchy. Rebellious leaders were usually branded traitors and outlaws, and were sentenced to ignoble deaths.

Religion was also an effective weapon in the monarchy's struggle with the powerful Shi'ah Hazaras, who rebelled in 1888. In subduing the Hazaras (1891), Abdur Rahman appealed to the orthodoxy and fanaticism of the Sunni Muslims, a move that secured him thousands of volunteers and *ghazis* (fighters for the faith).[11] He also used the stirrings of political consciousness in the Afghans as a weapon, evoking memories of the former greatness of the Durrani empire to muster the support of the Afghan tribes in his attempt to reestablish firm control over ethnically non-Afghan northern Afghanistan.[12] To the use of polygamy and marriage alliances, the playing upon religious and ethnic diversities, the appeals to patriotism, the resort to crude force, the Amir added still other measures. He adopted a feudal policy strikingly similar to that of Richelieu and Louis XIV, inviting various influential feudal chieftains to Kabul, granting them subsidies, destroying their strongholds and fortifications, and taking hostages.[13] He also initiated forced migratory movements. For instance, in the late 1880's he ordered some 10,000 Ghilzai families transferred from the Ghazni area to the region between the Oxus and the Hindu Kush, hoping thereby not only to strengthen the Afghan ethnic element in this region, but at the same time to weaken the powerful Ghilzai tribe.[14]

In the end, these policies were largely successful. By 1901, when he died, Abdur Rahman had managed to unify Afghanistan politically and to establish the first thoroughly centralized regime in the country.* He had consolidated Afghan rule in Afghan Turkestan, reestablished the monarchy's hold over Herat and Kandahar, and gained control over all ethnic

---

* Here is Curzon's description of the turbulent character and career of Abdur Rahman: "Born in 1844, [he] was ... the recognised head of the Barukzai clan. ... The Amir himself told me that up till the age of twenty he declined to learn either to read or to write, and that at a time when most European lads have their knees under a desk he was engaged in manufacturing rifled gun barrels and in casting guns. It was in 1864, the year following upon the death of the Dost [Muhammed], that he first appeared in public life, being appointed to a Governorship in Afghan Turkestan; and after that date there were few elements of romance or adventure that his career did not contain. Here victorious in battle (for he was a born soldier), there defeated; now a King-maker in his own country, anon a fugitive from its borders; for a time the powerful Governor of the Cis-Oxian provinces, and presently an exile in the courts of Meshed, Khiva, and Bokhara; later on a pensioner of the Russians at Samarkand, and, finally, the British nominee upon the throne of a recovered Afghanistan; for nearly forty years, whether in the forefront or the background, he presented the single strong figure whose masculine individuality emerged with distinctness from the obscure and internecine and often miserable drama of Afghan politics. ...

"His characteristics were in some respects even more remarkable than his features. This terribly cruel man could be affable, gracious, and considerate to a degree. This man of blood loved scents and colours and gardens and singing birds and flowers. This intensely practical being was a prey to mysticism, for he thought that he saw dreams and visions, and was convinced (although this was probably only a symptom of his vanity) that he possessed supernatural gifts. Generous to those who were useful to him, he was merciless to any whose day was past or who had lost his favour. But even in the most unpropitious circumstances his humour never deserted him" (*Tales of Travel*, pp. 56–57, 64).

groups in Afghanistan. "Tribe after tribe which had maintained some sort of independence was reduced to order, and scattered in colonies all over the country. Many nests of freebooters were extirpated, some of them very formidable strongholds."[15] Of special historical importance is the fact that, in the act of attempting to break the great political power of the tribes, he created a greater cohesion among the Afghans.

ADMINISTRATIVE REFORMS

While Abdur Rahman was pursuing the goal of unifying Afghanistan, he was also instituting administrative changes. The practice of selling public offices was discontinued, and a civil administration was created. The country was divided into four major provinces—Turkestan, Herat, Kandahar, and Kabul—and into seven administrative districts. Each province was governed by a hakim directly responsible to the Amir. Although the new governmental machinery was inadequate by contemporary standards, it represented a great advancement: at the time of Abdur Rahman's succession, administrative matters were handled by just ten clerks, who entered all financial and other governmental transactions on slips of paper.[16] The Amir instituted the use of ledgers and record books; to deface them was considered an offense so heinous as to be punishable by amputation. He also established trade and treasury boards, as well as departments of justice, communications, education, and medicine.

The Amir formed a constitutional government of a sort. He established a general consultative assembly made up of three categories of representatives: sardars (aristocrats, chiefly members of the royal family or clan), *khawanin mulki* (commoners, mainly khans or landed proprietors), and mullahs (religious representatives). The selection of the members of this assembly, which had no executive or legislative power, was subject to the Amir's approval. He had no intention of sharing his powers with such a body; its sole function, aside from symbolizing and promoting the concept of unity under the monarchy, was to serve in a consultative capacity to help the Amir gather war supplies and advise him in various state activities. The Amir also established a selected executive body (*khilwat*) as a supreme council or cabinet, but it was equally powerless. Not only was there no office equivalent to that of prime minister; the council could not give advice to the monarch unless he requested it to do so. The supreme council's only function was to execute the will of the Amir. It was not, nor was it intended to be, answerable to the general assembly.[17]

The quest for political absolutism, unification, and administrative reorganization led Abdur Rahman into a fierce struggle against the powerful and privileged Muslim religious establishment. The Amir considered Islam and its religious institutions essential for the health and strength of Afghanistan. In his words, "For the maintenance of a Kingdom and the strength and prosperity of a nation, religion, too, is a very good factor. A nation without religious belief would soon become demoralized and begin to decline until it fell altogether." The strength of both Islam and the Afghan state resided in unity, he declared; more important, that unity had to be conceived and sustained under the monarchy.[18] Starting from this premise, Abdur Rahman embarked upon a policy aimed at curbing the power of the mullahs and bringing them under secular authority.

As the "defender and champion of the Islamic faith in Afghanistan" and as the ruler of that kingdom by the "grace and will of Allah," Abdur Rahman assumed the dual role of leader and interpreter of Islam and Islamic laws, asserting that this step was essential to the preservation of orthodoxy and the true spirit of Islam. He attacked the Afghan mullahs, contending that they had taught "strange doctrines which were never in the teaching of Muhammed, yet which have been the cause of the downfall of all Islamic nations in every country." He held that, of all classes of people, the ignorant mullahs were the most dangerous.[19] The religious establishment was no longer to be allowed to prescribe the duties of the monarch or to call for a jihad or *ghazawat* (holy war). The Amir proclaimed that holy wars could not be fought except under the orders and instructions of the ruler of the country.[20] In his role of interpreter of the Islamic faith, he published various pamphlets and tracts as guides in theoretical religious questions. They dealt with such subjects as jihad, Takwim ud-Din (the foundation of religion), and Pand Namah (advice). In these publications he not only attempted to show himself as the champion of the faith but also tried to demonstrate the close interrelationship of temporal and spiritual power and to inculcate the concept of a religious duty to the Amir as the commander of the faithful.[21] To reinforce his role as the leader of the Islamic ummah (community), Abdur Rahman took control of the waqf, attempting thereby to destroy the economic self-sufficiency of the religious establishment and to reduce the mullahs to the status of mere bureaucrats, dependent upon his treasury.[22] Moreover, he forced the mullahs to take examinations to prove their ability and justify their eligibility for the privilege of becoming a functionary of the kingdom.[23]

Abdur Rahman thus succeeded in achieving a threefold control over the religious establishment: he preempted the right to interpret Islam; for all practical purposes he made the mullahs bureaucrats; and he checked their number and influence by imposing a procedural examination. Insubordination brought economic sanctions. One noteworthy instance was in 1888, when the Ghilzais revolted: for condoning the revolt and failing to preach obedience to the Amir, the religious leaders of the region were deprived of their stipends.[24] Still, the Amir made use of the religious establishment to rally his people and advance his political schemes, most notably during the conquest of Kafiristan. In undertaking the forcible conversion of the pagan Kafirs (1896), he had three goals: to consolidate his hold over that inaccessible and isolated province, to bar foreign political intrigues or Christian missionary activities there, and above all to gain the moral support of his people and of the religious leaders. The conquest of Kafiristan and the conversion of the Kafirs strengthened his position with respect to the religious establishment. He was given the title Ziya ul Millat wa Din, or "The Light of the Nation and of Religion."[25]

LEGAL AND SOCIAL REFORMS

Abdur Rahman made important reforms in the legal field, reforms that contributed significantly to his firm grip and control over the kingdom in general and the religious establishment in particular. Dividing the existing laws of his kingdom into three categories, Islamic laws proper (Shari'a), administrative or civil laws (*kanun*), and tribal laws, he established three types of courts: religious courts, which dealt with religious and civil affairs, criminal courts, which were administered by the chiefs of police (*kotwals*) and judges, and a board of commerce, which was made up of merchants, Afghan and non-Afghan, Hindu as well as Muslim, which settled business disputes.[26] In establishing the board of commerce, the Amir seems to have been motivated by a desire to remove commercial transactions as well as non-Muslim merchants from the jurisdiction of the religious courts.

Government officers called *kalantars* were responsible for order in various districts within the urban centers. They were empowered to deal with minor infractions and to arrest offenders. They were also responsible for obtaining the names of all males in their districts between the ages of sixteen and twenty-eight. The purpose of this measure was to establish a pool for the recruitment of members for the country's new police force. An elaborate criminal code was drawn up. It gave great authority to the kotwal, who combined the duties of a district chief of police and a judge of petty sessions. The police, too, were given great authority; they could deal with such problems as offensive language, the dishonest tradesman, the "indecorous father, the gambler, the purveyor of charms." They were also empowered to handle certain religious offenses, for instance cases involving misconduct in the mosque or failure to observe fast days.[27]

In general, the interpretation of law was vested in religious officials selected and appointed by the crown. The religious court, presided over by a *kazi*, was regarded as the highest provincial tribunal. Its authority extended not only to religious issues but to civil cases as well, However, civil cases could be appealed to district courts, which were presided over by the district governor or his deputy. Each province had a supreme court, which settled marital and inheritance cases. It was made up of a chief judge and a number of *muftis*, or interpreters of Islamic law.[28]

Although the decisions of the courts were based on Islamic law, they were subject to the Amir's approval. He retained the powers of a supreme court in his hands. His eldest son represented a court of appeals, and he himself the court of last resort. The Amir also heard cases that were not subject to appeal in the courts; these usually involved political disputes, cases of high treason, offenses against the throne, and matters of government revenue.[29] By reserving the right to appoint judges, by ensuring the participation of secular authorities in the judicial process, and by preserving jurisdiction over cases punishable by death, the Amir thus asserted the monarchy's supremacy and preeminent rights in the dispensation of justice: the Muslim jurists held office only under his sufferance and therefore, willing or unwilling, were bound to obey the crown.

Despite these reforms, Afghanistan was still far from possessing a uniform code of laws. Though the Amir established a degree of administrative unity, the legal system remained very complicated and anachronistic. Each law had to conform to Islamic law, to local custom (*adat*), and, in spirit at least, to the Afghan tribal code. To these considerations had to be added the interests of the Afghan government and the Amir. One of the Amir's chief concerns was establishing order within his kingdom. To this end, the new criminal code prescribed harsh punishments for cases threatening the welfare of the Afghan people or disrupting the peace and stability of the country.* In cases involving robbery and theft, the hand of the criminal

---

* There are many graphic accounts of the cruel punishments meted out by the Amir. One of the most colorful is by Curzon: "As I rode to Kabul, I passed on the top of the Lataband Pass an iron cage swinging from a tall pole in which rattled the bleaching bones of a robber whom he [the Amir] had caught and shut up alive in this construction, as a warning to other disturbers of the peace of the King's highway. He revelled in these grim demonstrations of executive authority.... After one unsuccessful rebellion he had many thousands of the guilty tribesmen blinded with quicklime, and spoke to me of the punishment without a trace of compunction. Crimes such as robbery or rape were punished with fiendish severity. Men were blown from guns, or thrown down a dark well, or beaten to death, or flayed alive, or tortured in the offending members...."

was amputated. Notorious highwaymen were often placed in iron cages fixed on the top of a mast along the roadside and were left to die of starvation. There were reports of bakers being baked for tampering with the quality and especially with the weight of bread.[30] In cases involving murder, Abdur Rahman altered the letter and the spirit of the old law, which had called for the imposition of a relatively small fine.[31] Under the new law, a murderer was left to the mercy of the relatives and friends of his victim, but even if they chose to forgive him, the government could still grant or withhold a pardon. If pardoned, the murderer had to ransom his life by paying a fine of 7,000 rupees.[32] In addition to prescribing severe punishments for the individual offender, the new criminal code imposed a fine, usually amounting to 20,000–50,000 rupees, on all villages within a ten-mile radius of the scene of a crime. If the villagers failed to pay, two or three regiments of soldiers were generally quartered in the village until they did. The effect of this was to make each villager chary of permitting his neighbors to interfere with travelers, since everyone suffered for the crime of one.[33]

Along with these harsh criminal laws, which had some success in pacifying the turbulent Afghan kingdom, the Amir enacted new laws and modified existing ones, in an attempt to effect a degree of social reform. He abolished a long-standing customary law, which in violation of Islamic law bound a wife not only to her husband but to his entire family as well: widows who wanted to remarry had to marry their husbands' next of kin, often against their will.[34] Abdur Rahman decreed that the moment a husband died his wife was to be set free. Unfortunately, there is no way to check to what extent this law was enforced. Among the Amir's other

---

One official who had outraged a woman was stripped naked and placed in a hole dug for the purpose on the top of a high hill outside Kabul. It was mid-winter; and water was then poured upon him until he was converted into an icicle and frozen alive. As the Amir sardonically remarked, 'He would never be too hot again.' A woman of his harem being found in the family way, he had her tied up in a sack and . . . ran her through with his own sword. Two men having been heard to talk about some forbidden subject, he ordered their upper and lower lips to be stitched together so that they should never offend again. A man came into the [palace] one day and openly accused the Amir of depravity and crime. 'Tear out his tongue,' said the Amir. In a moment he was seized and his tongue torn out by the roots. The poor wretch died" (*Tales of Travel*, pp. 65–67). The Amir's physician gave this description of the amputations performed on criminals: "The local butcher is called in. He knots a rope tightly just above the wrist of the criminal, and with a short sharp knife he severs the hand at the joint, plunging the raw stump into boiling oil. Then the criminal becomes a patient and is sent to the hospital to be cured. No flap of skin has been made to cover the end of the bone, and the skin has been scalded for two inches or more by the oil, so that months go by before the stump heals by cicatrization" (Gray, p. 343).

noteworthy measures was a law requiring the registration of marriages (*sabt*). He also modified a law pertaining to child marriages, permitting a girl who had been given in marriage before she had reached the age of puberty to refuse or accept her marriage ties, when she attained full age. Still another law allowed women to sue their husbands for alimony or divorce in cases involving cruelty or non-support.[35]

Another social ill that concerned Abdur Rahman was slavery, a practice that was commonplace when he ascended the throne. There were many slave markets in the northern and northwestern regions of the country, especially in the regions inhabited by the Uzbeks and Turkomans. The majority of the slaves of the Central Asian khanates, where slavery was a widely practiced and accepted institution before the Russian conquest, were drawn from northeastern Persia and Afghanistan. The Shi'ah Muslims, mostly Hazaras, and the poor sectors of the population of Badakhshan were especially subject to the raids of Uzbek and Turkoman slavers. As noted earlier, one report indicated that in 1883 nearly every well-to-do establishment in Afghan Turkestan had one or two Hazara slaves. Purchased with guns, ammunition, or horses, the Hazara slaves were valued on the basis of going food prices. The pagan Kafirs were also enslaved by the Muslim crusaders who invaded Kafiristan throughout the nineteenth century. Many of the Kafir slaves were to be found in Kabul, where they were sold according to height.[36]

Abdur Rahman abolished slavery in 1895, prohibiting any further use and abuse of human beings (slaves had sometimes been emasculated) as a violation of the tenets of Islam. However, his anti-slavery law failed to free those already enslaved from economic bondage, though it did provide that slaves who remained with their former masters had to be treated as members of the family.[37] Here, too, it is difficult to ascertain whether or not this legislation was strictly enforced.

THE NEW ARMY

Abdur Rahman relied heavily on a military autocracy to guarantee his absolutism. Perhaps the "Iron Amir's" greatest single achievement was the creation of a standing and centralized Afghan army. Despite the earlier efforts of Dost Muhammed and Sher Ali, Abdur Rahman inherited an army that was feudal and tribal in character. It relied for manpower on the tribal chiefs, landlords, and mullahs who could command the service of a number of followers. Moreover, despite the contributions of foreign advisers, the army was weak in administration, discipline, logistics, and armaments, and lacked a trained officer corps. The troops were mainly equipped "with discarded flint muskets, swords, belts, and bayonets of the British forces in India or a Kabul imitation of these weapons."[38]

Abdur Rahman retained the progressive features of his predecessors' reforms and instituted even wider and more comprehensive ones of his own. Using the Anglo-Indian army as a model, he organized his army into three branches, artillery (field and mountain), cavalry, and infantry, with territorial divisions, field columns, brigades, and regimental units.[39] The existing system of feudal levies was replaced with a single, central army, paid and controlled by the Amir. The *qomi* system (under which each clan was required to give a certain number of men), was abandoned in 1896; under the new system, the *hashtnafari*, each clan or tribe had to send one in every eight men to the Amir's army. Finding it impossible to apply this system throughout the country, the Amir attempted to tap feudal and tribal resources by organizing an auxiliary force of militiamen (*khassadars*) and cavalry (*khwanin sowars*). Tribal chieftains and feudal landlords were required to contribute men to this force in proportion to their landholdings.[40]

Abdur Rahman made still other changes in the army. He was at last able to institute the regular cash payments to his troops that had been a goal of his predecessors.* He also provided his troops with European-style uniforms, deducting the cost from their pay. Col. Charles E. Stewart reported that he was "much struck" by the uniforms of the Afghan army. Some of the troops, he wrote, wore a Mackenzie tartan like that of the Seaforth Highlanders, the regiment sent to Kabul under Lord Roberts: "The effect of the kilt was, however, decidedly spoilt by the men wearing white trousers in addition to their kilts. Instead of the highland bonnet, they wore brown felt forage caps with large black peaks."[41] Severe penalties (including the forfeiture of six months' pay) were imposed on soldiers who persisted in wearing their own "ugly trousers" instead of uniforms. The Amir assigned each regiment a mullah (as a chaplain), a hakim (physician), and a *jarrah* (surgeon). He also set up engineering and commissariat details in order to make each unit self-sufficient; his troops were supplied with Martini-Henry and Brunswick rifles and with a variety of guns: Krupp, Maxim, Nordenfeldt, Hotchkiss, and others.[42] The new

---

* Under the pay scale he established, a general of the first rank was to receive 600 Kabuli rupees a month, a brigadier 250, a cavalry colonel 200, a major 120, a cavalry captain 80, a corporal 10. The rank and file were to be paid partly in kind. See S. Wheeler, p. 217; and Angus Hamilton, *Afghanistan*, p. 272.

army even included military bands, which were fashioned after those in the British army, complete with bagpipes and bugles. They provided the music for the changing of the guard, another new feature of the army.[43]

Abdur Rahman paid special attention to problems of logistics. He allocated some 50,000 pack mules and ponies for military transport, and saw to it that great reserves of grain were stored at Herat, Kandahar, and Kabul.[44] In his view, both material self-sufficiency and a large standing army were essential to the peace of the kingdom. By the middle of the 1880's he had achieved both: he had a standing army of 50,000–60,000 men and enough military stores and equipment to undertake effective military campaigns against the recalcitrant tribes and non-Afghan ethnic groups.[45] Nevertheless, he did not feel that his forces were strong enough to defend Afghanistan against external aggression and hoped one day to build an army of one million men, equipped with the best and most sophisticated weapons. This was a forlorn hope (despite Angus Hamilton's assertions to the contrary).[46] The Amir had neither the money nor the trained officers and technical advisers for such an army, and he was opposed to direct Afghan-European contacts, even for training purposes, fearing that this might lead to the emergence of a politically conscious army, ready to serve foreign interests. He insisted that "a neighboring power, by offering military officers from its army, under the pretense of teaching the Afghan soldiers British military tactics might also teach them to attend to foreign interests."[47]

In such circumstances, the Afghan officers, products of a poor educational system, had to learn about modern military tactics and technology from Persian-translated books and manuals, and officer training remained at best haphazard. A few Indian Muslims provided some assistance, but their numbers and services were not enough to bridge the immense educational and technical gaps in the army. Their military knowledge was extremely limited, yet some of them were called on to perform a number of tasks. One Abdul Subhan Khan, for instance, was a brigadier in the artillery, an instructor in signalling, and the surveyor-general.[48]

ECONOMIC REFORMS

The Amir placed as much importance on the economic prosperity of Afghanistan as he did on the achievement of political unification. He encouraged the development of trade and internal communications, and hired European advisers in an attempt to introduce some European technology into the country. His first noteworthy measure in this area was the establishment of a single monetary unit, the Kabuli rupee; it replaced a number of regional currencies that had been artificially inflated to equal the Kabuli rupee.[49] To place his new currency on a sound basis, he opened a mint in Kabul and imported minting machinery. He coupled his monetary reform with a fiscal reorganization, hoping to regularize taxes and secure the country's revenues.* A revenue department was established to keep records and settle the accounts of the landlords, all of whom were legally required to pay taxes to the throne annually, and attempts were made to establish standard weights and measures. The land tax was fixed at one-third of the crop, a sizable increase over the taxes levied under Ahmad Shah and Dost Muhammed. With the systematic collection of land taxes, plus the proceeds derived from customs duties, exports, fines, registration and postage fees, and the revenues brought in by mines, government monopolies, and manufactures, the annual income of Afghanistan rose to more than one million pounds.[50]

Government workshops accounted for a substantial part of this revenue. Abdur Rahman reestablished the workshop program begun by his predecessors. (The workshops had been destroyed during the Second Anglo-Afghan War.) From both an economic and a psychological point of view, the establishment of these workshops and the hiring of foreign experts and technicians were among the most significant measures undertaken by Abdur Rahman.[51]

The primary purpose of the workshops and the other small-scale industries that were established was to meet military needs, but they also served as a source of revenue and prestige for the monarch. By closely linking the introduction of European technology to the country's military requirements, Abdur Rahman was able to overcome strong anti-European and traditionalist opposition to modernist measures. He persuaded the opponents of technological change that the defense and self-sufficiency of the nation were essential to the well-being and independence of the Islamic community of Afghanistan.

The Amir first entrusted the development of small industries in the country to a French electrical engineer named Jerome, who was to import European machinery from India. After this project failed, he turned, in

---

* Angus Hamilton, *Afghanistan*, pp. 243–44. Abdur Rahman explained his difficulties in gathering his land revenues as follows: "One quarter of the money, which is rightly mine, I get without trouble; one quarter I get by fighting for it; one quarter I do not get at all; and those who ought to pay the fourth quarter do not know into whose hands they should place it" (Munshi, *Life of Abdur Rahman*, I, 203).

1886, to an Englishman, Pyne (later Sir Salter Pyne), who was successful in establishing a number of state-owned workshops in Kabul.[52] Before long, sawmills, steam hammers, and lathes were producing a variety of military and non-military articles. The greatest emphasis, of course, was placed on military commodities, since that was the official and primary task of the workshops. Some of the products turned out were Martini-Henry and Snider rifles, cartridges, gunpowder, and musical instruments for the military bands. The output of cartridges was variously estimated at between 3,000 and 20,000 a day; the weekly output of rifles was 175, that of field guns two. By 1893, Afghanistan's small war industry had grown to the point where it was capable of casting some 50 muzzle- and breech-loading field guns.[53]

The workshops gradually enlarged their field of operations, engaging in such paramilitary and non-military activities as bootmaking, leatherstitching, soap production, and candlemaking. New machinery was imported, including stamps and dies for the mint and tanning and dyeing equipment. Eventually the workshops were capable of producing carpets, paper, glass, agricultural implements, needles, and even kilns.[54] Although the Amir was a devout Muslim, he was fully aware of the value of the vineyards in Afghanistan and attempted, with some success, to establish a large-scale (and lucrative) government monopoly for the manufacture of wine, whiskey, and brandy, which was exported to India.[55]

In connection with his workshop program, Abdur Rahman sought technical advice from a number of foreign experts. Besides Pyne, he employed 14 Englishmen, including experts in mining (Middleton), cartridge-making (Edwards), mechanical engineering (Stewart), minting (McDermot and Cameron), and tanning (Tasker and Thornton). He also employed a geologist (Griesbach), a studmaster (Collins), and even a piano tuner (Rich).[56]

In an effort to stimulate trade, the Amir attempted to improve the condition and security of the roads. He had new roads and bridges constructed and old ones repaired. The major trade routes—Kabul-Balkh, Kabul-Ghazni-Herat, Herat-Kandahar, Jalalabad-Kafiristan, and especially Kabul-Peshawar—were vastly improved. The inhabitants of villages and towns along the roads were held responsible for their upkeep and landscaping, as well as for the safety of travelers and merchants.[57] As an added security measure, and also to boost his income and augment his authority, the Amir restricted freedom of movement in Afghanistan. The people of Kabul, for instance, had to obtain permission and purchase a pass (*rahdari*) to travel outside a six-mile radius of the city.[58]

The Amir also attempted to improve the Afghan postal service, which was poor to begin with but considerably worse after the Second Anglo-Afghan War. During the reign of Sher Ali, the founder of the system, service had been confined mainly to Kabul-Peshawar. An attempt was now made to introduce techniques borrowed from the Indian system, including such innovations as registered mail and parcel post service. Carrier pigeons were used to establish daily communications between Kabul and Herat, in order to expedite government transactions.[59]

Afghan trade had been impeded not only by the insecurity of the trade routes but also by the excessive duties levied on goods, those intended for local consumption as well as those in transit or designated for export. The customs system had been one of utter confusion and chaos. Once the Amir had ensured a relative free flow of trade, he abolished the complicated system of tolls that had been required from province to province. He also created a caravan bureau, headed by a *kafila bashi* (chief or head of caravans). With the aid of a small militia task force and the cooperation of the board of commerce and the treasury and revenue departments, the bureau saw to the safety, supply, and transportation needs of travelers and caravans. To facilitate the flow of commercial traffic and give some measure of uniformity to Afghan customs duties, the Amir assigned a standard 2½ per cent ad valorem tax on all exports and imports.[60] (However, this figure was later raised considerably.) Thanks to these measures, something approaching normal trade began to flow between Afghanistan and India, Russia, and Persia, though it remained highly sensitive to the state of the country's foreign relations, which continued to be under British control.*

* There are no accurate figures that give a complete picture of Afghan trade. In large part this is because it is difficult to establish the exact volume of trade carried by the Powindahs (a collective name for all the migratory Pathans involved in caravan trade). The fact that trade was sometimes recorded by pack animal rather than by tonnage also makes it difficult to arrive at an accurate total figure. The Powindahs, who were mainly Ghilzais, Lohanis, Waziris, and Kakars, carried on a vast amount of trade between India, Afghanistan, Persia, and Central Asia. They banded together twice a year in large armed caravans, often mustering several thousand fighting men, and pushed their way between Bukhara and the Indus. In India they deposited their arms and, leaving their families and herds in the plains of the Punjab, generally took their goods by rail to Bengal, Karachi, and Bombay. They returned in the spring with goods purchased for the Afghan market. These statistics may offer some clues concerning the volume of trade they handled: in 1877 some 76,000 of them entered India, in 1878 some 58,000, and in 1880 some 50,000. Of those who entered in 1880, over 33,000 were males, more than half of whom were fighting men. In 1878 the Powindahs had with them over 77,000 camels and 188,000 sheep and goats. In a report to the Secretary of the State of India, the total value of import-export trade carried by the Powindahs in the 1870's was roughly estimated to be 500,000 pounds sterling a year. See Oliver, pp. 79–86.

Trade of Northern and Eastern Afghanistan with India[61]
(in tens of rupees)

Year	Imports from India	Exports to India
1890	796,500	325,300
1891	459,870	208,600
1892	653,639	218,120
1893	610,500	220,850
1894	405,200	188,800
1895	270,575*	152,791
1896	306,230	165,000
1897	290,162	151,538
1898	285,623	129,109
1899	312,266	217,235
1900	272,347	187,054
1901	299,051	190,049

* Jan.–March

In large part, Afghanistan imported basic articles of consumption. For example, three-fourths of the imports from India were cotton goods, the rest sugar, tea, and dyes, especially indigo. Cotton goods also accounted for much of the trade between India and Kandahar. In 1899–1900, 1,140,-910 rupees in a total of 2,874,510 went toward the purchase of European cotton goods from India, and another 721,950 rupees were spent on Indian-made cotton products.[62] Kabuli exports to India consisted mainly of horses, fruits, vegetables, raw wool, hides, ghi (fat), and other provisions.

The volume of trade fluctuated greatly during Abdur Rahman's administration. This can be attributed to a number of political and economic factors, the most important of which were the Anglo-Russian economic rivalry and the prohibitive tariffs the Amir himself instituted, ostensibly to aid "the ignorant and poor Afghan tradesmen." In the 1880's the Russians took a number of measures designed to exclude British-Indian commodities from Central Asian markets.* Certain foreign goods were banned al-

* Between 1868 and 1892 the Russian empire gradually consolidated its political and economic gains in the khanates of Bukhara and Khiva. In Bukhara, the Russians paid one-fortieth ad valorem in *zakat* (tax on animals, produce, and merchandise sold in the bazaar) compared to one-twentieth paid by Muslims. The Muslims paid one-sixtieth of the money they took into the khanate as tax, the Hindus and Jews one-twenty-fifth, the Russians nothing. By the terms of an 1873 Russo-Khivan agreement, Russian merchants trading in Khiva were exempt from zakat as well as all kinds of customs duties. They also obtained the right to establish commercial agencies in any location in the khanate and to own immovable property there. In 1888 the Russians established a consulate in Bukhara, which, among other things, was to deal with matters relating to

together from Russian Turkestan or their importation was discouraged through heavy taxation. By 1895, the flow of Anglo-Indian goods into Central Asia through Afghanistan and Bukhara had declined by 80 per cent, severely damaging Afghanistan's position in the transit trade.[63] The figures below reflect the Amir's attempt to achieve a favorable trade position for Afghanistan in the face of the Anglo-Russian economic rivalry and Russia's commercial advances in Central Asia.

Russian Trade with Afghanistan[64]
(*in rubles*)

Year	Exports to Afghanistan	Imports from Afghanistan
1888	3,983,270	3,944,568
1889	3,307,000	1,597,400
1890	4,059,000	1,612,000
1891	2,555,300	1,468,000
1892	1,971,000	801,000
1895	702,304	842,302
1896	906,571	2,093,366
1897	479,278	1,576,751
1898	727,637	2,208,974
1899	981,836	1,594,606
1900	898,604	2,116,070

The Amir attempted to promote the sale of his own products and to stop the outflow of Afghan capital in quantity to foreign countries. One plan involved the establishment of tea plantations near Jalalabad; the project was not successful.[65] In any case, such efforts were misguided, for though the Amir's *direct* income was increased by holding a royal monopoly on various items of foreign trade, in the end he suffered a decrease of much larger proportions in his indirect revenues. Nevertheless, that he was convinced of the soundness of his trade policies is evident in this statement: "Trade, in this lies the greatest source for enriching my country. In the past ... hundreds of foreign goods used to be imported into Afghanistan, for which money had to be sent out of the country; now these goods are manufactured at Kabul."[66]

Afghanistan. By 1892 the Russian customs frontier was extended to the Afghan-Bukharan border. Various commercial centers, notably Termez, New Bukhara, Chajui, and Kerk, were removed from the jurisdiction of Bukhara and put under a separate administration. The Russians also succeeded in collecting taxes from the nomadic population of the region. Despite these moves, the major weakness of Russo-Afghan trade was the lack of trade agreements and legal safeguards for the Afghan, Bukharan, and Russian merchants. See Woeikof, pp. 187–92; and Burnaby, Appendixes D and F.

The importation of salt was forbidden, as was the importation of many manufactured products. The Amir extended his personal monopoly over the timber industry, and further consolidated his hold over the Afghan economy by lending interest-free money to some Afghan merchants.[67] This measure, which was intended to promote foreign transactions, in effect placed the state in the position of supporting some Afghan businessmen and competing against others.

Afghanistan's precarious diplomatic position, and the fact that all the countries of the area used their commercial transactions as political weapons, contributed to a decline in trade. The absence of direct diplomatic relations and treaty arrangements with Russia was partially responsible for the especially sharp decline in Russo-Afghan trade. This lack of trade agreements, together with the high protective tariffs and stiff duties on transit trade the Amir imposed (seven pounds sterling per camel load weighing 450 pounds), had serious consequences.[68] One of the most serious was the diversion of a major item of Indo–Central Asian trade, Indian tea, to the sea route. Moreover, in spite of the Amir's program of roadbuilding and improvements, Indo-Afghan trade continued to be hampered by the poor transportation system. The major route between Kabul and Peshawar was open to caravans only two days a week, and even then, the use of the Khyber Pass on those days was virtually purchased from the fierce and independent Pathan tribes who guarded the pass.[69] Indo-Afghan trade was even further weakened because it was used by the Amir as a political weapon against the British government in India. When the British built a railway to New Chaman, hoping to increase trade between India and southern Afghanistan, Abdur Rahman gave strict orders that the Afghan traders were not to use that route. Consequently, they continued to transport their merchandise laboriously by camel over the Khyber Pass.[70]

THE AMIR'S SOCIAL PROGRAM

As previously noted, the city of Kabul—and in fact all Afghan urban centers—declined steadily in the nineteenth century. Kabul reached its lowest socioeconomic level in 1880. Like Sher Ali before him, Abdur Rahman hoped to build a new Kabul, one that would not be the "city of mud huts cramped into a corner among the mountains" Gray described, but a model city, serving as an example for the revitalization of the rest of the Afghan urban centers. Though he was not able to realize this dream, he made a notable start. A new *jumma masjid* (chief mosque) was built. The Amir had several furnaces for the production of baked bricks installed and encouraged the use of local cement.[71] Holdich reported that "new roads, new gardens, and palaces had sprung up. . . . The bazaars and streets were full of life and energy. . . . In the matter of planting, as in administration, there was most marked development. In short, the keynote of the whole scene was progress—progress everywhere."[72] Still, except for a number of new palaces and white-washed mosques, the majority of buildings in Kabul, as in most Afghan cities, were made of mud,[73] and though Kabul and the other urban centers made a steady recovery after the Second Anglo-Afghan War, they were still weak at the end of the nineteenth century. According to rough and often exaggerated estimates, the population figures around 1900 were as follows: Kabul, 75,000; Kandahar, 31,000 to 60,000; Herat, 25,000 to 50,000; Ghazni, 8,000; Istalif, 5,000; Charikar, 5,000; Jalalabad, 2,000 to 3,000.[74]

One area in which Abdur Rahman made noteworthy, though modest, gains was the field of public health. He brought a number of English professionals into the country, among them two physicians (Drs. John Gray and Lillias Hamilton), a veterinarian (Clements), a registered nurse (Mrs. Daly), and a surgeon-dentist (O'Meara). He also hired a number of Indian hospital assistants. The first public hospital in Afghanistan, a dispensary, was opened in Kabul in 1895, and the first European-trained Afghan dentist, Sufi Abdul Hak, started a practice in Kabul in this period. A few rudimentary military hospitals were opened to provide shelter, food, medicine, and treatment for the Afghan soldiers. European drugs were imported from India, and vaccination against smallpox was introduced under the supervision of Dr. Hamilton, who compiled a pamphlet on the vaccine for the use of the local hakims. This pamphlet, which was translated into Persian, was probably the first textbook on modern medicine in Afghanistan. As a sanitary measure, the Amir had public latrines built in Kabul and provided donkeys to cart the night soil from the city.[75] Health standards were also improved to some degree by the production of large quantities of soap in the Amir's workshops.

The impact of these progressive measures was limited, however. Afghanistan's health and sanitation needs were enormous; so were the obstacles. Superstition and ignorance continued to aggravate the already serious health problems. In cases of illness, the first recourse of most Afghans was still the mullah, from whom they purchased protective scrolls containing appropriate quotes from the Quran. In the event of recovery, the mullah was given great credit; in the event of continued sickness or death, *nasib*—one's lot as prescribed in the Book of Fate—was blamed. The medical knowledge of the hakims, whose services were very expensive, was severely limited. Bleeding remained their standard prescription for fevers, dyspepsia, gout, headaches, and other complaints.[76] The greatest damage was done by so-called eye doctors; in this respect, there was no perceptible improvement over earlier years.

In general, the Indian hospital assistants the Amir hired were of little use. With their limited training and almost total ignorance of European medicine, they did not alleviate the lot of the Afghan patients to any marked degree. Nor was the acceptance and use of European drugs by some of the hakims of much help; the hakims were unschooled in foreign languages and unable to understand the therapeutic properties of the drugs they prescribed. For the most part, the treatment of diseases remained empirical and shackled to medieval practices. The adoption of Western methods was obstructed by prejudice—both against the Europeans and against their drugs. Many Afghans were opposed to drugs on the grounds that they contained certain poisons; others were opposed on religious-traditionalist grounds to the use of alcohol. *Ex post facto* prejudice condemned the drugs, even though they were demonstrably helpful, because of their infidel source. The European medical practitioner was looked upon "as one who by the help of the powers of evil has in this world the gifts of knowledge, skill and wealth, but who in the next life must inevitably be consigned to eternal torment. Doubtless with his deadly poisons he can cure diseases if he wish, but it is not wise and indeed is scarcely lawful for a sick man to make use of him."[77] In short, European medicines were instruments of the Devil; retribution would, at some point in the future, strike those who used or received them.

Far more dangerous to public health than local prejudices was an almost total lack of knowledge of germs and the Muslim's firm belief in the purity of running water, a belief that has contributed to the outbreak of disastrous epidemics throughout the Middle East. The population of Kabul, for instance, was devastated time and again by cholera epidemics caused, in part, by the gross impurities in the drinking water.[78]

On the eve of Abdur Rahman's accession to the throne, the populace was almost wholly illiterate. According to the Amir, "There was no typewriting or printing press throughout the whole dominion of Afghanistan, and education was so neglected that I had to advertise all over the country for thirty clerks who could read and write their own language. I could, however, find only three to fulfill these conditions."[79] The Amir's statement is clearly an exaggeration (if only because he ignores the fact that being in his employ frequently proved fatal, ample enough reason for the dearth of applicants for the job). Nevertheless, his remarks indicate the sad state of the Afghan educational system and the extensive damage wrought by the economic and cultural stagnation that character-ized nineteenth-century Afghanistan. The small and antiquated village maktabs, without uniform curriculum or organization, were the basic educational units of the country. Essentially, only the mullahs and the *mirzas* (scribes) received instruction beyond the elementary level. Ac-cording to Dr. Gray, "Some of the latter study Persian sufficiently to write a well-worded and flowery letter; they learn, too, a certain amount of mathematics—arithmetic and Euclid. The *mullahs* learn some Arabic because the Quran is written in the language; otherwise foreign languages are not taught."[80]

Abdur Rahman's achievements in this field were not particularly note-worthy. He opened a few basic schools for Afghan soldiers, but they had neither trained personnel nor a definite program. There were also a few small educational facilities attached to the Afghan court. They offered little more than the traditional maktabs. Their curriculum was largely confined to some Arabic, the memorization of various verses or chapters of the Quran, and the study of moral lessons in Persian literary classics. Moreover, only male members of the royal family, page boys, some army officers, and the sons of certain feudal lords and tribal chieftains attached to the court were able to benefit from this education; it was, in short, an education for the elite.[81] The Amir attempted to establish a technical school in Kabul, with the English language as one of its subjects, and two Indian instructors were hired for that purpose. However, the school did not last long.[82] Abdur Rahman's most important contribution in the field of education was in bringing a Persian printing press to Kabul. In gen-eral, the press, which was under the direction of Munshi Abdul Razak of Delhi, was used to turn out stamps and legal forms, primarily contracts, deeds, promissory notes, and marriage settlements. However, some rudi-mentary school texts were also printed, though in extremely limited quan-tities.[83]

Abdur Rahman's educational activities were characterized by a random pragmatism and a lack of goals. Although he was aware of the need and value of a European-style higher educational system, as well as the desira-bility of a newspaper in the country, he failed to initiate either. A devotee of Persian literature, he adopted Persian as the official national language[84] and did not encourage the propagation and study of Pashto or, for that matter, any other language. Only a handful of Hindus and Armenians, educated by Christian missionaries or in the public schools of India, knew

English. The task of meeting the immense needs of adapting, copying, translating, and interpreting fell to them. Christian missionaries and foreign schools were barred from the country, and the government did not send students abroad to study. The resultant ignorance of foreign languages and cultures greatly impeded the development of an Afghan modernist movement.

Foreign trade introduced a great variety of European and Asian manufactured goods to Afghanistan. They included such items as clothing from England, boots from Russia and England, tableware from China, paraffin lamps from Germany, and soap from Austria, India, and Russia; even European sewing machines were available.[85] Though the number of these items was low and their prices too high to command more than a small market, they could not help but bring about a degree of social change. They were used mainly in court circles and by the upper class of Kabul, most of whom wore Western dress. The upper class gradually copied the Amir in adopting the use of European-style chairs and tables, which were manufactured in the government workshops or imported from India. An English tailor (Walter) was brought to court to outfit the members of the royal family and to teach the Kabuli tailors the cut of European clothing.[86] Corrugated iron roofs were imported from England for royal palaces; marble lions from India decorated the royal pavilion, which was guarded by European-style sentry boxes. Other innovations patterned after European practices included the adoption of a national anthem, "Salaam-i Padishah," presumably composed by an Englishman; the purchase of a piano for the royal palace (and, as previously noted, the employment of an English piano tuner);[87] the formation of brass bands, complete with pipers (they played Scottish tunes and "God Save the Queen");[88] and the use of Scottish kilts by the page boys of the infant prince. The Amir was one of the first Afghan rulers to allow himself to be photographed and have his portrait painted by Europeans. He was probably also the first Afghan monarch to display pictures in his palace (of the British House of Commons and House of Lords).[89]

The effect of these innovations and adaptations was felt mainly in and around Kabul; they did not represent a major intellectual challenge to traditional Afghan society. Most Afghan borrowings—Western military technology was an exception—remained faddish, unplanned, and superficial. Nevertheless, the fact that whims of this variety could be indulged was in itself significant.

THE POLITICS OF REFORM

The chief obstacles Abdur Rahman encountered in attempting to make reforms were financial and at the same time political. He was aware of his financial handicaps, just as he was aware of the potential of the natural resources of Afghanistan and of the benefits that European technical advice could bring. Nevertheless, even in the face of a very obvious need of adequate communications, he shrank from opening up his country and exploiting its natural wealth. Instead, he continued to rely on British subsidies, stiff taxes, and income derived from his workshops to finance his modernist schemes. His opposition to the unrestricted economic modernization and industralization of Afghanistan through European investment and technical advice was essentially political in nature. This is best illustrated in his refusal to allow railway and telegraph lines in the country.

In the closing decades of the nineteenth century there were various European plans to draw Afghanistan into a continental railway system linking Western Europe to India. One of these projects was conceived by Ferdinand de Lesseps, of Suez Canal fame, and a fellow countryman, Cotard. They proposed to link Paris (and Calais) with Calcutta, via Orenburg, Tashkent, Balkh, and Peshawar.[90] As presented to N. P. Ignatiev, the Russian ambassador at Constantinople, the plan envisioned dividing control of the Asian portions of the line between England and Russia, with Russia controlling the Orenburg-Samarkand section and England the Samarkand-Peshawar section. The plan was considered economically sound[91] and was favorably received by the Russian ambassador. However, it was rejected by the British, primarily for political reasons.[92] For the same reasons, the British authorities in India opposed General Annekov's proposal to extend the Russian railway system to India, which would have linked Paris with India, via Warsaw, Moscow, Baku, Herat, Kandahar, and Quetta. Col. C. E. Stewart submitted still another plan, proposing to connect the Indian railways with the Russian Central Asia line, via Herat.* His plan, too, was rejected in India.[93]

In the view of the British authorities, any intercontinental railway was

* In his book, Stewart discussed (pp. 422–28) what would be involved economically, politically, and physically in building such a line (about 560 miles). He felt that for a fair amount of money the Amir and his people would agree to the construction of the line and would protect it from harm. He cited the example of Persia, where initial opposition to telegraph lines had been overcome, and pointed out that Baluchistan, "certainly as savage as any part of Afghanistan over which this railway would run, ... is now perfectly safe."

strategically dangerous: it would facilitate a Russian military undertaking against India and require an enormous permanent garrison at the Indian frontier. The British also saw in the railway an excellent instrument for the extension and consolidation of Russian political and economic penetration of the entire region.[94] They feared that a strengthening of the Russian economic position in north and northeastern Persia and the opening of Afghanistan might be simply a prelude to a Russian rail link between the Caucasus and the Persian Gulf.[95]

The proponents of a forward policy, in India as well as in London, joined their political opponents in opposing an intercontinental railway. However, they advocated the extension of the Indian system to Afghanistan (at first to Kandahar, then to Herat). They argued that this would gain them political, strategic, and economic advantages in India, and would serve as an instrument for diplomatic and military pressure against Russia, thus guaranteeing the independence of Afghanistan and British interests there.[96] Some in India expressed an even more militant opinion. They urged that the buffer state policy in the region be abandoned in favor of out-and-out acquisition of Afghanistan. In their view, this would ensure peace between England and Russia by establishing a common frontier that neither country could cross without a declaration of war. These officials campaigned to push railways to Kabul and Kandahar, in the belief that this would end the prospect of costly and fruitless wars.[97] One argument they brought to bear was that a strengthening of central authority in Afghanistan with a corresponding decrease in the power of the tribal chieftains would lower the defensive capabilities of that country and make it—and India—more vulnerable to Russian attack.[98] To those who held this view, these were "sufficient and justified grounds" for extending the Indian railway to Kandahar and thence to Herat, with or without the consent of the Amir of Afghanistan.[99]

Abdur Rahman firmly resisted all efforts to introduce railways into Afghanistan. In this, he acted against the advice of some of his own advisers as well as the British government in India, who argued that Afghanistan could not fully exploit its natural resources or market its products unless modern means of transportation, production, and communications were available. Such arguments did not sway the Amir, as witness this passage from his autobiography:

I again advise my sons and successors not to listen to these people. I know what they say is quite true, but, at the same time, they do not consider that by making the country easily accessible, foreign powers would not find so much difficulty in entering and spreading themselves over our country. The greatest safety of Afghanistan lies in its natural impregnable position.[100]

The Amir vigorously condemned British railway-building activities at the borders of Afghanistan and the Indian government's avowed intention to push the line into his domains, an act, he wrote, that would be tantamount to "pushing a knife into my vitals."* However, Abdur Rahman (who was one of the first Afghan rulers to travel by train) did not rule out railway construction in Afghanistan altogether. On the contrary, he made it plain that the reason for his opposition was his country's inability to defend itself: "As long as Afghanistan has not arms enough to fight against any great attacking power, it would be folly to allow railways to be laid throughout the country."[101] Railroads and telegraph lines would be beneficial only when they served Afghan interests and only when the Afghans were sufficiently strong to foil the intrigues and aggressive designs of their neighbors.† Even then, the Amir advised his successors to build the first railway in the interior, far removed from the borders.

A constant fear of European imperialism, more than anything else, determined Abdur Rahman's economic and modernization policies. He once likened his kingdom and its serene isolation to a swan in the middle of a large lake. "On one bank of the lake," he said, "there lay, watching and waiting, an old tigress—the British Government in India. On the other was assembled a pack of greedy wolves—Russia. When the swan approached too near to one bank the tigress clawed out some of his feathers, and when the opposite bank, the wolves tried to tear him to pieces. He resolved therefore to keep secure from either foe in the middle of the lake."[102] (At another time, he said Afghanistan was like a goat on which a lion and a bear had fixed their eyes.)[103]

---

* Munshi, *Life of Abdur Rahman*, II, 154. J. D. Rees, a member of Parliament, wrote: "When the tunnel was made through the Chaman Range, in order to facilitate, if need be, the laying of rails to Kandahar, the Amir ... was very angry at what he regarded as a violation of his territory. The Viceroy invited him to the opening ceremony but he wrote back asking whether it was the custom of the English people when they bored a hole in a man's stomach to invite him to come and see the opening made" (as quoted by H. Mortimer Durand, p. 22). See also A. C. Yate, "Visit to India," pp. 33–35; Singhal, p. 137; and Rastogi, pp. 166f.

† The Amir felt that the extension of the Indian railway system to the Afghan borders was harmful to Afghan interests, because it would induce the Russians to extend their railway system to northern Afghanistan. He rejected the suggestion of Lord Curzon, who in 1897 had advised him to construct railways and install telegraphs as a means of bolstering Afghanistan's defenses. The Amir insisted that what Afghanistan needed was arms to defend itself. The Afghans would either reject or sabotage the railways and telegraphs, he declared, and besides, Afghanistan did not have enough money to bear the construction costs of such projects and was averse to the idea of seeking help from other nations. See Rastogi, pp. 203–4, 205.

Convinced that his powerful neighbors were hungry vultures, waiting for an opportunity to swallow their marked victim, Abdur Rahman faced a major dilemma: how to modernize his country and at the same time maintain its independence and his personal autocracy. Since he considered extensive foreign contacts, as well as any significant foreign presence in Afghanistan, threats to the country's independence, he adopted a policy of voluntary aloofness from the rest of the world, thereby delaying the exploitation of the country's natural resources. Great Britain, which considered Afghanistan her exclusive preserve, was opposed to any non-British presence or investment, in fact any direct contact, in Afghanistan, and was in a position to enforce this policy, because she controlled the country's foreign relations. For his part, the Amir was just as opposed to British financial activity in his country as he was to Russian or any other foreign activity. He made this clear in his autobiography: "I would most strenuously advise my sons and successors not to give the monopoly of their minerals to any foreigner, nor to let their mines be worked by any foreign companies, otherwise they will be immersed in many complications, thereby giving an excuse to foreign nations to interfere in the affairs of the country, for the sake of greed, which is growing unbearable from day to day." Not only should those who followed him refrain from giving contracts to foreigners, said the Amir; they should also bar foreigners from permanent residence in Afghanistan, especially those from countries that might raise questions of extraterritoriality. He regarded capitulations as nothing more than instruments of imperialism, declaring: "The destruction of a weak nation has been caused by a strong one, under the excuse of fighting for the rights of their subjects, who were interested financially in that weak country." Should Afghanistan ever find it essential to grant financial concessions to foreign powers, in order to meet its own needs, the Amir's advice was that such concessions be granted only to nations without common boundaries with Afghanistan, for instance, the United States, Italy, or Germany. Similarly, in hiring foreign technicians, preference should be given to nationals of those countries.[104]

Abdur Rahman was equally opposed to the presence of Christian missionaries in Afghanistan, on both political and religious grounds. He was opposed as well to the training of Afghan officers by the English. As for sending young Afghans abroad to study, he held that such a measure would cost the government huge sums of money, in return for which the students might acquire such vices as gambling and drinking, lose their faith, and, above all, become partial to alien interests.[105]

In instituting reforms, Abdur Rahman intended to adopt only such European skills and institutional forms as did not conflict with the vested interests of the monarchy, the independence of Afghanistan, or the tenets of the religious establishment; the three interests could not be separated. He opposed any measure or alien influence that could lead to a separation of religion and state or to a rejection of the concept of the unity and indivisibility of political authority. Reform and modernization were only the means, independence, under an absolute monarch, the end. Modernization had to be achieved as the country developed military might and economic self-sufficiency; above all, prolonged internal stability was essential.

Although Abdur Rahman Khan feared European imperialism, he effectively exploited Anglo-Russian rivalries to strengthen his diplomatic hand and Afghanistan's political position as an independent Muslim state.[106] Such was the case during the Panjdeh crisis, when he obtained and publicized a commitment on the part of the British to protect the territorial integrity and independence of Afghanistan.* The Amir was also fully aware of the political potential of Pan-Islamism and envisaged a Muslim triple alliance between the Ottoman Empire, Persia, and Afghanistan that would serve as a barrier against Russian advances in the Middle East.[107] He used the Islamic faith not only as a banner of unity for his ethnically heterogeneous kingdom but as a militant bulwark against foreign powers as well.[108]

In the end, however, despite Abdur Rahman's strenuous efforts to assert his personal rule and sovereignty, and his success in preserving the

---

* During his official visit to India in 1885, the Amir declined "politely but firmly" the viceroy's offer to send British troops and engineers to defend the northern and northwestern frontiers of Afghanistan. He replied "in a very explicit and determined manner that, though he himself was grateful for the offer, he could not answer for his people. They were ignorant, brutal and suspicious; he had fought with them himself for four years, and we [the British] must not suppose that he could control them, or move them about like pieces on a chessboard" (Forrest, *Lord Roberts*, pp. 139–40). Abdur Rahman had no intention of allowing his country to become a battleground for the English and the Russians. Instead, he wanted a firm public commitment from the British ("in plain and clear words") that they intended "to defend and protect the integrity of Afghanistan" and to provide the Afghans with whatever funds and arms were necessary to enable them to repel a Russian invasion without British intervention. On the eve of the Panjdeh incident, the Amir made public the viceroy's private assurances on these points, thereby committing the British government to this position. He thus attained the main objects of his visit. See Sir Alfred Lyall, *Life of the Marquis of Dufferin and Ava* (London, 1905, 2 vols.), II, 90–93.

de facto independence of his kingdom, he was unable to surmount the socioeconomic and political obstacles that constantly threatened the internal stability of the country and the evolution of an absolutist and economically self-sufficient monarchy: the entrenched and rebellious Afghan tribes retained their feudal and economic power, and Afghanistan remained a landlocked country, dependent for trade and communications on India, Central Asia, and Persia. The Amir's attempts to extend his spiritual and moral authority, if not sovereignty, over the Pathans of the Indo-Afghan borderland through lofty exhortations, financial subsidies, and marital alliances were steadily opposed by the government of India and were often bitterly resisted by the tribes. Had he been successful, he would have secured an Afghan footing on the Indian Ocean and, at the same time, gained a vast reservoir of soldiers, thereby improving both the economic and the strategic position of Afghanistan. In his view, Afghanistan's great opportunity to become permanently independent, and thus able to pursue its own brand of modernization, lay in access to the sea. Once the Afghans had access to the sea, they could maintain extensive but selective contacts with other countries, build or purchase their own freighters, and control their export-import trade.[109]

This, however, was a long-range program. Until such time as he could gain access to the sea for Afghanistan, Abdur Rahman pursued a practical policy aimed at the gradual reestablishment of total independence for his country. He pressed the government in India to allow him to establish direct diplomatic relations with Britain, a move that would have technically terminated the Indian government's hold over Afghan foreign relations, arguing that this would enhance the prestige of the monarchy, afford him an opportunity to employ British nationals (which would give the Afghans an opportunity to learn Western ways), and allow him to present his side of the story to the British Parliament, in case of conflicts with the Indian government.* The British government in India

---

* In a private court gathering the Amir declared: "After thinking it over for a long time, I have come to the conclusion that the affairs of my country will never be settled until I see the Queen and Ministers of England. I am sure I cannot get satisfaction in India." In 1892, with his chief engineer, Pyne, acting as intermediary, he transmitted his complaints to Lord Salisbury, proposing to submit his grievances about the attitudes and policies of the government in India directly to the British Parliament (see Singhal, pp. 136–37). According to Curzon (*Tales of Travel*, pp. 76–78), the Amir described in detail how he intended to make his accusations before Parliament: "I shall enter the hall, and the Lords will rise on the right, and the Commons will rise on the left to greet me, and I shall advance between them up the hall to the dais, where will be seated the Queen upon her throne. And she will rise and will say to me, 'What has Your Majesty come from Kabul to say?' ... I shall reply: 'I will say nothing'—and the Queen will

opposed any such plan, particularly in view of the Amir's announced intention to exert, if not complete political control, at least moral, spiritual, and some degree of feudal hegemony over the tribal belt.[110]

THE IMPACT OF THE DURAND LINE

In 1893, caught between Russian pressure, British intransigence, and his own unwillingness and unpreparedness to start a war with the government in India, Abdur Rahman signed the Durand Agreement.* In this pact (which increased his subsidy from 80,000 to 120,000 pounds), the Amir renounced Afghanistan's right to intervene in the tribal belt.[111] The Durand Line divided the allegiance of many tribes, without regard to the ethnography of the region.[112] It demarcated a no-man's-land, which became a haven for Afghan tribal chieftains and sometimes even for entire clans. Moreover, though the agreement pushed the British forward line into the tribal areas, it failed to modify the basic features of tribal life or to set up some kind of permanent tribal authority that might in turn have affected the position of the tribes in Afghanistan. In view of the military potential of the borderland and the close intertribal and family ties between some Afghan and Pathan tribes, the Durand Agreement resulted in a strength-

---

then ask me why I refuse to say anything; and I shall answer: 'Send for [Lord] Roberts. I decline to speak until Roberts comes.' And then they will send for Roberts . . . and when Roberts has come and is standing before the Queen and the two *Mejiloses* [the Houses of Parliament], then I will speak. . . . I shall tell them how Roberts paid thousands of rupees to obtain false witness at Kabul and that he slew thousands of my innocent people and I shall ask that Roberts be punished, and when Roberts has been punished, then will I speak."

* Afghan historians contend that the line of demarcation, the Durand Line, was imposed on Afghanistan under the threat of war and economic blockade. Mohammed Ali asserts that it deprived the country of "a quarter of a million Pathans of military age" (*The Mohammedzai Period*, pp. 140–41). British historians, for their part, maintain that the Durand Line was a negotiated settlement and cite as evidence both the Amir's public adherence to the agreement and his positive references to it in his autobiography (see Munshi, *Life of Abdur Rahman*, II, 166). As noted, the Afghans question the authenticity of these portions of the autobiography. An interesting idea has been advanced by Fraser-Tytler (*Afghanistan*, p. 189). He suggests that Abdur Rahman, unfamiliar with reading maps, did not understand all the implications when the line was drawn on a map before him, but was too conceited to say so. According to Singhal (pp. 152f), there were considerable differences between the map the Amir supplied his representative and the one on which the Durand Line was marked at Kabul. Says Singhal: "For the Amir it can properly be argued that the map drawn in 1893 had been prepared in a hurry and was not without inaccuracies." Rastogi also suggests that the maps varied (p. 180). According to Forrest (*Lord Roberts*, p. 172), "The Amir signed the treaty, but he did not sign the official maps indicating the boundary. He disliked the boundary because he considered it damaged his authority and prestige, and he determined by all the indirect means in his power to prevent its demarcation."

ening of the political position of the tribes of Afghanistan.[113] The policies of the Afghan rulers became more sensitive to the wishes of the major border tribes, on which they were dependent for the defense of the country. The stance of these tribes on any given issue became an important consideration in the successful implementation of domestic policies, especially those affecting eastern Afghanistan, the tribal homelands.

The Durand Agreement had other serious consequences for Afghanistan. It gave the British control of the border passes and thus the power to prevent Afghan nomads from entering India or re-entering Afghanistan. With this diplomatic and economic weapon, the authorities in India believed they could "induce the Afghans to compose any differences they might have with the British Government."[114] There was some justification for this assumption: the Afghan ruling elite had reason to fear the political consequences if the passes were to be closed, particularly since a halting of the seasonal migrations of the nomads and trade caravans would undoubtedly hurt the country's economy. Furthermore, constant British military activities, reprisals, and expeditions along the frontier kept alive a militant anti-foreign and anti-British feeling among the Pathan tribesmen.[115] This, in turn, affected the attitude of the Afghan tribes, reinforcing their traditional animosity toward the British and British institutions.

Following the Durand Agreement, the relations between Afghanistan and Great Britain deteriorated further. The government in India continued to oppose the establishment of direct diplomatic contacts between London and Kabul. Even so, Lord Elgin, the viceroy, extended an invitation to the Amir to visit India and England. In accepting, Abdur Rahman sent his reply directly to Queen Victoria, deliberately bypassing the viceroy. Curzon reported that the Amir was anxious to visit England, provided he could be assured of a welcome there "compatible with his own exalted conception of the dignity and prestige of the Afghan Sovereign, and . . . could safely be absent from his country for several months."[116] In the end, however, it was the Amir's son Nasrullah Khan who went to England (1895). However, his failure to obtain diplomatic representation in London only led to a further deterioration in the relations between the government of India and the Amir. There were constant disputes between the two countries over the tribal and forward policies of the Indian government (especially during the Tirah Campaign in 1897); they led to the viceroy's refusal to permit war materiel and imports of oil, iron, steel, and copper to pass into Afghanistan. In retaliation, the Amir repudiated his subsidy from the Indian government, and fired off an angry protest to Lord Curzon, rejecting a charge that he was responsible for the troubles the British were having with the Afridis and the peoples of Tirah, Bajawar, and Swat. He declared: "It is now eleven months since all caravans from my dominions have been stopped, and the implements which were necessary for my engine-workshop have been detained. They have caused my thoughts to incline to doubt India, so that enemy and friend are passed out of my memory (i.e., I confuse friends and enemies)."[117]

ABDUR RAHMAN: AN ASSESSMENT

Abdur Rahman's reign ended in 1901. In reviewing his 21-year rule, one can find both great accomplishments and major weaknesses. On the positive side, the Amir must be credited with bringing about the administrative, political, and economic unification of Afghanistan. He pacified the country; created a standing army; curbed the power of the religious establishment and of some tribal chieftains; introduced, on a small scale, modern machinery, European technology, and foreign technicians; brought doctors and some degree of medical knowledge to his country; increased interregional trade; and attempted to standardize weights and measures. However, one must note at the same time that his reforms were confined essentially to Kabul; the other important cities of Afghanistan were relatively unaffected. Herat, in 1885, for instance, was only a third-rate economic center, subsisting on a meager and irregular transit trade.[118] Moreover, the Amir's administrative and fiscal reforms were not accompanied by fundamental socioeconomic reforms affecting the structure of the rural economy of Afghanistan.[119] The Amir also failed to encourage modern education, to stimulate foreign trade and external contacts, to inaugurate modern communications, to establish banking institutions, and to exploit the natural wealth of Afghanistan.

Both internal and external factors contributed to the failure of his circumscribed moves toward the modernization and transformation of his country. The most important factor was the overwhelming number of divisive forces within Afghanistan itself: the ethnic differences, the religious animosity between Shi'ah and Sunni Muslims, the tribal jealousies, the feudal obligations and prerogatives, the conflict of regional interests, the traditionalist values. Another important factor was the lack of resources, both material and human, that a successful and sudden leap into modernity required. In an economically underdeveloped country, with few financial resources, the Amir tried to accomplish his reforms by relying on heavy taxation, especially of the urban and sedentary populations. Since most of the land tax was paid in kind and since many tribes, particularly the nomadic ones, enjoyed either complete or partial tax exemption, he had to depend on the merchant class, foreign trade, and British subsidies for the bulk of his cash income. That income was simply not sufficient to undertake major projects.

Yet the Amir was unwilling to compromise or jeopardize his power or the independence of Afghanistan in any way. Surrounded by large and small states, all acknowledging the rule, protection, or influence of either Great Britain or Russia, he adopted a policy of aloofness, isolation, and deliberate underdevelopment. He believed that this policy was the best way to guarantee the independence of his country, and that such a policy should be continued as long as Afghanistan was militarily weak. An underdeveloped Afghanistan would not whet the appetite of any foreign power. Nevertheless, total modernization was his ultimate aim, witness this passage from his political "testament":

> I hope and pray that if I do not succeed in my lifetime in the great desire for making railways, introducing telegraphs and steamers, working the mines, opening banks, issuing banknotes, inviting travellers and capitalists from all parts of the world, opening universities and other institutions in Afghanistan, my sons and successors will carry out these desires of my heart and make Afghanistan what I desire it to become.[120]

The question he left unanswered was: how, by what means and resources, did he intend to accomplish this lofty aim? His country was isolated by his will and by the will of Great Britain, and the fiscal policy that he fell back on alienated the merchants and urban class, the one important segment in the country that might have given the staunchest support to the monarchy, since it was to their interests to have a centralized, modernized regime at the expense of tribalism, regionalism, and feudalism. The Amir, however, did not intend to disturb the basic socioeconomic structure of his kingdom. His dependence on his Durrani kinsmen and on the other Afghan tribes made any such undertaking if not impossible at least highly dangerous. Furthermore, his reliance on Islam as a spiritual weapon against Britain and Russia, though it served Afghan interests by rallying disparate ethnic groups, promoted xenophobia and traditionalism. This, in combination with deep-seated Afghan fears about the ultimate aims of Britain and Russia, undermined the efforts and contributions of the few European technicians in his employ.* Thus, despite his patriotism and

---

* Griesbach, the geologist employed by the Amir, reported "how impossible it was made for him to do any useful work, for the whisper had spread that he carried a notebook and if he found a mineral of value, it was not the Amir to whom the fact was reported but the British Government." Griesbach resigned. His replacement, Arthur Collins, was followed constantly and "from whatever place he took a specimen, from the same

what he thought of as a benevolent despotism, despite his important contributions, Abdur Rahman Khan was not only unsuccessful in formulating a definite program of modernization, but indeed unable to find the means to bring such a program into being.

---

place an official in his ignorance took what he considered to be a similar specimen; this was to act as a check on the geologist.... [Collins] photographed some interesting geological formations.... At once it was reported that the new geologist was a political agent spying out the nakedness of the land. He was recalled to Kabul and kept for months doing nothing till in disgust he also resigned" (Gray, pp. 431–32). For an account of Afghan obstructionism in the operation of the tannery, see E. and A. Thornton, p. 25.

Mahmud Tarzi and "Siraj al-Akhbar"

Siraj al-Akhbar Afghaniyah (The Lamp of the News of Afghanistan), which was established during the reign of Abdur Rahman's successor, Habibullah, was the first successful news medium in modern Afghan history. Published biweekly from October 1911 to January 1919, it played an important role in the development of an Afghan modernist movement, serving as a forum for a small, enlightened group of Young Afghans, who provided the ethical justification and basic tenets of Afghan nationalism and modernism. The leading member of this group was Mahmud Tarzi, the journal's editor and chief contributor.[1]

Tarzi (1866–1935) was the son of Sardar Ghulam Muhammed Khan, a prominent leader of the Muhammedzai clan and a well-known poet (who wrote under the pen name Muhammed "Tarzi," or stylist).[2] In 1882, Abdur Rahman charged the Sardar with conspiracy against the state and banished him and his family from the country.[3] After a brief stay in Karachi, the Tarzis went to Damascus, where Sultan Abdul Hamid II, the Ottoman Emperor, allowed them to establish residence.[4] The years of exile, which lasted two decades, were important ones for young Tarzi. In the schools he attended in Damascus and Constantinople, he came into contact with European culture and institutions; he was exposed as well to the Ottoman nationalist-revivalist movement and the Pan-Islamic views of al-Afghānī.[5] He also gained administrative experience abroad, serving in the secretariat of the Ottoman provincial administration in Damascus.[6]

In 1902, after both Abdur Rahman and the Sardar were dead, the Tarzis returned to Afghanistan, under an amnesty promulgated by the new Amir, Habibullah.[7] Soon after, young Tarzi made his first efforts to initiate a program of reform in Afghanistan, calling the Amir's attention to the country's serious deficiencies in education, communications, and industry, and pointing out the undesirable effects of political, cultural, and intellectual isolation.[8] Tarzi was appointed chief of the Bureau of Translation for the royal court; his main task was to keep the Amir informed about events within the Muslim world and Europe.

Thanks to Tarzi's untiring efforts and the support of Inayatullah Khan, the Amir's eldest son (who supervised the administration of education and the operations of the royal press), Afghanistan became a country with a newspaper. Written in Persian, *Siraj al-Akhbar* was published under the auspices of the Amir and under the supervision of the court chamberlain.[9] During its first year of publication, the periodical was crudely printed, but later, after new printing presses were imported, the quality of the paper and of the printing and engraving was greatly improved, so much so, that in some respects *Siraj al-Akhbar* was superior to many current Afghan publications.

Tarzi's immediate aim was to provide Afghanistan with what, in his judgment, was "one of the most essential tools of modern civilization," a newspaper; except for the "bedouin and the savage tribes," he wrote, there were no organized societies without news media. To this end, he published both domestic and foreign news, either carrying translations of stories that had appeared in the English, Urdu, Turkish, and Arabic press or reproducing articles from Persian newspapers and journals. He also inserted photographs and drawings. He had, however, a greater ambition for the periodical. Under his editorship, *Siraj al-Akhbar* espoused the cause of modernization and nationalism, and undertook the political and social education of the Afghan ruling class.

In attempting to propagate the tenets of Afghan nationalism, Tarzi and his associates faced enormous tasks. Given a country in which almost half the population was ethnically non-Afghan, they had to try to redefine the term Afghan on a geographic and religious basis, and so allay any fears of the non-Afghans that modernization might lead to a strengthening of the Afghan hold over the country. Another important task was to convince Habibullah that a socioeconomic transformation of Afghanistan would not invite foreign intervention and domination or jeopardize the monarchy and its ruling dynasty; that, on the contrary, such a transformation, far from being dangerous to the monarchy, would reinforce the authority and power of the monarch, contribute to the stability of the country, and stave off external threats. Beyond that, the Young Afghans faced the difficult tasks of persuading the religious establishment that Islam, modernization, and secularism were compatible, of convincing the Shi'ah Muslims that modernism was not a mere device to undermine their weak position and establish total Sunni control, and of satisfying the Afghan tribal chieftains that a modern Afghanistan would not mean an end to their privileges or to Afghan ethnic rule.

The sociopolitical ideas of Tarzi and the Young Afghans were shaped to a considerable extent by a number of outside events and intellectual currents. The Russo-Japanese War, the Anglo-Russian Convention of 1907, the constitutional movements in Persia, the Ottoman Empire, and China (1906–11), the spread of Pan-Islamism, the Italo-Turkish (1911) and Balkan wars (1912–13), World War I, the Russian revolutions, and the proclamation of Wilson's Fourteen Points—each had great impact on Tarzi and his colleagues. They were also profoundly influenced by the great wave of Muslim revivalist-modernist thought that was sweeping India and the Middle East during these years.*

DECLINE OF AFGHANISTAN: A MODERNIST DIAGNOSIS

As proselytizers of modernism, Tarzi and his associates sought to analyze the factors that had caused the decline of Afghanistan and the Islamic world in general. Such an inquiry, Tarzi insisted, was not only the privilege but the duty of every devout Muslim and patriotic Afghan: only through self-examination and self-criticism could nations, like individuals, hope to overcome their shortcomings and avoid repeating past mistakes.[10] Tarzi contended that a thorough examination of Afghan history showed that one of the principal reasons the Afghans had fallen behind was the neglect of education and science. He pointed out that in 1918 there were more educated people in a single city in the Punjab than in all of Afghanistan.[11] In part, he said, this could be attributed to the Afghans' preoccupation with the defense of their fatherland and excessive reliance on physical force and might; however, the fact that education and learning were the exclusive domain of the mirzas and mullahs, whose own education was so sadly lacking, particularly in the scientific fields, was also a factor. For generations, said Tarzi, the Afghan people had been

* The general theses of Tarzi and the Young Afghans concerning Islam, reform, modernization, Pan-Islamism, and imperialism bear great similarities, indeed the imprint, of the works of al-Afghānī, Muhammad 'Abduh and his disciple Muhammed Rashid Rida, the Muslim Indian reformers Sayyid Ameer Ali and Sir Sayyid Ahmad Khan, and others. For the views of these men, see Jomier; Baljon, *Muslim Koran Interpretation*; Adams, *Islam and Modernism*; W. Smith, *Islam in Modern History*; H. Gibb, *Modern Trends*; Grunebaum, *Islam*; as well as Laoust; Cragg; Kerr; Vatikiotis; Vatikiotis and Makdisi; Rahman, "Muslim Modernism"; and A. Ahmad, "Les musulmans," and "Sayyid Ahmad Khan."

deprived of able and educated teachers. Superstition and tradition had prevailed, and the Afghans, like their fellow Muslims in general, had thus failed to tap a multitude of resources, human as well as natural. As a result, the light of science had shone in the West and darkness had engulfed the East. A veil of apathy had fallen on the Afghans, who, caught in their concern for private passions and appetites, had neglected their fatherland and endangered its independence and future development.[12]

Tarzi singled out the disunity of the Afghans and their anarchic concept of freedom and law as other factors that had contributed to the backwardness of the country. The disunity was such, he declared, that it had calamitously set city against city, village against village, street against street, tribe against tribe, brother against brother. Such divisiveness defied both the precepts of Islam, which ordained that all the faithful were brethren, and the dictates of reason, which taught that society functioned best within a framework of unity and mutual cooperation. Could Peshawar, Baluchistan, and Sistan have been wrested from the Afghans, if they had not been weakened by national disunity?[13]

In Tarzi's view, one important result of this disunity was that the majority of Afghans had developed a negative concept of freedom, equating freedom with the absence of restraint or governmental authority. He saw lawlessness as historically regressive and as alien to the spirit and elevated ethics of Islam. True freedom, he wrote, lay in adherence to a positive concept of law, a concept in which law is seen as a cohesive and constructive social force contributing to the development of religion, national genius, and civilization.[14]

Among the other causes of Afghanistan's decline, according to Tarzi, were the lack of contact with the outside world and the fanaticism of an unenlightened group of traditionalists in the country. Cut off from the main currents of modern life, the Afghans had not been able to borrow selectively from Western civilization; instead, only those products of European culture that were designed exclusively for European colonies had been accessible to them. These limited European cultural exports, which were permeated with materialism and political design, restricted the Afghans in their choice and prevented them from successfully grafting secular and foreign learning onto their own national and religious heritage.[15]

The Young Afghans rejected the contention of those in the West who held that Islam was the chief cause of the backwardness of the Muslims, and that, conversely, Christianity was the essential ingredient in the success and progress of Europe. They retorted that European material progress was attained precisely because of the separation of religion and learning, not because of their union. Muslim societies had declined as a result of the expansionist conflicts among Muslim rulers, which in the end caused the political disintegration of the Islamic world. Moreover, the gulf between secular interests and the ethical standards of Islam had grown ever wider, leading to the neglect and decline of the Muslim institutions of learning.[16] The superstitions and traditions that obstructed the rule of reason and learning had no basis in the fundamentals of Islam, Tarzi argued; the past achievements of Islamic civilization proved this. Therefore, the Muslims themselves, not their religion, were responsible for the decadence of their societies.[17] On this theme, he printed the following poem, which had appeared in the Persian paper *Nobahar* :[18]

> The black smoke rising from the roof of the fatherland
> Is caused by us.
> The flames that devour us from left and right
> Are caused by us.
> The disunity and weakness of Islam was not caused by
>   Christ or the Church,
> But was caused by us.

ON THE COMPATIBILITY OF MODERNIZATION WITH ISLAM

Tarzi was one of the first Afghans to argue that European predominance should not be attributed exclusively to European military might, but should be attributed also to Western cultural, economic, and industrial achievements.[19] Therefore, Afghanistan could not expect to meet the European challenge simply by adopting military technology. Only by thoroughly reorganizing their institutions could traditional societies like those of the Muslim world rejuvenate themselves. This applied as well to all emerging countries (e.g., the Russia of Peter the Great, and Japan).[20] The Afghans must not only transform their institutions, but also adopt electricity, chemistry, the telegraph, railways, and the like, along with military technology.[21] But, Tarzi warned, these borrowings should not be made solely for purposes of national defense, nor should the Afghans content themselves with unproductive copying. Instead, Afghanistan should make such cultural, scientific, and institutional borrowings as would allow science and learning to develop in the country, to the general benefit of the Afghan people.[22]

According to Tarzi and his colleagues, planned modernization was not incompatible with Islam. To demonstrate this, they offered their own interpretations of the "true" meaning and significance of the precepts of the Quran, the various Muslim holidays, and the sayings of the Prophet.[23]

Their assumption of such a responsibility was in itself an important step: for the first time, educated Afghan laymen publicly questioned the religious interpretations of the traditionalists and mullahs who violently objected to modernization. To those, for instance, who had raised doctrinal objections to the use of Western dress, Tarzi addressed this question: Were Muslims to be distinguished by their clothing or their faith? His own answer was that faith and ethics, not appearance and convention, constituted the important elements of Islam. Clothing was not an article of faith; if it were, a world convention of Muslims would or should have gathered to prescribe a uniform for all Muslims.[24] Tarzi castigated those of the religious establishment who condemned modern science as the product of infidels, declaring that such an attitude betrayed abysmal ignorance. He pointed out that in the West science and religion were treated and studied separately, while in Afghanistan, unfortunately, there was neither separation nor study. The ulama of the country had done a great disservice to the children of the fatherland through their negligence, indifference, and ignorance, Tarzi asserted. Moreover, their ignorance extended even to theology. Instead of studying the Quran and then enunciating the true precepts of Islam, the ulama recited memorized pages like parrots, and charged their critics with heresy and irreligion in order to hide their own ignorance.[25] The religious establishment, in insisting that all learning was their exclusive prerogative, had raised a formidable obstacle to the development of education and the dissemination of knowledge among their fellow Muslims.

Tarzi insisted that the maledictions and accusations of the religious establishment, arising as they did from ignorance, should not be allowed to distort or obscure the significance of modernism, which in essence and in principle was in harmony with the lofty teachings of Islam. How, he asked, could Afghan Muslims be asked to consider science and technology impious, when advances in these fields could greatly help consolidate the defenses of a Muslim country and preserve its independence? Acceptance of European technology did not necessarily presuppose the adoption of European mores.[26] Moreover, Tarzi argued, a study of Islam's history clearly indicated that in Islam's golden age the religious establishment preserved and propagated science and learning, deriving much of its vitality therefrom. Knowledge and efforts to acquire knowledge through education were not only compatible with the Quran, they formed an essential part of it.[27] By enjoining the faithful to work for the betterment of the Islamic community, the Quran was in concord with the spirit of each age and the needs of every era.[28] The Quran was not concerned with the eternal life alone. It also taught concern for this world, where good deeds were essential for personal, social, and national self-improvement. The cultural and material progress of the Islamic community had contributed to the strength and spread of the Islamic faith before; there was no reason to believe that further progress would undermine the position of Islam.[29] Furthermore, Tarzi argued, knowledge, and therefore science, was plainly held to be a necessity by the Prophet Muhammed, who suggested that ignorance could no more coexist with knowledge than could cleanliness with uncleanliness or light with darkness.[30] He pointed out that one of the *hadith* (traditions) of Islam was that "man's faith lay in his reason." Knowledge was therefore essential, if one were to know not only oneself but also God, man's creator.[31] Since the trait that distinguished man from the beasts and made him superior to them was his God-given reason, neglecting to cultivate and apply that reason was, by inference, a great disservice to oneself, to one's community, to Islam, and to God.[32]

Other contributors to *Siraj al-Akhbar* followed Tarzi's lead in invoking Quranic texts to demonstrate their points. One Abdul Hadi, for instance, attempted to endow travel abroad in pursuit of learning with Quranic sanction. He wrote that the Quran had acknowledged that non-Muslim peoples possessed knowledge that could be of benefit to the Muslims, in urging the faithful to travel "even to China" for the sake of learning. Surely, he reasoned, this passage by extension would also sanction travel to the West in pursuit of learning. He cited the extensive travels of famous Muslim geographers, sages, and navigators of the past as symbolic of Muslim open-mindedness and indicative of the universality of knowledge.[33]

The theme of the universality of knowledge interested Tarzi, too. In his view, that was what had allowed the West to borrow many of Islam's past scientific achievements. Science and knowledge, whatever the language or source, were beneficial: "A diamond encrusted with mud was still a diamond."[34] Why, Tarzi asked, should a firm belief in Islam as the best and most sacred of all religions deter the Afghans from trying to rid their country of ignorance, want, misery, disease, and dependency? Quite the contrary; efforts to mold a healthy, strong, free, and independent Islamic community in Afghanistan ought to be welcomed as acts of religious piety.[35] Another contributor to *Siraj al-Ahkbar*, identified only by the initials M. A., went even further in excoriating the "logical inconsistencies" of those who held that modern science and all its by-products were alien to Islam. If we accept such a conclusion, he wrote, we must stop importing all foreign goods, even matches and clothing, a move that would do nothing more than leave the Afghan people naked and without light.[36]

Since knowledge was beneficial and served the best interests of Islam and the Afghans, the teaching of foreign languages could not corrupt Afghan youth or harm the Afghan national genius, said Tarzi. Invoking the name of such incontestably patriotic Afghans as Dost Muhammed and Sher Ali, he reminded his readers that these rulers had permitted the English language to be used for military terms. He also pointed out that the acquisition of foreign languages along with modern technology by Japan, a major non-Christian Asiatic nation, had clearly advanced the development of her national institutions and genius.[37] Tarzi even used the anti-British sentiments of the Afghans to press home his argument for the teaching of foreign languages in Afghanistan. Knowledge of English, he asserted, would enable the Afghans to learn the secrets of British scientific and technological achievements and would, moreover, lead to a better understanding of Britain's policies and political designs on their country. For equally utilitarian reasons, Tarzi held that tourism and travel in general were beneficial. Not only would travel promote trade; it would also broaden the horizons of individual Afghans and strengthen their grasp of complex political and strategic problems.[38]

What was needed, Tarzi concluded, was a fundamental reformation of Afghan society, with a reorganization of its institutions and the introduction of modern science and technology. The achievement of this great task should be the joint responsibility of an enlightened Muslim religious leadership, the Afghan scholars, and the ruling elite. It was up to the religious leaders and the intellectuals to demonstrate the progressive spirit of Islam and free Afghanistan's Muslim community of a superstructure of superstition, customs, and habits that were essentially non-Islamic.[39] "Times of poetry are bygone," he wrote. "It is now the time of action and effort. The era is that of motor, rail, and electricity. The time of camels, oxen, and donkeys is bygone."[40]

ON THE IMPORTANCE OF EDUCATION AND OF
OTHER ASPECTS OF MODERNIZATION

In Tarzi's view, the first concrete step toward social change and reform should be the establishment of cultural contacts with the outside world. To this end, he assigned *Siraj al-Akhbar* the task of bridging the gap between Afghanistan and the rest of the world—of informing the Afghans of intellectual, scientific, and technological achievements in Europe and advancing their understanding of the nature of Western institutions. He devoted innumerable articles to new concepts and fields of study. Among the subjects discussed were the natural and evolutionary progress of humanity; the causes of cyclones; the human circulatory system; meteorology, geology, and cosmography; archaeology, geography, and historiography; international law, political science, and municipal government; and the importance of joint-stock companies. Other articles dealt with such technological achievements as trains, automobiles, and airplanes, the telephone, the microscope and the telescope, and photography. Tarzi also inserted hundreds of short items and poems on the nature of literature and on the history of science, all of them exalting modernity and stressing the enormous potential of scientific knowledge. The Afghans were exhorted to learn the lesson that Japan, the Ottoman Empire, and Persia had been forced to learn the hard way: that in the contemporary world no country could meet the challenge of modern European armies and Western technological superiority without borrowing techniques from the West.[41]

Tarzi published a great number of articles in *Siraj al-Akhbar* deploring the lack of modern educational facilities in Afghanistan. He also founded *Siraj al-Atfal* (Children's Lamp), the first Afghan publication aimed at a juvenile audience, in which he ran selected stories, moralistic and didactic tales, riddles, and puzzles, all designed to impress upon Afghan youngsters the importance of education. In a typical article, he bade young Afghans to strengthen their faith by obtaining knowledge, which alone would enable them to know God and His work, to understand the known and the unknown.[42] In *Siraj al-Akhbar* and in other works, Tarzi praised the greatness of true scholarship and science, which had conquered and enlightened the world; knowledge was the only source of social wealth and individual fulfillment.[43] He appealed to parents to recognize the worth and the rights of their children. Children, he wrote, were not objects or instruments of labor or capital investments. Their education was more important than achieving material success, which in any case was ephemeral; education alone was a lasting investment, an investment that benefitted the state as well as the individual.[44] Compulsory education was necessary, if Afghan progress and modernization were to be ensured, and to this end, public libraries and a network of modern schools with well-balanced curricula ought to be established.[45]

In order to generate popular interest in science and learning, Tarzi translated a number of European novels into Persian. Among them were Jules Verne's *Around the World in Eighty Days, Twenty Thousand Leagues Under the Sea,* and *The Mysterious Island.* He also translated two important Turkish works: *International Law,* by Hasan Fahmi Pasha, with which he probably introduced the concept of international justice and legal order into Afghanistan, and a five-volume *History of the Russo-Japanese War*, by the chief of staff of the Turkish army. Tarzi's original works include a personal journal entitled *Travel Across Three Continents in Twenty-Nine Days*, which he wrote in the the 1890's but did not publish until 1914, and various collections of essays and pamphlets; the most important of these are *What Is To Be Done?* and *Science and Islam*, in which he again attempted to demonstrate the compatibility of Islam and modern science and to enumerate the past scientific achievements of the Islamic world.[46]

Very few subjects were overlooked by Tarzi and his associates in their attempt to educate the Afghan public through *Siraj al-Akhbar*. One subject that especially concerned them was public health. They prepared articles explaining what germs were and stressing the necessity of using non-polluted water.[47] In others they emphasized the use of soap. Tarzi even invoked Quranic injunctions against uncleanliness, writing that uncleanliness invalidated prayers.[48] In still other articles, the meager and antiquated knowledge of the hakims was criticized. Tarzi contended that the local doctors knew nothing more than the ancient Greeks and the practitioners of the Middle Ages had, and insisted that the country needed doctors with modern training, pharmacies, and public clinics.[49]

Another of Tarzi's concerns was women's rights. Although he ridiculed the extremism and eccentricities of certain French feminists, he was the first Afghan to take a positive stand on this issue. He dedicated a series of articles to famous women in history, discussing the many abilities of women. He acknowledged the feminine contribution to science and human progress, and told his readers that in Europe there were women doctors, scientists, writers, lawyers, teachers, and government employees. But even as he supported the individual rights of women, including the right to an education, he maintained that a woman's primary duty still lay in raising a family and managing a household.[50] A monogamist himself, Tarzi never explicitly attacked polygamy, but he did so implicitly by constantly referring to the ideal family as a family in which there was one wife and a few children.[51] In his book *Raudat-i-hikam*, he noted that monogamy was universally practiced in Europe, and that the Europeans derided the Muslim custom of marrying as many as four women. Since, in his view, the health, welfare, and education of Afghan families was essential to Afghan progress, he attacked the extravagant expenditures incurred in connection with multiple marriages, which often financially ruined families.[52]

Another area of special concern was the Afghan economy. Tarzi urged his countrymen to adopt such innovations as the telephone, the telegraph, and the automobile, to import industrial machinery, to establish post offices, to form joint-stock companies; all he argued would assist in the economic unification of Afghanistan.[53] He insisted that railways were necessary to speed up this process. The railway would have an enormous impact on Afghan society; it would completely revolutionize the people's notion of time and distance in reducing, say, the Kabul-Herat journey of 35 days to three. Railroads would allow the Afghans to exploit their mineral wealth, transfer foodstuffs from one region to another quickly in case of famine, and market Afghanistan's chief export, fresh fruit, much more effectively; above all, railroads would vastly improve the country's defenses, especially since Russia and British India had extended their rail lines to the very borders of Afghanistan. Tarzi pointed out that Russia and India could, if necessary, instantly mobilize hundreds of thousands of soldiers against Afghanistan; in contrast, it would take an Afghan force an entire month to travel to the northern border by horse and camel.

However, Tarzi recognized that the question of a railway presented the Afghans with a dilemma, for the political drawbacks might outweigh the economic benefits. Railway concessions to great powers, or the scramble for them, could have dire consequences, witness China, the Ottoman Empire, Persia, and Morocco. There was even the possibility that a railway might lead to a division of Afghanistan into Russian and British spheres of influence. Tarzi found a plausible solution to this dilemma in international law: all the "interested parties" would pledge not to intervene in the internal affairs of Afghanistan. On this basis—and only on this basis— the Afghan government should permit construction of the railways the country so badly needed. Still, Tarzi was not so naive as to accept pledges of non-intervention and assurances of a belief in international law as adequate safeguards for preserving the integrity and sovereignty of Afghanistan. The Afghans, he said, valuing freedom more than material well-being, could simply destroy the rail lines, if their country were subject to interventionism. This was no light threat on his part; he went so far as to publish a manual for the Afghan army on the effective destruction of rail lines.[54]

Because of a deep-seated fear of capitulations and foreign intervention, Tarzi and some of his associates were unrealistic in suggesting that plans of modernization such as railway construction could be achieved without sorely needed foreign capital. Some of their proposals for indigenous financing of new programs were equally unrealistic. For instance, one Ali Akbar suggested that modernization programs could be funded through a nationwide system of individual, mandatory savings. He estimated that, given a population of 20 million, such a plan could bring in 20 million krans annually, enough to permit modernization without foreign assistance. Tarzi himself advanced a more ingenious, if equally impractical, plan. Every year, he said, thousands of animals were sacrificed for religious purposes. Were their skins to be contributed to the cause of Afghan education, a million or more rupees would be realized annually. This, he contended, would both serve the country and broaden the scope and meaning of religious sacrifices.[55] The fact is, the Afghan reformers had no immediate, concrete, practical solution to the dilemma that had plagued the Afghan rulers through most of the nineteenth century: how to modernize the country and at the same time preserve its independence and the monarchy. But, if they found no immediate solution to that dilemma, they thought they saw a long-range solution: in nationalism they foresaw a force mighty enough to protect Afghan sovereignty and permit Afghanistan to modernize itself unhindered.

NATIONALISM: ALLY OF MODERNISM

Finding the *raison d'être* of an Afghan state in the teachings of Islam, Tarzi attempted to link national aspirations with the cause of modernism. To support his contention that the very concept of an Afghan ethos and fatherland emanated from Islam, he quoted a saying of the Prophet Muhammed: *Hob ul watan min al iman* (patriotism derives from faith). Since the Afghans had accepted Islam by the grace and will of God, he reasoned, it followed that Afghanistan was a God-given country; thus, love for the Afghan fatherland was divinely ordained. The fatherland was the cradle of religion, and religion provided the foundation for freedom, honor, nationality, and individual identity. In an attempt to demonstrate that there was no contradiction between the concept of Afghan nationhood and the Quranic concept of a single Islamic community (ummah), Tarzi argued that, though all Muslims were members of one community, there were a number of political entities within that community. These constituted fatherlands (*watans*) for the communities living therein, who formed nations (*millets*). Since these political entities were Muslim by religion, the love each citizen bore his fatherland was perforce sanctioned by Islam and by God. To love one's country was to love one's religion and vice versa.[56]

Tarzi also attempted to link the legitimacy of the Afghan monarchy with the precepts of Islam, holding that religion, the nation, the fatherland, and the government were inseparable and sacred concepts.[57] If the fatherland were to be compared to a being, the nation would form its bones and flesh, the king its soul.[58] Therefore, it was the religious duty of every devout Muslim to serve not only his fatherland and his nation, but also his government and his monarch, for a "fatherland without a nation, a nation without a fatherland, both without government, and government without a king, would resemble inorganic substance."[59]

Tarzi's next step was to attempt to identify love of fatherland with the cause of modernism. He argued that, as patriotism was explicitly sanctioned and exalted by Islam as a religious duty, Islam almost by definition required a commitment to the defense of the fatherland. Since progress and modernization were indispensable in this regard, they were compatible with Islam. Only through modernization could the Afghan kingdom reorganize its army and bolster its defenses, and in so doing, protect its independence and Islam against the insatiable appetite of European imperialists.[60] True patriotism thus went beyond the willingness to fight in defense of the fatherland; it necessarily entailed the desire to reform and modernize the fatherland as well. It was clearly the duty of each true patriot to promote learning and to contribute to the development of educational institutions, which would ensure progress in Afghanistan.[61] Divinely ordained principles, as well as the cause of freedom and progress, required national unity. Therefore, those who opposed progress contributed to disunity and provided weapons to the enemies of Islam and the fatherland. Finally, Tarzi insisted that it was the supreme task of all Afghans to support the policies of the monarchy, whose aim was to unify the country and ensure its progress through modernization.[62]

The Young Afghans regarded the development of Afghan historiography as essential to the growth of Afghan nationalism. They urged scholars to develop historical rationalism, and by comparative study, discover the sources of the strength and weaknesses of various civilizations. Insight into the factors that undermine or strengthen a country would assist the Afghans in securing the future of their own country.[63] According to Tarzi, these studies ought to be accompanied by a concerted effort to raise the status of Pashto, which he and his associates regarded as "the Afghan language," in contrast to Persian, the official language. Pashto or "Afghani" was the manifestation of national genius and "the ancestor of all languages," a true national language. As such, it must be studied and taught to all the ethnic groups in Afghanistan.* Islam, Afghan history,

* Such a policy was adopted in the 1930's and was pursued vigorously in the 1950's, when Pashto became both the official and the national language of Afghanistan. Under the present constitution, however, both Pashto and Persian are considered official languages. For Tarzi's views on Pashto, see *SA*, 5th year, Nos. 1, p. 2, and 19, p. 5; 2d year, No. 9, pp. 9–12.

and Pashto together formed the mortar that would permit the country's ethnic mosaic to be molded into a single nation.

The Afghan reformers also attempted to link Afghan nationalism and modernism to the concept of Pan-Islamism.* Echoing the views of al-Afghānī, they attacked the position taken by various European writers that European imperialism was a progressive historical force. European colonialists, Tarzi contended, pursued both political and religious policies that propagated materialism and whose ultimate aim was to sap the strength of Islam. To this end, the colonialists supported the activities of Christian missionaries, capitalized on and even promoted divisions among the Muslims, and instituted educational programs in their colonies that were aimed at stifling the revival of the Muslim world.[64] In Tarzi's view, the Muslims could check European imperialism by adhering to the Pan-Islamic credo of al-Afghānī and promoting Muslim solidarity. In this connection, the Ottoman Empire, Persia, and Afghanistan, "the three remaining independent Muslim political entities," had an important historical role to play. In establishing close political, cultural, and economic ties, they could promote unity and solidarity within the Islamic world. Tarzi pointed out that such a political rapprochement had been prevented in the past by the particularism of the Shi'ah Persians, but that the threats now facing the Muslim world made unity both a religious duty and a political necessity.[65] The reconciliation of Shi'ah and Sunni differences in Afghanistan would in itself tend to consolidate the position of Islam; moreover, reconciliation would strengthen the defense of the Afghan fatherland and promote closer political and cultural ties with Persia.[66]

Tarzi was by no means the first to suggest that Shi'ah-Sunni differences had to be settled. In 1743, Nadir Shah, primarily for political reasons, had advanced a plan to reconcile the Muslim communities within his empire. He proposed that the Shi'ahs recognize the legitimacy of the first three Caliphs, in return for which the Sunnis would accept Shi'ism as a fifth legal school of Islam, to be ranked with the Hanafite, Malikite, Shafiite, and Hanbalite schools and to be known as the Jafarite school.[67] Shi'ah and

---

* Tarzi suggested that Turkish officers, technicians, and medical experts be hired to help implement Afghanistan's modernization programs, as an example of Muslim cooperation and solidarity. He argued that, as co-religionists, the Turks would not cause internal friction and therefore their presence would facilitate and accelerate modernization (*SA*, 1st year, No. 14, pp. 9–10).

ultra-conservative leaders alike opposed Nadir's plan, and it came to nothing.

A century later, al-Afghānī offered another plan to resolve the differences between the two groups. He suggested that the Shi'ahs recognize the Ottoman Sultan as the Caliph of all the Muslims, and that the Sultan recognize the Shah of Persia, the head of the leading Shi'ah state, as an independent and sovereign monarch. As a magnanimous gesture, the Sultan was to cede the Shi'ite holy places in what is now Iraq to the Shah. The two rulers were to discuss matters of common interest and coordinate their policies through consultation.[68] This plan failed, too.

The program Tarzi had in mind was much simpler. The three cardinal principles of Islam—the profession of faith ("There is no god but God and Muhammed is His Prophet"), the Quran, and the Ka'abah (the shrine at Mecca)—were non-controversial elements, and as such, provided a basis for Sunni-Shi'ah unity. This unity, moreover, was ordained by the teachings of the Quran and the Prophet, which held that all Muslims were brothers.[69] Tarzi simply left unanswered the question of Shi'ah recognition of the Caliphate. Unlike some of the Pan-Islamists, Tarzi did not believe that the revitalization of the Muslim world could be achieved through Muslim solidarity alone. He held that a Pan-Islamic program had to include plans for socioeconomic reform and should promote learning, intellectual freedom, and science.[70] The Pan-Islamic cause thus imposed a solemn duty upon Afghans to unify and modernize their country, which was an "anchor of hope for the Muslims of the East."[71]

Tarzi and his colleagues also used the concept of Asian solidarity in the face of European colonialism as an argument for the modernization of their country. Tarzi called upon the Afghans and other Muslims to awake and face facts. The Europeans had subdued almost all of Asia. "Peoples of India and Baluchistan, numbering five or six times more than the English nation, were being ruled by the will of a few hundred thousand Englishmen"; Russia, "like a spider, had extended itself from the Baltic to the Pacific, subjugating the Muslims of Turkestan and subjecting them to the most cruel exactions";[72] Russia and England together had launched an attack against Constantinople, "the political center of the Muslim world"; in Europe, Muslims had been slaughtered by the Italians, Greeks, and Bulgarians; in India, the British had demolished Muslim mosques and Indian temples;[73] and Afghanistan itself was flanked by governments that sought to destroy Afghan independence, governments that were inimical to both Afghan religion and Afghan honor.[74]

In the face of "Christian exactions and encroachments" in the East, particularly against Muslims, *Siraj al-Akhbar* called upon Muslims to join forces with the non-Muslim peoples of the East, whose awakening was manifest in Japan's victory over Russia. If China followed in the footsteps of Japan, the two powers would eventually join a struggle to liberate Asia, a struggle into which the Ottoman Empire, Persia, Afghanistan, and Arabia would inevitably be drawn under the banner of "Asia for Asians." Such a struggle could end once and for all the greed of Europe and perhaps even threaten Europe's very existence.[75] The socioeconomic transformation of Afghanistan was therefore indispensable in preparation for the coming struggle against European imperialists.

THE INFLUENCE OF "SIRAJ AL-AKHBAR"

Employing all of these elaborate arguments for a modern Afghan state, Tarzi and his colleagues used the pages of *Siraj al-Akhbar* to urge their compatriots and the ruling elite to embark upon a vast program of systematic and rapid social, cultural, and economic reform. In their endeavor to win the support of the ruling class, the most difficult obstacle they encountered was the fear that modernization could not be accomplished without impairing Afghan national, dynastic, and tribal interests. To allay these apprehensions, some, like Muhammed Barakatullah, a Muslim revolutionary who contributed articles to the periodical, stressed Pan-Asianism, suggesting that the modernization of Afghanistan be carried out with the assistance of "Asiatic and anti-imperialist Japan."[76] Tarzi and his colleagues, however, chose to emphasize the more narrow goal of Afghan independence. They insisted that genuine national development and progress were possible only when a society enjoyed complete independence, sovereignty, and freedom.[77] Full Afghan independence and Afghanistan's assumption of a rightful position in the family of nations were essential for the fulfillment of national aspirations and the rapid modernization of the country.[78]

The historical importance of *Siraj al-Akhbar* lies in its formulation of the tenets and goals of modern Afghan nationalism. Tarzi and his colleagues provided the first ethical justification for the modernization of Afghanistan and made modernism an integral part of Afghan nationalism. To be sure, the periodical did not have a large circulation. It was written in Persian (with an occasional verse in Pashto), which made it accessible essentially only to readers in the urban centers of eastern and western Afghanistan. Even then, widespread illiteracy prevailed. That, together with the absence of public libraries or reading rooms, the very novelty of the idea of a newspaper, a high annual subscription rate (one pound sterling), and the paper's numerous articles on abstract and unfamiliar subjects and consistent use of strange European words, prevented *Siraj al-Akhbar* from becoming a truly popular organ.

Still, the periodical reached an important audience. Persian was, after all, the language of the Afghan elite. Moreover, the Amir's active interest in and patronage of the periodical promoted its circulation among the country's prominent courtiers, educators and *literati*, members of the royal family, and even some representatives of the religious establishment. Some of the paper's readers who had previously been exposed to certain aspects of Muslim revivalist-modernist thought through pilgrimage, imported literature, or Muslim educators from India and the Ottoman Empire were especially receptive to the ideas of Tarzi and his associates. The paper thus had a degree of success, despite its limited circulation. It broadened the horizons of the Afghan elite, introducing them to many new concepts and acquainting them with developments in the rest of the Islamic world. It also stimulated the development of modern Afghan literature and journalism. Many poets and writers, notably Muhammed Amin (Andalib), Wadim, Abdul Ali Mostaghni, Abdul Ahad Dawi, Sardar Azizollah, Abd al Haq Betab, and Abdullah Khan Qari, as well as many important journalists, including Safa, Ali Ahmad Naimi, Sarwar Saba, and Aziz Rahman Safi, either found their first forum in the pages of *Siraj al-Akhbar* or were greatly influenced by its style and ideas.

Some of the aims of Tarzi and the Young Afghans were too ambitious for the time; many of their plans were, if not totally unrealistic, at least overly optimistic. Though their Pan-Islamic and nationalistic teachings and call for Afghan independence had widespread appeal among the masses, as well as widespread political and religious support, their proposals for modernization and reform lacked similar support. Many powerful tribal chieftains continued to oppose innovations and reforms, fearing that the central government would be strengthened at their expense. Similar fears preoccupied the religious establishment, which wholeheartedly supported the political goal of Pan-Islamism and the call for a struggle against European imperialism, but which in general opposed modernization programs that went beyond the improvement of the Afghan defense system. The religious leaders rightly saw in plans for socioeconomic reform a gradual end to their hold over education, tighter governmental control over the waqfs, increased secular regulation of Islamic law, and a general assault on the traditional Afghan way of life.

In the absence of a cohesive or strong middle class in Afghanistan, the monarchy was the only power that could usher in the tools and institutions of modern civilization. Tarzi and his colleagues therefore concentrated on reaching the Afghan ruling elite. They made a great effort to encourage the important families, especially those of the ruling Muhammedzai clan, to educate their children along modern lines. Each reform and modernization plan of the Amir, however modest, was hailed, publicized, and cast into historical perspective by *Siraj al-Akhbar*. Numerous articles lauded the Amir, who was characterized as an exemplary and progressive ruler, a man who had gained the respect and gratitude of the Islamic world, an "architect of progress," a "shining star."

Habibullah, of course, welcomed the enthusiastic support of Tarzi and his colleagues. He obviously especially welcomed their attempt to find the legitimacy of the monarchy in nationalism and Islam, their justification of his efforts to centralize political power and initiate some reforms, and their defense of him against foreign critics. Nevertheless, he curtailed the expression of extremely militant Pan-Islamic or nationalistic views within the *Siraj al-Akhbar* circle, which might have strained Anglo-Afghan or Russo-Afghan relations.[79] Beyond that, during World War I, he spurned the advice of those in the nationalist and modernist circles who urged him to commit Afghanistan to the cause of the Ottoman Empire and the Central Powers, and to attack the British position along the Indian frontier. In this he disappointed the Young Afghans, who believed that the Amir might have thus achieved the immediate and total independence of the country, an essential first step on the road to social and economic development. He disappointed them as well in his failure to meet their great expectations concerning the modernization of the country.

By late 1918, the avowed political and social aims of the Afghan nationalists were in sharp conflict with those of the Amir. Relations between the two camps became strained, and Tarzi was forced to cease the publication of *Siraj al-Akhbar*. However, in the end, he and his periodical proved to have been effective champions of Afghan nationalism and independence. Soon after the periodical was suspended, Afghan modernists and traditionalists temporarily united under the banner of Pan-Islamism and nationalism in support of a war against the British (1919). In the aftermath of that war (the Third Anglo-Afghan War), Afghanistan gained its complete independence.

In later years, Tarzi continued to play a major role in shaping government policies, wielding great influence as the father-in-law of the foreign minister and as the principal adviser of Habibullah's successor, King Amanullah.

Chapter Seven

Habibullah Khan: The Quest for Absolutism and Modernism

In his coronation speech, Habibullah Khan, Abdur Rahman's son, announced that he intended to pursue a policy of national unity, resistance against foreign aggression, and reform. To enlist popular support, the new Amir promised to abolish the much dreaded spy system that had been instituted by his father, and offered amnesty to many political prisoners and exiles, a category that included tribal chieftains, leaders of non-Afghan ethnic groups (notably the Hazaras), and a few intellectuals (among them, Mahmud Tarzi).[1] That the Amir could afford to make this magnanimous gesture indicates that the tribal chiefs no longer posed the immediate threat they once did, and that the central government was in a relatively strong position. The amnesty was also designed to prevent the exiles from uniting in opposition to the Amir or intriguing against him with foreign powers.[2]

Instead of relying on his father's forceful methods, Habibullah attempted to broaden the base of his power by improving the strained relations of the monarchy with the Afghan tribes, substituting cooperation for coercion. He relaxed the system of compulsory military recruitment, established a Council of State to handle tribal affairs, giving due consideration to the will and interests of the tribal leaders, and introduced a measure that permitted tribal representatives to participate in the adjudication of tribal cases by provincial authorities.[8] But despite these concessions, his goal was the same as Abdur Rahman's—an Afghan monarchy absolute in its authority.

In an effort to strengthen his position in the conquered province of Kafiristan, Habibullah allowed the Kafirs (Nuris) who converted to Islam to retain their lands, but confiscated the lands of those who would not adopt Islam, forcing them to move to the vicinity of Kabul. To mark the final establishment of Afghan rule and Islam in Kafiristan, he established a new Afghan holiday, National Unity Day.[4] The holiday, which was celebrated annually with much pomp and ceremony, had both a religious and a political character, honoring at the same time Afghan unity and the divinely ordained Afghan monarchy.

The same kind of religio-political character had attended the Amir's coronation. During that ceremony, the *khan-i-mullah* (chief religious dignitary), winding a head cloth of white muslin around the new Amir's head, presented him with a copy of the Quran, some relics of the Prophet Muhammed, and a flag from the tomb of an Afghan saint; the intention was to emphasize the Amir's religious duties as well as the divine source of his power.[5] A new and elaborate hand-kissing ceremony (*dastboosy*), designed to stress the sacredness of the office of monarch, was also adopted.[6] Both ceremonies indicate the degree to which the concept of monarchy had evolved since the simple and unsophisticated election and crowning of Ahmad Shah Durrani. Moreover, they reflected the efforts that had been made to link the monarchy as an institution to the defense of Islam and the fatherland, efforts that were to be carried even further by Tarzi and the *Siraj al-Akhbar* circle. In this light, the conquest of Kafiristan was hailed as a triumph of Islam over foreign intriguers and Christian missionaries, aliens who had been determined to convert the Kafirs and thereby subvert the territorial integrity of Afghanistan.[7] Similarly, the monarchy's suppression of tribal revolts was perceived as essential—not only to strengthen the institution of the monarchy but also to strengthen the fatherland and Islam.[8]

Once Tarzi and his associates had postulated an inseparable link between the monarchy, patriotism, and religion, Habibullah was in a position to undertake reformist and modernist measures that were "essential" to the well-being of the Afghan state and perhaps even win the support of the religious establishment. However, if appeals to religion and patriotism failed to check traditionalist opposition, he had other channels of control open to him. To those that had been used effectively by Abdur Rahman—the monarch's position as the defender of Islam and the supreme court of Afghanistan, exclusive right to proclaim jihad, control of the waqf, and ability to limit the number of mullahs through examinations—Habibullah added such measures as bribery and bestowal of robes of honor (*khalat*).[9] He also brought education under stringent government control, forcing the majority of the mullahs to remain salaried employees of the state.

These methods brought some positive results. Many mullahs decided to support, outwardly at any rate, the Amir's political and administrative reforms. Some even publicly welcomed his reformist measures as important steps in the further consolidation of the Islamic community, the Islamic law, and the Afghan fatherland. On one notable occasion, a group of mullahs bestowed upon him the title Siraj ul-Millat wa Din (The Light of the Nation and the Faith), in recognition of his "exemplary activities on behalf of Islam and Afghanistan."[10]

ADMINISTRATIVE AND MILITARY REFORMS

Habibullah retained some of the basic features of his father's administration and made further refinements. He divided Afghanistan into six provinces—Kabul, Kandahar, Herat, Farah, Afghan Turkestan, and Badakhshan (including Wakhan)—which were further divided into districts. Kabul, the capital, and Kabul province were administered by the Amir himself, though in 1907 a new office, that of *naib-ul-hukuma* (deputy governor), was given nominal control of the province. The other provinces continued to be governed by hakims. Under Habibullah, these governors had judicial as well as civil functions, presiding over provincial courts (*mahkame-ye hakim*) with jurisdiction over both civil and criminal cases. The religious courts (*mahkame-ye Shar'ia*) functioned under the provincial courts. They were headed by kazis, who were assisted by muftis, the number of kazis and muftis depending on the extent of the kazi's jurisdiction and the severity or complexity of a case. In the event of a deadlock or a precedent-setting decision, the religious courts referred a case to the khan-i-mullah at Kabul; if he was unable to arrive at a verdict, the case was sent to the Amir. Appeals against decisions of the provincial courts, both civil and religious, were also sent to the Amir.

The Afghan courts continued to use the codes of procedure drawn up by Abdur Rahman. The provincial civil and criminal courts followed the *Kitabche-ye Hukumati*, the religious courts the *Asas-ul-Kuzzat*, which was based on Islamic law. In general, the governors referred cases relating to Islamic law to the kazis, or at least consulted them. All disputes among merchants and traders, as well as most civil suits, were referred to a *panchayat* (council of elders). Cases involving treason, rebellion, embezzlement of state funds, forgery or bribery by officials, and other offenses against the state or against members of the royal family were dealt with by the Amir himself. He also heard cases involving adultery, theft, and murder, if the crimes had occurred in Kabul; elsewhere in the country, such cases were tried in the provincial courts. Death sentences passed by local authorities, even those that were in accordance with Shar'ia law, had to be confirmed by the Amir. In an effort to regularize civil suits, and as a source of revenue as well, Habibullah required the use of official stamps on documents and petitions pertaining to such suits.[11]

Like his predecessors, Habibullah concentrated first on modernizing his army. This priority was dictated by two considerations: the belief that a strong standing army was essential for the defense of the monarchy, and the fact that there was little opposition to military reforms. Even traditionalist elements could not protest too vigorously the reorganization of an army whose avowed purpose, among others, was the defense of Islam.

The Amir introduced modern weapons and broadened the program of military instruction begun under his predecessors. The first concerted attempt was made to train an officer corps with the founding in 1904–6 of the Royal Military College (Madrasse-ye Harbi-ye Sirajieh).[12] The cadets, who numbered only 80 in 1910, were mostly the sons of Durrani nobles or high-ranking court officials. (The college was an outgrowth of an earlier school, whose name, Maktab-e Malakzadeha, or school for the children of nobility, indicated the elitist character of both schools.)[13] The training of the cadets was entrusted in 1907 to a Turkish colonel, Mahmud Sami (known as Said Mahmud Efendi) and was under the general supervision of the heir apparent, Inayatullah Khan. The curriculum included the study of the Quran; courses in arithmetic, mensuration, geometry, and military logistics; and gymnastics and drill. The Persian and English languages, general and Afghan history, and geography were also studied.[14] Mahmud Sami was instrumental in introducing calisthenics into the Afghan army; he also compiled some military manuals, translating them from Turkish works, instituted the use of Turkish military terminology, and introduced the heliograph.[15]

The Amir took steps to strengthen his army against possible opposition within the country. He increased the pay of his soldiers (from eight Kabuli rupees a month to ten and later to thirteen) and recruited some 1,800 Nuris into the army.[16] In 1904, he also ordered the recruitment of a few regiments from among the Hazaras, who had not been subject to military service before.[17] In 1908 he granted large pay increases to the officers. During his reign, the basic needs of the army continued to be met by the state-owned workshops; on this point there was no change in the national policy: military self-sufficiency remained the ultimate goal.[18]

REFORMS IN EDUCATION

According to a contemporary estimate, at the time Habibullah ascended the throne, 98 per cent of the Afghans were illiterate.[19] In attempting to improve this situation, Habibullah laid the foundations of the present Afghan education system. In 1904, Habibiya College, the first secondary school (for boys only) was established.[20] Initially, the school offered mathematics, geography, calisthenics, and the English and Urdu languages, as well as traditional subjects. Eventually courses in education, physics, chemistry, botany, zoology, painting, drawing, history, and public health were added. The study of Pashto and Turkish, as well as English and Urdu, was officially encouraged.[21] At the Amir's behest, a modest library was established at the school; it represented the first public library in Afghanistan.[22]

Apart from Habibiya and the Royal Military College, the traditional Islamic system of education (consisting of four stages, primary, secondary, professional, and higher) remained in force, with no change in curriculum. Students in these schools continued to study the Quran, *fiqh* (juridical science based on theology), hadith, calligraphy, and Arabic and Persian classical literature.[23] Most of the students admitted to Habibiya had finished the first and second stages of the traditional education, and they continued to study traditional subjects after entering the college, for, despite Habibiya's modern curriculum, the major emphasis was still on these subjects.[24] This emphasis was the result of an effort to placate the traditionalists. From 1913 on, a student's promotion in lower level schools was made conditional on good marks in religion and Arabic.[25] The effect of this, together with an absence of common educational objectives between the traditional and modern educational systems (which in fact competed), was to severely handicap the Afghan students. Even after ten years of schooling, the Habibiya graduate had devoted only a small proportion of his time to modern subjects.[26]

The cost of maintaining Habibiya College, including the salaries of the teachers and the staff, was met by the royal treasury. At first, only small amounts were spent on non-military education, but the allocations gradually increased; in the years 1904–19, the government spent over two million rupees on education. The majority of Habibiya's teachers (some 55 in 1918) were Indian Muslims; most of them had received their training at the college at Lahore or at the Muslim modernist seminary at Aligarh. The teaching staff also included a few Afghans educated in India.[27]

At first the Afghan educational system was patterned after the Anglo-Indian system, but after the outbreak of World War I, it tended to follow the Turkish model, which was an adaptation of the French school system. This change reflected the Pan-Islamic sentiment that was prevalent in Afghanistan at the time. Moreover, the Afghans were impressed by the manner in which the Ottoman Empire, the spiritual leader of the Sunni Muslims, "had put to use the Western sciences," without rejecting its own traditions, a fact that made the Turkish system a suitable model for Af-

ghanistan.[28] The Turkish curriculum was gradually adopted, and a number
of Turkish instructors were hired.* This move was politically astute, if
not politically inspired, for it tended to counter traditionalist objections
to the adoption of modern techniques and ideas.

In the second decade of the twentieth century, the schools were still few
and the number of students small. In 1916, in the Kabul district—the most
advanced—only 130 pupils graduated from primary schools; in 1918,
only 324 of 665 pupils who had started a four-year elementary school program graduated.[29] Enrollment in the traditional schools far exceeded that
of Habibiya. In 1918, the new college had only 296 students against some
700 in five semi-traditional primary public schools in the Kabul area, and
an unknown number in mosque schools.[30] Outside of Kabul, children continued to attend the mosque schools, where supreme importance was attached to the memorization of the Quran. Those who did so were known
as *hafiz* (hafez); there were 214 hafiz in 1915–16. The majority of the
students who came out of these schools were poorly prepared to continue
their education in a modern school.[31]

During the first World War, the Afghan Department of Education,
which was founded in 1913, attempted to broaden the curriculum of the
traditional schools.[32] A special program for elementary-school teachers
was begun in 1914 with the founding of a teacher-training center (Dar-ul-
muallemin).[33] Uniform textbooks were adopted for certain subjects. Under royal patronage, a new organization, the Dar-ul-Ta'alif, selected,
translated, compiled, and published textbooks.[34] This same organization
also brought out the first books intended for public consumption; they included four books on religion, five Arabic and three Persian grammars,
and one book each on philosophy (an introductory textbook translated
from English), mathematics, and world geography. Between 1911 and
1918, the Dar-ul-Ta'alif published many of the works of Mahmud Tarzi,
among them his pamphlets "Learning and Islam" and "What Must Be
Done," a geography of modern Afghanistan (the first), and his translation
of the history of the Russo-Japanese War.[35] It also published the first
major Afghan work on the modern history of Afghanistan, *Siraj ul-
Tawarikh*, by Fayz Muhammad Kateb. All of these books were printed by
the government-owned press at Kabul.

With the exception of Habibiya College, the Afghan schools were poorly
administered and taught. Government attempts to improve and standardize the curriculum and to achieve tighter control over education by estab-

* This modified French-Turkish system was continued through the reign of Nadir
Shah (1929–33).

lishing the Department of Education were not totally successful. The mullahs, especially those outside Kabul, though they were state-employed, resented the government's control of education, the teacher-training center, and the teaching of English and of modern subjects in general, and vehemently resisted all further innovation.[36]

Habibullah and the modernists went to great lengths to convince the religious establishment that there was nothing incompatible between Islam and modern education.[37] The Amir made his position quite clear in a number of speeches. One of the most notable was made during a state visit to India in 1907. Addressing the students at Aligarh, he declared:

Let anyone who nevertheless still honestly thinks that religion and education are mutually antagonistic, and that religion must decline where education flourishes, come to this college, as I have come, and see for himself, as I have seen, what education is doing for the religious beliefs of the rising generation.... There is, I am told, a violent prejudice among many Indian Muhammedans against that particular kind of education which we call European education. What folly is this! Listen to me. I stand here as the advocate of Western learning. So far from thinking it an evil, I have founded in Afghanistan a college called Habibiya College after my own name, where European education is to be given as far as possible on European lines. What I do insist on, however, is that religious education is the foundation on which all other forms of education must rest.

If you cut away the foundations the superstructure will surely topple over. I say to you therefore, be ever careful to make the religious training of the students your first and foremost care. This all-essential condition I have imposed upon my college in Afghanistan, and I hope it will ever be strictly maintained there. But subject to this condition, I say again that I am a sincere friend and well-wisher of Western education.[38]

In another speech, on the occasion of the laying of the foundation stone of the Islamic College at Lahore, the Amir said:

O my Moslem brethren, endeavor to acquire knowledge, so that you may not wear the clothes of the ignorant. It is your duty to acquire knowledge. After your children have thoroughly acquainted themselves with the principles and laws of the faith of Muhammed, turn their attention towards the acquirement of the new sciences, as unless you acquire Western knowledge, you will remain without bread.[39]

On still another occasion, Habibullah summed up his feelings in this way: "In a single sentence, I give you my whole exhortation. Acquire knowledge." And he went on: "There are those who utter solemn warnings in your ears, who urge that Mohammedans have nothing to do with modern philosophy, who disclaim against Western sciences as though they are evil. I am not among them. I am not among those who ask you to shut your ears and your eyes. On the contrary, I say pursue knowledge wherever it is to be found."[40]

Prince Inayatullah, too, spoke out on this subject. The pursuit of learning, knowledge, and modernization would please God, the Prophet, and the King, he said; such learning could only bring honor to the Afghans and sustain the Afghan fatherland, people, and government.[41]

The Amir planned to send a number of Afghan students to Europe to pursue their education, but internal opposition and the outbreak of World War I prevented him from doing so. In 1917 he revived the plan, intending to send some Habibiya graduates to Europe or America to study medicine and engineering.[42] He was assassinated before the plan could be carried out.

IMPROVEMENTS IN PUBLIC HEALTH

Modest steps were taken to improve public health during Habibullah's reign. A Scottish engineer, James Miller, supervised the laying of a pipeline to bring water from Paghman to the city of Kabul.[43] After cholera epidemics broke out in Kabul, in 1903 and again in 1915, the government took the first steps toward assuming responsibility for public health. For instance, a municipal authority was set up to supervise the daily cleaning of the streets of Kabul.[44] However, many of the measures that were taken were only temporary, designed for the most part to meet emergencies. There were still no sewers in Afghanistan.[45]

The most important advance made in the health field was the establishment, in 1913, of the first state hospital. This was a major undertaking in a country that had only one Afghan doctor with modern training.[46] The new hospital, which was located in Kabul, was staffed by Indian attendants and supervised by two Turkish doctors, Munir Izzet Bey, the Amir's private physician, and Ahmad Fakhmi Bey. It had 30 beds and also served as a public dispensary and pharmacy. The hospital staff introduced the use of chloroform and prepared smallpox vaccine, inoculating thousands of children within a few years.* Though understaffed and too poorly equipped to tackle the immense needs of the Afghan people with real success, the hospital performed well within its limitations. In the course of a single year, 1914, 29,466 patients were reportedly treated and 95 major surgical operations performed; in the following year, the number of patients increased to 35,351. In that same year, the staff doctors gave some

---

* Afghans had previously inoculated their children by rubbing a little of the crust taken from the sore of an infected patient into the wrist of the person to be inoculated. According to T. L. Pennell (p. 43), the case of smallpox that resulted was usually mild, but sometimes was severe enough to cause the death of the patient. Berke (p. 4) credits the preparation of the smallpox vaccine to Munir Bey.

4,000 smallpox vaccinations. The hospital staff also served areas outside of Kabul. For instance, in 1916 hospital trainees were sent to Herat to vaccinate the local children.[47] Before the outbreak of World War I, the staff launched an official campaign to stop the spread of malaria. According to one account, the army and the people were given free treatment as well as regular supplies of quinine, Atabrine, and Plasmochin, and canals were dug to drain "hundreds of miles of marshland."[48]

The Amir employed Western professionals to take care of the medical needs at court: an English doctor (Winter), an American dentist, and two Englishwomen, Dr. Lena Brown and her sister, to attend the women and children.[49] In emergencies, he also secured medical aid from the British government in India.[50]

Despite the dedication of the hospital staff and the Amir's readiness to accept modern methods, the health standards of the country remained primitive. There was still just the one hospital and only a handful of doctors; health education was nonexistent; and superstitions in matters of medicine were widespread. The articles that appeared in *Siraj al-Akhbar* on health and sanitation had little impact. In general, the masses continued to rely on charms, omens, astrology, and similar practices, and to put their faith in the spiritual powers of the local mullahs and holy relics.* Most Afghans used the hospital only as a last resort.[51] Many arrived at the hospital after weeks of neglect and torment by the hakims, often after a long journey; the majority were all but dead on arrival. Because of this, and for other reasons as well, there was a high mortality rate among surgery patients (somewhere between 20 and 35 per cent).[52] Ignorance, superstition, and lack of adequate medical facilities took a heavy toll, especially among the children; the infant mortality rate was high. Fevers, rheumatism and catarrhs, lung ailments, venereal and urinary diseases, scrofula, smallpox, and all manner of skin and eye diseases were prevalent.[53]

To some extent, the progress of modern medicine was inhibited by the attitude of the government, which considered the hospital a charitable institution to be used only by those without other means. The greatest inhibiting factor, however, was the local hakim. It was to the hakim that the Afghan masses most often turned for the treatment of illness, and he pos-

---

* The graves of local saints, or *pirs* (whose shrines, or *ziarats*, were often located on hilltops, sometimes in the form of a domed tomb, sometimes as a mere heap of stones within a wall), were visited in cases of need. The masses, especially the tribesmen, believed that these saints could "avert calamity, cure disease, procure children for the childless, or improve the circumstances of the dead; the underlying feeling, apparently, being that man is too sinful to approach God directly, and that the intervention of some one more worthy must therefore be sought" (see India, *Imperial Gazetteer*, V, 49).

sessed little, if any, knowledge of medicine. The previously noted practices had changed very little. According to Dr. Pennell, as late as 1910 the Afghan hakims (like many of their colleagues in the Middle East) still resorted to talismans or to the two standard traditional Yunani (Greek) or Hippocratic medical practices, *dzan* and *dam*. Dzan was in effect "sweating" a patient with acute or chronic fever by wrapping him naked in the skin of a freshly killed sheep or goat; dam, or moxa as it was known in the West, was a method of cauterization, in which a burning oil-soaked cloth was applied to wounds. For other ailments, the local physicians continued to prescribe purges or periodic bleedings, and the standard medicines remained the herbs handed out by Indian drug merchants or purgatives.[54]

In the countryside, as well as in most urban centers, the barber performed ordinary surgical operations and the blacksmith extracted teeth. Though the barbers were often highly skilled, their surgical instruments were unsanitary and their methods of dealing with infection primitive. The circumcisions they performed accounted in good part for the high infant mortality rate.[55]

As noted, the Amir's plans to send students abroad to study medicine did not materialize. Throughout his reign, the Kabul hospital with its limited facilities remained the only modern medical institution in Afghanistan. There were no mental institutions at all and little thought of building one, since it was widely believed that the insane were possessed by spirits and should be allowed to roam as those spirits directed.[56]

BEGINNINGS OF MODERN INDUSTRY

In the period 1901–4, about 1,500 workers were employed in the government workshops at Kabul,[57] which included a steam-hammer shop, a mint (whose production capacity was 40,000 Kabuli rupees a day), iron and brass foundries, smithies and rolling mills, and boiler and engine houses. All in all, about 100 different kinds of machines were in use. In addition, there were a number of handicraft shops; they turned out guns, cartridges, wheels, black powder, bayonets and swords, tanned leather, distilled spirits, acids, tin and copper products, candles, soap (12 tons a week), and furniture.[58] Despite the variety of products, the primary task of these workshops continued to be to supply the Afghan army.[59]

Habibullah made important contributions to the expansion of local industry. He purchased equipment for a tannery and boot factory capable of producing 400 boots a day,[60] and established a textile mill. The fledgling textile industry was given wide publicity by the Afghan modernists, who stressed the point that the new mill and others like it would stop the flow of native capital to foreign lands by providing locally produced clothing for the Afghans.[61] Habibullah also established a distillery, intending to export alcoholic beverages to India. The plan was soon dropped, however, because such production was considered to be an encouragement of vice.[62] One of the Amir's most significant contributions was the construction of the first hydroelectric plant in the country. It was built between 1910 and 1913 at Jabal-ul-Siraj, near Jalalabad, and had a capacity of 1,500 kilowatts.[63]

By the end of Habibullah's reign, the number of industrial workers had risen to an estimated 5,000.[64] Nevertheless, Afghan industrial development was slow and difficult. The country still lacked skilled workers and, more important, capital. Banking facilities were virtually nonexistent, and there were no trade agreements with other countries. The government workshops, which were in fact royal monopolies, tended to stifle private initiative. The workers' wages were pitifully low: skilled workers earned 20–30 rupees a month and foremen, experts, and supervisors 20–100, but the majority earned only 8–10.[65] Moreover, working conditions were harsh. For instance, many fatal accidents occurred in the powder-making industry, in which highly volatile fulminate of mercury was used without safeguards or protective devices.[66] Wages remained static while the cost of basic commodities rose steadily. In the years of Habibullah's reign, for example, the price of bread in Kabul increased four times, but the workers' salaries remained unchanged. The plight of the workers became critical, especially in 1903, when a famine and a cholera epidemic together took the lives of thousands of Kabulis.

Industrial growth was also difficult because of a lack of fuel. Most industry was centered in Kabul, which had neither coal nor wood. In the period between 1890 and 1908, the wood supplies of the region were almost exhausted, and the workshops faced a fuel shortage. The situation was so critical that in 1908 two avenues of poplars lining the city streets were felled for government use. The police were ordered to protect the trees of the region and to fire on anyone seen cutting them for their own use, pack animals were muzzled to keep them from nibbling at the green branches, and a modest reforestation program was hurriedly set in motion,[67] but these haphazard measures did little to alleviate the immediate situation. As for coal, the nearest deposits were hundreds of feet below the surface and surrounded by water wells. Exploiting them would have required great sums of money and intricate machinery; neither was available. In any case, the cost of transporting the coal to Kabul by pack animal would have been prohibitive.[68]

Industrial development was also seriously impeded by the limitations placed on Habibullah in using European experts and technicians. For one thing, their services were costly, but more important, the employment of Europeans was highly objectionable to Afghan traditionalists. The Amir dared not alienate the Muslim conservatives or the influential anti-British faction of his brother Nasrullah, who was the commander-in-chief of the army and had both a priestly following and the sympathy of various tribes near Kabul.[69] Whenever possible, therefore, the Amir hired Muslims from India and later from Turkey, especially for such sensitive areas as the army, the schools, and the field of public health.

In the early years of Habibullah's reign, there were only three Europeans in Afghan service: Nurse Daly, the Amir's chief engineer (Martin), and an expert on guns (Fleischer). Martin was English, Fleischer was German; all three lived in Kabul. By 1904, only Martin was still in Afghanistan; Fleischer had been murdered, and Mrs. Daly had left the country.[70] After 1905, when a political agreement was concluded with the British, the Amir employed a few English experts, including two electricians, a construction engineer, and a tanner. During the next few years, he also employed several Europeans to serve at court. Besides the medical staff mentioned previously, there were a tailor and a chauffeur.[71] Miller, the engineer who supervised the laying of the water pipe, was in the Amir's employ from 1911 to 1914. During that period, he also built the textile mill at Kabul, a dam at Ghazni, and two or three golf courses. Four American and English engineers (Jewett, Kelly, Crawford, and Havner) built the hydroelectric plant.[72]

The work of these advisers was frustrated by the refusal of many Afghans to cooperate with them. One of them wrote that many Afghans, "being ignorant of the outer world's modern methods," resented the "introduction of [such methods] into their country by the unbelievers and always set their wits to prevent an Englishman succeeding."[73] The behavior of some of the Europeans (such as heavy drinking) intensified the already widespread popular resentment of their presence in the country. The situation was further aggravated by the sharp business practices and speculation of European merchants. Afghans were induced to buy steel for the construction of a steel mill, though there were no plans to exploit the known iron deposits. They were sold cooperage machinery, though there was no wood to make casks. They were persuaded to buy many symbols of modern technology, such as steam-operated smelting machinery, rock crushers, pianos, phonographs, clocks, even an electrically heated bath, most of them having no immediate practical use and sold at exorbitant prices. Often adventurers posed as engineers and accepted payment for expensive machinery that was never delivered. (In one instance alone, a man who was commissioned by the Amir to purchase the equipment for a soap plant made off with $47,000.)[74] Some foreign firms, taking advantage of the Afghans' economic isolation, lack of banking facilities, and ignorance of international marketing, made profits as high as 66 per cent of their original investments.

Abuses of this nature, which the American engineer Jewett called the "brown man's burden," increased the Afghans' distrust of Westerners and reinforced their suspicions that Europeans were merely interested in exploiting them. To prevent further waste and loss, the Afghan authorities installed a commercial agent in India and established banking facilities there. The Amir also ordered that a law be prepared permitting the formation of joint-stock companies in Afghanistan, in order to safeguard Afghan business interests.[75]

IMPROVEMENTS IN COMMUNICATIONS

Habibullah made some attempt to improve the principal Afghan trade routes. A road was built between Kabul and Dakka; others were opened between Kabul and Kohistan, Charikar, and Jabal-ul-Siraj; Kandahar and Quetta; and Kabul, Kandahar (via Ghazni), and Herat.[76] (This is one area in which the Amir made no concessions to the traditionalists; some of his roads ran through Muslim graveyards.)[77] During this period the first modern iron bridge was constructed, and other bridges were repaired. In this area, the Amir maintained the policy of his predecessors, holding villages responsible for the upkeep of their portions of the roads. Noncompliance or neglect on the part of the villagers brought either forced labor or heavy fines.

To build the new roads, Habibullah established what was in effect the first public works program, hiring a labor force of some 5,000–8,000 men, primarily Hazaras, for the project. However, the pay and working conditions were such that hundreds of workers ran away,[78] whereupon the Amir resorted to the traditional method of conscription to finish the job.[79] The road-building program was accompanied by an educational campaign, designed to inform the people of the value of good roads. Royal proclamations and posters were issued, and articles in *Siraj al-Akhbar* reminded the Afghans that roads were to be used for travel and transportation, not as meeting places.[80]

In 1905 Habibullah brought the first automobile into the country. He himself demonstrated its usefulness by making periodic drives from Kabul

to Jalalabad. *Tongas* and *tumtums* (wheeled vehicles for hire) also became
an increasingly familiar sight in the streets of Kabul. They were sometimes even used for travel to India.[81] The Amir helped found the Afghan
Motor Transport Company (or Association),* the first joint-stock company in the country, and appealed to well-to-do Afghans to invest in it.[82]
But though high hopes were placed in the company, there were still only
some 30 automobiles in the country in 1918.[83] The bulk of Afghanistan's
trade continued to be carried by pack animals. Heavy machinery had to be
carried by elephants, a slow and laborious process. About 1,200 cases of
machinery for the tannery were transported from Peshawar to Kabul by
this method; so was the equipment for the hydroelectric plant, which was
two-and-a-half months in transit and held up another five months at Jalalabad because of the weather.[84] Apart from the delays involved, caravan
transport was costly and afforded little protection against theft or damage.
Moreover, the Khyber Pass was still open only twice a week, and under
normal circumstances it continued to take some ten days to travel between
Kabul and Peshawar.[85]

Though Habibullah attempted to improve the Afghan postal system, it
remained primitive and inefficient. Postal communications with the outside world were completely unreliable. (Afghanistan did not become a
member of the International Postal Union until 1928.) Letters or parcels
from abroad had to be sent to an Afghan postmaster in Peshawar. They
were then forwarded to Afghanistan, but with endless delays. Only the
Amir's mail was carried regularly from India to Kabul. Although Afghan
stamps had been issued for some time, there were no fixed postal rates.†
There were no daily deliveries, even in Kabul. As a rule, letters could be
posted and delivered only in the larger towns; an exception was made for
state officials, whose letters were delivered everywhere. Postal dispatches
were limited to two per week.[86]

A telephone line linking Kabul and Jalalabad (the Amir's winter resi-

---

* The company, which proudly affixed "Ltd." to its name, had three or four automobiles and trucks. It was ostensibly established to make the run between Kabul and
India, hauling freight to Afghanistan one way and carrying Afghan exports the other.
In fact, it was used chiefly to serve the Amir's household. The engineer Jewett wrote
that he once pleaded with the Amir to send a truck to Peshawar to bring back an essential part, thereby avoiding a three-month delay. The Amir turned him down, a
refusal that Jewett attributed to the Amir's fear that the machinery might scratch the
truck's paint. See "An Engineer," p. 489.
† It was not until the end of Abdur Rahman's reign that the cancellation of postage
stamps was introduced. Before that, a small piece was torn off the stamp to indicate
that it had been used. The supply of stamps issued by Sher Ali and Abdur Rahman
was exhausted at the end of 1902. A few years later European-style stamps were introduced.

dence) was installed in 1908, and plans were made to extend the hookup to the other major urban centers.[87] In general, the line was reserved for the private use of the Amir and his staff. Occasionally, it was used to report official communications and news of the Amir's important audiences to *Siraj al-Akhbar.*

TRADE EXPANSION

Habibullah attempted to increase the volume of trade between Afghanistan and India, and reopened trade with Bukhara, which had declined badly in the final years of Abdur Rahman's reign. Trade with Russian Central Asia, which had been virtually suspended after the Panjdeh Incident and the Russian advance into the Pamirs, gradually returned to normal and even expanded prior to the Anglo-Russian Convention of 1907.

To encourage foreign trade, the Amir removed many of the official restrictions on the country's transactions with India and Russia. He remitted certain duties altogether and lowered the transit charges on "through" caravans, especially on those carrying indigo and tea, to a 2.5 per cent ad valorem tax.[88] As a result, exports from Kabul and Kandahar increased in the year 1904–5 by some two and a half million rupees. Although there are no complete figures available on the commercial transactions between India and Afghanistan for this period, the following official statistics indicate the general increase in the volume of trade between India and northern Afghanistan–Kabul in the years before the signing of the Anglo-Russian Convention:

Kabul–Northern Afghanistan Trade with India[89]
(*in tens of rupees*)

Year	Exports to India	Imports from India
1900–01	549,100	512,900
1902–03	459,100	715,600
1904–05	662,300	1,056,600
1906–07	970,400	1,124,800

As the Russians extended their railways to the Afghan borders (the Trans-Caspian and Orenburg-Tashkent lines), the volume of Russo-Afghan trade increased. In part, this increase reflected the lower freight rates, in part the concessions the Russians granted the Afghan traders. The Afghans were given a rebate on goods purchased in Russian territory equal to the tax levied by the Amir's officials, and the duty on their exports was cut in half:[90]

Russian Trade with Afghanistan[91]
(*in rubles*)

Year	Exports to Afghanistan	Imports from Afghanistan
1901	2,592,000	1,197,000
1902	2,384,000	1,903,000
1903	2,993,000	2,031,000
1904	2,666,000	2,548,000
1905	2,527,000	2,328,000
1906	2,184,000	1,893,000
1907	2,941,000	2,198,000
1908	2,730,000	3,015,000
1909	4,328,000	3,366,000

According to a Soviet source, this trade accounted for only 28 per cent of Afghanistan's foreign trade in the 1890's, 34 per cent in 1901–5, and 38 per cent in 1911–15.[92]

Even after the Anglo-Russian Convention and especially on the eve of World War I, the Russians continued to press the British for equal trade opportunity in Afghanistan, at least in northern Afghanistan, requesting the English authorities to try to persuade Habibullah to reduce the tariffs on various Russian goods. However, the Amir was unwilling to accord the Russians preferential treatment, both because of his apprehensions about the Anglo-Russian Convention[93] and because he feared the British would match the Russian demands with demands of their own. The lack of trade concessions is reflected in the figures for 1913–17, when Afghanistan exported more to Russia and imported less:

Russian Trade with Afghanistan[94]
(*in rubles*)

Year	Exports to Afghanistan	Imports from Afghanistan
1913	5,946,000	6,299,000
1914	2,936,000	2,943,000
1915	3,622,000	4,689,000
1916	2,431,000	6,782,000
1917	756,000	13,559,000

The Russian exports to Afghanistan were much the same as in the 1870's. They consisted largely of chintzes, glassware, sugar, linen, silk, cotton goods, cutlery, and paper; Russia imported mainly wool and karakul sheepskin.[95]

After the Anglo-Russian Convention was signed, Afghanistan contin-

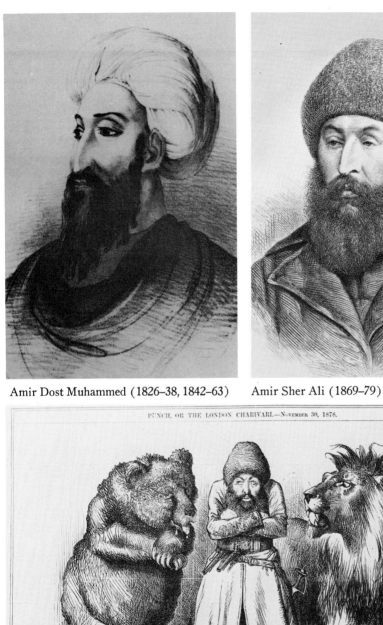

Amir Dost Muhammed (1826–38, 1842–63)   Amir Sher Ali (1869–79)

"SAVE ME FROM MY FRIENDS!"

"IF AT THIS MOMENT IT HAS BEEN DECIDED TO INVADE THE AMEER'S TERRITORY, WE ARE ACTING IN PURSUANCE OF A POLICY WHICH IN ITS INTENTION HAS BEEN UNIFORMLY *FRIENDLY* TO AFGHANISTAN."—*Times*, Nov. 21.

Punch's comment on the Second Anglo-Afghan War

Amir Abdur Rahman (1880–1901)

Map and proclamation prepared by Abdur Rahman (orientation is with west at the top). Afghanistan, center ; clockwise from top, Iran, Russia, China, India

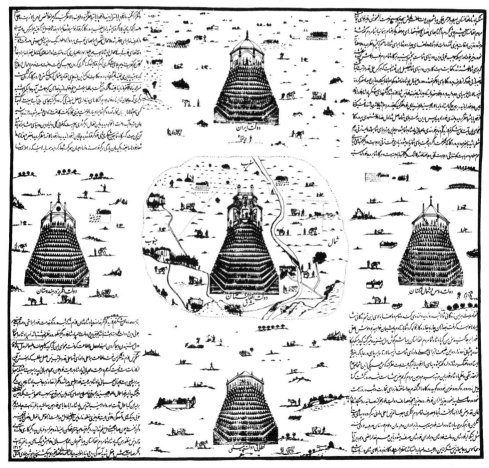

Amir Habibullah (1901–19)

Royal tiger hunt in India, 1907. Left to
right, Sir Henry MacMahon (behind
seated man), Habibullah, the Duke
of Manchester

Mahmud Tarzi

The first issue of *Siraj al-Akhbar*
(October 1911)

Queen Sorayya and King Amanullah
(1919–29) in London, 1928

Amanullah, with
President Kalinin,
reviewing guard
of honor in
Moscow, 1928

Above. Bacha-i-Saqao, the bandit Amir, at Independence Day festivities, August 23, 1929. Seated left to right, Bacha's brother, Bacha, a holy man of Kohistan, Amanullah's brother Muhammed Kabir. *Below*. The execution of Bacha and his relatives

King Nadir (1929–33)

King Zahir (1933–　　)

Prime Minister Hashim Khan (1933–46)

ued to carry on most of its trade with India, and the volume increased greatly:

Afghan Trade with India[96]
(*in pounds sterling*)

Year	Exports to India	Imports from India
1908	643,551	790,235
1909	570,459	764,274
1910	696,088	845,465
1911	610,102	974,396
1911–12	636,000	843,500
1912–13	847,000	1,660,000
1913–14	860,000	1,013,000
1914–15	806,000	909,000
1915–16	1,116,000	1,021,000
1916–17	1,144,000	1,150,000

Here, too, the items of trade had changed little from the nineteenth century. Afghanistan imported cotton goods, dyes, sugar, tea, iron, knives, scissors, needles and thread, paper, drugs, and machinery from India, and exported (in order of importance) fruits and vegetables, grain and pulse, wool, ghi, tobacco, carpets, and horses. The two items of Indian trade that increased the most were tea and sugar.[97] Used English uniforms of every description were also imported in increasing quantities. As one observer noted, "The country people kept their national dress but on cold days you see even them in overcoats, with 'Sussex' or 'Guard' or 'Ticket-Collector' on the collars."[98] According to Saise, it was because of Afghanistan's heavy dependence on English and Russian cotton goods and clothing that Habibullah was prompted to establish a textile mill.[99]

In this period, trade with Persia seems to have dwindled to a mere trickle. Herat, the major Afghan outpost of trade in Khorassan, was reported to be in a state of complete decay, its silk and carpet industries in decline and its artisans in serious trouble.[100]

On balance, Afghanistan's trade situation improved considerably, largely because there was relative internal stability, a degree of economic unity, some attempt to standardize customs fees,* improved relations with India and Russian Central Asia, and official encouragement of trade. Nevertheless, the Afghan economy continued to be hurt by the lack of adequate trans-

---

* See *Qawaid-e Siraj ul-Millat Dar Kharidari-ye Mal Az Dowal-e Kharijeh* (The Regulations of Siraj ul-Millat Regarding the Purchase of Goods from Foreign Governments), Kabul, 1904. To the best of my knowledge, this is the first set of laws regulating the import of foreign goods into Afghanistan. These regulations also had some protectionist provisions covering the products of the royal workshops.

portation and communications, banking facilities and trade agreements, and diplomatic and economic contacts, plus the restrictions on travel.[101] Though both Abdur Rahman and Habibullah attempted to introduce a uniform system of weights and measures, the units remained imprecise and often varied greatly from those of India, Persia, and Central Asia. Exact weights and measures were used only in government stores and workshops. This, combined with intermittent political quarrels between Afghanistan and its neighbors and the at best still chaotic Afghan customs system,[102] also impeded economic growth.

SOCIAL REFORMS

Habibullah took several steps in the field of social reform. However, he encountered stiff opposition when he attempted to institute measures that affected social tradition and, like his predecessors, was forced to seek accommodation with Islamic law and tribal custom. One early step was to open a public orphanage, the first in the land.[103] Another was to attempt to limit the burdensome expenses incurred in connection with marriage.* In 1911, he placed a ceiling on the amount that could be spent on marriages, urging his people to abandon the customary public celebrations in favor of private parties. The amounts he set varied according to class. Commoners were permitted to spend 100–500 rupees, tribal chieftains, feudal lords, and sardars up to 1,500, and members of the royal family up to 5,000.[104] Whether or not this law was strictly enforced is not known, but it *is* known that the royal family on a few highly publicized occasions attempted to set an example for the rest of Afghan society in this connection. The Amir himself also tried to set an example to the wealthy Afghans who exceeded the legal number of four wives. Officially banning the practice of keeping concubines and "female slaves," Habibullah publicly divorced all but four of his wives in 1903. There is, however, some question concerning his strict adherence to his own ruling.[105]

In the field of human rights, the Amir strengthened the anti-slavery laws and ordered that they be enforced.[106] He also banned the torture of prisoners on the grounds that Islam proscribed inhuman practices. The most dreaded dungeon in the country, Siah-Chah (Black Well), was abandoned sometime in 1912–13, and a relatively modern jail was built at Kabul.[107] The notion of rehabilitation was accepted in principle, and for the first

* In order to meet these expenses, most Afghans had to borrow money. At times they reportedly paid as much as 75 per cent interest on the loan. See Jewett, "An Engineer," p. 501.

time some attempts were made to teach prisoners handicrafts. Certain harsh punishments, including amputation of hands, cutting out of tongues, and blinding, were officially abolished.[108] However, this law was not always observed; moreover, it is not clear whether it was meant to apply to all criminals or only those in certain categories. It is a matter of record that the Amir himself, in dealing with certain types of crimes (e.g., tampering with such necessities as bread and meat), prescribed public and notably cruel punishments. One long-time English resident of Kabul reported that butchers who tampered with weights or who "ran out" of meat in order to inflate prices were nailed by their ears to the doors of their shops, that a baker whose wares were not finished on time was thrashed to death, and that an unrepentant thief lost an arm for stealing a second time. On at least one occasion, two highwaymen were caged and starved to death.[109] According to Jewett, a guard was stoned to death for collaborating with a thief, and as a rule, those guilty of serious offenses against Islam met a similar fate.[110]

Though harsh punishments in fact continued, the abolition of torture, if only in principle, was nevertheless an important development. So was a new concept by which prisoners were considered still members of the Islamic community, and as such possessed some rights, including the right to spiritual consolation.[111] It is also worth noting that the number of death penalties reportedly decreased, averaging about 20 a year in the Kabul province, during Habibullah's rule.[112]

The influence of the West became increasingly apparent in Afghanistan during this period. The Amir encouraged the use of Western dress. The Afghan soldiers wore tunics and coats that were at first patterned after English styles and then on Turkish clothes. The army officers and most of the court officials wore clothes of an English cut (riding breeches were popular), though some adopted Turkish frock coats and fezzes.[113] Habibullah also encouraged his people to wear astrakhan hats instead of turbans.[114] Earlier, Abdur Rahman had tried to persuade traditionalists of the virtues of Western dress by reminding them of Quranic injunctions against waste and extravagance;[115] the baggy trousers of the Afghan soldiers had been cast aside on this basis. Now, the justification for Western dress, at least for the members of the Afghan royalty, was that they could thus more honorably and properly represent their fatherland.[116] Moreover, as noted, the Afghan modernists insisted that clothing had never been an article of faith in Islam.

In order to enhance the prestige of the monarchy and "inculcate pride among the Afghans," Habibullah purchased a coach for use on ceremonial occasions. For similar reasons, he held a display of the goods produced in the government workshops in 1913; it was the first public exhibition in Afghanistan.[117] After visiting India in 1907, the Amir ordered the Afghan flag flown on all government offices.

Habibullah can be credited with introducing a number of technical innovations into Afghanistan. In 1911 the first clock tower was constructed. Until then, sundials were used, but the system involved reading tables in Persian to convert solar time to mean time and was so complex as to be accessible only to the learned; the masses had to depend on the sun's position and on a midday gun.[118] In 1905, the first cinematographic equipment was brought into the country. As noted earlier, that same year saw the first automobile in Afghanistan. Soon after, distance markers graced the roads to Kabul,* and the first traffic policemen were posted in the Afghan capital.[119] The Amir developed a great interest in photography and personally trained various Afghans in the use of cameras. He also encouraged the use of photoengraving. In this respect, he went a good deal further than Abdur Rahman, who had been the first Afghan ruler to permit himself to be photographed; Habibullah put his own portrait on sale (for the benefit of the orphanage). He also organized a photographic contest through *Siraj al-Akhbar*.[120] Among the other inventions that made their first appearance in the country in these years were the phonograph and the fountain pen (1909–11).

Along with the many innovations came an influx of European terms. The pages of *Siraj al-Akhbar* reveal these words in use: box, boot, seken kelass (second class), metr (meter), blok, estation, motor, ril (rail), telephon, apartman (apartment), rapor (report), address, mitrailleuse (machine gun), jeology, engenery (engineering), klishé, gimnastic, politik, zingografy (engraving), fabrik (factory), bomb, band, telegraph, statistic, dakter, minicipali (municipal), oonifurm, etnografia, jografia, metoorology, manover, alboom, panorama, gramafon, arkhelogy, zoology. These words entered the Pashto and Persian spoken in Afghanistan through three major channels: the Persian of Iran (which had incorporated a number of French, English, and Russian words between the seventeenth and early-twentieth centuries), Urdu, and Turkish.

Habibullah used Anglo-Indian architectural styles and Western furniture for his palaces. His winter palace at Jalalabad was decorated with

---

* According to Jewett, Habibullah was entranced to the point of obsession with distance markers, totally ignoring the question of their value for a largely illiterate population. Jewett reported that the Amir went so far as to order guardhouses built to protect the milestones against theft and vandalism. See "Off the Map," p. 28.

European pictures "cut from almanacs and common oleographs." He tried to keep abreast of European advances and to introduce as many of them at court as possible. For instance, he sponsored a pianola recital at court in January 1908. (The program, performed by Ernest Thornton, the English tanning expert, included selections from Gilbert and Sullivan's "The Gondoliers" and some Sousa marches.)[121] In these years the Afghan elite enthusiastically took up gymnastics and European sports, including golf, tennis, and ice-skating,* and even the workers in the royal workshops became interested in soccer.[122] The Amir's curiosity about and interest in all things European even extended to English jams and jellies, and in fact European cuisine; for some years he employed a French chef.[123]

Habibullah introduced new agricultural products into the country, notably cereal grains such as oats, and he imported various seeds and bulbs, including the daffodil, from England. He also initiated two agricultural projects, which though unsuccessful, were economically sound. One project involved the adoption of techniques used in California for the preservation of fruits, a plan that would have greatly benefited Afghanistan's important fruit industry. The other project was an attempt to grow cotton outside of Jalalabad, using seeds imported from the United States.[124]

FACTORS IMPEDING MODERNIZATION

Despite the Amir's interest in modern European inventions, he faced great obstacles in attempting to institute modernization in Afghanistan. One of the greatest was lack of capital. One estimate places the total annual income of the Afghan state under Habibullah at 12–13 million rupees, another places it a bit higher at 1–2 million pounds sterling.[125] (This was in addition to the Amir's annual subsidy from the British.) Revenues were irregular, and most taxes continued to be paid in grain and other produce, which had to be kept in government storehouses. Inadequate storage facilities, large staffs, inaccurate bookkeeping, inexact weights and measures, and extensive embezzlement cost the government almost half of the cash and goods it received. Moreover, an enormous amount of the totals collected had already been appropriated either by local tax collectors or by tribal chieftains.[126]

The Amir simply did not have enough revenue to underwrite major re-

---

* Habibullah was reported to be so great a golf enthusiast that he played a daily round for three years. He had links at both Kabul and Jalalabad. According to Jewett ("Habibullah Khan," p. 282), the Amir often found petitions stuffed in the holes; he gave orders that they be destroyed unread.

formist and modernization schemes and at the same time cover the expenses of the army, the court, and an inefficient and cumbersome bureaucracy. Yet he could not increase his revenues without leading the country out of its isolation, and he was decidedly reluctant to alter that traditional policy. He and his closest advisers, the sardars and tribal chieftains, consistently refused to countenance any foreign investment in Afghanistan or any firm commercial agreements with neighboring countries. Because of the political risks involved, many of those advisers were adamant on the question of the use of railways and telegraph lines in the country.

Until the conclusion of the Anglo-Russian Convention, the British authorities were as opposed to a rail link through Afghanistan as the Afghans themselves. On May 11, 1905, the British prime minister declared:

> Russia [is] making steady progress towards Afghanistan and railways [are] under construction which could only be strategic. . . . A war on the North-West Frontier would be chiefly a problem of transport and supply. We must therefore allow nothing to be done to facilitate transport. Any attempt to make a railway in Afghanistan in connection with the Russian strategic railways would be regarded as an act of direct aggression against us. . . . As long as we say resolutely that railways in Afghanistan should only be made in time of war, we can make India absolutely secure. But if, through blindness or cowardness, we permit the slow absorption of the country, if strategic railways are allowed to creep close to our Frontier, we shall have to maintain a much larger army.[127]

Even after 1907, British leaders and journalists were divided on the issue. There was almost general agreement on the economic value of such a railway, but apprehension about its military and political implications.[128] In order to secure the economic advantages that a railway in Afghanistan offered and, at the same time, avoid an extension of Russian influence in the region, some in Great Britain proposed a trans-Persian railway as an alternative. It was to eventually link Quetta and Kandahar with Herat and Meshed, thereby placing Afghanistan on a "direct path of communication between East and West . . . between Europe and India."[129] Others revived the idea of a South Asiatic railroad linking Europe and the Far East.*

---

* Two of the foremost proponents of the railways were C. E. D. Black, head of the Geographical Department of the India Office, and C. A. Moreing, a well-known British engineer. Black, in an article entitled "A Railway to India" (*Nineteenth Century*, January 1899), urged that the Hejaz railroad to Medina be completed and a new line built from Egypt to Quetta or Karachi. His proposed line was to cover some 2,200 miles and make a 66-hour trip of the journey from Port Said or Ismailia to Quetta. Moreing outlined his project, a much more ambitious undertaking, in the same magazine ("An All-British Railway to China," *Nineteenth Century*, September 1899). His argument was that since Russia was extending its influence in Asia and was building a trunk line to China, Britain should go one step further: the British should build a continuous line from the Mediterranean to the Yangtse. Moreing pointed out that part of this line was already built (in India) and could be quickly extended to Burma and to the Mediter-

Russian groups, too, hoped to see a rail connection between Russia and India via Persia. So as to avert friction and competition, they proposed that such a line might be international, possibly with French, German, and Belgian financial participation. It was their view that by linking the Baghdad and trans-Persian railways the interests of all the great powers would be safeguarded.[130]

There were some in England, however, who found the Afghans' fears of the political consequences of a railway justified. One was Sir J. D. Rees, who stated: "As to the Ameer's reluctance to admit railways into his territories, I confess, I sympathize heartily with it, for I believe the coming of the railways would mean the end of independent Afghanistan."[131] To dispel the Afghan fears, a British general, Sir E. Champan, proposed that the British adopt a new policy toward Afghanistan. He contended that British friendship with Russia had eliminated the necessity of massing large numbers of troops on the northwestern frontier of India, and that there was no longer an imminent Russian threat to Afghanistan. Therefore, the "buffer policy" had "died a natural death" and with it, "the supreme difficulty of gaining the Amir's consent to the advance of civilization and trade." Said Champan:

I believe that the Amir is chiefly concerned to secure his recognized independence as a sovereign ruler. We are no longer prepared to quarrel with Russia; we cannot, therefore, perform our part in an engagement by which he allows his foreign relations to be arranged through the Foreign Office of India. There would seem to be no objection to an acknowledgement of his independence being made by us, and to his being invited to a conference on a footing of equality.[132]

Unfortunately, no such policy was adopted, and in the face of continuing Afghan opposition, unresolved questions about Russian economic penetration into northern Afghanistan, and the outbreak of World War I, all plans to develop a railway in Afghanistan were set aside. The Amir could only have been relieved. Had the plans materialized, he would have been confronted with the prospect of a struggle with the many important tribes of southwestern Afghanistan, through whose territory the railway was to pass. These tribes saw the railway variously as a sinister plot to advance the centralizing schemes of the Afghan government at their expense or as a direct British military threat to the border tribes. For their part, the Afghan traditionalists were equally suspicious, and clung to Abdur Rahman's view that, until such time as Afghanistan possessed a

---

ranean. His proposed line was to run some 2,400 miles from Alexandria, via northern Arabia and Baluchistan, to Karachi. Other nineteenth-century plans envisioned a trans-Mesopotamian railway linking the eastern Mediterranean with the Persian Gulf.

well-armed, self-sufficient army, the best guarantee of Afghan independence lay in inaccessibility and economic underdevelopment. Finally, the majority of Afghans feared the economic consequences of a railway. One observer reported the average Afghan believed that "if you built a railway, away went the wheat and other food products to other countries." Popular prejudices were reinforced by the fact that in Peshawar the price of wheat had increased (from 24 seers per rupee to six per rupee), after the railway was extended there.[133]

The Anglo-Russian Convention of 1907 heightened the Amir's fears of British railway schemes.* (He had earlier declared that his subjects would regard it as "a spear pointed at the heart of Afghanistan" and asserted that if Britain's sole interest was in the protection of Afghanistan's northern frontier, he was prepared to allow the construction of a major road or railway through Sistan along the Helmand River to Hashtadan, which would constitute a genuine "shield for Afghanistan.")[134] Though he was privately inclined to go along with the modernists, hoping, as they did, that the Afghans could admit a railway but retain control of it and maintain their independence, he remained faithful to the policies of his father on this point. He also rejected a proposal to establish a telegraphic link with India.[135] He was, however, receptive to technological innovations that did not necessitate foreign financial investment and control. Witness his sponsorship of the building of the hydroelectric plant and of the installation of telephone lines in the country. (He even entertained the idea of stringing telephone lines between Kabul and Calcutta.)[136] The Amir did not oppose modernization as such; he opposed only those measures that might have jeopardized his own rule or Afghanistan's independence.

In the end Habibullah was no more successful than his father in resolving the dilemma of modernizing Afghanistan. He was reluctant to open the country to foreign assistance until such time as it was strong militarily, but he was unable to find the wherewithal to achieve such a position. He wavered on the question of admitting a railway, still hoping that instead he could fulfill his father's dream of obtaining a corridor to the sea. Like Abdur Rahman, he reasoned that this would permit him to deal directly with the external world and allow Afghanistan to free itself of its dependence on the good will of its neighbors. The Afghans could then develop

---

* In 1911 Keppel (p. 18) characterized the real purpose behind the Anglo-Indian railway projects for Afghanistan as one dominated by strategic and political considerations. The ultimate aim of the railway system was to free the British from the "inadequacies" of the Khyber roads, allowing the "rapid despatch of a large army into Afghanistan," and the provisioning of it while there.

their resources and sell their products directly, using the increased profits to strengthen the army and establish such industries and reforms as were necessary or desirable.[137]

Though Habibullah failed to fulfill this dream, he made important contributions to the emergence of a modern Afghanistan. His measures in the fields of education, public health, industry, and trade, though limited in scope, were of great significance. They assisted in the growth of the urban population and the rise of a small Afghan bourgeoisie. Most important, his reign saw the formation of the first educated and politically conscious Afghan generation, the *Siraj al-Akhbar* generation that contributed so greatly to the future course of Afghan development.

Chapter Eight

The Rise of Afghan Nationalism

In the years before World War I, Habibullah, supported by the Afghan nationalists and pressed by the anti-British faction in Kabul, made an effort to obtain international recognition for Afghanistan and to broaden its contacts with the outside world. Soon after his succession in 1901, he ordered his brother Nasrullah Khan to select 24 officers to serve as envoys to England, Russia, France, Germany, Japan, China, the Ottoman Empire, Egypt, Persia, and the United States.[1] In a bid to display his independence and to transform his father's personal agreement with Great Britain into an official recognition of the hereditary rule of his dynasty, he refused to renegotiate the treaty engagements between Afghanistan and the British government in India. He also declined an invitation to visit India and refused to draw the British subsidies that were his under the terms of the agreement with his father.

Several other developments made it clear to the British that they must rapidly resolve the question and the character of their future relations with the Afghans. In the years 1901–3, the Russians had made several attempts to reopen the question of establishing diplomatic relations with Afghanistan,[2] and the Germans had tried to make economic inroads in the area.[3] The British were also concerned that the outcome of the Russo-Japanese War might have great psychological impact on the Afghan elite, and were worried about the political influence an unfriendly Afghan ruler could wield among the frontier tribes.[4] Furthermore, military authorities in India advocated a "meaningful" British presence or close supervision of Afghanistan in view of the British commitment to defend the country against aggression.*

* Wrote Lord Roberts: "We are bound in honour, bound by solemn promise made seventeen years ago to protect Afghanistan, and between us and that nation there are two hundred thousand fighting men, who may either make the fulfillment of that promise easy or else most difficult if not impossible." See Forrest, *Lord Roberts*, p. 183. The same thoughts were expressed by Lord Kitchener: "We have solemnly guaranteed the

In an effort to reassert British influence over Afghanistan and to settle differences that might arise between the two countries, the British sent a mission headed by Louis Dane, foreign secretary of the government in India, to Kabul in 1904. Its main object, in the judgment of one German diplomat, seemed to be "to make England's influence predominant in Afghanistan and to induce the Amir to take such military measures under the British advice and supervision as will make a Russian invasion through Afghanistan impossible." Moreover, said the diplomat, Dane seemed bent on promoting trade between India and Afghanistan. "Thus, England has been quick in seizing the opportunity offered by the war in the Far East, to secure her position in India for a long time to come."[5]

The economic objectives of the Dane Mission took on even greater significance in view of a new Russo-Persian customs agreement. Concluded in 1903, this agreement imposed light duties on many articles of Russian origin, among them oil and sugar, and heavy duties on articles, such as tea and piece goods, that came mainly or wholly from British or Indian sources.[6] It was construed to be directed against the Anglo-Indian trade in Persia, and inaugurated a new era of intense Anglo-Russian economic rivalry.*

In three months of negotiations, the British failed to secure either economic concessions or new political undertakings from Habibullah.† The Amir merely consented to respect his father's agreement with the British government in India, in effect transforming that personal pact into a dynastic agreement.[7] A new treaty, known as the Dane-Habibullah Treaty, was concluded on March 21, 1905. It reaffirmed the annual subsidy granted in 1893, allowing the Amir to collect 400,000 pounds in undrawn subsidy payments, and reaffirmed as well Afghanistan's right to import arms without restriction.[8] The treaty implicitly guaranteed the territorial integrity

integrity of the Amir's dominions and have pledged ourselves to defend his frontier. If we are to fulfill our obligation in this respect, [the Afghan] frontier thereupon becomes in a military sense our own." See Sir George Arthur, *Life of Lord Kitchener* (London, 1920, 3 vols.), II, 152.

* According to the British consul general at Meshed, the Russians had begun selling wheat to the Afghans during a famine in 1903. The consul claimed that the Russians were offering cheap rates of credit and, in some cases, were obtaining mortgages on the Afghans' lands. Adamec, p. 34.

† *The Times* (January 26, 1905) intimated that the ultimate aim of the British proposals and objectives were the eventual link, by rail and telegraph, of Jalalabad and Peshawar, the training of Afghan troops by British officers, and the purchase of war materiel from England alone. Since Habibullah declined to discuss these proposals and instead raised the issue of establishing an Afghan legation in London and even touched on "an impossible request for a strip of land to the Baluch coast, for the purpose of founding an Afghan seaport," the Dane mission was considered a fiasco. See Keppel, pp. 47–48.

of Afghanistan[9] and officially recognized the Afghan ruler as "His Majesty, the independent King of Afghanistan and its dependencies." The Afghan monarch not only refused to grant the British trade concessions, he refused to countenance the introduction of railways into Afghanistan.[10] Though the British did not obtain the right to establish a diplomatic mission in the country, as they had hoped, they retained control of Afghanistan's foreign relations and considered the treaty a renewal of the Durand Agreement.[11]

British opinion was divided on the Dane-Habibullah Treaty. Some thought that the Amir, by dictating his own terms, had brought Afghanistan's status as a buffer state to an end.[12] Others argued that the treaty was a wise step, one that did not sacrifice Great Britain's vital interests to mere prestige. The opponents of the treaty were later somewhat mollified by the Amir's visit to India in 1907, which consolidated Anglo-Afghan ties and, as it turned out, was a major factor in the Amir's decision to remain neutral during World War I.[13] If the treaty did not end Afghanistan's isolation, it was nevertheless an Afghan diplomatic victory and important for both political and psychological reasons. It enhanced the position of the monarchy and Habibullah's personal prestige within Afghanistan, and it strengthened the hand of the Afghan modernists, who hailed Britain's recognition of Afghanistan as an independent country that had refused to compromise its freedom. The Amir's success in withstanding British diplomatic and economic pressure figured prominently in their arguments for modernization. They insisted that technological innovations need not be regarded as alien impositions upon a vassal country, but rather as borrowings freely adopted by an independent country to defend its territory and its moral and spiritual values.

THE IMPACT OF JAPAN

The Habibullah-Dane Treaty took on an additional importance because it coincided with the Russo-Japanese War. The defeat of a major European imperialist power by an Asian country had great repercussions, igniting highly inflammatory material in Asia as well as in Russia itself. Asian pride, hitherto battered by a continuous stream of Western conquests, was bolstered by the Japanese victory; moreover, the fact that the only Asian constitutional power had defeated the only major Western non-constitutional power seemed to show constitutionalism as "the panacea for internal ills and the secret of Western strength."[14] The modernization of Japan and its victory over Imperial Russia fired the imagination of

Asian nationalists and modernists. In India resurgent Japan became a symbol of hope. Tilak's paper *Kasari* wrote: "A knowledge of the history and the rise of Japan has kindled in the people's mind a strong desire for Swaraj [independence]." It advocated giving preference to Japanese manufactures above all imported goods. Rabindranath Tagore, the poet, wrote: "Japan's example has given heart to the rest of Asia. We have seen that the life and the strength are there in us, only the dead crust has to be removed." Similar views were expressed by Swami Vivekananda (the Bengali reformer), Gopak Krishna Gokhale, and others.[15] In the Ottoman Empire, the Young Turks and Islamist reformers hailed the Japanese blueprint for modernization as a model that guaranteed the adoption of Western sciences and technology without abandoning national traditions.[16] In Egypt, Mustafa Kamil, the famous ideologue of nationalism, wrote a book —*al-Shams al-Mushriqa* [The Rising Sun]—on the spectacular revival of Japan.[17] There was a similar reaction in Persia, where the three-volume *Siyahat-nama-ye Ibrahim Beg*, the first European-style Persian novel, attacked the socioeconomic backwardness of Persia and drew attention to Japan as a model of development. Many Persian poets also responded with enthusiasm to Japan's victory.[18] In Russia, the war sensitized the Muslims to Pan-Islamism and had an "unsettling effect" on the minds of the Russian-educated Muslim youth and intelligentsia of Central Asia.[19]

The reaction of the Afghan nationalists and modernists to the Russo-Japanese War seems to have been influenced by the prevailing climate in the nationalist circles in neighboring countries. The victory of a modernized Japan greatly impressed the ruling elite. Japan became a model for traditionalists and modernists alike. Both viewed Japan as a country that had freed itself of Western imperialism and assimilated Western technology without impairing its national culture or discarding its monarchy. Japan was held to be the best evidence that an Asiatic nation, once it possessed complete freedom and independence, could acquire the tools of knowledge and modern science, and achieve economic and political progress.[20] The nationalists and the modernists hoped for a rapprochement between Afghanistan and Japan. Barakatullah, who visited Tokyo in May 1913, wrote a letter to *Siraj al-Akhbar* proposing that a Muslim propaganda and missionary center be established in Japan.[21] He argued that the conversion of the Japanese to Islam could change the entire course of human history.*

* Others had doubts about such prospects. Sheikh Muhammed Rida, a leading disciple of Muhammed 'Abduh, reported the following conversation, which must have taken place shortly before 'Abduh's death in 1905: "We were at the home of the Imam

The modernists urged the establishment of close economic ties with Japan as a modest beginning toward an Asiatic cooperation that might eventually bring about the liberation of all Asia. The way to Eastern salvation was through unity, awakening, and progress.[22] However, they continued to insist that total independence was prerequisite to progress in Afghanistan, pointing out that Japan had not gained a preeminent political position simply because she had adopted modern techniques; she had also had sturdy foundations of freedom and independence. Japan was clearly a model for Afghanistan.

An article by Abdul Rashid Ibrahim Efendi praising the achievements and perseverance of the Japanese people was reprinted in *Siraj al-Akhbar*,[23] and, as previously noted, a five-volume study of the Russo-Japanese War was translated by Tarzi. (The translation was prepared for the private use of Habibullah, but was later released to the general public.)[24] *Siraj al-Akhbar* made reference a number of times to the fact that Japan was Asiatic and had become modernized only recently, yet had managed to become powerful enough to make even a great Christian power like Russia wary.

The military might and prestige of Japan particularly impressed Inayatullah. In an address to the Afghan cadets, he extolled "the sobriety, patriotism, and discipline of the Japanese soldiers and the ardour of the Japanese officer," contrasting them with "the drunkenness of the Russian soldier and the foppishness of the Russian officer, who spent his time twirling his mustache in Port Arthur, instead of being in his place with the Army."[25]

THE IMPACT OF POLITICAL EVENTS OUTSIDE AFGHANISTAN

The influence of the Russian Revolution of 1905 on the Afghan modernist and nationalist movements is difficult to gauge. According to Soviet historians, the 1905 revolution was largely responsible for the rise in Asia of progressive national-liberation movements, including the Young Afghan movement.[26] In the view of some, it played the same role in Asia

---

['Abduh] talking about what we had just heard concerning the desire of the Japanese nation to adopt the religion of Islam. Sheikh Hussain al-Jisr exclaimed, 'Now there will be hope for Islam to regain its true glory!'" To this, Rida reported, Sheikh Salman, another of 'Abduh's disciples, answered, "Leave [the Japanese] alone. I am afraid if they became Muslims like us we will corrupt them before they have a chance to reform us.... We shall yet see the result of your hopes in this dead [Muslim] nation and the outcome of the reforms you have attempted in these corrupt [Arab] people." Louis Shaiko, as quoted by Sharabi, p. 35.

as the French Revolution had in Europe,[27] deeply affecting the Ottoman Empire, Persia, China, Mongolia, India, and Afghanistan, "which sighed under the yoke of English capital."[28] There is, however, no good evidence that such was the case in Afghanistan.[29] The country was diplomatically isolated in 1905, had no important educational institutions (Habibiya College had barely made its start), and had no periodicals or newspapers. *Siraj al-Akhbar*, which was not founded until 1911, does not provide any direct clues about the influence of the revolution, and the Young Afghan movement itself was confined to an extremely narrow segment of society. There was thus no instrument by which the news and the historical significance of the revolution might have been spread in Afghanistan.*

Perhaps no single event gave as much impetus to the growth of Afghan nationalism as the Anglo-Russian Convention of 1907.[30] The agreement came as a shock to the Afghan nationalists. The ruler of Afghanistan had not even been consulted, though the implementation of the Afghan clauses was ostensibly contingent upon his "approval."[31] Both the monarch and the nationalists-modernists feared that the Anglo-Russian agreement threatened Afghan independence.[32] They saw in the agreement the possible elimination of a traditional aggressive rivalry that had had the effect of checking the designs of the two empires, and suspected that the agreement portended further agreements at the expense of Afghanistan.

The conclusion of the Convention intensified the fervor of the nationalist-reformist and revivalist elements—in Persia as well as in Afghanistan.[33] The fears of the nationalists were well expressed by the Persian poet Bahar Malik ul-Shoara, who dedicated a poem to the Convention. Entitled "A Critical Tribute to Sir Edward Grey," it read, in part:[34]

> Alas that thou, for all thy wits, has wrought
> A deed which, save regret, can yield thee naught.
> For India's gates, closed for a hundred years,
> To Russia now you open without fears.
>
> . . .
>
> Not Persia only feels the Russian squeeze;
> 'Tis felt by Afghans and by Kashgaris.
> "Russia her pact will keep," you answer me.
> Her records read, and wondrous things you'll see.

---

* If there was any impact at all, it must have been transmitted via Persia, where both the Russo-Japanese War and the Russian Revolution "had a most outstanding effect" (Browne, *Persian Revolution*, p. 120), or through important Persian-language newspapers like *Habl-ul-Matin* (published in Calcutta) and *Shams* (published in Istanbul), which commented on the significance of the war and the revolution (see Banani, p. 9). The Indian instructors at Habibiya College, as well as routine contacts with Central Asia, might also have served as channels of information. There is no indication that the Persian and Turkish periodicals published in the Caucasus reached Afghanistan.

Another poet, Iraj Mirza, wrote of the treaty: "The grocer's shop will be despoiled, owing to the agreement between the mice and the cat."[35] The bitter nationalist reaction was summed up in the Calcutta newspaper *Habl-ul-Matin*, which editorialized: "There is sweetness, kindness, and love in the Agreement. The Russian government will grant the English government opportunities for commercial activity in the northern sphere of influence, and the English will kindly grant permission to the Russians to do the same in the South. What right have the Russians in Persia to grant or not grant—from north to south—that which belongs to us? We aren't so youthful as to want a protector, and we aren't mad or insane and hence in need of one.[36]

The Afghans' fears concerning the threat to their independence seemed to be partially substantiated when the two colonial empires, disregarding the Amir's opposition, announced that they considered the Afghan clauses of the convention operative and binding.[37] The Afghan nationalists and modernists became convinced that they would have to formulate their limited reform projects within the framework of European *realpolitik*. In this sense, the Anglo-Russian Convention profoundly influenced the nature and the course of the politics of modernization in Afghanistan. It reinforced the position of those who called for a program aimed at strengthening Afghanistan's military, economic, and political position. At the same time, it reinforced the fears of the Afghan ruling elite about the serious consequences of foreign investment and concessions, and so had the effect of slowing the pace and distorting the character of that program.

The Persian, Young Turk, and Chinese revolutions that followed the Russo-Japanese War and the conclusion of the Anglo-Russian Convention encouraged the development of a constitutional movement (Mashroutia) in Afghanistan in 1907–9. In hopes of accelerating reform and modernization through political action, a militant minority among the Young Afghans pressed for the establishment of a constitutional assembly, founded on a national rather than a tribal basis, and circulated a petition addressed to the Amir to this effect. Habibullah, however, was firmly convinced that his attempt to establish a limited consultative legislative body in 1904 had failed because "the members were too ignorant for legislative work . . . and needed 30 years of education to be fitted for the post."[38] Moreover, his conception of constitutional government did not differ from that of his father. Constitutional government involved no more than a council of aristocrats, tribal chiefs (who were perceived as representatives of the people), and religious leaders acting in a purely consultative and advisory capacity. The Amir had no intention of broadening the basis of this council or of increasing its power at the expense of his own absolute authority. He quickly suppressed the constitutional movement and arrested its leaders,[39] leaving the arena open to the much larger and more influential moderate wing of the Young Afghans, who envisaged socioeconomic reform under the sponsorship and in the interests of the monarchy.

PAN-ISLAMISM

The humiliating defeats inflicted on the Ottoman Empire during the Italo-Ottoman War in Tripoli in 1911 and the War of the Balkan States in 1912 led to outbursts throughout the Muslim world against the "unprovoked aggressions of European imperialism and Christendom." Pan-Islamic agitation was especially strong among the Muslims of India, who in turn greatly influenced the Afghans. In this connection, a denunciation of Italy by the Muslim League Council in India and its call for a Muslim boycott of Italian goods were particularly significant. Important Muslim periodicals in India, notably *al-Hilal, Comrade, Zamindar, Hamdard*, and the *Aligarh Institute Gazette*, supported the Ottoman cause and argued for Muslim unity and solidarity.[40] The famous philosopher and poet Muhammad Iqbal also lent his voice to the protest, reading a poem dedicated to the Turkish struggle in Tripoli in the mosques of India. Revivalists and modernists alike mourned the past greatness of the Islamic world and expressed their hope that the onslaught of European imperialism, which had taken on the form of a modern crusade against Islam, "an attack of the Cross against the Crescent,"[41] would accelerate the process of Muslim awakening and unity.

In Afghanistan, the nationalists and modernists denounced the Italians, the Balkan peoples, and Christian Europe in general for unleashing a politico-religious assault against Islam. They held that Europe's aim was to deprive Muslims of the benefits of modern civilization and to undermine the foundations of their faith, in an attempt to subvert the power and independence of the Muslim states.[42] Numerous articles were published in *Siraj al-Akhbar* lamenting the sad fate of the Ottoman Empire, supporting the Turks against the Christians, and condemning the alleged atrocities of the Italians and the Bulgarians.[43] The paper also carried crude drawings of the "savages." One depicted a Bulgarian soldier who had "raped three Turkish women and cut off their heads" as souvenirs, another "a Balkan barbarian" who had cut open the womb of a pregnant Turkish woman to present the unborn child to its father.[44] Still others showed soldiers, politicians, and Greek Orthodox priests dining and drinking wine in churches converted from mosques. *Siraj al-Akhbar* also attacked the British.* One article pronounced the British "desecration of mosques and temples in India" a degree of barbarism surpassing that of the Spanish Inquisition.[45]

The wars of Italy and the Balkan states against the Turks gave fresh meaning to the Pan-Islamic teachings of al-Afghānī. The Young Turks' attempts to reform and revitalize the Ottoman Empire, and to check the growth of "parochial" nationalisms within it, inspired much of the Muslim world.[46] The Afghan nationalists and modernists exalted the Young Turks, hailing Enver Bey, the Young Turk military leader, as the "champion of Islam," the "hope of the Muslim world's salvation," a man dear to the heart of every Muslim from Balkh and Herat to India.[47] They emphasized the special role to be played by Afghanistan, Persia, and the Ottoman Empire, countries that had not yet fallen under the yoke of European imperialism. Afghanistan had to be modernized so that it might become a stronghold for the defense of Islam.

From an historical point of view, Pan-Islamism had both progressive and regressive effects on the Afghan modernist movement. The concept of Muslim solidarity made it possible for the traditionalists and the modernists to find common ground in the preservation of the fatherland and the defense of the Islamic faith.[48] Pan-Islamism was thus a successful tool in uniting an ethnically divided people and in promoting the cause of independence. Moreover, in the sense that it fostered Afghan nationalism, it served as a tool against possible Pan-Iranian or Pan-Turkic irredentist claims on the Afghan kingdom. Finally, Pan-Islamism provided the modernists a basis on which to justify innovation and reform; modernization was a legitimate means of strengthening the monarchy and of defending both Afghanistan and Islam. On the negative side, Pan-Islamism contributed to Afghan xenophobia and religious fanaticism, and hardened the position of those who opposed reform in the country or cultural contacts and political cooperation outside it.

The Afghan modernists hoped to overcome the objections of the traditionalists through education. They also hoped for the help of the Young Turks and the influential Muslim reformers of India, but in this they were disappointed. Their attempts to promote modernization under the banner of Pan-Islamism met serious obstacles in the Pan-Turkic programs of the Young Turks and the relative indifference of the Indian reformers toward

---

* Habibullah warned Britain of the danger of remaining neutral in the Italian and Balkan wars. Neutrality was not in Britain's national interest, since her Muslim subjects were no longer passive: "The eyes and ears of all have become open and sentiments of freedom and self-government have kindled their brains." (As quoted by Adamec, p. 82.)

Afghanistan. The modernists were especially disillusioned by the general attitude of the Indian Muslims.

In an article in *Siraj al-Akhbar*, the Afghan reformers took issue with the Indian Muslims on several counts.[49] They began by attacking certain Indian journalists who were urging the Afghan monarch to purchase a dreadnought for the Ottoman navy. Reminding the Indians that the Amir had contributed some 6,000 gold sovereigns to the Ottoman cause during the Italo-Turkish War, the Afghans pointed out that India's Muslims, "although eighty million strong and opulent," had not purchased a dreadnought for the Turks, yet expected such an act of generosity from an Afghan monarch whose economic resources were very meager. They then launched into a general attack, chiding the Pan-Islamists of India who, despite lofty aims, had not provided Muslim educators or assistance to Afghanistan, a stronghold of Islam. Moreover, they said, the passive, possibly "neutral," Pan-Islamic views of the Indians did not contribute to the spread of militant nationalism, whose end was India's liberation "from the British yoke." The Divine injunction to Muslim solidarity was not to be honored only in the breach; it required commitment and action. *Siraj al-Akhbar* questioned the general attitude of the Muslims of India, who could stand aside as British regiments with Indian Muslim troops attacked fellow Muslims in the Sudan, Egypt, and Afghanistan. What, the writers wondered, was the stand of the Indians on the past sufferings of the Afghan nation? What were their feelings on the subjugation of Merv by Russia and Baluchistan by England?

In this same article and in others, the Afghan modernists made it clear that they considered the defense of the Ottoman Empire essential. Not only was it the Islamic world's "window on Europe," the head of the Muslim world, and the seat of the holy places of Islam; it was also the citadel of Islamic modernism and reform, the only major Muslim country with significant military might and all the advantages of modern civilization. Seeing in the Ottoman Empire the hopes for a transformation of the entire Muslim world, the Afghan modernists construed European intervention in the internal affairs of the empire as a deliberate attempt to prevent the spiritual and political rebirth of the Muslim world.

WORLD WAR I

The First World War had great impact on the Afghan nationalist and modernist movements. As the Afghans saw it, the Ottoman Empire's entry into the war on the side of the Central Powers created a seemingly impossible situation for the tens of millions of Muslim subjects of Great

Britain, France, and Russia, "who were torn between their consciences and duties."[50] In addition, the war destroyed several myths: the myth of a united Christendom, the myth of a militant West engaged in a concerted onslaught against the East, the myth of a monolithic Muslim world. The Ottoman commitment to the Central Powers, the Japanese alliance with the Allies, and the Arab Revolt violated some of the cardinal tenets of Pan-Islamism and dealt a blow to the concept of Asiatic solidarity against European imperialism.

The destruction, misery, and bloodshed wrought by "the most civilized peoples," by those who considered themselves the guardians of civilization and the rest of mankind barbaric,[51] shocked the Afghan modernists, shattering their illusions about the greatness and superiority of modern civilization.[52] The holocaust in Europe gave weight to those who insisted that Western civilization was decadent and materialistic, devoid of spiritual and moral values.* Nevertheless, accounts of the great technological innovations and revolutionary methods of modern warfare brought home to the Afghan modernists the extent to which their country had fallen behind the "caravan of progress."[53]

At the outbreak of the war, Habibullah proclaimed his country's neutrality for "as long as the honour, existence, independence, and freedom of

---

* In an article in *Harper's Weekly* (December 11, 1915, p. 571), the Amir's nephew Sheikh Achmed [Ahmad] Abdullah wrote: "We [Afghans] are unmoved by the slaughter, the losses, the untold sufferings, the wholesale destruction. The reason for this is sweetly simple and obvious. Whatever hurts the Occident helps us. Therefore it pleases us. Asia and Europe play the game from opposite sides of the board. The losses of Europe are the gains of Asia. Each killed European is a killed potential enemy." The Afghans, he wrote, wanted nothing of their fellow whites in Europe and in America except rifles and ammunition. "We prefer to clout out our destiny alongside of yellow Japanese and Chinese, brown Moros, chocolate-colored Dravidians from the south.... The common basis of [our] steadily growing Asian solidarity is hatred of the whites, the Christians.... This hatred is universal from the Siberian tundras to the burnt south of India. We hate the European because we consider him an intolerable barbarian, who bullies where his wheedling is unsuccessful. We hate him because, according to us, he is tortuous and cannot speak the truth; because he prates about his new-found hygiene, but is personally unclean compared to the majority of Asians. We despise him as a hypocrite who ships whiskey, rifles, diseases, and missionaries in the same mixed cargoes. We dislike him because he is a recent parvenu. We are convinced that in spite of his present leadership in mundane affairs, he is our inferior physically, morally, and mentally."

He concluded with these words: "We are glad of this war. Whatever the outcome, it will weaken Europe in treasure and blood. It will kill the flower of their fighting men. It will reduce their birth rate. Europe will not get over the effects of this conflict in fifty years. Asia will be strong and ready in less than fifty years. The Europeans have taught us with the sword. Presently we shall teach them with the sword. And if the sword be simitar, yataghan, kurkree, or kris, it will not dull the sharpness nor weaken the swish of the steel."

Afghanistan were in no ways jeopardized or threatened."[54] The entry of the Ottoman Empire into the conflict, however, aroused widespread Pan-Islamic and nationalist sentiment in the country (despite various officially inspired articles in *Siraj al-Akhbar* advising Muslims that they could remain faithful to both their religious convictions and their governments without contradiction).[55] The overwhelming majority of the Afghan nationalists and modernists were sympathetic to the Turkish cause. Though a few questioned the wisdom of the Turks' move and ascribed it to German attempts to manipulate Pan-Islamism as a political weapon,[56] most found the move justified, on the grounds that the Turks had to avenge themselves on the Italians, Greeks, and Serbs, and put an end to foreign capitulations. They argued that the Ottoman Empire was forced to seek a rapprochement with Germany, in the face of the Anglo-Russian Convention, which threatened the empire's existence. In their view, the Turks' fears of Russia were historically justifiable, and the Anglo-Russian Convention an act of diplomatic shortsightedness on the part of Great Britain.[57]

Siraj al-Akhbar increasingly reflected the widespread pro-Turkish feeling in the country and became the voice of those who hoped for Afghanistan's entry into the war. Despite Habibullah's policy of benevolent neutrality toward the British, Mahmud Tarzi and some of the Young Afghans (primarily products of Habibiya College) joined with traditionalist-clerical Pan-Islamists to launch an anti-British and anti-Russian propaganda campaign. In carefully chosen, hypothetical articles or reprints from other Muslim periodicals, they posed a number of questions in *Siraj al-Akhbar*. Were there gains to be derived from German-Afghan mutual assistance and cooperation?[58] What were Afghanistan's strategic and political advantages? Could the Afghans play a truly great role in promoting Pan-Islamism, if they so desired? Tarzi answered this last question by asserting that Afghanistan had the opportunity to become the torchbearer of freedom for the millions of Muslims in Baluchistan, Turkestan, and India, but instead had chosen to remain neutral and observe its treaty obligations.[59]

Siraj al-Akhbar printed enthusiastic accounts of Persia's readiness to enter the war on the side of the Ottoman Empire,[60] and argued for an Afghan entry on the grounds that the Anglo-Russian Convention and alliance had jeopardized Afghanistan's independence. In the past, a Russian thrust into India would have caused England to go to war to protect Afghanistan, but under the present agreement, Afghanistan had no such assurance.[61] Because the Afghan nationalists saw in the war an unequalled opportunity for the rejuvenation of the Muslim world, revenge on the infidels, and liberation from European imperialism,[62] they disavowed the Arab Revolt, condemning it as a deterrent to the Muslim dream and an act of insubordination against the Caliphate. They expressed shock and disbelief that Sherif Hussein, the Guardian of the Holy Places of Islam, had not only sanctioned but even led the revolt.[63]

In providing a basis for agreement, however short-lived, between the Afghan modernists and the Afghan traditionalists, the war helped advance the cause of modernism. The modernists had long promoted technological change as essential to the military and economic strength of Afghanistan;* now even the traditionalists began to regard technological change as an integral part of a policy aimed at Great Britain and as a prerequisite for the liberation of their Muslim brothers from the yoke of the infidels. This situation permitted the legitimization and implementation of certain limited reforms.

IMPACT OF MUSLIM THOUGHT AND WARTIME AGITATION

The periodicals and writers in other Muslim countries took an even more Pan-Islamic line after the Caliph issued a call for jihad against the Allies in 1914; Afghan nationalist sentiment grew accordingly. In Constantinople, *Jihan-i-Islam*, an aggressively Pan-Islamic newspaper, carried articles praising the indomitable fighting spirit of the Afghans; the editors expressed their certainty that the Afghans would respond to the Sultan's appeal.[64] In Persia, articles appeared (and were reprinted in *Siraj al-Akhbar*) that called on the Afghans to take up the struggle and "not to wash their hands of their freedom."[65] The Persian poets Adib Pishawari and Vahid-e Dastgardi wrote in praise of the Kaiser and in denunciation of the Allies.[66] From Tokyo, *The Islamic Fraternity*, a paper published by Barakatullah, spread anti-British, Pan-Islamic, and Pan-Asiatic propaganda.[67] Though this paper was eventually suppressed by the Japanese government, Barakatullah was able to continue airing his views in *Siraj al-Akhbar*.

By far the largest amount of Pan-Islamic literature reached Afghanistan from India. The Muslim publications of India greatly influenced Afghan thinking. Among the most important were the politically and religiously radical *al-Hilal* (published in Calcutta by Abul Kalam Azad) and its suc-

---

* In selecting which letters to the editor to print, *Siraj al-Akhbar* frequently chose those pleading for modernization of the army, railways, new roads, stronger defenses, improved industries, and similar measures. See, for instance, a letter written by one Aziz Ahmed Qureishi, in *SA*, 3d year, No. 18, p. 8.

cessor, *al-Balagh*; the profoundly anti-British *Zamindar* (published in Lahore by Zafar Ali Khan); and the militantly activist *Comrade* and *Hamdard* (both published in Delhi by Muhammed Ali, *Comrade* in English, *Hamdard* in Urdu).[68] Although the British suppressed these nationalist and Pan-Islamic publications during the war, their message was carried on by two Calcutta papers, *Habl-ul-Matin* and the *Muslim Chronicle*.[69]

The impact of Indian Muslim thought on Afghanistan was in general far-reaching. The Afghan religious establishment and ruling elite had ties with the Muslim community of India going back to the days of Ahmad Shah Durrani. In the early twentieth century, Afghan revivalist and modernist thought was divided along essentially the same lines as these schools in India: in India, too, the traditionalists and modernists agreed on the weak and degraded state of the Muslim world; in India, too, the traditionalists attributed that decline to the Muslims' disunity, religious heterodoxy, and accretion of non-Islamic religious elements;[70] in India, too, the modernists found the reason for that decline in the Muslims' refusal to accept modern European education, science, and civilization.[71] The Afghan fundamentalists were undoubtedly also influenced by the Indian Muslims' deep distrust of the British and tendency to associate Western culture with British political interests, a tendency that caused them to cling the more tenaciously to orthodox Islam. The Afghans had also come into close contact with the religious and political revivalist movement of Sayyid Ahmed Barelvi (1796–1831), whose Wahabi followers, seeking the religious reformation of Islam and the eventual restoration of Muslim political supremacy in India, attempted to win both Afghanistan and Bukhara to their cause.[72] Some of these Wahabis (dubbed "Hindustani fanatics" by the British) had fought on the Afghan side during the First Afghan War; others had become *mujahidin* (fighters in a holy war) in the 1897–98 wars between the British and the Pathan frontier tribes.[73]

Two Muslim religious institutions in India particularly influenced Afghan thinking. In general, the Afghan traditionalists and religious establishment were affected by the religio-political teachings of the faculty at Deoband, which was known for its orthodoxy and anti-British activism. The theologians at Deoband, who "stood in the forefront of the movement to discard Sufi (mystic) and Hindu accretions to Islam," sought to resurrect the religious orthodoxy of the Abbasid period and to grant genuine, rather than titular, authority over the entire Muslim world to the Caliph.[74] The Young Afghans, for their part, were influenced by the teachings of the Muslim modernists of Aligarh. The so-called Aligarh movement, which was begun by Sir Sayyid Ahmad Khan, foresaw an extension of Western education among Muslims without any weakening of their allegiance to Islam.

World War I and Pan-Islamic sentiment tended to narrow the political gulf between the Muslim traditionalists and modernists in India, as it did in Afghanistan. The ulama of Deoband advocated closer ties with and support of the Ottoman Empire and the Caliph, and the concepts of Muslim solidarity, revivalism, and self-assertion were popularized by leading intellectuals like Abul Kalam Azad, the editor of *al-Hilal*.[75] More important, the All-India Muslim League, which was originally founded in 1906 to protect Muslim rights and promote loyalty to the British government, joined the Indian Congress Party in demanding self-rule for India (Lucknow Pact of 1916).[76]

THE TURKO-GERMAN MISSION IN AFGHANISTAN

As the Pan-Islamic movement was gaining momentum in the Muslim world, the Turks and the Germans began actively seeking to draw Persia and Afghanistan into the war. The German High Command hoped to profit greatly from any "religious and political union of Islam" that might result from the Caliph's call to jihad.[77] In general, public opinion in Afghanistan was on their side, as it was in India and Persia, where even the peasants and tribesmen seem to have been anti-British and anti-Russian.[78] The three most influential families in Afghanistan, nationalist and modernist in outlook, were sympathetic to the Turkish cause. One was the Musahiban family (Yahya Khel), whose members were the descendants of Sultan Muhammed Khan, a brother of Dost Muhammed. Five brothers—Muhammed Aziz, Nadir Khan, Hashim Khan, Shah Wali, and Shah Mahmud—were its leading members. (The family had been exiled to India, where the brothers were educated; they had been permitted to return to Afghanistan in 1901.) The other two were the Charki family, the descendants of Ghulam Hyder Khan, the commander-in-chief of Abdur Rahman Khan,[79] and the Tarzi family.

There were three factions within the royal court itself: the anti-British conservative-clerical faction headed by Nasrullah Khan; a moderate but pro-Turkish faction led by Inayatullah, who was Tarzi's son-in-law as well as the Amir's son and heir-apparent; and the modernist-nationalist faction led by Tarzi himself, which was the most radical and pro-Turkish of the three. Amanullah Khan, the Amir's youngest son, also a Tarzi son-in-law, belonged to the last group.[80]

Given the generally pro-Turkish sentiment in the country and at court,

Habibullah's position was an extremely delicate one : the Caliph had called for a holy war, the Muslims in India were agitating for Muslim solidarity, and the Persian liberal-nationalists were overwhelmingly pro-German and pro-Turkish. At home, the political situation was especially serious because of the temporary unity of the Afghan modernists and traditionalists under the banner of Pan-Islamism. The nationalists became even more restive after the arrival of a Turko-German mission in Kabul in September 1915. Headed by Oscar Niedermayer and Kazim Bey, the mission was sponsored by the Ottoman war minister Enver Pasha, and was armed with credentials from the Sultan and a letter from the Kaiser.* (Several Indian revolutionaries, including Mahendra Pratap,[81] 'Obaid-ullah Sindhi, and Barakatullah, joined the group later.)† The mission attempted, through religious and moral pressure as well as promises of military and financial assistance, to draw the Afghan ruler into the war; specifically, the Germans and the Turks wanted Habibullah to cause a major upheaval in the tribal belt along the Indian frontier.[82]

Habibullah firmly resisted these pressures and those of his own countrymen as well. After protracted consultations with tribal chieftains and with his advisers, he took the position that the history of events leading to the outbreak of the war was obscure and the outcome problematical. In these circumstances, he urged his subjects to remain united and vigilant.[83] According to the Afghan writer Ikbal Ali Shah (who seems to have rationalized the actions of various Afghan rulers while they were in power and condemned them afterwards), the Amir's policy of neutrality was "entire-

---

* According to Adamec (p. 83), after Turkey entered the war Enver Pasha reported that he had received a message from Habibullah asking if the Afghans ought to attack Russia or Britain. Adamec does not specify in what form the message was sent. Given Habibullah's grasp of the realities of the situation, it seems quite unlikely that he took such an initiative. It is more likely that Enver used some sort of verbal report to impress upon the Germans the necessity of sending a mission to Kabul.

† Ghadr (mutiny), an Indian revolutionary organization with which the mission was in contact, apparently succeeded in establishing a network that extended from the Punjab to Kabul, Rangoon, and Singapore. See India, Sedition Committee, pp. 169–78; and W. Smith, *Modern Islam*, p. 237. The founder of the organization was Har Dayal, a native of Delhi and a graduate of Oxford University. In 1913 he founded an anti-British periodical in San Francisco from which the group took its name. He attempted to politicize the Indian residents up and down the Pacific coast of Canada and the United States, and to rally the Indian students at the University of California at Berkeley to the cause of India's independence. He was at one time a lecturer at Stanford University but was discharged because of his political activism. In 1914 the United States government arrested him as an undesirable alien. Jumping bail, he went to Geneva. See T. Walter Wallbank, *A Short History of India and Pakistan from Ancient Times to the Present* (a Mentor book), New York, 1958. See also Great Britain, General Staff, *Daily Review*, June 19, 1916, pp. 3–4, for some interesting details about Ghadr's activities.

ly in keeping with the public mind." Shah claims that at a meeting of the Afghan ulama "it was resolved that the war could not be regarded as a religious one, and that there was no obligation on Afghanistan to uphold the cause of the Central Powers." He continues: "The truth is, the Afghans remained quiet because they had a very poor opinion of the religion of modern Turkey, the Turks being regarded as indifferent Moslems, degenerate followers of the Prophet who no longer set store on the rigid essentials of their faith."[84] In fact, there is no evidence suggesting that the Afghan ulama took this position, nor are there any indications of widespread anti-Turkish sentiment among the general population.

The Amir's policy of benevolent neutrality toward the British was motivated primarily by political and economic considerations. Entry into the war would have exposed Afghanistan to a combined Anglo-Russia attack. Not only was the country too weak to withstand such an attack militarily, it was too weak economically and, moreover, depended largely on trade conducted through India and Russia. There were other considerations as well. Pan-Islamism had not proved to be a political movement with sufficient force to jolt the Muslim countries and the communities under colonial control into taking concerted action, and in fact the Arabs within the Ottoman Empire had revolted, which had been a great psychological blow. The avowed Pan-Turkic goal of the Young Turks also had to be considered. Finally, British military successes in southern Persia and the Russian capture of Erzerum, in eastern Turkey, in 1916 no doubt dampened whatever enthusiasm Habibullah may have had for the cause of the Central Powers. Kut al-Amarah fell in February 1917, and with the evacuation of Turkish forces from Persia in that same year, all Turko-German hope of success in Persia and Afghanistan was dispelled.[85] Through skillful diplomatic maneuvering,* the wily Amir managed to both check the increasing influence of the nationalist, anti-British faction and maintain his policy of benevolent neutrality: he renewed his assurances to Great Britain of his continued friendship and at the same time managed to conclude a tentative

* Mahendra Pratap, who provides interesting details about the Amir's handling of the mission, reports that the Amir asked the visitors to "show your wares and then we shall see whether they suit us." In the course of the many bargaining sessions, which were often day-long affairs, the mission members spoke of giving Baluchistan and "Persian-speaking Central Asia" to the Amir, and a treaty was negotiated. Various members of the mission met secretly with what Pratap terms the "Amanullah party" and its influential members Inayatullah and Nadir. According to Pratap, it was evident in the summer of 1917 that "the King of Afghanistan and the Crown Prince [Inayatullah] had become especially pro-British. Seeing that Turkey was defeated in Iraq, they did not consider it in the interest of the State to oppose their powerful neighbour" (Pratap, *My Life*, pp. 49–56).

treaty with Germany, making Afghan participation in the war contingent upon the arrival of a large military force, huge supplies of armaments, and a sizable amount of gold.[86]

Most of the members of the Niedermayer mission left Kabul on May 22, 1916. Though the mission had failed in its immediate object—to win Afghan support in the war—it had some success in stirring up trouble within the tribal belt, where there were scattered outbreaks against the British. Two of the most serious were a Mohmand attack, led by the Haji of Turungzai, and a Waziri revolt.[87] Despite the mission's failure, its place in the history of the Afghan nationalist-modernist movement is important. The modernists were more convinced than ever that complete political independence from Britain was essential before Afghanistan could successfully initiate modernization programs. Moreover, their position was greatly strengthened by the presence of Germans in Afghanistan in the role of champions of Pan-Islamism, providing tangible evidence that it was possible not only to collaborate with a Western power but also to obtain its assistance for the achievement of national goals.

THE RUSSIAN REVOLUTIONS OF 1917

Most of the reports of the February Revolution in Russia reached Afghanistan through the medium of the censored press of India, making details few and confused. However, two important points were clear: the Romanov dynasty had fallen, and the goals of the revolution were avowedly pacifist and non-imperialist.[88] Afghan nationalists greeted the revolution with enthusiasm, believing that it greatly increased the prospects of the Muslims of Russia. They expressed their hope that the Russian Muslims would attempt to take advantage of their new political opportunities to shape their own future.[89]

The revolution sharpened the desire of the modernist-nationalists to secure Afghanistan's complete sovereignty. It also led them to step up their agitation for the liberation of India from colonial rule. In this connection, *Siraj al-Akhbar* printed the text of a telegram sent by the Indian National Committee to the Muslims of Russia (August 22, 1917), in which the Indians thanked the Russian Muslims for their offer to assist in the liberation of the Muslims of Asia and Africa, expressed their gratification at the Provisional Government's pledge to bring about the liberation of captive nations, and denounced the British for their continued subjugation and exploitation of some 315 million Indians.[90]

The actions of the Kerensky government and those of the Bolshevik regime that followed, as well as the general disintegration of the tsarist empire, had important implications for the Afghan nationalist movement. The Provisional Government's abolition of restrictions based on nationality and religion, endorsement in principle of the right of national self-determination, and renunciation of all imperialist designs in the East,[91] the Bolsheviks' "Appeal of the Council of People's Commissars to Muslims of Russia and the East" (November 24/December 7, 1917),[92] together with their disclosure of Allied wartime agreements and understandings,[93] denunciation of the Anglo-Russian Convention,[94] and withdrawal from the war—all seriously weakened Habibullah's argument that Afghanistan, caught between two contending empires, had to tread carefully both in international diplomacy and in pursuit of modernization, so as not to jeopardize its independence. The Amir's once legitimate fears of a two-front Anglo-Russian war against Afghanistan, which were in large part responsible for the country's neutrality, were no longer justified.*

The Afghan traditionalists and nationalists attacked the Anglo-Russian wartime understandings on Afghanistan, denouncing the British for their betrayal and ingratitude for Afghan neutrality.[95] Many Afghans began to realize that their "splendid isolation" had denied them the opportunity to capitalize on their unique strategic position between India, Persia, and Russia, and that, unless they combined socioeconomic development with political independence, Afghanistan's future was in jeopardy.[96] The modernists pressed publicly for an about-face, continuing to insist that total independence was essential before any steps toward modernization could be taken. They completely rejected the notion that any nation could maintain its internal independence and at the same time not control its own foreign relations: there was only one kind of independence—total independence. The *Siraj al-Akhbar* group denied that they were official or even semi-official spokesmen for the monarchy, but they readily accepted the role of spokesmen for the Afghan people.[97] They urged Habibullah to take advantage of the world political situation to free Afghanistan from British tutelage and to champion the cause of the Pathans of the North-West Frontier Province, the Ottoman Empire, and Pan-Islamism. They maintained that the Treaty of Brest Litovsk was the first international recogni-

---

* According to Toynbee (*Survey, 1920–1923*, p. 32), "After the breakdown of the Russian Empire in 1917, the sole inducement for Afghanistan to remain within the British orbit was removed (at any rate, for the time being), and events were to prove that the sudden cessation of pressure from the north had made a much greater impression on the Afghans than the victory of Great Britain and the remaining Allies in the General War, which occurred in the following year."

tion of Afghanistan's independence and a symbol of Ottoman-Afghan solidarity.[98] (The signing of that treaty, the Bolsheviks' endorsement of the principle of national self-determination, and Woodrow Wilson's formulation of his Fourteen Points had great impact on the Afghan intellectual community, where discussions of concrete political problems gave way to study of the larger question of the rights of men and nations under international law.)[99] Nationalist feeling grew even more intense when it appeared that there might be a Turkish-German push from the Caucasus to Transcaspia, a drive that might have carried the military activities to Herat itself.[100] The prospect of such an advance reinforced the nationalists' dreams of liberating Afghanistan.

In 1918, the writer Ikbal Ali Shah, claiming that his "views were shared by other patriotic and progressive Afghans," advanced a program that he hoped would divert Afghan nationalism and modernism from its anti-British course and save the Amir's personal power and prestige. That program foresaw the economic and military development of Afghanistan through close Anglo-Afghan cooperation and partnership. Modernization under British sponsorship would strengthen the country, counter Turko-German political influence, and reduce anti-British sentiment. As a concrete step, Shah proposed that Britain provide facilities in India (at the military college at Quetta) for the training of Afghan officers, a move that would help establish closer Indian-Afghan commercial ties and partially compensate for the losses in Afghan trade caused by the disintegration of the Russian Empire. These British-trained officers, Shah felt sure, would become "missionaries of British friendship in high and influential circles."[101] Implicit in this proposal was the hope that the creation of a British-trained officer corps would be a modernizing influence in Afghanistan. (In 1919, Shah renewed his plea for British investment and assistance in the economic development of the kingdom, including the extension of the Indian railway system into Afghanistan.)[102]

Shah's proposals do not appear to have had any significant support in Afghanistan. Nor was any support likely as long as Afghan demands for total independence were not met. Habibullah sought to appease the Pan-Islamists and traditionalists by reviving the hope of a Central Asian Confederacy under the aegis of the Afghan monarchy.[103] He also wrote the viceroy of India on February 2, 1919, seeking cooperation in obtaining international recognition of the "absolute liberty, freedom of action, and perpetual independence of Afghanistan" at the Paris Peace Conference.[104]

The British, who on January 21, 1918, has suspended the Anglo-Russian Convention of 1907, met this request with an expression of gratitude for the Amir's wartime neutrality* and a declaration that Britain looked forward to Afghanistan playing a continued positive role in the defense of India, possibly even a role of political leadership in Central Asia. There were, however, some among the British who spoke out in favor of granting Afghanistan full independence and helping the country in its modernization program.[105]

Habibullah's belated move to enlist British cooperation in achieving Afghanistan's independence did not satisfy the impatient Afghan nationalists. As Sykes noted, "with the complete defeat of Turkey by a Christian power and the occupation by the victors of some of the Holy Places of Islam, fanaticism was aroused, together with bitter feeling that Afghanistan had failed Islam in the hour of need."[106] The nationalists were all the more dissatisfied because the Amir considered independence an end in itself, whereas they considered it only a beginning. In their view, Habibullah's dilatoriness indicated that he had failed to appreciate fully the great changes in the international situation, especially in Russia, and to take advantage of new political opportunities by supporting and encouraging the nationalist movement.

In the end, Habibullah was to pay with his life for his determination to observe his treaty obligations with the British and for his failure to heed the demands of the Afghans for full independence. He was assassinated on February 20, 1919, at Jalalabad.†

* Wrote Barton: "But for his support, Britain might have been compelled to divert three or four divisions of British troops from the Western front at what might have been a critical period. Reactions in India, especially on the Moslems, would have been serious if we had let the borderland go" (*India's NW Frontier*, p. 141).

† Marin ("L'Entrée," p. 141) suggests that the assassination of the Amir was the belated result of the Turko-German mission's intrigues. Raskolnikov, a Soviet envoy to Afghanistan, in a very interesting article entitled "The War in Afghanistan," attributed the assassination to the Amir's failure "to take into consideration the changes and developments which the World War and the October Revolution had brought about in the international position of Afghanistan." He asserts: "After the October Revolution the Soviet Union was practically at war with Great Britain [but] Habibullah did not understand how to exploit these international differences in favour of the national interests of his country, and for this incompetency he paid with his life" (p. 181). Shah Wali Khan Ghazi concurs, noting (p. 5) that despite numerous promises of aid and changes in the international situation, the Amir failed to solve the problem of independence.

Chapter Nine

Amanullah Khan, Ill-Fated Champion of Modernization

The assassination of Habibullah sparked a struggle for power between the reformist-modernist and conservative-traditionalist forces in Afghanistan. The Amir's youngest son, Amanullah Khan, led the reformist group, Nasrullah Khan, the Amir's brother, the conservative opposition. Nasrullah spoke not only for the anti-British faction at court but also for those who opposed technological innovation and change, especially institutional change.

The outcome of the power struggle was determined as much by political circumstances as by ideological considerations. Amanullah's mother, Ulya Hazrat, was the chief wife of the assassinated ruler and a member of the powerful Barakzai clan ;[1] her influential position considerably increased the young prince's political prospects. Moreover, Amanullah, who was the governor of Kabul province, was in Kabul at the time of the assassination and controlled the Kabul garrison, arsenal, and treasury.[2] Finally, the traditionalists made serious tactical errors : in the confusion following the assassination they failed to initiate a thorough investigation of the crime, and at Jalalabad hurriedly proclaimed Nasrullah Amir, neglecting to consult the tribal chieftains. These mistakes provided Amanullah powerful psychological and political weapons. Describing himself as a legitimist, he denounced as suspect the late Amir's entourage at Jalalabad and demanded an investigation of the regicide.

Thanks to Amanullah's personal popularity, the rallying of the Barakzais, and the support of the army (gained in part by a pay hike for both regulars and officers),[3] he was proclaimed Amir of the Afghan kingdom (February 21–22, 1919). Maintaining that his legitimacy and his mandate to rule emanated from the "Afghan nation,"[4] the new ruler addressed his first proclamation to the nation and the army, deliberately omitting any mention of the religious establishment. One of his first acts was to order the arrest of his uncle and most of the members of Habibullah's entourage, pending investigation of the assassination, an astute move that immobilized the leadership of the traditionalist forces, and, for a time, even the moderate forces : among those arrested were many members of the Musahiban family, including Nadir Khan, the commander-in-chief of the Afghan forces; they were soon found innocent, however, and released. Nasrullah died in jail. Amanullah, after gaining full control of the country, addressed himself to the task of achieving full independence for Afghanistan, a task that resulted in the Third Anglo-Afghan War.*

Afghan, British, and Russian historians disagree on the origin, course, and outcome of this third Afghan war. The Afghans claim that war was forced on them by the British, but they are ambiguous on the question of who started the actual hostilities.[5] All Afghan historical literature claims a total Afghan military and political victory.[6]

The official British position, set forth in state papers at the time[7] and elaborated on by a number of British writers since, is that the war had its genesis in the wild hopes and plots of the Afghans. According to this view, the Afghans wanted to make use of Indian nationalist movements and Pathan strength and support to regain the Punjab.[8] Other British writers assert that internal political considerations prompted Amanullah to initiate the conflict. Sykes, for instance, writes that Amanullah's condemnation of Nasrullah and release of the suspect Musahiban family so alienated the mullahs and the army that "the young and impetuous monarch" decided he could unite the nation only by proclaiming a jihad against the British.[9] Molesworth, too, finds the immediate cause of the war in the internal situation in Afghanistan. He maintains that Amanullah was strongly suspected of complicity in his father's murder, and that he attacked India as a "suitable and popular diversion."[10] All British sources claim a military victory for Great Britain.

Recent Soviet accounts of the war place the blame squarely on British imperialism, contending that the British launched an aggressive war, forcing the Afghans "to take up arms for the defense of their native land and their freedom."[11] Soviet historians give their country a good deal of credit

---

* Inayatullah Khan, who had been groomed by Habibullah as his successor, became a victim of the Nasrullah-Amanullah rivalry. A political moderate and a "Westernizer," Inayatullah chose upon the death of his father to recognize Nasrullah, his uncle, as Amir. Nasrullah then named him vice-regent. Consequently, in the ensuing power struggle he was ignored as the rightful heir to the throne. However, Amanullah directed his struggle not against Inayatullah but against Nasrullah, though Inayatullah was arrested along with the other members of Habibullah's entourage. Later freed from house arrest, he became reconciled with Amanullah and recognized him as Amir. In 1929, when Amanullah abdicated, Inayatullah became the ruling monarch, but only for a few days. His remaining years were spent in exile.

for the success of the Afghan war of independence. A. Kh. Babakhodzhaev, for one, asserts that it was the Red army's "liberation of Merv" (May 23, 1919) and the Soviet Republic's diplomatic recognition of Afghanistan that thwarted British plans to renew the war by launching an attack from Persia or Bukhara.[12]

These various schools of thought notwithstanding, the genesis of the Third Anglo-Afghan War must be found in the development of Afghan nationalism and the rising social and political expectations in the country. Amanullah made a point of promising to lead his subjects to "total liberation" in his first royal proclamation, and this promise did much to rally Afghan public opinion to his support.[13] Because of it he was able to woo the traditionalists and to channel nationalism into the path of modernism. He was therefore firmly committed to obtaining, either by negotiation or by military action, total independence. The route by which he came to the throne had been a departure from the traditional patterns of succession established by the tribal code and Islamic law; that in itself implied a sense of national urgency. In 1919, no ruler could have succeeded in establishing a strong hold over the Afghan nation without pledging himself to the cause of total Afghan independence. Sykes tacitly recognized this in writing that after World War I, in view of Habibullah's "inestimable services, the independence of Afghanistan should surely have been promptly acknowledged. By such a statesmanlike act the Amir, who had lost his popularity owing to his loyalty to our cause, might well have recovered it and have escaped assassination. This tragedy undoubtedly led to the Third Afghan war."[14]

The method Amanullah chose to obtain total sovereignty was to present the British government in India with a *fait accompli*: he informed the viceroy of his accession to the Afghan throne and proclaimed the full independence of Afghanistan.[15] The viceroy was slow to reply; when he did so, his answer was evasive and made no direct reference to the proclamation of independence. The British took the position that the Dane-Habibullah Treaty was a dynastic agreement and not subject to unilateral abrogation. This position came as no great surprise to the Afghans; they took it for granted the power that had "taken the Afghan independence would not surrender [its] rights easily without war."[16]

The Afghans made intensive preparations for the forthcoming struggle and attempted to make use of postwar political developments in Central Asia and nationalist sentiment in India to further their cause. They campaigned vigorously among the Pathan tribesmen, spreading nationalist-religious propaganda and distributing arms in the tribal belt. These efforts were greeted with great enthusiasm by the Afghan public and raised the hopes of the army and of those border tribes that favored total Afghan independence.[17] Afghan leaders urged all Afghans who were true Muslims and patriots to prepare themselves for the struggle against Great Britain, "the traditional foe of Afghan independence."[18]

The British prepared themselves as well, and when negotiations between the two countries failed, hostilities began.* For a number of reasons the timing of the war was favorable to the Afghan cause. The Russian Empire had disintegrated. The Germans, Turks, and Soviets had already recognized Afghanistan's independence by the Treaty of Brest Litovsk. There were widespread social and political disturbances in Egypt as well as in India. The Indian nationalists were protesting the use of Indian troops and money for British imperialist purposes,[19] while the British public and army were demanding demobilization and a reduction of the financial burden of supporting imperial commitments.[20] According to Harold Nicolson, the Afghans—and other Asian nationalists—seemed to realize that the Great Power system had collapsed, that "the Allied powers had surrendered to President Wilson and Russia in accepting the principle of self-determination and no annexations." Said Nicolson: "Even to the simplest minds, imperialism, however disguised, was a violation of that principle. That old trade-union, the Concert of Europe, had been dissolved. A tribunal had suddenly sprung into existence to which an appeal could be made against the machine guns of the Western Powers. The tribunal was the tribunal of world, as distinct from European opinion."[21]

During the war, the British Royal Air Force bombed Jalalabad and Kabul. At Jalalabad, which was bombed twice, the military installations were partially destroyed; at Kabul a powder factory and the city's fort were hit.[22] Despite the Afghans' intensive preparations, they were not ready for this type of warfare. Their army, weak in organization and logistics, could not stand a major and protracted military conflict. As a result, the war was fought in a series of small engagements. The Afghan army was unable to make a general advance. Its only noteworthy military success was the capture of the fort of Thal by the forces of Nadir Khan, an achievement that drew the support of Waziri and Mahsud tribesmen.[23] However, the Afghans did not receive the massive support of the Pathan tribes, as they had hoped. Thanks to an energetic political and military

---

* War broke out when regular Afghan troops crossed the frontier at several points and occupied strategic positions in the Khyber Pass. The government of India counteracted with military measures, and the viceroy sent a strong protest to the Amir, asking him to take "immediate steps to restrain his subjects." See the May 8 communiqué of the India Office, in *The Near East*, May 16, 1919, p. 449.

campaign conducted by the British authorities* and an Afghan defeat in Khyber, a general uprising of the Pathan tribes was forestalled.

The Afghans, unwilling and unable to carry on a prolonged war against a technically superior foe, sued for an armistice on May 28, 1919. In the face of stiff Afghan resistance and the constant threat of a general uprising in the tribal belt, the British accepted the armistice, and in the Treaty of Rawalpindi signed on August 8, 1919, recognized Afghanistan as a fully sovereign state.[24] (The British subsequently revoked their subsidy to the Amir and halted the import of arms through India.) Amanullah paid a price for Afghan independence, however: he was forced to recognize the Durand Line.[25] The effect was to allow the British to strengthen their position in the Pathan tribal belt and to dim the Afghan hope of establishing moral and political control in that region.

AMANULLAH'S FOREIGN RELATIONS

After some confusion and hesitation, Amanullah's foreign policy followed three distinct paths: he established diplomatic relations with Soviet Russia, gradually normalized Afghanistan's relations with Britain, and strove for solidarity within the Muslim world. He was able to reestablish the balance of power that had been destroyed by the provisions of the Anglo-Russian Convention. More important, Afghanistan's new freedom of action allowed him to check the ambitions of Soviet Russia and the British by playing off one against the other.

Even before Afghanistan had gained its independence, Amanullah had communicated his desire to Russia to establish "permanent, free and friendly relations." On April 7, 1919, soon after his accession, two letters were sent to Moscow. One was from Mahmud Tarzi, who had been named foreign minister. Addressed to the Commissariat of Foreign Affairs of Russia, it informed the "Great President of the Russian Republic [Lenin] of the enthronement of the benevolent Amir Amanullah Khan." The second letter was a personal note from Amanullah to the "Honorable President of the Great Russian Republic." In it, Amanullah stressed the fact that Afghanistan was free and independent, and pointed out that the Afghan "psychology had always contained in it ideas of equality, humanity and liberty."[26]

Lenin replied on May 27, 1919, congratulating the Amir and the Afghan

---

* Most of the Mohmands and the Afridis stayed neutral during the war, and the British authorities managed to secure the cooperation of various Indian rulers and tribal leaders. See the May 15 communiqué of the India Office, in *The Near East*, May 23, 1919, p. 477, and *ibid.*, June 13, 1919, p. 560.

people for their heroic defense of their liberty and accepting the proposal
to establish diplomatic relations.[27] That same month an "Afghan" mission headed by one Maulvi Barakatullah arrived in Moscow. Disclaiming
any official status or relationship with the Afghan government, Barakatullah asserted that he was neither a communist nor a socialist, but an Asian
nationalist interested in ousting the British from India. In that respect, he
declared, the Russians and the Asian nationalists were natural allies.[28]

The Soviet authorities held precisely the same view. They saw great
possibilities in an alliance with Afghanistan against Great Britain, especially in view of Afghanistan's strategic position as a gateway to Asia and
the great nationalist-religious influence the Afghans could bring to bear on
the Muslims of India.[29] Mindful of the important repercussions an Anglo-
Afghan conflict might have in the Muslim world, Lenin even encouraged
Amanullah to continue pursuing Pan-Islamism as a goal.* In a letter to
the Afghan ruler dated November 27, 1919, Lenin wrote that Afghanistan was "the only independent Muslim state in the world, and fate sends
the Afghan people the great historic task of uniting about itself all enslaved
Mohammedan peoples and leading them on the road to freedom and independence."[30]

The two countries signed a treaty on September 13, 1920, at Kabul; it
was ratified by the Soviets on February 28, 1921, and by the Afghans in
August 1921.[31] The treaty placed Afghanistan in a much stronger bargaining position in its relations with Great Britain. The Afghans were
given free and untaxed transit through Russian territory of all goods,
whether purchased in Russia or abroad (Article 6), and were promised
one million gold rubles a year and other aid (Article 10). In Article 8, "The
actual independence and freedom of Bukhara and Khiva, whatever form of
government may be in existence there," was recognized. This provision
was a concession to the Afghans and greatly enhanced Amanullah's position as a champion of Islamic solidarity. The Afghans, for their part,
agreed not to enter into military or political agreements that might be
prejudicial to the interests of either party (Article 3), and gave the Russians permission to open five consulates in Afghanistan (Article 4). According to *The Times* of London, Russia was also to establish a powerful
radio station at Kabul and to supply engineers to improve Afghanistan's

---

* According to M. N. Roy, Lenin saw in colonial liberation movements led by the national bourgeoisie an objective, historically progressive revolutionary force. In this
context, even Pan-Islamism was seen as a revolutionary movement and thus deserving
of the support of the world communist movement. The success of Kemal Ataturk in
Turkey was considered to be of ultimate benefit to the Bolsheviks. See M. N. Roy, pp.
390–411, 538. Stalin regarded Amanullah's struggle as a revolutionary one, since it
tended to weaken, disorganize, and undermine imperialism. See M. G. Reyser, p. 27.

communications. *The Times* speculated that such improvements might include a better road between Turkestan and Afghanistan, a telegraph line between Kabul, Kandahar, and Kushk, on the Soviet-Afghan border, and the creation of an Afghan air force, with Soviet planes and instructors.[32]

Concurrently, Amanullah moved to establish diplomatic relations with other European countries and the United States, and instructed Tarzi to send a diplomatic mission to various states expressly for that purpose. The mission, headed by Muhammed Wali Khan, visited Belgium, France, England, the Baltic States, Poland, Italy, and the United States.[33] Between 1921 and 1922, the Afghans succeeded in establishing diplomatic ties with France, Italy, and Germany. In the United States, the mission was received by President Harding on July 26, 1921, an act that constituted official recognition of both Amanullah and Afghanistan's independence.* Harding also forwarded a letter to the Amir advising him that the question of diplomatic representation in Afghanistan would be given serious consideration.[34]

Afghanistan's establishment of diplomatic relations with Turkey and Persia was particularly important. The Turkish nationalists, especially Jemal Pasha, had played a great role in cementing Soviet-Afghan relations: they had made a great effort to allay the Afghans' distrust of Russia and to convince them that Russia could help the Pan-Islamic cause in the East.[35] Amanullah himself made the importance of the Turkish role clear. In a letter to Lenin in December 1920, he stated that Jemal Pasha had explained to the Afghans "the noble ideas and intentions of the Soviet Republic regarding the liberation of the Eastern world" and had told them of the moral and material assistance Turkey had received from the Soviet Republic.[36]

A Turko-Afghan treaty was concluded on March 1, 1921, affirming Turkish independence and recognizing Afghanistan "as independent in the most real and complete sense of the word" (Article 1). The right of all Oriental nations to absolute freedom and independence was acknowledged (Article 2). Afghanistan and Turkey agreed not to make agreements with a third state, if either country objected, and to inform each other before concluding a treaty with any state (Article 5). In theory, this provision gave each country a voice in the other's foreign policy. The Turks

---

* In 1925, Nadir Khan, then minister to France, discussed a treaty of friendship with the United States ambassador in Paris. A draft treaty was forwarded to Secretary of State Kellogg, who advised the ambassador to inform Nadir that the draft would be studied. There is no record of further negotiations on the subject. See United States, Department of State, *Papers*, pp. 557–58: Nadir to Herrick, October 30, 1925; and pp. 559–60: Kellogg to Herrick, January 26, 1926.

promised to send educational and military missions to Afghanistan for at least five years and to renew them thereafter if the Afghan government so desired (Article 8). The treaty had very definite Pan-Islamic overtones. The two signatories hailed the awakening of the Orient as the handiwork of Almighty God, recognized the independence of Khiva and Bukhara, acknowledged the necessity of establishing close contacts and relations with all the Muslim powers, and specifically recognized Turkey as the guide of Islam and the upholder of the Caliphate (Article 3).[37]

This treaty was a most important one for Amanullah and the Afghan modernists, for Turkish military and cultural assistance was consonant with Islamic solidarity and thus represented a channel through which modernity could be ushered into Afghanistan. As the seate of the Caliphate, Turkey had great prestige and could help neutralize the opposition of the traditionalists.

On June 22, 1921, Afghanistan concluded a Treaty of Friendship and Neutrality with Persia. Its economic clauses were especially important (particularly Article 7): they represented the first customs and postal agreements between the two countries.[38] In concluding a treaty with Persia, Amanullah not only greatly strengthened Afghanistan's diplomatic position in the Middle East but also enhanced his personal prestige, particularly among the Shi'ah Muslims of his own country. Both of the new treaties were hailed by the Afghan nationalist-modernists. Moreover, Pan-Islamists everywhere welcomed the political rapprochement of the three countries, seeing in it the beginning of a moral and political reconstruction of the Muslim world.[39]

AMANULLAH AND PAN-ISLAMISM

In the early years of his reign, Amanullah pursued a militantly Pan-Islamic policy. Soon after his accession to the throne, an attempt was made to improve Afghanistan's relations with neighboring Bukhara. In this connection, the Amir's mother addressed a long letter to Said Mir Alim-Khan, the Emir of Bukhara, in which she argued that renewed Muslim solidarity was essential to the peoples of Bukhara and Afghanistan, as well as to the rest of the Muslim world. In this regard, Afghanistan had demonstrated its good will and sincerity, she wrote: Amanullah had made his treaty with Russia conditional on Russian recognition of the independence of Bukhara.[40]

In a speech delivered on the first anniversary of his father's assassination, Amanullah declared that he saw "the shadow of a great and terrible calamity hovering over" the Muslim world: the Great Powers of Europe were contemplating the destruction of the Caliphate as an institution. He was pleased, he said, that the Muslims of India, who enjoyed the support of the Hindus, had resolved either to declare holy war or to emigrate from India, if the issue of the Caliphate was not resolved according to the wishes of the Muslims. He pointed out that he himself had written the British to inform them that "no Muslim can tolerate any interference in the affairs of the Caliphate no more than he can witness his Caliph submitted to any controls. A combination of such sort is not compatible with the pride and dignity of Afghanistan." Amanullah noted with favor that both the United States and France were inclined to disassociate themselves from the anti-Caliphal policy of Great Britain, and he warmly praised the Russians for their policy toward the Muslim world. Expressing his determination to support the Caliphate and to die for the cause of Allah, he called for Muslim unity. At the same time he also pleaded for Muslim dedication to the cause of progress and modernism, which alone would save the Islamic world from destruction or impotence.[41]

In an attempt to promote his stature as a champion of Pan-Islamism, Amanullah took credit, at least tacitly, for securing Russia's commitment to the independence of Bukhara and Khiva.[42] In October 1919, responding to the appeal of the Emir of Bukhara, he sent men and material to help the Bukharan principality in its struggle against revolutionary forces and the Red army. To enhance Afghan political influence and to bolster the Emir's position, Amanullah established diplomatic relations with the ruler of Bukhara. He also established contacts with the leaders of the anti-Soviet religious-nationalist Basmachi movement in Turkestan, helping them with arms and possibly with men as well. Afghan policies in Central Asia went beyond the confines of mere Pan-Islamic solidarity: an independent Bukharan emirate could have served as a buffer against Russia and its interests in Afghanistan; the Afghans could use their support for Bukhara as a bargaining point in their relations with Britain and exploit the fears of a "Red menace" to India; and, if the secession of Turkestan from Russia became a permanent reality, Bukhara could become a focal point for an Afghan-dominated Central Asian Confederation.[43]

Amanullah also supported the religio-political Khilafat movement in India, whose adherents called for the right of self-determination for all peoples and for the preservation of the temporal and spiritual authority of the Ottoman Sultan; they also fought against the breakup of the Ottoman Empire. Many of these Indian Muslims, who regarded the preservation of the Ottoman Empire and the spiritual leadership of its ruler as essential to the unity and welfare of all Muslims, finally denounced the British for their policies toward the empire and the Caliphate, and for their oppressive and "infidel" rule in India, and left India in the summer of 1920.[44] During this *hijrat* (emigration), more than 18,000 Muslims poured into Afghanistan, where they were welcomed by Amanullah. The majority of them were poor. Because they had been so promised by their leaders, they expected not only hospitality but land as well.[45] In the midst of the Afghans' alarm over these expectations, almost demands, Amanullah was invited by some of the refugee leaders to invade India and liberate the Muslims. In India, Muhammad Ali, one of the leaders of the Khilafat movement, proclaimed that were the Afghans to invade India, it was the duty of the Muslims to join the struggle.[46]

Meanwhile, the establishment of a Soviet government in Bukhara (September 1920), ending in the flight of the Emir of Bukhara to Afghanistan, and the continued struggle of the Basmachi movement offered Amanullah new opportunities to enhance his position as a Pan-Islamic leader. He spurned the friendly overtures of the Soviet government of Bukhara, resisted the diplomatic protests and pressures of Soviet Russia, and gave refuge to the Emir of Bukhara. Material, political, moral, and perhaps even financial support were given to the Basmachis,[47] who used northern Afghanistan as a base of operations. Amanullah also established contact with Enver Pasha, by this time leader of the Basmachi movement.*

Amanullah's nationalist, anti-British, and Pan-Islamist actions and exhortations won him praise throughout the Muslim world. Muhammed Iqbal, the renowned Muslim philosopher-poet of India, dedicated his famous poem *Payam-i-Mashriq* [The Message of the East] to the Afghan Amir. Another poet, Vahid-e Dastgardi, a Persian, hailed the Amir's devotion to Islam and Pan-Islamism in a work entitled *Chekame-ye ittihad-e Islami* [Qasida on Islamic Unity].[48] The Amir also reaped great political and psychological rewards from his active support of the Pan-Islamic cause. During the Third Anglo-Afghan War, for instance, this policy reinforced Afghanistan's religious bonds with the Pathan border tribes and

---

* Driven out of the Ottoman Empire following World War I, Enver sought refuge first in Germany and then in Soviet Russia, posing as a "national-bolshevist." He proposed to the Bolsheviks that he help incite and organize the Muslims of the Middle East for a revolt against British imperialism. He also volunteered to establish contact with the Khilafat and other Pan-Islamist movements, as well as with the Pathan tribes of the North-West Frontier Province, with the thought of using Afghanistan as a base of operations for a revolutionary movement in India. See M. N. Roy, pp. 298ff, 404–12, and *passim*. Once in Turkestan (1921), he double-crossed the Russians, becoming the leader of the Basmachis. As such, he issued an ultimatum to Russia demanding the restoration of Bukharan and Khivan independence. He died in battle in August 1922. For details on his activities in Turkestan, see Castagné, *Les Basmatchis*, pp. 45–55; and Baymirza Hayit, *Turkestan im XX. Jahrhundert*, Darmstadt, 1956, pp. 185–97.

the Muslims of India, which in turn strengthened the country's military and political position in the struggle with the British government of India. The Amir was also more easily able to promote closer relations with Turkey and Persia and to gain the moral support of other Muslim leaders of the Middle East. More important, the Amir's Pan-Islamic policies united the Afghans themselves. Some of the most influential Afghan religious leaders, who had received their training at Deoband, and were both militantly Pan-Islamic and actively anti-British,[49] joined the modernist-nationalists in support of Amanullah's Pan-Islamic policies.

Nevertheless, after 1922 Amanullah was forced to curb his militance in this area. Economic and political considerations required that he seek a normalization of relations with Great Britain and abandon his policy of active intervention in Soviet Central Asia. His limited financial resources and the country's landlocked position precluded long-range and expensive Pan-Islamic activities. In simultaneously alienating the Soviets and the British, he would have isolated Afghanistan once again, thereby retarding its socioeconomic development.

A major political consideration was the triumph of the Soviets in Central Asia. After the fall of the Emir of Bukhara, Amanullah's fears of a Soviet-sponsored revolutionary or irredentist movement among the ethnic minorities of northern Afghanistan understandably increased. He and his advisers may also have been concerned about the possibility of a communist revolutionary movement in Afghanistan. Indeed, the Comintern had already made some futile attempts in 1919 to penetrate and create revolutionary cadres in the country.[50] Afghanistan had been one of the targets of a general propaganda campaign that the Comintern had launched from Germany. As part of that campaign, lithographed pamphlets written in native languages and advocating national and social liberation movements and uprisings had been distributed in quantity in various Eastern countries. An Afghan representative had attended an Eastern Communist Central Committee meeting held in Berlin in December 1919. Afghans had participated as well in the Comintern-sponsored Congress of the Eastern Peoples held in Baku in September 1920,[51] and, in fact, had a representative, Kara Tajiev, on the presidium of that congress. A recent Soviet study states that the "Afghan delegates, upon returning [to] their fatherland, did a great deal of work in carrying the liberating ideas of [the] October Revolution to the people."[52] Some reports indicate that a few Bolshevik agitators were active in the early 1920's in Herat and other urban centers, including Mazar-i-Sharif, one of the sites chosen by the Comintern Executive Committee (in 1924) as a propaganda center.[53] According to Fatemi, the flight of the Emir of Bukhara to Afghanistan and the many stories published in the papers about the Baku Congress convinced Amanullah "that his Bolshevist friends were merely waiting for a propitious moment to liquidate him and set up a Soviet government in Kabul."[54] Whether or not this was in fact the case, news of some of these activities undoubtedly reached the Afghan government, which energetically resisted the dissemination of Bolshevik propaganda on Afghan soil, even as it sought to maintain friendly diplomatic relations with Soviet Russia and the Soviet regimes in Central Asia.[55]

Despite British alarmists, who tended to regard Amanullah as a Soviet "Trojan horse," the Afghan ruler insisted that all Russian arms sent to Afghanistan for eventual use in a national liberation movement in India be transported by the Afghan government, and that all Indian revolutionaries entering Afghanistan be disarmed. According to the Indian communist M. N. Roy, the Afghans made it clear that they had no intention of allowing any Soviet force to enter their territory and use it as a base of operations against India, nor did they desire to participate in such an operation.[56]

In the end, Amanullah drifted back to the traditional policy of seeking a balance of power in the area. In part he was led to do so by his increasing apprehensions about Soviet intentions, in part by Britain's consolidation in the North-West Frontier Province and strong diplomatic protests, even threats, to the Soviet government over Soviet activities (real or not) in Afghanistan against India.[57] This shift in policy meant a rapprochement with Great Britain, an idea that was repugnant to many Afghan traditionalists and some nationalists. (It also was bitterly opposed by Jemal Pasha, the former Young Turk minister, who in 1920–21 was engaged in the reorganization of the Afghan army and in anti-British political activities.)[58] Despite these objections, Amanullah signed a treaty with Britain on November 22, 1921. It provided for the establishment of legations in London and Kabul, and granted Afghanistan tax exemptions on materials destined to help modernize the country. One important feature was Afghanistan's agreement to keep Soviet consulates out of eastern Afghanistan.[59] Once this treaty was concluded, though Amanullah continued to lend moral support to various Pan-Islamic activities, he concentrated on internal reforms within Afghanistan. Anti-British revolutionaries like Mahendra Pratap, 'Obaid-ullah Sindhi,* and Mohammed Barakatullah

---

* 'Obaid-ullah asserts that Amanullah recognized him as a member of the "Provisional Government of India" and admitted him into his inner council, which decided matters relating to war and peace with India. He also intimates that his relations with Soviet Russia began at the initiative of Amanullah (Siddiqi, p. 384).

(the "president," "prime minister," and "foreign minister," respectively, of the "Provisional Government of India") no longer found a haven in Afghanistan.[60] Amanullah assured his admirers throughout the Muslim world that the Anglo-Afghan pact would in no way make him indifferent to the fate of the Muslims, the Pathan tribes, and the Caliphate. Nevertheless, the Afghan periodical *Ittihad-i-Mashriqi* on June 17, 1922, set the tone of the new Afghan foreign policy: Afghanistan was to seek friendly relations with all countries.

REFORMS IN EDUCATION

Amanullah's nine-year reign was a period of major reforms. As early as February 1919, he made it clear that his ultimate goal was the transformation of Afghanistan into a modern state:

By the Grace of God our sublime Government will employ such measures of reform as may prove suitable and useful to the country and nation so that the Government and nation of Afghanistan may make and gain great renown in the civilized world and take its proper place among the civilized powers of the world. For the rest, I pray to God for his favors and mercy and seek his help for the welfare and prosperity of you Muslims and all mankind. From God I seek guidance and the completion of my wishes.[61]

His first reform measures were in the field of education, to which he attached paramount importance. In order to reorganize and strengthen the educational system, the Amir hired Egyptian and Turkish teachers and negotiated for the establishment of a permanent French educational mission in Afghanistan. In the meantime, Alfred Foucher, a Sorbonne professor and the head of the first French archaeological mission to Afghanistan (1922), was assigned the task of designing a new system of higher education.[62] Three new secondary schools were founded; all were along the lines of Habibiya, though each used a different foreign language as the medium of instruction.[63] The first, Amaniyeh, was founded in 1922. Named after Amanullah, the school was renamed Lycée Istiklal (Independence) after his fall. It was patterned after the French schools, and classes were taught in French. The staff consisted of five French professors (one of them a woman) and 12 Afghan instructors.[64] By 1926, Amaniyeh had some 300–350 students.[65]

In 1923, Amani, a school modeled after the German schools, was established. Like Amaniyeh, it was named for Amanullah; it, too, was later given a new name—Najat (Liberation). Amani was under the supervision of one Dr. Iven, whose staff included three German professors and a few Afghan teachers.[66] In the period 1924–26, the school had about 100 students.[67] In 1927, the third school, Ghazi (Victor), was founded; its classes were taught in English. The first baccalaureate examinations were offered at Habibiya in the same year.[68]

Amanullah founded other schools as well. In 1924, he established a four-year school of administration (Maktab-i-hukkam). Its emphasis was on accounting and arithmetic. Turkish was taught as a second language, since Amanullah intended to pattern the Afghan administrative apparatus along the Turkish model.[69] Future government workers were also taught administrative techniques by the governor of Kabul, who was required to conduct courses in administrative law.[70] In order to improve the quality of the teachers and to train new ones, the teacher-training center founded by Habibullah was expanded and given a systematic curriculum. English was the principal foreign language used there.[71]

Once the teacher-training program was under way, the government began to focus its attention on other professional schools. A small School for Fine and Applied Arts was organized, and other specialized schools were founded from 1924 on. Among them were schools for the instruction of foreign languages (notably English, French, German, Russian, and Turkish) and schools offering courses in telegraphy, glassmaking, masonry, and accounting. In general, all of these small schools were ill-equipped and poorly organized.[72] In 1928 a junior college was founded. Its student body was recruited from among the graduates of Afghanistan's four secondary schools. After completing the requirements of this institution, some of the students were sent abroad to continue their education, but the institution itself did not last long.[73] By 1928, according to Dr. Ténèbre, then director of Amaniyeh, there were 14 intermediary and secondary schools in Kabul as well as a secondary school in each of the provincial administrative centers.[74]

The goals of the new Afghan educational system, as described by Amanullah and Mahmud Tarzi (by this time Amanullah's principal adviser) were twofold: to cultivate an enlightened intellectual class in Afghanistan, an essential ingredient for successful reform and modernization, and to provide a group of able administrators for the monarchy. The Amir attempted to end public apathy toward education, using both persuasion and coercion: he had notices posted in public places advising his subjects to send their children to school and ordered all government servants to set an example by enrolling their own children; those who did not were subject to fine or dismissal.[75]

Both primary and higher education were free, and in fact students beyond the primary level were paid a small sum and reportedly clothed and fed, as an inducement to continue their schooling.[76] Efforts were made to establish government-supported maktabs in provincial areas, with modern subjects as part of the curriculum.[77] There are no records to indicate how much success the Amir's administration had in this area. What *is* clear is that in all the maktabs of the country the traditional curriculum continued to be given top priority and occupied at least half a school day, if not more. The modern courses that were added were apparently mathematics and the geography of Afghanistan.[78]

In general, the effect of the expansion of the modern educational system was to increase the competition between the traditional and modern institutions. It was still commonly believed that the only goal of education, whatever the level, was to reinforce the teachings of Islam, and the traditionalists continued to frown on the introduction of new subjects into the curriculum.[79] Amanullah, like his predecessors, had the enormous task of convincing the religious establishment that modern secular education and Islam were not incompatible, and that the new schools did not threaten the sanctity or spiritual message of Islam in Afghanistan. He was quite aware of the difficulties he faced, as is evidenced by this statement he made in an interview with Lowell Thomas:

We are keenly alive to the value of education. But to bring learning to my people must be a slow process. . . . We hope to lay our plans well and truly but not too fast. Religion must march hand in hand with learning, else both fall into the ditch. This country is rich in fine men and magnificent material resources, both as yet undeveloped.[80]

The hard line taken by the religious establishment prevented the implementation of some other educational plans. For instance, when consideration was given to establishing a university (Dar-ul-Ulum) in Kabul, no agreement could be reached on the basic orientation of the institution: was it to serve only the Muslim theological sciences and scholasticism, or was it to welcome the study of modern subjects, too?[81] However, the opposition of the traditionalists was only one of many problems Amanullah faced. Fierce national pride and sensitivity soon brought the Afghan modernists, even Amanullah, into conflict with the French and German educators who were in charge of the highest educational establishments of the country.[82] Moreover, though the Amir wanted to broaden the scope of the modern educational system and institute compulsory education for children between the ages of six and eleven,[83] he was confronted with a lack of qualified teachers; even if he had been able to win over the die-hard traditionalists, he would not have been able to institute compulsory primary education.[84] The school facilities were generally inadequate, and in many regions of the country there were none at all. Amanullah had neither the funds to implement his programs nor the wholehearted cooperation of the public that he sought: the most generous estimates place the total enrollment of the Afghan primary schools in 1928 at 40,000.[85]

There were a few other noteworthy developments in this and related fields under Amanullah's administration. One was the founding of an open-air theater in Paghman, where the first theatrical performance in Afghanistan was held ("The Conquest of Andalusia").[86] Also worthy of note was the conclusion of a cultural agreement with France. Signed in 1922, it gave a French archaeological mission the exclusive right to carry out excavations in Afghanistan and led to the founding of a modest museum in Kabul. Two other developments were even more important: the first Afghan students were sent abroad to study under government sponsorship, and the first schools for girls were opened in Afghanistan.

The principal reason for the introduction of three different educational systems into Afghanistan and for the teaching of new languages was to prepare Afghan students for study abroad.[87] In 1921, Hidayatullah Khan, the heir apparent, and 44 other Afghan youths, all from upper-class families, were sent to Paris to study at the Lycée Michelet.[88] (The French government provided the young Afghans interpreters and otherwise attempted to help them adjust to their new environment.) In 1922, another 40 students were sent to Europe, this time to Germany.[89] Still others were sent to Turkey, Persia, Switzerland, and England; one of Amanullah's brothers attended Oxford University. The Amir planned eventually to send a total of 300 students out of the country, 100 to Europe and the rest to India, but this plan was not realized.[90] Even so, the program as operated cost the Afghan government, at a conservative estimate, some 50,000 pounds a year. To their conservative critics, the Amir and the partisans of modernization justified both this expense and the sending of students to Western Europe on the basis of the Islamic dictum that bade the faithful to go "even to China" in pursuit of knowledge.[91]

Once the students were outside the country, many restrictions were placed on their conduct. They had to promise to fast during the month of Ramazan and to keep the other religious and national holidays of Afghanistan. When Christian students went to church or read the Bible, the Afghan students were to read the Quran to strengthen their own faith. They were to observe the restrictions imposed by the Quran on food and drink; they were forbidden to dance or to watch immoral shows or to have intimate relations with women. To defy any of these injunctions or to engage in activities contrary to the policies of the Afghan government meant a revocation of the student's scholarship and his recall to Afghanistan. To ensure compliance, a supervisor was assigned to keep track of the students and report on their activities to the Afghan government,[92] the government taking the position that the students could help reconstruct and advance their society only if they were true Muslims and upright Afghans.

An even more significant development was the attempt to initiate public schooling for girls in Afghanistan. This program, which began in 1921 with the founding of Essmat (later renamed Malalai), was not made a part of the regular educational system, but was operated autonomously under the patronage and guidance of the Amir's wife, Queen Sorayya, and Mrs. Mahmud Tarzi.[93] At the Essmat opening-day ceremonies, the Queen described the high social position that women had held throughout the history of Islam. It was her hope, she said, that the education of Afghan women would improve their social status and permit them to play a more useful role within the community, thereby contributing greatly to the health and happiness of Afghan society as a whole.[94] By 1928, there were about 800 girls attending schools in Kabul (Amaniyeh began accepting a few women that year),[95] and there were even some Afghan women studying abroad, notably in Turkey, France, and Switzerland.[96] At that time, Amanullah had plans to build five more schools for girls and intended his planned compulsory education system to apply to girls as well as boys.[97] Both projects were dropped after his fall in 1929.

Amanullah's efforts to provide educational opportunities for girls was only part of a more general program to improve the position of women in Afghanistan. At the time he took the throne Afghan women had few rights. Child marriages were common, and the laws of inheritance were most unjust. A widow had no legal rights; she had no control of her dead husband's goods and did not even have custody of their children. Veiling in public was strictly adhered to and rigidly enforced.[98] Amanullah, determined to improve this situation and maintaining that his support of the feminist cause was based on "the true tenets" of Islam, took more steps in this direction in his short rule than were taken by all his predecessors together.

One of the most important legal measures he enacted was the Family Code of 1921, which undertook to regulate marriages and engagements. Some token efforts at reform had been made in this area by Abdur Rahman and Habibullah, but none of their measures were as great in scope or as earnestly applied as those of Amanullah. Child marriage and intermarriage between close kin were outlawed as contrary to Islamic principles. In the new code Amanullah reiterated Abdur Rahman's ruling that a widow was to be free of the domination of her husband's family, followed his father's example and placed tight restrictions on wedding expenses, including dowries, and granted wives the right to appeal to the courts if their husbands did not adhere to Quranic tenets regarding marriage. One source reports that in the fall of 1924, Afghan girls were given the right to choose their husbands, a measure that incensed the traditionalist elements.[99]

In an effort to promote social consciousness among Afghan women, the Queen founded, in 1921, the first women's magazine in Afghanistan.[100] The weekly, *Irshad-i-Niswan* (The Guide for Women), was edited by Mrs. Mahmud Tarzi and provided recipes and useful tips (such as the formula for preparing face-powder); it also discussed social problems and the role of women in society. A few Afghan women began submitting articles to other publications in which they dwelt on the historical role of women in Islam and the great contributions of Afghan women during the war of independence. A typical article appeared in *Aïne-ye-Irfan*, the organ of the Ministry of Education. The same publication also carried accounts of feminine progress in Egypt and of the role of women in Europe.[101]

The presence in Kabul of a considerable number of unveiled women, especially Turkish women who had abandoned the veil and adopted modern dress, undoubtedly encouraged the efforts of the few Afghan feminists. However, their greatest support came from Amanullah himself. It was his belief that "the keystone of the future structure of new Afghanistan would be the emancipation of women."[102] Some of the steps he took were totally without precedent, most notably when he appealed directly to women and personally addressed women's groups to promote the feminist cause.[103] The Afghan press, including the bulletins of the War Office, took part in the emancipation campaign.[104] In 1928, during the final months of his rule, Amanullah made a frontal assault against the institution of *purda*, or veiling, "which hid half of the Afghan nation."[105] Because of his efforts and the personal example of Queen Sorayya, some 100 Afghan women had reportedly discarded the veil by October 1928.[106] Two incidents, unimportant in themselves, nevertheless had a symbolic significance bordering on the revolutionary: in 1927, *Anis* (Companion) began publishing a column on family and marital happiness, and in the same year, a group of Afghan women were taken for an airplane ride in the skies over Kabul.[107]

THE AFGHAN PRESS

Amanullah's administration made a major contribution in encouraging the importation of printing presses and assisting in the establishment of an Afghan press. Tarzi's *Siraj al-Akhbar* reappeared in Kabul in October

1919 under a new name, *Aman-i-Afghan* (Afghan Peace), and assumed the role of a semi-official paper.[108] Privately owned and operated papers began to appear soon after. In February 1920 *Ittihad-i-Mashriqi* (The Eastern Union) began publication in Jalalabad,[109] and that same year *Faryad* (The Clamor) and *Ittifaq-i-Islam* (The Concord of Islam) appeared in Herat. All four of these papers were written in Persian, though they occasionally carried articles and poems in Pashto. In northern Afghanistan, *Bidar* (The Wakeful) and *Ittihad-i-Islam* (The Union of Islam) began publication at Mazar-i-Sharif in 1920, *Ittihad-i-Baghlan* (Unity of Baghlan) was started in Baghlan in 1921, and *Ittihad-i-Khanabad* appeared at Kataghan in 1922. In Kandahar, *Tulu-e-Afghan* (The Afghan Sunrise) was started in 1921, and *Setare-ye-Afghan* (The Afghan Star) was begun in Kohistan. Kabul gained a second periodical, *Haqiqat* (The Truth), in 1923, and a third, *Anis*, four years later.[110] *Anis* was written in Pashto and was, in this sense, the first national paper.*

Under orders from the government, a number of ministries started publishing their own professional magazines. In addition to the Ministry of Education's *Aïne-ye-Irfan* (The Mirror of Knowledge), there were the Finance Ministry's *Majalle-ye-Sarwat* (Journal of Wealth) and the Ministry of War's *Askariyeh* (The Military).[111] Most of the new publications were issued monthly, fortnightly, or weekly; Afghanistan did not have a genuine newspaper until 1927, when *Aman-i-Afghan* began daily publication.[112] All of the papers were subject to government censorship,[113] and in reflecting the Amir's commitment to the reform and modernization of the country, were used to help rally public opinion in support of that goal.

The Afghan writers of the period continued to dwell on the three major themes that had so concerned the *Siraj al-Akhbar* circle: independence, nationalism, and, above all, modernization.[114] In stressing a nationalism that transcended ethnic and religious differences, they compared the nation to a family, united by the innumerable ties of common heritage, soil, climate, and way of life.[115] The concept of national unity as a religious duty remained a favorite subject, and it was made clear that, thanks to this unity, the Afghans had overcome the British.[116] Following in the

---

* The program of *Anis*, which was published in its first issue (May 5, 1927), read in part: "Anis is a newborn child in the world of publicity. It wants to become a friend in times of recreation, a helper during the hours of work, a counsellor in matters of difficulty, a comforter in circumstances of sorrow and grief, and in general, a companion and a servant in the intellectual and material life of everybody, especially of the class of Government functionaries." See Bogdanov, "Notes," p. 152.

best tradition of *Siraj al-Akhbar*, the Afghan journalists extolled science
and learning: unity without science was like an engine without fuel; only
through education could the Muslims regain their self-confidence, overcome the prevailing apathy, and catch up on lost time to reach the level
of civilization enjoyed by other nations; education could raise an ignorant
child to the level of an Aristotle or a Plato; education was the cure-all
for ignorance and misery, and Amanullah, its champion, was a great re-
deemer who had delivered his country from foreign rule and was hero-
ically trying to free his people from ignorance, want, and poverty.[117]

PUBLIC HEALTH AND COMMUNICATIONS

Comparatively little was achieved in the realm of public health under
Amanullah's rule. A few Turkish and German doctors were added to the
Kabul hospital staff, and one of Habibullah's palaces was converted into
a sanatorium for tubercular patients. Though the fruit sellers of Paghman
were ordered to protect their wares from flies with mosquito netting, it is
not clear whether the earlier anti-malaria campaign and the drainage of
marshlands continued.[118] The most significant development in the health
field was Amanullah's attempt to bring medical practice under state control. An examination and licensing system was instituted in an effort to
curb the practices of the unlettered hakims, and those who, through ignorance or negligence, prescribed the wrong medicines were subject to punishment, including loss of license, under a new penal code enacted in
1924.[119] In 1923 a German sanitation mission opened two hospitals, one
for men, the other for women.[120] In general, the few advances that were
made were confined to Kabul and had little impact; a shortage of doctors,
a lack of hospital facilities, and an almost total disregard for the most basic
principles of sanitation continued to be major national problems.

Amanullah was quite conscious of the importance of good communications. Among other things, he expanded the telephone system and introduced the telegraph. He evidently obtained the telegraph equipment itself
from Soviet Russia and other material with which to build a link between
Kabul and Herat from Britain. Telegraphic communication was also established between Peshawar and Kabul.[121] The postal, telegraphic, and
telephone services remained primitive, however, and the roads were still
in poor condition. After Afghanistan joined the International Postal
Union in 1927, Amanullah hired a French engineer to reorganize the en-

tire postal, telegraphic, and telephone system,[122] but the revolt of 1928 put an end to this project. In 1925, the first Afghan radio station began operating in Kabul, and in 1927 the government began negotiating with a French company for the purchase of two 100-watt transmitters similar to the one already in use; that project, too, was abandoned after the 1928 outbreak.[123]

In 1924 the Afghan government obtained its first five airplanes, which were purchased from Russia and were flown to Kabul by Soviet pilots; the occasion was hailed as one of great historical significance.[124] Later, the government purchased three Junkers from Germany and two planes from Great Britain,[125] and some 25 young Afghans were sent to Soviet Russia and Central Asia to be trained as pilots.[126] By 1928, an air link had been established between Soviet Central Asia and Afghanistan, and in the same year, the first flight between Kabul, Kandahar, and Herat was made by a Soviet pilot.[127] At one point, Amanullah considered establishing an Afghan civil aviation agency and discussed the project with the Turks, who had such an agency.[128]

During Amanullah's reign, old roads were repaired, and plans were made for new roads to link the capital with Afghan Turkestan, Peshawar, and Kandahar. Hotels were built in Kandahar, Jalalabad, Herat, and Kabul.[129] Once these plans were completed, Amanullah intended to establish a railway system in the country. In fact, his preoccupation with this question in part explains why relatively little was done in the way of roadbuilding in these years. American, German, and Russian engineers were at various times assigned to study the possibilities of connecting India and Central Asia,[130] but whatever the system, Amanullah intended to follow the advice of Abdur Rahman and build the first lines well in the interior: Kabul was to be the hub of any system, and only later were the tracks to be extended outward to the borders. The Amir built a small station in Kabul and set up a project for laying a track between Kabul and Dar-ul-Aman, a city that he hoped to make his new capital. The line was later to be extended from Kabul to Jalalabad.[131]

Like Abdur Rahman and Sher Ali, Amanullah was excited by the idea of building a new capital, a "metropolis" near Kabul.[132] What he obviously had in mind was a "scientific city"; when the first stone of Dar-ul-Aman was laid, he declared that the growth of a healthy urban population was conditional on an observance of the laws of hygiene, and that the cleanliness of the streets and the purity of the water were absolutely essential.[133]

ADMINISTRATIVE AND LEGAL REFORMS

Amanullah faced enormous administrative problems. Trained personnel were in short supply, and corruption and inefficiency were major concerns. Habibiya graduates had provided the main body of Afghan civil administrators in the World War I period and were in effect in charge of the political machinery of the government. The government attempted to raise the level of efficiency by instituting administrative training courses, and made an effort to eliminate corruption by ordering all civil servants to list their property holdings.[134] The first group of foreign-trained Afghans returned to the country after 1927,[135] but both the number and the training of the personnel remained inadequate. The police force, too, was inadequate, and Amanullah was led to fall back on the system of making villages collectively responsible for crimes committed in the region, a measure that had been primarily designed to maintain the security and safety of the trade routes.[136] The government helped organize municipal councils in various urban centers. The councilmen—the military commander, the mayor, and a prominent merchant of the area—were to address themselves to welfare and security problems.

The basic administrative structure of the country remained much as it was under Habibullah, though where he had divided the country into six provinces, Amanullah established five: Kabul, Kandahar, Afghan Turkestan, Herat, and Badakhshan. As before, there was a further division into districts.[137] Amanullah continued to centralize and institutionalize the administration of justice, a process that had begun during the reign of Abdur Rahman and was carried further by Habibullah. Under the supervision of the governors, justice was administered by government-paid district judges and magistrates. The Amir continued the practice of making the monarchy the final court of appeal, setting aside one day in the week to receive his subjects and hear their legal and administrative difficulties.[138]

Between 1921 and 1925, efforts were made to codify the Afghan criminal laws. The result was the Penal Code of 1924–25. The Amir clearly intended to bring the entire administration of justice under the direct and immediate control of the monarchy, as the preamble of the new code indicates: "Just as the right to pass sentences for crimes against the state belongs to the state, those crimes which are committed against an individual come under the jurisdiction of the state; so do religious and political crimes."[139] The new code had 308 provisions and separated crimes into three categories: serious crimes, such as adultery, consumption of alcoholic beverages, and theft, for which the code specified the punishments (*hadd*) already prescribed by Islamic law; major crimes, such as murder and intentional bodily injury, for which it also provided specific punishments (*qesas*); and lesser crimes, for which public and exemplary punishments (*ta'zirs*) were to be fixed by judges at their own discretion.

A notable innovation was a clause that allowed prisoners to apply to the government for a commutation of sentence or release. Such prisoners were required to produce evidence of their genuine remorse and rehabilitation, including witnesses who could testify to that effect and assure the authorities the convicts would be welcome back in their own communities. Orders for the release of prisoners sentenced to one year had to be approved by the provincial governor; for those sentenced to longer terms, the approval of the Ministry of Justice (terms of three to ten years) or of both the Ministry of Justice and the Afghan monarch (over ten years) was needed. There was another important innovation in Article 26, which read: "Persons under 15 years are not responsible for their crimes and shall be turned over to their parents. Above 15, they are responsible, but cannot be punished until they are 17. If the criminal is a woman, her latest year of responsibility is 15, but can be as early as 9 years. If she is pregnant, or shows other signs of maturity, she is considered responsible."[140]

A number of provisions dealt with civil and property rights. Officials resorting to torture to extract confessions were subject to dismissal; those meting out harsher sentences than prescribed by law or those entering private property without the owner's permission were subject to punishment (Articles 226–28). Private property was to be protected against exactions and demands for bribes on the part of government officials (Articles 229–33); soldiers and government officials were to pay for their food, and forced labor (*begar*) was outlawed (Article 234). There were also provisions against gambling, against story and fortune tellers, and against religious-legend singers. The penal code even attempted to prevent cruelty to animals: there were prohibitions against hanging live chickens by the feet in the bazaar, against bird and animal fights, and against overloading pack animals (Articles 274, 277, 279).

The monarchy retained the power to extend the death penalty to crimes that were not punishable by death under Shar'ia law (Article 15). A vaguely worded clause (Article 22) attempted to exclude a range of activities from the direct control of the religious establishment: "In situations where the carrying out of business breaks a law, or causes someone to break a law, canonically prescribed punishments are not to be applied." The penal code placed most crimes in the category of ta'zir, apparently in an attempt to extend the discretionary power of the judges and thereby allow the monarchy to extend its authority and its power to intervene or control the judiciary process.

Despite these attempts to modernize the judicial system and, in a few instances, to institute more humane laws, the penal code remained harsh and archaic. Prisoners who had been sentenced to terms of from one to three years were to sit in prison with one leg shackled and to be kept busy with work; "notoriously mean prisoners" were to have both legs shackled and were to be forced to work (Articles 10, 11). Public whipping remained a suitable punishment, though when women were involved, another woman was permitted to hold the victim's head during the punishment; whipping was to continue until the skin was broken (Article 13). Persons who drank, either publicly or privately, were to receive 80 strokes of the whip (Articles 86, 87). There were strict punishments for those who smoked hemp, hashish, or opium (Article 91) and for those who danced, professionally or otherwise; fathers or other relatives who allowed boys to dance were subject to punishment (Article 96). Sodomy with a young boy could bring the death penalty for both participants, if the boy was over fifteen (Articles 132–34). Adultery between a married man and a married woman brought death by stoning to both (Article 138). In cases of adultery between unmarried men and married women, the man was to receive 100 strokes of the whip and the woman was to be stoned to death (Articles 134, 142). In cases involving single people, both offenders were to be whipped 100 times (Article 143).

The new code extended the range of crimes against the state (Articles 33–45). Articles and speeches inciting unrest among the population were banned in Article 54, in effect the first censorship law in Afghanistan. Members of outlawed Muslim religious sects (Sabi, Zendiq, and especially Qadyani) were to be killed (Article 123).* Foreigners living in Afghanistan were to be subject to the same punishments as Afghan citizens (Article 18).

The importance of the new penal code lay in the fact that it represented a major attempt to increase the power of the secular authority at the expense of the religious establishment. Moreover, by providing a detailed

---

* On August 25, 1924, a Qadyani sheikh was stoned to death in Afghanistan, touching off major protests in India. On that occasion, *Aman-i-Afghan* stated that unrestricted liberty of conscience could not exist in Afghanistan; at the same time it affirmed a policy of tolerance toward Hindus, Christians, and Jews, on the condition that they paid the special tax levied on them and did not attempt to proselytize. See Pernot, *L'inquiétude de l'Orient*, pp. 38–39.

code for personal, social, and political crimes, it attempted to institutionalize many features of the Pushtunwali, thus bringing tribal justice, too,
under the control of the monarchy. In establishing a uniform code, Amanullah also attempted to bring the Shar'ia law and the Pushtunwali in line
with each other, for there were certain provisions of religious law, notably
those on inheritance and vendettas, that some tribes did not observe.[141]

Another of Amanullah's attempts at administrative reform, the drawing
up of the first national budget in 1922,[142] was noteworthy in that it represented the first effort to clearly distinguish between a public treasury and
the monarch's private funds. Even more important, however, was the pro-
mulgation, in 1923, of the first Afghan constitution. (It was officially
named Nizam-nama-e-Asasi-ye-Dovlat-e Aliyya-e Afghanistan and was
amended the following year.)[143] Made up of 73 articles, the constitution
institutionalized not only a cabinet system of government but also the Afghan monarchy. Articles 1 and 4 upheld the principle of an absolute and
hereditary monarchy, with the Afghan crown passing on to the direct male
descendants of the reigning Amir. Islam was declared the official religion
of the country, but the Hindu and Jewish communities were to enjoy religious freedom (Article 2). There was, however, a provision that required
them to pay a special tax and to wear distinctive emblems. The Amir was
declared the Defender of the Faith (Article 5), and his name was to be
mentioned in *khutbahs*, or sermons (Article 7). The constitution prohibited slavery (Article 16) and made elementary education both compulsory
and universal (Article 68). Foreigners were barred from teaching and
journalism, unless they were employed by the government (Articles 11 and
14) ; missionaries were forbidden entry into the country.

Although the monarchy remained essentially an absolutist institution,
the constitution provided for the formation of an advisory Council of State
and a number of other consultative bodies (Articles 39–49). These included the Durbar Shahi, which was composed mainly of Afghan noble-
men, predominantly Durrani tribal leaders, and the Khawanin Mulki,
which was made up of khans and maliks representing the people. Membership in the Durbar Shahi was hereditary, subject to the Amir's approval ;
half of the delegates to the Khawanin Mulki were nominated by the ruler,
the rest were elected by the people. For national emergencies and important
decisions, the Amir could, at his discretion, call a Great National Council,
or Loe Jirga ; this was essentially an extension of the traditional procedure provided by the tribal code. Amanullah retained full executive powers, including the position of supreme commander and that of last court of
appeal. A cabinet made up of ministers of education, commerce, war, jus-

tice, finance, and public security was chosen by him and was responsible only to him, although they were to give an account of their work and achievments to an Assembly of Notables once a year (Article 27).[144]

MILITARY AND ECONOMIC REFORMS

The Amir reorganized the army almost entirely along Turkish and German lines. He also established additional plants to manufacture military items, among them munitions factories equipped by the Krupp Company of Germany.[145] In addition to the airplanes he purchased from Russia, Germany, and Britain, he ordered some 100 trucks and small cars from Milan in 1928. His ultimate goal was a modern army of eight divisions.[146] As noted, some Afghans were sent to Soviet Russia and Central Asia for flight training; others were trained by Italian instructors brought to Afghanistan for that purpose, and still others were sent to France and Italy. Though the Italian government sent a team of military advisers and instructors to train an Afghan artillery corps (1927), and Germany, too, provided a few military instructors,[147] the overall supervision and training of the Afghan army was entrusted to Turkish officers. The main responsibility fell to a military mission headed by Gen. Kazim Pasha, a former chief of staff of the Turkish army. In addition, some 50 Afghan officers were sent to Turkey for advanced training.[148] (Earlier, in 1919–21, Amanullah had attempted to enlist the services of Turkish officers who had been prisoners in Siberia and wanted to return home.)[149] The Afghan officer corps was outfitted in new uniforms that included a black astrakhan cap, a Sam Browne belt, and Turkish cavalry boots.[150]

The Afghan tribes deeply resented the Amir's attempts to democratize the conscription system by making it universal[151] and, in fact, resisted conscription of any kind. Because of this and probably because of the Amir's own wish for an army that would transcend tribal and feudal loyalties, the regulars were recruited chiefly from among the ethnic minorities.[152] These recruits usually served two years.

The strongest elements in the Afghan economy were trade and the government workshops. Though Amanullah had some new workshops built, notably soap and match factories, and imported large quantities of tools from Japan and Germany,[153] little genuine economic progress was made during his regime, primarily because he followed no systematic plan for industrial development. Machines of all kinds were ordered, but when they arrived, no one knew what to do with them: Afghanistan became a mausoleum of unused machinery and factories. No important industrial projects were completed in Afghanistan in the 1920's, nor were there any significant accomplishments in agriculture in that period.[154]

As for trade, the customs duties remained inconsistent and continued to be a major stumbling block. This, despite Amanullah's efforts to eliminate the more flagrant abuses caused by taxes like the *chilyaka*, which, by imposing an assessment of one-fortieth per load, per weight, per cost price, per number of articles, or per piece, offered considerable temptation to the customs officers; officials charged with appraising the value of commodities collected as much as 10 per cent commission on the import duty they assessed.[155] Corruption was further encouraged by the absence of uniform and standard weights and measures.* In 1925 the Amir introduced the decimal and metric systems,[156] but his efforts to achieve a degree of standardization do not seem to have extended beyond the government factories.

Amanullah took several steps in an effort to improve the flow of trade and end the widespread corruption in the customs service. All imports were divided into three categories: (1) religious literature, war materiel, and a few other items, which were duty-free; (2) European-made luxury items, which were subject to 100 per cent duty (among these were cards, marbles, cigarettes, pictures, sugar, honey); and (3) non-luxury items, which were taxed at varying rates. In this last group were tea, on which there was a 40 per cent tax, wearing apparel, on which there was a 15 per cent tax, and an entire category of "useful items," such as shoes, kerosene, oil, and gas, on which there was a 25 per cent tax.[157] (According to one source, even pictures of relatives were liable to taxation.)[158] The Amir appointed "respectable and propertied merchants" as customs officials and provided each customs office with a register for receipts and reports; tampering with them was made a criminal offense.[159] These steps, however, were hardly cures for a badly antiquated system.

Although the goods produced in the government workshops were protected against foreign competition, no protection was afforded the native handicraft workers, who could not compete with the products imported from the West, still cheap despite the huge import duties on them.[160] Concern over the plight of the native artisans was expressed in various Afghan periodicals, but nothing was done to remedy the situation.[161] The only change Amanullah made that genuinely advanced Afghanistan's trade was the reduction of the duty on Afghan exports and interregional trade items to a 5 per cent ad valorem tax.[162] Given the absence of standard tariffs and

---

* See Appendix B for details on the various weights and measures in use in the country in the nineteenth and twentieth centuries.

the lack of accurate information on the value of merchandise, most of his other measures in this field were all but useless. The steady development of Afghan trade continued to suffer because of the uncertain customs situation. There are no complete and accurate statistics available for the volume of trade in this period. The following figures give only a general picture of Afghan trade.

Afghan Trade with India[163]
(*in pounds sterling*)

Year	Exports to India	Imports from India
1918–19	1,194,000	2,020,000
1919–20	1,975,000	1,607,000
1920–21	1,543,200	1,328,500
1921–22	809,500	1,353,700
1922–23	1,606,160	1,575,240
1923–24	943,350	1,725,850

Afghan Trade with Russia[164]
(*in rubles*)

Year	Exports to Russia	Imports from Russia
1923–24	1,314,000	69,000
1925–26	3,271,000	2,541,000
1926–27	4,160,000	3,422,000
1927–28	6,698,000	6,849,000
1928–29	11,718,000	7,007,000

Amanullah's grandiose but nebulous modernization projects required far greater capital investment than the monarchy was able to raise. In 1926 the entire revenue of the Afghan kingdom was an estimated 45 million afghanis (2.5 million pounds).[165] Nor were the Afghan communications and transportation systems such as would attract foreign investors.[166] In any event, the Amir refused to allow any major foreign investment,[167] and that fact, together with the absence of laws protecting foreign companies and the lack of banking and credit facilities in Afghanistan, made the prospects of any investment at all very dim.

THE KHOST REBELLION

The first organized reaction against Amanullah's reforms was directed against a controversial administrative code, the Nizamnama, which he passed in 1923.[168] Among other things, that code attempted to liberalize the position of women and to permit the government to regulate various family problems formerly dealt with by the local mullah. A few traditionalist mullahs inveighed against the new code, asserting that it was contrary to the precepts of Islamic law and the spirit of the holy Quran. Their cause was picked up in 1924 by the Mangal tribe of the Khost region and soon assumed dangerous proportions. By March armed warfare had broken out.[169] The religious and tribal leaders of the revolt were particularly exercised over the sections of the code that deprived men of full authority over their wives and daughters, an authority that had been sanctioned by time-honored custom. They were further incensed at the opening of public schools for girls.[170]

The Khost rebellion continued for more than nine months, lasting until January 1925, and it dramatically illustrated the weakness of the Afghan army. Amanullah was forced to fall back on tribal levies from the Mohmands, Shinwaris, Waziris, Afridis, and Hazaras, and to proclaim a jihad, before he was able to suppress the revolt. The rebels suffered enormous losses: some 3,500 houses were bombarded and burned, 1,575 rebels were killed or wounded, and 450 women and children died of cold and hunger.[171] Presumably, the losses on the government side were as great. The cost of the rebellion, an estimated five million pounds, represented the total government receipts for two years. The Amir was thus forced to postpone various modernization projects, and his prestige fell accordingly.[172] He was also forced to revoke or modify many important sections of the Nizamnama; the schooling of girls, for instance, was limited to those under twelve.[173]

From a psychological point of view, the Amir's use of airplanes piloted by Russians and Germans against the rebels was at the least ill-advised. The intrusion of "infidels" into an internal feud was not only regarded as a sign of weakness but considered irreligious as well. The Soviets, who suspected the British had a hand in stirring up the revolt, accused Britain of furnishing "money and arms" in order "to overthrow the liberal Amir."[174] They, in turn, supported the cause of the Afghan monarch; in fact, Chicherin, the Soviet commissar for foreign affairs, boasted that Soviet military assistance had played a decisive role in the Afghan government's victory over the tribesmen of Khost.[175] The British, for their part, claimed that the rebellion was suppressed largely through British aid, pointing to the rapprochement between Afghanistan and Britain in 1925 as evidence of their support of Amanullah.[176]

The Khost rebellion was important for two reasons. First, it revealed the weaknesses of the Afghan army, which remained poorly trained, underpaid, and sadly lacking in medical facilities. Furthermore, there was increasing discontent among the older officers, many of whom had been superseded by younger, European-educated men.[177] They deeply resented the fact that various modernization schemes had depleted the Amir's meager resources at the expense of the army, which until 1919 had held a privileged position. Second, thanks to the Amir's impolitic action in using tribes that had long-standing feuds with the Mangals,[178] inter-tribal feuds were rekindled. Moreover, Amanullah's dependence on the tribes to put down the rebellion only increased their already considerable power.

THE GRAND TOUR

Once a measure of stability had apparently been reestablished in Afghanistan, Amanullah set out on what has been called his Grand Tour. Between December 1927 and July 1928, the Amir, Queen Sorayya, and an official party, which included the ministers of foreign affairs and finance, the governor of Kabul province, the president of the Afghan "parliament," and five senior officers, paid state visits to India and various countries in Europe and the Middle East. In Amanullah's words, this extensive trip, the first of its kind for an Afghan monarch, was "not a voyage of pleasure but one of study and social exploration," a trip that would allow him "to take back to my country the best things that I discover in European civilization and to show to Europe that Afghanistan has her place on the map of the world." Said Amanullah: "I have so far tried to raise my country to the level of the Western civilization, according to what I have hitherto learnt through books. The time has now come to complete my studies by personal observation and experience."[179] The Amir sincerely believed that his visit to Europe would result in a respect for Afghanistan, a respect that would in the end contribute to the country's commercial success and prosperity.[180]

In India, where Amanullah spoke of Islamic solidarity and was in turn hailed as the King of Islam,[181] his visit aroused widespread nationalist and Pan-Islamic sentiment. In Egypt he was enthusiastically welcomed by King Fuad and the Egyptians, who considered him "a champion of the Orient in its struggle with the West." In a statement to the Egyptian press, Amanullah declared that Afghanistan's independence had been achieved because of the Afghans' determination to be free; he reminded the Egyptians that the Afghans had gone to war five times in defense of their independence even before the concept of a fatherland was clear in their minds.[182] In Italy Amanullah was welcomed by King Victor Emmanuel, who decorated him with the Collar of the Annunziata. He also received the Order of the Golden Spur from the Pope. The Italian monarch took his royal guest to various points of interest, including the cavalry school and an army camp. The royal party also attended an air show at Campino.[183]

The Amir was extended similar courtesies in France and Germany. His stay in France included an official welcome by President Doumergue and a tour that took him, among other places, to Versailles, the Hôtel des Invalides, the Pantheon, the Louvre, and Saint-Cyr. In his official statement in France, the Amir declared that the efforts to meet the demands of modern life and achieve progress had brought the Afghans closer to France. He specifically praised the work of the French archaeological mission in "reconstructing [the] Afghan national past," and expressed his hope that France would extend the same disinterested collaborative effort to the economic domain.[184] In Berlin, where in honor of his visit school children were given a holiday, the Amir was received by President von Hindenburg and was awarded an honorary doctorate by the University of Berlin.[185]

The Amir was also decorated during his trip to England, receiving the Collar of the Royal Victorian Order from King George. While there, he visited the British fleet at Portsmouth and Southampton, inspected a submarine, and made a flight over London. He also visited Manchester, Liverpool, and Sheffield. At Oxford University, he was awarded a degree (doctorate of civil law) and was made an honorary member of the Royal Geographical Society. In a speech at Oxford, Amanullah spoke of his great admiration for education and for those engaged in the noble cause of science, expressing his conviction that his attempts to promote education in Afghanistan would bring lasting results.[186] *The Times* compared Amanullah's visit to that of Peter the Great of Russia; the vice-chancellor of Oxford spoke of the Amir and Queen Sorayya as a second sun and moon that had come from the East to illuminate this distant kingdom in the West.[187]

The next stop on the tour was the Soviet Union. The Amir delayed three days in Warsaw en route, judiciously avoiding the May Day celebrations in order to spare his hosts embarrassment (as a representative of the "old order") and in order to mollify the British.[188] In Moscow he was received by Kalinin, Chicherin, Voroshilov, Lunacharsky, and other Soviet leaders. He also visited Leningrad, the Ukraine, and the Crimea. Some have described Amanullah's visit to the Soviet Union as anti-climactic,[189] but others have contended that it made a great impression on him. According to Fischer, in Russia the Amir saw "an East that was yet of the West—his ideal for Afghanistan.... Industrialization, art, sports, military prowess, the Lenin Institute—all were displayed to him."[190]

Amanullah's Grand Tour was a personal triumph: he gained first-hand

knowledge of modern civilization and signed dozens of treaties, important
and unimportant, that secured Afghanistan a place in the world community. Only his desire to gain recognition for Afghanistan can account for
his eagerness to sign extradition agreements and formal treaties of friendship with Finland, Switzerland, Bolivia, Latvia, Liberia, and Poland.[191]
He also had some success in generating German, Italian, and French interest in the economic development of Afghanistan and in the country's
strategic position as a window on India.[192] In the course of his travels, he
purchased war materiel and enlisted the services of various Italian, German, and French technicians. He also received generous gifts from his host
countries: 13 airplanes, two tractors, and a Rolls Royce.[193]

The climax of Amanullah's tour came on his way home, when, during
his visit to secularist Turkey and Westernizing Iran, he witnessed the steps
Mustafa Kemal and Reza Shah had taken to modernize their countries
in the face of traditionalist opposition. Upon his arrival in Constantinople
on May 19, 1928, he hailed the friendship between his country and Turkey,
referring to the Turks as elder brothers and guides. In response, Ataturk
praised the dauntless Afghan spirit of independence and pointed out that
the Turks and the Afghans had a common goal and could consider themselves the heirs of the same nation. Amanullah, he declared, was just the
leader that Afghanistan needed.[194]

AMANULLAH'S SECOND REFORM PROGRAM

The Amir returned to his capital in July 1928—at the wheel of his Rolls
Royce. In many ways, he was a changed man. The European tour and his
visits to Turkey and Iran had induced in him a sense of pessimism and
near failure: he now recognized the enormity of the task of modernizing
Afghanistan. According to Roland Wild, a *Daily Mail* correspondent who
accompanied Amanullah to Europe, "He became infected with the germ
of the West so seriously as to lose his sense of proportion."[195] The Amir,
impressed with the forceful, sometimes dictatorial methods Mustafa Kemal and Reza Shah were using to thrust their countries into the twentieth
century, became determined to broaden the scope of reforms and accelerate, if necessary, the pace of modernization in his kingdom.

On the return trip to Kabul, Amanullah had everywhere harangued the
Afghan masses about progress and attacked the reactionaries and traditionalists who wanted to keep Afghanistan shrouded in ignorance. Once in
Kabul he addressed an emotional appeal to the Afghan nation, which read
in part:

My beloved people! I can hardly express to you the measure of my devotion to my country, and to you. I have seen most of Europe, and you will be pleased to know that I was everywhere warmly welcomed and esteemed. But it was not my personality that was so highly honoured: rather it was in the fullest sense the Afghan nation.

My purpose in going was to understand thoroughly the secrets of Europe's wonderful progress, my one idea being to formulate the proper means for our own advancement. I earnestly desire to see our sacred country progressing in every way by leaps and bounds. It was my part to chart the path of progress, to devise measures for the uplift of our general condition—moral, mental, social, economic. . . .

The surest way [to progress] is to make every effort to have our sons and daughters educated according to modern standards. I am compelled to say that the great secret of progress for our country lies in discarding old, outworn ideas and customs, and as the proverb goes, march with the times. Rest assured that it rests with our generation to rebuild this country in the fullest sense. In truth, the rise or fall of our country depends largely upon our rising generation, and you are in duty bound to bring up your children in the light of modern education. Therefore, I ask you to make a solemn promise that you will do your best to support the cause of education throughout the length and breadth of Afghanistan. We must show [other countries] that we are no longer an ignorant people and that we are determined to stand upon our own feet, without leaning upon others.[196]

In August, soon after his return, Amanullah convened a Loe Jirga, summoning some 1,000 notables from all over the kingdom to hear a report on his tour. Over a period of five days, he described his trip and his impressions of Europe, speaking in glowing terms of the attempts of the Turks, Persians, and Egyptians to modernize their societies.[197] He reportedly concluded this enthusiastic account by embracing a soldier, a government official, a civilian, and a student to indicate the forces with which he intended to build a new Afghanistan.[198]

The most important part of Amanullah's report, however, dealt with his proposals and programs for the rapid socioeconomic transformation of Afghanistan.[199] He suggested that substantial changes be made in the 1923 constitution, amendments that were to make the government genuinely representative, though the monarchy, under the hereditary rule of the Amir's family, was to be retained. These amendments provided for the dissolution of the Council of State and of the two consultative chambers, all of which had long represented the interests of the feudal lords and the powerful Afghan tribes, especially the Durranis. These bodies were to be replaced by a cabinet, including a prime minister, and a parliament with limited legislative powers. The new body was to be made up of 150 deputies, who were to be elected for three-year terms by direct vote. It was to sit for eight months a year, with 81 deputies representing a quorum. Under the new provisions, citizens under twenty-one, government officials, military personnel, and naturalized citizens were to be barred from serving as deputies, and the vote was to be extended only to men twenty years old or over, convicts whose terms had exceeded three years and illiterates excepted. (Illiteracy was not defined.)[200]

Amanullah also proposed to make a number of changes in the army. In order to create a well-trained standing army and one of truly national composition, he asked that military service be made compulsory, that the age of those eligible for the draft be lowered to seventeen, and that the length of military service be extended from two to three years.[201] He reported that he had purchased 53,000 rifles from France and argued for his military reforms on the grounds of national defense, the sacred duty of every Afghan. On the same grounds he asked for the imposition of a new tax, specifically for the purchase of an additional 50,000 rifles and some five million rounds of ammunition.[202] In general the new tax, to be levied on every male over fifteen, was to be from three to five rupees, but government officials were to pay a month's salary.

In the economic field, the Amir's suggestions were primarily concerned with communications. He asked for the installation at some future date of telegraph stations at Maimana and Khanabad in northern Afghanistan. For the present, he expressed his determination to begin immediate construction of railways, with the assistance of French and German companies.[203] In education, he called for the founding of public libraries and the implementation of a program of free and compulsory education for boys and girls between the ages of six and eleven; his stated aim was to achieve free universal education throughout the country.[204] Among the other reforms he proposed was the discontinuance of the use of hereditary titles, of extravagantly designed ceremonial uniforms, both in the army and in government circles, and of all military decorations and medals except the Afghan Order of Independence. He also advanced a number of strict administrative measures designed to curb corruption among government employees.

The Loe Jirga accepted the Amir's constitutional amendments, even though those amendments meant a curtailment of the authority of the khans and tribal chiefs. It also reluctantly approved his military reforms, including the request for a new tax. However, the Afghan notables fiercely resisted the Amir's proposed social program. They rejected, for instance, a proposal to set an age limit on marriages, which the Amir suggested should be eighteen for girls and twenty for men. They also vehemently opposed the notion of a modern, Western education for Afghan girls, either in Afghanistan or outside it.[205]

Opposition to social reform soon came from a number of other quarters. The Amir issued three orders that created a great public uproar: he attacked polygamy, outlawing the practice among government officials; he declared that women were free to discard the traditional veil; and he decreed that all Afghans visiting or residing in Kabul were to adopt Western dress.[206] These measures, which affected every segment of Afghan society, provoked widespread discontent and provided rallying points for an opposition that was led by the religious establishment and some tribal chieftains.

AMANULLAH AND THE RELIGIOUS ESTABLISHMENT

As a class, the mullahs were alienated from Amanullah almost from the start. From 1919 on, they opposed many of his measures, most of all those designed to emancipate women legally and socially. Amanullah's attempts to secure the right of public education for women and the right to go unveiled in public were particularly distasteful to the religious elements. Even the Amir's wish to grant women the right to cut their hair as fashion dictated ran afoul of Afghan tradition: a woman's hair was to be cut solely as a mark of disgrace.[207] To most mullahs, the Amir's advice—and sometimes his orders—to Afghan men to adopt Western clothing was tantamount to blasphemy (this was particularly true with respect to European-style hats), and they especially resented the element of compulsion. Moreover, Amanullah had taken certain steps that directly affected the mullahs themselves. For instance, he denied them the right to study at the orthodox Deoband school in India, and he had refused to grant important jobs or subsidies to certain mullahs from Central Asia, also known for their rigid orthodoxy.[208] He had also continued his father's practice of maintaining control of the waqf, and had even lowered some of the subsidies.[209]

Amanullah's attempts to limit the legal authority of the mullahs and to divest them of all control over education backfired.[210] The religious establishment was not likely to be appeased by his trips to the Great Mosque of Kabul to pray for help in serving the Afghan people and Islam when he used those occasions to speak out against the abuses and prejudices sustained in the name of religion.[211] Nor did his reputation in other parts of the Muslim world as a champion of Islam and Muslim solidarity do much to soften the opposition of the mullahs at home; on the contrary, his friendship pacts and treaties with Turkey and Persia, countries that pursued secularist and modernist policies and had abandoned Pan-Islamism as a political goal, only weakened his position. Furthermore, his image as a militant Pan-Islamist was to a large extent destroyed with the collapse of the Basmachi revolt, the failure of the Khilafat movement, and the subsequent normalization of Afghanistan's relations with Soviet Russia, Soviet Central Asia, and Britain.

The abolition of the office of Sultan and Caliph by a republican, secularist, and modernizing Turkey transformed the character of the Turko-Afghan alliance, eliminating the Pan-Islamic element that had been part of its appeal for many Afghans. In view of Amanullah's close association with the Turks and his use of Turkey as a model for the modernization of his own kingdom, the abolition of the Caliphate came as a great shock. The Afghan ruling elite made a valiant attempt to placate the traditionalist, Pan-Islamic elements and to keep the alliance and cooperation between Turkey and Afghanistan from becoming a liability to the Amir. This was most evident in the actions taken by a Loe Jirga convened in 1924. At that meeting, though the Afghan minister of education delivered a tirade against the Turkish government's abolition of the Caliphate, the resolutions the assembly passed, probably drafted by Mahmud Tarzi, were quite mild. They simply stated that if an Islamic conference gathered to discuss the issue of the Caliphate, Afghanistan would participate, and that the "competent men of the Empire" (Ottoman Empire?) should study the question of whether or not a Caliph was "absolutely necessary" for the growth and progress of Islam. In an interview, Tarzi explained why, apart from issuing these resolutions, Amanullah's administration refused to become the hub of a Caliphate movement:

Our Amir is first of all a soldier and an Afghan patriot. He has placed all his intelligence and activity at the service of his country. I do not think that he will be willing to be tempted by the functions of that of a Spiritual Leader that would bother him in the accomplishment of his duties as a sovereign. And then, the Shi'ites, would they ever be willing to recognize the authority of the Sunni?... No, the Amir will not rally himself to a solution in which both the country and himself will have much to lose and nothing to gain.

In the same interview, Tarzi emphasized once more that Afghanistan's major preoccupations were domestic ones: "Having become free, [Afghanistan] aspires to occupy in the world an honourable place, hence its hurry to establish contacts with the most civilized nations or to accept from them the needed assistance in order to advance rapidly on the road of progress." There was a time, he continued, when religions set peoples against one another. "Those times are bygone. Certainly, we are proud to be Muslims, and we will not allow any blows against the honour of Islam. But today we do not see that honour to be in peril. Assured on that side, ... we are directing our efforts toward a new goal; we would like to live, be strong and make Afghanistan a modern state. We are terribly behind, we know it and we would like to make up for the lost time."[212]

THE FALL OF AMANULLAH

By 1928, Amanullah had little public support. His taxes and reform measures had alienated the urban population as well as the peasantry, the religious establishment as well as many Afghan tribes. His social reforms became the focus of attacks against him, many of them personal. His opponents questioned his loyalty to Islam, and after his audience with the Pope, spread the rumor that he had converted to Roman Catholicism. The Amir's agreements with France, Germany, and especially Great Britain were interpreted as not in Afghanistan's best interests.[213] The visit to Europe was roundly criticized. The rumor spread that the trip had cost one million pounds, and that the Amir's conduct in Europe had been impious: he had danced, drunk alcoholic beverages, even eaten pork.[214] The traditionalists were outraged because the Queen had traveled unveiled in foreign lands;[215] moreover, her picture had appeared in many newspapers, including the Persian papers *Settare-ye Iran* (The Star of Iran), *Koushesh* (Effort), and *Iran*. They also took exception to an administrative order making Thursday a public holiday;[216] In their view, this was an impious act that detracted from the religious atmosphere and holy significance of Friday, the Islamic day of rest and prayer. Under these circumstances, Amanullah's announcement of a new set of reforms after his return from Europe created an extremely dangerous situation. The situation grew even more tense when two of the most prominent religious leaders of Afghanistan, Hazrat Sahib of Shor Bazar and his nephew, were jailed for agitation and for collecting signatures for a petition against the Amir's reforms.[217]

On October 2, 1928, there were violent anti-government demonstrations in Kabul. Although they were quickly suppressed by the Afghan army, a major revolt started in November, when the Shinwari tribe rebelled and was soon joined by the Khugianis, Mohmands, Jadrans, and Jajis.[218] The immediate cause of the revolt is unclear. One explanation is offered by Fletcher, who writes that in November 1928

a caravan of Suleiman Khel Ghilzai on their winter migration to India met a band of Shinwaris whom they mistook for (or perhaps recognized as) bandits. The Suleiman Khel resisted, and several of the Shinwaris were killed before a company of soldiers arrived and arrested the Ghilzai nomads. They were able, however, either to convince the local commandant of their innocence or to satisfy his avarice, and were released. Soon afterward the Sangu Khel clan of the

Shinwaris, to which the dead men had belonged, rose in revolt and captured the military posts of Achin and Kai. These successes brought out other Shinwari clans. . . . The Khugianis and Safia, who had been watching with interest, now joined in the rising.[219]

A more plausible explanation is advanced by Taillardat, who reported at the time (in January 1929) that the storm broke out on November 10, when Amanullah's tax collectors and army recruiting officers arrived in Shinwari territory, and were met with gunfire. According to him, the Kabul garrison, moving to suppress the revolt, recruited the services of the Khugiani tribesmen, who were rivals of the Shinwaris; but for reasons unknown, the Khugianis, who had been armed by the government, deserted the Amir and joined the rebels.[220] In any case, the rebellious tribes cut the road between Jalalabad and Dakka, thereby halting the flow of munitions and other supplies through the Khyber Pass. They then captured Jalalabad and destroyed the royal palace. The Amir's grip over the eastern provinces was shaken off. The army, poorly paid and ill-trained, was not equipped for a winter war and failed to regain control of the area.

Meanwhile, the shaky political situation became more menacing when Kabul itself was attacked by the followers of a notorious and daring Tajik highwayman, Bacha-i-Saqao (Water-Carrier's Son). Bacha's forces were driven from Kabul after a bloody struggle, but with the assistance of certain influential mullahs, he gradually assumed the leadership of traditionalist elements. Entrenching himself in Kohistan, he again pushed the struggle against Amanullah to the outskirts of Kabul, where he was able to remain, despite the efforts of the royal troops. Amanullah was forced to negotiate to protect the capital and his throne. Between January 2 and January 14, the Amir was compelled to cancel most of his social reforms and to suspend his controversial administrative measures. The Afghan girls studying in Constaninople were to be recalled, and the schools for girls in Afghanistan were to be closed; the ulama of Deoband were to be allowed free access to and the right of residence in Afghanistan; women were not to go unveiled or cut their hair; the mullahs were no longer to be required to obtain teaching certificates; compulsory military recruitment was to be abandoned and the old tribal system reinstated; *muhtasibs* were to be appointed for each province to ensure that religious precepts were observed. The Amir also cancelled his order making it mandatory (after March 31, 1929) for all Kabulis and visitors from outlying areas to wear Western dress, including hats, when walking or riding on the main roads of the city; the Afghans were to be left free to wear whatever they chose, as long as they did not offend religious sensibilities. A ruling that

Afghan military personnel could not belong to religious orders was annulled. Thursday was no longer to be an official holiday. Amanullah also promised to appoint inspectors in each Afghan province to ensure the honest use of weights and measures. As a last, desperate concession, the unhappy Amir agreed to the formation of a council of 50 notables, to be chosen from among "the most respected religious luminaries and tribal chieftains," and promised to abide by their advice as well as to conform to Islamic law as interpreted by the orthodox religious leaders. Any measure the government proposed to enact was to be ratified by this council.[221]

In the end, all of these concessions were to no avail. On January 14, 1929, Bacha's forces launched another attack against the city of Kabul. With the help of disloyal members of the royal army, Bacha took over the Amir's artillery, and according to an authoritative source, a Mahsud auxiliary force deserted to the rebel camp, placing the government troops under a crossfire.[222] Amanullah abdicated, declaring: "The welfare of the country demands that I should withdraw from public affairs, for all the bloodshed and risings in the country are due to a general hatred of me." Consigning the throne to his brother Inayatullah, he fled to Kandahar.[223] Bacha, however, refused to accept this new state of affairs. On January 17, his troops surrounded the citadel, which enclosed the royal palace, the treasury, and the arsenal, threatening to bombard it. At this point, the prominent religious leader Hazrat Sahib sought the help of the British minister at Kabul, Sir Francis Humphreys, in arranging a cease-fire. Inayatullah, too, abdicated. A safe-conduct was procured by the Muslim leader, and Sir Francis arranged for the royal party to be evacuated by air to Peshawar.[224] (The British diplomat also arranged for the air evacuation of most of the foreign residents of Kabul in these months.[225] Between December 12 and February 25, approximately 585 aliens, including Englishmen, Germans, Italians, Japanese, Frenchmen, Turks, and Persians, were airlifted from Kabul to Peshawar. The operation was an extraordinary feat in view of the immense technical difficulties that had to be faced.)*

After Inayatullah abdicated, Bacha was proclaimed monarch. Assuming the name and title Amir Habibullah Ghazi, or Habibullah the Victor (he modestly declined the title Shah, which had been assumed by Amanullah and his father), he promised to reestablish the rule of Islamic law "in all its purity."[226] Amanullah, still in Kandahar, was overwhelmed at this turn of events. "Responding to the wishes of the populations of Kandahar,

---

* According to Sir Francis, there was only one casualty: a German woman, concerned about her luggage, stepped into a propellor.

Farah, Herat, Maimana, and Kataghan," he rescinded his abdication and appealed to the Afghan tribes to unite under his banner and defeat the rebels and the usurper.[227] The Hazaras, Mohmands, Safis, and Vardaks rallied to his cause, and in northern Afghanistan, Ghulam Nabi Charki (the Afghan envoy to Russia) recruited an army to come to his aid, reportedly with the blessing and support of Soviet Russia.[228] However, Amanullah's only real hope of success lay in swiftly rallying the Durrani tribe behind him and winning the support or at least a promise of neutrality from the Ghilzais, and this he was unable to do.

Despite a two-month period of military inactivity during the harsh Afghan winter, Amanullah was not able to organize his newly assembled 15,000-man army into an effective force. His troops were in no better shape than before his hasty abdication, and their loyalty was further undermined by the propaganda of Bacha and the traditionalist elements behind him. (In Kandahar, some of the mullahs ceased mentioning Amanullah's name in their Friday prayers and sermons.) Amanullah had other problems as well: he was short of money; his forces suffered a sharp setback near Ghazni; and the support of the Ghilzais, tenuous at best, ended in the open hostility of the Suleiman Khel against him. Disheartened and faced with constant rumors of assassination plots, he abandoned the struggle. In late April 1929 he left Afghanistan for India, proceeding from there, via Bombay, to Italy.[229] Afghanistan plunged into political anarchy.

SOME CONCLUSIONS

The underlying causes of Amanullah's downfall have been the subject of a variety of interpretations and a great deal of speculation on the part of contemporary historians and journalists. Much of that speculation is disguised as fact in various historical studies, and has inhibited critical study and obscured the importance of the internal socioeconomic factors that contributed so much to the events of 1928.

Soviet authorities then and now have placed great emphasis on "external factors precipitating the outbreak" of the rebellion in 1928, attributing Amanullah's fall largely to British machinations. They describe Bacha-i-Saqao as an anti-Soviet, pro-Basmachi Muslim reactionary and a stooge of British political interests.* In their view, Great Britain attempted to

---

* The British completely reject the charge of sponsorship of Bacha as both ridiculous and unrealistic. The greatest fear of the British government in India was not Amanullah but political anarchy or the division of Afghanistan into rival principalities. Moreover, Britain could not afford to alienate the Durrani tribe. Sir Francis Hum-

crush an Afghan national liberation movement and aroused the border tribes against Amanullah. At the time, *Pravda* charged that Col. T. E. Lawrence, the famous Lawrence of Arabia, had masterminded the entire anti-Amanullah uprising,* while *Izvestia* saw in the outbreak the spirit of Disraeli: a British pretext to extend the frontier of India and to launch an attack against the Soviet Union.[230]

These charges were not confined to the Soviet press. There were similar conclusions and accusations in the European press, notably in the German and French newspapers. The German press interpreted the overthrow of Amanullah as a British maneuver to reestablish Britain's pre-1919 hold over Afghanistan, thereby preventing the emergence of any strong polities in the neighborhood of India. The French papers offered a different interpretation. They held that Amanullah's downfall was long and patiently planned by the British in revenge for the Amir's role in the Third Anglo-Afghan War, his close relations with Soviet Russia, and his distrust of the British government in India.[231] Even the British papers questioned Britain's part in the affair. The *Daily Herald*, which had warmly championed Amanullah's reforms, joined the *Daily News* in taking the British government to task about the "mysterious activities" of "Aircraftsman Shaw" (the alias of Lawrence) in the North-West Frontier Province of India and his possible connection with the Afghan upheaval. Similar questions were raised in the House of Commons by Labour deputies.[232] The unprecedented move of Hazrat Sahib in seeking the help of Sir Francis Humphreys, and the British diplomat's role in arranging a truce and the evacuation of the royal party and foreigners from Kabul, caused the European and Indian press, as well as the Soviet authorities, to question his role in the affair.†

---

phreys adds these points: he himself never met Bacha, Amanullah was a close personal friend, and Britain remained strictly neutral and did not recognize Bacha's government. On British neutrality, see A. Qadir, "The Outlook," p. 466.

* Lawrence was indeed in India at this time, but there is no evidence or even a hint in his letters that he was involved in any subversive activities concerning Afghanistan. For a collection of his letters, see Garnett. Lawrence was offered an opportunity to become the clerk of the British air attaché in Kabul, but declined. See Weintraub.

† Amanullah's image in India remained untarnished. In an interview with the Associated Press (February 19, 1929), Aga Ahmed Khan, characterizing Amanullah as "an ideal ruler," said: "He regularly prayed for the amelioration of Afghanistan after every Namaz (prayer). He was noble-hearted and a patriotic King, the like of which the Afghans had never seen. The ex-King's love for his nation overpowered him so much that all the reforms were introduced in rapid succession, though his councillors were in favor of introducing them by installments" (as quoted by N. N. Ghosh, pp. 180–81). Ghosh himself described Amanullah as a person "misunderstood by his coun-

To many of the contemporary British observers, the fall of Amanullah was to be attributed to the impatience of some Afghans and the fanaticism of others. Comyn-Platt, for instance, declared that "it is the old story again of young men in a hurry and if there is one thing the Afghan dislikes it is haste and change." In a similar vein, Sir Michael O'Dwyer wrote in the *Daily Mail* and *Sunday Express* that Amanullah had attempted to "hustle the East," and had thus "wrought his own ruin by reckless and ill-judged attempts to upset the customs and religion of conservative and fanatical tribesmen, most of whom never paid more than a nominal allegiance to Kabul." Emanuel had this to say: "The Afghans are perhaps the most fanatically religious people on earth and the mullahs were the principal agents in the overthrow of Amanullah."[233]

As for the Afghan view of the revolt, Amanullah himself held that it was "a reaction and not a revolution," a judgment with which Hidayatullah Khan, the heir apparent, agreed. Inayatullah, on the other hand, felt that Amanullah's overthrow ought to be attributed to "the curse of the departed spirit" of his father (and Amanullah's) on those responsible for his assassination.[234]

Afghan historians later found it difficult to explain the causes of the upheaval: if they ascribed Amanullah's overthrow to a reaction or revolution against his ambitious programs and far-reaching socioeconomic reforms, they would in effect be admitting that the Afghans were either not ready for modernization or unwilling to accept progress; if, on the other hand, they argued that the revolt was engineered by outside forces, namely Great Britain, they feared they might weaken the case for a legitimate change in the Afghan ruling dynasty and alienate the religious establishment by implying that it was used as a tool. Consequently, they found a formula whereby the causes of the outbreak are attributed primarily to shortsightedness—to the haste with which Amanullah acted and to the poor advice of his counselors—but with external intrigue playing a role.[235]

---

trymen" and asserted that "the career of that great man, indeed greater than any other Afghan, was cut short by ignorant, obstinate and factious opposition which... is common with the most Eastern countries (p. 178). Kātrak (pp. 105–6) wrote of Amanullah's fall: "The reasons are not very far to seek. An independent, war-like, bigoted nation, with a staunch faith in religion which debarred all foreign education, manners and customs from entering into their hearth and home, could not brook interference even from a monarch, when he wanted to strike at the very root of their social manners and customs. How can a nation so staunch in its faith, as to be almost bigoted, tolerate the change of its social manners and customs?" Among the Muslim Indian writers, Mohammed Yunus alone ascribes Amanullah's overthrow to his eagerness to copy Ataturk. He contends that the Amir "lost his balance, and ill-digesting some of his impressions, he turned the tables against himself in his own country" (p. 64).

Because of their preoccupation with ideological and political problems, they have been led to ignore the internal factors that precipitated the Amir's downfall.

Amanullah's reform program suffered from the same weaknesses that had characterized the much more limited programs of his predecessors. The tragic fact is, he undertook the enormous task of rapidly transforming Afghan society without a definite plan, without the necessary financial resources, and without the requisite technological skill and manpower. Moreover, it was impossible for him to modernize the country without transforming its socioeconomic structure, and it was equally impossible to do so without sharply curtailing religious and tribal authority. But to retain the Afghan character of his kingdom and to secure the hereditary rule of his dynasty, he needed the support of the Afghan tribes, particularly the Durranis; and to give homogeneity and cohesion to the peoples of Afghanistan, he needed Islam as a religious and cultural bond.

Furthermore, the Amir's timetable of reform was unrealistic, given the weakness of his financial base. He opposed feudalism as a political force, but he had nothing to substitute for it and did not attack its economic base. In order to wage a successful campaign against the religious establishment and the reactionary tribal leaders, he needed popular support. That support was forthcoming only when the political objectives of Afghan nationalism were involved; it could not be mustered for social reforms that infringed on traditional values and institutions. The constant attacks on the Amir's social reforms effectively obscured the significance of his economic, educational, and political programs, which otherwise might have won him some support. In the face of a tribal-feudal-religious-traditionalist coalition in opposition, he was unable to find the necessary support in a strong urban middle class or in an economically healthy peasant class.

As early as 1929, Raskolnikov, the Soviet envoy to Afghanistan, noted this situation. He wrote that there was "practically no middle class at all in Afghanistan." There was no question of an industrial bourgeoisie, he said, and "even the commercial bourgeoisie [was] still at an embryo state," with "the entire foreign trade (with negligible exceptions) . . . in the hands of Indian merchants." Raskolnikov concluded that "the tragedy of Amanullah's case lay in the fact that he undertook bourgeois reforms without the existence of any national bourgeoisie in the country. . . . The organic fault of all the reforms of Amanullah lay in the fact that they were devoid of an economic basis."[236]

Raskolnikov also asserted that, in order to implement his progressive

reforms, Amanullah relied not only on the royal army but also on the peasant masses and the Young Afghans, "who were for the greater part descended from the more progressive of the small landowners." Such an
assertion cannot be supported. For that matter, Raskolnikov himself re-
futed this statement in his own reports, as did other contemporary Soviet
authorities. In fact, Amanullah undertook no major socioeconomic programs, such as land reform, that might have won him the support of the
peasantry. The majority of his measures dealt with urban problems. The
Afghan peasants, already burdened with a variety of taxes, had to underwrite a large share of the cost of reforms that were of no real and immediate advantage to them. Zelenski, secretary of the Central Asiatic Bureau
of the Central Committee of the All-Russian Communist Party, warned
as early as 1928 that "from the point of view of class, the measures outlined or enforced by Amanullah Khan tend to create most favourable conditions for the development of a bourgeois state, for the normal development of trade and industrial capital. Compared to feudalism, capitalism
is of course a sign of cultural and economic development.... Yet capitalism in Afghanistan will be fed by blood, by toil, by the exploitation of the
working people and the ruin of the village."[237]

The Soviet Central Asian press, in its analysis of the underlying causes
of Amanullah's downfall, dwelt on the same point. Said *Pravda Vostoka*:[238] "The chief part of the yearly increasing taxes required for the
development of industry and the maintenance of the centralized state departments and the army is borne by the peasantry. The discontented peasants, unable to formulate their demands, follow the feudal and clerical elements—who incite them to act against the government."*

In 1928, about 30 per cent of Amanullah's revenue was derived from
land tax.[239] Wild described the situation in these words:

Since the tussle with the British, increased pressure had been brought to bear
on the landowners. Their taxes were steadily mounting.... The tax-gatherers
were more pressing than ever they had been in the past. Hardly a month went

---

* The 1928 revolt came at a time when the peasants' economic position had deteriorated badly, primarily because of the increased taxes but also because the taxes had
to be paid in cash. In the nine years Amanullah was on the throne, the tax on horses
and donkeys rose 400–500 per cent, the tax on land increased three to four times, the
tax on short-horned cattle more than quadrupled (from seven puls to 30), and the tax
on long-horned cattle tripled (20 puls to 60). The requirement that taxes be paid in
cash not only led to bureaucratic abuses but also increased the indebtedness of many
peasants, who reportedly were forced to rely heavily on moneylenders. Even after
there were crop failures in 1925, the government did not ease the peasants' tax burden.
See Chokaiev, "Bolsheviks and Afghanistan," pp. 507–10, and "Situation in Afghanistan," p. 326; and Raskolnikov, "The War in Afghanistan," p. 183.

by but they came with news of a new valuation. There were new taxes on houses, and new demands made on weddings and funerals and village ceremonies. There seemed to be more taxation officers than tax-payers. Gradually the peasant began to know the other side of the "reform." ... There was a new education tax, and an added tax for building. There was a tax to pay for the war, and a tax merely labelled "development." ... The peasant paid, and when he could not, suffered the annexation of his land in the cruel winter.[240]

The Amir also taxed the urban population heavily and his increases in the duties on exports and imports hit hard at the merchant class. Theoretically, the customs duties ranged from 100 per cent on luxury items to 15–40 per cent on useful or necessary items (with some exceptions). In practice, however, the duties were much higher, ranging more often from 20 per cent to 200 per cent.[241] Even internal trade was subject to at least a 5 per cent tax. Ignorance about the value of manufactured or imported goods opened the way to arbitrary decisions and corruption, thus alienating the tradesmen and the merchant class. In need of money, Amanullah "found himself baulked on every side just when he wished to forge ahead with his most grandiloquent schemes. He could not conduct with severity his campaign against corruption while he was unable to pay his officers sufficiently to keep them from the temptation."[242] Venality among the bureaucrats was widespread and was encouraged by the fact that the pay of the government officials was very low; some high officials, even district governors, had to purchase their offices, and even low-paid officials were forced to provide themselves with European clothing. The establishment of compulsory military service, accompanied by a special tax to cover the expenses of modernizing the army, not only antagonized the tribes; it also led to new abuses. In a country without central records or an accurate census, the local maliks and district governors were assigned the task of implementing the provisions of the conscription law. They often exempted the sons of influential or rich families, recruiting among families who could not afford to bribe them or among those with whom they had feuds. In various districts, the control of water rights by the local authorities also encouraged venality. Afghan, French, and Soviet sources all agree that the combined weight of taxation and administrative abuses encouraged brigandage in the countryside and contributed to social disturbances. One notable example was in 1927, when the finance minister was attacked by some 30 peasants.[243] The appeal and success of the outlaw Bacha-i-Saqao in the region of Kohistan can be easily explained by the prevalent socioeconomic conditions in the region. Amanullah's tactics were also partially responsible for the alienation of the important Mohmand tribe. During the Khost rebellion, a large sum of money was promised to the Mohmand chieftains, in return for their promise that the Mohmands would not join the Mangal tribe. The Amir's officials not only reneged on this promise but also vilified the Mohmand leaders for their lack of patriotism. Significantly, in the 1928 uprisings, the Mohmand tribe's stand against the Afghan government proved to be fatal to the cause of Amanullah.

The Amir's already limited financial resources were often drained away uselessly. In the absence of trained commercial agents abroad, necessary equipment was often purchased at ten times its worth. Furthermore, in hiring foreign advisers and experts, little thought was given to future plans or even to projects in progress: "There were Italian wireless engineers on the payroll ready for a wireless station. There were engineers for road-making, come to teach the Afghan contractors the latest methods of the West. There were German mining engineers, idling their time away in Kabul, waiting for orders that never came."[244] Amanullah's orders and purchases from Europe were similarly haphazard; he established mills for the manufacture of cotton and woolen yarn, an electric power station, paper mills, laundries, and printing plants[245]—all without first making a general survey of the nation's needs and resources. A country with such limited resources could scarcely afford this kind of random profligacy.

Armed with ambitious and costly, if unstudied projects, and at the same time fearful of jeopardizing the independence of Afghanistan, Amanullah was unwilling to give major concessions to other countries or to allow foreign investments. Therefore, though he followed an open door policy, political considerations overrode economic necessities. Although he hired a number of European geologists, he refused to give mineral rights to Europeans, so as "not to make a mockery" out of the newly won Afghan sovereignty by "enticing the greed of foreigners."[246] Even when he did consider the possibility of granting concessions to foreign companies or negotiating foreign loans, he was moved by political rather than economic motives, giving preference to German, French, Italian, or American firms and nationals rather than to Soviet or British companies. In any case, the poor communications, lack of skilled labor, and absence of banking and credit facilities were not likely to attract great numbers of foreign investors. The uncertain legal status and rights of the non-Muslim foreign residents of Afghanistan further complicated the problems of prospective investors, and in some instances created serious diplomatic incidents.*

* In one case, an Italian engineer, Piperno, shot and killed an Afghan policeman who had attempted to serve him with a notice to appear before the police authorities. Piperno was tried and condemned to death, but Italian officials persuaded the victim's family to accept blood money, thus voiding the death sentence—an old Afghan custom that had been retained in the administrative code. Unwilling to wait out the long for-

In an effort to overcome some of these financial handicaps, Amanullah laid the foundations of an Afghan bank and tried to set limits for foreign investments in his administrative code. In 1927 a Loe Jirga debated the question of whether the functions of a bank conflicted with the principles of Islam. Although the assembly seems to have agreed in principle to the founding of a bank, the project was put off indefinitely.[247] In general, the Amir's attempts to institute legal and financial reforms were frustrated by the opposition of the religious establishment, which continued to stress that Islamic law derived from God and needed no elaboration.[248]

Thus, Amanullah, dependent on the revenues gained by overtaxing the rural and urban populations of the country and in a precarious position with respect to the religious establishment and many of the tribes, was obliged to rely on his army to strengthen his position and enforce some of his unpopular social reforms. However, unlike his father and grandfather, he did not make the army, potentially his best weapon, the focal point of his reforms. Instead, he spent his limited funds on education and other socioeconomic programs, leaving little money with which to train and completely re-equip the inefficient Afghan army.

Although many of the Amir's reforms were progressive, large numbers of Afghans found them obnoxious. His methods were often exceedingly tactless. Only a small, enlightened elite was committed to the ideal of a modern Afghanistan and to the Amir's ambitious, if nebulous, program for realizing that ideal. Nevertheless, in the face of all these difficulties, Amanullah made important contributions. He reasserted the independence of Afghanistan, established diplomatic relations with many European and Asian countries, and opened the doors of the Afghan kingdom. He founded modern schools, encouraged the study of foreign languages, and sent many students abroad for advanced study. He lent his support to the improvement of communications and to the archaelogical explora-

---

malities involved in his release, Piperno escaped from prison and attempted to reach Soviet Central Asia; he was captured and executed in 1925. The Italian government not only demanded a formal and personal apology from the Afghan foreign minister but insisted that the Italian flag be saluted by the Afghan troops, that the blood money be returned, and that an indemnity of 7,000 pounds be paid. After long negotiations, the Afghan government agreed to pay an indemnity of 6,000 pounds and to extend a formal and personal apology through the Afghan undersecretary for foreign affairs. The affair was thereby declared closed. See *The Times*, June 15 and August 19, 1925; and Caspani and Cagnacci, pp. 135–36. Soviet Russia saw in the Italian demarche a covert attempt by a capitalist country to secure extraterritorial and capitulatory rights, and thus prepare the ground for a massive Italian penetration of Afghanistan. See *Izvestia*, June 27, 1925. The fact remains, however, that there were no special laws or provisions regarding the status of Europeans in Afghanistan. A similar incident marred Afghan-German relations. See Stratil-Sauer.

tion of Afghanistan. Even his unpopular feminist reforms provided a needed psychological shock. Perhaps one of his greatest failings was that instead of concentrating on the economic development of the country, he dissipated his efforts and resources by introducing mere symbols of progress: thus, he purchased phonographs and microphones, built bandstands and hotels, opened a café and a movie house, issued passports, insisted on the adoption of Western dress.[249]

Amanullah's major mistakes are well summed up by Mustafa Chokaiev:

> Amanullah chose to follow in the footsteps of Ghazi Mustafa Kemal but forgot that the Turks had been for centuries in contact with the cultured world of Europe and that the governing class in Turkey had been long since Europeanized. Amanullah forgot also that Turkey knew not the tribal regime, and that she had a comparatively well-ordered centralized apparatus of power, such as did not ... exist in Afghanistan. Mustafa Kemal had an army that was loyal and devoted to its leader. Nothing of the kind existed in Afghanistan. ... We have on one side the King-reformer considering the Afghans as a united, single political organism, as a unified state-nation; and on the other side the Afghan tribes, who looking at the state can comprehend it only from the point of view of the tribal interests, to the defence of which the principles of the "sacred Shariat" are put forward.[250]

Sir Francis Humphreys, who later became the British ambassador to Turkey, states that Mustafa Kemal himself agreed with Chokaiev's analysis.[251]

The fall of Amanullah and the rise of Bacha-i-Saqao were serious setbacks on the road to modernization. The religious establishment and the tribes, the two forces that were largely instrumental in the downfall of the Amir, threw off a considerable portion of the administrative, legal, and financial restraints that had been placed on them by Abdur Rahman and Habibullah, along with those imposed by Amanullah. The ensuing civil war and the rule of Bacha plunged Afghanistan into anarchy and destroyed most of Amanullah's achievements. An exciting dream had vanished.

Chapter Ten

Bacha-i-Saqao, the Bandit Amir

Bacha-i-Saqao's hold on the throne of Kabul lasted from January 17 to October 13, 1929, a period that was marked by political anarchy and severe economic dislocation. His program, as enunciated on the eve of his accession to the throne, was clearly reactionary.[1] After attacking Amanullah's "sacrilegious and impious" acts, the new Amir promised the Afghans a complete return to the principles of the Quran and Shar'ia law, and the reestablishment of ancient customs regarding marriage, the status of women, and the function of education. Following through on this pledge, he halted all of Amanullah's progressive measures. All of the modern schools were closed, female students were recalled from Turkey, foreign military advisers were forced to leave Kabul, and the polygamy laws were reinstated. Laboratories, libraries, palaces, and the royal museum in Kabul were sacked. According to the Afghan historian Mohammed Ali, "Rare books and articles of value were either destroyed, burnt, or sold at ridiculous prices. For one *kran* (about 3 pence) down, one could buy as many books as one could carry on one's shoulders. . . . Confiscation of property, exile, or simple death were deemed uncommon instances of . . . leniency. Most of the unfortunate victims were either blown up from the cannon's mouth, or shot down; others were either beaten, bastinadoed, impaled, bayonetted, or starved to death. . . . [Bacha's] chief victims were the officials of King Amanullah Khan, and wealthy merchants or influential and learned men. . . . He suspected the students most and regarded them as his secret enemies."[2] These charges in substance were supported by Andrée Viollis, a correspondent of *Petit Parisien,* who was the only foreign reporter in Afghanistan at the time. She wrote that the destruction even extended to the felling of the trees of Kabul as a form of payment for Bacha's partisans.[3] According to the Peshawar correspondent of the *Daily Telegraph,* "Kabul is a city where rioting and sabotage are a daily feature, a city where the inhabitants are living in daily terror of more terrible occurrences, and where no one knows who rules, nor what may occur at any moment." The new Amir was reported to be "looting and doing everything to provide himself with funds and material against the coming spring when the capital will be attacked from several fronts."[4]

The reign of terror, however, was followed by decrees that were designed to enhance the new ruler's popularity: he promised to lower the burdensome taxes, and he abolished the conscription law. He also dissolved the ministries of education and justice, both of which were regarded as unnecessary and unwelcome infringements on the power of the religious establishment.[5] The sole responsibility for the courts and schools reverted to the Muslim religious leadership.

After the initial chaotic phase of his rule, Bacha made an attempt to legitimize his reign. In this he enjoyed the support of many Afghan religious leaders, who proclaimed their fidelity and bonds to Amanullah severed and announced their endorsement of Amir Habibullah Ghazi, "the servant of God and the Nation and the ardent partisan of the pure faith of the Prophet and the doctrines of Hazrat Sahib."[6] Bacha himself felt that he represented the "true faith" and attempted to lay the causes of his rebellion as well as the reasons for his former occupation as a brigand to Amanullah's "ridiculous innovations regarding clothes, beard, veil, and head dress and reforms of [a] much [more] serious type calculated to injure the sanctity of Islam"; because of these innovations, he claimed, he had been forced to take a vow to "serve the cause of God by opposing the irreligious Amir and helping the cause of the *ulama* and *Shariat* and of the Holy Prophet."[7]

Bacha set out to consolidate his power and assert his rule over other areas. In this he had some success, managing to occupy Kandahar, Mazar-i-Sharif (the capital of Afghan Turkestan), and Herat.[8] To restore some kind of order, he formed a regular government made up of relatives and friends. His younger brother Hamidullah was given the title assistant to the Amir; Seyed Hussein, his closest companion, became minister of war; Sher Jan, another close friend, was made chamberlain; and Ata ul-Haq, a brother of Sher Jan, was appointed minister of foreign affairs. The new Amir followed the same practice in filling the other cabinet posts. Of the eight members of the new Afghan cabinet, four, including the Amir himself, were illiterate.[9] None of them had administrative experience.

Bacha had been undecided on the question of whether or not to retain a ministry of foreign affairs. However, he not only decided that the ministry was necessary but even tried to promote better relations with foreign powers, hoping to enhance his prestige and possibly legitimize his rule.

His attitude toward foreign residents during the two months of bloody civil war was one of benevolent cooperation: no injuries were inflicted on any foreigner, and it was thanks to his assistance, whether voluntarily given or forcibly obtained, that the more than 500 foreign residents had been evacuated to India by the British Air Force. Despite the mass exodus of diplomatic personnel and technical advisers, Afghanistan did not lapse into its pre-Amanullah diplomatic and physical isolationism; the Turkish, Persian, and Soviet diplomatic missions were not withdrawn from Kabul, and Germany sent its consul-general in Calcutta to Kabul to act as chargé d'affaires.[10] Bacha thus had avenues through which he might have normalized relations with foreign powers and gained international recognition of his *de facto* regime. His greatest asset, however, was Afghanistan's strategic position, which made it too important for its neighbors, especially Great Britain and Soviet Russia, to allow it to revert to isolationism or to remain in a state of internal political uncertainty for any period of time. However, Bacha's cancellation of Amanullah's reform program made the presence of foreign technical advisers unnecessary, and by August 1929, there were reportedly only some 30 foreigners in Afghanistan, a number that included 14 members of the Soviet diplomatic mission, three French citizens, and a few Turkish and Persian diplomats.[11]

In a speech during the Afghan independence day festivities, Bacha made overtures to the foreign powers, declaring that he was dedicated to the safeguarding of Afghan independence, but was ready to reestablish good relations with other countries. He announced that he was receptive to the idea of reopening the schools at some future date and spoke of his determination not to oppose any reforms that did not conflict with the tenets of Islam or threaten the strict principles of Muslim orthodoxy that guided him. As part of the festivities and evidently to prove his open-mindedness, a theatrical performance was staged in honor of the foreign guests. A two-act didactic play entitled "How Islam Conquered Spain and How It Lost Her" was the offering.[12]

Under this "liberalization," Bacha allowed the publication of a paper, *Habib-ul-Islam*, which was dedicated to strengthening his rule and promoting conservative Islamic principles.[13] He even permitted the school for the instruction of foreign languages to reopen. At the reopening ceremonies, Qiamuddin Khan, one of his close associates, went so far as to emphasize the importance of learning "the languages of the unbelievers, without the knowledge of which it was impossible to have normal relations with foreign states."[14]

REACTION OF THE GREAT POWERS

The foreign powers, especially the major ones, were noncommittal and cool to Bacha's diplomatic overtures. Though they did not break diplomatic relations with Afghanistan, they did not grant *de jure* recognition to the new regime. According to certain unconfirmed reports, Bacha's rebellion presented the Soviet authorities with a dilemma, causing the decision-making bodies of Soviet Russia to split over the course of action to follow after Amanullah's abdication. As these reports have it, the Comintern and the O.G.P.U. (Soviet secret police) favored supporting Bacha-i-Saqao, arguing, among other things, that his revolt was a social one, which had "sprung from the people," and that "his power was based on the peasants whose champion he was." The Commissariat of Foreign Affairs, on the other hand, argued for the support of either Amanullah or Inayatullah on the ground that Bacha, a Tajik, would not be accepted by the Durranis, or, indeed, by most of the Afghan and Pathan tribes. Moreover, in the view of the Soviet diplomats, if Bacha was indeed a British puppet who had come to "restore feudal authority as a necessary condition for the British colonization" of Afghanistan, he might, as a Tajik, represent a danger for the security of Soviet Central Asia: he could disseminate anti-Soviet propaganda among the Tajiks of Central Asia and possibly encourage pro-Basmachi political activities in the region. Agabekov, the major source of this information, asserts that the Politburo decided to take the advice of the foreign affairs office and champion the cause of Amanullah.[15] Accordingly, in 1929 Soviet authorities reportedly aided Ghulam Nabi, the Afghan ambassador to Moscow, who crossed the Afghan-Soviet border at the head of a small army detachment in an attempt to mobilize the people of Afghan Turkestan and transform the area into a pro-Amanullah base of operations.

Nabi's attempt failed. Hearing of Amanullah's flight to India and of the collapse of resistance in Kandahar and Mazar-i-Sharif, and unable to withstand Bacha's forces, he was forced to recross the Oxus into Soviet territory and to go into exile.[16] The Soviet press, meanwhile, kept up a steady attack on Bacha and his alleged alliance with Great Britain. The Soviets contended that Great Britain had sent arms, military instructors, and financial aid to Bacha in an effort to strengthen his hold over Kabul; in their view, this was the second move in a policy that had sponsored the reactionary uprising against Amanullah in the first place.[17] The evacuation of the British diplomatic mission from Kabul was only a ruse, declared *Izvestia*: "After sponsoring the revolt, they are afraid that they may find themselves in a very delicate situation if the victory went to the adversaries, hence the urgent evacuation of the Mission and especially the recall of Humphreys, who was implicated in the Afghan uprising." The Moor had done his job, said *Izvestia*.[18] A few days later it renewed the attack, charging that the ultimate aim of Great Britain was to split Afghanistan into a number of hostile provinces, which would consume their energies in internecine battles and thus be powerless to oppose the designs of the Anglo-Indian government and British imperialism.[19] A favorite Soviet theory held that Bacha had been planted in Afghanistan by the British in order to establish a close alliance with Saïd Alim, the former Emir of Bukhara, and Ibrahim Beg, the Basmachi leader. The goal of such an alliance was either the rekindling of the Basmachi revolt in Central Asia or the preparation of an aggressive move against Tajikistan.[20] One Soviet paper asserted that Bacha's rule represented the darkness of the Middle Ages in a struggle against a modern bourgeois culture and suggested that the unholy alliance between British imperialism, Bacha, the mullahs, and the feudal lords was perhaps simply the prelude to a military adventure against the Soviet state.[21] The Soviet government's press attacks were extended to Iran, which was warned not to entertain any hopes of a partition of the Afghan kingdom or a reconquest of Herat. Such designs, the Soviets asserted, would be beneficial only to British imperialism.[22]

The British government's position was a very difficult one, and its policy most complex. Though the British were fearful that Amanullah's disappearance from the Afghan political scene would plunge the country into anarchy, creating a vacuum that would allow the Soviets to establish a base for revolutionary operations in India, they were unwilling to intervene openly: "Warned by the painful experience of the past century against intervention in Afghan internal affairs, they had refused Amanullah's requests for help, and ignored hints thrown out by Bacha that he should be accorded official recognition as the ruler of the Afghan state."[23] The British government devised an extremely delicate policy: to prevent a possible extension of Soviet influence or inroads in Afghanistan and to preserve the 1921 Anglo-Afghan treaty, Great Britain quickly granted *de facto* recognition to the new government (and was, in fact, the first European state to do so) ;[24] at the same time, she withdrew her diplomatic mission, leaving herself open and noncommitted, in a position to avoid alienating the tribes, especially the Durranis, and free to deal with any future contender who might successfully challenge Bacha.

Despite the apparent strength of the bandit Amir, his authority had shallow roots. The Shinwari tribe, which had led the uprising against Amanullah, refused to accept him and continued their struggle against the neighboring tribes, infesting the caravan route between the Khyber Pass and Kabul. More important, most of the Afghan tribes, both within the country and across the frontier, either refused to take a stand or were openly hostile to him. The Durrani tribe and its powerful ruling class resented the loss of political preeminence they had held since 1747, and especially resented the usurpation of the throne by a non-Afghan, a lowly and illiterate Tajik bandit. Faced with this strong opposition, Bacha, who had initially gained the tacit and at times even the active support of the powerful Durrani rivals, the Ghilzais, failed to forge a strong alliance with them and, by sharing his power with them, to use them to counterbalance the Durranis. Meanwhile, the Hazaras, who had actively supported Amanullah in his bid to recapture the throne, remained aloof. Nor was Bacha able to win the support of the Shi'ah Muslims. Reportedly even those in the transfrontier areas, notably in Tirah, supported Amanullah, the first Afghan ruler who had not capitalized on or manipulated Shi'ah-Sunni religious antagonisms for political ends.[25]

Bacha's difficulties were compounded by his fiscal plight. Faced with the virtual independence of the major Afghan tribes, a ravaged urban population, a dislocated central administration, and a disorganized army, he needed financial resources to set his kingdom in order. His treasury, however, was depleted. He resorted to the expediency of striking new coins, but this was of no help: the new money had little real value. Metal was scarce, since the Afghan mines had been idle during the civil war. In desperation leather coins were devised to supplement the nickel and silver money. According to Morrish, this desperate measure was coupled with "pressing appeals ... to merchants to pay into the state treasury all that could be afforded. [Though] high rates of interest were offered, and every inducement was held out to persuade the more wealthy to come to the aid of the state ... the Kabuli was not anxious to sink his savings in government 'security' which might easily prove to be waste paper within a few months."[26]

Bacha was unable to restore order to the point where normal trade might resume. Tribes that had fought against Amanullah were demanding to be rewarded and were plundering caravans with impunity. The bandit Amir, who had capitalized on the corruption of the Amanullah administration, was unable to uproot dishonest tax collectors or to regularize the archaic and erratic customs system. In order to consolidate his power, he had increased the pay of the officers of the royal army, promised a 200 per cent raise to the common soldiers, and agreed to increase the state's financial contributions to the members of the religious establishment. He was not only unable to fulfill these commitments; he was not even able to provide pay regularly. In urgent need of money, but unable to get it by the usual methods, e.g., forcible loans, or pressing the Afghan tribes for their overdue taxes, Bacha reverted to another familiar practice, extortion, forcing the well-to-do merchants and citizens of Kabul to contribute to his treasury. Again according to Morrish: "For months life in Kabul was terrible. None was safe, houses were pillaged indiscriminately, women were ravished, and a reign of terror was established unprecedented in the annals of bloody Afghan history."[27] Outside the city Bacha selected members of his clan to act as informers, stationing them throughout the country to compile reports on the approximate wealth of the citizens of various districts, the volume of trade, and the income of prospective victims.[28] The devaluation of Afghan money and the large-scale extortions alienated not only the merchants of Kabul but also the powerful Afghan merchants of Peshawar, who in fear of their own ruin as well as that of Afghanistan, adopted a resolutely anti-Bacha posture and began searching for a new candidate for the Afghan throne.[29] It was under these conditions that the cause of the Durrani tribe and the leadership of the anti-Bacha forces were assumed by the four brothers of the powerful Musahiban family—Shah Wali Khan, Mahmud Khan, Hashim Khan, and the driving spirit of the opposition, Sardar Muhammed Nadir Khan.

NADIR KHAN

Born in 1883, Nadir Khan was related to both Afghan royal dynasties. On his father's side he was a Muhammedzai, on his mother's a Sadozai. He was a kinsman of Dost Muhammed and a third cousin of Amanullah by marriage. In addition, the second wife of Amanullah's father was Nadir's sister. He and his brothers were born in India (in Dehra Dun, according to one source)[30] during the family's exile. Like the Tarzis, the Musahibans returned to Afghanistan after the death of Abdur Rahman; like the Tarzis, they rose to important positions within the Habibullah administration.

Nadir, for instance, was appointed a colonel in the elite royal guard at the age of twenty, and by 1906 was a brigadier-general in the royal army; by 1913 he had assumed the office of commander-in-chief.[31]

Nadir's role in the Young Afghan movement is not clear. According to some accounts, as early as 1917 there were two schools of thought within the Afghan nationalist-reformist movement, one led by Mahmud Tarzi, the other by Nadir.[32] The major disagreement between the two seems to have been on the question of timing. Tarzi, representing the more radical wing, wanted extensive and rapid social change, using the Turkish blueprint for modernization as a guideline, whereas Nadir opposed draconian measures and, taking into full account the problem of the religious establishment and the Afghan tribes, advocated a more moderate indigenous program and a more leisurely timetable.[33]

Though Nadir had been among those arrested for complicity in the assassination of Habibullah, he was soon released and was reinstated as commander-in-chief of the army. In the Third Anglo-Afghan War, his command was the only one that fared well militarily. His troops advanced through Khost to the Kurram Valley and, according to Fraser-Tytler, "seriously upset the British defensive system from the Khyber to the Gumal."[34] During the war, he was instrumental in enlisting the support of some of the transfrontier Pathan tribes to the cause of Afghan nationalism and the war effort. In the years 1919–24 he was an outspoken critic of the British consolidation and forward policies in the Pathan tribal belt, and it was largely at his insistence that in the peace settlement a clause was inserted in the agreement granting amnesty to the transfrontier tribesmen who had fought against the British. For all these reasons, he had great repute and influence among the frontier tribes.[35]

In this same period there were marked personality and policy conflicts between Nadir, Mahmud Tarzi, and Muhammed Wali Khan, the minister of war. There is also evidence that there was increasing friction between Amanullah and Nadir over both the tempo of Afghan modernization and the governmental policies in dealing with tribal opposition to that modernization, Nadir apparently advocating conciliation and the use of intra-tribal jirgas instead of force.* These differences culminated in Nadir's demotion

---

* Fraser-Tytler (*Afghanistan*, pp. 224–25) attributed the rift to Amanullah's desire to surround himself with "yes men." Mohammed Ali, an apologist of the Musahiban family, provides the following unsatisfactory explanation of the conflict: "The ... worthless and selfish courtiers seized every opportunity to poison the mind of the King against them [members of the Musahiban family]. What they wanted was that no honest and capable men should be allowed to retain office under the government, so that they might be able to fish in the troubled water and fatten themselves on bribes

and virtual exile to France, where from 1924 to 1926 he served as the Afghan envoy. Because of deteriorating health and continued disagreements with the Amanullah administration, he resigned and retired to Nice, where he was joined by two of his brothers, Hashim Khan and Shah Wali Khan.[36]

After the Afghan revolt and the ascendancy of Bacha-i-Saqao, the three brothers ended their self-imposed exile in southern France and at the end of February 1929 returned to Afghanistan. In the meantime, Bacha, mindful of the power of the Musahiban family, had sent two delegates to France to invite Nadir to return to Kabul, reportedly as premier.[37]

On reaching Peshawar, Nadir had to decide on a course of action. He had, of course, been invited to enter the service of the new Amir; that invitation he declined with contempt. He had also been invited by Amanullah to join him in Kandahar; he rejected that invitation, too. Instead, he decided to proceed to Khost in order to rally the Afghan tribes and make them the basis of an anti-Bacha campaign.[38]

On March 19, 1929, Nadir challenged Bacha to submit the question of the legitimacy of his claim to a national jirga to be made up of all the Afghan tribal chieftains.[39] The issue was an important one, since Bacha's hold on the throne had been legitimized by the religious establishment, but had not been officially sanctioned by the tribal chiefs. Nadir's challenge angered Bacha, who responded by imprisoning all the members of Nadir's family and confiscating their property.[40] The bandit Amir put a price on Nadir's head, distributing leaflets in southern and eastern Afghanistan that read:

Whereas we have received intimation that Muhammed Nadir Khan has set on the path which borders on to treason against the paramount Muslim state, and whereas he wishes to sow the seeds of discord and disunion among Muslims, I hereby make it known to you that he is the same Nadir whose brothers and relatives were the Amir's assistant commanders and advisers.

It was his party which was responsible for the murder of the late Amir, an established fact to which the whole of Afghanistan bears witness. Having done with the Amir, the general and his men turned their kind attention to Amanullah, and because of their machinations against the commandments of Islam and the rules of Hijrat migrated from a Muslim Kingdom to the infidel land [France]. Now, wherefore I being Amir of the Muslims and Defender of the Faith took mercy upon them and being unaware of their evil intentions allowed them to come back to their country, the brothers were summoned with honour from Europe. But because during their stay in Europe they had been partaking

---

and embezzle public money to their heart's content.... The King, being young and raw, could not see through their destructive designs. He soon forgot the meritorious services of this family and began to depend upon the advice of these selfish courtiers" (*The Mohammedzai Period*, pp. 168–69).

of ham and bacon which has permeated their blood vessels and blackened all their fibre and veins, they on arrival in Afghanistan rose up against me and instigated the people to rebel. For the above reasons I consider it lawful to take their blood. Be it known therefore to all and sundry that anyone capturing Nadir Khan alive will get a reward of 40,000 rupees and one gun, and anyone bringing his head will get 30,000 rupees and one gun. For the capture of each of his brothers I promise a reward of 10,000 rupees and a gun.*

In the Khost region, meanwhile, Nadir Khan and his three brothers attempted to organize an effective opposition against Bacha's regime. Their strategy was to win the alliance of the important Pathan transfrontier tribes as well as the support of the Afghan tribes of the Kabul-Kandahar-Jalalabad region. Mahmud Khan was sent to woo the Jajis, and Shah Wali Khan was sent to win over the Mangals, while Nadir himself tried to get a commitment from the Jadrans. It was, however, the support of the Durranis that was critical. Nadir appealed to the tribes through *Islah*, a weekly paper he established (which was printed in Jaji territory). In it he focused on the question of the legitimacy of Bacha's rule and emphasized Bacha's lower-class origin, his career as an outlaw, and especially his non-Afghan ethnic background. The paper termed the bandit Amir's assumption of the throne an affront to Afghan and Pathan honor, and a defiance of the tribal code, which required that a jirga be convened and consulted. *Islah* carried the latest details of Bacha's tyrannous and capricious rule, giving prominence to particularly alarming news, for instance, reports that Bacha was about to institute a heavy taxation system in order to form a strong royal army with which to fight against the Afghan people.[41]

Nadir ran into many difficulties. The initial response of the tribes to his appeals was disappointing. Jirgas that were assembled at Gardez and at Mukur were not successful in swinging a powerful Afghan tribal confederation behind Nadir. The former Afghan commander-in-chief did not have enough money and arms to recruit an army. The Durranis were divided, the Ghilzais remained aloof. The fact is, many tribal chieftains were not anxious to see law and order reestablished.[42] Amanullah's repudiation of his abdication and his effort to recapture the throne made Nadir's situation even more difficult. However, since he had proclaimed himself for legitimacy but had not thrown in his lot with Amanullah, his

* *Pioneer*, April 24, 1929. According to Bacha's "autobiography," he "intensified [his] propaganda regarding the General's intrigue on behalf of Amanullah, and so bitter was the feeling against the ex-King that Nadir Khan found plenty of tribesmen only too anxious to bar his progress" (Habib-Allah, p. 221).

own struggle was not discredited by Amanullah's failure. On the contrary, in his role of mediator he was in a position to court both the pro-Amanullah and the anti-Amanullah tribes.

THE FALL OF BACHA

Nadir's initial military ventures were marked with frustrations and failures. The tribal levies he had managed to recruit among the Waziri, Mohmand, Mangal, Jaji, and Jadran tribes were divided by traditional hostilities; suspicions at times led to defections. These tribal rivalries were exploited by Bacha, who had some early success and managed to occupy Gardez.[43] However, the tide turned against him in June 1929, when Sher Agha, a Ghilzai tribal chief and a brother of the famous Hazrat Sahib, assembled a jirga of southern and western tribes and threw his support to Nadir.[44] On September 25, 1929, the Musahiban brothers launched an offensive (their fifth) against Bacha's forces. The three-pronged attack was successful, and on October 6 the troops of the bandit Amir were defeated. Three days later a tribal force led by Shah Wali Khan and Allah Nawaz Khan, the chief of the Waziri tribe, entered Kabul, and on October 13 the citadel where Bacha had taken refuge fell,* though Bacha himself escaped.[45] Two days later Nadir entered Kabul to the cheers of the tribesmen, the relief of the townspeople, and the welcome of the Persian, Turkish, and Soviet diplomatic representatives.[46]

The 12,000 tribesmen, mostly Waziris, who had defeated Bacha's forces, demanded to be rewarded for their services. However, Bacha had either looted the treasury or effectively concealed any remaining cash, and Nadir did not have the money to reward them. Consequently, the tribesmen sought their own reward: Kabul was plundered. Writes Fraser-Tytler: "There was neither an army to restore order, nor police order, nor police to maintain it if restored, and there were several thousand triumphant tribesmen, undisciplined and hungry for loot, demanding either a just reward for their services or permission to seek it for themselves." He adds: "Permission was granted, and Nadir had to stand by while all government buildings and even the French legation were stripped of every article of

---

* The attack on the citadel was a risky one, since members of the Musahiban family were being held hostage there. According to Ghazi (p. 76), Nadir's wife wrote to her husband, urging him to do his duty and attack Kabul: the family was ready to die for the liberation of the fatherland. Nadir's answer to Bacha's blackmail, says Ghazi (p. 40), was to the effect that the honor of Afghanistan could not be negotiated with the life of his family.

value."[47] By all evidence, there is no justification for such an assertion (and that evidence includes the testimony of Andrée Viollis, the only foreign correspondent in Kabul at the time). It appears rather that the plundering took place during the five days preceding Nadir's entry into the city, and that it was not officially condoned. Indeed, Nadir had issued a manifesto specifically ordering the tribesmen, under penalty of death, to respect the lives and property of foreigners. His orders were simply ignored. The Turkish, Persian, and Soviet legations suffered only minor damage, but the French Legation was thoroughly looted, as were the houses of the few Europeans who remained in Kabul.[48] Kabul itself was ransacked. The citizens of the capital thus paid a high price for their liberation from Bacha-i-Saqao. In all, according to Shah Wali Khan, in the five major battles as well as in the occupation of Kabul, Bacha lost some 15,000 followers.[49]

Meanwhile, the bandit Amir, a fugitive with a huge price on his head, was betrayed by his followers and handed over to Nadir Khan. Writing of his capture, Bacha said: "I underestimated the power of greed. Large rewards were offered for my capture, and it was unarmed hillmen who eventually took me, and not sabre thrusters from Kabul."[50] The fact is that the circumstances of his surrender and execution are not clear. Some sources report that before fleeing from the citadel, his last line of defense, Bacha killed his elderly father in order to save him from the expected humiliation and vengeance of his enemies; they further claim that Bacha spared the lives of the women and children he was holding hostage.[51] To this reported act of generosity, some modern historians add still another note: they assert that Bacha was not captured but instead surrendered himself to Nadir, after receiving a promise of pardon. Fletcher, for one, advances this view, stating that Nadir was, however, "unable to restrain the tribesmen or to resist their demand for the death of the bandit."[52] Fraser-Tytler, for his part, subscribes to the view that Nadir played little or no part in the execution of Bacha. "Subsequent information," he says, "showed that the brigand surrendered unconditionally after being deserted by his followers, and that his execution was demanded by the tribal army then in complete control of Kabul."[53] In an attempt to satisfy the demands of the southern tribes and to restore the honor of Afghanistan, the victors ordered the execution of several of Bacha's closest followers as well, notably his brother Hamidullah; Muhammed Siddik, the ex-governor of Kabul; Seyed Hussein, the ex-minister of war; Sher Jan, the court chamberlain; Abdul Wakil and Abdul Ghiyas, two of his generals; and two or three Kohistani chiefs.[54]

THE QUESTION OF A SUCCESSOR

With the deaths of Bacha and his followers, Afghan rule was ensured. However, the question of legitimacy and succession proved vexing. According to Viollis, many Afghan notables had begged Nadir to accept the throne as early as October 16, the date on which he had come to the ransacked and looted palace of Dilkusha to thank God and his supporters for the victory against the enemies of the Afghan fatherland, "who had ruined and dishonoured Afghanistan." On that occasion he reminded his countrymen of the past great services of Amanullah and urged the tribes to remain united for the task of reconstructing Afghanistan. Viollis reports that Nadir, referring to his own poor health, recommended that a jirga choose the next Amir, indicating he would then support that choice wholeheartedly. Nadir, she says, even asked the foreign diplomats to assist him in the choice of a candidate. The notables insisted, however, and the tribal warriors brandished their rifles, shouting that if Nadir Khan was not the Amir, they would leave. In the face of such overwhelming enthusiasm, Nadir gave in, saying simply: "Since the people do designate me so, I accept. I will not be the King but the servant of the tribes and the country." As he then prayed for divine guidance, his prayers were punctuated by a salvo of cannons announcing the election of a new Amir.[55] Toynbee asserts that Amanullah wired Nadir his congratulations, but he is mistaken on this point: Amanullah sent only congratulations on Nadir's victory.[56] In fact Nadir Khan's election to the throne soon became a matter of bitter and protracted controversy.

The supporters of Amanullah and his dynasty challenged the legitimacy of Nadir's rule and questioned his loyalty to Amanullah. They argued that Nadir's success against Bacha could be attributed in large part to various tribes shifting their allegiance to Amanullah, in whose name Nadir had professed to be fighting. This charge was spread by the Afghan trade agent at Peshawar who, in an interview in *Pioneer*, claimed that he had given financial assistance to Nadir on the understanding that it would help restore Amanullah to his throne. Stating that the jirga was "a flagrant contravention of Nadir Khan's solemn promise that he would support Amanullah Khan" and "a farce," the agent declared: "Nadir Khan, who from the beginning appears to have cherished the desire for Kingship, has by present act created more troubles for Afghanistan and wiped off all the good work hitherto done by him."[57] The pro-Amanullah elements charged that Nadir Khan had not made a strong plea for the case of Amanullah.

Furthermore, the small jirga that nominated and elected him had not spoken for all the tribes; in fact, only a few tribes were represented, and the gathering had not waited for the arrival of the representatives of the pro-Amanullah tribes of the west, who were on their way to Kabul. Amanullah's supporters rejected the contention that in restoring the ex-Amir to the throne, the jirga would have rekindled the Afghan civil war; it was highly unlikely that a war-weary Afghanistan, having rid itself of Bacha-i-Saqao, would embark anew on such a destructive course.[58] Some of the younger members of the pro-Amanullah forces were particularly unhappy, fearing that the election of Nadir meant a triumph of reaction and an appeasement of both the religious establishment and the British government in India.[59]

Amanullah's own reaction to Nadir's accession was at first one of conciliatory bewilderment. This was followed by a cautious wait-and-see attitude coupled with an optimistic expectation he would eventually be asked to return to his homeland and reassume the throne. With this in mind, he issued a statement in which he attempted to explain to the Afghans the "true circumstances" that had forced him to abandon his kingdom. In it he sought to refute the arguments of his opponents, who held that in the face of defeat he had dishonored himself and the Durranis by abandoning the struggle and the country, and that he had thus forfeited his claim to the throne. Amanullah declared that his departure from Afghanistan was not caused by the defeat of his armies at Kandahar and Ghazni; on the contrary, the battle of Ghazni had resulted in his victory. He had left Ghazni because he was faced with bloody quarrels between the two most powerful tribes in the country, the Durranis and the Ghilzais, the one supporting him, the other regarding him as an enemy of the Ghilzai race. A similar situation awaited him in Kandahar, he claimed, whereupon he had left, not wishing to have Afghan blood uselessly spilled in his name. It was not military force but intrigue that had defeated him, he declared. After hinting that his reforms, which had been approved by an all-Afghan national assembly, could be nullified or modified only by such an assembly, he appealed to world opinion and especially to other Muslim countries to take note: the forces that had triumphed in Afghanistan had nothing to do with Islam as a religion and were motivated only by "ignorance and gain." He ended this explanation on a note of self-abnegation: "I do not care whether I put on the crown or a feather on my cap—whether I sit on a throne or on a plank. All I care about is service for my country."[60]

Though Amanullah concluded his statement with a farewell to the Afghan people ("I leave you; you will not hear my name again. My wish is that this may bring you happiness"),[61] he was soon expressing his readiness to return to Afghanistan and assume the throne, if the Afghan people called him back. He is reported to have declared in Istanbul that, in such an eventuality, he would attempt once again to implement his modernization programs.[62]

The case against Amanullah and for the new ruler was best summarized in an article signed by Muhammed Amin in *Islah*. Entitled "Refutation of Futile Declarations of Amanullah Khan," the article declared an all-Afghan tribal jirga had rejected Amanullah's contention that Nadir had achieved victory by fighting in the ex-Amir's name. Said Amin:

> The noble Afghan nation will not allow itself once again to be cheated by the lies of Amanullah Khan.... At the time, the hatred of the Afghan nation for Amanullah was so strong that nobody... could pronounce the name of Amanullah Khan. All the circumstances of the fall of Amanullah Khan at Kabul, his flight to Kandahar, his defeat at Ghazni followed by his flight to Italy were well known. If the military operations against Bacha-i-Saqao and his partisans ... lasted for some time, that was because people had some doubts as to whether Nadir Shah was making war on behalf of Amanullah Khan. It is surprising that such an impudent lie could come out of the pen of Amanullah Khan. If Amanullah Khan was so much loved by his nation, how could the Great Revolution of Afghanistan take place? Nadir Shah and his family did not arrive in Afghanistan to reign but rather to save the country. He did not want to become a King. Kingship was thrust upon him "in the presence of delegates of the nation and the diplomatic corps." It was under the repeated pressures of the jirga that he accepted the burden of reign.

After reviewing Amanullah's "crimes" and outlining his "cowardice" and his "vices," Amin concluded with the statement that only "Nadir Shah could have saved Afghanistan from the revolution and the civil war."[63]

Shah Wali Khan offers substantially the same argument, writing that Nadir faced an almost impossible and desperate situation: Amanullah's army had been defeated at Ghazni; the important Ghilzai clan of Suleiman Khel had sided with Bacha (mullahs of the clan had argued with Nadir that to oppose the bandit Amir was to oppose the principles of Islam and Islamic law),[64] Amanullah and his brother Inayatullah had left for India; Ali Ahmad Khan, who had proclaimed himself Amir in Kandahar, had been captured; Ghulam Nabi had been forced to return to Soviet Russia, and northern Afghanistan had fallen to Bacha; the Afghan minister to London, who had assumed control of Herat, had fled to Iran, and Herat, too, had acknowledged Bacha's sovereignty; and the British were opposing the active participation of the transfrontier tribes in the internecine struggle of Afghanistan.[65] Shah Wali Khan asserts that Amanullah's standing was extremely low among various Afghan tribes and the religious establishment, so low in fact that many tribal leaders (notably those of the Ahmedzai, Mangal, and Suleiman Khel tribes) insisted that Nadir first proclaim himself Amir to prove he was not in Amanullah's service, a condition that Nadir refused to accept. Amanullah was thus a liability, not an asset, in Nadir's struggle to liberate Afghanistan from the rule of the usurper, Shah Wali Khan insists.

Looking back at the political developments and the record of the activities of Nadir and his brothers during the crucial period between February and October, 1929, one is forced to agree with the observation of Professor Ghosh that Nadir, on his arrival in India, was "wonderfully discreet in all his replies to welcome addresses or the interviewers' queries."

He had his own reason for not committing himself absolutely one way or the other. He would first see how far Amanullah had alienated the sympathies of the tribes before he chalked out his line of action. Only at Lahore station, perhaps moved by the unprecedented enthusiasm of thousands of Muslims, Hindus, and Sikhs ... did the General in an unguarded moment declare that "he would not rest until he had seen Amanullah back on the throne of his ancestors." Otherwise his general line was that "he would do or say nothing for Amanullah until he had received a verdict of the tribes in a jirga."[66]

Morrish, at the time a close observer of the Afghan scene, agrees:

Nadir Khan was fully aware of the mistakes which Amanullah had made. He knew that he had become utterly discredited by those who exerted influence in Kabul, and he feared that were he again to be given the throne which he had deserted, even then the Afghan trouble would not be ended but a second revolution, probably more fierce and even more extensive, would result. Nadir Khan made his policy plain. He stated openly that he was prepared to attempt to defeat the Bacha, but if successful, then the people—the masses—must choose their King. He neither bound himself to support nor oppose the ex-monarch.*

---

* According to Morrish (pp. 18–19, 45), it was this policy that kept Nadir from receiving the financial support of the pro-Amanullah merchants of Peshawar in the early stages of his struggle. Chokaiev ("Situation in Afghanistan," p. 326) sees Nadir's acceptance of the throne as "resulting from and justified by the course of events," rather than as the fulfillment of his personal ambitions. Says Fraser-Tytler (*Afghanistan*, p. 226): "It is very doubtful whether from the outset any such intention had crossed his mind. Nadir Shah was a patriot who loved his country with a fervour which was fanatical in its intensity, and who believed that he himself had been chosen by God to lead the Afghans along the path of prosperity and peace." In a personal interview, Sir Francis Humphreys agreed with this assessment. According to Ghazi (p. 38), Nadir consistently stated that his sole aim in returning to Afghanistan was to serve his fatherland. He had also stated that he could not accept the rule of anyone who was not acceptable to the Afghan people as a whole, and that he himself was not a candidate for kingship. His position was that once the civil war had ended, the Afghans ought to choose their monarch in the time-honored way. Within that context, he was not opposed to Amanullah: Amanullah's future depended on the will of the Afghan people. In this connection, see also Muhieddin, pp. 270ff. Ghazi further asserts (p. 94)

THE SPLIT IN THE MODERNIST CAMP

The Afghan revolution and civil war exposed a deep rift among the Afghan modernists, a rift that found the advocates of gradual modernization pitted against those advocating rapid change, a rift that separated the supporters of Amanullah and his dynasty from those championing Nadir, a rift that revived family and personal feuds between the Tarzi and Charki families on the one hand and the Musahibans on the other. For some two decades following Nadir's accession to the throne, the members of the Charki and Tarzi families and many supporters of Amanullah lived in exile in Turkey, India, or Europe. However, some who had once supported and praised Amanullah and his reformers shifted their loyalty to Nadir. Prominent among them was Ikbal Ali Shah, who asked:

Is it either possible or fitting to apply to the Eastern hemisphere the whole apparatus of Western civilization without making allowances for psychology and environment? Is even the partial adaptation of Occidental culture to Oriental life wise or politic? Would it not be more judicious, more scientific to allow the East to develop in its own way and along its own lines, of course, under proper safeguards, both administrative and commercial?

The pessimism of the ex-Amanullah supporters led them to glorify the virtues of the East against modernization and Westernization and to denounce the West. Again in Shah's words:

In the "waiting East" Asians are striving with their souls rather than their bodies to achieve mental and moral perfection. To such men the merely material endeavors of European civilization are as vanity and worse than vanity. ... It is in spirituality that the West is unquestionably inferior to the East. ... It is difficult for a cultivated Oriental to comprehend the arguments of the Westerner that it would be to the benefit of Asia to adopt the Occidental mode of existence. The European points to such things as quick transit, sanitation, police, and "settled government" as among the blessings bestowed by his civilization. The amusing thing is that he possesses them himself only superficially, as the slums of any great European city show. ... Rapid transit of the West ... has merely given more time to waste in other ways. ... Machinery has brought into being a generation of toilers who work merely that they may be kept in life, whose leisure, if any, is spent in useless and stupid amusements, people who have no higher outlook whatsoever. ... We are divided by psychological gulfs so profound as can scarcely ever be surpassed. Our destinies lie in totally different directions, and this we must accept. Only Europe's most enlightened minds are capable of recognizing the eventual superiority of our system of psychic thought and effort. ... No, we cannot follow Europe where Europe is going, because our path has not only been clearly defined for us ages ago but we feel it instinctively to be the true one for us.[67]

---

that Nadir insisted the Assembly of Notables reelect Amanullah or select a member of his family as monarch, but the Assembly rejected the suggestion and pressed for Nadir's candidacy.

As previously noted, most Afghan students and modernists who returned to Afghanistan and accepted the rule of Nadir Shah had (and still have) difficulty explaining the nature and causes of the Afghan revolution and the success of Bacha-i-Saqao. Disinclined to interpret the revolution as a popular uprising against modernization and Westernization, they have thus come to attribute the causes of the anti-Amanullah movement to haste and to external factors and intrigues. Typical in this regard is the noted Afghan historian and diplomat Abdur Rahman Pazhwak (who was the president of the UN General Assembly in 1966). He writes:

By the time Amanullah returned from Europe, the impression of all he had seen there made him eager to introduce the western way of life into his country with revolutionary swiftness. Although the King's reforms were resisted by a certain group of reactionaries who were strongly opposed to the modernisation of their country, this opposition was confined to but one section of the population too weak to maintain its stand. The fierce civil wars which broke out in the country had their cause not, as some writers have tried to represent, in the reluctance of the Afghan people to see their country develop along modern lines, but rather in the political maneuverings of outside elements.[68]

Writing in a similar vein, Roashan maintains that Amanullah was determined to Westernize Afghanistan almost overnight. This, says Roashan, brought some opposition from a section of the population, "but the ensuing revolt against him was really hastened by the intrigues of foreign elements rather than a lack of desire on the part of the nation to see Afghanistan develop along modern lines."[69]

The immediate aim of the Afghan nationalists and modernists was to go beyond the question of legitimacy and dynastic feuds and defend the future of Afghan modernism. In general, on the eve of Nadir Shah's accession to the Afghan throne, many modernists were hopeful that his rule would not be one of reaction but would usher in a period of socioeconomic and political reconstruction—and ultimately a modern Afghanistan.

Chapter Eleven

Nadir Shah: From Anarchy to Selective Modernization

Following his accession to the Afghan throne, Nadir Khan outlined a program aimed at reestablishing political stability in the country and effecting a socioeconomic reconstruction of Afghan society. In interviews with the correspondents of *Petit Parisien, Hamburger Nachrichten,* and the *Daily Mail,* he outlined his immediate preoccupations and future intentions. His first priorities were to repair the ruins of Afghanistan and "to preserve jealously its independence." Then, without intruding on religious beliefs and time-honored traditions, he intended to help his people find material and intellectual progress. "I am for a certain progress and for cultural reforms in the Western sense: but I want such reforms to be introduced with a slower pace than those adopted by Amanullah. The fact that Amanullah's reforms brought his downfall does not prove in any way ... that they were bad. If in order to cure himself fast the sick absorbed a potion tenfold stronger than [that] prescribed by the doctor, he certainly may become sicker. That, however, does not prove in any way that the medicine itself was bad." The government, he said, should not impose upon the Afghan people new ideas and institutions; new programs ought to develop naturally.[1] Within this context, Nadir saw no reason "why religion and progress should disagree. Islam, one of the world's greatest religions, does not constitutionally prohibit progress. The two can march side by side.[2]

Nadir's policies—as elaborated by his supporters in *Islah,* the semiofficial Afghan newspaper, and in speeches before tribal assemblies—were based on the belief that Afghan independence rested on the cornerstones of security, prosperity, and science. Education, military reforms, and the development of commerce, agriculture, and industry were all necessary for both the material and the spiritual strength of the Afghan people. To be a good Muslim and a good Afghan one had to contribute to the stability, prosperity, and progress of Afghanistan under the guidance of the monarchy, but also "under the shadow of the sacred law of Islam."[3] It was his belief that conservatism and progress could be reconciled, that Afghan conservatism would be a miraculous element both "adamantine, yet fully sensitive to and assimilative of new cultural forces."[4]

To institute his program and consolidate the rule of his dynasty, Nadir relied heavily on his brothers as well as on the cooperation of the religious establishment and the Afghan tribes. His government was virtually a family circle: Hashim Khan was premier, Shah Wali Khan was minister of war and commander-in-chief, and Shah Mahmud Khan was minister of the interior. To please the moderate Afghan modernists (and possibly to please Muslim modernists and nationalists abroad as well), Nadir retained two ministers from Amanullah's government. Faiz Muhammed Khan, the former minister of education, became minister of foreign affairs, and Ali Muhammed Khan, the former minister of commerce, was named minister of education. At the same time, Nadir sought to ensure peaceful coexistence with the Afghan religious establishment, and as a gesture of conciliation to conservative and anti-Amanullah forces, made some rather large concessions. He named Sher Agha, the brother of the religious leader Hazrat Sahib, minister of justice and Muhammad Saïd, another brother, minister of state. Hazrat Sahib himself became the Afghan minister to Egypt.[5] Nadir also absolved the anti-Amanullah forces of any blame in the former Amir's downfall, hoping thereby to win the support of the conservative and at times reactionary elements who so opposed Amanullah's social reforms. In 1931 he declared:

As for those persons and people who cherished hostility towards the government of Amanullah Khan, as well as the ministers and the officers and the spiritual leaders and respectable members of the public who were not agreeable to the personally harmful activities of Amanullah Khan, it is certain that their want of agreement with Amanullah Khan was for the good of the motherland and the happiness of the nation. They desired to keep him back from those thoughtless and vainglorious activities which did not take into consideration the sentiments of the Nation or of Religion.[6]

In an effort to allay the suspicions of tribal chieftains and religious leaders that he meant to centralize political power at their expense, Nadir attempted to attribute a paternalistic character to his rule. In a proclamation issued on October 25, 1929, he declared:

The royal private property of Afghanistan is not personal in the real sense of the word. In other words, the private property has been so altered that from the beginning up till now a great deal has every now and then been taken from the public treasury and added to it; and as it stands today . . . the whole affair has assumed such an intricate form that it is impossible to distinguish the real property from that added afterwards. We therefore, considering all such properties as rightly belonging to the public treasury, ordain that all such lands, shops, etc., which now are included in the private royal assets be transferred to the public treasury of the nation and the office relative to the private property be abolished.[7]

A year later, in September 1930, an Afghan jirga rejected the demands of Amanullah that his properties and assets in Afghanistan be restored to him.[8]

Nadir went to great lengths to win over the Afghan religious establishment. He periodically made public statements repeating his complete support of and devotion to Islamic law. A notable example was on the occasion of the first anniversary of his rule (October 16, 1930), when he offered his thanks to God for changing the dark and perilous days of Afghanistan into happy ones, and declared that God, who was great, just, and merciful, rewarded only those individuals and communities who followed His fundamental laws: "According to Muslim beliefs, the success and the decadence of nations and governments depend on their observance or negligence of the divine law."[9] In another conciliatory move, he rescinded Amanullah's measures secularizing the law and established a tribunal of ulama at Kabul charged with the interpretation and administration of Islamic law.[10] He also ordered the first printing of the Quran in the Afghan kingdom, an act that was hailed by the Society of Ulama of Afghanistan as both pious and important in its commitment to the cause of the moral and religious education of the Afghans.[11]

Nadir, who often consulted the Society of Ulama on social, educational, and political issues, reinstated all customary and religious laws regarding the social position and appearance of women. Heavy veiling was again mandatory; strict purda and seclusion were reestablished; women had to wear the *chaderi* (an all-enveloping garment that covered the body from head to foot, with only a latticed opening allowing the wearer to see without being seen).[12] Bacha had cancelled a number of social reforms that had embittered and alienated the conservative ulama, and had closed the schools for girls, recalled the female students from abroad, and reinstated the laws of polygamy. Nadir now reaffirmed Bacha's rulings.[13] Honorary titles, which were abolished in 1928, were revived.[14] The government undertook to direct and conduct the affairs of state in strict accordance with "the tenets of the holy and sacred religion of Islam," according to the Hanafi school. The Ministry of Justice was assigned the responsibility of enforcing Islamic law throughout Afghanistan. A department of Ihtisab, which supervised the strict adherence of Muslims to the moral codes of Islam, was made "an essential feature of the government."[15] The

King denounced every breach of Muslim dietary restrictions, singling out the consumption of alcohol as particularly repugnant, "since it destroyed both the physical and spiritual forces of the individual" and his community.[16] A royal proclamation ordered severe punishment for drinking: "sale of liquor, public or private, was prohibited throughout the Afghan kingdom and the inhabitants were not allowed to brew liquors. If any employee of the government was found drinking, in addition to legal punishments prescribed under religious law, he was to be dismissed from his post."[17] All of these measures represent the price Nadir had to pay for national unity and political stability within the Afghan kingdom. In effect, he brought to a halt the efforts of his predecessors to undermine the power of the Afghan clerics; any reformist and modernization programs were now to percolate through the religious establishment.

Once Nadir had reached a *modus vivendi* with the religious and conservative forces, he was ready to initiate a cautious program of socioeconomic reconstruction. To prepare public opinion for new measures, the Nadir administration encouraged the formation of "conciliation and progress" committees in various urban centers. The committee of Kandahar was typical. It was made up of 28 of the town's most prominent citizens, whose tasks were to promote a spirit of national conciliation and unity, to attempt to eliminate the differences and distrust among the Afghan tribes of the region, and to seek ways to achieve happiness and progress within their area.[18]

THE REORGANIZATION OF THE ARMY

Nadir's most urgent tasks, once the ground was prepared, were to reestablish the army and to organize a functioning administration. The new army was to be recruited partly by annual draft calls and partly on a voluntary basis. Voluntary enlistment was for life; compulsory service was for two years active and eight years reserve duty, but conscripts were subject to call for additional military service until the age of sixty in case of national emergency.[19] Nadir abandoned Amanullah's unpopular recruitment policy in an effort to satisfy Afghan tribal interests, leaving the recruitment of soldiers among the tribes to the discretion of the chieftains or a tribal council. In case of need, the tribal leaders were required to help the Afghan monarchy with levies of tribesmen, but they retained the command of their units. Thus all attempts to tap, control, and gradually centralize the military resources of the tribes, as Amanullah had envisioned, were halted. Nadir also abandoned the traditional *makoolat* system, whereby the cost of a soldier's food was deducted from his pay. Under the new program, the soldiers received a ration allowance, and wages were paid in cash and on a regular basis. An attempt was made to provide medical facilities for the troops, with a central military hospital and rudimentary dispensaries under the supervision of a physician in each military cantonment.[20] To help build up a modern officer corps, students were sent to France and Germany for military training;[21] others received basic training in Afghanistan. In 1933 a preparatory military school, the Maktab-i-Ihzariah, was opened in Kabul for the sons of tribal chieftains who wanted to take up a military career. The army was provided with some mechanical transport, and the small Afghan air force, which had been established under Amanullah's administration, was reactivated; it was manned by Afghans who had been trained in Europe.[22]

The new army was built around a nucleus of some 12,000 men, mostly Hazaras, Mangals, and Mohmands. They were eventually joined by many of the soldiers who had served in Amanullah's army.[23] By 1933 the regular army was variously estimated to number between 40,000 and 70,000 men.[24] In order to arm the royal force, Nadir at first relied on appeals to wealthy merchants; later, after order was restored, customs duties and taxes provided additional revenue.[25] In addition, Nadir received great help in the early years—1929–31—from the British government in India. In his inaugural speech to the Afghan parliament, he referred to that assistance: "Great Britain last year, without any condition, rendered help to Afghanistan. This help consisted of a loan of 175,000 pounds without interest and 10,000 rifles and five lakh cartridges." Nadir was also able to take over existing credits and loans from Germany, which Amanullah had not used fully at the time of the revolution of 1929. The German government transferred the balance of the funds to him and extended the period of repayment from six to eight years. As part of the transaction, Germany provided some 5,000 rifles and half a million cartridges to Afghanistan. These were supplemented with 5,000 rifles purchased from Great Britain and some 16,000 rifles and 1.8 million cartridges purchased from France. Nadir justified these loans and gifts from the West on the grounds of necessity as well as historical precedent, pointing out that Amanullah had accepted similar assistance when the kingdom was torn by a revolt and later during his Grand Tour.[26]

Nadir's ultimate aim was to form a modern standing army of 100,000 men, with 15,000 men stationed in the southern province, 15,000 at Kandahar, 15,000 in northern Afghanistan, 10,000 at Jalalabad, 5,000 at Ghazni, and the remainder at Kabul.[27] His hope was that thus strategically deployed, the Afghan royal army could effectively guarantee internal stability and, through the help of tribal confederations, defend the independence of the kingdom. However, according to him, the real task of the army was to foster Afghan national unity and secure progress. In a speech at the inauguration of the military school at Kabul, he declared that in the past the country, "thanks to the bravery and courage of its inhabitants, has been considered throughout Asia as one of the most powerful countries." Unfortunately, he said, "an era marked by discords and civil wars has ruined and weakened our native land, and it is only after a series of coordinated efforts that it will be possible to reestablish its might and prosperity. I hope, with the help of almighty God, that Afghanistan may possess a strong and well-organized army that will constitute a beautiful rose on the head of its friends and a thorn in the eyes of its enemies—an army that would assure peace and prosperity in our country."[28]

ADMINISTRATIVE AND JUDICIAL REORGANIZATION

Nadir also focused his attention on reestablishing an administrative structure for the country. He divided Afghanistan into nine areas, consisting of five major provinces (*vilayat*), which were centered around the major urban centers of Kabul, Kandahar, Herat, Mazar-i-Sharif, Kataghan, and Badakhshan, and four minor provinces (*hukumat-i-ala*), which included Farah and Maimana provinces and the eastern and southern sub-provinces.[29] The provinces and sub-provinces were divided into first-, second-, and third-class prefectures (*hukumat*), depending on their size and importance; these were in turn divided into cantons (*ilaqadhari*). At the head of each of the five major provinces there was a governor (*vali*); the minor provinces were headed by chief administrators (*hakim-i-a'la*). Various prefectures were grouped together to form an administrative district (*hukumat-i-kalan*); its chief administrator (*hakim-i-kalan*) was subordinate to the provincial government. Each province and district had executive councils, which were to help in the maintenance of law and order and to counsel the governors and the district administrators on local and legal matters. The councils were made up of the heads of various governmental departments and the members of a consultative assembly (Majlis-e-Mashwarah) who were the elected representatives of the inhabitants of the area. The governors or the regional administrators presided over these councils. Below the canton level, towns with 10,000 or more inhabitants were formed into municipalities (*baladieh*), with elected mayors (*raïs*) and municipal councils. Municipal elections were subject to the approval of the provincial governors.[30]

A nationwide police force was also established. It was organized on a district and regional basis, but the overall authority was vested in the Ministry of Interior at Kabul. Since there were no trained police administrators in the country, the government sent a few Afghans to Birmingham, England, for training; they in turn were expected to train recruits in modern police methods. In the meantime, soldiers were used to supplement the police force.[31]

Nadir made significant concessions to the religious establishment in the legal field. He rescinded most of Amanullah's secularist measures, so that civil and criminal law were once again based wholly on Islamic law. Justice was administered through 106 lower or prefectural courts (*mahkame-ye ibtidaieh*), 19 courts of appeal (*mahkame-ye murafiah*), and a Supreme Court (Mahkame-ye Tamiz). The appeals courts sat in the provincial centers, the Supreme Court in Kabul. The executive councils, district and provincial assemblies, and tribal jirgas also had some juridical responsibilities, but their main function was one of counsel and arbitration. In effect, all justice was administered through religious courts; only minor breaches of the law were dealt with in the local police courts, and then the decisions were subject to appeal to the governor of the province.[32] The records the courts were required to keep show that in 1934 alone there were some 160 cases tried by the Supreme Court, 5,612 cases heard in the appeals courts, and 73,084 cases tried in the lower courts.[33] The Jamiyat-ul-Ulama (The Society of the Learned Muslim Interpreters of Law) was entrusted with the interpretation of existing law. All proposed governmental regulations and laws were also to be submitted to the society in order to ascertain their compatibility with holy writ.[34]

In an effort to combat administrative corruption and red tape, Nadir had a complaint box placed at the Ministry of Defense. The Kabulis were urged to help the government fight corruption but not to abuse this direct line to the rulers of the country for false accusations. The Amir's brother Shah Mahmud was reported to have been personally charged with handling citizens' complaints and to have had full powers to order inquiries if necessary.[35]

The Nadir administration also made a few attempts to correct the archaic and inhuman practices in the Afghan prisons. A central prison, which was built near Kabul, adopted elementary rules of hygiene, and medical officers were appointed to care for the prisoners. The idea of the rights of prisoners and of the prison as a corrective institution, concepts that had been pioneered by Amanullah but discarded by Bacha, gained currency again. A vocational school was established in the new prison, and the government for the first time undertook to feed the prisoners.* Theoretically, torture and cruel punishments were outlawed, and the anti-slavery laws enacted under Abdur Rahman, Habibullah, and Amanullah were revived.[36] Again, it is difficult to establish whether all these measures were enforced uniformly throughout the kingdom.

THE CONSTITUTION OF 1931

Nadir made a major attempt to restructure the entire legal framework of the Afghan state. In this area, his most noteworthy contribution was a constitution—the Usul-e Asasi-ye Dovlat-e Aliyya-e Afghanestan (The Fundamental Laws of the Government of Afghanistan)—which was promulgated on October 31, 1931.[37] It was divided into 16 sections with 110 articles, many of them retained from the constitution of 1923. One important change concerned the status of the non-Muslim communities in the country. Whereas the constitution of 1923 had a statutory provision requiring the Hindus and the Jews, as *dhimmis*, to pay a special tax and to wear distinctive emblems, the new constitution dropped all mention of such discriminations against non-Muslims. These communities were to be allowed to follow their own religious beliefs and instruction.[38]

The new constitution proclaimed that Afghanistan's religion and the religion of her monarch was the Hanafite rite of the "sacred religion of Islam." Non-Muslims were assured of religious tolerance and protection, "provided they did not infringe upon the ordinary rules of conduct, propriety, and public customs" (Article 1). By implication Articles 2 and 3 abolished tribal claims to territorial or regional sovereignty: all of the regions of the kingdom formed an organic whole under a monarch who enjoyed complete internal and external authority; all of the inhabitants of Afghanistan were equal in the eyes of the government. Article 5, which constituted a kind of compact between Nadir and the "noble Afghan nation," legitimized Nadir's rule and his dynasty. According to this article, in recognition of the meritorious services of Nadir, who had saved his people "from injustice and despotism," the Afghan people (the "entire Af-

---

* "Formerly the prisons of Afghanistan were a blot on humanity. The prisoners were lodged in dark chambers filthy beyond measure, and daily marched in chains through the streets to beg for their food, and to serve as a public warning" (Ahmad and Abd al-Aziz, pp. 109–10; see also Mohammed Ali, *Progressive Afghanistan*, p. 189).

ghan nation") accepted him as their true, worthy monarch. They further agreed to make the throne of Afghanistan hereditary, provided that Nadir's descendants executed the laws of the country in conformity with both the prescriptions of Islamic law, as interpreted by the ulama, and the established constitutional principles. There were other conditions as well: Nadir's successors must consider their "most important duty the protection of the independence of Afghanistan" and must remain "faithful to the people and the fatherland." Article 5 thus placed the source of sovereign power in the crown with the implied consent of the people. The next article required those ascending the throne to take a solemn oath before God and on the Quran "to defend the independence of Afghanistan, to protect the rights of the Afghan people," and to strive for the happiness of the fatherland and its progress, "in conformity with the holy religion of Islam and the legal advice of religious luminaries of Islam."

Article 7 listed the following royal prerogatives: the right to select and control a cabinet and all civil servants; a veto power over the legislative branch; the command of all armed forces (including the right to appoint the commander-in-chief); the right to conduct foreign policy, declare war, conclude peace, and make treaties; and, in the monarch's role as a last court of appeal, the right to grant royal pardons and commute sentences "in conformity to the rules of holy religion." The monarch was also to be mentioned in all Friday sermons and to have currency coined in his name.

Though all subjects of the kingdom were proclaimed to be equal, "without any distinction of creed and religion" (Article 9), all were required to respect and observe the injunctions and prohibitions of the government pertaining to political matters and religion, including those concerning the official rite (Article 10). These two seemingly contradictory articles were apparently designed to satisfy the Sh'iah minority of the kingdom without alienating the orthodox religious establishment. Article 15 tried to reconcile the two by proclaiming that all Afghans were equal before the holy religion and the laws established by the state. The constitution guaranteed personal liberties and property rights. Arrests and punishments could be made only in accordance with Islamic or state law (Article 11). Freedom of action in commerce, industry, and agriculture were guaranteed "within the limits of the appropriate regulations" (Article 12). Though private property was guaranteed, property necessary to the state, "for reason of public interest and in conformity to the prescriptions of sacred Shar'ia and established laws," could be expropriated; in such instances, compensation was mandatory (Article 15). Citizens' homes were to be inviolable; no person, even a government agent, could enter a house without legal authority or the permission of the owner (Article 16). Confiscation of property was outlawed, except in the case of Afghan subjects "residing abroad and making propaganda and intrigues against the Afghan government" (Article 17); this article was apparently directed against the pro-Amanullah forces (notably the Tarzi and Charki families) who were continuing to question the legitimacy of the rule of the Musahiban family. Torture was outlawed; no one was to be punished except by ways prescribed by law (Article 19). By implication, this article was an attempt to bring the administration of tribal justice under the religious establishment and the Afghan government. It was also a move to make a crime an offense against the state, rather than simply an offense against a particular person or family. Levies and forced labor were prohibited "except during the time of war" (Article 18).

Articles 20–22 pertained to education. Primary education was proclaimed compulsory, and Article 21, which authorized Afghan citizens to teach Muslim scholastic and moral sciences either in public or in private, removed the restrictions that Habibullah and Amanullah had imposed in an effort to limit the role of the Muslim clerics in education. The same article prohibited foreigners from opening or directing schools in the country. Only foreigners who were hired by the government to teach "sciences, industries, and foreign languages" were to be allowed to work within the Afghan educational system. Article 22 was a dubious attempt to justify a public education system without offending the religious leaders. Afghan schools were placed under the supervision of the government on the grounds that education could then be made compatible both with Islam and with science, art, and industry. Article 23 set guidelines for the press. The news disseminated could not be contrary to Islamic principles, and the right to publish was restricted to the government and Afghan citizens. Foreign newspapers were permitted free entry and circulation, provided they did not contain materials offensive to religion or the government. Beyond these restrictions, the press was to be free. In Article 109, the inviolability of private correspondence was recognized. Letters and other correspondence could not be opened except by court order.

Articles 27–70 covered the rights, prerogatives, and duties of a bicameral parliament consisting of a National Consultative Assembly (the Majlis-e Shura-ye Melli) and a House of Peers (the Majlis-e Ayan). The constitution declared that the parliament was organized "in conformity to the decision and the will of His Majesty the King and approbation of the jirga of 1930, gathered at Kabul" (Article 27). Parliamentary authority therefore emanated from the King and the will of the Afghan people, as represented by that jirga. This same point was made by Nadir in his inaugural speech before the parliament: "I open this Assembly of Muslim *Councillors* [italics mine]. . . . May God be praised that you and I are Muslims. Conferences are the foundation of all our actions. By the injunctions of the Holy Quran, we were and are bound to hold consultations and in future too it shall be incumbent on us to act accordingly." In this same speech, Nadir attempted to justify the institution of parliament on the grounds of historical precedent and religious sanction. Consultation had been a basic feature of Islamic society and a cause of its success from the time of the Prophet Muhammed and the Orthodox Caliphs. After the Abbassid period, however, the Muslim Sultans considered consultation incompatible with their power and prestige, and therefore paid little attention to the practice, disregarding the fact that consultation had been responsible for progress and spiritual elevation. This neglect had contributed to the decline of the Islamic world. "In Afghanistan the recourse to consultation has existed for many centuries—and we can say that the Afghan jirgas are regular governmental channels of the people of Afghanistan. For us, for the entire nation, consultations . . . do not constitute something new. If the previous sovereigns did not act according to the councils of the people, the people themselves did not abandon the institution; until these very days, the decisions of their jirgas are listened to and executed by the tribes."[39]

The rights and prerogatives of the National Consultative Assembly included the election of its president; the approval and ratification of legislative bills or proposals, subject to the King's veto or approval; the study and approval of the budget; the chartering of commercial companies and the approval of treaties and arrangements granting commercial, industrial, and agricultural monopolies (both foreign and domestic); the approval of domestic and foreign loans; and the approval of the building and expansion of railroads. When the parliament was not in session, the administration could pass certain ordinances, but they had to be approved, rejected, or modified by the consultative assembly later. The assembly also had the right to petition the King, though it first had to request the minister of court (a position equal to the office of chamberlain) to arrange an official audience (Article 49). Members of the assembly were to enjoy complete freedom of expression in parliamentary debate, and all "ordinary debates" were to be open to the press and the public. Half of the members were to constitute a quorum; decisions were to be carried by a simple majority. The assembly had 116 deputies, elected by male Afghan citizens over the age of twenty "who possessed sound moral character, who were neither bankrupt, nor convicted of criminal offences, nor legally incapable of managing their own affairs, and who had resided within their respective constituencies for at least one year." Theoretically, each constituency of about 100,000 inhabitants had the right to elect a member to the assembly.

The upper house, or House of Peers, was made up of "experienced and foresighted" members selected and appointed by the King. Legislative proposals drafted by the government were to be sent to this house for discussion and vote. Measures passed by the National Consultative Assembly required the approval of the House of Peers and vice versa. However, if the upper house was not in session, royal assent alone was sufficient for a bill to become law. If the upper house passed a measure that was rejected by the lower house, a joint committee of both houses was to try to find a compromise solution; in the event of a deadlock, the King was to decide the outcome.[40] Thus, though Nadir had granted great power to the National Consultative Assembly, he could block its measures either through his own veto or through his handpicked senate. Furthermore, the constitution granted the King broad emergency powers; in case of social unrest and rebellion threatening public order, he had the power to adopt all "necessary measures to put down the insurrection and restore the peace" (Article 104).*

The great authority of the King was manifest also in his complete control of the cabinet. In language Amanullah's constitution and Nadir's differed considerably on the relationship between the cabinet and the parliament. In the constitution of 1923, the cabinet was responsible only to the monarch, whereas in the new constitution the ministers, both individually and collectively, were answerable to the National Consultative Assembly and the House of Peers, a provision that theoretically reduced the power of the monarch. In practice, however, the King could block assembly-initiated measures against his ministers through the House of Peers. Moreover, the prime minister, who was appointed by the King, was not responsible to the parliament, and only he or the King could dismiss members of the cabinet. The cabinet, not the assembly, held the primary responsibility for initiating new legislation. The legislative prerogatives of the assembly were further curtailed by a constitutional provision that "regulations approved by the consultative assembly could not go counter to prescriptions of Islamic religion (which explains everything) and the policies of the country" (Article 65). Most important of all, jurisdiction over taxes was not vested in the assembly or included in the constitution of 1931. Eventually, in a special law, the parliament was given consultative powers on

* According to I. A. Shah (*Modern Afghanistan*, p. 253), it was the King's right not only to open, close, postpone, or extend the national assembly but also to dissolve it.

revenue questions, but even then it was not given the right of veto or the right to initiate legislation.

Nadir made very real concessions to the Afghan tribes. Under a new law, a national Loe Jirga was to be convened at least once every three years, and no new taxes could be imposed or radical changes made without the consent of this extralegal body,[41] which in the view of the monarchy represented the national consensus of the Afghans. The powerful Afghan tribal chieftains were thus given a strong voice in financial policies that affected their interests as well as the power to veto foreign policy commitments or radical modernization plans made by the government. The new law also represented an attempt to institutionalize the supremacy of the Afghan ethnic element over the non-Afghan elements, thereby guaranteeing the Afghan character of the kingdom. The fact that the constitution contained no provisions for amendments was also a concession to the tribes. By unwritten law, only the Loe Jirga could make changes in the constitution. Moreover, since the interpretation of the constitution was not assigned to any designated authority, controversial or important cases were submitted to the Loe Jirga.[42]

In the domain of the judiciary, the new constitution made a distinction between civil courts (*mahakim-e-adliyya*) and religious courts (*mahakim-e-shar'ia*). Great concessions were made to the religious hierarchy. Articles 87–96 confirmed and institutionalized the rights and prerogatives of the religious establishment. The supremacy and orthodoxy of the Hanafi school of jurisprudence was recognized, and the complete autonomy of Shar'ia courts was guaranteed. In general, lawsuits were to be tried in the religious courts, though commercial disputes were to be referred to special courts for arbitration, and cabinet members charged with misdemeanors were to be tried by a temporary supreme court organized for that purpose. In granting the Muslim ulama broad powers but reserving for the monarchy the right of final appeal, Nadir seems to have made a deliberate though indirect attempt to make use of the religious establishment's powers to extend the jurisdiction of the monarchy over the tribal territories. In this connection, Article 93 prohibited the establishment of "any special tribunal to settle particular cases out of court." Similarly, though Articles 71–72 and 102–5 guaranteed some degree of local self-government, through either provincial consultative assemblies or municipal councils, the government could intervene and reverse any injustices or breaches of laws within the provinces (Article 104). The government was thus given the power to oversee the administration of law, and, by extension, to intervene in the affairs of tribal territories.

To allay the fears of the tribal chieftains and soften the opposition of the Muslim clerics, conservative elements, and xenophobic nationalists, the rights of foreign subjects were greatly circumscribed. They could not operate schools or be admitted to the ranks of the Afghan armed forces, except as doctors or military instructors (Article 108), and they were not allowed to own land. Two amendments to the constitution made in February 1933 barred army officers, officials of the Ministry of Foreign Affairs, and young Afghans studying abroad from marrying aliens.[43] No non-Muslim Afghan subject could become a member of the cabinet. Missionaries were forbidden to enter the country or to distribute material there. A major concession was made to conservative anti-Amanullah elements in the 1931 constitution: there was no mention of Afghan women or their rights. Legally and theoretically, as Afghan nationals women could claim full rights, including the right to vote. However, by tradition and common consent, and in the absence of a mandate on the part of the Loe Jirga (which in 1930 had revoked most of Amanullah's measures in this area), women were denied this tacit right. Moreover, the Jamiyat-ul-Ulama interpreted Islamic law as specifically prohibiting women from voting.

In 1932 the Nadir administration enacted additional statutes further defining Afghan citizenship and the rights of citizens. One was the "Statute Regarding Identity Cards, Regulations for Passports and the Law Regarding Citizenship," which read in part:

Persons born on Afghan soil or those born abroad whose parents (or father) are Afghan citizens are held to be Afghan citizens, and are obliged to take out an Afghan card of citizenship [Article 91].

If foreigners born in Afghanistan desire, when they reach their majority, to become Afghan citizens, their requests will be granted [Article 92].

Women of foreign nationality married to Afghan citizens are considered to be Afghan citizens.

Widows of Afghan citizens, if of Muslim origin, are free to revert to their original nationality. Widows converted to the Muslim faith can revert to their original nationality after the Government has assured itself that in returning to infidel countries they will not apostasize. Those non-Muslim widows whose Muslim marriages are legal, cannot change their Afghan citizenship [Article 96; this refers to marriages between non-Muslim women and Muslim men; marriages between Muslim women and non-Muslim men were forbidden by tradition and Islamic law].

Afghan women married to non-Afghan Muslims are not considered to be Afghan citizens unless their husbands become naturalized Afghan citizens. Otherwise, on the death of their husbands they can revert to Afghan nationality by petitioning the government [Article 97].

Afghan women married to foreign citizens cannot own any property (other than movable) ... and are excluded from all privileges of Afghan citizenship [Article 100].

Afghan women possessing property in Afghanistan are obliged to sell all property and land on their marriage to a foreigner [Article 101].

As for male Afghan citizens,

Change of nationality on the part of the father, however, does not necessarily imply change of nationality on the part of children, whether they are minors or of age. A son born after his father has changed nationality takes the nationality of his father [Article 99].⁴⁴

The laws of citizenship thus institutionalized the inequalities in the rights of women and men, of Muslims and non-Muslims, and of Afghans and non-Afghans. In general, these laws, too, represented great concessions to the Afghan traditionalists and conservatives. The new constitution and the subsequent legislation formalized tribal, religious, and dynastic interests, fusing them into a clear conception of the Afghan monarch as the personification of the state and the government. The entire membership of the parliament consisted of khans and *begs* representing feudal, tribal, religious, and commercial interests. Through the cooperation of the parliament and the Jamiyat-ul-Ulama, Nadir tried to provide a legal framework and a basis for consensus, as well as the machinery for a program of limited, guided reform and modernization. The parliament also afforded the administration both the opportunity and the means to bring many powerful tribal leaders to Kabul, where they stayed from May to October, dabbling in the art of lawmaking and establishing contacts with each other. In this way, they were effectively kept from seriously disrupting the peace of the country. Their urban sojourns, which coincided with the crucial summer months when uprisings were most likely to occur, and their frequent moves reportedly made caravan routes less hazardous.⁴⁵

EDUCATION

Nadir attached great importance to education, which in his judgment had to pave the way for the people's acceptance of social reforms. He made this clear in any number of speeches and interviews. "You can not build a nation," he said, "anymore than you can build a house by starting at the top. Amanullah tried to change the minds of people by changing their hats. The painstaking, difficult tasks involved in preparing the ground take as much time as sending the structure into the sky. Such work at first does not make a big display."⁴⁶ Convinced that without education the country could not take a step forward, he reopened the Afghan schools, including the German and French secondary schools.⁴⁷ However, he opposed the immediate reopening of schools for women or the precipitate launching of a coeducational system before the nation "seemed ready for it."⁴⁸

As noted, elementary education as a right and a duty was made part of the new constitution. A Bureau of Education (Dairah-i-ta'lim-o-tarbiah) was created with six members to oversee the operation of the system. They had both deliberative and judiciary powers. Administratively, each province was a unit operating under a director (*mudir*); education in the sub-provinces was under the direction of a superintendent (*mamur*). Both the mudirs and the mamurs were subject to the direction of the Ministry of Education.[49] The primary schools were to cover six years and were to teach "literacy and certain elementary knowledge about daily life; also to prepare pupils for secondary schools."[50] In practice, however, the government established six-year schools only in the district centers as models. Compulsory elementary education was not universally practiced; such a measure was not and could not be enforced because of the shortage of teachers, schools, and money.

In areas without primary schools, village schools provided a rudimentary education. They generally had one teacher and a three- or four-year program that included religious instruction, reading, and writing. Instruction was in Pashto or in Persian. In many of the villages, the only schools available were the traditional maktabs.[51] In a majority of the village schools, the teachers were mullahs, who generally had no better than a sixth-grade education and no professional training in teaching.[52] Eventually, all four secondary schools of Kabul were reopened. This was a step of major importance, for these schools were responsible for the literate, modernist class that in large part staffed the Afghan army, civil service, education system, and foreign ministry.[53] (It was during this period that the names of two of these schools were changed.) After order was restored in the kingdom, graduates of the secondary schools, usually members of the ruling elite or from other influential families, were again sent abroad to study, notably to France, Germany, England, the United States, Turkey, and Japan.[54]

The educational system as Nadir envisioned it was a compromise that would hopefully be based "on the solid foundation of public good-will and national life, traditions, and institutions."[55] Apart from making religious instruction a central preoccupation and conceding local control to the mullahs, he also tried to effect a compromise by virtually banning the teaching of Western languages at the primary and intermediate levels (ages seven to fourteen).[56] In this he apparently sought to ensure a more solidly based primary education conducted in the mother tongue as well as to forestall opposition from conservative elements.

The financing of the Afghan school system was intricate. Elementary mosque schools were supported in part by local contributions and in part by the government.[57] Primary, secondary, vocational schools, and later schools of higher education were wholly financed by the government. Books and stationery for all the schools, lunches in the secondary day schools, and board and lodging plus a stipend to "deserving students" were provided by the state. The government also encouraged philanthropic-minded firms and individuals to follow the example of Nadir and other members of the royal family in making donations for educational purposes.[58]

As for women's education, only one of the schools for girls, Malalai, was reopened, and then not until two years into Nadir's administration. In an effort to soften the opposition of the mullahs and the other traditionalists, the government promoted it as a special school for nurses and midwives. It was to be some two decades before Malalai would become a true secondary school and produce its first graduates.[59]

As part of the Nadir administration's higher education program, the Teacher Training School (Dar-ul-Muallemin) of Kabul was reopened. When it was established in 1913, the school had only three grades beyond the six-year primary education. Later, under Amanullah's administration, the standards were improved, and those who entered the school had graduated from ninth grade. Upon completion of a three-year course, they were certified as teachers.[60] Now a new system was established. Those who completed ninth grade and then took a two-year training course were qualified as intermediary-school teachers; those who took an additional two years of schooling at the Teacher Training School became secondary-school teachers.[61]

In 1944 the government established a school for the instruction of Islamic law, which by 1950 had become the Faculty of Theology and Islamic Law of the University of Kabul.[62] The foundations of Kabul University itself were laid in 1932, when what was to become its first faculty, the School of Medicine, was established. The medical school had a seven-year program. No fees were charged and, according to one source, nearly 20 per cent of the students received monthly stipends of 50 afghanis. They also received free books and supplies, and reportedly free meals and clothing as well. The students in the secondary schools were also given stipends, receiving some 20 afghanis a month in their first year, 30 in their second, and 40 in their third.[63] Studies at the School of Medicine were carried on under the guidance and supervision of foreign professors, primarily French and Turkish.

Under the constitution, the employment of foreign technical experts by the government was permissible, and because of the shortage of qualified teachers the state was forced to employ foreign teachers in the secondary schools.[64] Teachers from India, France, and Germany once again assumed teaching posts in the four secondary schools in Kabul. Specialized schools also began operating. The School of Fine and Applied Arts was reopened and was expanded to include instruction in native arts and crafts.[65] A vocational technical high school was also founded to teach carpentry, carpet-making, weaving, masonry, and other crafts.[66]

Even though the modern schools were reopened, Islam continued to permeate the curriculum of the entire Afghan educational system. Says one authority: "The number of traditional subjects was decreased in the primary level but it was made up for in the curriculum of intermediate schools. The history of Islam and the history of the Prophets became a part of the general program of history. The integrity of the traditional subjects was thus secured in various levels of education."[67] Sciences and scholasticism may have coexisted within the secondary educational system, but in the traditional mosque schools scholasticism reigned supreme. Aside from the Quran, the basic text used in most of these schools was the *Panj Ganj* (Five Treasures), which had sections devoted to didactic moral lessons, Persian classics, and religious precepts and laws.[68] Given this type of education and the absence of both a uniform traditional-school curriculum and qualified teachers, the Afghan students continued to have great difficulties in making the transition from the elementary to the secondary schools. Adding to their difficulties was the fact that the medium of instruction for religion was Arabic, whereas Persian was used for the classical Muslim education and Pashto for subjects drawn from the national culture. Despite these concessions to the ethnic diversity of the country, no provisions were made to institute Turkish as a language of instruction for the benefit of the Turkic groups of northern Afghanistan.

In connection with schools and youth, Nadir Shah issued a royal proclamation in 1931 establishing the Afghan Boy Scouts Association in Kabul (Anjuman-e kashshafan). The group, which was placed under the patronage of Zahir Khan, the heir apparent, had about 1,000 members by 1932, when it became affiliated with the International Boy Scouts Association. The Nadir administration also encouraged sports and included them in the curriculum of the secondary schools. In 1932 a National Olympic Association was formed under the presidency of the King's brother Shah Mahmud Khan. It sent teams to the Western Asian Olympic games in Delhi in 1934,[69] and to the Olympic games in Berlin in 1936. These were the Afghans' first international athletic contacts.

In the general area of culture and the arts, a few developments during this period are worth noting. The Kabul Museum was reopened, and small museums were established at Kandahar, Herat, and Mazar-i-Sharif. Public libraries were established, and literary societies were organized in Kabul, Kandahar, and Herat,[70] which attempted to encourage the development of modern Afghan literature by establishing prizes for poetry, drama, literary criticism, and linguistics.[71]

THE PRESS, COMMUNICATIONS, AND PUBLIC HEALTH

During the brief rule of Bacha-i-Saqao, the Afghan press, which had blossomed under the rule of Amanullah, all but disappeared. There was only one paper in Kabul—*Habib-ul-Islam*—which was the creature of the bandit Amir, although some anti-Bacha lithographed papers appeared in various provinces for a time. They included *Ghayrat-i-Islam, De Kor Gham* (published in the eastern province), *Ittihad-i-Afghan*, and *Islah* (Nadir's paper, which was published in the southern province). During Nadir's rule, the Afghan press was reestablished. Some of the papers and periodicals published during Amanullah's reign reappeared, notably *Anis* (which later became a bilingual daily), *Bidar, Ittihad-i-Khanabad, Tulu-e-Afghan, Ittihad-i-Mashriqi, Aïne-ye-Irfan, Sahiyyah* (Health, a monthly published in Kabul), and *Ordu-ye-Afghan* (The Afghan Army, a military monthly). In addition to *Islah*, which began as a weekly and then became a semiofficial daily, several new publications appeared. *Iqtisad* (Economics), a monthly published by the Ministry of National Economy, *Al-Falah* (Salvation), a monthly published in Kabul first under the auspices of the Jamiyat-ul-Ulama and later as an organ of the Ministry of Justice, and *Majalle-ye-Adabi-Kabul* (Literary Journal of Kabul) all began publication in 1930. Herat soon (in 1932) had a literary magazine as well. Other new publications were *Majalle-ye-Pashto* (Pashto Journal) and *Salna-me-ye-Majalle-ye-Kabul* (Annual of the Kabul Review).[72] There are no accurate circulation figures for these periodicals, nor is there any breakdown on the audience they reached. It is clear, however, that few of them added materially to an Afghan cultural nationalist movement.

In 1930, the Post, Telegraph, and Telephone Department was expanded and separated from the Ministry of Interior, becoming instead a Directorate. The postal bus service that had begun operating in 1925 between Kabul, Jalalabad, and the Khyber Pass, and between Kabul, Kandahar, and Herat, was resumed, as was air passenger service between Afghanistan, Soviet Central Asia, and Europe (via Central Asia). Fortnightly and later weekly air service was established between Kabul, Termiz (on the Soviet bank of the Oxus), and Tashkent, via Mazar-i-Sharif. The primitive airports at Kabul, Herat, Kandahar, Jalalabad, Ghazni, Badakhshan, and Mazar-i-Sharif were reopened. Nadir confirmed a contract originally granted by Amanullah to the firm of Junkers, giving the company a monopoly on the air service between Kabul, Kandahar, and Herat.[73]

Airmail letters were accepted for the first time,[74] and branch offices were opened at the eastern, western, and northern frontiers to handle international mail. Simultaneously, the Nadir administration attempted to expand, repair, and improve the roads of the country. Most of the Kabul–Khyber Pass road was resurfaced, and the Kabul–Kandahar road was improved greatly. Even so, in 1933 Afghanistan possessed only 1,800–2,000 miles of roads. Nadir's chief contribution in this area was to finish the Great North Road that linked Kabul and northern Afghanistan. The construction of this road, which was completed in 1933, was supervised by a Hungarian engineer and was built by "Afghan brains and labour"; it permitted year-round crossing of the Hindu Kush for the first time.[75]

In 1934 the postal service was expanded again, the Directorate of Post becoming part of a new Ministry of Post, Telegraph, and Telephone. Most of the country's telegraph and telephone lines had been destroyed during the revolution. New lines were now laid and attempts were made to enlarge the system. The link between Herat, Farah, Kandahar, and Kabul was restored, as were those between Kabul and Torkham (Khyber Pass), and Kabul and Mazar-i-Sharif. The country renewed its ties with the International Cable Union (which it had joined in 1928). By 1935 the major urban centers of the country had been linked telegraphically with Kabul.

During Amanullah's reign, Kabul had a 50-line telephone cable that connected the capital with Jalalabad, Kandahar, Farah, and Mazar-i-Sharif.[76] Now a 120-line cable was installed at Kabul, and service to these cities was restored. Service to Peshawar and Termiz was also reestablished through wireless stations at Kabul and Mazar-i-Sharif. Another wireless station was planned for Herat to provide a link with Kandahar, Kabul, and possibly Iran.[77] It is not clear whether or not the Afghan government resumed radio broadcasting, which had been initiated in 1925.* It would seem that not until 1936 was serious thought given to

---

* According to one report, there were some 1,000 radio sets by 1928. The Kabul transmitter operated on standard wavelengths, and an indeterminate but in all likelihood very small number of Kabulis were able to listen to the fledgling radio station through earphones or battery-operated amplifiers. See Roashan, p. 40, and Reshtiya, "Kabul Calling," p. 1.

resuming broadcasting, and that Radio Kabul, newly equipped and reorganized, did not begin operating until 1939.[78]

The Nadir administration made some attempts to improve the health standards of the country. According to one report, during the civil war there were only two qualified Afghan doctors in Afghanistan. The breakdown of governmental machinery and the educational system, and the period of political anarchy, allowed the hakims to regain lost ground and to operate freely. Sanitary conditions, especially in the countryside, were appalling.[79] The government upgraded the former Public Health Department to a Ministry and tried to reorganize and standardize the existing hospitals. Simple, even crude, hospitals and clinics were established in the headquarters of each province and major administrative district, and a Medical Department in the Afghan army maintained a few military hospitals. Theoretically, in remote regions the army also attended to the medical needs of the civilian population.[80] There is, however, no indication that the army's medical services to the public were extensive.

Nadir's establishment of the Faculty of Medicine was an important first step toward providing the medical services the country so desperately needed. The various hospitals were affiliated with the medical school and made use of its diagnostic laboratory.[81] Other important advances were also made in these years. A well-equipped X-ray and electrotherapy institute, a mental institution, dental clinics, and a hospital for women were opened, and as previously noted Malalai, the school for girls, was converted into a nursing school.[82] The King also founded Rifqi Sanatorium, which was named after his personal physician, Dr. Rifqi Kamil Urga, who practiced in Afghanistan for 18 years.[83] Another sanatorium, this one for women, was opened at Darul Aman.[84] Both of these institutions were small; the Rifqi Sanatorium had only 20 beds, the women's facility only 30.[85] The vaccination department of the Ministry of Health prepared serum, conducted courses at the nursing school, and began a public inoculation program.[86] Even so, in 1930 cholera and other epidemic diseases took the usual heavy toll of victims. By 1938, however, a newly founded Bacteriological and Hygiene Institute and the efforts of Afghan medical students and doctors had achieved a degree of success in controlling epidemics, most notably of smallpox. Schoolchildren, government employees, and soldiers were all vaccinated, and medical teams were sent to the provinces in an attempt to check the disease, which had often reached epidemic proportions.[87]

The government renewed the campaign against the use of opium that had been started under Amanullah. Articles and didactic poems appeared in Afghan literary magazines and newspapers depicting the moral, physical, and social ills resulting from the use of the drug.[88] Following the lead of other Muslim countries, Afghanistan also at this time formed the equivalent of a chapter of the Red Crescent (Red Cross). The Afghan group, the Mihrab-i-Ahmar, was organized by royal decree and was given an annual grant of 100,000 afghanis (5,000 pounds). It became affiliated with the International Red Cross and sent representatives to the international conferences.[89]

In general, most measures in the domain of public health were very elementary and limited in scope. For the most part, they were limited to Kabul and a few other major urban centers. Qadir Khan's assertion that by 1934 "in every village of any size public dispensaries were opened," is clearly an exaggeration.[90] Afghanistan continued to lack even minimum standards of health, and the steps taken under Nadir represented only the most basic groundwork for the massive reforms that were needed.

THE AFGHAN ECONOMY

One of the most urgent tasks facing Nadir's government was the reorganization of the country's royal workshops, which had been neglected under Bacha and gutted during the civil war. In 1930 Afghanistan possessed only a small complex of workshops at Kabul. Only a munitions factory, the tannery and boot factory, a wool mill, and a button plant were in operation, all devoted primarily to the needs of the Afghan army and owned by the government. The hydroelectric station at Jabal-ul-Siraj remained the only facility of its kind in the country.[91]

In order to promote the development of industry and trade, the monarchy permitted the establishment of a bank in 1930. When it opened for business in 1931, its name, Shirkat-i-Ashami-i-Afghan, indicated that it was a joint-stock company. The intent evidently was to avoid conflict with the religious establishment by emphasizing that profits were to be derived from trade rather than exclusively from interest or usury.[92] Still, when the institution was reorganized and expanded in 1932, it was renamed the Afghan National Bank (Bank-i-Milli).[93] It opened branches in Herat, Kandahar, Mazar-i-Sharif, Khanabad, Jalalabad, Quetta, and Peshawar, and later established either correspondents or offices in Karachi, Delhi, Bombay, Calcutta, London, Paris, and Berlin. The bank was not a state enterprise; it drew upon both public and private resources. However, it held a monopoly on handling government business and was allowed to issue drafts payable at government treasuries. It also held monopolies for the purchase of foreign currency, bullion, and government imports, such as sugar and trucks.[94] Moreover, it was given the first option on the development of the country's natural resources. With this kind of government support, the bank was in a strong position, and it grew rapidly. At the end of its first year, it paid a dividend of 28 per cent to its shareholders.[95] The creation of the bank ended not only the ancient methods of currency exchange but also the virtual monopoly held by the Hindu and to a lesser extent the Jewish merchants on the financial transactions of the kingdom.[96]

The initial capital of the new bank was 35 million afghanis, a sum that was later increased to over 63 million (approximately 1.3 million pounds).[97] The founder and director was Abdul Majid Zabuli, a wealthy merchant.[98] After the bank was established, the Afghan government was empowered to issue banknotes in sums of 5, 10, 20, 50, and 100 afghanis, up to 19 million afghanis. In 1932 the government increased its capital investment in the bank from 30 million afghanis to 36 million, setting aside 35 per cent of that sum as reserves for the Afghan Treasury. Only Afghan citizens were allowed to purchase shares in the bank.[99] Since the principal stockholders were rich and well-known merchants, the bank managed to attract a great part of the national capital, which was then reinvested in joint-stock companies under its control.[100] The underwriting of the bank by the Afghan government apparently added an extra element of security and led to a greater investment of local capital in industry and trade.

The establishment of the bank was part of a so-called Overall Economic Development Plan, which was adopted by the Afghan government in 1932. The basic aims of the plan (the work of a group of businessmen and government officials with little experience in economic planning) were: (1) to draw up a financial and currency report; (2) to promote foreign and domestic trade; (3) to improve the level of health, education, and communications; (4) to encourage industrial development; and (5) to institute progressive reforms in agriculture.[101]

Encouraged by the bank, some 30 large private joint-stock companies were set up between 1932 and 1934. The principal companies in Kabul, all engaged in exporting karakul, were Saber (capital 6 million afghanis), Tawakul (1 million), Baradaran (1 million), Ghanaat (1.25 million), and Kushesh (1.5 million). In northern Afghanistan, there were several companies that also exported lambskin: the Eybek, Salamat, Saadat, Sadakhat, Ikhlass, and Maimana companies, all having a million or more afghanis in capital. One of the largest import companies was the Petroleum Company of Kabul, which had a monopoly on the importation of oil and on the right to maintain contacts with foreign oil companies. Other major companies were the Etminan Company (initially capitalized at 2.5 million afghanis), which controlled the wool and lambskin export trade in Herat, the Ittehadieyeh Shomali (10 million), which also exported karakul and imported cement, among other things, and the Pashtun Company of Kandahar (1.673 million), which exported dried fruits.[102] A few state enterprises, notably the textile mill at Jabal-ul-Siraj and the match and leather factories at Kabul, were leased to private interests.[103]

The effect of this attempt to turn a significant amount of the country's economic activities over to the private sector was to stimulate individual interest and participation in the development of the Afghan economy. The activities of the joint-stock companies and the Afghan National Bank contributed both to the growth of foreign trade and to the accumulation and local reinvestment of capital. The government was able to put several small light industries into operation. Among them were a textile factory, which was established in Afghan Turkestan, where cotton was plentiful; a raw sugar factory, which was set up in Jalalabad; and a shawl factory, which was established in Kandahar.[104] However, the growth of the infant Afghan industry was slowed by the difficult process of transforming former peasants and artisans into a labor force capable of coping efficiently with modern machines.[105]

The national bank also received the full cooperation of the Afghan government in its efforts to promote foreign trade. The Nadir administration appointed a trade agent in London, and later had agents in Leipzig, Moscow, and Paris.[106] A new customs law in 1931 attempted to standardize customs duties and to regularize and increase government revenues. Class A (luxury) imports, such as coffee, cocoa, cotton and silk underwear, towels, handkerchiefs, toilet articles, and mirrors, were subject to a 30 per cent ad valorem tax, crude sugar to a 25 per cent tax, soap, copper wire, combs, scissors, hats, hand mirrors, boots, chemicals, medicines, matches, lamps, iron, and steel to a 20 per cent tax, and carpets, rugs, woolen mats, maps, charts, photographs, and postcards to a 10 per cent tax.[107] No alcoholic beverage of any kind could be imported. Anyone violating this injunction was liable to three years imprisonment and a fine equivalent to half the value of the contraband, which was to be destroyed.*

On some luxury items, notably Persian and Central Asian silk thread, the tax was low, only 2 per cent ad valorem; on others, notably jewelry and foreign currency, the rate was still lower: one-half of 1 per cent. The

---

* An exception was made for non-Muslims and foreign subjects, who were allowed to import alcoholic beverages according to quotas set by the Afghan Foreign Ministry.

new customs laws tried, apparently for the first time (and then a bit whimsically), to limit the amount of money that Afghan pilgrims could take with them to Mecca. Pilgrims were divided into three categories: those accompanied by three servants, who were allowed to take along 2,728 afghanis; those accompanied by two servants, who were allowed to take 2,182 afghanis; and those with "one servant or more" (!), who were allowed to take 1,364 afghanis.

Afghan exports were also subject to customs duties. Although opium could not be imported, it could be exported, subject to a 10 per cent ad valorem tax. The duty on fruit, both fresh and dried, ranged between 25 and 80 per cent. In general, duties were levied on all articles except ordinary wearing apparel, necessary toilet articles, and writing materials. The export of gold and silver coins and bullion, as well as of manuscripts and antiquities of all kinds, was forbidden.[108]

The provisions of the new customs law reveal serious weaknesses in Afghan trade policy. No real distinctions were made between genuine luxury items and essentials. Consideration was not given to possible obstacles to foreign capital investment. There was no provision for the protection of either Afghan industry (with the exception of matches) or the Afghan export trade.[109] The basic reason for most of these weaknesses was the government's great reliance on customs duties for its revenues. The revenue from other sources—stamp duty, seigniorage, and taxes on land and animals—represented only a little more than one-third of the total income of the government; customs accounted for all the rest.[110]

This precarious situation had plagued both Habibullah and Amanullah. Like his predecessors, Nadir remained dependent on the major Afghan tribes for the defense of the kingdom and his dynasty, and for the preservation of the country's Afghan character. Enjoined by the constitution from increasing the land taxes without the consent of the Loe Jirga, he, too, taxed the export-import trade heavily, thus overburdening the merchant class and the urban sectors, whose efforts and cooperation he needed to implement his modernization programs. Even modest modernization became difficult when the United States and European economies were hit by the depression of the 1930's. Afghan exports declined accordingly, as did the afghani. Between November 1 and December 23, 1930, the exchange rate of the afghani dropped from 38.6 in a pound sterling to 45.4.[111]

The total value of Afghan trade in 1931 reportedly remained the same as in 1901 (some five million pounds), even though there had been a substantial increase in the volume of trade.[112] In general, Afghan imports in

this period exceeded exports, creating a balance of payments deficit that
further weakened the Afghan currency.[113] The reversal of the Afghan-
Soviet trade balance in the period 1932–34 and the decline in volume indicate the serious difficulties that beset Afghan foreign trade.

Russian Trade with Afghanistan[114]
(*in rubles*)

Year	Exports to Afghanistan	Imports from Afghanistan
1928–29	7,000,000	11,700,000
1929–30	7,300,000	10,300,000
1930	7,800,000	9,200,000
1931	11,500,000	11,600,000
1932	14,600,000	11,800,000
1933	7,100,000	5,600,000
1934	3,100,000	2,800,000
1935	3,500,000	3,900,000

A similar situation existed in the case of Afghan-British trade. In 1932,
for instance, Afghan exports to Britain were valued at 15,535 pounds
against imports valued at 65,935 pounds.[115] Because Afghanistan's chief
exports were luxury articles, such as karakul, rugs, and lapis lazuli, whose
value fluctuated greatly in the world market, the government faced great
difficulties in economic planning. This situation was aggravated by the
fact that much of the country's private capital was increasingly committed
to commerce rather than to industrialization. As one authority notes:
"With the rate of profit in export and import operations continuing substantially higher than in industrial enterprise, Afghanistan's private capital virtually strove to curtail to the utmost its participation in investments
in industrial or other capital construction yielding little profit."[116]

Though trade and the infant industry of Afghanistan received official
assistance and encouragement under Nadir's administration, agriculture
was neglected. Some minor irrigation projects were started under the supervision of Italian and German engineers,[117] and a number of model and
experimental farms, which had been established by Amanullah's government, were reopened. These included a model dairy, a horticultural station, experimental vegetable farms, and institutes for animal husbandry,
sericulture, and forestry,* all centered in Kabul.[118] However, in general
these establishments were too ill-equipped in both materials and trained

---

* According to A. Qadir ("Afghanistan in 1934," p. 213), the government had "established colleges for forestry, etc." This is a complete exaggeration: the government had
merely planned to form a department for afforestation. See Morrish, p. 37.

personnel to be of genuine value. The most important contribution of Nadir Shah's government in this area was the continued encouragement of the cultivation of cotton in northern Afghanistan. Cotton subsequently became a major export,[119] and later cotton mills and a textile industry developed in the north. In the absence of major water projects, the country was unable to yield agricultural surpluses, though in any case, there were no facilities for storage. Wheat remained the chief agricultural commodity; three-fourths of the estimated five million acres under cultivation was devoted to it.[120]

Though the monarchy attempted to effect a few changes, they were only superficial, and the basic structure of the country's land tenure and property system was left virtually intact. According to Cervinka, land was divided into five categories: privately owned land; land under cultivation by tenant farmers; land held as waqfs, or religious endowments; public or state lands; and tribal lands, both cultivated and pasture. Arid lands belonged to the state, which also possessed vast areas of cultivated lands. Theoretically, all undiscovered and unexploited mineral resources, too, belonged to the state. The waqf lands, which reportedly did not represent a major percentage of the cultivated land, were controlled by the state.*

Much of the land was held by the tribes and the *latifundias* (large landholders), though there was a substantial number of middle and small landowners as well as tenant farmers. As previously noted, some of the tribes had preserved a collective form of ownership. In such tribes, a jirga periodically redistributed the land among the tribesmen. In many tribes, feudalism continued to prevail; tribal lands and herds were the personal property of the khan, who claimed various clans as well as individual farmers as vassals or clients. In these tribes, land was divided among the various cultivators, and the harvest was divided according to five variables: land, water, seeds, field animals, and human labor. For the most part, the feudal tribal chieftains and big landholders owned the country's water rights

---

* Since the time of Abdur Rahman, the Afghan monarchs, in their role of Defender and Protector of Islam, had assumed the prerogative of appointing the staff of the waqfs. Apparently the state maintained the major mosques and paid the salaries of religious luminaries out of the waqf funds. See Ahmad and Abd al-Aziz, pp. 107–8. According to Alizo (pp. 29–30), there were three categories of state ownership: Matrukah, Amlak, and Khalisa. Matrukah is "land which is reserved for public purpose," Amlak in Afghanistan is land owned by the state or national government and operated through the Department of Amlak, and Khalisa designates crown lands: "The term is used in Iran and Afghanistan probably to make a theoretical distinction between ruler's property and state property. Even today the terms are in use, especially for the land and property of the monarch and his family." Unfortunately, Alizo does not give details about the delimitation of the categories and their actual use.

and controlled the great bulk of the agricultural product.[121] According to the estimates of Soviet Afghanists, some 70 per cent of the cultivated land and a great percentage of the irrigation facilities and water rights belonged to the big and moderately well-to-do landowners. The peasants, who represented an estimated 90 per cent or more of the population of Afghanistan, owned less than one-fifth of the cultivated land. About 30 per cent of them were landless, and most of the others cultivated at least part of their lands as tenants.[122]

Chapter Twelve

Nadir Shah: Foreign Policy

As Nadir Shah pursued a cautious modernization program at home, he followed a delicate foreign policy, a policy that was more or less molded by the traditional Afghan attitudes toward Russia and Britain. His general foreign policy aims were enunciated on the occasion of the opening of the Afghan National Consultative Assembly: "In my opinion the best and most useful policy that one can imagine for Afghanistan is a policy of neutrality. Afghanistan must always entertain good relations with its neighbors as well as all the friendly powers who are not opposed to the national interests of the country. Afghanistan must give its neighbors assurances of its friendly attitude while safeguarding the rights of reciprocity. Such a line of conduct is the best one for the interests of Afghanistan."[1]

The most delicate task he faced was to make Afghan neutrality a reality and to convince all elements, including the Soviets and the Muslim nationalist-modernists inside and outside the country, that he was not a tool of British imperialism. The controversy surrounding the fall of Amanullah and the suspicions concerning Britain's role in it made this difficult. Before the Musahiban brothers set out to wrest Afghanistan from the grip of Bacha, Nadir had met with Richard Maconachie, a former counselor of the British Legation in Kabul and, at the time, the British political agent in the Kurram Valley. That meeting undoubtedly caused some apprehension among the Afghans, and British aid to Nadir in 1931 (10,000 rifles, five million cartridges, and some 180,000 pounds)[2] seemed to be a further indication of a British endorsement of Nadir.

In acknowledging the British aid, Nadir emphasized that it was not accompanied by conditions, and that Amanullah had accepted similar British materiel and monies when Afghanistan was in the grip of internal political difficulties.[3] He vehemently denied that he and his brothers had received British assistance in their struggle to overthrow the bandit Amir:

"It was only through the exclusive help of the Almighty God, and thanks to the sacrifices of the people of Afghanistan unassisted by any foreign power, that I took Kabul. It was only the divine help and the zeal of the entire Afghan nation that saved our fatherland."[4] His brother Shah Wali went even further. He claimed that during the initial and crucial stages of the anti-Bacha struggle, the British authorities, far from helping Nadir, had in fact obstructed him.[5]

In any event, the whole question of whether or not Nadir received British assistance in ousting Bacha was academic, since in general the policies Nadir pursued were highly compatible with British interests and plans in India. Unlike Amanullah, he adhered to a policy of non-involvement both in India and in Central Asia, seeing in "positive neutralism" the best means of securing internal political stability, consolidating the new royal dynasty's power, and guaranteeing both the flow of Afghan trade and the success of a modest modernization program. Such a policy made it essential for him to stay on friendly terms with both the British and the Soviets. Otherwise, the consequences could be disastrous; the Soviets could conceivably champion irredentist or revolutionary movements in northern Afghanistan, the British could stir up tribal opposition to the Afghan monarchy, and either or both could champion the cause of Amanullah against the Musahiban family.

As a first step, Nadir made his brother Shah Wali an envoy to London and sent another brother, Muhammed Aziz, to Moscow. In May 1930 Afghanistan confirmed the Anglo-Afghan treaty of 1921 and the trade convention of 1923 (which stipulated that goods destined for Afghanistan were to have free transit through India). In reaffirming the 1923 agreement, Nadir embraced the tacit understanding that had accompanied it: no Soviet trade agencies were to be opened in the eastern provinces of the Afghan kingdom adjacent to India.[6] As far as Great Britain was concerned, the major test of Afghan intentions and the future course of Anglo-Afghan relations depended on Nadir's attitude toward and activities in the tribal belt. As Fraser-Tytler puts it, the question that interested the British authorities in India was whether or not Nadir would resume "where he had left off the championship of his fellow tribesmen's cause in their desperate struggle to preserve their freedom against the forward policy of Britain, and in so doing disregard all international boundaries and treaty obligations as Amanullah had done? Or would the years of exile have taught him that there are issues more vital than the brief popularity deriving from support of some local interest, and that no country and particularly no country so lately entered into the comity of nations, can long prosper which disregards the sanctity of international obligations." In short, the British wanted to know if Afghanistan intended to champion national-liberation movements in India and press for the rights of the Pathan tribesmen on the other side of the Durand Line. To their relief, Nadir's actions, specifically the line he took with respect to the "Red Shirt" movement and the Afridi and Mohmand tribal struggles in India, persuaded them that the "whole frontier policy of the Afghan government would be actuated by a desire for peace on both sides of the frontier and a spirit of true friendship towards His Majesty's Government."[7]

THE RED SHIRT MOVEMENT

The Khudai Khidmatgaran (Servants of God) or the Red Shirts were Pathan nationalist-reformists, members of a movement that began in the Peshawar district and gradually spread to rural areas, ultimately making its headquarters in the village of Utmanzai. When founded in 1921, the group was known as the Society of Afghan Reformation, but it later took the name Afghan Youth League.[8] In 1929–30, after administrative cells had been established in most Pathan villages, the movement officially became known as the Central Afghan Jirga and organized a body of volunteers, the Khudai Khidmatgaran.[9]

The founder and leading spirit of the movement was Abdul Ghaffar Khan. Born in 1890 into a leading family of the Muhammedzai tribe of the Peshawar district, he attended the mission high school in Peshawar, but "unfortunately did not pass the matriculation examination."[10] According to Maheva Desai, young Abdul was so impressed by the character and self-sacrifice of the school's principal, the Reverend Mr. Wigram, that he then and there made "some kind of a resolve to serve his community as his Principal had served his faith in a missionary spirit."[11] The Afghan journalist Benawa offers a less idealistic and more anti-British explanation for Abdul Ghaffar Khan's turn toward social reform, tracing it back to a time when the young man gave up the idea of joining the Anglo-Indian army after seeing a British junior officer mistreat an Indian superior.[12] In any case, it is clear that as early as 1911 he became interested in establishing a network of Pathan schools in the North-West Frontier Province. After a brief flirtation with the Khilafat movement, he and his British-educated brother, Dr. Khan Sahib Khan, emigrated to Afghanistan during the Hijrat movement. In 1921 he returned to India and pursued his dream of founding a Pathan school system.[13] His overall aim seems to have been to combat, through education and social action, the widespread ignorance of his fellow tribesmen and to bring about the religious and social reformation of the tribal societies.* Above all, his goal was to inspire a sense of national consciousness in the Pathans, and ultimately to achieve Pathan autonomy.[14]

The Khudai Khidmatgaran were guided by seven basic rules: (1) every adult was eligible to become a member; (2) those who believed in the caste system could not enter the party; (3) each member had to dress in national attire; (4) each member was to be ready to serve the people; (5) members were to be prepared to travel about the country on party affairs at their own expense; (6) all members were brothers; (7) members had to follow the orders of the party to the letter. In addition, the Red Shirts took this oath:

> To be loyal to God, the Community and the Fatherland.
> To lead a pure life.
> To dedicate oneself to the faithful service of the party.
> To avoid any contacts with organizations hostile to the Khudai
>   Khidmatgaran.
> To support the interests of the people, and the liberty of the
>   fatherland with one's entire power, and if need be, to
>   sacrifice one's goods and life for that cause.
> To expect no reward for service.[15]

The remarkable thing about this movement is that its members, drawn from the traditionally militant tribesmen, adhered to the Gandhian doctrine of non-violence in pursuit of their revolutionary goals. Abdul Ghaffar Khan's insistence on non-violence as both a tactic and an article of faith is clearly reflected in his speeches and writings. For instance, in *The Pukhtun*, a Pashto periodical the party established to spread its message, he wrote: "O thou my brethren, bravery does not consist in beating others; rather it consists in developing the power to bear and to berate beating."[16] Elsewhere he asserted:[17]

My non-violence has almost become a matter of faith with me.... The unparalleled success of the experiment in my province has made me a confirmed champion of non-violence. God willing, I hope never to see my province take

---

* Clearly, he was concerned with raising the status of women, as witness these remarks made to a group of women at Togh, in the Kohat district: "Let me assure you that when freedom has been won, you will have an equal share and place with your brothers in this country. We are like two wheels of a big chariot, and unless our movement has been adjusted, our carriage will never move, and even if it does there will be a constant fear of some type of disaster. Islam has given you equality and you did enjoy it during the days of the Prophet.... But in order to secure that position again, you must exert and prepare yourself for the same status. As for myself, you may trust me to uphold your cause which I believe to be just. Our independence would be a farce and a fake if it deprived half of its population of an equal share in its orbit" (M. Yunus, p. 172).

to violence. We know only too well the bitter results of violence from the blood feuds which spoil our fair name. We have an abundance of violence in our nature. It is good in our own interests to take a training in non-violence. Moreover, is not the Pathan amenable only to love and reason? He will go with you to hell if you can win his heart, but you cannot force him even to go to heaven. Such is the power of love over the Pathan. I want the Pathan to do unto others as he would like to be done by. It may be I may fail and a wave of violence may sweep over my province. I will then be content to take the verdict of fate against me. But it will not shake my ultimate faith in non-violence, which my people need more than anybody else.*

To promote the Pathan cause within the larger framework of the national self-determination of India, Abdul Ghaffar Khan established an alliance with the Gandhian movement[18] and actively promoted the notion of Muslim-Hindu unity. Accordingly, he tried to redefine the basic tenets of Islam so as to stress its common bonds with other religions. "I do not measure the strength of a religion by counting heads," he said. "For what is faith until it is expressed in one's life? It is my inmost conviction that Islam is *amal, yakeen, mahabbat* [right conduct, faith, love], and without these one calling himself a Musalman is like sounding brass and tinkling cymbal. The Koran-e-Sharif makes it absolutely clear that faith in One God without a second and good works are enough to secure a man salvation." In attempting to present the concepts of one God, right conduct, good works, and love as the foundation of Islam, he hoped to demonstrate that the "fundamental principles of all religions are the same though details differ, because each faith takes the colour and flavour of the soil from which it springs." Since die-hard orthodox Muslims were unlikely to be convinced by this argument alone, Abdul Ghaffar Khan offered another: Hindus also possessed a revealed book—the Gita—and therefore, like the Jews and Christians, should be considered People of the Book. He asserted that "Hindus and their books are not mentioned in the Koran-e-Sharif, because the list there is not exhaustive but merely illustrative. The Koran-e-Sharif simply lays down the principle."[19] If one read carefully, he wrote, one would find out that "all the Holy Books of all the religions teach loyalty, love, justice, and honesty. They all teach service to humanity."[20] Contending that no religion sanctioned the killing of children or permitted

---

* This and similar statements refute the argument of those who contend that Abdul Ghaffar's non-violence was nothing more than a tactic. Edward Thomson, for one, wrote (p. 477): "It is very doubtful if 'A. G. K.' understands what non-violence is. He has grasped one thing, that it calls for much patience, and, as he points out in his speeches, the whole history of Islam has been marked by patience and endurance; but apart from that fact I do not think that 'A. G. K.' understands what non-violence means." M. Desai, however, points out (pp. i–ii) that Gandhi himself in effect acknowledged the non-violence of the Red Shirt movement in stating "The brave Khudai Khidmatgars will carry on Satyagraph [non-violent disobedience] even if my Hindu Satyagraphis fail." See also Shridharani, p. 470.

massacre and plunder, he denounced wars that made use of religion to rationalize and mask their true motivations, and condemned the "interested parties" on both sides who "fanned flames of passion and prejudice" among the Muslims and the Hindus. On this basis he defended his own cooperation with the Congress party: "People criticize me for having joined the Congress. The Congress is a national, not a Hindu body. It is an organization composed of Hindus, Jews, Sikhs, Parsis and Muslims. The Congress as a body is working against the British. The British nation is the enemy of the Congress and of the Pathans. I have therefore joined and made common cause with the Congress."[21] To those Muslims who doubted the wisdom of his moves, he retorted: "I want you to read the history of Islam and ask you to consider what the Prophet's mission was. It was to free the oppressed, to feed the poor and to clothe the naked. Therefore the work of the Congress is nothing but the work of the Prophet, nothing inconsistent with Islam."[22] Since India was the fatherland of both Muslims and Hindus and belonged collectively to all,[23] the Congress party's aims were liberation and social justice for all: "The Congress aims at liberating the people from slavery and exploitation, or in other words, the Congress aims at being able to feed India's hungry millions and clothe India's naked millions."[24] Though non-violent, the Khudai Khidmatgaran movement pursued a militantly anti-British policy. According to Abdul Ghaffar Khan, all the misfortunes of the Hindu and Muslim communities of India should be placed at the door of the British, who had pitted one group against the other in order to convince them that a British presence was necessary in India.[25]

BRITISH, SOVIET, AND AFGHAN REACTION

The appearance of the Khudai Khidmatgaran and their alliance with the Congress party, coinciding with uprisings and unrest in the strategic tribal belt, alarmed the British authorities in India. In the program and tactics of the Servants of God they saw a dangerous and politically inflammable element that could easily be ignited and manipulated either by the Soviets or by the Afghans, the one in pursuit of revolutionary goals, the other seeking recovery of the Peshawar region and some degree of authority over the transfrontier tribes. Under the circumstances, the uniforms of the Servants of God seemed an ominous sign to the British and a hopeful one to the Soviets. Significantly, Abdul Ghaffar Khan, who was widely read in the history of various revolutionaries and an admirer of Lenin,[26] eventually chose to outfit his followers in brick-red uniforms.[27]

At first the Soviet press was enthusiastic in support of the Red Shirt movement, and this reaction only increased the British fears that the movement was Communist-oriented or could easily become so. One Soviet paper reported that the Red Shirts, a revolutionary organization in the North-West Frontier Province with some 25,000 members, had an emblem that included a hammer and sickle as well as the Persian (*sic*) inscriptions "Long Live Revolution" and "Workers and Peasants of All Countries Unite."[28] *Pravda*, which placed the number of Red Shirts at 100,000, saw in the organization the potential of a revolutionary peasant movement.[29] Within a year or two, however, these high hopes were dampened, and by the end of 1931 the Soviets were attacking the Red Shirt movement: far from acting as Servants of God, the Red Shirts were "Servants of Imperialism" who had betrayed the Pathan peasantry. The Russians charged that the organization listened more and more to its religious and mystical elements, who had drowned out the objective revolutionary demands of the peasant masses against the dominant classes. The lack of assertive revolutionary leadership was attributed chiefly to Gandhi and his partisans and to the bourgeoisie of India, who had succeeded in taking over the direction of the peasant movement.[30]

Despite this change of attitude on the part of the Soviets, the British still considered the Red Shirt movement dangerous. In proclamations issued in various districts of the North-West Frontier Province, they warned the tribesmen to "prevent Congress volunteers wearing red jackets from entering your villages. They call themselves Khudai Khidmatgaran (Servants of God). But in reality they are the servants of Gandhi. They wear the dress of Bolsheviks. They will create the same atmosphere as you have heard in the Bolshevik dominion." The British leveled official charges at the Red Shirts: it was a subversive revolutionary organization whose objective was to drive the British out of India by force. "Though stress was laid on the observance [of] non-violence, people were encouraged to expect some great event, to be united in anticipation of it, and to be ready to resume the struggle which was described as war."[31] To back up this charge, they cited Abdul Ghaffar Khan's declaration that

If I do not die, I will prevent the English from ruling my country and with the help of God I shall succeed. . . . We and the Congress have two purposes: first, to free our country, and secondly, to feed the hungry and clothe the naked. Do not rest till freedom is won. It does not matter if you are blown up with guns, bombs, etc. If you are brave come out onto the battlefield and fight the English, who are the cause of our troubles. . . . The English are the common enemies of the Congress and the Pathans.[32]

In such circumstances, the British authorities carried on a campaign of constant harassment against the Red Shirts. Abdul Ghaffar Khan and his followers were frequently arrested. For lack of other charges, the leaders were accused of "interfering with the law, administering justice on their own, withholding evidence,"[33] or general non-cooperation.*

The Khudai Khidmatgaran, denounced as betrayers of the revolution by the Soviets and as subversives by the British, did not receive any encouragement from Nadir and the Afghan government either. In part Nadir's coolness can be attributed to Abdul Ghaffar Khan's close ties with Amanullah, whose leadership of the Afghan liberation movement and modernization program had won the admiration of the young reformer. In 1919 Abdul Ghaffar Khan had actively promoted the Afghan cause,[34] and it was reportedly on the advice of Amanullah that he had returned to his homeland.[35] There he continued to follow Amanullah's activities with sympathy, and during the civil war he attempted to help the Afghan ruler by stopping the flow of supplies to Bacha. When Amanullah abdicated, Abdul Ghaffar Khan placed most of the blame on the British.[36]

Given Abdul Ghaffar Khan's pro-Amanullah sentiments, in supporting him Nadir risked not only angering the British but also establishing a potentially inimical base on his own frontier. In addition, his support would have seemed to encourage the secular educational plans and social reforms of the Red Shirts, and in 1930 he could ill afford to alienate the Afghan religious establishment and conservative elements. Furthermore, in view of the putative pro-Bolshevist tendencies of the Red Shirts, Nadir had reason to suppose that the movement might be used against the Afghan monarchy and Afghan interests.[37] Still, his major concerns seem to have been the first named: he did not want to become involved in a military conflict with the British, and he did not want to see the tribal belt made into an ideological or political base for a movement that might easily turn against the Afghan throne. There were even fears that such a movement might develop a kind of reverse irredentism by attempting to extend a democratic, modernizing regime over Sind, Kashmir, Afghanistan, and the North-West Frontier Province—and at some later date over other portions of Central Asia.[38] The constitutional experiment in the North-West Frontier Province was a double-edged sword threatening the absolutism that ruled in Afghanistan as well as the autocracy of the militarized frontier region of India.[39]

Nadir's government went to great lengths to discourage the activities of

---

* P. Sykes writes ("The Present Position," pp. 158–59) that Abdul Ghaffar and his brother joined the Congress Party and "organized an unscrupulous campaign of hatred and vituperation against the British Raj. The result was a serious attack on Peshawar by tribal lashkars in 1930." Thus the charge is not that of organizing a revolt but of inspiring one.

the Red Shirt movement and disassociate itself from them. In the judgment of one British official, "The present ruler, King Nadir Shah, has honourably lived up to his engagements and shown himself most fair and loyal. Indeed he has kept his firebrands on his side of the border much better than we have ours. It is greatly due to his influence that the Red Shirt movement has not spread into independent territory to a greater extent than it has."[40] Thus, the same man who had mobilized the frontier Pathan tribes for the cause of Afghan independence in 1919 failed to support them actively in this period of open revolts and civil disobedience.*

NADIR AND THE FRONTIER TRIBES

By 1929 it was clear to the British that some 40 years of British administration had failed to stabilize the frontier region, and that unless they exercised control and influence beyond the border, such stability was impossible to achieve. They needed either the active cooperation or the benevolent neutrality of the Kabul government. Even so, their problems were many. The region was a strategic stronghold : the Pathans were armed, the terrain a difficult one. The cost of effective military occupation would have been prohibitive. In the border districts, where there was a complicated administrative structure modeled on the British-Indian system, resistance and resentment over what the Pathans regarded as unnecessary encroachments on their autonomy and time-honored laws were high.[41] Traditionally, the British had sought to control the tribes across the administrative border by paying generous subsidies and by using force when necessary. By 1930 the authorities in India were paying out 885,790 rupees annually in subsidies alone,[42] and were using both air bombardments and military expeditions to back up their agreements with the tribes.[43]

In 1930, as the Pathans grew more restive and the Red Shirt and Congress propaganda flourished, the British government in India continued to pursue a forward policy, establishing military installations and consolidat-

---

* He had outlined quite a different policy in his inaugural speech before the Afghan parliament. At that time, describing the problem of the free Pathan tribes of the frontier as "a question of equal importance to Afghanistan and the British Government," he had declared : "Afghanistan is not free from anxiety about the border tribes. . . . The frontier tribes and ourselves are united with the ties of Islam and tribal spirit. The British Government has probably experienced, during the long years, this mutual sympathy of the tribes and Afghanistan. We cannot possibly renounce this sympathy. The distress of the free tribes of the Frontier having repercussions in Afghanistan, we always wish the well-being and prosperity of these free tribes." See *Islah*, August 7, 1931, and Mohammed Ali, *Progressive Afghanistan*, pp. 216–17.

ing their position along the frontier. This was bound to cause a reaction. More important, however, there was a developing sense of self-awareness among the Pathans and a rekindled confidence in the power and destiny of the Pathans.[44] Other circumstances combined to worsen the relations between the government and the tribes. The powerful Afridis were disappointed in their failure to reap any permanent benefits from the Indian railway and were further alienated by the British support of the Shi'ah Muslims against the Sunnis. The Mohmand tribe grumbled that its subsidy had not once been increased in the past 30 years. The Sarda Act, passed by the Indian government in 1930, also aroused the apprehensions of the Pathan Muslims, who feared that it represented a further encroachment on Islamic law and Muslim traditions in stipulating, among other things, age limits and the consent of both parties for marriages.[45]

The first of several transfrontier tribal uprisings in 1930 was led by the famous Haji of Turungzai (a kinsman of Abdul Ghaffar Khan), who led a Mohmand tribal lashkar against the British authorities in the Peshawar district, requiring the intervention of the British army and air force. In May of that year, further agitation shook the city itself, after a soldier accidentally killed a Hindu woman and her two children. At this point, the incensed citizens were ready to welcome the tribesmen. Lashkars of Orakzais and Afridis soon followed the Mohmand lashkar, and in July a Mahsud force invaded the district. The inhabitants of the region gave the invaders every possible assistance, while the invaders, for their part, posing as liberators, refrained from looting and even from firing on Indian troops. In this critical period, the government of India sought to divert the growing political consciousness in the province into constitutional channels of thought.[46]

Meanwhile, the Nadir administration remained aloof, and the appeals of the tribes to Kabul for help against British measures received no positive response: "The tribes were coldly advised to make their peace with the British."[47] Fraser-Tytler confirms that the Afghan government followed this line both at this time and later, in 1933, when there were more troubles: "Deputations of tribesmen who had come to ask for help against the British were sent back from Kabul with nothing to show for their trouble but some salutary advice. . . . No tribesman, disturbed at British penetration of the frontier areas, received either help or encouragement to take up arms against this relentless pressure on his freedom."[48] And Sir Percy Sykes commented: "For the first time the Afghan Government had ceased to encourage the warlike, fanatical tribesmen to give trouble to the British."[49]

RELATIONS WITH THE SOVIET UNION AND THE MUSLIM STATES

In adopting this policy, the Afghan government alienated many tribes-men and played into the hands of the pro-Amanullah elements, who sought to discredit Nadir. Moreover, the Afghan neutrality troubled the Soviets, with whom the new Afghan government wanted to reestablish normal and correct relations. Indeed, the Afghans intended "to cultivate friendship with the Soviet Union as the nearest and most useful neighbours of Af-ghanistan."[50] The passivity of the Nadir administration toward the Pathan tribal revolts and the Indian national-liberation movement was construed by the Soviets as a betrayal of Amanullah's policies and a tacit collabora-tion with British imperialism, designed to safeguard the vested interests of the landlords and ruling classes from the influence of the revolutionary ideas and currents in India. The Soviets regarded the Afghan monarchy's decision not to intervene in the struggle of the transfrontier tribes as proof that "Nadir Shah had justified the hopes placed in him by British imperial-ism" and that feudal and reactionary elements lent their support to im-perialism in colonies and semicolonies.[51]

In the emergence of the new Afghan royal dynasty and British consoli-dation along and across the Indian frontier, the Soviets also saw a general imperialistic design to encircle the Soviet Union in preparation for a mili-tary adventure against it. In a Plenum of the Executive Committee of the Comintern, Marcel Cachin denounced the attempts of Anglo-French im-perialists to recruit the military services of various states bordering the Soviet Union: "India and Afghanistan are being transformed into mili-tary bases for an attack on the U.S.S.R."[52]

Despite these apprehensions and accusations, the Soviet Union re-sponded favorably to the diplomatic overtures of the Afghan government. At first, when the internal situation in Afghanistan was in flux and the final outcome uncertain, the Soviets seem to have accorded limited *de facto* recognition to Nadir's government without becoming involved in the ques-tion of the legitimacy of the dynasty. On October 19, 1929, the Soviet For-eign Ministry "acknowledged the information that Marshal Muhammed Nadir Khan *has been recognized by the national representatives of Af-ghanistan* [italics mine]. The People's Commissariat for Foreign Affairs notes with satisfaction your statement, made in the name of the Afghan Government, that the friendly relations existing between the two Govern-ments will be continued in the best manner and on the firmest founda-tions."[53] The Soviet Foreign Minister, Maxim Litvinov, announced a policy of non-intervention in the internal affairs of the Afghan kingdom and called for other governments to adopt a hands-off policy too. The Soviet Union, he said, intended to continue to be a good neighbor to Afghanistan and hoped to develop relations with her on the basis of existing agreements, that her independence and progress might be ensured.[54]

This expressed readiness to establish friendly relations was coupled with an indirect admonition: the Russians pointed out the weaknesses of the Afghan government in order to deter it from any tempting anti-Soviet ventures. As *Izvestia* put it, "The government will be stable and will lead the country back to peace if it has profited by the lessons of Civil War, if it takes a decisive stand against the feudal and clerical reaction, if it gives satisfaction to the immediate needs of the peasants, if it guarantees the rights of its national minorities, and if it adopts in its foreign policy a conduct which will systematically and surely lead to the complete independence of Afghanistan." Otherwise, *Izvestia* warned, there were many difficulties in establishing a stable government: the treasury was empty, the national economy was disorganized, the peasant population had been ruined, there were divisions among the tribes, and there was the possibility of British aggression from India.[55]

The Afghan government, in an effort to demonstrate its good will, concluded a non-aggression pact with the Soviet Union in 1931,[56] and, like Turkey, showed marked sympathy for the Soviet viewpoint at the Disarmament Conference in 1932. A section of the non-aggression pact that anticipated a ban on activities in one country by organizations hostile to the other seems to save been rigorously observed by the Afghan government. Though the emigrés from Turkestan who had settled in northern Afghanistan were allowed to remain in Afghanistan, where they had a good deal of public sympathy as persecuted Muslims, they were transferred to the southern provinces and their activities were curtailed.[57] More important, from the Soviet point of view, the Nadir administration not only prevented any activities in support of the Basmachi movement but also expelled Ibrahim Beg, one of the last Basmachi leaders and an associate of Enver, refusing to allow northern Afghanistan to be used as a springboard for anti-Soviet, Pan-Islamic, or Pan-Turkic activities. The relations between the two countries were further improved by the signing of a Soviet-Afghan agreement on the definition of aggression.[58]

Nadir's decision to adopt a policy of non-intervention in Soviet Central Asia indicates his grasp of *realpolitik*. Because the roads through the Hindu Kush remained virtually impassable, northern Afghanistan, a region whose population was ethnically tied to Central Asia, was isolated, and the Afghan government had neither the financial means nor the military power to cope with revolts that might be fomented there under the banner of national self-determination and cultural autonomy.[59] A weak Afghanistan had to put its house in order and bring about the socioeconomic integration of the kingdom, not embark upon irredentist movements that might result in its own disintegration.

The normalization of diplomatic relations between Afghanistan and the Soviet Union was accompanied by an expansion of trade between the two countries. The main Afghan exports to the Soviet Union were wool and carpets, the main imports, oil, gasoline, sugar, and tea.[60] Between 1928 and 1932, the Soviet Union gained a greater share of the Afghan market, and in Herat and northern Afghanistan, goods made in Bukhara and Tashkent dominated.[61] In 1933 Strickland observed that "business with India is not likely to diminish but Russian goods have driven the British articles out of all but the highest grade market, and the imports from India are now Indian or Japanese rather than British. British prices are simply too high; where the British machinery is indispensable the price is paid, but in other lines a cheaper substitute is preferred."[62] In an effort to increase the volume of Afghan-Soviet trade and to reestablish contact with Europe through the Soviet Union, the Nadir government initiated negotiations with Soviet Russia that resulted in both a commercial treaty and postal and telegraphic ties between the two countries.[63]

The new Afghan monarch also attempted to maintain the same level of cordiality with Turkey and Iran as had been achieved under the administration of Amanullah. When the Afghan ambassador to Turkey presented his letters of accreditation to Mustafa Kemal, he went beyond mere formalities in his official speech. Declaring that the "fraternal relations between the two countries are based on great historic and social tradition," he asserted:

No force, no hand will be able to dissolve those ties. We even think that the two nations have the same spirit in their hearts.... The Revolution, the success and the development of the noble Turkish nation under the direction and auspices of Your Excellency, are inscribed in golden letters in the pages of Universal History in general and the East in particular. It is thanks to you that this courageous and valiant nation has been led from material and spiritual oppression to the road of progress. The noble Afghan nation, which has followed with joy the progress of its Turkish brothers, presents them its congratulations.[64]

Meanwhile, Nadir wrote a personal letter to Reza Shah, expressing his sympathies for the "untiring efforts" of the Iranian monarch and stressing his best wishes for the well-being and progress of all Muslim nations. He praised Reza Shah for the progress and elevation of Iran: "Iranian history will inscribe your name in golden letters." Nadir assured the Iranian monarch that he intended to make every effort to ensure the well-being and progress of Afghanistan, and announced his desire to continue the friendly relations between the two countries. In reply Reza Shah echoed these sentiments, wishing Afghanistan continued progress and assuring the Afghans that there were no ulterior motives or designs in the friendship he and his country extended to the Afghans and to Nadir.[65]

Nadir's efforts to reassert good and friendly relations with Turkey and Iran went far beyond the exigencies of normal diplomatic relations. He seems to have made a deliberate effort to preclude the possibility of either Turkey or Iran being made into a base of operations for pro-Amanullah elements, and to dissuade Iran from making any irredentist claim on Herat. In addition, both he and the Afghan modernists seem to have been anxious to prevent any assumption being made that in rejecting Amanullah Afghanistan had also rejected progress. Overt admiration for Turkey and Iran would be helpful in this connection.

Though the Afghan monarchy declined to join in the Basmachi and tribal struggles, it championed a platform and program of Pan-Islamism that was mild enough not to offend the country's giant neighbors, yet lofty enough to please Muslims both at home and abroad. An Afghan delegation sent to the kingdom of Hejaz to establish official relations presented a declaration that emphasized the unity of interests and solid bonds of friendship among the Muslim states. Good and friendly relations, it read, "were recommended by God when God said 'the believers are brothers.' " That was also the teaching of the Prophet Muhammed: "The believer is for a believer like the material of an edifice which they hold between them." In addition, there were other "authentic traditions which show the necessity of establishing wider moral ties and official relations to guarantee such ties." To sow the seeds of Islamic union and harmony through official relations was to be commended and this was the course of the Afghans who, by taking the initiative in establishing diplomatic relations with the Hejaz, were promoting Islamic concord between the Afghan and Arab peoples. This duty, the delegation observed, had been neglected by Nadir's predecessors.[66] As a result of these overtures, the Afghans signed treaties of friendship with Saudi Arabia and Iraq in 1932.[67]

RELATIONS WITH EUROPE AND THE UNITED STATES

In Europe, Nadir continued Amanullah's policy, seeking to establish diplomatic ties with as many countries as possible. Apart from a desire to assert Afghanistan's sovereignty, legitimize his own rule, and secure his dynasty, he was interested in reopening Afghanistan to the presence of European powers other than Great Britain and the Soviet Union. In this context, he concluded treaties of friendship with Estonia, Lithuania, Finland, and later Austria, Denmark, Holland, Sweden, Norway, Spain, and Hungary. Still later, he signed agreements with Estonia, Lithuania, Poland, Rumania, and the Soviet Union on the definition of aggression.[68]

Nadir was particularly anxious to secure the help and support of France, Italy, and Germany. On October 18, 1929, soon after his triumph over Bacha, he told Andrée Viollis, the French journalist, that his first goal was to expand the country's education and road systems, after which he would perhaps build railroads in order to encourage industry and the exploitation of Afghanistan's natural resources. In all this, he declared, he counted on the help and sympathy of foreign powers.

I count especially on France. . . . I hope that the intellectual cooperation established by King Amanullah between our two countries will continue and will grow. Amanullah, along with all our enlightened compatriots, regarded your country as one of the spiritual forces of the world. I will seek that cooperation not only in the archaeological mission, which has given brilliant results, and in the existing schools but in all our scientific establishments. Could not France send us teachers, engineers, all kinds of technicians who could help us exploit our riches?[69]

Nadir confirmed the archaeological monopoly granted to the French by Amanullah, permitted the teaching of the French language again, and renewed the services of French teachers and professors. Similar relations and contacts were restored with Italy and Germany. In the case of Italy, he thanked the Italian government, which was the first European power to recognize Afghan independence and to extend its help: "The Afghan people and history of Afghanistan will never forget that gesture." Praising Mussolini for his efforts to rebuild Italy, Nadir especially hailed the achievement of progress within a framework of respect for national customs and habits. "This should serve as an example to the heads of various countries of the world who desire to lead their country towards progress, while at the same time preserving their religion and national traditions and customs."[70] In 1933 the government made a major gesture to Italy, authorizing the establishment of a chapel in the Italian Legation and the residency of a priest to minister to the spiritual needs of the diplomatic corps.[71]

Nadir was also eager to interest two non-European states in the development of the Afghan kingdom: the United States and Japan. The American position on his government was unclear and confusing. In 1921 the United States had granted *de jure* recognition to Afghanistan. In the years 1925–28, upon the initiative of Nadir, then the Afghan envoy to Paris, the United

States entertained the idea of concluding a treaty of friendship with Afghanistan, but the matter was dropped after the overthrow of Amanullah. The United States was the last major power to recognize the new dynasty, doing so only in 1934; even then, it did not establish a diplomatic mission in Kabul. This reluctance was explained by William Phillips, the acting secretary of state by "the primitive condition of the country, the lack of capitulatory or other guarantees for the safety of foreigners, and . . . the absence of any important interests."[72]

Nadir solicited the support of American visitors in his effort to secure United States representation in Kabul and assistance in exploiting Afghanistan's resources.[73] To one visiting American he declared: "We prefer to have our resources exploited by capital from countries which have no colonial ambitions in the East. Our country is rich in oil, coal, copper, and other precious and commercial minerals. But we do not see fit to sell Afghanistan piecemeal by concessions to European powers who have aggressive interests."[74] The United States government was not unaware of the Afghans' interest in obtaining maximum American participation and cooperation in the guided modernization of their country. Wallace Murray, the chief of the Division of Near Eastern Affairs of the State Department, later wrote: "The Afghans themselves are naturally the best judges of what they desire from this country. It may be surmised, however, that their wants include: the establishment by the U.S. of a diplomatic mission in Kabul; *the development of Afghanistan by American enterprise and American capital* [italics mine]; American teachers and experts to advise and to work with the Afghan authorities; an assured supply of American automobiles and accessories; treaty alien status for Afghan merchants who travel to the U.S. on business; continued fair treatment of Afghan exports to this country." He pinpointed the basic dilemma of the Afghan government: the reluctance to grant the United States "most-favored-nation treatment in trade and customs matters is not due to a desire to place our goods at a disadvantage but is to avoid affording certain other countries, of whom the Afghans entertain suspicions, opportunity to press for equal advantages which could be used for political ends. There is the added difficulty that a foreign trade monopoly system exists in Afghanistan as in Iran, and that Afghanistan, like its western neighbor, has entered into certain compensation arrangements." Under the circumstances and even with the knowledge that the Afghans were disposed to give a favorable reception to American enterprise and capital, the State Department left it to the discretion of American "private interests themselves to determine whether or not Afghanistan is a suitable field for their endeavors."

Murray suggested that since the Afghans were unwilling to permit American eleemosynary or missionary activities in their country, the only direct American presence in the country apart from businessmen might be archaeological missions.[75]

The efforts of the Nadir administration to maintain the tradition of not granting concessions to Afghanistan's two major neighbors, the Soviet Union and Great Britain, and instead to use the offices of the United States to modernize the country were thus unproductive. A similar effort was made to secure the cooperation of Japan. On November 19, 1930, an Afghan-Japanese treaty of friendship was concluded in London.[76] Diplomatic missions were exchanged; Sardar Habibullah Tarzi, the first Afghan minister to Japan, arrived in Toyko on October 6, 1933, at which time he stated that the ever-growing industrial importance of Japan and the great demand for Japanese products (cloth, chemical products, and machinery) in Afghanistan had made his appointment necessary.[77] Though these contacts paved the way for future Japanese trade and economic expansion in Afghanistan and led to limited technical assistance, they did not bring about a revolutionary change in the scope, pace, or direction of modernization in Afghanistan. The Japanese ran into the same reservations and difficulties that faced the United States.

From time to time Nadir accepted some technical advice and help from the British government in India and the Soviet Union, but the activities of the two governments in the kingdom were sharply curtailed. He insisted that all Soviet personnel be withdrawn from the Afghan air force, and though he permitted a Soviet trade exhibition in Kabul (1933), he refused to allow the Russians to establish commercial missions in various regions of Afghanistan. His restriction of British activities was equally severe. All British nationals were barred from employment in the kingdom: "Even in education matters, while the French and German schools established by Amanullah were reopened and restaffed from Europe, the teaching of English was entrusted to Indian teachers, with the result that while many young Afghans spoke excellent German and French, very few knew more than a few words of English. But fewer still knew any Russian."[78] In all there were only about 70 Europeans in Afghanistan during Nadir's reign, a number that included, aside from diplomatic personnel, a French archaeologist, a German director of the postal system, and two Italian officers attached to the artillery school.[79]

To the Afghan tribal representatives Nadir unequivocally announced: "My government up to this day has given concessions or rights to no state, and so long as I am alive, no such transaction will receive my signature."[80]

Clearly he had no intention of making a radical departure from the policies of his predecessors on the exploitation of the country's natural resources. He was thus unable to bring to Afghanistan the railway system that would allow it to tap those resources. He did not want British or Soviet help in this area; instead he expected "politically disinterested" foreign powers and investors to participate in this enormous undertaking. Such help was not forthcoming. In 1931 a group of Japanese capitalists visited Kabul and held conversations with the government concerning the construction of a railway linking India (probably Chaman) to Kandahar and Herat;[81] nothing came out of the discussions. Earlier, in 1930, *Pravda* announced that Nadir had approved a contract allowing various German firms to build a railway system linking India with the U.S.S.R.;[82] this proved to be mere speculation. In the end, the Afghan monarch fell back on the old formula: in order to safeguard the independence of Afghanistan and avoid alienating the powerful Afghan tribes by granting major foreign concessions, the Afghans must realize the railway project through their own efforts.[83]

THE END OF NADIR'S REIGN

From 1932 on, Nadir's government was seriously shaken by a series of events. The sequence began in November, when the administration, fearful of the possible activities of Ghulam Nabi, asked the former Afghan envoy to Moscow and ardent supporter of Amanullah to accept a suitable pension, leave Afghanistan, and abstain from politics. According to Afghan official sources, Ghulam Nabi, while pretending to consider the offer, attempted to foment a rebellion in the southern province. Summoned before the King, he was charged with high treason. Nadir ordered his instant execution. According to Fraser-Tytler, "Such precipitate action was a cardinal error, perhaps the only error in judgement on a major issue made by Nadir Shah. . . . At the time he tried to repair his mistake by placing the undoubted proofs of Ghulam Nabi's guilt before three separate bodies, who affirmed that he had been justly executed. But the King's autocratic action aroused much feeling against him throughout the country."[84] Nadir's clear violation of the processes of legal redress granted under the constitution of 1931 provoked widespread resentment; he had made the execution seem a matter of personal vengeance. The political struggle between the pro-Amanullah elements and the ruling dynasty thus took on an additional dimension, that of a blood feud between the Musahiban family and Ghulam Nabi's family, the Charkis.

The anti-government opposition, which now included partisans of Amanullah, impatient modernists, and disillusioned nationalists, took its first victim in July 1933. Nadir's brother Muhammed Aziz, the Afghan envoy to Germany, was assassinated. The assassin, Kemal Seyed, a graduate of the Najat secondary school who was in Germany for advanced studies, was a member of an Afghan student circle. Upon his arrest he declared that his action was a protest against the predominance of British influence in Afghanistan and against the betrayal of the frontier tribes by the Afghan government,* which through its passivity in the face of British forward policies, had permitted Britain to tighten her control over the free Pathan tribes of the North-West Frontier.[85] Not long after, another Najat student, driven by the same motives, made an attempt on the life of the British envoy in Kabul. Entering the British Legation, the would-be assassin was thwarted of his main victim but killed the legation's chief clerk and two servants. The Afghan government adopted stern measures: the young man was executed, a number of arrests were made, and 32 students and friends of the assassin were given jail terms ranging up to 14 years.[86] These developments culminated in the assassination of Nadir Shah himself on November 8, 1933, the anniversary of Ghulam Nabi's execution, during a school prize-giving ceremony. The assassin, Muhammed Khaliq, also a Najat student, was, according to varying reports, either a natural or an adopted son of Ghulam Nabi. His motives were thus both personal and political.

The assassination of Nadir widened the gulf between the Musahiban family and the Amanullah supporters, especially the Charki and Tarzi families. Amanullah tried to make political capital of the assassination and to interpret it as a repudiation of Nadir's policies, declaring:

Today's event is the result of anxieties among the Afghan people, provoked by the policy of Nadir. This policy has resulted in assassinations and imprisonments. Many young Afghans have been sacrificed, and their loss has chagrined me. Nadir was an Afghan. Nevertheless, I cannot affirm that my sorrow is relieved by the thought that for the past 10 years I have fought to give the Afghan people independence and liberty. The policies of Nadir were dangerous for both Afghan independence and foreign countries. Afghans realized it. If the Afghan people invite me to return and put into action my program for progress, I shall be ready to serve my country.[87]

Shah Wali brushed this offer aside: Amanullah could never retake his place on the Afghan throne because he had shown disdain for the historical traditions of the country and affronted the Afghans. The succession of events in Kabul confirmed this judgment. The pro-Amanullah and anti-

---

* Charges that Nadir had sold out to the British may have been spread among the Afghan students abroad by *Fougani Afghan*, the organ of the Alliance for the Defense of National Rights, a revolutionary group. The periodical, which began publication in 1933, was written in Persian and was probably published in Switzerland. It may have been supported by Amanullah. See *Revue des Etudes Islamiques*, 1934.

Nadir elements were unable to exploit the situation. Even though only one of the Musahiban brothers, Shah Mahmud, the war minister, happened to be in Kabul at the time Nadir was killed, he acted promptly and was able to preserve the continuity of the Musahiban dynasty. On that same day, Zahir Shah, Nadir's only son and the heir apparent, ascended the throne.

SOME CONCLUSIONS

Nadir Shah's major contribution lay in the liberation of the kingdom from the reactionary and chaotic rule of Bacha-i-Saqao and in the political reunification, centralization, and pacification of the country. Slowly the foundations on which a modern Afghanistan could be built under the guidance of the ruling elite were restored. However, as Nadir acted to destroy Bacha's regime and consolidate his rule, he had to make major concessions to the religious establishment and the tribal interests, and in so doing, he placed himself and his modernization plans in the ancient straitjacket that had bound the previous Afghan rulers. He, too, faced the apparently insoluble problem of modernizing without jeopardizing the dynastic rule, Durrani domination, and Afghan ethnic preponderance, and without encroaching on the vested interests of the powerful Afghan tribes and the religious establishment or disturbing the precarious strategic balance in the area. Strung tight between these conflicting forces from within, the fabric of Afghan society was also threatened by dynamic social movements in the territories of its two powerful neighbors: communism in the north and the national-liberation and democratic-constitutional movements in India.

Under these circumstances, Nadir adopted a policy of "make haste slowly." He pursued socioeconomic progress with circumspection, administering small doses of reform that would not lead to domestic upsets. Under his administration, economic policies were institutionalized, and the apprehensions of the Afghan people and conservative elements about the potential ills of modernization were somewhat eased.[88] The country's economic and diplomatic contacts with the external world were reestablished, and the monarchy even provided the kingdom with its first banking institutions. The constitution of 1931, which institutionalized the power of the religious establishment, also had provisions that were to permit gradual reforms in the juridical system in keeping with the requirements of a modernizing state: cases involving commercial and industrial activities and those involving the duties of government officials were removed from the jurisdiction of the Shar'ia courts and placed under the authority of special courts. The reopening of the secondary schools and the resumption of the program of sending students abroad for higher education were also historically significant, adding new members to the small but highly conscious Afghan intelligentsia who provided the main body of administrators and who in general championed the cause of modernization.

Despite his many achievements, Nadir failed to find a formula for the exploitation of the country's natural resources, failed to bring about major agricultural and land reforms, and failed to placate the powerful nomadic and seminomadic tribes. Though many of his measures were important, they were limited in scope and were generally confined to the Kabul-Kandahar-Ghazni triangle. They did, however, provide the nucleus and guidelines for the reform programs of future Afghan administrations.

Chapter Thirteen

Hashim Khan: Nationalism and Gradualism

Nineteen-year-old Zahir Khan ascended the Afghan throne on November 8, 1933. Born in Kabul, the young ruler had attended Habibiya and Istiklal, and later, during his father's stay in France, several French lycées. Upon his return to Afghanistan in 1930, he underwent military training and graduated from the military school in Kabul. At age eighteen he was first named acting minister of defense and then acting minister of education by his father, in order that he might become familiar with "the arts of government and administration of the state."[1] His accession to the throne ensured the legitimacy and continuity of the Musahiban dynasty. The real power, however, lay in the hands of his three paternal uncles, Shah Mahmud Khan, Shah Wali Khan, and particularly Muhammed Hashim Khan, who as prime minister assumed complete control of the country's domestic and foreign policies.[2]

Under the Hashim administration, the Afghan nationalists and modernists continued to formulate (and where possible to update) the tenets of Afghan nationalism, and to defend the principles of reform and modernization. Their writings on these subjects, scattered widely in the literary, economic, and historical journals of the day, are intricate, and their rationalizations and conceptualizations are often confused, redundant, didactic, and moralistic. Those who were apologists of Islam placed the major blame for the "backwardness" of Afghanistan (and other Islamic societies) on the disunity of the Muslims and their failure to observe and adhere to the laws and true spirit of Islam.[3] Others endeavored to explain that "backwardness" by historical factors, placing the burden of responsibility on foreign elements, especially the Turko-Mongol invasions of the thirteenth and fourteenth centuries,* which in their view irreparably undermined the

* The historian Ghubar wrote: "Until the onslaught of Gengiz Khan ... Afghanistan was the shining star of the Islamic world. Neither in cultural level nor in the stage of civilization had she any equal among the Muslim countries" ("Role of Afghanistan," p. 32).

material civilization of the Afghans for the following six centuries and perverted "the lofty moral fiber of the Afghan people."[4]

In the tradition of Tarzi and the modernists of the 1920's, many of the Afghan writers, poets, and historians of this period regarded modernization as the prescription for an Afghan cultural renaissance, spiritual renovation, and national rebirth. They attempted to demonstrate not only the individual benefits of modern education and learning but also the desperate need for knowledge in all Islamic societies.[5] The new generation of modernists especially praised science and technology, and exhorted their countrymen to view modern civilization as the result of unceasing effort and applied knowledge. Without the accoutrements of technology—machinery, factories, industries, skilled workers, training programs—Afghanistan would constantly be dependent on outsiders and could never achieve real independence: "The individual without knowledge and the nation without technical know-how and machinery will find itself in the role of a patient confined to bed."[6] The alternatives facing the Afghans were very clear: either modernize and meet the challenges of the times or witness the erosion of Afghan power and the loss of Afghan sovereignty.[7] Nor, they insisted, was the modernization of Afghanistan a utopian dream. Some of the nationalist-modernists pleaded with the representatives of the new Afghan educated elite, especially those educated in Europe and America and "dazzled and overwhelmed by their civilizations," not to be pessimistic about Afghanistan's ability to bridge the technological gap: progress was not indigenous to Europe, nor was it the exclusive preserve of the peoples of that continent. Just as the rise and decline of societies and civilizations are subject to natural phenomena, so are the dynamics of modernization.[8] By inculcating self-confidence among Afghans and patiently working to give them a sense of national purpose, the Afghan elite could transform Afghanistan into a modern state. Following the example of Japan, Afghanistan must industrialize and must mobilize its manpower and natural resources.[9]

Like their predecessors, the Afghan nationalists and modernists of the 1930's argued long and ardently that Islam, progress, and modernization were not incompatible, and in fact emphasized many of the same themes: the ability to learn and to acquire knowledge were divine attributes and basic to all men; no man had the right to perpetuate ignorance; the welfare of Islamic societies and the defense of the fatherland were incumbent on all good Muslims; no true Muslim could knowingly and willingly oppose reform and modernization, whose goal was the harmonious blending of modern civilization with tradition.[10] The new generation of modernists, like the older one, held that the principles of Islamic law were guides to social welfare, progress, and justice, and that those principles could be discovered only through reason, which could be cultivated through learning and education alone. Islam and modern education were therefore not only compatible but essential to the welfare and independence of the Afghan people. Without independence, Afghanistan would be like a house without light, like an organism without a soul, like a plant without water.[11]

The theme that Islam was the religion of reform and progress was not confined to literary and historical journals. Even *Al-Falah*, the organ of the Society of the Learned Muslim Interpreters of Law, published articles to that effect. Ibrahim Khan Pardis, for example, wrote that the high ethical precepts of Islam and the lofty tenets of the Quran made them at one and the same time guides and sources of inspiration for social reform; after all, did not the Quran specifically instruct the faithful to help the poor and the hungry, to promote hygiene, to institute and uphold the true rules of equal justice?[12] *Al-Falah* even reprinted an article castigating those who believed that any attempt to improve one's fate and institute social reform was impossible or undesirable. From the very beginning, Islam had been interested in and committed to the welfare, happiness, and defense of the Muslim community.[13] In this modern day, the only way the Muslims could preserve their societies and their spiritual legacy was with military power, which must be achieved through the application of knowledge. The sword was essential, but Islam also needed knowledge and progress to defend itself.[14]

Some Afghan modernists went so far as to maintain that faith was a matter of individual conscience and heart, an intimate relationship between man and his Creator that no one has the right to disturb. Some even expressed a desire to see this idea, "prevalent in Western countries, gain ground in the East as well," so that in the future religion would not be a source of discord and animosity but would perform its true function, that of a spiritual force.[15] A few others championed the right of Afghan girls to receive an appropriate education: as future mothers, they were responsible for the moral education of Afghan youth, and therefore their education was essential to the welfare of the Muslim community and the strength of Afghanistan.[16] In general, though, such pronouncements were rare in the 1930's and 1940's. In that period the major concern of the Afghan modernists was to reconcile Islam with reform and modernization, and to neutralize the opposition of the Muslim religious establishment. Hopefully, the Afghans would preserve their spiritual and moral values in their pursuit of progress, and would resist the creeping materialism, capitalism, and moral decay that prevailed in the modern world and carried with them the seeds of perennial discord and war.[17]

The new generation of writers also dwelt on the subject of nationalism. Again they reiterated earlier themes: love of the fatherland was sanctioned by Islam; patriotism was the duty of every devout Muslim; modernization and progress were beneficial to the fatherland, making the pursuit of those goals the sacred duty of every patriotic Afghan.[18] The nationalists of the 1930's were concerned with the problem of ethnic diversity in the country. Where the early Afghan chroniclers and nineteenth-century historians had been mainly interested in the genealogies of the individual Pathan tribes and the uniqueness of the Afghans, the writers of this period became preoccupied with establishing a common history, religious background, and ethnic origin for all the peoples of Afghanistan.[19] They tried hard to promote the notion that though there were many tribes and races in Afghanistan, all of them had a common ancestry, and that in fact the country's two languages, Persian and Pashto, derived from the same source. History was invoked as proof that the majority of the inhabitants of Afghanistan, whatever their name, whatever their class, whatever their race, were descended from Aryans and had no fundamental difference in blood. Centuries of common history and culture, together with Islam and its sense of community and brotherhood, had erased whatever differences there may have been and had tied together the fate of the inhabitants of Afghanistan.[20] In this context, the Afghan nationalists welcomed the invaluable work of the French archaeological team in Afghanistan, which had uncovered the richness of the country's Bactrian and Kushan heritage.[21] The Afghan nationalists took great pride in the fact that Kushan rule had had a far-reaching impact on the destinies of the peoples of eastern Iran and India, especially in the fields of religion and art.[22] Moreover, they contended that the contributions of their ancestors were not confined to the Kushan period but also had affected Islamic civilization:

The country of the Ancient Aryans, or the Islamic country of Khurasan, that is the Afghanistan of today, presented the Islamic world with as many men of science and letters as any single constituent of the Islamic world has.... The contribution of the people of Afghanistan to the civilization and culture of the Islamic world is outstanding and significant. The Afghans introduced the Arabs to the philosophy and religion of the people of India long before the Arabs had even made the slightest infiltration into the land of the Indians. The contribution of the Afghans to astronomy, geometry, mathematics, philosophy and theology of that time is admitted by all the Muslim historians.... In the ninth century the political and administrative influence of the Afghans was so obvious in the imperial hierarchy that the Arab scholars and historians were forced to admit that the period of the Abbassid Caliphate was more Khurassani than Arabic. This assertion was correct, because the Abbassid Caliphs were backed mostly by the Afghans. . . .

Afghanistan's contribution has not been only to the civilization of Islam. All along, during the rise of the Muslim Empire she struggled to retain her own national individuality and she was the first among the Muslim countries to declare her political independence by organizing the Tahiriia [Tahirid] Empire of Khurasan. . . . She was the first among the occupied nations of the East to give impetus to her native language (Persian of today) against the mighty and well-established language of the Arabs, and it was she who presented the world with a new and amazing literature, the Persian literature. Sanai, Mawlawi, Ansari, Farrukhi and Anwari are some of the outstanding representatives of the Afghan literature of that time. . . . Islamic and Afghan culture and civilization [spread] all over Central Asia and it was due to the Ghaznawids and the Ghurids, that from the tenth century until the sixteenth century Islam was spread and the Afghan literature was made popular in the subcontinent of India.[23]

Some of these claims have invited the criticism of many scholars—Iranian, Arab, Soviet, and others—who question the existence of a distinct Afghan culture at such an early stage of history, and the classification of such writers as Mawlawi, Farrukhi, and Ibn Sina (Avicenna) as Afghans.

In any event, the Afghan claims must be seen in the light of the rise of the modern Afghan state and the need to legitimize the continuity and unity of the country. This emphasis is especially evident in the attempt to attribute an Aryan origin to most of the inhabitants of Afghanistan, a preoccupation of most of the Afghan historians then—and now.* These historians contend that the ancient Aryans, the ancestors of today's Afghans and Pathans, founded their first kingdom near Balkh, in northern Afghanistan, somewhere between 3,500 B.C. and 1,500 B.C., and that from there they spread east to India and west to Persia. The most interesting aspect of this theory is the claim that the ancient kingdom of Bactria was the first *Afghan* kingdom because the word Paktun is derived from the word Bactria.[24] The readiness with which Afghan official spokesmen have accepted this theory reflects their strong desire to refute the contention of the historians of "neighbouring countries," who "tried to show that the

---

* According to some, at least for a brief period in the 1930's, and perhaps under the influence of Nazi racial theories, the proponents of the theory of Aryan descent went beyond nationalism and flirted with racism. Robert Byron claims that racial theories played some part in the forced exodus of the Jews of northern Afghanistan. There were plans to rebuild the city of Balkh, which was hailed as the mother of Aryan cities and the home of the Aryan race, says Byron, and on that account the presence of Jews there might have been unwelcome. See *Road to Oxiana*, pp. 119, 237, 294-95. Such assertions are difficult to substantiate; nor was I able to verify that there were anti-Jewish riots in Kabul in 1934, as reported in *The Universal Jewish Encyclopedia*, I, 106.

Afghans had no history," and that modern Afghanistan consists of a collection of heterogeneous peoples. By maintaining that the origins of the Afghan kingdom began some 3,500–5,000 years ago, Afghan historians have sought to prove that the Afghans demonstrated state-building qualities long ago, and that modern Afghanistan is the product of a continuous historical process, not simply a "political accident."[25]

The Aryan descent theory was used not only to unify the peoples of Afghanistan but also to consolidate the historical and cultural ties of the Pathans "living in Afghanistan and the borderlands."[26] The exposition of this theory was accompanied by a plea for the study of the Pashto language, along with Pashto literature and history. These studies were considered to be of paramount importance, for in addition to promoting solidarity within the country, they would also refute the "distortions" of those who "attempt to divide the Pathans or to link them to themselves."[27] Various authors of the period wrote surveys praising the outstanding cultural and artistic heritage of the Pathans;[28] others started a systematic survey and translation of various European works on the history, language, and literature of the Pathans.[29]

In order to illustrate the inherent superiority of the Pashto tongue and Pashto letters, and still demonstrate the unity of all the languages of Afghanistan, some authors argued that the language of the Avesta (the holy book of Zoroastrianism), the language of the ancient states of Sogdiana and Khwarezm, and the language of the Sakas and other peoples all belonged to the Afghan linguistic group. Of all these languages, however, Pashto was the most important, the purest of living languages. Even under the Achaemenid and Sassanid rule, Pashto remained pure, free of either the Pahlavi Persian or Sanskrit influence, evolving in its own cultural milieu.[30]

According to the Afghan nationalists, the Avesta and the earliest Vedas were the greatest masterpieces of Afghan and Pashto literature. In order to stress the indigenous nature and development of Afghan civilization, and to minimize the impact of any Persian influence, they insisted that even Zoroastrianism spread to Persia from Afghanistan.[31] Other nationalists made equally extravagant claims, contending that "the most famous and important dialect of the ancient Persian language, Darri, which became the foundation of the modern Persian, originated in Afghanistan."[32] The Afghan writers were thus not content merely to demonstrate the historical continuity of their people and their country; they also stoutly maintained that historically Afghanistan had been more a cultural exporter than an importer.

These efforts were encouraged by the Afghan government. The Ministry of Education, various semi-official publications, such newly established organizations as the Historical Institute and the Pashto Tulana (Academy), and the *anjoman-e adabi* (literary circles) pursued four aims: to study and clarify the Afghan historical heritage; to study and promote Afghan literature and folklore; to study and promote the Pashto language; and to spread knowledge about Afghanistan and its culture abroad.

The ultimate objective of the nationalist-modernists was to achieve the economic and political independence of Afghanistan. The highest goal of any people and any country was to be free, independent, and sovereign. Over and over again they stressed that only a truly free country could modernize effectively, and that modernization would strengthen the Afghan spirit of independence and love of liberty. Since the Afghans had already wrested their freedom and independence from the foreigners, they had a secure base for genuine modernization, modernization that would go hand in hand with their national interests and strengthen their independence and sovereignty.[33]

Political independence, however, was not the sole end of modernization. According to modernists, Afghanistan had another need: a cultural renaissance that could be achieved through knowledge and technology.[34] (There were even attempts, reminiscent of those of Tarzi's period, to link the Afghan national and cultural revival to the general awakening of the East, and to regard modernization as a protective shield against imperialism.)[35] But political independence and a revitalized culture could be sustained only if they were accompanied by economic development and independence. Without this, the process of modernization would not be complete. Afghanistan was a rich country; all it needed was peace, security, and modernization to achieve economic progress.[36]

In the best traditions of Mahmud Tarzi and *Siraj al-Akhbar*, the Afghan nationalist-modernist journalists began a campaign to school their readers in the intricacies of modern economics and politics, and to make them more aware of the need of various social reforms. Some Afghan periodicals covered such subjects as bacteriology, psychology, and other scientific disciplines, and dwelt on the benefits of various scientific discoveries.[37] Others explained the nature of commerce and attempted to present the views of Adam Smith, as well as those of Karl Marx.[38] Still others dealt with the contributions of Socrates, Voltaire, Goethe, Lamartine, Kant, and Bergson, or with the achievements of important scientists like Faraday and Edison.[39] The Afghan periodicals also reprinted the works of contemporary Middle Eastern and Indian writers and poets, among them Tagore, Namik Kemal, Malik ul-Shoara, Iqbal, and Taha Hussein.[40]

Like Tarzi and his colleagues, the modernists of the 1930's and 1940's deplored the indifference, even the active opposition, of many traditionalists toward European scientific thought and technology. They maintained that science and knowledge were products of man's collective effort, and that modern science and Western technology would in no way undermine Islamic traditions or the cultural legacy of the Afghans. Moreover, they asserted, there was an urgent need for the systematic translation of European works into Persian and Pashto to bridge the gap between Eastern and Western civilization. To sneer at European culture and label European achievement superficial was unhealthy; in any case, even those who wished to confine their studies to Eastern civilization and ancient Afghanistan were indebted to and needed the works of European orientalists and other scholars.[41]

Still, crucial as such translations might be in stimulating socioeconomic change, in the opinion of most of the Afghan writers they were no substitute for the development of a modern national culture. Many urged that Afghanistan's folklore and traditional music be collected, and called for the development of a new literature reflecting both the nation's historical legacy and its present social realities, needs, and aspirations. Poets and writers were exhorted to see themselves as vehicles of social change and their role as the awakening of the Afghan people.[42] Some took up the challenge, most notably in the effort to secure more rights for Afghan women. One writer compared women to "a sacred book sent by God," who taught man to love and to be kind; women were partners, companions, and friends, the foundation of the Afghan family. Another admonished fathers to pay due attention to the upbringing and education of their daughters.[43] The poet Fekri Seljuki lamented the fact that the Afghan women were unschooled and ignorant; educated women were essential in preparing future generations and in the socioeconomic and cultural renovation of Afghan society.[44] In some cases, these writers indirectly endorsed monogamy;[45] a few went so far as to advocate equal rights for men and women. With proper education, women could contribute to all spheres of modern civilization, even science and trade. Since morality and reason (a divine attribute) were closely related, educating women could in no way make them immoral; on the contrary, it would make them conscious of their duties as individuals, as members of society, and as Afghans. Many of these authors deplored the fact that the rights accorded women under Islamic law were not respected in

Afghanistan. They were careful, however, not to lay the blame for this on the religious establishment or the government, but instead attributed this negligence to Afghan national traditions, which had placed undue emphasis on the honor of women. Because of this emphasis, women were often denied any voice in the selection of their husbands, making most marriages mere business transactions or, more bluntly, the "sale of girls." One writer, Shayegh, focused on the laxity of the courts in enforcing the legal rights of women in regard to marriage, divorce, and property, attacking the tyranny of mothers-in-law and sisters-in-law in this connection. He even made an indirect attack on purda, which he found discriminatory and non-Islamic, placing women in the position of second-class Muslims. Shayegh felt that all these problems could be solved if women were properly educated and received instruction in Islamic law before marriage.[46]

Shayegh also attempted to make economic justice a national goal. In his view, agriculture was the basic source of the country's wealth, the very foundation of its trade. Nevertheless, it was an area that had been largely neglected. He deplored the socioeconomic condition of the peasantry, the exactions of the great landlords, the lack of educational facilities and opportunities in the rural regions, and the ignorance of the peasants concerning their legal and social rights.[47] Few of the other modernists shared his concern in this respect, however. Socioeconomic justice was not a dominant theme in the writings of the period.

The preoccupations and arguments of the Afghan nationalist-modernists were echoed in the speeches of King Zahir and Hashim Khan. "It is well-established that the progress of humankind depends upon such scientific and other knowledge that help the acquisition of wealth and power," Zahir declared in his inauguration speech before the third session of the Afghan parliament, adding: "We should unite our common efforts and proceed on the road of progress, that is to say, to develop and acquire more and more useful knowledge."[48] At the ceremonies marking the twentieth anniversary of Afghan independence, he spoke of independence and freedom, terming them divine gifts that were to be preserved through modernization and national unity. On still another occasion, he argued that the modernization of Afghanistan in no way conflicted with Islam, "a religion which had proved itself as the source of happiness and reformation of Muslim societies." Modernization would secure the independence of Afghanistan and promote the well-being and unity of Muslim society, he said; therefore it should be welcomed by everybody.[49] The King often invoked Islam's past history and cultural achievements, along with its ethical standards and spirit, to prove that Islam was a social religion, concerned with the general well-being, unity, and progress of its adherents.[50]

These arguments were also used by Hashim Khan. The Afghans, he said, were naturally favorably inclined toward modernization, since they had always sought to defend their fatherland and sustain their freedom.[51] In the tradition of *Siraj al-Akhbar*, Hashim and others in his administration quoted sayings of the Prophet Muhammed and passages from the Quran (notably the Quranic injunction to "travel even as far as China" in search of knowledge) in an effort to overcome the traditionalist opposition to modernization.[52]

POLICIES IN EDUCATION

Hashim Khan placed great emphasis on modern education, for reasons that he made clear in a 1937 interview: "This year ... we are devoting a sum to public education equal to half our war budget. In this way we are forming the men who tomorrow will have to watch over the independence of their country. We must transform the thoughts of the Afghans before we can build an ultra-western capital, as Amanullah tried to do. We saw only the outward forms of modernization."[53] King Zahir, too, believed that education was the most crucial and fundamental item in the government's modernization program. According to him, only the establishment of a good school system could provide the Afghan kingdom with a solid base for modernization.[54]

Modernization, however, was not the only goal of education. Education was also perceived as an instrumentality to achieve national unity, promote national consciousness, and institutionalize Pashto as the national language.[55] According to Hashim Khan, by 1938 Pashto was to become "the language of our officials, doing away with Persian. Our legends and our poems will then be understood by everyone. We shall draw from them a pride in our culture of the past, which will unite us."[56] The policy of making Pashto co-equal with Persian as a national and official language had been advocated during Amanullah's reign; the supremacy of Pashto had been affirmed soon after Nadir's accession, however, and in 1930 the issue had become the subject of a debate between the Persian and the Afghan press.

The case for the use of the Persian language in Afghanistan was best defended by the Calcutta paper *Habl-ul-Matin*, which warned the Afghan government against the disastrous effects of imposing "an artificial national language, which may be harmful to the national unity of the people of

Afghanistan." Pashto was spoken by a minority of the inhabitants of Afghanistan, wrote the paper, whereas Persian was the language of the majority. Instead of forcing everyone in Afghanistan to learn Pashto, *Habl-ul-Matin* suggested, the government might encourage the Afghan tribesmen to learn Persian and thus partake in and benefit from the treasures of Iranian culture. To institute Pashto as the official language of Afghanistan would set the Afghans apart from their neighbors and divorce them from their literary and scientific language.[57]

The Afghan government was not persuaded, however. In fact, it was precisely in order to give the Afghans a distinct and unique national language, and to consolidate their ties with the transfrontier Pathans, that the government proclaimed Pashto the official language of Afghanistan (1937).[58] The institutionalization of the study of Pashto in all Afghan schools and the preparation and publication of Pashto textbooks and grammars were major preoccupations of the Afghan Ministry of Education into the early 1940's. Teachers attended classes designed to give rapid instruction in Pashto, and government officials were obliged to take night courses in the new national and official language.[59] There was even some talk in 1937 of abandoning the use of the Arabic-Persian alphabet in favor of the Latin alphabet for Pashto,[60] but the plan never advanced beyond the talking stage.* The proposal to teach Pashto throughout Afghanistan revealed many problems to the Afghan government: the shortage of teachers, the absence of modern teaching techniques, and the predominance of the Persian language in most of the important urban centers of the country.[61]

Retaining the basic educational framework developed under Nadir, the Hashim administration tried to increase the number and the quality of the modern schools and, in a few instances, to expand their social base. It was unable, however, to implement the provisions of the constitution of 1931 calling for free and compulsory education throughout the kingdom. Primary education during the period 1933–46 was therefore neither universal nor compulsory. The general socioeconomic conditions in the country, the shortage of classrooms, schools, and teachers, the lack of economic resources, and the opposition of traditionalist elements—all worked to prevent the realization of this goal. The presence of an estimated two million or more nomads in the country added to the difficulties.[62]

The three major aims of Afghan primary education, as formulated by the Ministry of Education, were to impart literacy and a basic fund of

---

* Such proposals have been revived periodically since World War II. In 1958, for instance, both "Afghanistan News" (No. 10, p. 19) and *Anis* (March 15, 1958) announced that the Pashto Tulana had decided to adopt the Latin alphabet.

knowledge to all children, to equip them for secondary education, and especially to make them into useful and patriotic members of Afghan society. Future generations were to be taught "subjects of importance in this modern age, so that they may not only grow up into good Moslems and staunch nationalists, but also be enabled to play their part as decent citizens of the world. The success of this venture and achievement of these aims devolve to a great extent upon primary school teachers.... It must therefore be understood that Afghanistan's development in other fields is an integral and indivisible part of the progress achieved by primary school teachers."[63]

ACHIEVEMENTS IN EDUCATION

Despite the government's avowed hopes and goals, the traditional village maktabs still constituted the basic framework of the Afghan primary educational system in this period. There are no accurate estimates of the total number of village schools at the time (or even at present). Some of these schools, but only a few, covered a three-year curriculum. (As late as 1959 there were only 504 three-year village schools in all Afghanistan, 90 per cent of them for boys; it was only in 1957 that similar institutions were established for girls.)[64] The teachers of the maktabs, still primarily mullahs in the 1930's and 1940's, were usually paid by contributions from the parents of their pupils. The Ministry of Education sometimes provided textbooks, writing materials, and desks, but apparently neither the Ministry nor, for that matter, the Jamiyat-ul-Ulama controlled the curriculum.[65]

The number of modern, public primary schools was equally limited. In the period 1919–30 there were only about 300 such schools in the country.[66] As noted, these schools were not co-educational and generally covered a basic four-year term of study. After 1936 and into the 1950's, the curriculum included compulsory courses in three languages, Persian, Pashto, and Arabic; courses on the Quran and on Muslim theology were compulsory as well. Side by side with these traditional subjects, the curriculum provided by the Ministry of Education included arithmetic, geography, history, basic natural sciences, drawing and handicrafts, and physical education.[67]

Until 1940, the Afghan public education system was based on a ten-year program consisting of four years of primary school, three years of middle school, and three years of secondary school.[68] In the school year 1940–41 Hashim lengthened the term of study in the primary schools to six years in an effort to improve the quality of elementary education and provide a smoother transition to the secondary level.[69] Technically, students who successfully passed their elementary school examinations qualified for admission to a middle school, which either prepared them for the academic secondary schools or gave them vocational training. Completion of some of the middle schools qualified students for government employment, and a few upper middle schools, grades 10–12, trained teachers for the lower middle schools.[70] As in the primary schools, the curriculum of the middle schools included compulsory instruction in Persian, Pashto, Arabic, the Quran, and theology. Among the other subjects offered were foreign languages, arithmetic and geometry, the natural sciences, economics, history, geography, and physical education.[71]

Some of the graduates of middle schools entered the vocational schools of Kabul, either the older schools, such as the Agricultural School, the Primary Teachers Training School, the Industrial School (or the School for Fine and Applied Arts), and Dar-ul-ulum Arabiyah (the School for Arabic Studies, which was established in the 1920's and reopened by Nadir after Bacha's fall from power), or new ones established by the Hashim administration. Among these were the Kabul Mechanical School (1937), the Secretarial School and the School of Commerce (both 1938), the Teachers Night School (1942), the Teachers Training Institute for Intermediary Schools (1943), and the Theological School (1944).[72] The government recruited foreigners to staff these vocational schools; French, Italian, and Japanese teachers, for instance, were on the staff of the Agricultural School.[73] The Kabul Mechanical School, which prepared skilled workers for industry, was founded with the help of German specialists; its equipment was presented to Afghanistan as a gift of the German government.[74]

The Afghan government paid special attention to increasing the number of secondary schools and extending the system outside Kabul, where the four major lycées—Habibiya, Istiklal, Najat, and Ghazi—continued to grow. Secondary schools were opened in the provinces of Kandahar, Kabul, and Herat, and in northern Afghanistan.[75] The general aim of these schools (called colleges), which covered grades 10–12 and which were patterned on the French and German secondary schools, was "to offer education up to the [French] baccalaureate standard and to prepare students for University education."[76] Their curriculum included the same compulsory courses required in the lower schools, along with such subjects as mathematics, chemistry, physics, biology, geology, foreign languages, logic, history, geography, and physical education.[77]

In 1940 there were 324 primary public schools, with an enrollment of

60,000 and 1,990 teachers, in the country; by 1945 the number of schools had increased to 346, the number of students to 93,000, and the number of teachers to 2,546.[78] In part the rather substantial increase in the number of teachers and students was due to the lengthening of the course of study to six years.*

In both the academic secondary schools and the technical schools, special encouragement was given to the study of European languages. According to official Afghan estimates provided to Dr. Stolz, by 1955 almost 80 per cent of the foreign language instruction was in English.[79] The government employed a number of foreign experts to implement its educational program. Six French educators were in charge of advising and preparing the best students of Istiklal for the French baccalaureate examinations.[80] German teachers were hired to advise the administrators of Najat on curricular matters and to teach German; during World War II the Afghan government dismissed them and the instruction of German was entrusted to Najat graduates. English was taught chiefly by instructors from India, though by 1943 the Afghan government was attempting to replace them with American teachers.[81]

The University of Kabul was officially inaugurated in 1946, but even before that the Hashim administration founded a number of faculties and departments. These included the Department of Political Science and Law (1938), the Faculty of Natural Sciences (1941), and the Faculty of Letters (1944). The Faculty of Natural Sciences eventually branched out into various divisions: physics, mathematics, and a third branch subdivided into departments of chemistry, biology, and geology. A new central laboratory was also built. All the faculties and departments were completely subsidized by the Afghan government and were under the control of the Ministry of Education. Many of the advisory and teaching posts in them were filled by Europeans.[82]

As part of the effort to improve and centralize the public education system, the Ministry of Education published a series of textbooks, among them works on religion, theology, and ethics. That the government sponsored the publication of books on such topics indicates an indirect attempt was being made to control the curriculum of the village schools and the teachings of the mullahs. In cooperation with the Historical Institute and the Pashto Tulana, the ministry also provided a series of historical and

---

* In these years emphasis was also placed on opening new elementary schools in the provinces. According to the *Kaboul Almanach* (1942–43, p. 66), in 1942 there were 53 elementary schools in Kabul province, 59 in Kandahar, 39 in Herat, 34 in Mazar-i-Sharif, and 31 each in Kataghan and Badakhshan.

literary studies and texts on the Pashto and Persian languages and on science. It also furnished translations for the Afghan secondary and teachers' schools, along with a variety of books in Pashto.[83] The Pashto Tulana, which had four sections—history, literature, linguistics, and press–publication—played an important role in the effort to promote Pashto as the national language. To help institutionalize the instruction of Pashto throughout the kingdom, the academy published a general dictionary, a standard grammar, and textbooks patterned after the Berlitz method. Since a royal decree in 1936 had ordered all government officials to learn Pashto within three years, the Pashto Tulana printed a weekly instruction booklet, which along with the textbooks, was distributed throughout the country.[84]

An important advance was made with the formation of a Health Center within the Ministry of Education. The center instituted a biannual physical examination for some 12,000–14,000 students, teachers, and school employees, and attempted to establish minimum rules of hygiene in the schools. However, the problems it faced were enormous, particularly in combating malaria and trachoma, the two diseases most prevalent among students; according to a ministry report, half the cases examined were incurable.[85] In 1941–42 the Health Center gave smallpox vaccinations and typhoid shots to some 14,000 students.[86] Another notable addition to the Ministry of Education was the Directory of Physical Education and Sports, which instituted such sports as soccer, volleyball, basketball, and boxing, arranged track and field competitions, and initiated systematic programs of physical exercise in the schools.[87]

Despite important achievements, the needs and shortcomings in the realm of education in Afghanistan were staggering. According to both Soviet and Western estimates, by 1948 only an estimated 8 per cent of the population was literate. At that time there were only 2,758 teachers and 98,660 pupils.[88] According to a UNESCO mission, in 1949 less than 10 per cent of the school-age girls were in educational institutions.[89] As late as 1954, the total student enrollment in Afghanistan, excluding the students at Kabul University, was 114,266, or about 4.5 per cent of the approximately 2.4 million school-age children.[90] At that time there were only 13 primary schools, one middle school, and two secondary schools for girls, most of them in Kabul, and only an estimated 8,625 girls were receiving any kind of education. There were reportedly no girls in the village schools.[91] This was the period when the Malalai school for girls, which had been reopened by Nadir as a school for nurses and midwives, was converted into a ninth-grade school. Its teaching staff included French women, and French was its foreign language specialty.[92]

In assessing the state of education in the period 1933–46, we see a continuation of the pattern that developed during the reigns of Amanullah and Nadir: the majority of the educational facilities were in the capital and in the province of Kabul. Later figures provided by the sociologist Eberhard indicate the general educational imbalance. According to him, as late as 1959 Kabul (with an estimated population of 213,345, or 1.8 per cent of the estimated total population) had 73.8 per cent of all the secondary school students in the country.[93] His estimates, and Spencer's as well, indicate another major problem area: in 1958 only 3 per cent of the students were in vocational schools and only 1 per cent were in secondary schools or in Kabul University. Another serious problem was the small number of secondary students completing their studies, some 26 per cent.[94] Finally, the shortage of qualified teachers continued to be a major obstacle. As late as 1950, Afghanistan had only 3,007 teachers, half of whom had no special training.[95] Until 1955 the students admitted to the Teacher Training Institute had only an elementary school education. Only after that were graduates of the ninth grade admitted for a three-year program before going into teaching. The total number of graduates of the teachers' school from its foundation to 1959 did not exceed 2,500.[96] Because of financial and political difficulties during World War II, as well as the teacher and classroom shortage, the Afghan government was unable to launch a major, nationwide campaign to extend the educational system and broaden its social base.

CULTURAL ACTIVITIES

A noteworthy development in the 1930's was the attempt of the teachers and staff at Istiklal and Najat to form theatrical troupes in their schools. In the same period a few members of the Afghan educated elite worked hard to revive the Afghan theater, which had existed for a short time during Amanullah's reign. In 1937 Muhammad Rejaii, the director of the Literary Circle of Herat, published an article emphasizing the importance of the theater as an educational and socially beneficial force. In it, he advocated the foundation of a national theater and the formation of theatrical groups throughout the country. During that year two theatrical shows were presented in Herat. Both were didactic works; one was entitled "Learning and Ignorance," the other "Union and Disunion."[97] There were also theatrical performances in Kandahar and Mazar-i-Sharif in 1937. Despite these efforts, a national Afghan theater, the Puhani Nandari (Theater of Wisdom or Erudition), was not established until 1941. The moving spirit behind the theater, which was under the sponsorship and control of the Directorate General of the Press, was its director Rashid Latifi. The initial repertoire consisted primarily of plays in Persian depicting the struggle of the Afghan nation for freedom and independence, although there were occasional performances of the works of Molière and of plays written by Latifi himself. The difficulties the new theater faced were many: the religious traditionalists were bitterly opposed to female actresses, there were financial problems and a shortage of technicians, and the theater lacked a general, sophisticated audience. In these circumstances, it was forced to close in 1944. Theater did not become truly established in Afghanistan until after World War II. In 1947 Latifi's theater was reopened under the direction of Abdul Rashid Gelia, and in the same year the Municipal Theater of Kabul was founded.[98]

Hashim Khan's government followed a policy of limited expansion, centralization, and governmental control in the field of communications, a policy that extended to all cultural societies as well as to radio and the press. Under a five-year plan to expand the country's communications, the government attempted to establish a national radio station, to increase the number of radios in the country (an estimated 1,000 in 1936), and to form a national news agency. In 1937 the Marconi company built radio stations at Kabul, Maimana, Khost, Khanabad, and Dujazuugi, and in the same year the Telefunken company of Germany was given a contract to install a 20 kw. transmitter. Radio Kabul began experimental broadcasts in 1939 and was officially inaugurated the next year. The government assigned the new station a number of tasks. Apart from spreading the message of the Quran, it was to attempt to reflect the national spirit, to perpetuate the treasures of Afghan folklore, and to contribute to public education by reaching those who were deprived of educational opportunities. A number of small receiving sets, equipped with loudspeakers, were set up in various provincial centers, allowing the Afghans to gather in the main public squares for an evening of news, music, and popular programs. The Bakhtar News Agency, the Afghan official news agency, was established in this same period. It was initially equipped with three wireless Marconi receivers and a dozen radio monitoring sets of its own and was also given the use of the government's telegraph and telephone facilities.

According to Reshtiya, the Hashim administration was severely handicapped in its planned expansion of the country's communications during World War II, when it was difficult to import new equipment or even spare parts to maintain the old. More important, the Afghans were unable to avail themselves of German credits that had been extended, and German contracts could not be fulfilled. Nevertheless, by 1948 the Afghans owned some 8,000 radios, eight times as many as in 1930.[99]

The Afghan press continued to grow steadily under the Hashim Khan administration. The Kabul papers *Islah* and *Anis* began daily publication and became bilingual in these years; with the incorporation of more articles in Pashto, they began reaching greater segments of the Afghan population. Outside of Kabul, the provincial weeklies *Bidar* (Mazar-i-Sharif), *Ittihad-i-Baghlan*, *Ittihad-i-Mashriqi* (Jalalabad), and *Ittihad-i-Khanabad* continued publication, and two former weeklies, *Tulo-e Afghan* and *Ittifaq-i-Islam*, became dailies. Most of these publications, too, began to carry articles in Pashto and to emphasize the Pashto heritage. New papers that were begun in this period include *Waranga* [Beam of Light] (Gardez, 1942), *Paktya*, and *Badakhshan* (1946). A number of journals and periodicals were also started, among them *Zerai* [Good News] (1938), a monthly of the Afghan Academy; *Aryana* (1942), the organ of the academy's Historical Society; *Aryana Dairat-ul-maarif* (1941), an Afghan encyclopedia published quarterly in both Persian and Pashto; *Paktoon Jhag* (1940), a publication of Radio Kabul; *Storai* [Star] (1943), a biweekly published in Maimana; *Hughugh* [Laws], a publication of the Faculty of Law of Kabul University; and *Afghanistan* (1946), a quarterly written in English and French and published by the Afghan Academy's Historical Society. There was also a popular but short-lived magazine in Kandahar—*Pashto*—which was published between 1932 and 1936.[100]

Though the number of publications increased, their circulation remained limited. For one thing the illiteracy rate in Afghanistan was still high. Beyond that, the printing facilities of the Afghan press, poor at best, suffered from serious shortages of equipment and paper during the war; many Afghan publications were forced to limit their circulation and to reduce both the size and the number of their pages. Moreover, though the government allowed students to purchase periodicals at a considerably reduced rate, the generally high price of newspapers and journals helped to limit their circulation; so did the lack of public libraries and reading-rooms. As late as 1958, the Kabul dailies each circulated about 15,000 copies; the provincial newspapers distributed no more than 1,500 each. Most of the press, as well as Kabul Radio and the Bakhtar News Agency, were subsidized by the government and were supervised by the Department of Press and Publication, which controlled at least the general tenor and direction of all releases.

The government recognized the value of the cinema as an educational tool, but was apprehensive about the introduction and widespread use of motion pictures, both because of the reaction of the conservatives in the country and because of the possibility that movies might introduce liberal social ideas or serve as a propaganda medium. Primarily for these reasons, it seems, motion pictures were permitted only in Kabul, and then only to a limited extent. On the eve of World War II, there was only one public cinema in Kabul. There was also a movie theater in the Ministry of Defense, where on national holidays and other special occasions, technical or "moral films" were shown to a select audience, in order to increase "the knowledge of the Afghans, without harming the national culture or character." Even after the war, the cinema was slow to come to Afghanistan; in 1956 there were only seven public movie houses in the entire country.[101]

As part of the effort to study and preserve the heritage of Afghanistan, the Hashim administration helped to reestablish and maintain the country's five museums, two of which had been gutted during the civil war. These museums—the central museum in Kabul and the provincial museums in Herat, Ghazni (founded 1935), and Kandahar and Mazar-i-Sharif (both founded 1933)—were rudimentary, lacking in trained personnel, physical facilities, and funds. However, the wealth of material they contained was impressive. The Kabul museum, located in Dar ul-Aman, became an important repository of rich archaeological and ethnographical collections of the Hellenistic, Graeco-Buddhic, and Ghaznawid periods, thanks to the efforts of the French archaeological mission (1922–46). Among the mission's finds were some 20,000 artifacts from the Gandharan school (unearthed in 1923); a significant number of works dating from the fifth century A.D., including a collection of Buddhist murals and statues of Buddha, and the painted temples of Bamian (found in the Kakrak Valley from 1930 on); and numerous Greek artifacts and statues dating back to the first century A.D., as well as additional pieces of Buddhic art (unearthed at Begram and Ghorband between 1937 and 1942). The museum housed a rich selection of some 40,000 coins from various historical periods, and a number of rare and valuable Oriental manuscripts. The Press Department had jurisdiction over the country's museums.[102]

The number of libraries in Afghanistan remained limited, despite high hopes in government circles ever since Amanullah's administration. Most of the libraries had been ruined in the civil war, but some of them were reopened during Nadir's rule and were able to increase their holdings in the 1933–46 period. In addition to the library at Habibiya, the two major libraries of Kabul were the Ministry of Education Library (founded in 1920), which had some 10,000 works in Persian, Arabic, Russian, English, French, German, and Turkish, and the Library of the Press Department (founded in 1931), which at the end of the war had some 20,000 books and

300 Persian, Arabic, and Pashto manuscripts. With the founding of the various faculties of higher education, the nucleus of a university library was built; it contained a few thousand volumes, primarily technical and legal works. The Afghan Academy also maintained a library of Persian, Pashto, Arabic, Turkish, and European works on the history and heritage of Afghanistan, and there was a library in the royal palace. The French archaeological mission had a small but good collection of books and periodicals on the history of Afghanistan at its headquarters in Kabul.

Though there were many private libraries in the provinces (as well as in Kabul), only Herat, Kandahar, and Mazar-i-Sharif had public libraries; they were quite small. The library of Herat, for instance, had less than 3,000 volumes. There were also Persian, Pashto, and Arabic manuscripts in the provincial museums. In general, as in the case of the educational institutions, especially the secondary schools, the majority of the libraries in the country were concentrated in and around Kabul. As late as 1957, nine of the 20 public libraries in the kingdom were located in the capital. For the most part, the quality of the cataloguing and maintenance in the libraries was poor; like the museums, they lacked trained personnel, adequate physical facilities, and funds.[103]

Hashim, like Nadir, encouraged and sponsored sports and athletic competitions. The Afghan Olympic Committee remained active and, as previously noted, sent teams to the Olympic Games in 1936. In Kabul the Afghans organized teams for tennis, hockey, soccer, volleyball, basketball, track and field events, boxing, and other sports, sending some of them to Soviet Central Asia and Iran for competitions. Between 1936 and 1946, the Directory of Physical Education and Sport made a concerted effort to make physical education and sports an integral part of the curriculum in the intermediate and secondary schools. The success of the program was limited. There were few sports fields and stadiums in the country, and most of the schools did not have the money to spend on equipment or instructors' salaries. Again much of the government effort was directed to the major Afghan urban centers, especially Kabul. In 1957, 12 of the 13 athletic clubs in Afghanistan were in Kabul.[104]

ECONOMIC POLICIES

The Hashim administration strove to make the country less dependent on its powerful neighbors, to integrate its economy, and to give it a small industrial base. As *Iqtisad*, the journal of the Ministry of Economy observed, if a country like Afghanistan did not modernize its agriculture and industrialize, its economy would remain dependent on other countries;

this, in turn, could jeopardize its independence.[105] According to one Afghan spokesman, every state in the world followed a policy of supporting national industries against foreign competion. Industrialization and the protection of national industries was the duty not only of private individuals but of the government as well. The Afghans, he wrote, intended to build gradually and protect constantly such essential industries as would make them more and more independent of foreign goods. To buy Afghan-made goods was therefore a patriotic act, the protection of these goods by the government a historical and national necessity.[106]

The government's policy on industrialization, according to another writer, lay somewhere between laissez-faire and German state socialism: governmental intervention was called for only when individual action and initiative was deficient or absent.[107] The government's goal continued to be the development of the country's resources as rapidly as possible on a "pay-as-you-go" basis; its policy was still to avoid heavy indebtedness for capital investments or the granting of major concessions to foreign firms. The process of accumulating, centralizing, nationalizing, and "Afghanizing" the nation's commercial capital was carried on in two stages: the first was the formation, in 1932, of the Bank-i-Milli; the second was the creation of major companies that not only controlled the chief export-import commodities of Afghanistan but also invested heavily in the country's growing industry.

The Bank-i-Milli, which began with a capital of 35 million afghanis (about 3.5 million dollars), had about 2,000 shareholders and a capital of 454 million afghanis (about 40 million dollars) by 1948. Two years later that sum had grown to 660 million afghanis. In 1939 Da Afghanistan Bank, a government bank, was founded. By the end of World War II, its capital holdings amounted to some 200 million afghanis. In 1949 the combined capital of the two banks was 1.2 billion afghanis. The Da Afghanistan Bank acted as the fiscal agent of the Ministry of Finance, controlling the Afghan currency and supervising foreign exchange transactions, functions previously handled by the Bank-i-Milli. However, the government left the Bank-i-Milli in charge of the private sector of the Afghan economy, and retained only a 5 per cent share in the bank's holdings (increased in 1949 to 25 per cent). The Bank-i-Milli invested in both private and government projects, and controlled personal, commercial, and foreign credit. Through both banks the government oversaw investments in national industries and exercised overall control of Afghan exports and imports, attempting to maintain a favorable trade balance in the purchase of industrial machinery and the payment of foreign technical experts. A favorable balance of payments was considered an essential feature of Afghan foreign and economic policy—a safeguard for Afghan independence and a way to ensure a "pay-as-you-go" industrialization program.[108]

Between 1933 and 1946 the Bank-i-Milli managed to attract the greater part of the private capital in the country, and to invest it in some 50 trading and industrial holding companies. The same important merchants who held shares in the bank were the majority stockholders of these companies. In addition to a virtual monopoly in the major commodities of the Afghan export-import trade, the Bank-i-Milli and its president, Abdul Majid Zabuli, gained control of most of the industry of the kingdom, both the well-established state-owned enterprises and the budding new firms.[109] The bank mobilized and concentrated the national capital in its hands, establishing a mutually beneficial cooperation with the Afghan ruling dynasty. Some members of the ruling elite were shareholders.

In cooperation with the bank, the Afghan government formulated a general plan for economic development. Out of this grew a renewed interest in cotton and textiles, especially in northern Afghanistan, where the developing textile industry had been interrupted by the Bolshevik revolution and the loss of steady Russian markets. The fall of Amanullah, the civil war, and the lack of banking facilities and investment capital had also impeded the growth of the textile industry. The renewed interest in the cultivation of cotton in the north was primarily due to the efforts of the enterprising Bank-i-Milli and its president, who recognized that the province of Kataghan was especially suited for the purpose: it had good soil and a favorable climate, known coal deposits, water for electricity and irrigation, and rich wheat and rice fields. The government, however, had more than economic motives in attempting to provide northern Afghanistan with an industrial base. The policy of relocating Afghan ethnic groups in the northern regions (the government offered land in Kataghan Province to landless or unemployed Afghans), the opening of the Great Northern route to link Kabul directly with the region, and the encouragement of industry in the region—all seem to indicate the government was trying to achieve a degree of economic independence with respect to the Soviet Union in the north. (Beyond this, the bank and the government, by developing indigenous industry in northern Afghanistan, avoided alienating the Afghan tribes and yet placed the industries outside their control.) A similar effort was made in the south, where the Afghans sought to free the local markets of their dependence on India by providing some basic commodities.

The cotton-growing projects, especially those in northern Afghanistan, were carried on under the auspices of the Cotton Joint-Stock Company, an organization directly linked to the Bank-i-Milli. The company, which was founded in 1934, began by reclaiming marshlands and surveying coal deposits; an irrigation project was started in the north. Prior to 1935, the annual output of cotton in northern Afghanistan was less than 400 tons (the estimate for the entire country was 4,500 tons). This figure increased sharply, reaching the 10,000-mark by 1946 (with the country's total production at 36,000 tons). In 1936 the cotton company imported machinery from England and started construction of a textile mill at Pul-i Khumri; full-scale operations began in 1942. By the 1950's the mill produced, on the average, some 15 million yards of cloth yearly. Between 1934 and 1938, the company founded another cotton mill, this one in Jabal-ul-Siraj; its annual production capacity was over one million yards of cotton cloth. The company's control extended from seed to finished product: it supervised the cultivation of cotton, provided seeds to the peasants, purchased the cotton from them, and ginned, baled, and exported the raw cotton, or processed it in the new mills.

Following the lead of the Cotton Joint-Stock Company, other companies entered the growing textile industry. In 1937 the Vatan Joint-Stock Company, of Kandahar, imported equipment and installed cotton gins and presses in Mazar-i-Sharif, Taliqan, Balkh, and Khanabad. The Kandahar Woolen Textile Mill was founded in 1943 with an annual production capacity of about 120,000 yards of material; within a decade this figure had increased sixfold. Various new units were added to the Kabul woolen factory in 1943, allowing it to increase its production to something like 170,000 yards of goods a year. Small cotton and silk industries developed in Laghman, Kabul, and Herat. The mill in Herat had 100 silk looms and 1,000 cotton looms, which turned out some 10,000 pounds of silk yarn yearly; half was exported, the rest was used for turbans. To improve the quality of Afghan silk, an Institute of Sericulture was founded in Kabul in 1936. A similar attempt was made to improve the methods used in the cultivation of cotton. The cotton and textile companies of Kunduz and Kandahar, in cooperation with the Ministry of Economy and its General Directory of Agriculture, established experimental farming stations in northern and southern Afghanistan.[110]

Another joint venture of the Bank-i-Milli and the Afghan Ministry of Economy was a ceramic plant, the property of a joint-stock company that held a virtual monopoly. Established in Kunduz in 1940, by 1944 the plant was producing tiles, plumbing equipment, and china. Another plant was built later in Kabul. In 1938 the cotton company of Kunduz extended its activities, founding a soap factory in the province of Kataghan; by 1953 it was producing one million pounds of soap annually. Under the auspices of the Bank-i-Milli, still another joint-stock company assumed a monopoly over the cultivation of sugar beets and the processing and sale of sugar, thus reviving Amanullah's dream of making Afghanistan self-sufficient in the production of a major basic commodity.* In 1938 the company established a sugar factory in Baghlan; in 1940 equipment was imported from the Skoda company of Czechoslovakia at a cost of one million dollars, and by 1946 the factory was supplying nearly one-third of the country's sugar. The Bank-i-Milli controlled 85 per cent of the factory's assets.

The cement plant Amanullah had established in Kabul, which had been shut down after his fall because of a shortage of raw material, was re-opened in 1938, again as a monopoly of a joint-stock company controlled by the Bank-i-Milli. Another of the bank's companies established a match factory in Kabul in 1943. The tannery and the shoe factory in the capital were expanded; the tannery reached a maximum capacity of 600 hides a day, and the shoe factory a capacity of 500 pairs of military boots and 100 pairs of shoes a day. A major spare parts and automobile repair shop was established at Jangaalak, a suburb of Kabul. The central workshops of Kabul were expanded, and several new ones were built. Among other things they produced furniture, buttons, and soap. A canning plant was established in Kandahar to process the fruits of the region. Some trading joint-stock companies attempted to encourage the Afghan rug industry; a small rug factory was founded in Herat, and in 1935 the government established a school of carpet-weaving, which was attached to the School of Fine Arts in Kabul.[111]

An attempt was also made to exploit the rich mineral resources of the country (which included iron, lead, silver, gold, copper, zinc, beryl, chromium, coal, salt, sulphur, oil, and semiprecious stones, such as lapis lazuli). As always, enormous difficulties stood in the way. The lack of adequate transportation and production facilities, together with the expense of hiring foreign geologists and technicians, made the production costs prohibitive. In 1939 the Directorate of Mines was expanded into a Ministry of Mines. The new ministry continued the major project of its predecessor, the preparation of a general survey of the country's mineral deposits, and was charged with overseeing all mining operations. In this period, attempts were made to exploit the nation's gold and coal deposits; both projects

---

* The equipment Amanullah purchased in 1928 to process sugar cane in the Jalalabad region was left unused for over 20 years. A factory was finally built in the years 1952–58.

proved to be uneconomical. Between 1939 and 1943, a bare 70 pounds of gold a year were extracted from the Kokcha and Amu river regions; the costs far outweighed the value of the ore, and the project was abandoned in 1948.[112] The mining of coal, although expensive, was continued because of the country's desperate need for fuel. The only profitable mineral resource seems to have been lapis lazuli, a government monopoly; it was exported chiefly to Germany until the outbreak of the war.[113]

The lack of good roads, means of transportation, and power remained major problems in the 1930's, despite the efforts of the Hashim administration and the Bank-i-Milli to overcome some of the difficulties. Between 1933 and 1946, nearly 2,000 miles of roads were laid, and for the first time the trip from the northern provinces to Kabul could be made by automobile. The semi-circular route between Kabul, Kandahar, Farah, Herat, Maimana, and Mazar-i-Sharif was improved. In addition to these all-weather roads, there were some 3,000 miles of secondary roads at this time. Two new highways were started, one toward the Sino-Afghan border, the other toward Termez, the railway terminal on the Afghan-Soviet border. The rebuilding of bridges destroyed during the civil war of 1929 continued. Nevertheless, until the late 1940's, most of the trade of Afghanistan continued to be carried by caravan (estimates place the length of the caravan routes at 18,000 miles).[114] The question of a railroad was again shunted aside for political, strategic, and economic reasons.

With the improvement of the roads, the Afghan Post Office began providing regular bus service, for passengers as well as for mail. A monopolistic motor company, another business dependent on the Bank-i-Milli, increased its imports considerably: about 1,000 trucks and automobiles and more than 5,000 bicycles were imported in the years 1937–39. By 1938 there were 3,000 trucks in the kingdom. (In the World War II period, imports declined, but after the war, the import of trucks and automobiles grew steadily.) Thanks to the improved roads, at the end of the war, trips between the major urban centers (Kabul-Kandahar, Kandahar-Herat, Herat–Mazar-i-Sharif, Mazar-i-Sharif–Kabul) could be made in two days.[115]

Between 1934 and 1946, a supplemental unit was added to the 1,500 kw. power plant at Jabal ul-Siraj, providing an additional 900 kw. Through the cooperation of a Bank-i-Milli company and the Afghan government, a 4,000 kw. plant was built at Chak-e-Vardak. The country's other power stations were at Pul-i-Khumri (4,800 kw.), Kandahar (250 kw., with an additional 275 kw. provided by the textile mills there), Herat (725 kw.), Maimana (36 kw.), and Mazar-i-Sharif (36 kw.). The government started plans for two major installations: a plant at Sarobi, which, with a projected capacity of 24,000 kw., was to be the largest in the country, and an Argandab River plant, which was to provide some 6,500 kw. However, in the mid-1940's, Afghanistan still had only about 22,000 kw. of power, most of it serving Kabul.[116]

According to Akhramovich, the well-known Soviet Afghanist, though the accelerated accumulation and centralization of capital made it possible to take the initial steps toward building up a national industry, "the few light industry plants . . . the country had could meet but 10 to 15 per cent of the home demand for textiles, sugar, footwear, and so on."[117]

TRADE EXPANSION

In contrast to the limited expansion of industry, Afghanistan's trade, both foreign and domestic, increased sharply in the 1933–46 period, under the auspices of the Bank-i-Milli and the encouragement of the government. The leading joint-stock companies and their subsidiaries, which enjoyed either monopoly or preferential rights in purchasing and exporting agricultural products and in importing and marketing foreign consumer goods, controlled as much as 80 per cent of the country's export-import trade. Some of them were also engaged in manufacturing; it was not unusual for a company to build a textile mill and at the same time import foreign textiles. The same situation obtained with other products as well, sugar, soap, and footwear, for example. This duality of interests created difficulties: the imports often guaranteed more financial gain but were not always in the national interest, which required increased industrialization in order to use the country's raw materials and reduce, if not end, its dependence on foreign imports; moreover, these imports sometimes damaged or prevented the development of local industries.

The Bank-i-Milli, through its control of the export-import trade, industry, and most of the credit system and foreign exchange of Afghanistan, managed to increase its capital a hundredfold between 1932 and 1938. Its shareholders gained enormously, in some cases increasing their investments by a third. Over the years the relationship between the powerful merchants' group behind the bank and the government had its ups and downs, alternating between cooperation and semi-conflict. In 1938, when many of the ventures of the bank and its trading companies proved to be yielding great margins of profit, the government rescinded some of the bank's monopoly rights and ordered an investigation into its activities, as well as those of a few of its major shareholders. Attention was particularly focused on the karakul trade and foreign exchange. (Among other things, the investigation led to a six-year prison sentence for one of the prominent shareholders.) It was in order to offset the Afghan government's complete dependence on the Bank-i-Milli that the Hashim administration organized the Da Afghanistan State Bank, withdrawing the government's investments in the private bank and taking control of Afghan currency and foreign exchange. After 1938 the Bank-i-Milli began to pay dividends to the government, and between 1938 and 1940 gave it two loans totaling 21.1 million afghanis (1.6 million dollars). According to Cervin, these "loans" were to be construed as a net profit for the Afghan government.[118]

Despite these conflicts, which were compounded by the rivalry between groups of Herati, Kandahari, and Turkestani merchants, the private capital of the Bank-i-Milli continued to play an important role in the Afghan economy and to control the greatest part of the import-export trade. One of the most important of the new companies was Sherkat-e Saderat-e Karakul (Karakul Export Company), of Kabul. Founded in 1938, it grew quickly and by 1946 was one of the country's major corporations. (In the next decade its capital reached 44.2 million afghanis.) In 1939 the company purchased and exported some 889,000 karakul hides; its nearest competitor, Sherkat-e-Rushtiya, exported 85,000, and the remaining companies, about 25 in number, exported between 10,000 and 15,000 each.[119]

Karakul was the most important foreign exchange source of the country, constituting between 40 and 50 per cent of all Afghan exports in the years 1936–46. Both Abdur Rahman and Habibullah had tried to make the karakul trade a government monopoly, setting arbitrary prices for the hides and overseeing their export. Before the 1917 revolution in Russia, the major markets for karakul were Moscow, Bukhara, and Peshawar, and the trade was mainly in the hands of Jewish, Hindu, and Bukharan merchants. Between 1880 and 1917, an estimated 50,000–70,000 skins were exported each year. Because of the loss of Russian and Central Asian markets following the Bolshevik revolution and the Sovietization of Bukhara, the merchants of Afghan Turkestan were forced to place a greater emphasis on the Indian market, and later on West European markets. The Afghan monarchy had relinquished its monopoly over the karakul trade in 1918, charging only a 5 per cent export tax, and under the Amanullah administration the annual export figure had reached the 700,000 mark. In 1931 a conference of Afghan merchants was convened under the auspices of Nadir Shah, for the purpose of seeking more foreign markets for karakul, increasing its output, and preventing non-Afghan control of the country's most profitable export item. Between 1935 and 1945, exports of karakul more than doubled, increasing from some 1.5 million skins to 3.3 million.[120]

Fruits, grains, cotton, and wool were the other major export items of Afghanistan, together representing about 40 per cent of the export trade. The major exporters of these commodities were Sherkat-e Pashtan and Sherkat-e Vatan, both of Kandahar, Sherkat-e Miva, of Kabul, Sherkat-e Ittihad-e Shumali, of northern Afghanistan, and Sherkat-e Ittihadie-ye Herat and Sherkat-e Panba, of Herat. There were also many small private and joint-stock companies dealing in these items. Between 1935 and 1944, a joint-stock company, Sherkat-e Tiryak, exported opium.[121]

In the years 1937–44, 88 per cent of the Afghan exports were agricultural products; the imports were mainly textiles, oil, tea, cement, iron, utensils, and machinery. In most of those years, the country had a favorable balance of payments.

Afghan Trade, 1936–1944[122]
(*in millions of afghanis*)

Year	Afghan Imports	Afghan Exports
1937–38	324	258
1938–39	332	411
1939–40	394	492
1940–41	512	444
1941–42	308	461
1942–43	340	578
1943–44	627	734

A breakdown of the Afghan export-import trade by countries is difficult. According to Fazl Ahmad, during World War II, 80 per cent of the Afghan trade was with India and the United States. Here are the figures for Afghanistan's trade with the Soviet Union before the war.

Soviet Trade with Afghanistan[123]
(*in rubles*)

Year	Imports from Afghanistan	Exports to Afghanistan
1933	7,100,000	5,600,000
1934	3,100,000	2,800,000
1935	3,500,000	3,900,000
1936	16,300,000	22,000,000
1937	17,000,000	17,000,000
1938	14,800,000	13,700,000

(From 1936 on the figures should be divided by 4.38 for purposes of comparison.)

Despite the growth of capital, the mushrooming of joint-stock companies, the increase in the volume of commercial traffic, and a favorable balance of payments, the structure of the Afghan economy remained weak. According to Peter Franck, Afghanistan's economic life depended on foreign trade in three fundamental ways:

An interruption of the flow of its two important products [animal skins and fruits] causes a substantial drop in income and employment in important agricultural sectors of the economy; because of the absence of any significant domestic market for skins (especially karakul) or alternative uses for labor and land devoted to fruit growing, no other income-producing activity can be substituted in an emergency. ... In the second place, export surpluses are an important source of capital. Economies in which are produced only enough goods to meet the people's basic requirements, with no resources available for the enhancement of productive capacity, tend to stagnate. The procurement of equipment and plants to produce more goods requires capital which the government or the community or both must provide. In Afghanistan the export surplus substitutes for the ordinary source of funds of the capitalist type. The profits from export activities have provided the liquid funds, which investors, including Bank Melli [Bank-i-Milli], need to promote new productive enterprises. ... In the third place, exports provide Afghanistan with its only foreign exchange. ... Since all modern consumer durable goods, petroleum products, steel and non-ferrous metal supplies, all transportation equipment, and machinery have to be imported, the level of exports is one of the important determinants of the country's standard of living.[124]

Such dependence on foreign trade, as well as on the goodwill of neighbors for the flow of transit trade, necessitated both a delicate foreign policy and a plan for economic development. The Overall Economic Development Plan, the guideline for the Afghan government in the years 1932–38, was replaced in 1938–39 by a Seven-Year Economic Plan. Its objectives were to improve the agricultural economy of the country through major irrigation projects and new agricultural industries and processing facilities; to expand the transportation and communication systems; and to develop hydroelectric power and the country's mineral resources.[125] The outbreak of World War II interfered with the timetable of this plan.

MILITARY AND ADMINISTRATIVE REFORMS

In the years following Zahir's accession to the throne, the Afghan ruling elite continued Nadir's policy of modernizing the Afghan army. The modernization and mechanization of the army was considered to be of utmost importance and urgency; to serve in the army, it was proclaimed, was to serve the Muslim faith and the Afghan fatherland.[126] Because the Afghan army was regarded as an instrument for achieving and maintaining internal stability and prosperity, it was perceived as an instrument of progress. It was also perceived as an instrument of peace, its sole aim being the defense of Afghanistan's territorial integrity and political independence.[127]

The army was under the complete control of the monarchy and the ruling oligarchy. The King's uncle, Shah Mahmud, was the minister of war. Under his supervision the army was equipped with German, Italian, British, and Czech arms, the small air force was maintained, a few tank units were formed, and the transportation units were mechanized to some extent. Pilot-training courses were started, and the curriculum of the military academy was revamped. The ministry added a logistics department to the army, reorganized its translation department, placing great emphasis on the translation of military manuals, opened a general repair shop for military vehicles, and built army hospitals near the major camps. Military training became more systematic; large-scale military maneuvers and sports became regular features. (An army stadium was built near Kabul.) For the most part, Turkish officers were in charge of military training, although prior to 1939 there were also German and Italian military instructors and advisers in the country. From 1935 on, schools for artillery, cavalry, and infantry officers were opened at Maimana and Mazar-i-Sharif, and the artillery schools in Kabul and Herat were enlarged. Afghan officers were sent to India, the USSR, Italy, Japan, and Turkey for further training. According to Forbes, the pay of the soldiers quadrupled between 1930 and 1937; by 1937 they were receiving 27 afghanis (13 shillings) a month.[128]

The Ministry of War made every effort to recruit the sons of Afghan tribal chiefs for the military academy. Clearly guided by political considerations, the administration hoped thereby to train an ethnically Afghan officer corps, to please the tribes that regarded the army as a national institution, and to appease the others. The thought was that some tribes might view the presence of their members in the army hierarchy as a new way of sharing power with the monarchy.

Officers were recruited for life. Nadir's compromise in the matter of military conscription, a combination of compulsory service for 24 months and voluntary enlistment for life, remained in effect. Each Afghan tribe supplied a certain number of recruits; other soldiers were conscripted "by casting lots in the villages, where out of every group of eight able-bodied men one [was to] serve two years and two months with the colours."[129] In 1934 there were an estimated 70,000 men in the Afghan army, in 1936, 80,000, and by 1941, 90,000. Before 1937 almost 50 per cent of the country's revenue was devoted to military expenditures: in 1935–36 out of an estimated total national revenue of 150 million afghanis, 71 million went to defense. The defense budget became proportionately higher in the following years.[130]

The government also reorganized the police and the gendarmery, making them national forces under the jurisdiction of the Ministry of the Interior. Manuals and criminal codes, covering everything from hunting regulations to the laws of arrest, were translated from Turkish into Persian to serve as guidelines for the police units.[181] Military and police courts were established and operated under secular legal codes, effectively removing them from the jurisdiction of the religious establishment.

The process of centralizing the judiciary power in Kabul, bringing uniformity to the application of laws, and codifying state and religious laws continued under the Hashim administration. By 1936 the Ministry of Justice supervised a judiciary system that incorporated a Supreme Court in Kabul, 19 courts of appeal in the provinces, and 106 lower courts throughout the country. The monarchy's long-time hope of having commercial disputes placed in a separate civil category (as a way to avoid applying Islamic law to Jews, Hindus, and Europeans) became a reality. Permanent local boards, composed of merchants, adjudicated and arbitrated these cases. In cases involving complicated intra-tribal disputes, however, the Afghan government continued to move carefully, reluctant to alienate any of the parties. The administration left major cases to tribal arbitration committees, which were often assisted by tribal jirgas or district and provincial assemblies.[182] If the government took any position at all in such affairs, it tried to be more an umpire than a partisan (except of course in cases involving the vital interests of the ruling clan and the Durrani tribe).

In 1936 the government reorganized the internal structure of the courts, issuing a decree that defined and delimited the powers of the judges, and made mandatory the registration (*sabt*) of proceedings (such as marriages and divorces) in the Shar'ia courts; the registers of the religious courts had to be forwarded to the Ministry of Justice. The decree also specified that a good knowledge of Shar'ia law was requisite for those administering the religious code, and that uniform language must be adopted, "in order to facilitate the appeals."[183] By such means, and through a variety of other administrative measures, the monarchy attempted to concentrate the administration of justice in its hands and curtail the power of ignorant or independent-minded judges and mullahs. In another decree, issued in 1938, the government attempted to regulate the expenses incurred in marriages, divorces, and funerals. Since the excessive expenditures customarily involved in these ceremonies were considered to be in violation of the spirit of Shar'ia law, government control in this area was not considered an interference with the administration of justice by Islamic principles. The decree also put controls on inheritance laws and real estate transactions. In an effort to prevent unscrupulous people (or relatives) from taking over the property of a deceased person as self-appointed guardians or executors, the government decreed that all legal documents and wills had to be drawn up on standard forms. In cases where there were no appropriate and lawful heirs, the courts were to serve as guardians of the estate, and any income from it was to be used for the public benefit—for roads, schools, mosques, and the like.

The Hashim administration also directed some attention to the country's archaic prison system. New prison buildings, bathhouses, and workshops were built in Kabul; the prohibitions against torture were reiterated. By government order, all prisoners were to be issued food and clothing (both summer and winter), and their moral and religious needs were to be attended to. The avowed goal of the prison workshops was to console, occupy, instruct, and rehabilitate the criminals.[134] There is no way to measure the extent to which these lofty measures were carried out. In view of the still-rudimentary nature of the Afghan administrative apparatus, and the country's limited resources, it is unlikely that they were strictly followed, particularly in the provinces.

Despite some noteworthy measures, the country's health standards remained low throughout the administration of Hashim Khan. The Ministry of Health was faced with a herculean and highly frustrating task. In 1935 alone the few small hospitals in Kabul treated 93,168 patients and those in the provinces treated 105,907. Several new facilities were opened the next year: a general 150-bed hospital, a 20-bed wing at Rifqi Sanatorium, a 100-bed hospital for women, a 30-bed sanatorium for women (all in Kabul), and three small hospitals for women (in Mazar-i-Sharif, Herat, and Kandahar). However, in view of the enormity of the medical problems in the country, these few improvements were scarcely noticeable. The Faculty of Medicine tried to meet some of the more urgent needs by giving crash programs to train pharmacists, dentists, midwives, and other paramedical personnel. In the first year of a five-year plan to improve public health (which was begun in 1939 but was interrupted between 1941 and 1945), an X-ray Institute was established in Kabul, dentistry courses were inaugurated for men and women, arrangements were made to distill alcohol for medicinal purposes, and some elementary drugs were prepared. Antirabies serum was made in the country for the first time in 1937. A village for lepers was built in the Hazara region. In all these efforts the Ministry of Health relied heavily on Turkish medical experts and on the small number of Afghan doctors trained at the Faculty of Medicine in Kabul or abroad. Whenever possible, the Turkish doctors were replaced by Afghans.

Within the limitations imposed by World War II, which made medicines both expensive and scarce, the Ministry of Health tried to cope with the epidemics that ravaged the population; cholera, typhoid, typhus, and smallpox were the most serious threats. In 1938 some 400,000 people were inoculated against typhoid, and 164,000 were vaccinated against smallpox. In the following year, 725,000 Afghans received cholera shots.

By the end of World War II, Afghanistan had a total of 67 hospitals (a figure that does not include the few military hospitals and clinics in the country). Twenty-eight of these hospitals were in the province of Kabul, most of them in the capital city itself. In one year alone (1945), the 67 hospitals cared for some 372,000 patients.[135]

Chapter Fourteen

Hashim Khan: Foreign Policy

The general foreign policy aims of Afghanistan, as stated by King Zahir in a speech in 1934, "were shaped by the desire of the King and his government for world peace so that Afghanistan could continue to combat its socioeconomic retardation and catch up with progress."[1] In the speech he emphasized three points: his desire to maintain friendly relations with all countries, his hope to live in peace and friendship with neighboring countries, and his intention not to raise political difficulties or obstacles for other governments, a policy he expected other governments to adopt for Afghanistan. In practice the Hashim government was guided by the same principles as Nadir in foreign policy: correct relations with the Soviet Union and Great Britain; close relations with Turkey, Iran, and other Muslim countries; greater international recognition and wider contacts; and a continued attempt to secure the assistance of distant industrial powers in modernizing the country. Safe and cautious economic development continued to be one of the chief aims of Afghan foreign policy.

The Hashim government took steps, as Nadir had, to satisfy the Soviet government that the Basmachis and other emigré elements from Turkestan, who continued to enjoy the support of the Afghan religious establishment and Pan-Islamists, would be prevented from engaging in anti-Soviet activities. Some of the prominent anti-Soviet leaders were "encouraged" to emigrate to Turkey or Europe. (In a corollary move the Afghans also placated Great Britain by closing the Afghan frontier "to Indian rebels," and reportedly promised the British government they would "prevent the Afghan tribes along the Indian border from participating in acts hostile to British authority.")[2]

Possibly to conciliate its neighbor to the north, Afghanistan did not join the League of Nations until the Soviet Union decided to do so; both became members in 1934. The two countries signed an agreement on an anti-locust campaign in May 1935 that provided a basis of cooperation and an excuse for the convening of annual conferences.[8] In 1936, to the great satisfaction of the Soviets, the Afghan government renewed the 1931 Soviet-Afghan Mutual Pact, which was extended until March 29, 1946.[4] This was followed by a Commercial Agreement (May 1936) providing transit rights for Afghans and a financial arrangement between the Soviet Commissariat for External Commerce and the Bank-i-Milli.[5] The Afghans seem to have assured the Soviets that in the economic development of northern Afghanistan, especially with respect to cotton, Afghanistan would try to take advantage of Soviet technology and expertise; to this end, they placed various orders for Soviet machinery and tools.[6] In an attempt to allay mutual fears of interference in each other's internal affairs, Afghanistan and the Soviet Union decided to close their respective consulates in Tashkent and Mazar-i-Sharif.[7] This move pleased Great Britain, which had campaigned since 1921 against the establishment of Soviet consulates in Afghanistan.

After joining the League of Nations and settling Afghanistan's frontier dispute with Iran,* the Hashim government, through bilateral and multilateral negotiations (1934–37), paved the way for the conclusion of the Saadabad Pact (July 1937), an alliance between Iran, Iraq, Turkey, and Afghanistan. In the preamble to the pact, the four powers declared that they were "actuated by the common purpose of ensuring peace and security in the Near East by means of additional guarantees within the framework of the Covenant of the League of Nations." They agreed to abstain from interference in each other's internal affairs; to respect the inviolability of their common frontiers; to consult in cases involving international disputes affecting their common interests; to refrain from aggression against one another, either singly or jointly with one or more powers; to bring any violation or threat of violation of this provision before the Permanent Council of the League of Nations, without prejudice to their own exercise of the right of self-defense; and to have the right to terminate the pact with any signatory who committed an act of aggression against a third power. In addition, each of the signatories agreed to take active steps to prevent the formation or activities of armed bands, associations, or organizations in their territories that might have as an objective the subversion of established institutions or of the order and security of another power, or that

---

* The Iranian-Afghan frontier dispute was finally settled in 1934, when both countries, in conformity with the provisions and the spirit of their Treaty of Friendship and Security (1927), agreed to submit their dispute to a mutually acceptable neutral power. The verdict of the umpire (Turkey) was accepted by Iran. For the text of the agreement, see Tavakulli, pp. 81f.

might attempt to change the constitutional system of such other power.[8]

The Saadabad Pact provided for the establishment of a permanent council and a secretariat, and for annual meetings at which the parties would consult and coordinate their policies. Hailed by its signatories as the first regional security and friendship pact among the independent Middle Eastern countries,[9] it was the first (and last) regional agreement Afghanistan made. The actual and potential benefits of the Saadabad Pact were limited. It represented an attempt by the signatories to ensure greater solidarity among themselves in meeting aggression from any European power and in forestalling the possibility of an attack against another Middle Eastern state. According to George Kirk, the Saadabad Pact nations represented "a regional bloc strong enough to withstand Great Power interference whether from the growing Mediterranean ambitions of Fascist Italy or from the traditional Middle Eastern rivalry of Britain and Russia."[10] For the Afghans the pact provided added benefits: at home the monarchy could (and did) portray the agreement as an example of Pan-Islamic solidarity, an opportunity for cultural and economic cooperation between "independent and progressive" Muslim states; outside the country, the specific application of broad provisions of the pact enabled the Afghan government to relax its guard against the possibility that either Iran or Turkey might champion the cause of Amanullah or become a base of operations for pro-Amanullah forces. Furthermore, the rapprochement with Iran settled the border disputes between the two countries, obviating the revival of an Iranian irredentist movement, and at the same time served as a friendly gesture to the Shi'ah community in Afghanistan.

The public reaction of the Great Powers to the Saadabad Pact was mixed. The Soviet Union welcomed it, as did Great Britain. The Soviets considered the pact an extension of the collective security system of the League of Nations, which would hopefully "bring stabilization of peace in the region" and usher in an era of closer political coordination among the pact members.[11] Contemporary political commentators disagreed about the origins, motivations, and eventual impact of the arrangement. Some saw it as a triumph for Soviet diplomacy (since the Soviet Union had non-aggression agreements and other treaty arrangements with Turkey and Afghanistan), or as an attempt of the four Middle Eastern countries to limit the power of Great Britain in the region. Others viewed it as a coup for British diplomacy (because Britain had treaties with Iraq and Egypt, the latter a power that cooperated closely with the Saadabad Pact members), and as an attempt by the British to safeguard their political and economic interests in the region against Soviet self-assertion and Italian expansion.[12] In fact, it is very likely that the Saadabad Pact was concluded with the tacit approval or even the active encouragement of both the Soviet Union and Great Britain.[13]

Nazi Germany's initial reaction to the pact was a favorable one, but Fascist Italy's was not: Italy considered it an instrument of British imperialism in the Middle East.[14] For Afghan diplomacy, however, the important fact was that Afghanistan had joined a regional pact without alienating either of its two powerful neighbors.

The pact inaugurated a new era of cooperation between Iran and Afghanistan. In July 1938 the two countries concluded a postal convention, which was followed in January 1939 by an agreement covering the telephone and telegraphic connections between them.[15] Most important of all, in 1939 the two governments settled their differences over the division of the waters of the Helmand River. That same year Iranian and Afghan authorities worked together in combating a cholera epidemic in Afghanistan near the Afghan-Iranian frontier.[16] Relations with Turkey, too, continued to improve: the Turko-Afghan Treaty of Friendship and Mutual Assistance of 1928 was renewed (December 31, 1937) for ten years.[17]

RELATIONS WITH THE WEST

Outside the Muslim world, the Afghans reaffirmed their friendship agreements with Estonia, Lithuania, Finland, Austria, Denmark, Holland, Hungary, Sweden, Norway, Spain, and Brazil, and concluded a similar treaty with Czechoslovakia.[18] The desire to formalize and broaden their relations with the United States remained a major preoccupation. Continuing the efforts of Nadir, the Hashim government attempted to obtain more than token United States recognition of Afghanistan, pressing for an exchange of diplomatic missions and an increase in trade. The search for a suitable formula for the investment of private American capital in Afghanistan and for the employment of American experts was intensified. To the gratification of the Afghans, the United States officially recognized King Zahir's government in 1935 and appointed the American minister to Iran to act also as the accredited United States representative to the Afghan court.[19] Soon after, in 1936, a provisional agreement, with clauses on friendship and diplomatic representation, was concluded between the two countries.[20] According to Murray, the chief of the State Department's Near Eastern Affairs section, the conclusion of a more far-reaching agreement at that time was prevented "by the discovery that the text first proposed to the Afghans did not take account of their ineligibility to American citizenship and the legislative structure based thereon," and "by the refusal of the Afghans to enter into an agreement providing for reciprocal and unconditional most-favored-nation treatment in regard to commercial and customs matters." Murray drew the conclusion that as long as American interests continued to be slight, there was no likelihood of the United States establishing a permanent diplomatic mission in Kabul.[21]

On June 27, 1941, Dreyfus, the United States minister in Iran, sent a report to the State Department on his visit to Kabul. "Our reception was unusually cordial," he wrote, continuing:

The Afghans have a sincere and deep-rooted desire, in the absence of a friend or neighbor to whom they can turn, to have a disinterested third power friend to assist and advise them, and they have always hoped that the U.S. would be willing to fill such a role. This desire on their part is not opportunistic because of the war, although war conditions have made it more acute. I venture to recommend the immediate opening of a legation at Kabul for the following reasons: first and most important, the U.S. should accept the hand of friendship offered it by this small and independent nation in keeping with its world responsibilities. Secondly, this is an opportunity which should not be missed of establishing ourselves solidly in a strategic position in Asia. Thirdly, our interests in Afghanistan should increase, since negotiations are now under way to bring a number of American teachers and technical advisers, and many more are contemplated if all goes well.[22]

Dreyfus also assured the Secretary of State that while "justice is administered exclusively . . . on the basis of Islamic law, . . . in practical application foreigners are accorded suitable treatment." Furthermore, he added, the Afghan government had expressed its willingness to sign a more comprehensive treaty with the United States, which could include a most-favored-nation clause with certain reservations. Despite the recommendations of Dreyfus, the United States did not establish a permanent mission in Afghanistan until 1943.

The reluctance of the United States to become economically or politically involved in Afghanistan was not matched by the German government, which continued its efforts to establish close ties with the Afghan government. In November 1937 Lufthansa German Airlines established a route between Berlin and Kabul, via Tirana, Athens, Rhodes, Damascus, Baghdad, and Tehran, and by 1938 was accepting a few passengers on its flights to and from Kabul.[23] The considerations leading to this air link, a real achievement for the time, were more political than economic: it was a step in Nazi Germany's concerted drive to penetrate the Middle East politically and culturally, as well as economically. Germany offered Afghanistan financial credits and technical advisers. Because the German companies received subsidies and guarantees (including a clearing system of some 60 million marks), they had a competitive edge in Afghanistan.[24] In 1937–38, according to Ernest Fox, an American geologist who worked in Afghanistan, "One met German salesmen in Kabul, and German highway engineers in the field. German steel was going into the new bridges on the highways. The Deutsche Lufthansa Co. was the only commercial airline [that] landed on the Kabul airport."[25]

In 1937 The Afghanistan Mines, Ltd., an Afghan-German company, was established to survey and exploit the mineral resources of the kingdom. In the same year, the Bank-i-Milli opened a branch in Berlin in order to promote German-Afghan trade and German investments in Afghanistan. By 1939 there were somewhere between 100 and 300 German experts and technicians in Afghanistan, most of them engineers in charge of road-building projects, hydroelectric plants, and factories. Germans also occupied important teaching and planning posts, not only in the various industrial projects of the country but also in the Bank-i-Milli, the post, telegraph, and telephone system, the Kabul police department, and the Afghan army, where they helped train the officer corps. Several German business houses opened branches in Afghanistan and sent German nationals to staff them. Some of these firms successfully outbid other foreign interests for the right to supply machinery and mining experts to exploit the Afghan coal fields; in some instances, the German bids were half those of their closest competitors. In August 1939 Germany concluded an extensive financial and commercial agreement with Afghanistan: Afghanistan was given long-term credits for the purchase of German machinery for new textile mills and hydroelectric plants, and in return agreed to repay all advances over a ten-year period by furnishing cotton to Germany. Under the terms of this agreement 80 per cent of the materials bought by the Afghan government (through its state bank) were to be financed by the German Reich. The agreement—which the Nazi economic journal *Südostecho* saw as opening unlimited possibilities for German trade and capital in Afghanistan (August 25, 1939)—was a great triumph for Nazi diplomacy. At a time when Great Britain, the USSR, France, and the United States were either unwilling or unable to make long-range financial commitments to Afghanistan, Nazi Germany, for political reasons, was "prepared to accept the risk involved in the provision of long-term credits to a country which could offer little or no tangible security for repayment."[26]

The Afghan ruling elite and modernists, always apprehensive of colonialism, did not regard the German economic expansion and financial credits as a form of neo-colonialism, but saw in them only their overt purpose: a means of industrializing and modernizing the Afghan economy.

In the words of Hashim Khan, the Germans were employed "to build our bridges, our roads, and our new town districts. They prospect for us, oversee the cotton factories, teach at the German college [Najat], at the Art College, at the Agricultural College, and at the Professional College, a magnificent present made by Germany to this country."[27] Well aware that despite such pronouncements the British and the Soviets were apprehensive about the German advances in Afghanistan, the Afghan government attempted to attract investors and technical advisers from other countries. In an effort to demonstrate a policy of even-handed neutrality in such matters, the government hired Indian Muslim and Persian doctors, some 150 Turkish military experts, medical personnel, and other technicians to work with the Afghan army,[28] and a considerable number of Polish, Czech, Italian, and Japanese engineers, as well as Japanese agricultural specialists. An Italian served as a financial and economic adviser to the Afghan government. Soviet technicians built plants in Kunduz, and Soviet nationals were stationed in Mazar-i-Sharif in connection with the anti-locust campaign. A few Englishmen were also employed; some built radio and telegraph stations, others taught in secondary schools. The Afghans themselves sent a substantial number of students to India, the Soviet Union, and Italy for training as pilots. On the average, from 1933 on, the Afghan government sent 20 to 30 students to Europe and America for higher education each year.[29]

The Afghans continued to make special efforts to attract American capital and experts. In May 1937 the Afghan government granted its first concession to a foreign company, giving the American Inland Exploration Company a 75-year option on the exploration and exploitation of the oil resources of the entire country.[30] The company was also granted the right to explore the kingdom's mineral deposits and, subject to further negotiations, concessions to any discoveries. For its part, American Inland agreed to pay 330,000 pounds in the first five years of the concession and 20 per cent of its annual profits thereafter. Three American geologists began carrying out explorations in 1937. (They had to be accompanied by Afghan subjects and submit copies of their reports to the Afghan government.) Within a year, however, even before the geologists had completed their preliminary studies, the company surrendered its concession. By way of explanation, it pointed out that the rich oil deposits of the kingdom were virtually inaccessible and would require, by some estimates, nearly 300 million dollars to exploit; that the communications of the country were poor; and that the cost of constructing a pipeline to the Arabian Sea was prohibitive in itself. In any case, the world situation was scarcely conducive

to major American investments in Afghanistan. By 1938 it was clear that
hostilities in Europe were inevitable. In the event of war, oil fields in Afghanistan would be vulnerable to a Soviet or Iranian attack and could be
protected only by British action, a guarantee Britain would not give. According to Ernest Fox, one of the three American geologists, the Afghans
were bewildered and disappointed at the company's withdrawal. He wrote:

Several reasons for the withdrawal were given ... none of which was plain to
Afghans. They knew that their first experience with peaceful foreign penetration had backfired in a way that might even have startled the canny old Abdur
Rahman; and it was bewildering to them that Americans should give up so
easily a favor that others had fought so hard and long to gain.[31]

The American action was obviously a blow to the policy of seeking support, services, and investments from distant and, hopefully, politically disinterested industrial countries. Since the United States and France were
not ready for large-scale, long-term investments, Afghanistan, determined
to refuse concessions to the Soviets and the British, and equally determined
not to allow Soviet and British nationals into the country in significant
numbers, was forced to fall back on German, Italian, Japanese, and Czech
investments and technicians.[32] This tendency greatly alarmed the country's
two powerful neighbors, the Soviet Union and British India, especially
after the Munich Pact. Under these circumstances, the Afghan government
desperately attempted to keep its developmental policies clear of the political events and alignments of Europe, and to continue the urgent task of
modernizing Afghanistan.

POLITICAL DIFFICULTIES IN WORLD WAR II

The Afghans' heavy dependence on the financial and technical assistance
of the Axis powers in their economic development program placed them in
a precarious position on the eve of World War II. That such dependence
was understandable made it no less objectionable to the Soviet Union and
Great Britain. Clearly, the best way for the Allies to have ended the dom-
inance of the Axis in this strategic country was for the United States and
Great Britain themselves to have extended technical assistance and long-
term credits to the Afghan kingdom. Neither chose to do so. The Afghans
had another alternative: they could have turned to the Soviets for assistance. But not only was such a move anathema to them; it would have
been highly unwelcome to the British, who might then have felt obliged to
press for an equal influence or presence in Afghanistan. A British presence
was no more acceptable to the Afghans than was a Russian presence. Sir

William Barton proposed another course of action for the British, a plan that would at one and the same time eliminate Axis influence in Afghanistan, contribute to the defense of India, and gain the gratitude of the Afghans. He argued that "a strong and friendly Afghanistan" was essential in the pacification of India's turbulent border area, and that economic development was "of the first importance" in working to this end. "Why," he asked, "should Britain not play her part in the economic field in Afghanistan?"

The country is landlocked, its foreign trade, except on the Russian side, has to move nearly 1,500 miles to the sea across India; in such conditions rapid expansion is impossible. The obvious remedy is a port and an approach corridor on the Arabian Sea. To have such a port is an ambition of the Afghan Government. Why does not Britain offer the concession? Doubtless as a *quid pro quo* the Afghan Government would give Britain special trade facilities.[33]

Barton's plan fell on deaf British ears. In any case, such a concession would have been conditional on a most-favored-nation clause and capitulatory treaties for Britain. At the very least, the Soviet response would have been demands for reciprocity. Both consequences were unacceptable to the Afghan ruling elite. Under the circumstances, then, the Afghan government could only continue to walk a tightrope in 1938.

The most fundamental tenets of Afghan foreign and economic policy were jolted by the outbreak of World War II and the conclusion of the Nazi-Soviet non-aggression pact in 1939. The possibility that Afghanistan's independence might be jeopardized, or that the country might become a battleground of European diplomacy—even a theater of war— seemed very real. The Hashim government, hoping to salvage its modernization programs and safeguard the country's independence, followed the traditional guidelines of Afghan foreign policy, proclaiming the neutrality of Afghanistan in September 1939. Serious internal and external pressures were brought to bear on that neutrality, however. There were Afghan nationalists and modernists who could not see how Afghanistan could stop its defense efforts, interrupt its modernization programs, and sever its diplomatic and commercial ties with the Axis powers without jeopardizing its independence and sovereignty. The frustrating position of the Afghan ruling elite is well described by George Kirk:

The plan of industrial development and military re-equipment was just coming into full operation. Much material, ordered from Czechoslovakia and Germany, had arrived, but there was much still to come. Textile mills were half-finished, hydro-electric installations lacked essential parts, there were guns without ammunition and ammunition without guns. Nothing could have been more unfortunate than a severance of relations with Germany, at least until the delivery of all recent purchases had been completed.[34]

The Afghans were able to complete some of their programs in the 1939–41 period, since the Soviets did not pressure them to sever their connection with the Axis while the Nazi-Soviet pact was in effect. The British, for their part, were in a poor position to make such a demand. A confrontation with Afghanistan would have played into the hands of Nazi Germany and seriously threatened the British defenses in India. Since 1938 Britain had been trying to prevent an eruption in the North-West Frontier Province, where the Pathan tribesmen did not need much prompting to assert their autonomy, a fact that had always created difficulties in Anglo-Afghan relations and continued to do so. One particularly explosive situation developed in Waziristan in the spring of 1938, when a Syrian adventurer, Said al-Kalani, known as the Shami Pir, denounced King Zahir as a usurper and called on the Pathan tribesmen to restore Amanullah to the Afghan throne. Recruiting a tribal force, al-Kalani attacked an Afghan frontier fortification. He was unable to capture it, but the Afghan government lodged strong protests with the British government over the incident. (Some Afghan circles saw in the incident a British hand applying pressure against the Afghan government for its extensive ties with the Germans.) The Indian Political Department managed to defuse the situation, reportedly by persuading the "holy man of Damascus" to accept 20,000 pounds and go home.[35]

The Shami Pir story was but one episode in the turbulent history of the tribal belt. From 1937 on, periodic anti-British uprisings in Waziristan, led by Haji Mirza Ali Khan, the famed Fakir of Ipi, drained both British wealth and manpower, and "acted as a magnet to draw adventurous Germans and Italians."[36] After the war, it was revealed at the Nuremberg Trials that the Italians had tried to induce the Fakir of Ipi (with large sums of money) to carry on pro-Axis activities in the frontier area and to create difficulties for Britain.* It was also revealed after the war that Quaroni, the Italian minister to Kabul, had prepared a major plan for the insurrection of the North-West Frontier tribes, which the Italian government had communicated to the German High Command. In the belief that

---

* The Italian negotiations with the Fakir of Ipi were carried on by Anzilotti, the counselor of the Italian legation in Kabul. In February 1941 the Italians and the Germans gave the Fakir 160,000 afghanis, promising him an additional 25,000 English pounds every two months thereafter. In June 1941, after a visit to the Fakir's camp, Anzilotti reported that the Fakir was willing to intensify the border fighting and to accept Axis nationals as radio technicians. In order to intensify hostilities, however, he would need a large amount of money. The Italians were not able to provide the necessary amounts promptly. The German legation in Kabul made a new proposal: instead of 25,000 pounds every two months, the Fakir should be paid 300,000 rupees

Britain was about to succumb anyway, the Germans shelved the project, explaining that "they did not want to diminish further the prestige of the whites in the Middle East or India."[37]

The correspondence between the German legation in Kabul and the German Foreign Ministry during the years 1934–41, as well as the latest study of two East German scholars* (which unfortunately was received while this book was in press), reveals that the German government was unhappy about Afghanistan's normalization of relations with the Soviet Union and British India, a normalization that was marked by improved economic relations and by a renewal of the Afghan-Soviet non-aggression treaty. By supplying economic and technical assistance and helping the Afghans in their modest industrial undertakings, the Nazi authorities had hoped to secure the cooperation of the Afghan ruling elite in neutralizing Soviet and British influence in Afghanistan, securing a pro-German base there, and forging a strong pro-German alliance. But the Afghan government, though it actively encouraged German economic assistance and even allowed the Germans to train the Afghan army, resisted the efforts of the Nazi government to enlist its support for an official anti-Soviet and anti-British campaign; nor did it allow the Germans to supervise the exact dispensation of German credits in Afghanistan. Piqued by the "correct neutrality" of the Hashim government, the Nazi regime between 1939 and 1941 attempted to enlist the support of ex-King Amanullah and his partisans for a *coup d'état*, in which the Musahiban dynasty would be overthrown and Amanullah restored to the throne. The "Amanullah Project," sponsored by the Nazi Abwehr (counterintelligence) and Foreign Ministry, was opposed by Alfred Rosenberg, the head of the foreign affairs office of the Nazi party,[38] who recommended instead the cultivation of a mutually advantageous political alliance with the Hashim government. Moreover, the success of the project depended on the cooperation of the Soviets. Taking advantage of the Nazi-Soviet pact, the Third Reich attempted to

---

a month to keep up his "petty hostilities," double that amount if he extended the hostilities to other areas, and triple the amount if he could stir up a general uprising in the North-West Frontier Province. See U.S. Department of State, *Documents on German Foreign Policy*, XIII, 136–37: German Legation in Afghanistan to Foreign Ministry, July 14, 1941. For Italian activities in Afghanistan and the border area, see also Quaroni, pp. 120–28.

* Johannes Glasneck and Inge Kircheisen, *Türkei und Afghanistan. Brennpunkte der Orientpolitik im zweiten Weltkrieg* (Berlin, 1968), pp. 161–278. Photostatic copies of some of the unpublished documents of the German Foreign Ministry are available at the Hoover Institution, Stanford, Calif. (See British Foreign Office and U.S. State Department's Document Field Team, Data on Documents Transmitted: Serial Nos. 344, 2195, 2195H, 2277H, 2824.)

obtain transit rights and covert or overt Soviet support for the proposed coup. However, the Soviets refused to participate in the plan. Frustrated, the Germans turned to Abdul Majid Zabuli, then Minister of Economy and president of the Afghan National Bank, hoping that he could find support either in the Afghan government or among dissident Afghan elements for the German cause. Zabuli offered to mobilize enough anti-British and tribal resistance in the North-West Frontier Province to prevent Indian armed forces being sent to the Mediterranean. His initial price for this and other services was threefold: the Germans were not to upset the delicate balance of power between Great Britain and the Soviet Union with respect to Afghanistan, were to guarantee Afghan territory against the USSR, and were to furnish Afghanistan with heavy armaments (including airplanes, tanks, and artillery). The German moves to win over Zabuli were prompted not only by his own eager overtures but also by reports based on hints of the Afghan commercial attaché in Berlin that Zabuli was considering "whether or not he should turn away from the present Afghan Government."[39]

The Axis activities were scarcely confined to this incident. There were German plans in 1939–40 to divert the British in India by encouraging the Soviet Union to move into Afghanistan.* Brauchitsch, the commander-in-chief of Germany's land forces, revealed in January 1940 that the Reich was intent on channeling Soviet expansion into Afghanistan and India. But even as the Nazis were thinking in these terms, the German envoy in Kabul was making further overtures to win the Afghans to the Axis cause. In 1940 he confidently announced to them that Hitler would be in London by August. He reportedly offered Afghanistan a restoration of the Durrani Empire, proposing that she be given Baluchistan, Sind, Kashmir, and the western Punjab, including the port of Karachi.[40]

In 1941 the Germans renewed their efforts, attempting to enlist the Afghan government to the cause of the Rashid Ali al-Gailani government in Iraq, which was carrying on a nationalist, anti-British campaign. Encouraged by the popularity the Gailani cause enjoyed among some Afghans, the Germans devised a plan to supply modern arms to the Iraqi army: Afghanistan (or Iran) was to be made the consignee of an arms

---

* Ribbentrop suggested that "the focal points in the territorial aspirations of the Soviet Union would presumably be centered south of the territory of the Soviet Union in the direction of the Indian Ocean." See R. J. Sontag and J. S. Beddie, eds., *Nazi-Soviet Relations, 1939–1941: Documents from the Archives of the German Foreign Office*. U.S. Department of State, Washington, D.C., 1948, p. 250. See also *Völkisher Beobachter*, December 6, 1939.

shipment, which would be sent through Iraq and there "seized" by the Iraqi army. In this the Germans thought they would have the support of Abdul Majid, who had let it be understood that he was ready to help Iraq.* However, both Zabuli and Faiz Muhammed Khan, the Afghan envoy to Turkey (another Gailani sympathizer), decided to inform the Afghan government of the German project.[41] The plan was dropped. The Afghan government was weary of costly adventurism. It decided to maintain its neutrality, adhering to a position much like Habibullah's during World War I. The government adopted a correct attitude toward British India and the Soviet Union, reiterating often and loudly its devotion to peace and neutrality, and the Neutrality Act promulgated by Zahir was approved by both houses of the Afghan parliament.[42] The Afghans rejected the suggestion of the Iraqi government that they take up its cause under the terms of the Saadabad Pact. Such a move, they replied, should have come before, not after, the hostilities. Another Iraqi suggestion, that Afghanistan take the initiative and call a jihad against Britain, was also rejected.[43] Fraser-Tytler, then the British envoy to Kabul, described the situation as one in which "the Afghans figuratively buttoned their coats and turned their backs to the blast, crouching behind the frail shelter of their international frontiers, and their proclaimed neutrality . . . hoping that the whirlwind would pass them by."[44]

Such was not to be the case, however. After the German invasion of the Soviet Union, it became evident that neither Great Britain nor the Soviet Union, now allies, would tolerate the presence and activities of hundreds of German and Italian (as well as Japanese) nationals in Afghanistan. Moreover, the Allied fears of Axis activities were not unfounded. In 1941 Ribbentrop instructed Dr. von Hentig, the newly appointed German minister to Afghanistan, to coordinate the activities of German teachers, officers, engineers, and doctors, to establish contacts with Afghan nationalist circles in order to use them ("if necessary against the Government"), to coordinate the German intelligence services, and to contact the frontier

---

* Abdul Majid and some Afghan envoys kept in close touch with the German government. According to Nazi documents, in a series of meetings with the German government from March to June, 1941, Zabuli offered to discuss "the possible territorial changes resulting for Afghanistan from the war." What the Afghans had in mind, wrote Baron Ernst von Weizsäcker, state secretary of the German Foreign Office, were "the British possessions in the southeast and south, to Karachi, and the Indus as the new Afghan border." Abdul Majid's talks with the German Foreign Office were not official, but he believed that if they went well, he could obtain instructions from the Afghan government to formalize their substance. See U.S. Department of State, *Documents on German Foreign Policy*, XII, 283, 729, 971–72: Weizsäcker to Foreign Minister, March 12, May 6, and June 6, 1941.

tribes and their nationalist leaders. He was also instructed to spread German propaganda in India, to note British military measures in Baluchistan and along the Iranian frontier, and to support the national independence movements in Iran and Afghanistan, "particularly in so far as these are connected and cooperate with one another."[45] More concretely, the Nazis hoped for permission from the Afghans to establish a short-wave radio transmitter in the Afghan-Indian border area, to allow "inconspicuous German participation" in using the transmitter of Kabul Radio, and to tolerate "a certain amount of smuggling of arms."[46] As for the Italians, as noted, their negotiations with the Fakir of Ipi were carried on through their legation in Kabul.

Both Britain and the Soviet Union had separately expressed concern over the presence of Axis subjects in the Afghan kingdom earlier; now they were in a position to take concerted action. In October 1941 they sent similar notes to the Afghan government demanding the ouster of German and Italian citizens.[47] The Afghan reaction to this ultimatum was apprehension, bitterness, and public outcry: apprehension because the Afghans feared the issue might be a pretext for the invasion of their country, as a similar demand had been in Iran;* bitterness because even in 1940, when Britain "stood alone," the Afghans had kept their correct neutrality; and public outrage because the Afghans saw the demand as an infringement on their sovereign rights and a violation of their neutrality. The Afghan government summoned a Loe Jirga for consultation. It agreed to comply with the demand but it also expressed Afghanistan's will and determination to preserve its strict neutrality, independence, and territorial integrity.[48]

In order to curtail the range of Axis activities in the country, the Afghan authorities not only placed the Kabul area under strict surveillance but in July 1941 began restricting travel by imposing gasoline rationing (three gallons a day per car). In the same month Afghan border guards shot two German agents on their way to the camp of the Fakir of Ipi, killing one and wounding the other. Hashim Khan conveyed his regrets to the Germans. The Afghan guards, he said, had mistaken the two agents for Ama-

---

* The Anglo-Soviet attack and invasion of Iran had thoroughly alarmed the Afghans. The German envoy reported, in September 1941, that "the hostile feeling against England and Russia on the part of the Government and people, produced by the Iranian events, still persists. Although the Government has taken account of this feeling by sharply criticizing what has happened through public statements in the newspaper *Anis* and the Radio, nevertheless it is dominated by its original fears that the Iranian events could be repeated here." See U.S. Department of State, *Documents on German Foreign Policy*, XIII, 463–64: Pilger to Foreign Ministry.

nullah's son and the nephew of Ghulam Sidiq Khan. He also told the Germans, "in strict confidence," that the British, who had previously protested the appointment of the "agitator," Dr. von Hentig, now had filed a protest "almost in the form of an ultimatum," demanding not only on behalf of the British government but on behalf of the Soviets as well that the German colony's activities be restricted. Hashim Khan reassured the Germans that he had rejected these protests; nevertheless, he demanded that Afghanistan's neutrality be observed, and that such incidents not be repeated, for they could be used by *agents provocateurs*.*

The convening of the Loe Jirga was an astute and timely move on the part of Hashim Khan. It gave a national mandate to his foreign policy, eliminating the possibility of the charge of appeasement of the Allies and contributing to a greater sense of national unity and purpose. An aroused Afghan nationalism allowed Hashim Khan to push forward measures that at any other time would have been highly unpopular, among them a new national conscription law making military service obligatory for all male Afghan citizens over the age of seventeen and a special tax to help the government increase the size of the army, purchase arms, and improve the country's communications.[49]

ECONOMIC IMPACT OF WORLD WAR II

Though Afghanistan escaped the fate of Iran during World War II, it still paid a high price. Its reform and modernization programs were inter-

---

* In filing an account of the friendly "démarche" of Hashim Khan, the German minister in Kabul reported that the Afghan prime minister had "stressed several times his friendly feelings toward us. However, he replied to all my remarks that Afghanistan's situation as a buffer between two allies was so unfortunate that the Government requested urgently that everything be avoided that could give the English an occasion for exerting any sort of pressure." Reminiscent of the promises of Habibullah to the Turko-German mission in 1915 were Hashim Khan's promises to the Nazi minister that the Afghan "government was ready, when the moment for intervention had arrived as a result of the approach of German troops [to Afghanistan], to let all of Afghanistan take up arms on our side. In that case he would then mobilize about 500,000 men, including the border Afghans." See U.S. Department of State, *Documents on German Foreign Policy*, XIII, 269–71: Pilger to Foreign Minister, July 31, 1941. See also *ibid.*, p. 137. Hashim Khan, apprehensive of the possibility of German or Italian support of Amanullah's cause, gave similar explanations about Afghan foreign policy to Quaroni, the Italian minister. See Quaroni, pp. 128–34. The efforts of Hashim Khan brought some positive results: on August 9, 1941, Ribbentrop instructed the German legation in Kabul to "make it incumbent on all Reich Germans in Afghanistan that they observe complete restraint, for the time being, so as not to aid and abet English and Soviet Russian efforts through any kind of incidents." See U.S. Department of State, *Documents on German Foreign Policy*, XIII, 301.

rupted, its plans for development were abandoned or postponed, and its economy was dislocated. The abrupt exodus of hundreds of technicians left many of the industrial projects in disarray. Most of the annual wartime revenues (an estimated 150–220 million afghanis)[50] were earmarked for national defense. Because of the economic scarcities created by the war, Afghanistan was hard hit by inflation. In the first year of the war the price of most commodities increased, by as much as 20 per cent in some cases. On the basis of the 1936–37 price index, by 1946 the price of clothing had increased 325 per cent, food 361 per cent, housing rents 313 per cent, and all prices an average of 355 per cent. The government imposed strict price and foreign exchange controls, but these measures, which were largely circumvented by the big merchants and companies, were not enough to stem the tide.[51] The government itself contributed to the inflation by issuing enormous quantities of paper money. In 1935 there were 20 million afghanis in circulation; by 1938 the figure had grown to 60 million, and by the end of 1939 to 180 million. In 1946 the total sum of afghanis in circulation had climbed over the 600 million mark,[52] spinning the wheels of the country's economy through the rounds of spiraling inflation.

The war not only cut off the sources of machinery, equipment, and manufactured goods, but also greatly reduced the markets for Afghan exports. An important portion of the country's foreign trade, notably the trade carried on with Germany, Czechoslovakia, and Japan before the war, had to find new markets, since the Allied occupation of Iran had cut off the route of that trade. The most serious development in this field was the collapse of the karakul trade, the most important source of foreign exchange for the country. In 1939 only 29,176 skins were exported to London, one of the chief outlets for karakul. The cost of shipping insurance, the British wartime taxes on luxury items, and the lack of demand virtually destroyed the market. A similar situation prevailed in the other major market, the United States. In the years 1943–45 there were millions of unsold skins in the United States and in Kabul.[53] To earn foreign exchange, the Afghans had to rely on exports of agricultural products, further inflating their cost.

The Afghan government hoped to resolve some of its economic difficulties by establishing closer diplomatic and economic relations with the United States, thinking to compensate at least in part for the loss of German, Japanese, Czechoslovakian, and Italian markets, technicians, machinery, and credits. In 1941 the Afghans proposed that the two countries sign a treaty of friendship. The draft read, in part, as follows:

There shall be a firmly established and lasting peace and sincere friendship between His Majesty the King of Afghanistan, his descendants and subjects on the one hand and the U.S.A. and her citizens on the other, in all their territories and dominions [Article 1]. . . . As to their persons, property, rights and interests, the treatment accorded will not be less favorable than that accorded the nationals of any other country [Article 3]. . . . The government of the U.S.A., in its dominions and possessions in commercial and customs matters, shall receive the rights and facilities given by the Royal Government of Afghanistan to a third foreign government or to be given in the future [Article 4].

The Afghan government even expressed its willingness to sign a more comprehensive treaty, including a "most-favored-nation clause with certain reservations," as touched upon above.[54] Consideration of such a treaty, however, remained in abeyance during the war. Thus United States markets were not able to take up the slack in Afghan exports.*

The Afghan economy was further weakened by the flight of Afghan capital to Peshawar. The business community, interested in quick profits in such unstable times, invested its surpluses not in industrial expansion but in large farms and real estate, contributing to the inflationary trend of the Afghan economy.[55] The consequence was greater deterioration in the economic status of the peasant and urban populations. The hardships and deprivations of the Afghan masses during the war, coupled with the frustrations of the Afghan nationalist-modernists, carried the seeds of a politically and socially explosive situation.†

At the end of the war Afghanistan faced staggering social and economic needs. Moreover, the war had demonstrated how fragile the political independence of the landlocked country was without socioeconomic development, as well as the precariousness of a developmental policy that did not take into account a diversification of markets and the cooperation of neighboring countries. The war thus confirmed the case of the Afghan national-

---

* In 1943, when the two countries finally exchanged diplomatic missions, President Roosevelt told the Afghan envoy: "I know that those of my countrymen who have visited Afghanistan have been deeply impressed by the courage and fortitude of the Afghans, by their love of freedom and their determination to tolerate no acts of aggression against their country. You will find, I am sure, Mr. Minister, that the love of freedom upon which we in the United States so pride ourselves is similar to your own, and that there is much in the mutual idealism of our two peoples to cement the friendship now being manifest." See L. M. Goodrich and M. J. Carroll, eds., *Documents on American Foreign Relations*, Boston, 1944, V, 605. The immediate and practical benefits of the diplomatic exchange were limited: Afghanistan became a signatory of the Interim Agreement on International Civil Aviation (1944) and in the same year agreed to prohibit the cultivation of opium in Afghanistan. See *ibid.*, VII, 699.

† Even *Islah*, the semi-official newspaper, carried gloomy reports about the state of the Afghan economy. The paper pointed out that agricultural output was on the decline, the number of livestock was decreasing, inflation was unchecked, and small shopkeepers faced economic ruin. In short, the Afghan economy was in a most precarious state, and the discontent of the masses, who were the major victims of the economic dislocation, was rising. See *Islah*, October 9, 1946.

ist-modernists and strengthened their determination to press for fundamental socioeconomic reforms. Reform and modernization were not only
desirable but absolutely necessary if social upheaval was to be averted, if
the independence of Afghanistan and the power of the ruling elite were
to be sustained.

In the aftermath of the war, the Hashim administration tried to return
Afghanistan to normalcy, counting on American markets and technicians
to provide the necessary means for his administration to undertake reforms. The Afghan parliament busied itself in deliberations on provisions
for retirement, labor laws, travel regulations, and similar matters. A commission was named to study to what degree Persian technical words were
in use in the country in the fields of law, political science, sociology, philosophy, economy, and finance: making Pashto a truly effective national
language was still on the government's agenda. In an effort to alleviate the
financial hardships of the Afghan bureaucracy, a budget of 16 million afghanis was allocated for a Cooperative of Government Employees, which
was to import goods and provide items to government employees at cost.
Two hospitals were opened, one at Badakhshan, the other at Farah.[56]

But these measures were not far-reaching enough for the new breed of
Afghan modernists, men who had been trained in Europe, Turkey, and the
United States, and who were, largely, members of the most influential
Afghan families. They proposed a massive program of social and economic
reform, including the allocation of land to poor peasants and the development of light industry,[57] and pressed for an end to the paternalistic
and autocratic regime of Hashim Khan. There were reports of anti-government plots and of the arrest of various journalists and writers—even
of the deputy prime minister.[58] In May 1946 Hashim Khan, already in
failing health, resigned as prime minister. He was succeeded by his brother
Shah Mahmud Khan, who announced a new and ambitious program of
socioeconomic development. Thus began a new phase in the history of
modern Afghanistan.

CONCLUSION

Afghanistan is one of the few countries to resist successfully the tidal
wave of European imperialism that swept Asia and Africa in the nineteenth
century. Like Persia, Ethiopia, Nepal, and Siam, she was able to retain
a degree of political independence because of a "stand-off" between competing European imperial powers, in her case, in the Great Game (as it
came to be called) between Britain and Russia. There were, however,

other important reasons for her success in staving off foreign domination: the strategic advantages of her eastern territory, the military strength and fighting spirit of the Afghan and Pathan tribes, and especially the astute post-1880 foreign policy of her rulers, who skillfully exploited the Anglo-Russian imperialist struggle. Though the Afghan rulers conceded control of their foreign relations to Great Britain, they tried to minimize the burden and significance of that control through isolationism, which was perceived as the best means of protecting both the dynasty's rule and the country's independence. Isolationism, the foundation of Afghan policy throughout the period 1880–1919, together with the shrewd manipulation of Anglo-Russian rivalries, permitted the Afghans to consolidate their rule where it was most vulnerable: in the west and in the north, the one area a target for Persian irridentism, the other a potential target for Russian political and economic expansion. Throughout this 39-year period, the Afghan rulers firmly resisted British pressures for diplomatic and military representation, economic concessions, and the extension of rail and telegraph lines into Afghan territory. At the same time, they incorporated Kafiristan, thus preventing that region from becoming a center of Christian missionary work, which in the Afghan view would inevitably be followed by economic and political penetration.

The Afghans paid dearly for their political independence and sovereignty, however. Two Anglo-Afghan wars were fought, control of the country's foreign relations was sacrificed, and the Durand Line was reluctantly accepted. Beyond that, though isolationism was a successful weapon against European political domination and economic exploitation, it was highly detrimental to the socioeconomic development of the country, which was isolated culturally as well as politically and economically.

The task of maintaining Afghan ethnic and Durrani dynastic rule over an ethnically and religiously heterogeneous Afghanistan, with its entrenched and strong tribal structure, was not easy. Like Japan and the Ottoman Empire, Afghanistan undertook what Cyril Black has termed a "defensive modernization,"[59] at first against the Persians, the Bukharans, and the Sikhs, then against the British and the Russians. At the same time and equally important, modernization became a political and economic instrument, a tool to unify the country politically, to consolidate the dynasty's power, to lessen the monarchy's dependence on the tribes, and to achieve a degree of military and economic self-sufficiency. In adopting a limited and eclectic modernization program, then, the Afghan monarchy was primarily concerned with military preparedness. A well-armed, modern standing army was regarded as the key to political stability and political power. Economic development was simply a subsidiary benefit of the effort to meet military exigencies. In this context, the Afghan rulers from 1880 on used their power and the offices of the state to usher in limited socio-economic reforms, largely borrowed from the West. To achieve its aims without antagonizing the powerful Muslim religious establishment or alienating the powerful Afghan tribes (whose military strength was still needed for defense and for the preservation of Afghan ethnic rule), the monarchy adopted a policy of guided, limited, and gradual modernization. This policy was wedded to the monarchy's policy of isolationism: the Afghan rulers refused to open the country to foreign capital, to grant most-favored-nation clauses to any power, to allow the extension of British or Russian railways or telegraph lines into Afghanistan. In this they followed the guidelines for modernization laid down by Amir Abdur Rahman Khan, believing, with him, that as long as Afghanistan was not militarily power-ful, the removal of natural barriers would rob the country of its strategic advantages and upset the delicate balance of power so necessary to the continued independence of the kingdom. Pandora's box, once opened, would bring disaster to Afghanistan.

During Abdur Rahman's rule, the legitimacy of reforms and of the cen-tralization of power depended solely on the ruler's personal authority; he used the Afghan religious establishment in an effort to achieve that legitimacy. Under Amir Habibullah, however, a handful of Afghan mod-ernists formulated an ideology of nationalism and modernism that gave the throne historic legitimacy, but at the same time sought to give a larger role to an educated elite in determining the future course of the Afghan nation. In it, the monarch was conceived to be the historical representative of a nation-state, rather than the institutional embodiment of political power. The legitimacy of political power and of socioeconomic reform (which was aimed ultimately at modernization) derived from the mandate of a nation and its people, held in trust by the ruler. The Afghan monarchy was now seen as a national rather than a feudal institution; in theory at least, the Afghans were citizens, not subjects. The modernists attempted to provide a rationale for the "backwardness" of the Afghans and to pro-mote development as national self-realization: through economic advance and a cultural-political renaissance, the Afghans were to achieve a new place of dignity and equality in a fast-changing world.

Under Amanullah, the political elite (made up of the ruling oligarchy, educated members of the landed and tribal aristocracy, and a few im-portant merchants), together with the modernist-nationalists, sparked na-tionalism in Afghanistan into what Rupert Emerson has termed a "positive and creative response," a "new dynamism" that began "to insist on taking control of its destiny into its own hands."[60] Whereas the main goal of the monarchy under Abdur Rahman and Habibullah was to organize the country's military power and achieve political unification and stability, under Amanullah the Afghan political elite sought to end the country's isolationism and dependence, and to expand the goal from limited military and technological acquisitions to a fundamental transformation of economic and political institutions. Essentially, Afghan nationalism followed the patterns of development outlined by Emerson and others. That is, the ideology of nationalism was used to further social mobilization, rationalization, secularization, politicization of the masses, attainment of independence, consolidation of territory, and economic and cultural integration; to hasten modernization; and to give priorities and direction to the process of social change.[61] Moreover, Afghan nationalism, by adopting the defense and welfare of the fatherland as its major platform (and in the case of Pan-Islamism, a form of proto-nationalism, stressing not only the unity of the Muslims but the reformation and defense of the Islamic world as well), managed to circumvent the opposition of the Afghan religious establishment to European technology and institutions. Though nationalism was used by the political elite to sustain its entrenched position, it also served as the means for a redefinition of the relationship between Islam and society and as the rationale for the secularization and expansion of the Afghan educational system, the introduction of various reforms, and the concentration of political power, including the administration of justice.

Initially, Amanullah abandoned the traditional policy of isolationism in favor of active Pan-Islamism. After 1922, however, he adopted a policy of "positive neutralism," a posture that recognized the national aspirations of various Muslim and non-Muslim Afro-Asian peoples but required correct relations with Afghanistan's powerful neighbors, British India and the USSR. His neutralist policy was dictated by his desire to avoid jeopardizing the country's newly won political independence while she worked out her economic problems undisturbed. Since Afghanistan, a landlocked and underdeveloped country, had to rely on foreign imports for a substantial portion of the raw materials and practically all of the machinery needed for development projects—and most of its essential consumer goods as well—Amanullah's lofty developmental plans were largely dependent on the goodwill of his neighbors. Neutrality and internationalism were thus regarded as necessary to the successful modernization and continued independence of Afghanistan. However, though Amanullah broke with tradition in attempting to obtain international credits and foreign assistance for the modernization of his kingdom, he followed his predecessors in refusing to grant financial and commercial concessions to foreign powers and companies. The granting of capitulations, with the possible consequence of foreign economic and political domination, was not considered a necessary price for modernization.

The Afghan reformist and nationalist movement was similar to those of Persia, the Ottoman Empire, Ethiopia, and Siam, in that the decisive breaks with the past were led by the traditional leadership itself.[62] In a country in which tribalism, traditionalism, and regionalism combined to perpetuate illiteracy and inertia, hindering the development of a solid middle class or other national entity capable of forcing change, foreign policy considerations and vested economic interests led the Afghan dynastic elite to become the vehicle of guided socioeconomic reform. In this the Afghan rulers came to enjoy an alliance with a small group of nationalist-modernist writers and intellectuals. These men saw in the Afghan monarchy and the state apparatus the only effective agencies for reform and modernization, and hoped either to become part of the ruling oligarchy and guide the process of reform and modernization themselves or to influence the ruling elite's decisions to their own persuasion.[63]

The revolt of the traditionalist-reactionary forces in 1929 and the bloody civil war that ensued demonstrated to the nationalist-modernists how precarious reforms and modernization were without the active support of the ruler and the power of the Afghan state. The shadow of reaction and the potential threat to Afghan independence obliged the Afghan nationalists and modernists to seek an alliance with the new Musahiban dynasty. The lesson the modernist-nationalists drew from the triumph of traditionalism in 1929 was that reform and modernization in Afghanistan had to be gradual. However, World War II was to teach them another, and contradictory, lesson: that rapid reform and modernization were necessary, if the ruling dynasty and the elite were to preserve their rule and Afghan independence and at the same time solve the country's staggering socioeconomic problems. Moreover, the war destroyed the ruling elite's naive dream of modernizing the country with the help of distant and politically disinterested industrial powers. It was finally brought home to the landlocked Afghans that they were dependent on their neighbors, and that the success of their programs was impossible without the support and help of the USSR and the British in India.

Although reform and modernization in Afghanistan has been a jerky, uneven, and frequently interrupted process, we have seen important and fundamental changes in the period under study. Among the most significant were the increased centralization of power, the emergence of the state as a national institution, the differentiation and specialization of political institutions, the weakening or transformation of traditional sources of authority, the addition of the army as a new national institution, and the development of nationalism as a force working for socioeconomic reform. In this period, the state assumed new responsibilities; education, public health, roads and communications, the national economy—all came to be considered properly within the sphere of the state's activities. Though motivated by the monarchy's desire to legitimize its rule, constitutions and legal codes were promulgated that followed the form, if not the practice, of European parliamentary systems, and that guaranteed, in theory at least, the individual and participatory rights of Afghan citizens. The Afghan constitutions marked "the decline of traditional legitimation of the rulers with reference to powers outside their own society (God, reason) and . . . the establishment of some sort of ideological or institutional accountability of the rulers to the ruled, who are alleged to be the holders of the potential political power."[64]

This period witnessed the establishment of modern schools, a slow interaction of European and Afghan cultures, and the secularization and rationalization of education and thought, accompanied by an increasing rejection of the providential interpretation of historic events in favor of a rational interpretation, based on physical and psychological forces. In the realm of health, it saw a growing concern for public health and a rejection of the notion that disease was natural to the human condition, but instead was subject to preventive or curative control. Perhaps most dramatic of all was the development of the monarchy's role in the stimulation and direction of the national economy. Initially interested primarily in improving the royal army, the Afghan monarchy eventually assumed responsibility for the health of the country's economy, and by introducing industries, encouraging the development of a modern banking system, and promoting the formation of joint-stock companies, contributed significantly to the growth of a vigorous entrepreneurial and middle class, which ushered modern capitalism into Afghanistan.

Still, the Afghan reform and modernization programs were weak in many respects. The monarchy, ever fearful of disturbing vested tribal-feudal interests and alienating the religious establishment, attempted to fit modern technology and institutions into existing feudal arrangements, without upsetting their foundations. Furthermore, the reforms were confined to the urban centers, which were intended to serve as models and as sources of power, wealth, and prestige. Consequently, the agricultural system of the kingdom remained virtually untouched, and reform and modernization came to be regarded as strictly urban processes. Moreover, despite a degree of social ferment in the wake of the efforts of the political elite and the intelligentsia to effect some reform, the process of social integration was slow. In 1946 upward social mobility was still to be achieved only in the educational system, the army, and the small bureaucracy, and horizontal mobility was still inhibited by traditional values and loyalties, especially family, clan, and tribal loyalties.

The position of the Afghan monarchy at the end of World War II is perhaps best described in the words of Huntington, who observed that "power which is sufficiently concentrated to promote reform may be too concentrated to assimilate the social forces released by it."[65] The monarchy, autocratic under Abdur Rahman and Habibullah, oligarchic under Amanullah and the Musahibans, was capable of providing avenues of individual mobility for the intelligent and the talented. It remained, however, basically traditionalist and incapable of creating new institutions to accelerate the processes of cultural integration, social mobility, and group participation in the political and economic life of the kingdom. Having successfully completed the first phase of modernization, the achievement of modern statehood, and well into the second, guided and planned economic growth and industrialization, the Afghan ruling elite has, since 1946, been trying to cope with this very problem, to lead Afghanistan into a third phase of modernization, one of social and political integration.

Appendixes

Afghan Currencies

In writing about the economy of Afghanistan in the nineteenth century, one is faced with enormous difficulties. Not only were different monetary units in use in Bukhara, Khiva, Persia, Afghanistan, and India, but the currencies and their values differed within each country as well. The fluctuating exchange rate of these currencies in relation to the British pound and the Russian ruble adds to the difficulties.

Before 1835 the prevalent monetary units in use in India and their average rate of exchange were:

mohur (Bengal) = £1/13/6¾
mohur (Bombay) = £1/10/1¼
rupee (Bombay and Madras) = £1/9/2½
star pagoda of Madras = 4s/¾d
East India Company rupee = 1s/10¼d

By acts of 1835 and 1870, the British administration created a uniform currency for all of British India. Under this system the Madras (silver) rupee became the basic Indian monetary unit, with 16 *annas* to the rupee and 12 *pies* to the *anna*. There were one hundred thousand rupees to a *lakh* (*lak* or *lac*), ten million to a *crore*. Until 1873 one rupee equaled about two shillings. Sixteen rupees, or one gold *mohur*, had a value of £1/12. Because of a world monetary crisis (and a depreciation of silver after 1873), the gold value of the rupee dropped, reaching at one point a low of one shilling. For the next two decades, its value fluctuated; by 1893 it was worth 1s/4d (against 2s/3d in 1870). In 1893 the gold standard was introduced and the rupee was pegged at 15 to the pound sterling; its value then became stabilized at between 1s/2½d and 1s/4d. In the years 1893–1914, then, three rupees were equivalent to two pre-1873 rupees, with 1,000 rupees equivalent to £67 against a value of £100 in 1873. The rupee reached its highest exchange rate in 1920, when it was worth 2s/8d. After that it declined; between 1927 and 1939 it had a value of 1s/6d (U.S. $.30).

In Persia the basic monetary unit was the *toman* (*touman* or *tuman*), which was subdivided into *krans* (*qrans*), *shahis*, and *puls*. There were ten *krans* in a *toman*, 20 *shahis* in a *kran*, and two *puls* in a *shahi*. Four *shahis* were called an *abbasi*. The silver content of the *kran* varied; at times it contained as much as 88 grains of silver, at others as little as 71. Its price fluctuated accordingly. In 1871–72 the *kran* was worth between 9½ and 11½ pence, with about 20 *krans* to the British pound. Between 1874 and 1893, the *kran* declined in value, dropping from 25 to a pound in 1874 to 34 in 1888, and to 42 in 1893. By 1894 the *kran* was worth only 6⅓d.

The monetary units of Bukhara and Khiva were the *tanga* (a silver coin) and the *tilla* (a gold coin), both widely used in northern Afghanistan. Their value also fluctuated, not only because of the rise and fall of the price of silver but also because of Russian expansion in the region. Eight to nine *tangas* were equal to one *tilla*. In the 1870's the *tilla* was worth 10s. (The Russian ruble at the time was worth 2s/9d.) In the 1880's and the 1890's, there were five to six *tangas* to the ruble.

In the nineteenth century, the Kabuli rupee was subdivided as follows:

10 *dinnars* = 1 *paisa*
5 *paisas* = 1 *shahi* (copper)
2 *shahis* = 1 *sannar* (*saddinar* or *misqali*, silver)
2 *sannars* = 1 *abbasi* or *tanga*
1½ *abbasis* = 1 *kran*
2 *krans* = 1 rupee
2½ rupees = 1 *nim sanad*
5 rupees = 1 *sanad*
20 rupees = 1 *toman*

The Kabuli rupee, which was worth 1s/1d in the 1870's, declined in value in the years 1890–1914, when it was worth only 5d. It then climbed in value to 8d in the period 1914–19.

The Kabuli rupee was not the only currency in circulation. In Kandahar Province the Kandahari rupee was the prevalent monetary unit until Amanullah's administration. Its units were:

6 *puls* = 1 *shahi*
26 *shahis* = 1 *kran*
2 *krans* = 1 rupee

The Kandahari rupee's rate of exchange also fluctuated. In the 1860's it was worth about 1s, in the 1870's 1s/8d.

Two other currencies in use in nineteenth-century Afghanistan were the *bajoglee* and the Tabrizi rupee. The *bajoglee* (the Belgian ducat) was the dominant currency in Herat in the 1840's. It was worth two Herati *tomans* (or 40 Herati rupees, with three rupees equaling one East India Company rupee). The Tabrizi (*kham, khawa*) rupee was used in both eastern and western Afghanistan in the middle of the nineteenth century. There were 20 rupees in a Tabrizi *toman* (just under 15 East India Company rupees).

The Kabuli rupee gained ground from 1890 on, but in 1927 it was abandoned for a new monetary unit, the *afghani*. The new currency was subdivided into *puls* and *krans*.

> 50 *puls* = 1 *kran*
> 2 *krans* = 1 *afghani*
> 20 *afghanis* = 1 gold *tilla*

The old Kabuli rupee was worth 91 *puls* (11 Kabuli rupees = 10 *afghanis*).

In 1936 the exchange rate was 3.65 *afghanis* to the Indian rupee, 35.22 *afghanis* to the U.S. dollar. During World War II the official rate of exchange was 13 *afghanis* to the U.S. dollar.

Here are some figures that may provide a useful basis for comparison with the figures on Afghan trade and revenues I have used in the text. In 1872–73 the total revenue of the United Kingdom (Great Britain and Ireland) was £76,608,770. India's revenue at the time was £48,286,400, her exports worth £64,661,940. The United Kingdom's budget for 1892 was £90,430,000.

In 1908 common laborers in the major towns of Afghanistan earned about 100 *dinnars* (about 4½d) a day, plus food. In Kandahar, the average was three *shahis*, twelve *dinnars* (6½d–7d). At this time, flour cost about 2d a pound.

This information is based chiefly on *Statesman's Yearbook* for the years 1874–1919 and 1927; India, *Imperial Gazetteer*, IV, Chap. 16, and V, pp. 54, 61–62; G. H. MacGregor, "Valley of Jalalabad," p. 880; White-King, pp. 324–27; Ferrier, *Caravan Journey*, p. 121n; Marsh, pp. 30, 46, 86, 109; Vambery, *Travels*, p. 268; Mitford, pp. 91, 93; Lal, *Dost Mohammed*, I, 236, 241–42; Hyder Khan, Part 2, p. 99; Lumsden and Elsmie, p. 156; A. Conolly, II, 9; Thomas Gordon, *A Varied Life*, p. 100; Angus Hamilton, *Afghanistan* (London, 1906 ed.), p. 307; Furon, *L'Afghanistan*, p. 61; I. A. Shah, *Modern Afghanistan*, p. 339; Caspani and Cagnacci, p. 36; U. N. Sarkar, p. 61; Franz Pick, *Pick's Currency Yearbook: 1955* (New York, 1955), p. 19; René Sedillot, *Toutes les monnaies du monde: dictionnaire des changes* (Paris, 1955), pp. 15, 452, 456–57; Baudet, "La philatélie," p. 12; and Nowrozjee Furdoonjee, "Report on the Weights, Measures and Coins of Cabul and Bukhara," *JASB*, October 1838.

Unless otherwise specified, the figures used in the text are in Indian rupees, sometimes bracketed with the equivalent value in British pounds.

Afghan Weights and Measures

Throughout the nineteenth century, there were a variety of weights and measures in use in Afghanistan. The Afghan units varied widely from region to region, as did those of India and Persia, which were widely used in Afghanistan. The prevalent unit of weight in northern India was the *maund* (about 82 lbs.), which consisted of 40 *seers*. The common unit of land measure in India was the *bigha* (generally about five-eighths of an acre in northern India).

In Kabul and Jalalabad, the basic unit of weight was a *nukhut* (*nokhud, nakhud*), or the size of a pea:

24 *nukhuts* = 1 *misqal*

6 *misqals* = 1 *pukhtah bar* = approx. 1 oz.

4 *pukhtah bars* = 1 *khurd*

4 *khurds* = 1 *pao* (*pow*)

4 *paos* = 1 *charak*

4 *charaks* = 1 *seer* (*ser*) = approx. 16.3 lbs

8 *seers* = 1 *man*

10 *mans* = 1 *kharwar*

In Kandahar and Herat:

2 *misqals* = 1 *seer* = approx. .21 lb.

40 *seers* = 1 Kandahari *man* = approx. 8.5 lbs.

100 *mans* = 1 Kandahari *kharwar*

1 Herati *man* = approx. 7 lbs.

In northern Afghanistan, Mazar-i-Sharif weights were in general use:

1 Mazari *seer* = 1.75 Kabuli *seers* = approx. 28.5 lbs.

15 Mazari *seers* = 1 Mazari *man*

3 Mazari *mans* = 1 Mazari *kharwar*

Persian weight units were used extensively in the western regions of Afghanistan. The basic units in Persia were also the *misqal* and the *man*. However, the Persian *man* varied from region to region throughout the nineteenth century. The main Persian unit in use in western Afghanistan was the Tabrizi *man*:

256 *misqals* = 1 *charak*

2.5 *charaks* = 6 *abbasis* = 1 Tabrizi *man*

100 Tabrizi *mans* = 1 Tabrizi *kharwar* = approx. 649 lbs.

The *gaz* (*guz*) was the standard unit for linear measurement in Afghanistan, India, and Persia. The Bengali *gaz*, which was in common use in India, measured 38 inches. In Afghanistan the most widely used unit was the Kandahari *gaz*, which varied according to use. The *gaz-e shahi* (1.066 meters or approximately 42 inches) was used in the measurement of goods and lumber; the *gaz-e rayati* (.737 meter or about 29 inches) was a land measure.

The usual large unit of land measure was the *jarib* or the *tanab*. One *jarib* = 3,600 sq. *gaz-e rayati* (or *gaz-e jarib*) = about half an acre. In Kabul the *jarib* was equal to about 1,918 sq. meters. In Herat the land was also measured by *jarib*, but there the *gaz* equaled about a yard. Larger parcels of land were measured in *zauj*. In some regions the *zauj* was the equivalent of 80 *jaribs*, in others the equivalent of 100 or more.

In northern Afghanistan the basic unit of linear measure was the *kadam* (pace).

1 *tasu* = approx. 1.75 inches

16 *tasus* = 1 *kadam* = approx. 28 inches

12,000 *kadams* = 1 *sang* (*farsakh*) = approx. 5.5 miles

The *farsakh* (also called *kos*, *farsang*, *karoh*, or *kuruh*) was used throughout Afghanistan, but represented widely varying distances. Generally, it was the equivalent of about four miles, but in Sistan it was about six miles, in northern Afghanistan, as noted, about five and a half miles, and in other places slightly under two miles. Other common land measures were the *biswasah* (9 sq. *gaz-e rayati*) and the *biswah* (20 *biswasah*). Twenty *biswahs* equaled 3,600 sq. *gaz* or a little more than 2,417 sq. yds. Still other measures were the *kulach* (about 6 ft.) and the *kulba* (a less precise unit consisting of some 40 *jaribs*). The standard cubic measure was also called the *gaz-e shahi*.

In addition to these measures, some Persian units were used in western Afghanistan. The most common were the Persian *gaz* or *zar* (40.95 inches) and the Tabrizi (or Azerbaijani) *gaz* (44.09 inches). There were 6,000 *gaz* in both the Persian *farsakh* (3.88 miles) and the Azerbaijani *farsakh* (4.18 miles).

My information on Afghan weights and measures is based chiefly on *Statesman's Yearbook* for 1874, pp. 675, 695; 1894, p. 817; 1928, pp. 645–

46; 1934, p. 656; 1935, p. 660; and 1939, p. 685; India, *Imperial Gazetteer*, I and V; Bogdanov, "Afghan Weights"; G. H. MacGregor, "Valley of Jalalabad," p. 880; A. Conolly, II, 7; Angus Hamilton, *Afghanistan* (London, 1906 ed.), pp. 306–7; F. A. Martin, p. 245; Jewett, *An American Engineer*, p. 28; I. A. Shah, *Modern Afghanistan*, p. 339; Caspani and Cagnacci, pp. 37–38; and Nowrozjee Furdoonjee, "Report on the Weights, Measures and Coins of Cabul and Bukhara," *JASB*, October 1838.

Notes

Notes

Complete authors' names, titles, and publication data are given in the Bibliography, pp. 503–69. Abbreviations used in these notes and in the Bibliography are:

BSE	Bolshaia Sovetskaia Entsiklopediia
BSOAS	Bulletin of the School of Oriental and African Studies
CAR	Central Asian Review
EB	Encyclopaedia Britannica
EI	Encyclopedia of Islam
GLE	Grand Larousse Encyclopédique
IHRC	Indian Historical Records Commission Proceedings
JASB	Journal of the Asiatic Society of Bengal
JCAS	Journal of the Central Asian Society
JRCAS	Journal of the Royal Central Asian Society
JWH	Journal of World History
KSIV	Kratkie Soobscheniya Instituta Vostokovedeniia
KSINA	Kratkie Soobscheniya Instituta Narodov Azii
MEJ	Middle East Journal
MES	Middle Eastern Studies
MH	Majalle-ye Herat
RMM	Revue du Monde Musulman
SA	Siraj al-Akhbar
SV	Sovetskoe Vostokovedenie
TDPMKV	Trudy dvatsat piatogo Mezhdunarodnogo Kongressa vostokovedov

INTRODUCTION

1. See, respectively, Price, "Present Situation," p. 103; and Fletcher, *Afghanistan,* p. vi.

2. See Toynbee, *World and the West,* especially the chapter on "Islam and the West"; Cooke; Fairbank, pp. 381–406; and Sinai, pp. 206–50.

3. Emerson, pp. 8, 12; and Boeke.

4. See, respectively, Kohn, *Nationalism in the East,* pp. 7, 15; Bonné, *State and Economics,* p. ix; Maunier, I, 90, 96.

5. See Lerner, 1964 ed., pp. vii–ix; Fougeyrollas, p. 7; and Deutsch, "Social Mobilization," pp. 494–95, and *Nationalism,* pp. 100ff.

6. Almond and Coleman, p. 53 and *passim;* Ward and Rustow, pp. 3–4; Fougeyrollas, pp. 8–9; Jansen, *Japanese Attitudes,* pp. 19, 27; C. Black, *Dynamics of Modernization,* pp. 5–8; Thompson and Reischauer, p. v; Eisenstadt, *Modernization,* p. 1; Richard Lowenthal, "The Points of the Compass," in John H. Kautsky, ed., *Political Change in Underdeveloped Countries: Nationalism and Communism,* 4th ed. (New York, 1965), pp. 341–42.

7. On the shortcomings of the term Westernization, see Rustow, pp. 4–6; C. Black, *Dynamics of Modernization,* pp. 6, 54, and *Russian Society,* p. 8; H. Gibb, "Social Change"; and Janowitz, p. 25.

8. Benjamin Schwartz; cited in Jansen, "Modernization of Japan," p. 3.

9. This characterization of the process of modernization is based on Halpern, *Politics of Social Change,* pp. 35–36; Jansen, *Japanese Attitudes,* pp. 19, 27, and "Modernization of Japan," pp. 3–5; Ward and Rustow, pp. 3–4; Almond and Coleman, pp. 387–89; Hitti, pp. 86, 89, 93, 99; Shils, pp. 379–411; Biggerstaff, "Modernization," pp. 607–18; Frey, "Political Development," pp. 298–305, and *Turkish Elite,* pp. 406–19; Eisenstadt, *Modernization,* pp. 2–8; C. Black, *Dynamics of Modernization,* pp. 6–8, 14–15, 67–68; Fougeyrollas, pp. 8–12 *passim,* 18; Shinomura, pp. 8–9; Kishimoto, pp. 871–74; W. R. Polk, "The Nature of Modernization," *Foreign Affairs,* October 1965, pp. 100–110; Burkes; and Micaud, pp. ix–x.

10. The only attempts to assess the character of the new Afghan social structure and the makeup of its elite are Poulada's "Problems of Social Development in Afghanistan" and Eberhard's "Afghanistan's Young Elite." Serious post–World War II anthropological studies have dealt mainly with the Hazaras and the Mongols, e.g., the works of Bacon and Schurmann. Such scholarly studies as Rustow, "The Politics of the Near East," in Almond and Coleman, eds., *The Politics of the Developing Areas,* and Halpern, *The Politics of Social Change,* make only passing references to Afghanistan, and Haddad's work on the military in the Middle East gives a very general and unsatisfactory treatment of the role of the Afghan military establishment. Well-known studies on Islam and modernism—for example, *Whither Islam?* and *Modern Trends in Islam* by H. A. R. Gibb; *Islam in Modern History* by W. C. Smith; *Near Eastern Culture and Society* by Young; *Islam and the West* by Frye; *Unity and Variety in Islamic Civilization* by von Grunebaum; *The Middle East in Transition* by Laqueur—and even the current second edition of the *Encyclopedia of Islam* do not discuss the Afghan nationalist and modernist movements or the ideologues and ideologies of these movements.

11. Mohammed Ali, *New Guide to Afghanistan,* p. 2.

12. See, for instance, Kohzad, "Les manuscrits"; and Beaurecueil.

13. For some important publications of Afghan historians and the Afghan Historical Society, see Ghubar, *Ahmed Shah;* Benawa, *Hotakiha;* Fofalzai, *Timur* and *Dorrat-ul-Zaman;* Khafi; Kohzad, *Men and Events, Highlight,* and *Tarikh-e Afghanestan.* A particularly interesting primary source is *Vagheat-e Shah Shuja,* a work written jointly by Muhammed Hussein Herati and the Afghan monarch Shah Shuja.

14. Reshtiya, *Afghanestan.*

15. For a bibliography of Russian works on Afghanistan, see Kukhtina, *Bibliografiia,* and Central Asian Research Centre, *Russian Works on Afghanistan.* For the works and achievements of Soviet historiography pertaining to Afghans and Afghanistan, see Romodin; and Dianous, "La contribution récente." On the Soviet studies on Turkic ethnic groups in Afghanistan, see Löewenthal, *Turkic Languages.*

16. The number and scope of the post-1940 non-Soviet studies on Afghanistan, both European and American, are limited. The historical and descriptive studies include: P. Sykes, *History of Afghanistan,* a detailed political account of the region from antiquity to World War II; Fraser-Tytler, *Afghanistan,* also political and diplomatic in its emphasis; Clifford, *The Land and People of Afghanistan*; Fletcher, *Afghanistan, Highway of Conquest*; Klimburg, *Afghanistan*; Griffiths, *Afghanistan,* which, like the works of Clifford and Fletcher just cited, is a general survey dealing mostly with political history; Furon, *L'Iran, Perse et Afghanistan,* a very general historical survey; Caspani and Cagnacci, *Afghanistan,* the best descriptive survey in Italian on the geography, demography, and customs of Afghanistan; Humlum, *La géographie de l'Afghanistan,* the only comprehensive geographic account. Among the studies on Pathans, Spain's *The Pathan Borderland* and *The People of the Khyber* are good general surveys, and Caroe's *The Pathans* remains by far the best post–World War II scholarly work in English on the Pathan tribes; however, all three works are confined in their scope and do not deal with all of the Afghan tribes.

There are only six general surveys of contemporary Afghanistan: Cervinka, *Afghanistan*; Wilber, *Afghanistan*; Watkins, *Afghanistan, Land in Transition*; the latest economic surveys of Rhein and Ghaussy; and the works of Abawi and Resai. (The last three are in German.) Monographic studies dealing with various developmental phases of the Afghan economy are very few. Diplomatic history, dealing mainly with Anglo-Afghan and Anglo-Russian relations in the nineteenth century and with the Anglo-Afghan wars, has produced various good monographic studies, including those by Munawwar Khan, Singhal, Adamec, and Norris.

17. For a discussion of the problems facing the student of Middle Eastern history, see Sinor, *Orientalism*; H. Gibb, "Problems of Middle Eastern History," pp. 2–5, and "Problems of Modern Middle Eastern History"; Brunschvig, "Perspectives"; and Cahen, "Histoire de l'Orient musulman," pp. 93–115.

18. Davison, pp. 13–29.

19. C. Black, *Dynamics of Modernization,* p. 57.

CHAPTER ONE

1. For varying estimates of the area, see East and Spate, p. 183; *Statesman's Yearbook: 1966,* p. 789; *Britannica Book of the Year: 1965,* p. 104; U.N. *Statistical Yearbook: 1965,* p. 88; Humlum, p. 16; Stamp, p. 177. The highest estimates, ranging between 711,000 and 800,000 sq. km., are made in *GLE,* I, 131; *Collier's Encyclopedia 1959 Yearbook,* p. 26; Anjoman-e Aryana, p. 1; and Afghanistan, Press Department, *Afghanistan,* p. 5. Estimates of Afghanistan's population vary widely. Various sources give the following estimates: Furon,

L'Iran, p. 200, 7–9 million; Wilber, *Afghanistan,* 1st ed., p. 62, 8 million; Humlum, p. 95, 12 million; *Statesman's Yearbook: 1966,* p. 789, 13.8 million; *Britannica Book of the Year: 1965,* p. 104, 14.5 million; U.N. *Demographic Yearbook: 1964,* p. 124, 15.2 million.

2. On geopolitics and Afghanistan, see Humlum, pp. 13–14, 82–83; Wilber, *Afghanistan,* 2d ed., pp. 25–26; Fraser-Tytler, *Afghanistan,* pp. 3, 9, 13–14, 19; Roueck, pp. 14–17; Reshtiya, "Au point de vue géographique," pp. 16–22; Wilber, "Independent and Encircled," pp. 486–94; Michel, "Foreign Trade"; and P. Franck, "Economic Progress," pp. 43–59.

3. Broadfoot, p. 358.

4. Vavilov and Bukinich, p. 500; Pikulin, *Afganistan,* p. 69; Humlum, pp. 130, 165.

5. See U.N. *Economic Survey,* p. 57; *Stateman's Yearbook: 1966,* p. 791; *Oxford Economic Atlas,* Appendix, p. 3. There is no exact statistical breakdown of the urban-rural population. Afghan official sources have indicated that there are somewhere between 2 and 2.5 million nomads in Afghanistan (see, for example, Pazhwak, *Afghanistan,* p. 62; and *Statesman's Yearbook: 1966,* p. 789). According to Prince Peter of Greece, an estimated two-thirds of the population are "practically nomads" (see his "Post-War Developments in Afghanistan").

6. On the contributions of the Kushans, see V. Smith, *Oxford History,* 1920 ed., pp. 133–35; Grousset, *L'empire des steppes,* p. 69; Altheim, pp. 388–89; Tsukamoto, p. 551; J. Marshall, *Buddhist Art,* p. 112. For various distinctive features of the Gandharan school, see J. Marshall, *Taxila;* Foucher's in certain respects exhaustive study *L'art gréco-bouddhique;* Godard *et al.;* and Deyder.

7. Arnold and Guillaume, p. 79.

8. Schacht, "Islam," p. 341.

9. Lopez, pp. 594–622; Goitein, "Near Eastern Bourgeoisie," pp. 597ff.

10. On the role of Islam as transmitter and molder of various cultural heritages of the region, see Barthold, *La découverte,* p. 50; W. M. Watt, *Islam and Integration,* pp. 191–99, 228–35, and *Islamic Philosophy,* pp. 37–48; H. Gibb, "An Interpretation," p. 97; Wiet, pp. 63ff; Spuler, "Iran," pp. 171–79; Schacht, "Islam," p. 341; and particularly Dubler, pp. 47–75.

11. Browne, *A Literary History,* I, 347–49, 353–54; Buchner, pp. 121–24. On the advanced administrative techniques and contributions of the Samanids, see Bosworth, *The Ghaznawids,* pp. 27–34.

12. Bosworth, "Development of Persian Culture," pp. 35, 39.

13. Chorpa, p. 371; Spuler, "Ghaznawids"; and Longworth-Dames, "Ghaznāwids." On the use of the Afghan tribesmen by the Ghaznawids, see al-Utbī, in Elliot and Dawson, pp. 20–33; Bosworth, *The Ghaznawids,* p. 114; Caroe, *Pathans,* p. 120; and M. Prasad, pp. 84, 85, 93, 110, 134. For the administrative system of the Ghaznawids, see Nazim, pp. 126–50; and Bosworth, *The Ghaznawids,* pp. 48–97.

14. Cahen, "L'évolution de l'*iqta.*"

15. The historian Imad-ad-Din, writing on the Seljuk period, stated that allowing the feudal lords to retain large amounts of royal revenues was the only way to interest the turbulent Turkish tribesmen and soldiers in the prosperity

of agriculture and the attractions of the sedentary life (cited by B. Lewis, *The Arabs*, p. 148).

16. Bosworth, *The Ghaznawids*, pp. 86–89, 259–61. On the eve of the Mongol invasion, the term dihqān had taken on the meaning of "peasant" (see Lambton, *Landlord and Peasant*, pp. xxiv, xxvi).

17. Caroe, *Pathans*, pp. 125–33; Brockelmann, pp. 241–42. On the Ghurid dynasty, see Defrémery, "Histoire des Ghourides," pp. 167–200, 258–91; and Juzjānī.

18. Ibn'l Athir, *Chronicle*, Cairo ed., IX, 128; cited in Browne, *A Literary History*, II, 105. For measures the Ghaznawids took to uphold orthodoxy, see also Brockelmann, p. 170; M. Prasad, p. 115; Minorsky, "Iran," p. 187; and W. Watt, *Islamic Philosophy*, pp. 91–92. On the persecution of "Shi'ah heretics," see al-Utbī, pp. 24, 27.

19. Minorsky, "Iran," p. 187; Cahen, "Body Politic," pp. 152–53. On the attempts and measures of the Seljuk sultans to stamp out heresy and foster religious orthodoxy, see Nizām ul-Mūlk, Chap. 8, p. 84; Lane-Poole, *Muhammedan Dynasties*, p. 149; Browne, *A Literary History*, II, 168.

20. B. Lewis, "Significance of Heresy," p. 62. See also Lambton's excellent study, "Quis Custodiet Custodes," Part 1, pp. 125–48, and Part 2, pp. 125–46.

21. See W. Watt, *Islam*, pp. 236, 238–51, and *Islamic Philosophy*, pp. 151–52. Watt illustrates this cleavage by citing al-Ghāzāli, who maintained that ordinary men should not be allowed to engage in or hear theological discussions, since such discussions could result in misunderstandings and thus weaken the belief of the masses in the orthodox doctrines of Islam (*Islam*, p. 244). According to B. Lewis, Ibn Taymiyya (d. 1328), too, preferred a "quarantining of suspect groups and individuals, followed where necessary by admonition and even coercive action" ("Significance of Heresy," p. 53).

22. Grunebaum, *Medieval Islam*, pp. 143, 169, and *Unity and Variety*, p. 154. See also H. Gibb, *Islamic Society*, p. 31. Instances of such intellectual compromises can be found in the writings of Ibn Jāmāa (d. 1333), who wrote: "The sovereign has a right to govern until another stronger shall oust him from power and rule in his stead.... A government, however objectionable, is better than none at all." (Quoted by Lambton, "The Unrighteous Ruler," p. 62.) Similar views were expressed by al-Ghāzāli (II, 124). For an exposition of his views, see Lambton, "Theory of Kingship," pp. 47–55.

23. Khadduri, *Islamic Jurisprudence*, p. 44. See also his *War and Peace*, p. 16.

24. Ibn Khaldūn, III, 246–58; H. Gibb, "Constitutional Organization," p. 13.

25. D'Ohsson, I, 387.

26. For the Mongol destructions in Afghanistan, see Juvainī, I, 131–33, 135; Nessawī, pp. 138–41; D'Ohsson, I, 350–51; Barthold, *Turkestan*, pp. 444, 446–49, 459–60; and Grousset, *L'empire mongol*, pp. 239–46.

27. Juvainī, I, 97. Barthold (*Four Studies*, I, 304) estimates that Genghis Khan killed approximately four-fifths of the urban population of the regions he conquered.

28. Ba'hadour Khan, p. 104.

29. See Grousset, *L'empire des steppes*, p. 316; Power, pp. 107, 127, 155; Howorth, I, 11; Minorsky, "Iran," p. 191. According to Barckhausen (pp. 93–

94), the religious tolerance of the Mongols was most likely the result of indifference.

30. Ibn Battuta, Introduction, p. 16.

31. Barthold, *Histoire des Turcs*, p. 151, and *Four Studies*, I, 55. For the writers of the Mongol period, see Browne, *A Literary History*, II, 467–88. For Mongol patronage of poets and scholars, see *ibid.*, III, 43–44.

32. Grousset, *L'empire des steppes*, p. 305; Barthold, *Four Studies*, I, 49, 55; Minorsky, "Iran," p. 191. On the state of agriculture and agrarian relations following the Mongol invasion and rule, see Belenitskii, "Les Mongols," pp. 614ff, and "K voprosu o sotsialnikh otnosheniiakh," pp. 111–28; Petrushevskii; and Yakubovskii.

33. Barthold, *Four Studies*, I, 50, and *Histoire des Turcs*, pp. 151–52, 160. Khan Baraq ordered his own fiefs—Samarkand and Bukhara—plundered, in order to raise funds for his new army (see D'Ohsson, III, 436).

34. Ibn Battuta, pp. 178–80.

35. Yazdi, I, 360, 368–69, 379; II, 8–16.

36. For details on the Timurid cultural renaissance, see Bouvat, "Essai," pp. 193–299; J. Aubin, pp. 71–88; E. J. W. Gibb, II, 10–11, 29–31; and Barthold, *Four Studies*, I, 63. On the observatory, which was founded by Ulugh Beg, see Barthold, *Four Studies*, II, 43–177.

37. Arberry, *Legacy of Persia*, pp. 137–39; Skrine and Ross, p. 180; P. Sykes, *History of Afghanistan*, I, 272–73.

38. See Grunebaum, "Studies," pp. 16–18, 20–21, and "Arabic Literature," pp. 63–65; see also Brunschvig and Grunebaum.

39. As Barthold notes, "His [Ulugh Beg's] only pupil left Samarkand and died in Constantinople" (*Four Studies*, II, 133–34, and *Histoire des Turcs*, p. 185).

40. Bābur, I, 126, 200, 229–40.

41. Barthold, *Istoriia Kulturnoi*, pp. 67, 79, 96–97, 100, 103, 107, 110, and *Four Studies*, II, 65.

42. H. Gibb, "An Interpretation," p. 60. According to Saunders (p. 716), "The atrophy of Muslim civilization in the late Middle Ages must be at least partly attributable [to] the breakup of its cultural and linguistic unity."

43. Vambery, *Sketches*, pp. 202–3.

44. B. Lewis, "Significance of Heresy," p. 61.

45. Erskine, pp. 319–20; Browne, *A Literary History*, IV, 63, 94–95. For a good discussion of Uzbek-Persian and Persian-Moghul struggles involving various regions of Afghanistan, and ensuing diplomatic moves and countermoves to form an Ottoman-Moghul-Uzbek united Sunni front against Persia, see A. Ahmad, *Studies*, pp. 30–40.

46. The Moghul Emperor Akbar's advisers had even issued a legal opinion that the *hajj* (pilgrimage to Mecca) was no longer binding on Indian Muslims, since the land route was controlled by the "heretical" Safawids and the sea route by the Christian Portuguese (see A. Ahmad, *Studies*, p. 30). Though the rise of the Safawids in Persia greatly reduced the volume and nature of the contacts of the Sunni Muslims of Central Asia and Afghanistan with Mecca and Medina, it did not stop those contacts altogether. Petty commerce and interchange were carried on via the Indian Ocean. See Gibb and Bowen, p. 302.

47. Saunders, p. 715; see also Barthold, *La découverte,* pp. 50, 129, and *Four Studies,* I, 65.

48. According to W. Watt (*Islam,* p. 34), the Islamic prohibition of usury retarded industrial development in Muslim countries during the last century, since it was interpreted as forbidding the formation of joint-stock companies. For a modern Muslim apologist interpretation of Islam's position toward banking and usury, see A. I. Qureshi, pp. xx–xxi.

49. In 1585, the Moghul Emperor Akbar ordered the construction of a road for wheeled traffic through the Khyber Pass in order to consolidate his rule over the Afghans (A. Ahmad, *Studies,* p. 31). However, the road does not seem to have been completed.

50. Chorpa, p. 373; Barthold, *La découverte,* p. 129.

51. Ferrier, *History,* p. 67. During the reign of Aurangzeb (1658–1707), Moghul subsidies to the tribes ran about 600,000 rupees annually. See Spain, *Pathan Borderland,* p. 32.

52. E. T. Tavernier, II, 140.

53. Schacht, "Mirāth," pp. 511–17, and "Shariā," pp. 673–78; Arin, pp. 277–318.

CHAPTER TWO

1. Percentage estimates for each ethnic group vary. *EI* (2d ed., I, 230) puts the figure for the Afghan ethnic group at 50–55 per cent of the total population, whereas other post-1940 Western and Soviet sources put it at 50 per cent or less. See, for example, P. Sykes, *Afghanistan,* I, 16; Furon, *L'Iran,* p. 201; *GLE,* I, 131; *BSE,* 2d ed., III, 496; Mamayev, p. 207; Bochkarev, p. 34; and Dvoriankov, p. 40. Afghan sources, however, raise the figure to some 60 per cent, probably in order to stress the Afghan character of the country (see Pazhwak, *Afghanistan,* p. 59; Roashan, p. 39; Ahmad and Abd-al-Aziz, p. 39), and some Western sources accept the Afghan estimate (see Wilber, *Afghanistan,* 1st ed., pp. 40, 62; Humlum, p. 95; *Britannica Book of the Year: 1965,* p. 104).

2. Schurmann, p. 40.

3. For a monographic study of Pashto, see Penzl, *A Grammar of Pashto.* For a differentiation between Pakhtu and Pashto, see Caroe, *Pathans,* p. xvi.

4. Caroe, *Pathans,* pp. xiv–xv.

5. There is no monographic study dealing with the origin and development of this theory. The main Afghan source for the Beni-Israel tradition is Nematullah, who relates the story of Jacob and Saul and writes of the migration of the Afghans to Ghor, their earliest known habitat. See al-Harāwī; for an abridged English version, see Dorn, *History of the Afghans,* Chap. 2, and his annotations in Part 2, pp. 59–65. For a genealogical account of the Afghans, see Shir Muhammed Khan. For English summaries of the legend of the Afghan descent from the Beni-Israel, see Elphinstone, pp. 155–57; C. Masson, *Narrative,* I, x; Lal, *Amir Dost Mohammed,* I, 408; Bellew, *Journal,* pp. 49–77; *The Jewish Encyclopedia,* pp. 223–24; Caroe, *Pathans,* pp. 3–5; and Holdich, "Afghan Claim" and "Beni-Israel."

6. Burnes, *Travels,* II, 141; Bellew, *Races,* pp. 23–24; Raverty, *Pukhto Grammar,* Introduction, p. 19n; and Holdich, "Beni-Israel," pp. 193–95. C.

Masson (*Narrative,* I, 81) reports an Afghan legend to the effect that Jesus Christ—"Hazrat Isa, our Saviour"—was an *"assil* or genuine Pathan." Elphinstone (p. 157) and Lal (*Amir Dost Mohammed,* I, 9ff) record two other legends pertaining to the origin of the Afghans: one legend holds that the Afghans were descended from a Caucasian tribe (either Armenian or Georgian); the other, that they were descended from Copts and Moghuls.

7. Among the writers who have advanced this explanation of the Afghan tradition are Darmesteter (*Chants populaires,* pp. clvi–clviii); Longworth-Dames ("Afghanistan," p. 50); P. Sykes (*Afghanistan,* I, 13); and Wilber (*Afghanistan,* 1st ed., p. 40). Elphinstone (pp. 152, 156n) and Malcolm (II, 596–97) were among the first to cast doubt on the Jewish origin of the Afghans on the basis of linguistics and genealogies. Later authorities who agreed with them include Dorn (Chrestomathy, p. ii); Darmesteter (*Chants populaires,* p. clvii); and Caroe (*Pathans,* p. 176).

8. *EI,* 2d ed., I, 223.

9. Cited in P. Sykes, *Afghanistan,* I, 54. See also *EI,* 2d ed., I, 233; and Foucher, *La vieille route,* II, 217n, 235, and "Notes sur l'itinéraire," p. 274.

10. Browne, *A Literary History,* IV, 133.

11. *Hūdūd al-'Alam,* pp. 91, 115; al-Utbī, pp. 467–71; al-Bīrūnī, I, 99, 208; Juzjānī, I, xii–xiv, and II, 852; A. Siddiqi, ed., *Tarikhnama-i-Herat* (Calcutta, 1944), pp. 169, 198, 267 (cited in Schurmann, p. 40); Ibn Battuta, p. 180; and Qāzwinī, pp. 161ff.

12. Schurmann, p. 40.

13. The only major account of the early expansion of Afghan society is given by Reysner, *Razvitie feodalizma,* pp. 35–61. For some observations questioning certain of Reysner's conclusions, see Schurmann, pp. 41–49.

14. There are no accurate statistics on the numerical strength of various Afghan tribes. The earliest estimates were made by Nadir Shah and Ahmad Shah Durrani. The works of Hayat Khan and Elphinstone served as the chief sources in determining the tribal strength of the Afghans in the 19th century and are still used today. Elphinstone in 1815 (p. 400), W. Hamilton in 1820 (II, 545), Dubeux and Valmont in 1848 (p. 24), and *La grande encyclopédie,* 1887–1902 (p. 708) all estimate the number of Durranis at about 800,000. Here are some of the more recent estimates of their numbers:

Source	Year	Estimate
Huffmann	1951	1.2 million
Humlum (p. 90)	1959	1–2 million
Dvoriankov (p. 35)	1960	1.4–1.5 million
Fletcher (*Afghanistan,* p. 289)	1965	1 million

15. On Durrani tribal structure, see Elphinstone, p. 397; Dubeux and Valmont, p. 24; J. Fraser, *Historical and Descriptive Account,* p. 320; and Vigne, p. 334.

16. For early sources on the Turkic origin of the Ghilzais, see C. Masson, *Narrative,* II, 207–8. See also Bellew, *Afghanistan,* pp. 220–21, and *Races,* pp. 56, 97. (Masson also reported [pp. 208–9] a tradition to the effect that the Ghilzai tribe was at one time Christian, with its members' allegiance divided be-

tween the Armenian and Georgian churches, but there is no evidence to corroborate such an assertion.) W. Crooke (*Natives of Northern India*, London,
1907, p. 59) goes so far as to claim that "the Afghans to be seen in the Indian
plains are largely Ghilzais, Turks ... by race ... not akin to Afghans except in
language and religion." Raverty (*Notes*, pp. 52, 346n, and *passim*) describes
them (in 1220) as a small tribe dwelling near the Suleiman Range, the cradle
of the Pathans, which they left two centuries later. Caroe (*Pathans*, pp. 17–19,
131) also declares that the Ghilzais are of foreign stock, but not necessarily
Turkish: "The Khaljis were no longer Turks when they entered India ... and
they are, whatever their rootstock, frequently bracketed with Afghans."

17. Caroe, *Pathans*, pp. 18–19, 131. Among the early estimates of the number
of Ghilzais, Elphinstone in 1815 (pp. 437–40), J. Fraser in 1833 (*Historical
and Descriptive Account*, p. 322), and P. Sykes in 1915 (*Persia*, II, 307) all
cite the figure 100,000 families. Dubeux and Valmont in 1848 (p. 27) estimated
a population of about 1 million, and *La grande encyclopédie*, 1887–1902, a population of about 600,000. Here are some of the recent estimates of the Ghilzai
tribe's numerical strength:

Source	Year	Estimate
Huffmann	1951	1 million
Humlum (p. 90)	1959	1–2 million
Dvoriankov (p. 35)	1960	1.5 million
Fletcher (*Afghanistan*, p. 291)	1965	1 million

For details on Ghilzai tribal structure, see Elphinstone, pp. 437–40; C. Masson,
Narrative, II, 204–5; Broadfoot, p. 291. On the economic power of the Suleiman
Khel in the 19th century, see C. Masson, *Narrative*, II, 212. For a monographic
history of the Ghilzai tribe until 1738, with emphasis on its leading subtribe, see
Benawa, *Hotakiha*.

18. Here are some estimates of the numerical strength of the other major
Afghan tribes. AFRIDIS—Irwin (1840 estimate), Part 5, p. 59: 50,000. C. M.
MacGregor (1871), *Central Asia*, Part 2, p. 32: 85,000. *La grande encyclopédie*
(1887–1902), p. 708: 50,000. Davies, "Afridi," p. 245: 50,000 fighting men.
Spain, *Pathan Borderland*, p. 46: 250,000. Fletcher, *Afghanistan*, p. 289:
250,000. WAZIRIS—C. M. MacGregor, *Central Asia*, Part 2, p. 32: 128,000.
La grande encyclopédie, p. 708: Utmanzai only, 80,000. Spain, *Pathan Borderland*, p. 51: 200,000. Fletcher, *Afghanistan*, p. 296: 115,000. Dvoriankov, p.
36: 800,000. MAHSUDS—Spain, *Pathan Borderland*, p. 52: 100,000. Fletcher,
Afghanistan, p. 293: 50,000. MOHMANDS—Todd (1838), "Report: 1906," p.
31: 40,000 families. C. M. MacGregor, *Central Asia*, Part 2, p. 32: 80,000.
Spain, *Pathan Borderland*, p. 44: 400,000. Fletcher, *Afghanistan*, p. 294:
130,000. KHATTAKS—*La grande encyclopédie*, p. 708: 100,000. Fletcher, *Afghanistan*, p. 292: 160,000. SHINWARIS—C. M. MacGregor, *Central Asia*,
Part 2, p. 32: 50,000. Fletcher, *Afghanistan*, p. 295: 80,000. YUSUFZAIS—W.
Hamilton, II, 545, and *La grande encyclopédie*, p. 708, cite the 1815 estimate
of Elphinstone: 700,000. C. M. MacGregor, *Central Asia*, Part 2, p. 32:
400,000. Fletcher, *Afghanistan*, p. 296: 500,000. Dvoriankov, p. 36: 750,000.

19. The Waziri tribe provides a good example of the extensive subdivisions

of the Afghan and Pathan tribes. One of its branches, the Ahmedzai, is divided into 18 major clans; the other, the Utmanzai, into nine. See M. Yunus, pp. 90–92; Fletcher, *Afghanistan,* p. 296.

20. Spain, *Pathan Borderland,* p. 56.

21. For the location and estimated numbers of the smaller border tribes, see Fletcher, *Afghanistan,* pp. 289–97; Spain, *Pathan Borderland,* pp. 48–54; and Dvoriankov, p. 36.

22. Estimates of the numbers of Tajiks vary. At the turn of the century, *La grande encyclopédie* (p. 709) placed their number at 1 million; some three decades later, Massignon (*Annuaire,* p. 158) placed it at 1.5 million. More recent estimates in *EI,* 2d ed., I, 230, and *Britannica Book of the Year: 1965* set the figure at about 31 per cent of the population, a figure that is in harmony with official Afghan estimates (see Pazhwak, *Afghanistan,* p. 59; Wilber, *Afghanistan,* 1st ed., pp. 45, 62; Humlum, p. 95). Furon (*L'Iran,* p. 202) gives the lowest estimate, 25 per cent. Soviet sources, who have paid particular attention to statistics that relate to Tajiks, Uzbeks, and Turkomans—"the same peoples that inhabit our Central Asian Republics"—estimate there are 2.1–3.0 million Tajiks in a total population of 9.5 million. (See M. Maklakov, "Afghanistan," *New Times,* Moscow, April 1, 1946, p. 24; *BSE,* 2d ed., III, 496; Bochkarev, p. 34; Dvoriankov, p. 36.)

23. Schurmann, pp. 74–80. A 19th-century traveler reported that the Mountain Tajiks "live secluded without foreign trade or traffic through their territory [and] carry on agriculture to such an extent as their rugged country and limited wants admit and require, with breeding of cattle and horses, gold washing, salt mining and a manufacture of excellent iron" (cited in John Wood, p. lxx). See also Humlum, pp. 84–85. Because of their seclusion, the Mountain Tajiks until recently preserved their ancient Iranian language, known as Pamiri or Galcha. (See *EI,* 2d ed., I, 231; Badakhshi, p. 46.)

24. *EI* (2d ed., I, 230) and Pazhwak (*Afghanistan,* p. 59) assert that the Hazaras constitute 3 per cent of the population. Fraser-Tytler (*Afghanistan,* p. 56) and Humlum (p. 86) put the figure at 500,000 or more, Fletcher (*Afghanistan,* p. 17) at 600,000, *BSE* (2d ed., III, 496) and Dvoriankov (p. 37) at 1 million.

25. Schurmann, p. 77. For the conclusions of modern scholarship about the Hazaras, see Bacon, "Hazara Mongols," pp. 230–47; Shinobu and Schurmann, pp. 480–515; Schurmann, pp. 17, 25, 110–55; Dianous, "Hazaras," Part 1, pp. 71–97. For a review of Schurmann's work and differences between him and Bacon, see *Central Asiatic Journal* (The Hague), VIII, 1 (March 1963), pp. 62–67.

26. Burnes, *Cabool,* pp. 229–33; John Wood, pp. 127–28. The subdivisions of the Hazaras are many and complex. According to Fofalzai (*Dorrat-ul-Zaman,* p. 445), in the early 19th century the Dai-Kundi had 27 subdivisions, the Dai Zengi 30, and the Bahsud 34. See also Schurmann, pp. 125–40.

27. Schurmann, pp. 119–20. See also Thesiger, "Hazaras," pp. 312–19.

28. Burnes, *Travels,* II, 165; and Dubeux and Valmont, pp. 103–4.

29. In the case of the Uzbeks, too, population figures vary widely. Among the most recent works on Afghanistan, Fletcher (*Afghanistan,* p. 16) puts their number at 800,000; Wilber (*Afghanistan,* 1st ed., pp. 57–62), 700,000–800,000;

BSE (2d ed., III, 496) and Bochkarev (p. 34), 1 million; Humlum (p. 95) and Dvoriankov (p. 37), 1.2 million. In terms of percentages, Reysner (*Afghanistan*, p. 32) and *EI* (2d ed., I, 230) put the figure at 6 per cent, Wilber and Humlum at 10 per cent. *Britannica Book of the Year: 1965* (p. 104) and most official Afghan sources give the figure of 5 per cent (see, for example, Pazhwak, *Afghanistan*, p. 28).

30. On the distribution and habitat of the Afghan Uzbeks, see Jarring, pp. 57–64; Schurmann, pp. 96, 101; Humlum, pp. 92–93; and Zadykhina, pp. 154–58. For a monographic study, see Kushkaki.

31. Dianous ("Hazaras," Part 1, p. 77n) asserts that it was in the middle of the 19th century that various Turkoman tribes settled in Afghanistan. I could not find corroborating evidence for this statement. For information on the Turkomans of Afghanistan, see Vambery, *Travels*, pp. 301–28; Tumanovich, pp. 83ff; Jarring, pp. 35–51; Schurmann, pp. 85–96; and Vasiléva, pp. 158–63.

32. Bonvalot, p. 103.

33. Most recent sources have estimated the number of Turkomans at 200,000. See Reysner, *Afghanistan*, p. 266; *EI*, 2d ed., I, 230–31; Wilber, *Afghanistan*, 1st ed., p. 62; Humlum, pp. 92–93; Fletcher, *Afghanistan*, p. 16. Soviet sources generally provide higher estimates. For example, *BSE* (2d ed., III, 496) and Bochkarev (p. 34) offer the figure 380,000, and Dvoriankov (p. 37) estimates 400,000.

34. Jarring, pp. 76–78; Fraser-Tytler, *Afghanistan*, pp. 59–60, 66; *EI*, 2d ed., I, 230; Wilber, *Afghanistan*, 1st ed., p. 52.

35. Hackin, "In Persia," pp. 359–63. For information about the Qizil-Bash, see Elphinstone, pp. 320–21; E. Thornton, *Gazetteer*, I, 312–14; Dubeux and Valmont, pp. 34–35; Lal, *Amir Dost Mohammed*, I, 204–5, and *Journal*, pp. 266ff; Burnes, *Travels*, II, 314; Vigne, pp. 167, 355; Bellew, *Journal*, pp. 16–17; Gray, p. 209; and Huart.

36. Dianous, "Hazaras," Part 2, pp. 109–10; Humlum, p. 85; Wilber, *Afghanistan*, 2d ed., p. 52; and Fletcher, *Afghanistan*, p. 18. In addition to Jarring (pp. 79–81), there are a few post–World War II studies that have shed some light on the Chahar Aimak. See Bacon, "Hazara Mongols," pp. 230–47; Dianous, "Hazaras," Part 2, pp. 91–113; Ferdinand; Thesiger, "Hazaras," pp. 312–19; and Schurmann, pp. 49–73. For Soviet contributions, see Gafferberg, "Narody Afganistana," pp. 107–48, and "Zhilish Dzemshidov," pp. 124–43.

37. Wilber, *Afghanistan*, 1st ed., p. 52; Humlum, p. 51; and Fletcher, *Afghanistan*, p. 19.

38. Robertson, *Kafirs*, pp. 376, 380–81; and Hackin, "Les idoles," pp. 258–62.

39. On the conquest and Islamization of Kafiristan, see Robertson, in *EB*, 11th ed., XV, 634; and Amir Habibullah Khan, in Saise, pp. 13–15. See also the panegyric account of Jalalabadi. On the frequent jihads against the Kafirs before 1895, see C. Masson, *Narrative*, I, 202–25; and Schérzer and Léger, p. 375. Before the Islamization of the Kafirs, their external contacts were limited to a little trade with the Afghans and Indians, which was transacted through an intermediary group called "Neemdu Musulmans," or half-Muslims (Burnes, *Travels*, II, 142; C. Masson, *Narrative*, I, 231). In the 1890's their few commercial contacts were made in Islamicized Kafir villages (Robertson, *Kafirs*, p. 540).

40. C. Masson, "Journals," p. 129; C. E. Stewart, pp. 271–72, 275ff; and Martineau, I, 145–53. On the origin, history, and tribal structure of the Baluchis, see Longworth-Dames, *The Baloch Race*. For a study of the Baluchi languages, see Morgenstierne, *Indo-Iranian Languages*, I.

41. My estimates for the Baluchis and other small ethnic groups are based on figures found in Wilber, *Afghanistan*, 1st ed., pp. 56, 62; Humlum, p. 95; and *EI*, 2d ed., I, 231. On other minor groups, such as the Arabs and the Qazakhs, see Schurmann, pp. 101–10, and Dvoriankov, pp. 38–39. For the linguistic divisions of the small ethnic groups, see Morgenstierne, *Indo-Iranian Languages*, II; Gauthiot, pp. 239–70; and Badakhshi, p. 46.

42. Mohammed Ali (*Manners and Customs*, p. 80, and *New Guide to Afghanistan*, p. 112) regards almost all the Afghans, as well as the Tajiks, Turks, and Uzbeks of Afghanistan, as Sunni Muslims. Pazhwak, in his book *Afghanistan*, does not even mention the presence of a Shi'ah Muslim community. Dianous ("Hazaras," Part 1, p. 73) expresses doubts concerning official estimates on the number of Shi'ahs. He cites a figure of 2 million Shi'ahs "provided by an Afghan holding an important post." Cornelius van H. Engert (*A Report on Afghanistan*, U.S. Dept. of State, Series C, No. 53) gives the figure 1.2 million for all the Shi'ahs in the kingdom. Dorothea Franck (*The New International Yearbook*, p. 5) estimates 1 million; so does a confusing account by Massignon (*Annuaire*, p. 158). Fletcher (*Afghanistan*, pp. 20–21) states that "probably about 80 per cent of all Afghans are members of the Sunni sect of Islam." In view of the numerous 19th-century reports about major Shi'ah strength in western Afghanistan among the Hazaras, the Chahar Aimak, and the Qizil-Bash (see C. Masson, "Journals," p. 124, and *Narrative*, II, 260; Lal, "Description of Herat," p. 9; C. E. Stewart, pp. 369–70; and Bellew, *Races*, p. 115; see also Angus Hamilton, *Afghanistan*, pp. 148, 215), it seems safe to take Fletcher's 80 per cent as a minimum. In determining the number of Shi'ahs, one thing is overlooked by almost all students of Afghan history: the article of faith that allows a Shi'ah to conceal his religious denomination in order to escape punishment or persecution. For current estimates on the numerical strength of Shi'ahs, see Humlum, pp. 97–98; Wilber, *Afghanistan*, 1st ed., p. 62; Dianous, "Hazaras," Part 1, p. 89; *EI*, 2d ed., I, 232; Caroe, *Pathans*, pp. 202–3; Schurmann, pp. 154–56, 158, 253; and Dvoriankov, p. 39.

43. The sectarian movements in Afghanistan remain unstudied. There are, however, some scattered sources dealing with their origin and development. See Elphinstone, pp. 209–10; "Notice of Peculiar Tenets"; J. Fraser, *Historical and Descriptive Account*, p. 305; W. Hamilton, II, 548. On Sufism and one of its major representatives, al-Ansari al-Harawi, respectively, see *EI*, 1st ed., IV, 681–85, and *EI*, 2d ed., I, 515. On Muhammed Baha al-Din al-Bukhari Nakshband (1317–89), founder of the Nakshibandi order, see *EI*, 1st ed., III, 841–42.

44. See J. Fraser, *Narrative of a Journey*, pp. 328–29; A. Conolly, I, 156–83; Burnes, *Travels*, II, pp. 12, 54; Lal, *Journal*, pp. 105–6, 156–57; John Wood, pp. 133–34; Vambery, *Sketches*, pp. 212–13; Gray, pp. 211–12; Holdich, *Gates of India*, p. 253; Angus Hamilton, *Afghanistan*, pp. 168–69.

45. Rose, "Customs," pp. 4ff.

46. Elphinstone, p. 164.

47. The discussion in the text dealing with the Afghan tribal structure, tribal code, and customary law is largely based on Elphinstone, especially pp. 159–71, 360–63. W. Hamilton (II, 542–49) and Dubeux and Valmont (pp. 11–16, 37–38) make a few additions on the information provided by Elphinstone. Broadfoot (pp. 359–62), J. Fraser (*Historical and Descriptive Account,* pp. 300–314), Bellew (*Journal,* pp. 23, 37–39, 44), Barton (*India's NW Frontier,* pp. 14–18), and Warburton (pp. 23ff) provide additional details on tribal structure and government. A fairly good summary of the 19th-century scholarship on Afghan tribes is presented in Reclus, pp. 62–65, 104. The best Western studies of the Afghan tribes are C. C. Davies, "Afridi," "The Amir and the Frontier Tribesmen of India," and *The Problem of the North-West Frontier*; Caroe, *The Pathans*; and Spain, *Pathan Borderland* (pp. 63–84). Among the Soviet works on the subject, I have relied on the survey of Masson and Romodin (II, 117ff) and especially on the standard works by Reysner (*Razvitie feodalizma,* pp. 190–297, 323ff) and L. R. Gordon (*Agrarnye otnosheniia,* Appendix I). Unfortunately, there are no monographic or even general surveys dealing with the interrelation between Islamic law, the tribal code, and customary law in Afghanistan. In addition to the above sources, there are only a few studies that contain pertinent and valuable information on the topic, among them Pazhwak, "Taamelat-e hughughi," pp. 341–58; Khadem, *Pushtunwali*; Boulnois and Rattigan; Rose, "Customs"; Ridgeway; Lumsden, "Report on the Yusufzai"; Bolton, *The Tribal Custom*; and Lorimer, *Customary Law.*

48. Reysner, *Razvitie feodalizma,* p. 226.

49. The Roshania movement included elements from both Isma'ilism and Sufism intermingled with a belief in the transmigration of souls, which was borrowed from Hinduism, and in the manifestation of divinity in the persons of the *pirs* (holy men). The information in the text dealing with the Roshanis is based on Elphinstone, pp. 209–11; Darmesteter, *Chants populaires,* pp. clxxv–clxxxvii; Shafi, pp. 1121–24; Abdulhayy Khan Habibi, "Tarikhcha," pp. 194–202; Caroe, *Pathans,* Chap. 13; and Morgenstierne, "Khushhal Khan," pp. 49–57. Among the Soviet sources that I have relied on are Aslanov, "Narodnoe dvizhenie roshani," pp. 121–32, and "Roushanity"; Reysner, *Razvitie feodalizma,* pp. 284–86, 292, 304–7; and Gankovskii, "Nezavisimoe afghanskoe gosudarstvo," pp. 164–79. These Soviet scholars see in the Roshani movement the first manifestation and the foundation of an Afghan national struggle for independence.

50. Morgenstierne, "Khushhal Khan," p. 55.

51. For information on Khushhal Khan, his poetry, and his historical role, see Elphinstone, pp. 192–97; Biddulph, "Afghan Poetry," pp. 103–14; Caroe, *Pathans,* pp. 236–42, 306; Morgenstierne, "Khushhal Khan"; and Majrouh. Majrouh (p. 250) compares the *Dastar Nama* of Khushhal Khan with Machiavelli's *The Prince.*

52. The information in the text on the ascendancy of the Ghilzais and their decline is based chiefly on Sultan Muhammad Durrani, pp. 5–6, 68–69, 97–98; Hanway, I, 22, 104–5; Ferrier, *History,* pp. 28–29; Browne, *A Literary History,* IV, 122ff, 186–87; Lockhart, *Nadir Shah,* pp. 6–8, and his exhaustive study *The Fall of the Safavi Dynasty,* pp. 85–96; Reysner, "Padenie"; and Benawa, *Hotakiha.* On the rise of Durrani power in Herat, see Sultan Muham-

mad Durrani, pp. 5–6; Browne, *A Literary History,* IV, 125ff; Arunova, pp. 153–63; and P. Sykes, *Persia,* II, 311.

53. Lockhart, *Nadir Shah,* p. 120. On Nadir Shah's battles and policies in Afghanistan, see *ibid.,* pp. 51–54 and Chap. 11; Astarabadi, pp. 156–79, 324–29; Sultan Muhammad Durrani, pp. 109–18; Irvine, pp. 324–25; and P. Sykes, *Afghanistan,* I, 329–38. Gankovskii ("Istorii osady Kandagara," pp. 27–33) attributes the fall of the Ghilzais to the sharp divisions among the western Afghan tribes, especially between the Abdalis and the Ghilzais, and the discontent of the non-Afghan urban populations, who were crushed under the burden of heavy taxes.

54. Caroe, *Pathans,* p. 255; Kohzad, *Men and Events,* p. 2. For details on the rise of Ahmad Khan, see J. Scott, II, 200–221; Alami, pp. 5ff. On his election and coronation, see Ferrier, *History,* pp. 68–69; Malleson, *History,* pp. 274–75; Kohzad, "Two Coronations," pp. 38–40; Gankovskii, *Imperiia Durrani,* pp. 36–37. For an early biographical sketch, see "Life of Ahmed Shah," pp. 17–25. Among the valuable post–World War II studies, see Ghubar, *Ahmed Shah,* and Singh, *Ahmad Shah.* For a Russian translation of Ghubar's work, see Ghubar, *Akhmad Shakh,* and for an analysis of the work in English, see *CAR,* VIII, 2 (1960).

55. Elphinstone, pp. 397–402, 513, 518–19; W. Hamilton, II, 546; Singh, *Ahmad Shah,* p. 33; Ghubar, *Akhmad Shakh,* pp. 205–15; Reysner, *Razvitie feodalizma,* p. 345; and Gankovskii, "Nezavisimoe afghanskoe gosudarstvo," pp. 171ff.

56. Reysner, *Razvitie feodalizma,* pp. 346–51. See also H. C. Rawlinson, "Dooranee Tribes," pp. 825–28.

57. P. Sykes, *Afghanistan,* I, 353; Fraser-Tytler, *Afghanistan,* p. 65.

58. The information in the text on the relationship between the Afghan tribes and the monarchy is based mainly on Elphinstone, pp. 401–2, 511, 521, 524–25, 530, 544; J. Fraser, *Historical and Descriptive Account,* pp. 302–3; J. Scott, II, 93; Hayat Khan, pp. 225, 317–37; Rahim, "Afghan Monarchy," pp. 116–32; Kaye, *History of the War,* I, 15n, 16–17; Ferrier, *History,* p. 93; and Barton, *India's NW Frontier,* p. 14. On the army and the military system of the Durrani Empire, see Elphinstone, Chap. 6; Ferrier, *History,* pp. 69–70, 93–95; Malleson, *History,* pp. 276–77; Gankovskii, "Armiia i voennaia sistema," pp. 57–87; and Reysner, *Razvitie feodalizma,* pp. 361–62.

59. Elphinstone, pp. 214–15, 512–13, 527, 540; J. Fraser, *Historical and Descriptive Account,* pp. 305–6.

60. The information in the text on Afghan imperialism is based on Elphinstone, pp. 544–45; Ferrier, *History,* p. 69; J. Scott, II, 226–27; Broadfoot, p. 360; J. N. Sarkar, I, 228ff, 434; V. Smith, *Oxford History,* 2d ed., p. 484; Singh, *Ahmad Shah,* pp. 34–35; P. Sykes, *Afghanistan,* I, 355–57; Caroe, *Pathans,* pp. 256–58; and Gankovskii, *Imperiia Durrani,* pp. 20–31. The Afghan invasion of India and Ahmad Shah's championship of the cause of Islam stirred the pan-Islamic hopes of Indian Muslim religious luminaries. Among them was Shah Wali Ullah, who asked Ahmad Shah's help in combating the non-Islamic elements in India. See A. Ahmad, "Mouvement des mujahidin," p. 113, and *Studies,* pp. 208–9.

61. Elphinstone, p. 199; Ghubar, *Ahmed Shah,* pp. 176–77; Singh, *Ahmad*

Shah, p. 335; Caroe, *Pathans,* p. 259. On poets and writers of the time, see Abdulhayy Khan Habibi, "Tarikhcha," pp. 210–13; and Gerasimova and Girs, pp. 51–56.

62. The information in the text on Timur Shah is based on Elphinstone, pp. 199, 559–60; Fofalzai, *Timur;* Kohzad, *Men and Events,* p. 3, and *Highlight;* Reshtiya, *Afghanistan,* pp. 2–7; Abdulhayy Khan Habibi, "Tarikhcha," pp. 212–13; P. Sykes, *Afghanistan,* I, 368–69; and Caroe, *Pathans,* pp. 260–63. Vincent Smith has apparently confused the Barakzais with a non-Durrani subtribe in writing that Timur, "distrusting the Durranis, leaned on Payandah Khan, chief of the Barakzai clan" (*Oxford History,* 2d ed., p. 599).

63. Reshtiya (*Afghanistan,* p. 4), Kohzad (*Highlight,* p. 5), P. Sykes (*Afghanistan,* I, 370), and V. Smith (*Oxford History,* 2d ed., p. 599) set the number at 24; Fraser-Tytler (*Afghanistan,* p. 67) and Caroe (*Pathans,* p. 260) at 23; Fofalzai (*Dorrat-ul-Zaman,* pp. 9–10) at as many as 31; and Vigne (p. 336) at 50 or 60.

64. For the elaborate distribution of the important posts of the Durrani empire among the Durrani clans, see Elphinstone, pp. 518–68; Fofalzai, *Dorrat-ul-Zaman,* p. 16.

65. For the policies of Zaman Shah, see Caroe, *Pathans,* pp. 264, 266, 270; Fofalzai, *Dorrat-ul-Zaman,* pp. 11ff and *passim;* Elphinstone, pp. 199, 568ff; P. Sykes, *Afghanistan,* I, 373–74; and V. Smith, *Oxford History,* 2d ed., p. 599.

CHAPTER THREE

1. Elphinstone, pp. 175, 257–58, 312; Broadfoot, p. 346.
2. G. Meyendorf, p. 35.
3. In "Itinerary from Yezd to Herat," p. 8, and A. Conolly, II, p. 3, the number of caravanserais during the first quarter of the 19th century is given as 17; this figure, however, seems clearly exaggerated, and in view of the general economic state of Herat, the number seven recorded by Lal (*Journal,* p. 237, and *Travels,* pp. 263–64) seems more realistic. For details about Herat during this period, see J. Fraser, *Historical and Descriptive Account,* pp. 62–63; C. Masson, "Journals," p. 124; Lal, *Journal,* pp. 245–47, and *Travels,* pp. 271–74. According to a manuscript of Eldred Pottinger (cited in C. Masson, *Narrative,* I, 203n), "about two-thirds of this magnificent bazaar still [1837] remains, but so choked up with rubbish and so ruinous, that it has lost much of its attraction to the eye." A. Conolly (II, 61) described Herat as "one of the dirtiest [cities] in the world.... No drains having been contrived to carry off the rains, which fall within the walls, it collects and stagnates in ponds which are dug in different parts of the city. The residents cast out the refuse of their houses into the streets, and dead cats and dogs are commonly seen lying upon heaps of the vilest filth."

4. Elphinstone (p. 489) quoted this estimate, but it is contested by Boukhary (p. 7), who has advanced the figure 300,000 rupees. In the 1830's Herat's income, according to A. Conolly (II, 9), was 21,429 pounds. On the eve of the First Anglo-Afghan War the revenue of Herat and all its dependencies was estimated to be somewhere between 38–40,000 pounds. See Eastwick, II, 244; and Kennedy, I, 289.

5. In 1828–29, cholera killed thousands, and during the Persian siege, Herat suffered famine, fever, and a "scurvy reign of terror." Thousands more died or emigrated. See Kaye, *History of the War*, I, 259–60, 267f. See also A. Conolly, II, 5; and Ferrier, *Caravan Journeys*, pp. 173–75. The already depressed economy of Herat was further damaged by the migration of rug weavers and other artisans during the Afghan-Persian and Anglo-Afghan wars. See A. Conolly, II, 12.

6. Elphinstone, p. 489; "Itinerary from Yezd to Herat," p. 8; Ferrier, *Caravan Journeys*, p. 172. According to C. Masson (*Narrative*, I, 205), the "general appearance of the inhabitants [of Herat] was that of a poor and oppressed people, dirty and ill-clad." He estimated that the population was about 45,000. However, A. Conolly (II, 3), writing a few years earlier, estimated that the number of inhabitants in the city of Herat proper was 12,000.

7. My material on the economic state of the city and province of Herat is based mainly on "Itinerary from Yezd to Herat," pp. 3–8; Lal, *Journal*, pp. 259–61, *Travels*, pp. 287–89, and "Description of Herat," p. 10; J. Fraser, *Historical and Descriptive Account*, pp. 49, 66; C. Masson, "Journals," p. 123, and *Narrative*, I, 205, 311; A. Conolly, II, 2–12, 61, 70–77; Abdul Kerim Munshi, p. 274; E. Conolly, pp. 319–40; Leech, "Description of Seisthan," pp. 115–34; Todd, "Report: 1844," pp. 339–60; Ferrier, *Caravan Journeys*, pp. 144, 171–75, 392–94; Marsh, pp. 91, 93f; and W. W. Hunter, *Imperial Gazetteer*, I, 35, 39.

8. Much of my information on Kandahar is based on Elphinstone, pp. 424–25; Boukhary, pp. 6, 17f, 269; W. Hamilton, II, 560–61; "Itinerary from Yezd to Herat," pp. 13, 15; C. Masson, *Narrative*, I, 279–82, 284, 287, 295, and II, 287, and "Journals," pp. 113, 123; Vigne, p. 167; Dubeux and Valmont, p. 29; A. Conolly, II, 105–7; Bellew, *Journal*, p. 9; and Ferrier, *Caravan Journeys*, pp. 320–22.

9. Bellew, *Journal*, pp. 9–11, 270, 383. On the famine, see Bellew, pp. 228–29; and Lumsden and Elsmie, pp. 157–58.

10. C. Masson, *Narrative*, II, 203–4. See also I, 288–89, and II, 199.

11. Taylor, p. 105. My information on the population of Ghazni is based primarily on Boukhary, p. 270; Todd, "Report: 1906," p. 28; Broadfoot, p. 353; W. Hamilton, II, 556; Dubeux and Valmont, p. 30; C. Masson, *Narrative*, I, 219; and Vigne, p. 127. According to Vigne (pp. 114, 126), a large proportion of the population of Ghazni at the time was Hazara. However, the account of C. Masson (*Narrative*, II, 224) indicates that the Afghan tribes were gradually displacing the Hazaras from the region, and Todd corroborates this, noting that the inhabitants of the town were mainly Durranis or Tajiks ("Report: 1844," p. 355).

12. My information on the economic state of Ghazni is drawn chiefly from Broadfoot, p. 346; C. Masson, *Narrative*, II, 212, 219; Vigne, p. 105; Abdul Kerim Munshi, p. 368; Irwin, "Memoirs," Part 5, p. 64; and Bellew, *Journal*, pp. 185–86. C. Masson (*Narrative*, II, 222) estimated that the revenues of the province of Ghazni totaled 404,000 rupees, and that duties and caravan transit fees brought in 65,000 rupees, agricultural taxes on Tajik lands 70,000, agricultural taxes on Anduri and other Afghan tribal lands 90,000, agricultural taxes from the district of Wardak (between Kabul and Ghazni) another 90,000, and

tribute from the Hazaras 89,000. It is very difficult, however, to ascertain whether these assessed taxes were actually collected.

13. Much of my data on the economy of Kabul is drawn from Elphinstone, p. 294; Boukhary, pp. 6, 270; W. Hamilton, II, 554–55; C. Masson, "Journals," pp. 116, 123, and *Narrative*, II, 260, 263, 267; Vigne, pp. 165, 167; Hyder Khan, Part 2, pp. 98, 100; Burnes, *Travels*, II, 124; Abdul Kerim Munshi, p. 366; and Irwin, "Memoir," Part 5, p. 49. At the outset of the First Anglo-Afghan War, Taylor (pp. 155, 157) described Kabul as a town that "covers a considerable extent of ground, and the streets are in general regular and well built as compared with the other cities of Asia.... Principal articles of merchandize which attracted our notice were Cashmere shawls of the richest and most expensive patterns and costly silks of every description. A considerable trade is also carried on in preserved fruits." According to Kennedy (II, 98–100), the great bazaars of Kabul were well kept, swept and watered regularly.

14. A number of 19th-century travelers, emissaries, and authors wrote of the insecurity of the Khyber Pass and of the power of the Afridi or other tribes to hinder traffic and collect fees. See, for instance, Elphinstone, p. 292; Broadfoot, p. 289; C. Masson, *Narrative*, I, 162–66; Vigne, pp. 82–83, 105, 111; Lal, *Travels*, pp. 57–66, and *Journal*, pp. 51–56; Abdul Kerim Munshi, pp. 361–62; Bellew, *Journal*, pp. 126–27; and Dubeux and Valmont, p. 38.

15. John Wood, p. 103.

16. C. Masson, *Narrative*, II, 261–65, 289.

17. Hyder Khan, Part 2, p. 95; C. Masson, *Narrative*, I, 176. Boukhary (p. 6) reported that the income of the province of Jalalabad was 400,000 rupees in the early 19th century.

18. My material on the decline of Jalalabad is drawn from Burnes, *Travels*, II, 105; Vigne, p. 23; Irwin, "Memoir," Part 5, p. 52; C. Masson, "Journals," p. 116; Broadfoot, pp. 360, 363; Dubeux and Valmont, p. 103; and India, *Imperial Gazetteer*, XIV, 13.

19. On the situation in central Afghanistan, see Burnes, *Travels*, II, 152; Broadfoot, pp. 389, 396; C. Masson, *Narrative*, II, 206; Lal, *Travels*, pp. 324ff, and *Journal*, pp. 294ff; India, *Imperial Gazetteer*, XIII, 85; and Ferrier, *Caravan Journeys*, p. 221. Hazarajat being a mountainous region, the Hazaras had a strategic advantage and were well situated to withstand Durrani attempts to subdue them. According to Dubeux and Valmont (p. 103), sugar and salt were the only major articles the Hazaras sought.

20. My information on conditions in Balkh during the first decades of the 19th century is based on Boukhary, pp. 7, 261; Elphinstone, pp. 463–65, 473ff (both of whom report the limited revenues of the district in 1809); C. Masson, *Narrative*, II, 305–6; Dubeux and Valmont, p. 49; Gerard, "Peshawar to Bokhara," pp. 10–14; Ferrier, *Caravan Journeys*, pp. 207–8; W. W. Hunter, *Imperial Gazetteer*, I, 53–56; and John Wood, p. 106.

21. John Wood, p. xxxvii. See also Gerard, "Peshawar to Bokhara," p. 10. According to Marsh (pp. 72, 76), similar devastation was inflicted by the rulers of Khiva and by Turkoman tribesmen in northwestern Afghanistan. Kohsan, an Afghan frontier fort and trade center, was abandoned by its inhabitants in 1827, because of the increasing Turkoman raids.

22. Vigne, pp. 220–21, 329.

23. On conditions in Kunduz, see Burnes, *Travels*, II, 196; Dubeux and Valmont, pp. 92, 101. On those in Tashkurgan and Badakhshan, see Burnes, *ibid.*, p. 200; Dubeux and Valmont, pp. 92–95; and Boukhary, p. 231. See also Ferrier, *Caravan Journeys*, pp. 198, 205, 210.

24. W. Hamilton, II, 540; Elphinstone, pp. 188, 295.

25. Hyder Khan, Part 2, pp. 98f; Vigne, pp. 69f.

26. W. Hamilton, II, 540; E. Thornton, *Gazetteer*, I, 310. See also Lal's letter in *The Asiatic Journal*, September 1834, pp. 14–15.

27. Hyder Khan, Part 2, pp. 40, 98–99.

28. W. Hamilton, II, p. 541; Broadfoot, p. 396; J. Fraser, *Historical and Descriptive Account*, pp. 210–11, 243. According to Fraser, since the only means of transporting goods in Afghanistan was by pack animal, the price of all commodities was greatly raised by the transportation costs.

29. W. Hamilton, II, 540; Elphinstone, p. 295.

30. Broadfoot, p. 396; Burnes, *Travels*, II, 142; Bellew, *Journal*, p. 10.

31. Elphinstone, p. 295. Commerce between Persia and Afghanistan, already difficult because of Shi'ah–Sunni religious animosity and precarious trade routes, also suffered because there was a lack of confidence among the traders: "Though a few of the longest established merchants of different cities have correspondents in Meshed, they only trust each other to a limited extent, and few traders requiring a sudden advance of money could obtain it otherwise than at a ruinously exorbitant rate of interest" (see A. Conolly, I, 347). Shi'ah pilgrims also carried a considerable amount of petty trade.

32. Elphinstone, p. 296; W. Hamilton, II, 541; C. Masson, *Narrative*, I, 231. According to Vigne (p. 234), "No persons but the vendors of salt and itinerant workers of golden ornaments [were] allowed by the Kafirs to enter their country." Barter economy persisted among the Kafirs until the late 1890's. See Robertson, *The Kafirs*, pp. 540ff.

33. A. Conolly, II, 271–72. My information on the Afghan-Bukharan and Indian–Central Asian transit trade is based on Hyder Khan, Part 2, pp. 98–99; Burnes, *Travels*, II, 125; John Wood, p. 137; Vigne, pp. 22, 32; and Lal, *Journal*, pp. 294ff, *Travels*, pp. 324ff, and letter cited in note 26 above.

34. Herati and Shuja, p. 14. Another indication of the scarcity of European goods is the fact that in the 1830's there was only one artisan in Kabul who could repair watches and other European articles. See Lal, *Amir Dost Mohammed*, I, 211. In 1841, British linen was reported to yield a 100 per cent net profit, and broadcloth, shoes, and such metals as lead and copper were "eagerly sought." See "On Tabular Returns of the N.W. Frontier Trade with Afghanistan," *JASB*, May 1841, pp. 251–52, 255.

35. Although Peshawar was weakened by a major cholera epidemic, protracted civil wars, and Afghan-Sikh animosity, it still yielded an estimated annual revenue of 1.1 million rupees in the 1830's. See C. Masson, *Narrative*, I, 126, 129, 135. According to Boukhary (p. 6), in 1810 Peshawar yielded a revenue of some 600,000 rupees annually and Kashmir 2.4 million.

36. On Durrani and Baluchi relations, see C. Masson, *Narrative*, II, 101–2. On the economic position of Dera Ghazi Khan, Dera Ismail Khan, and Dara-

band, see Boukhary, p. 6; C. Masson, *Narrative*, I, 29, 32, 40, 46, 72–73; and E. Thornton, *Gazetteer*, I, 163.

37. For a general account of Afghan contacts with Europe from the 16th century to the early 19th century, see Gregorian, pp. 121–43. On the presence and influence of Europeans and European technology in the Moghul army of India in the 17th and 18th centuries (and their probable impact on Moghul Afghanistan), see Abdul Aziz, *The Mughal Court and Its Institutions*, Lahore, 1942, pp. 216–17, 234–35; and William Irvine, *The Army of the Indian Moghuls: Its Organization and Administration*, London, 1903.

38. Halpern, *Politics of Social Change*, p. 46.

39. For information on the activities of Hindu merchants in various regions, see the following works. PERSIA, 17th–18th centuries: Herbert, *Travels in Persia*, pp. 41–42; Fryer, II, 216, 248; Pinkerton, IX, 27; E. T. Tavernier, II, 140ff. HERAT AND KANDAHAR, 17th–18th centuries: report of Joseph Salbanck to the East India Company, in Purchas, III, 85; Forster, "Extracts," pp. 279, 291; Elphinstone, p. 317. JALALABAD, GHAZNI, AND KABUL, 17th–early-19th centuries: Goëz, p. 580; G. H. MacGregor, p. 878. (The Hindu merchant community had already established itself in eastern Afghanistan in the 16th century; according to Habib [pp. 397–98], as early as 1554 the Afghans borrowed money from Banyas, the Indian commercial caste.) BASRA, MUSCAT, AND THE ARAB MIDDLE EAST: Francklin, pp. 236–37; P. Masson, p. 507. ASTRAKHAN: Antermony, p. 283; Jean Potocki, p. 267. According to Potocki, there were 75 Hindu merchants in Astrakhan in 1797; they were mostly from Multan and were Afghan subjects.

40. My material on the economic position of the Hindus in 19th-century Afghanistan and its dependencies is based mainly on Boukhary, pp. 258, 269; Forster, "Extracts," p. 285; Todd, "Report: 1906," p. 278; Agha Abbas, pp. 564–621; Nubee, pp. 667–706, 786–826; C. Masson, *Narrative*, I, 287, II, 139–40, 154–65, and III, 185; G. Meyendorf, p. 35; Dubeux and Valmont, pp. 31, 34, 93, 101; Schérzer and Léger, pp. 225, 230, 365; J. Fraser, *Historical and Descriptive Account*, pp. 68, 70; E. Conolly, p. 320; Burnes, "Description of Bokhara," p. 227; A. Conolly, II, 36; and Ferrier, *Caravan Journeys*, pp. 45, 121, 321. According to Hyder Khan (Part 2, p. 38), most of the bankers of Peshawar in the 1820's were Hindus. Burnes (*Travels*, II, 144) reported that in the 1830's the Hindu merchants had "eight houses of agency" in Kabul alone, and Honigberger (p. 176) wrote that during the same period the Lohani merchant caste of Sind was in charge of the transit trade, which amounted to "ten thousand camels of burden." These Lohani merchants exported Indian products from Multan to Khorassan and Bukhara, paying an estimated 400,000 rupees in duties annually to Afghan authorities in Kabul, Ghazni, and Bamian (Bamiyan). E. Thornton (*Gazetteer*, II, 191–94) reported that the credit of the Hindus of Shikarpur (Shikarpore) stood so high that their bills were honored in every part of India and throughout central and western Asia, from Astrakhan to Calcutta. Ferrier (*Caravan Journeys*, p. 321) reported in 1845 that the Hindus exerted considerable control over the trade of Kandahar with India. As late as 1876–77, the trade in wool, one of the principal items of Indo-Afghan commerce, was in the hands of Shikarpuri merchants. "Indeed, nearly all the

trade from southern Afghanistan [was] managed by Hindus" (W. W. Hunter, *Imperial Gazetteer*, I, 40).

41. C. E. Stewart, pp. 98f. See also Angus Hamilton, *Afghanistan*, pp. 165–66, 316.

42. Cited in Martineau, II, 440. The Second Anglo-Afghan War saw an exodus of Hindus from eastern Afghanistan. Some 2,000 were reported to have left for India (Augustus Abbott, p. 341), but this exodus does not seem to have been permanent, nor does it appear to have seriously affected the economic position of the Hindus in the Afghan kingdom.

43. Angus Hamilton, *Afghanistan*, pp. 151, 165–66, 211, 217, 316; Holdich, *Gates of India*, p. 331; India, *Imperial Gazetteer*, XIV, 375.

44. Forster, "Extracts," p. 291; Dubeux and Valmont, p. 34; Vambery, *Travels*, p. 250; Keppel, p. 6. According to Ferrier (*Caravan Journeys*, pp. 322, 454), Hindus were highly regarded in Herat, but were subjected to various exactions in Kandahar.

45. C. Masson, *Narrative*, I, 287, and "Journals," pp. 110, 123; A. Conolly, II, 180–81; Angus Hamilton, *Afghanistan*, pp. 211, 287, 316–17; L. Thomas, *Khyber Pass*, p. 155. Discriminatory practices against the Hindus were also prevalent throughout Central Asia during the first half of the 19th century. Burnes ("Description of Bokhara," p. 233) wrote that in Bukhara the Hindus were not allowed to build temples, set up idols, walk in processions, or ride within the city; that they had to wear distinguishing clothes, pay a capitation tax, and "never abuse or ill-use a Muhammedan"; and that they were not permitted "to purchase female slaves, as an infidel would defile a believer, nor do any of them bring their families beyond the Oxus." See also p. 227.

46. Brauer, p. 121; Robinson, p. 27; Slousch, "Juifs en Afghanistan," pp. 502–11; Wolff, *Researches*, p. 225. On the immigration of Bukharan Jews to Afghanistan, see Benjamin, p. 157. According to Ferrier (*Caravan Journeys*, pp. 122–23, 453), around 600 Jews were forcibly converted to Islam in Meshed in 1839, but some emigrated to Herat and returned to their ancient faith.

47. A. C. Wood, pp. 214f.

48. Charles-Roux, *Les echelles de Syrie*, pp. 48–49, as quoted in Gibb and Bowen, I, Part 1, pp. 308–9.

49. For a bibliographical note on the Jews in medieval Afghanistan, see Baron, pp. 110 fn44, 282–83; Fischel, "Rediscovery." For a survey of Judeo-Persian literature, see Fischel, "Israel in Iran," pp. 1149–90. On the presence and position of Jews in Persia and the Middle East from the 16th century on, see Herbert, *Travels in Persia*, pp. 41–42; Fryer, II, 216, 247f; Francklin, p. 232; Alexander Hamilton, p. 293; Antermony, p. 308; Longrigg, p. 8. In the early 16th century, Barbosa (I, 54) mentioned a Jewish colony in Aden. As for the Jewish community of India, we know that their numbers increased in the 16th century as a result of an influx of Jews driven from Spain. In a letter to the King of Spain (December 15, 1513), Albuquerque asks leave to exterminate these emigrants one by one, "as I come across them." Quoted by Danvers, *Portuguese in India*, I, 287; and W. Hunter, *British India*, I, 190. According to Strizower (*Jewish Communities*, pp. 48–49, and "Bene Israel," pp. 127–31), the Jews of India came mainly from Baghdad, Aden, and Afghanistan, and were known as Baghdadis.

50. S. A. Khan, p. 249. In Surat, a major Indian trade center, Jewish and Armenian merchants paid less duty than Muslim and Hindu merchants. See Milburn, I, 162–63. The Jews also served in official capacities. According to C. Masson (*Narrative*, II, 4), the agent of the Bombay government in Muscat in 1831 was a Jew, one Reuben Ben Aslan.

51. My information on the contacts of various Jewish communities is based mainly on Gerard, "Peshawar to Bokhara," p. 3; G. Meyendorf, p. 35; Schérzer and Léger, p. 230; Radolff, p. 298; Vambery, *Travels*, p. 372; Polovtsoff, pp. 88, 157, 159, 164; Loëwenthal, "Juifs de Boukhara," p. 108; Fischel, "Leaders," pp. 533–47; and Strizower, *Jewish Communities*, p. 96.

52. Vambery, *Travels*, p. 373.

53. Brauer, p. 123; *The Universal Jewish Encyclopedia*, II, 444.

54. Vambery, *Travels*, p. 250; *The Jewish Encyclopedia*, I, 224; Federbush, pp. 320–21. C. Masson (*Narrative*, II, 246) claims that the Jews were tolerated; the majority of other sources, however, speak of a number of discriminatory practices. (See G. Meyendorf, p. 59; Dubeux and Valmont, pp. 12, 103–4; Radolff, pp. 298–301 *passim*; Bonvalot, pp. 36–37; and Robinson, p. 27.) According to A. Conolly (II, 180–81), exactions against Jews and Hindus were "partly induced by anarchy and dislocation of central power." Discriminations against the Jews in various regions of Afghanistan seem to have followed the general practice in 19th-century Central Asia, where the Jews were not allowed to ride horses, were barred from building new synagogues, were prohibited from wearing turbans or kamarbands, were obliged to wear distinctive clothing, and were forced to pay a heavy head tax. Reports indicate that in some towns they were not allowed in the streets after curfew. See G. Meyendorf, pp. 35–37, 41; Schérzer and Léger, p. 230; Burnes, "Description of Bokhara," p. 228; Woeikof, p. 127; Polovtsoff, p. 89; and Federbush, p. 320. Most of the discriminatory practices continued after the Russian conquest of Central Asia. Jews were prohibited from owning land in Tashkent and later in all of Russian Turkestan, and their freedom of movement was restricted. On the eve of World War I, the Bukharan Jews were still living under oppressive conditions. Those under direct Russian rule were subjected to the same discriminations and restrictions as those practiced in Russia itself. See Bonvalot, p. 36; Woeikof, p. 127; Polovtsoff, p. 89; Slousch, "Juifs à Boukhara"; and Itzhak Ben-Zvi, *The Exiled and the Redeemed*, Philadelphia, 1957, pp. 78ff.

55. Federbush, p. 324; Niedermayer, *Afghanistan*, pp. 15–17, 59–60; Dollot, pp. 37ff; Brauer, pp. 123–24; *The Jewish Encyclopedia*, I, 224. For details about the position of the Jews as distillers, see Hyder Khan, Part 2, p. 98; C. Masson, *Narrative*, II, 246–47; Wolff, *Researches*, p. 225; Burnes, *Travels*, II, 127–28; and Holdich, *Gates of India*, p. 252. According to Brauer (p. 126), Jews were legally allowed to produce wine and arrack in Afghanistan until 1928 and had a virtual monopoly.

56. For various figures on the dwindling Jewish population of Afghanistan, see *The Jewish Encyclopedia*, I, 223; Massignon, *Annuaire*, pp. 157f; Federbush, p. 319; and Hans, p. 167. Some authors, notably Furon (*L'Afghanistan*, p. 59) and Massignon (*L'Islam*, p. 13), have erroneously dated the end of the Jewish community in Afghanistan. Furon puts it in the middle of the 19th century, Massignon in the year 1926. However, elsewhere Massignon asserts

that some of the Afghan Jews were expelled in 1933 (*Annuaire*, p. 15). Though it is true that in the 1930's increasing Afghan nationalism and greater efforts on the part of both the government and the Afghan merchants to control the country's foreign trade gave rise to some official anti-Jewish policies (including a forced exodus of the Jews from the region of Balkh), there is nothing to substantiate the allegation that the Jews were expelled from Afghanistan because of Aryan or Nazi racial theories. See Byron, *Road to Oxiana*, pp. 119, 237, 268, 280; *The Universal Jewish Encyclopedia*, I, 106; Brauer, p. 122; and Robinson, p. 28.

57. W. N. Sainsbury, I (1513–1616), 23; Manrique, II, 361; Pinkerton, IX, 191–92; Alexander Hamilton, p. 293; Antermony, p. 28; A. C. Wood, p. 147; P. Thomas, p. 122; Bruce, II, 618; and Willan, p. 60. For a survey of the Armenian settlements in Persia and India, see Abrahamian, pp. 234–63, 436–85.

58. Buxton, pp. 195–96; Mill, p. 128; S. A. Khan, p. 294n; W. N. Sainsbury, II (1617–21), 256, 304–5; and Roe, pp. 51, 74, 372, 406, 459. See also "The Journal of Sir Thomas Roe," in Pinkerton, VIII, 56; and Manrique, II, 361.

59. Manrique, II, 342–44; see also Henry Bornford's account of a journey from Agra to Tatta in 1639, in Birdwood and Foster, pp. 134f; and Forster, "Extracts," p. 280. In 1738, on the eve of Nadir Shah's occupation of Jalalabad, an Armenian merchant, resident there, sent a report to the Russian ambassador to Persia, in which he described economic conditions in the city. See Brosset, Part 2, p. 369. Armenian commercial activities extended as far as Dacca, where, according to Henry Walters ("Census of the City of Dacca," *Asiatic Researches* [Calcutta], XVIII [1832], 548) there were 42 Armenian houses.

60. Seth, p. 207; and *Azgaser* (Calcutta), I (1845), 16, 125.

61. Hyder Khan, Part 2, p. 98; Seth, pp. 207, 210; Burnes, *Travels*, II, 127–28; Ayvazian, III, 64. In a letter to the Armenians of Calcutta, Abdur Rahman set the original Armenian population of Kabul at 500. See Davidson, pp. 10–11; and Seth, pp. 214–16. I. N. Allen (pp. 312–13) described the church as small and unpretentious, "with a small picture of the Holy Family, much dimmed by smoke and dust. [It was] carpeted and kept clean, apparently with great care. Upon the altar were six candlesticks, two small crosses, and two copies of the Holy Gospels."

62. My information on Armenians in Afghanistan is drawn from Aghanian, III, 298, 553–54, and VIII, 521, 567–69; Rev. N. Sayeghian, in *Avetik* (Beirut), 7th year (1938), Nos. 17–19, pp. 289–90; Hyder Khan, Part 2, p. 98; C. Masson, *Narrative*, I, 44–45, 237, and II, 275; Sale, p. 12; Dubeux and Valmont, p. 30; Taghiadianz, p. 224. On the activities of Armenian merchants in Bukhara and Khiva, see Strong, I, 167, 248; Burnes, "Description of Bokhara," p. 228; and Gerard, "Peshawar to Bokhara," pp. 13f.

63. Burnes, *Travels*, II, 127–28; I. N. Allen, p. 313; Gray, p. 209; Ayvazian, III, 64; Davidson, pp. 4f.

64. C. Masson, *Narrative*, II, 246; Holdich, *Gates of India*, p. 377. According to Holdich, the Armenians were treated with "more than toleration and intermarried with Mahomedans."

65. Gray, p. 209. In the 1870's some Armenian merchants of Persia carried on trade with the province of Herat via Shahrud, Abbasabad, and Sabzawar. See Marsh, pp. 50ff.

66. Gray, p. 44; Davidson, pp. 4f. Burnes (*Travels*, II, 127–28) attributed the decrease of the Armenian population to the measures of Dost Muhammed, especially his prohibition of the distillation of spirits, which eliminated one of the chief occupations of the Armenians and the Jews. According to Davidson (p. 10), the last Armenians of Kabul were expelled as the result of an interpellation of the "Red Sultan," Abdul Hamid II. There is no evidence to substantiate this assertion, nor that of Field, who states (pp. 170–71) that, "after the Armenian massacres in Turkey, the Amir probably fearing a similar outburst in Kabul ordered Armenians to leave it." I believe the expulsion must be attributed in part to the Amir's determined effort to please the religious establishment and in part to his attempt to remove all justification for the admittance of Christian missionaries. Furon (*L'Afghanistan*, p. 59) places the end of the Armenian colony somewhere in 1830–40; Massignon (*L'Islam*, p. 13) states it came in 1926; both are in error, as is Massignon's later assertion (in *Annuaire*, p. 159) that the Armenians were expelled in 1933.

67. We possess only fragmentary information concerning Georgians in Afghanistan. Manrique (II, 346) noted that there were 12,000 Georgian cavalrymen in the Persian army stationed in Afghanistan in the 17th century. There are also some references in 18th-century Armenian historical texts to Georgian merchants engaged in Persian-Afghan trade. See, for example, Aghanian, IX, 569; and Forster, "Extracts," p. 279. In 1809, Elphinstone (p. 322) wrote about Lezgis who had been established in Farah by Nadir Shah. Masson wrote about a centuries-old tombstone of a Georgian bishop in the graveyards of Kabul's Assa Mahi hill (C. Masson, *Narrative*, II, 275). As far as I know, Dubeux and Valmont (p. 35) is the only source that mentions the presence of Georgians in Kabul in the 1830's.

68. Elphinstone's study is so thorough that even now, some 150 years later, it must still be consulted on various tribal subdivisions and the development of the economy and institutions of the Afghan kingdom. For an assessment of Elphinstone's work, see Barthold, *La découverte*, p. 165, and Caroe, *The Pathans*; for a commentary on the importance of Elphinstone's journey and mission, see Cotton. Another important contribution was Sir John Malcolm's *The History of Persia*; for an assessment of this work and a discussion of its impact, see, respectively, Yapp, "Two British Historians," pp. 343–56, and Gail, Chap. 10. The work of Sir William Jones was also important; for his contributions and an early biographical sketch, see "Account of Books," in *The Asiatic Annual Register*, pp. 1–16, 56–62; and Arberry, *British Contributions* and *Oriental Essays*, pp. 48–87.

69. Izzet Ullah, an emissary of William Moorcroft, made a journey through Kashgaria, Fergana, Samarkand, Bukhara, and Kabul, and recorded his impressions in *Travels in Central Asia*. Some of his material was also published in *Calcutta Quarterly*, 1825. For an assessment of his work, see H. W. C. Davis, p. 234. For an appraisal of Moorcroft's reports from Bukhara, see *ibid.*, p. 246, and Maclean, p. 28. Evaluations of Pottinger's contributions can be found in Holdich, *Gates of India*, pp. 330–32, and Barthold, *La découverte*, p. 165.

70. For an assessment of Masson's work and contributions, see Holdich, *Gates of India*, pp. 344–410. Masson gathered 15–20 thousand coins in the area; they were later given to the East India Company and contributed much to our

knowledge of chronological events in Central Asia. See Atkinson, pp. xi–xii, and Lal, *Travels*, pp. 325ff.

71. This account, entitled "Itinerary from Yezd to Herat and Herat to Kabul via Kandahar," was translated by Maj. Neil Campbell in 1839. The French officer who wrote it was in the service of the Sikhs at that time. Campbell believed that the report was written at the request of the Russian governor of Georgia (as cited by Forrest, *Selections from Travels and Journals*, p. 2).

72. For an evaluation of A. Conolly's contributions, see Maclean, p. 38; Baker, p. 257; and H. W. C. Davis, pp. 243–44. For an assessment of the work of Alexander Burnes, see Barthold, *La découverte*, p. 165; Holdich, *Gates of India*, p. 376; and Caroe, *The Pathans*, pp. 308–9. Gail (pp. 113–19) deals not only with the travels of Burnes but also with the impact his reports had on Matthew Arnold and other English writers. According to H. W. C. Davis (p. 236), Gerard also prepared the first military map of Afghanistan.

73. H. W. C. Davis, pp. 236ff. For an evaluation of John Wood's work, see Barthold, *La découverte*, p. 165; and Baker, p. 254.

74. Field, pp. v, 77; Wherry, p. 131.

75. Rao, pp. 70–71.

76. On Wolff and his activities, see Burnes, *Travels*, I, 133–34; Gerard, "Peshawar to Bokhara," p. 3; Lal, *Journal*, pp. 59–63, and *Travels*, pp. 67–73; Ferrier, *Caravan Journeys*, p. 128; Maclean, pp. 17–21; H. S. Edwards, p. 87; and Field, p. 77.

77. H. S. Edwards, p. 86. The Russian bans were continued into the 1880's. Foreigners, especially missionaries, were discouraged from visiting Central Asia, and special permission was required to visit the region. See Moser, p. 11; Burnaby, p. 329; and Bonvalot, p. 268. On the eve of World War I, agents of the British and Foreign Bible Society were allowed to sell multilingual Gospels, Bibles, and Testaments in Turkestan and along the Trans-Siberian Railway; however, only 10 annual passes were granted for the entire area. See Kemp, pp. 173–74. Even after the Russians had gained significant political and economic concessions and influence in Khiva (1868) and Bukhara (1873), the rights of missionaries remained restricted. See Burnaby, pp. 399–401, 406–7; and Woeikof, pp. 187–91, 210–14, 239ff.

78. Wherry, pp. 131, 133. On the attempts of missionaries to penetrate Afghanistan from India, see Stock, IV, 121, 209–10; and A. Lewis, pp. 305ff. For a Pashto text of the Bible, see *The New Testament in Pashtu* (translated by T. J. L. Mayer), London, 1890.

79. See Barthold, *Four Studies*, II, 65–66, 121. The process of cultural decline had already begun in the 18th century. In 1752, Tunfato l'Chani reported that Samarkand was desolate, and that its madrassa was used for storage (*Si Yu T'On Tche*, Paris, 1870; cited by Holdsworth, p. 32).

80. On the curriculum and general organization of a typical madrassa (in this case, the madrassas of Balkh) in the 18th century and before, see Davydov, pp. 82–128. For the Afghan educational system at the beginning of the 19th century, see Elphinstone, pp. 188f. Bellew (*Journal*, p. 26) indicates that attendance at the maktabs was very limited during the first half of the 19th century.

81. Vambery, *Sketches*, p. 188. Vambery states (p. 200) that scholasticism, formalism, and fanaticism spread from Bukhara to Afghanistan, India, and Kashmir, largely because the whole region was isolated from Istanbul and Mecca. However, this is clearly exaggerated: these "isms" were in evidence in other regions, as Vambery is forced to concede elsewhere in his work (see p. 196). Khanykov (pp. 105–10, 273–94) also noted the stagnancy of the Bukharan educational system, describing it as permeated with superstition. Dubeux and Valmont (p. 71) observed that in Khiva very few Muslim clerics knew how to read Arabic and understand the prayers; those well versed in Arabic or Persian literature were rare indeed. In Peshawar, too, there were reportedly very few who could read Arabic and Persian. Moorcroft reported that there were no colleges in Peshawar in the 1820's. See Hyder Khan, Part 2, p. 41.

82. Elphinstone, p. 189; Dubeux and Valmont, pp. 43–44.

83. Behruz, pp. 304–39; Holdsworth, p. 35; Dubeux and Valmont, pp. 31–34 *passim*, 43–44.

84. Elphinstone, p. 249; Adivar, p. 122.

85. Bellew, *Journal*, pp. 374–75.

86. Mouraviev, p. 386; Dubeux and Valmont, pp. 72f.

87. Hyder Khan, Part 2, p. 98; C. Masson, *Narrative*, II, 265.

88. H. Gibb, *Studies on Civilization*, p. 127, and *Modern Trends*, pp. 124–25.

89. Khadduri, *Islamic Jurisprudence*, p. 44.

90. K. Hakim, pp. 286–87.

91. B. Lewis, *Modern Turkey*, p. 34.

92. Démorgny, pp. 27–28; Toynbee, *A Study of History*, VIII, 222.

93. For a survey of the literature of the period, see Behruz, pp. 304–39; and Abdulhayy Khan Habibi, "Tarikhcha," pp. 208–13.

94. Barton, *India's NW Frontier*, p. 13.

95. Gerasimova and Girs, pp. 51ff; Abdulhayy Khan Habibi, "Tarikhcha," pp. 210–14; Dianous, "Littérature afghane," Part 1, pp. 134ff; Behruz, pp. 307–12 *passim*. See also Boldyrev's preface in Vasifi, *Tārikh-i-Badakshan*.

96. Behruz, pp. 309, 311f, 316.

97. *Ibid.*, pp. 320, 337–38; Rahmany, "Deux poètesses," pp. 39–44.

98. Lichtenstadter, p. 136.

99. Afghannevis, Part 1, pp. 59–60, Part 2, pp. 39–41, Part 3, pp. 28–31. See also Beaurecueil.

100. C. Masson, *Narrative*, I, 431f; MacMunn, *Martial Races*, pp. 137f. For details on the attempts of the Sikhs to modernize their army, see Cunningham, pp. 155–57; and Ganda Singh, ed., *The Panjab in 1839–40*, Amritsar, 1952, pp. 24–27.

101. See J. Fraser, *Historical and Descriptive Account*, pp. 218–19; Kaye, *History of the War*, I, 138–48; and C. E. Stewart, p. 222.

102. For material on the limited reforms undertaken in the Central Asian khanates, see Becker, pp. 5f, 85, 202–8 *passim*; and Strong, II, 58f, 69–70.

103. On the internecine struggles in the Afghan kingdom, see Kaye, *History of the War*, I, 19–21; Burnes, *Travels*, II, 163; John Wood, p. 106; Caroe, *The Pathans*, pp. 266–68; and especially Herati and Shujah, pp. 2–86; and White-King, pp. 280–94.

104. Lal, *Amir Dost Mohammed*, I, 183, 225, and II, 307; Vigne, p. 220.

105. C. Masson, *Narrative*, III, 23–24. White-King (p. 284) gives a similar characterization.

106. For details on the Amir's marriage alliances and religious policies, see Lal, *Amir Dost Mohammed*, I, 164, 193, 200–205 *passim*, 223–24, 307; C. Masson, *Narrative*, I, 253, II, 229–30, 298–302 *passim*, III, 24ff; and Vigne, p. 229. Masson reports (*Narrative*, III, 36–37) that the Amir separated his many sons into three major groups: those whose mothers were Muhammedzai, the principal branch of the Barakzai subtribe; those whose mothers were non-Barakzai Durranis; and those whose mothers were not Durranis. The non-Durranis were further divided into two categories: those with mothers of Qizil–Bash descent and those with mothers from lesser tribes.

107. Burnes, *Travels*, II, 118, 120, 123, 141.

108. My information on Harlan is based on Harlan, *Central Asia*, pp. 7, 9f, 17; Lal, *Amir Dost Mohammed*, I, 173–74, 177, 240; Kaye, *History of the War*, I, 130n; C. Masson, *Narrative*, III, 335–36; F. E. Ross; *Dictionary of American Biography*, VIII, 272; Cunningham, p. 187; and Caspani. Caspani states (pp. 37, 39) that Harlan was hired by Shah Shuja, the deposed Afghan ruler, who wanted the adventurer to disguise himself as a fakir and visit several Afghan tribes in an attempt to enlist them for Shah Shuja's cause. I could not corroborate this information. Caspani also asserts that it was Harlan who introduced the use of artillery into the Afghan army, but he is incorrect in this. Reshtiya (*Afghanestan*, p. 65), writing of a "Dr. Harlan," refers to him as an instigator of war and an adventurer in the service of Runjit Singh. Later in the same work (p. 153), Reshtiya writes of a certain Larhan (sic), the American in the service of Dost Muhammed; the author has probably taken the two to be different men. Harlan's claim that he was commander-in-chief of the Afghan army was made in his book *Central Asia* (p. 17). H. S. Edwards (p. 66) refers to him as chief of staff; it is more probable that he held this position, if he held any at all. In 1842 Harlan returned to the United States, where he published a book, *A Memoir of India and Avghanistaun* .... He died in San Francisco in 1871.

109. C. Masson, *Narrative*, III, 261–62; Lal, *Amir Dost Mohammed*, I, 162; Vigne, pp. 388, 391, 393.

110. "Asiatic Intelligence," p. 52; Angus Hamilton, *Afghanistan*, pp. 264–65. According to Sir Harry Lumsden, Campbell "was conspicuous for gallantry, integrity and judgement; but being severely wounded and taken prisoner in the battle lost by his master near Kandahar, he renounced his faith and declared himself a Muhammadan. He subsequently took service with the Barakzais, for whom he laboured long and faithfully, but later he gave himself up to drunkenness and debauchery.... [He] commanded Sirdar Muhammad Afzul Khan's troops in Balkh and died there in 1856" (Lumsden and Elsmie, p. 165).

111. John Wood, p. 39.

112. *Ibid.*, pp. 41, 101f. According to C. Masson (*Narrative*, III, 479), in 1838 there was a Frenchman (Carron) in Kabul who was in communication with the British authorities in India.

113. Vigne, p. 128.

114. C. Masson, *Narrative*, III, 10–12; Vigne, p. 184; Lal, *Amir Dost Mohammed*, I, 160–61.

115. Kaye, *History of the War*, II, 620.

116. John Wood, pp. 41, 101–2. See also Enriquez, pp. 69–70.

117. On the military reforms of the Amir and the contributions of Campbell, see Lal, *Amir Dost Mohammed*, I, 220–33; Munshi, *Life of Abdur Rahman*, II, 55; Angus Hamilton, *Afghanistan*, p. 265; and Mahmud Tarzi, in *Siraj al-Akhbar*, 2d year, No. 12, p. 4. Some have asserted that uniforms and other reforms were introduced into the Afghan army after the First Anglo-Afghan War, but they are mistaken. See C. Masson, "Journals," p. 116.

118. My information on the structure of Dost Muhammed's army is based on Todd, "Report: 1844," p. 357; Lal, *Amir Dost Mohammed*, I, 220–33, 239–42, and II, 307; Vigne, p. 378; C. Masson, *Narrative*, I, 252; W. W. Hunter, *Imperial Gazetteer*, I, 48; and Reshtiya, *Afghanestan*, p. 153.

119. C. Masson, *Narrative*, III, 307–10 *passim*, 381–82. For references to Dost Muhammed's use of the frontier tribes, see *ibid.*, III, 76; Lal, *Amir Dost Mohammed*, I, 226; Kaye, *History of the War*, p. 12; Henry Marion Durand, p. 167; and Cunningham, p. 188. According to Cunningham, Dost Muhammed also chose the title Amir instead of Shah so as not to offend his brothers, whose allegiance he sought and whose assistance (against the Sikhs) he needed.

120. Kaye, *History of the War*, I, 119. On the Amir's administration, see C. Masson, *Narrative*, II, 255–56; Lal, *Amir Dost Mohammed*, II, 308; Vigne, p. 374; and Lumsden and Elsmie, p. 149. Dr. Gerard, a member of the Burnes mission, was favorably impressed with the Amir. He wrote: "Kabul is rising into power under his republican spirit of government and I should say is destined to an importance.... It is astonishing how much the country is relieved by the overthrow of the royal dynasty and with respect to the latest reigns of Timur's family.... In Shah Shuja's haughty career there was little security in all we most value, and robberies and bloodshed disgraced the precincts of his court. Dost Muhammed's citizen-like demeanor and resolute simplicity have suited the people's understanding; he has tried the effect of a new system, and the experiment has succeeded" ("Peshawar to Bokhara," p. 2).

121. Lal, *Amir Dost Mohammed*, I, 233–35. The volume of trade between Bukhara and Kabul in the late 1820's and in the 1830's was estimated at 3–3.5 thousand camel loads annually. See Dubeux and Valmont, pp. 21f, 75.

122. For material on the collection of taxes, see C. Masson, *Narrative*, I, 250f, 291, and II, 212; Vigne, pp. 106–7; and Broadfoot, pp. 363, 367. According to Masson (*Narrative*, III, 379), a modern battalion led by Abdul Samad Khan was used to collect taxes.

123. C. Masson, *Narrative*, I, 141–42; Vigne, pp. 239–40.

124. Kaye, *History of the War*, I, 121–22.

125. Burnes, *Travels*, II, 128; A. Conolly, II, 46–47. For details about Dost Muhammed's regulations against drinking, gambling, etc., see C. Masson, *Narrative*, III, 87; and Lal, *Amir Dost Mohammed*, I, 237f. According to Lal (*ibid.*, p. 92), the Amir himself was at one time very fond of drinking.

126. C. Masson (*Narrative*, I, 250) gives the lowest of these estimates; Vigne (p. 373) and Lal (*Amir Dost Mohammed*, I, 232–33), the highest. W. W.

Hunter (*Imperial Gazetteer*, I, 47) provides a much higher estimate. According to him, Dost Muhammed's annual revenue in 1857 was some 4 million rupees (about 400,000 pounds). This figure was for all of Afghanistan except Herat province, which was autonomous. In 1863, after Herat was reincorporated, the revenue of the Afghan kingdom was estimated to be some 710,000 pounds, the cost of the Afghan army being some 430,000 pounds. According to Reshtiya (*Afghanestan*, p. 155), custom duties brought in a net amount of half a million rupees.

127. See Lal, *Amir Dost Mohammed*, I, 170, and II, 308; and C. Masson, *Narrative*, III, 314. The Amir was often forced to borrow money from the Hindu commercial houses to pay his troops. See "Asiatic Intelligence," pp. 51–52. According to Masson, he even confiscated his wives' jewelry to raise funds.

128. C. Masson, "Journals," p. 114; Broadfoot, p. 354.

129. During his exile, Dost Muhammed spent some time in Ludiana, Calcutta, Mussoorie, and Lahore. In Calcuttta he was shown arsenals, ships, industries, courts of justice, and troops "simply to impress him with the British power" (Chopra, p. 84).

130. Reshtiya, *Afghanestan*, p. 149.

131. Bellew, *Journal*, p. 44. On the practices of the hakims, see also Vigne, pp. 91–93, 96, 211. The only treatment one important hakim could offer for cholera (and he claimed it was effective) was to recite the 99 attributes of God three times in the presence of the patient. See Ferrier, *Caravan Journeys*, pp. 205, 392, 451; and Lumsden and Elsmie, p. 233. Belief in the malignant effects of the "evil eye" was widespread in the Middle East throughout the 19th century, though it was not confined to that region. The same belief persists in various forms in the Middle East today and in other societies as well. In 19th-century Afghanistan, the destruction of property, the illness of one's horse or camel, and especially certain illnesses of children were attributed to the evil eye. See A. Conolly, II, 171.

132. Bellew, who was a medical officer, reported (*Journal*, p. 125) the case of a hakim who blinded a boy by using sulphuric acid. See also C. Masson, *Narrative*, I, 118, 151; and Lal, *Amir Dost Mohammed*. I, 205.

133. Vigne, p. 371; Bellew, *Journal*, p. 36; and Reshtiya, *Afghanestan*, p. 148.

134. Dubeux and Valmont, p. 31.

135. Vigne, p. 173.

136. Lumsden to Governor General, April 23, 1857, in Lumsden and Elsmie, pp. 151–52. For details of the unification of Afghanistan, see *ibid.*, pp. 131–34; and White-King, pp. 282, 284–88, 293–94.

137. Lumsden and Elsmie, pp. 151–52.

138. *Ibid.*, p. 174.

139. *Ibid.*, pp. 137, 187f, 219.

140. *Ibid.*, pp. 221–22.

141. Bellew, *Journal*, pp. 42, 245, 267; Vambery, *Sketches*, pp. 243, 276–77. According to Bellew, most of the Afghan uniforms consisted of castoffs or obsolete clothing of British regiments in India, which were purchased at Peshawar by a special Afghan agency. Lumsden and Elsmie (p. 164) attribute the use of discarded clothing to the fact that the British uniform carried with it a certain prestige, rather than to an inability to pay for better clothing.

142. Frere to Elphinstone, February 22, 1858, in Martineau, I, 229.

143. Lumsden and Elsmie, p. 163.

144. On the organization of the army during Dost Muhammed's second reign, see Ferrier, *Caravan Journeys*, pp. 454–55; Lumsden and Elsmie, pp. 163–68; and W. W. Hunter, *Imperial Gazetteer*, I, 48. For a survey and assessment of Dost Muhammed's rule, see Haye, "Amir Dost Muhammed," pp. 235–44; White-King, pp. 284–88; and India, *Imperial Gazetteer*, V, 39.

145. Kateb, II, 258–60; Kohzad, "Emir Cher Ali," p. 59; Banerjee, "British Policy," pp. 9–20, 143–52.

146. Baudet, "La philatélie," p. 12. On Azam Khan's rule, see Kateb, II, 258–60; and Reshtiya, *Afghanestan*, pp. 173–88.

147. Chahardehi, p. 10; Reshtiya, *Afghanestan*, pp. 173–88. Unfortunately, our information about the periodical *Kabul* is scanty: as far as I know, there are no copies available or any contemporary Afghan, British, or Russian accounts that might corroborate or refute al-Afghānī's role in editing it.

148. Reshtiya, *Afghanestan*, pp. 177–78; see also Chahardehi, p. 11.

149. Munshi, *Life of Abdur Rahman*, I, 7–8; P. Sykes, *Afghanistan*, II, 79.

150. Reshtiya, *Afghanestan*, p. 188, and "Journalism," p. 72. See also Bertels, p. 12; Karimi, "Maaref," p. 395; and Azmi, "Moshahir-e rajal-e vatan," pp. 34–35.

151. Vigne, p. 6.

152. On the school system during Sher Ali's reign, see Karimi, "Maaref," p. 395; and Stolz, "Langues étrangères," pp. 25, 27.

153. On Sher Ali's military reforms and related programs, see Munshi, *Life of Abdur Rahman*, II, 55–56; S. Wheeler, p. 216; Roberts, pp. 412–13; Mahmud Tarzi, in *Siraj al-Akhbar*, 2d year, No. 13, p. 5; Marsh, p. 109; Angus Hamilton, *Afghanistan*, pp. 266–68; P. Sykes, *Afghanistan*, II, 78; Reshtiya, *Afghanestan*, pp. 187–88; Banerjee, "Ambala Durbar, 1869," pp. 19–20; and Mitford, pp. 67–68, 82, 118–20. According to Mitford (p. 123), one of the Amir's innovations was the introduction of a culinary department and a mess system in the army.

154. See *Parliamentary Papers*, LXXX (Central Asia, No. 1, 1878), 97–98, 160, 162; Grodekov, pp. 5–6; and Iavorskii, II, 213, 369–70.

155. Reshtiya, *Afghanestan*, p. 200. In his autobiography, Abdur Rahman is most unfair to Sher Ali in claiming that before his own rule the division of the government into departments was unknown in Afghanistan (see Munshi, *Life of Abdur Rahman*, II, 49–50).

156. P. Sykes, *Afghanistan*, II, 78. The customs system remained disorganized and confusing. According to Marsh (pp. 98–99), the commercial traffic between Kandahar and Herat was still taxed five times as late as 1872.

157. Kohzad, "Maskukat," p. 247; Baudet, "La philatélie," p. 12. On Sher Ali's coinage, see Mitford, p. 91; and White-King, pp. 318–28.

158. Kohzad, "Emir Cher Ali," pp. 63–64.

159. *EB*, 13th ed., I, 312; W. W. Hunter, *Imperial Gazetteer*, I, 47; S. M. Ahmed, p. 195; Tate, *Afghanistan*, p. 168; and *Statesman's Yearbook: 1901*, p. 363.

160. *Parliamentary Papers*, LVI (Afghanistan, 1878–79), 466.

CHAPTER FOUR

1. Howard, pp. 232–33. See also Charles-Roux, *L'Angleterre*, I, 175–79, 228–29, 256.

2. Leibnitz, *Mémoire*. For details about earlier French interest in the area, see Charles-Roux, *Autour d'une route, L'expedition d'Egypte*, and "Un projet français."

3. Dubois and Terrier, p. 44. For details about Peter the Great's alleged political "testament," see Lockhart, "Peter the Great," pp. 438–41; and Sumner.

4. Barthold (*La découverte*, p. 250) discusses Russian plans in the 18th century to establish an Oriental Academy to study Central Asia and the East, and to set up commercial agencies in Bukhara, Samarkand, and Afghanistan. Ideas and projects for sending an expeditionary force to India were advanced by A. M. de St. Génie (who sent a memorandum about it to Catherine II of Russia) and by Marshal de Castries. In a 1781 memorandum, the French consul at Baghdad also promoted the case for an expedition. See Krausse, p. 149. A plan was presented to Catherine II in 1791 that envisioned a Russian invasion of India via Bukhara and Kashmir, but she rejected it as both "non-practical and impossible." See Terentiev, *Istoriia zavoevaniia*, I, 43. For information on French activities in Mesopotamia in 1796, see Longrigg, pp. 253–54.

5. Krausse, pp. 149, 152. Much of the information on this "Indian Project" is questionable. For details, see Strong, I, 135–36, 143–45; Anderson, p. 31; and Popowski, p. 71n. According to Krause (pp. 149–50), Paul had gone so far as to order the Ataman of the Don Cossacks to mobilize for a march against India to attack the English "in their most vulnerable part, where they least expect it." See also H. S. Edwards, pp. 34–42; Snesarev, p. 216; Marriott, p. 171; and Lefebvre, pp. 175–79. Some Soviet historians attempt to link Paul's murder to the British, implying there was a connection between his death and the French-Russian plan. See Potemkin, I, 356–57.

6. See "Instruction to Décaen (February 1803)," in Prentout, p. 27. The landing of a British army in South Africa made the success of the plan to sail around the Cape highly questionable.

7. See India, *Treaties*, XI, 287–88. In their attempts to frustrate the French plans in India, the British even attempted to use the services of the Ottoman Sultan, the Caliph of all the Muslims. The Caliph asked Tipu Sultan not to join the camp of "faithless France," the "enemy of Islam and the Ottoman Empire" (M. Martin, I, 159). See also Bowring, p. 187; Bayur, pp. 619–54; and A. Ahmad, *Studies*, pp. 53–54. For Tipu Sultan's correspondence and relations with the French and the Afghans, see *Asiatic Annual Register*, pp. 161–285. For Tipu's rule, his relations with the British, and his fall, see Bowring, Chap. 13; Hutton, Chap. 3; P. E. Roberts, *India Under Wellesley* (London, 1929), pp. 34–52; Daniel, pp. 116–21; and Mahmud Husain, I, 427–90.

8. For details on Wellesley's policies, see M. Martin, I, 61–64; C. H. Phillips, I, 130, and II, 263, 277; P. E. Roberts, cited in note 7 above, Chap. 13; and Joshi, pp. 120–66.

9. Kaye, *History of the War*, I, 3n.

10. *Ibid.*, I, 66; Owen, pp. 577, 582.

11. M. Martin, I, 286, 432; Owen, pp. 585, 607–8; Joshi, pp. 120–66; Gupta, "Shah Zaman's Accession," pp. 129–37. For Afghan studies on Zaman Shah and his relations with India, see Fofalzai, *Dorrat-ul-Zaman*, pp. 147–71; and Kohzad, *Men and Events*, pp. 5–7.

12. Kaye, *History of the War*, I, 10. For details concerning British diplomatic activities in Persia, see Kaye's two-volume work, *Sir John Malcolm*, and his *History of the War*, I, 4–10; see also Bina, pp. 94–96; and Munawwar Khan, pp. 15ff. For the text of the treaty, see India, *Treaties*, XII, 38; and Hurewitz, I, 68–70.

13. My information on Franco-Persian relations is drawn from Gardane, pp. 71, 81ff; Driault, *La politique orientale*, pp. 172–73, 318; Charles-Roux, *L'Angleterre*, II, 213–14; Lebrun, p. 8; Bina, p. 107. For the text of the Treaty of Finkenstein, see Hurewitz, I, 77–78. For a Persian account of the Gardane mission, see Nafisi, pp. 100–121.

14. Driault, *La politique orientale*, p. 320; H. C. Rawlinson, *England and Russia*, p. 19; Bina, pp. 115–28. On French diplomacy in the East, see Kaye, *History of the War*, I, Chap. 3.

15. For details on the British mission, see Brydges, *Account of Transactions*; Bina, pp. 132–34; Kaye, *History of the War*, I, 61–74. For the text of the treaty, see Kaye, *History of the War*, I, 637–40; Malcolm, I, 395ff; India, *Treaties*, XII, 46.

16. India, *Treaties*, XII, 54; Great Britain, *State Papers*, Part 1, Vol. I, pp. 261–64. For the text of the Definitive Treaty, see Kaye, *History of the War*, I, 643–46; and Hurewitz, I, 86–88.

17. India, *Treaties*, XI, 336; Kaye, *History of the War*, I, 83–89, 641–42. Marguerite Wilbur states (p. 373) that the royal permit to Elphinstone was granted only reluctantly, because "the Afghans disliked the idea of foreign contacts." However, she does not cite a source to substantiate this observation. For the text of the treaty with the Sikhs, see Kaye, *History of the War*, I, 640–41.

18. H. W. C. Davis, p. 230; Bina, pp. 173–74. See especially Sir Harford Jones' letter to Robert Adair (September 1809), as quoted by Bina, p. 139.

19. Wellesley to the Secret Committee of the Court of Directors, in Owen, pp. 607–8. See also Kaye, *History of the War*, I, 4; and H. W. C. Davis, p. 230.

20. Bina, Chap. 4, and pp. 236–47. For the texts of the treaties, see *ibid.*, pp. 259–86; and Hurewitz, I, 96–102. See also Kazemzadeh, "Russia and the Middle East," pp. 491–92. For the economic advantages Russia obtained from Persia, see India, *Treaties*, XI, 297–98.

21. Bina, pp. 241–42; Mosely, *Russian Diplomacy*, pp. 3–4.

22. H. W. C. Davis, p. 230.

23. See McNeill's *Progress and Present Position of Russia in the East*. For an example of the anti-Russia pamphlets, see Evans, *Practicability of an Invasion*. For a detailed study of British Russophobia, see Gleason, Chap. 5. There were some Russophobes (notably Henry Ellis, a prominent member of the Board of Control of India) who feared that Muhammed Ali's rise in Egypt might lead to an Egyptian-Russian alliance for the partition of Persia. The possibility of Egypt becoming an important naval power in the Indian Ocean was also considered a threat. See Véreté, p. 149.

24. For details of Palmerston's policies, see Public Record Office, F.O. 60

(Persia), 42, 44, 47: Palmerston to McNeill, June 2 and 13, 1836; see also Ellis to Palmerston, April 16, 1836, in *Parliamentary Papers*, XL (1839), 101; and Webster, II, 738–74.

25. *Parliamentary Papers*, LXXX (1878), 1, 44. See also "Considerations on the Invasion of India," pp. 18–24.

26. Ghose, p. 3.

27. Dodwell, V, Chap. 28, and p. 491.

28. H. W. C. Davis, p. 240.

29. Public Record Office, F.O. 60 (Persia), 42: Palmerston to McNeill, June 2, 1836. For an account of Palmerston's diplomatic moves to nullify the Treaty of Unkiar Skelessi, see Anderson, pp. 94ff; and Puryear, *Economics*, Chap. 2. On the implications of the treaty, see Temperley, pp. 66–74; and Crawley, pp. 46–73.

30. V. Smith, *Oxford History*, 1958 ed., p. 591.

31. *Ibid.*, p. 603. See also Ward and Gooch, II, 203–4; Colvin, pp. 86–88, 124.

32. Kaye, *History of the War*, I, 165–66, 176–77; Lal, *Amir Dost Mohammed*, I, 251–59. For a discussion of the aims of the Burnes mission and of Burnes' negotiations with Dost Muhammed, see C. Masson, *Narrative*, III, 430–68.

33. See Burnes' letters of October 30 and December 30, 1837, in Kaye, *History of the War*, I, 179, 180n, 343n.

34. *Ibid.*, pp. 293ff. See also V. Smith, *Oxford History*, 1958 ed., p. 603; and Munawwar Khan, p. 36.

35. McNeill to Auckland, March 13, 1837, in Kaye, *History of the War*, I, 193. For the opposing views of McNeill and Wade, see *ibid.*, pp. 293–97. See also *Parliamentary Papers*, XXV (1859), 283; and Habberton's comprehensive study *Anglo-Russian Relations Concerning Afghanistan*, p. 10.

36. Ellis to Palmerston, in Lal, *Amir Dost Mohammed*, I, 277–78; see also McNeill to Palmerston, in Ferrier, *Caravan Journeys*, p. 161n. For similar views about the British interests in Herat, see Forrest, *Selections from Travels and Journals*, pp. 9–10, 82ff; and A. Conolly, II, 322.

37. Kaye, *History of the War*, I, 166–210; H. S. Edwards, pp. 63, 73; Public Record Office, F.O. 60 (Persia), 55: Palmerston to McNeill; and Habberton, p. 14. The British intervention in the struggle between the Afghans and the Persians, even for mediation purposes, violated the 1814 Anglo-Persian treaty, Article 9 of which prohibited intervention unless mediation was sought by both parties.

38. Kaye, *History of the War*, I, 273; and Norris, pp. 74–80. See also Habberton, pp. 14ff. The British took an anti-Persian position in the Persian-Afghan conflict, even though they privately agreed that the government of Herat might be the real aggressor, that there was ample reason for a Persian intervention, and that a Persian war against Herat was "fully justified." See McNeill to Palmerston, February 1837, in Dutt, p. 6.

39. Ashley, II, 25. For details, see Puryear, *Economics*, pp. 78–84.

40. Hertslet, VIII, 719.

41. Wilbur, p. 401.

42. Kaye, *History of the War*, I, 320, 332–35; Webster, II, 747–48; Munaw-

war Khan, pp. 41–43. For the treaty between Runjit Singh and Shah Shuja, see Kaye, *History of the War*, I, 319–23; for the texts of the Anglo-Sikh–Shah Shuja agreements (known as the Tripartite Treaty), see Lal, *Amir Dost Mohammed*, I, 371–78. Most of the official correspondence pertaining to the evolution of British political and economic aims in 1832–38 has been published. However, the Pakistan Government Archives at Karachi contain some correspondence that has not been fully utilized. This material is included in "Pre-Mutiny Records of the Commissioner in Sind," in Files (Political) 300–307. For an account of the events leading to the First Anglo-Afghan War based on Russian sources, see Mosely, "Russian Policy in Asia."

43. Kaye, *History of the War*, I, 355–59. The text of the manifesto, known as the Simla Manifesto, appears in most of the official and secondary works on the history of the First Anglo-Afghan War. Norris, in his recent study, has attempted to provide a much-needed historical perspective on the events leading to the war. He has studied its causes in terms of Britain's interests and official policies, rather than as "Auckland's Folly" (Norris, Chaps. 8 and 9). Despite the official policy, there were many statesmen, both in England and in India, who questioned the wisdom of an "adventure" in Afghanistan. The Duke of Wellington predicted that the consequences of such a move would be "a perennial march into that country." Sir Charles Metcalfe argued that the "surest way to bring Russia down upon ourselves is for us to cross the Indus, and meddle with the countries beyond it"; and Mountstuart Elphinstone wrote to Alexander Burnes, "I have no doubt you will take Kandahar and Kabul, and set up Shah Shuja, but for maintaining him in a poor, cold, strong and remote country, among a turbulent people like the Afghans, I own it seems to me to be hopeless. If you succeed, I fear you will weaken the position against Russia." See Augustus Abbott, pp. 63–64. See also Dutt, p. 7.

44. Most of the official correspondence on the events of 1838–43 is published in *Parliamentary Papers*, XXXIX (1843). However, some unpublished material can be found in the Pakistan Government Archives at Karachi (in Political Files 203, 211, 224, 287–90, 306–13). For the course of military events, see Kaye, *History of the War*, II, 218–46; Fortescue, Chaps. 22–29; and Norris, Chap. 15.

45. For details on the liquidation of Lord Auckland's policy and the reexamination of the British position on Afghanistan, see Munawwar Khan, Chap. 5.

46. Nechkina, p. 597; Barthold, *La découverte*, p. 250. For a discussion of Russian interests in Central Asia in the 17th and 18th centuries, see Strong, I, 18–24, 103f, 212. For details on Russian trade with Central Asia between 1773 and 1848, see *ibid.*, pp. 218–32; and Khanykov, pp. 217–30. In 1840–50 the value of Bukharan-Russian trade was 2,065,697 rubles; in 1853–60 the figure was 4,234,412 rubles (Vambery, *Sketches*, pp. 248–49). The bulk of the trade was in cotton. By 1864 the cotton exports from Central Asian khanates to Russia were valued at 6,521,000 rubles. For statistical data on the Russian and Central Asian trade in 1850–67, see also M. K. Rozhkova, "Iz istorii torgovli Rossii so Srednei Aziei vo 60 Kh godakh XIX v.," *Istoricheskie Zapiski*, LXVII (1960). On Russian economic interests in Bukhara and the Anglo-Russian economic rivalry, see Becker, pp. 59–64; and Strong, I, 307–12.

47. V. Smith, *Oxford History*, 1958 ed., p. 591; and Schiemann, *Geschichte Russlands unter Kaiser Nikolaus I*, III, 297–98, as quoted by Habberton, p. 11. See also Schuyler, II, 95.

48. Public Record Office, F.O. 181/488: Buchanan to Granville, May 24, 1871, No. 705; and Kuropatkin, pp. 4–5.

49. The seriousness and the soundness of British undertakings in Central Asia were questioned by many. For instance, the proponents of the stationary policy and the directors of the East India Company held Moorcroft's journey into Central Asia to be unnecessary; his reports on Central Asia were "appreciated more in London than in India." The stationary school also opposed Burnes' mission to Afghanistan, fearing entangling commitments. See H. W. C. Davis, pp. 246–49. According to Davis, "Burnes had no doubt that on all grounds, military, political, commercial, the time had come when Great Britain ought to cultivate alliances in Central Asia." This is not entirely true. Initially, Burnes thought that the formation of a league of the Sunni Muslim principalities of Central Asia with Afghanistan, under British guidance, might stop Russian advances and foil "Russian and Persian designs in the region" (see Fraser-Tytler, *Afghanistan*, p. 96); later, however, he seems to have dismissed the plan. Captain Conolly suggested that Britain provide financial assistance to the Central Asian khanates to strengthen them and prevent Russian expansion in the region. See C. Masson, *Narrative*, I, 540n. Capt. James Abbott, who led a mission to Khiva in 1839–40, was another who advocated containment of the Russians in Central Asia. Otherwise, he wrote, the balance of power in the region would be upset and a world war might ensue. See James Abbott, I, 82; and H. C. Rawlinson, *England and Russia*, pp. 158–59.

50. Maclean, pp. 28–29, 39–47 *passim*. On British attempts to secure a Khivan alliance, see Henry Marion Durand, p. 239; and Norris, pp. 306–10. On British missions to Central Asia and adjacent regions, see C. Masson, *Narrative*, I, 167–69, II, Chap. 5, and III, 473; and Strong, I, 97–116.

51. *Parliamentary Papers*, XL (1839), 200ff.

52. Habberton, p. 21. Some in Britain felt that Palmerston's policy toward the Russians was one of "appeasement." See, for example, Urquhart; and Bolsover. Vigne suggested (p. 468) that the British retaliate against a Russian seizure of Bukhara by taking over Kabul and Kandahar. "And if we do not make ourselves masters of Herat," he wrote, "we should allow no foreign power to do so. It might be regarded as neutral ground."

53. Krausse, pp. 247–48. On the Straits Convention of 1841 and the aims of Palmerston's policy toward the Ottoman Empire, see F. S. Rodkey, *The Turco-Egyptian Question in the Relations of England, France, and Russia, 1832–1841* (Cambridge, Mass., 1934); and Anderson, pp. 106–7. In 1844, in the so-called Nesselrode Memorandum, the English and the Russians reached a secret, though vague, agreement, which tended to normalize their relations. The two powers undertook to maintain the integrity of the Ottoman Empire and to seek an understanding about what action should be taken, if it became clear that the empire could not be kept alive. See Anderson, pp. 110–13; and Puryear, *England*, pp. 439–44.

54. Ghose, pp. 4, 6. Jacob proposed that a military and commercial base be established in Quetta, that Baluchistan be made a buffer state, and that the area's

communications be improved. By making the khanate prosperous and peaceful and yet preserving its sovereignty, he argued, the people would be "cordially friendly to us." Quetta, thus, would "give us complete command of all Afghanistan, without at the same time our giving the least offence to anyone around us." In such circumstances, Amir Dost Muhammed "or whoever might be the ruling Afghan Chief" would "be delighted to enter into a closer alliance with us if we wished it," and "Britain would have the support of Baluchistan and Afghanistan in any subsequent move on Herat that might be found necessary." See Lambrick, pp. 304, 343; and Pelly, p. 349.

55. Roberts, p. 29. See also Besant, p. 93. For the text of the treaty, see H. C. Rawlinson, *England and Russia*, Appendix III. For background on the treaty, see Munawwar Khan, Chap. 4, especially pp. 86–93; Lumsden and Elsmie, pp. 133–36; and H. B. Edwardes, *Memorials*, I, 236–45.

56. The subsidy was paid for some 15–16 months. See Martineau, I, 202.

57. Roberts, p. 31. See also P. Sykes, *Afghanistan*, II, 70; Lumsden and Elsmie, p. 188; and Martineau, I, 202, 239.

58. C. E. Stewart, pp. 9–10.

59. Martineau, I, 204; H. B. Edwardes, *Memorials*, I, 360–475, and II, 1–25. For a detailed study of the policies of Charles J. Canning, viceroy of India at the time, see Sir H. S. Cunningham, *Earl Canning* (London, 1891).

60. Curzon, *Persia*, II, 229, 340; Tavakulli, pp. 40–62. For details on the Anglo-Persian war, see Standish, pp. 18–45. For the text of the treaty, see Tavakulli, pp. 56–59; Afschar, p. 19; and Bushev, pp. 235–36. Bushev, a Soviet historian, argues (pp. 75–79 and *passim*) that the British "concern" for the defense of Herat and the integrity of Afghanistan was only a pretext for the British imperialists to advance their position in the entire East and was part of their designs on Khiva, Bukhara, and Kokand.

61. Vambery, *Travels*, pp. 2, 32.

62. R. B. Smith, II, 620ff.

63. W. Hunter, *Earl of Mayo*, I, 283–84. According to Lord Dalhousie, the arrangements made with Afghanistan in the 1855 and 1857 treaties provided real advantages for India, in that they afforded complete security for India's northwestern frontier, without entangling the Indian government in an inconvenient reciprocity. See Singhal, p. 6; and Munawwar Khan, pp. 95–96.

64. Martineau, I, 113–15, 166. See also Lambrick, pp. 242–43.

65. India, *Treaties*, XI, 212–14; Martineau, I, 157; and Lambrick, pp. 260–62. According to Article 1 of the 1841 treaty between India and Kelat, the Khan of Kelat was an acknowledged vassal of the rulers of Kabul; however, in concluding the 1854 treaty, the British dealt with Kelat as an independent state. See Munawwar Khan, p. 83n.

66. Besant, pp. 107ff; Boulger, *Central Asian Questions*, p. 62; Kapur, pp. 4–6. The British attitude toward the internecine struggles in Afghanistan is discussed in Banerjee, "British Policy," pp. 143–52, and "Neutralization of Afghanistan," pp. 469–72; R. B. Smith, II, 624f; and Wyllie, pp. 24–173 *passim*.

67. For a thorough account of the Russian advance in Central Asia, see H. C. Rawlinson, *England and Russia*, Chaps. 3, 5, and 6. See also Pierce; Becker; and G. Wheeler, Chap. 4. On the impact of the Crimean settlement on Russian foreign policy, see Anderson, pp. 145–46.

68. H. C. Rawlinson, *England and Russia*, pp. 14, 263–92, 362; Besant, pp. 109–10; Martineau, I, 240. See also A. P. Thornton, "Central Asian Question," pp. 122–36.

69. Martineau, I, 240–41, 488.

70. Lawrence to Frere, in *ibid.*, pp. 488–89; Wood to Frere, pp. 482f.

71. Habberton, pp. 24, 32–35; H. C. Rawlinson, *England and Russia*, pp. 309–10. See also *Parliamentary Papers*, LXXV (1873), 1, 1–16: "Correspondence with Russia Regarding Central Asia." For an analysis of the diplomatic moves leading to the agreement, see A. P. Thornton, "Afghanistan."

72. *Parliamentary Papers*, LXXV (1873), 1 ("Central Asia"); Public Record Office, F.O. 65 (Russia), 1202.

73. *Parliamentary Papers*, LXXX (1878), 39–40: Gortchakoff to Schouvaloff, February 1876; also quoted by Habberton, p. 36. The acting director of the Russian foreign ministry told the British chargé d'affaires in St. Petersburg that Russia eventually would have to annex Bukhara and Khokand, and that India would eventually have to annex Afghanistan. *Parliamentary Papers*, LXXX (1878), 1 ("Central Asia"), 45: Doria to Derby, July 13, 1875. For additional information, see Munawwar Khan, Chap. 9.

74. Potemkin, II, 63; Kazemzadeh, "Russia and the Middle East," pp. 496–97, 505.

75. Monypenny and Buckle, VI, 155; Salisbury to Disraeli (confidential), October 31, 1874, in *ibid.*, V, 434. See also Anwar Khan, pp. 232–40. For a detailed study, see Goriainov.

76. *Globe*, May 11, 1880; Marvin, pp. 61, 67f; M. F. Martens, *La Russie et l'Angleterre*.

77. Popov, "Iz istorii zavoevaniia," p. 211; Terentiev, *Istoriia zavoevaniia*, II, 428, 431.

78. Marvin, pp. 87, 207.

79. Lacoste, pp. xvi–xviii.

80. Terentiev, *Russia and England,* II, 114, and *Istoriia zavoevaniia*, II, 428ff; Marvin, p. 105; Giers to de Staal, June 8, 1884, in A. Meyendorff, I, 26; *Parliamentary Papers*, LXXX (1878), 1 ("Central Asia"), 141; Tcharykow, pp. 159–60. In the past, Soviet historiography, following the Pokrovskii school, recognized the aggressive character of Russian imperialism and colonialism in the Middle East and Central Asia (see "Afghanistan," in *BSE*, 1st ed.; Reysner, *Afghanistan*, pp. 74–85; Potemkin, II, 32; A. Pankratova, *Histoire de l'U.R.S.S.* [Moscow, 1948], Part 2, pp. 250–52). However, since 1948 and especially since Stalin's death, Soviet historians have attempted to prove that the Russian conquest of Central Asia and Russia's forward policy were in part a response to the aggressive policies of Great Britain. They hold that Great Britain, if unchecked, would have added Afghanistan and the Central Asian khanates to her possessions in India. See Pankratova, *Razivitie Kapitalizma*, pp. 34–35. Soviet historians contend that the "alleged British fears" of a Russian "threat" to India and Afghanistan were only pretexts to cover the British conquest of Central Asia. See "Afghanistan," in *BSE*, 2d ed.; Shteinberg, "Angliiskaia versiia," pp. 47–66; and Reysner and Rubtsev, I, 303–4. Khalfin acknowledges that the policies of tsarist Russia in Central Asia were "indisputably aggressive," but he asserts that Russia did not have plans to invade

India or Afghanistan, nor could she have done so even if she wanted to. He maintains that the British fears of Russia were based on Russia's proximity to India, which "might have contributed to the development of independence movements" among "the enslaved populations of colonies." He asserts: "It was in order to prevent any external assistance to the aspirations of colonized peoples that Britain embarked upon an aggressive forward policy and engaged in a policy of establishing buffer states in order to keep Russia away from the proximity of British possessions." For a fuller exposition of this view, see Khalfin, *Proval britanskoi agressii*, especially pp. 146–54. In general, current Soviet historiography regards the "Russian threat to India" and the "defense of India" as slogans designed to conceal the expansionist aims of British imperialism. See Tikhomirov, pp. 109–11.

81. For details on the various plans, see H. S. Edwards, pp. 262ff, 271–95; Marvin, p. 79; and Krausse, pp. 165ff.

82. Middleton, p. 11.

83. Martineau, I, 492–93; United States, National Archives, *Persia*: Benjamin to Frelinghuysen, October 26, 1884. Some Russian diplomats, too, were apprehensive of the influence of the Russian military on the formulation of foreign policy in Central Asia. See de Staal to Shishkin, 19/31, May 1899, in A. Meyendorff, II, 171. The British authorities in India were frustrated (especially after 1857) by the limitations of representative government and their inability to send armies beyond the frontiers of India without the sanction of the British Parliament. See Martineau, I, 245–46.

84. Curzon, *Russia in Central Asia*, pp. 275–76; *Parliamentary Papers*, XCVIII (1880), 1 ("Central Asia"), 100; D. Fraser, "Strategic Position," pp. 11, 17. General Annekov even proposed to extend the railway to the Indian subcontinent (via Kizil–Arvat–Herat–Kandahar–Quetta), thereby linking Europe with India. See Marvin, pp. 174–79.

85. Martineau, I, 493–98. As noted, some of these policies (though with many modifications and reservations) had been proposed by Gen. John Jacob in 1856–57. See Lambrick, pp. 304–408, and Appendix B.

86. Martineau, II, 145–46, 148–49.

87. *Ibid.*, II, 154–55.

88. Lady Balfour, p. 8. For the instructions of the British government to the viceroy of India, see *ibid.*, pp. 88–93. For the major guidelines of the Conservative government's forward policy, see Kapur, pp. 1–8.

89. Cecil, II, 72. See also *Parliamentary Papers*, LVI (1878–79): "Correspondence Respecting the Relations Between the British Government and that of Afghanistan, since the Accession of the Ameer Shere Ali Khan."

90. Layard to Derby, Telegram, No. 32, April 31, 1877, as quoted in Lee, "A Turkish Mission," p. 340; Layard to Lytton, June 14, 1877, *ibid.*, p. 341. See also Lee, *Great Britain*, p. 184.

91. Lee, "A Turkish Mission," p. 344.

92. H. C. Rawlinson, *England and Russia*, p. 283; Taillardat, "Politique anglaise," pp. 273–74; and T. E. Gordon, p. 135.

93. *Parliamentary Papers*, LVI (1878), 1 ("Afghanistan"), 183.

94. Lady Balfour, p. 255. For a detailed account, see Munawwar Khan, Chap. 10.

95. *Parliamentary Papers*, LXXX (1878), 1 ("Central Asia"), 159.

96. Roberts, p. 386. For the text of the treaty, see India, *Treaties*, XI, 344ff; and India, Army Intelligence Branch, Appendix V. For a detailed and comprehensive history of the Second Anglo-Afghan War, see Hanna.

97. Dawson, pp. 72–91; Monypenny and Buckle, VI, 475.

98. J. Allen, "British Policy."

99. Buckle, 2d series, III, 56; Monypenny and Buckle, VI, 482.

100. Ghose, pp. 154–55. Lord Roberts, Rawlinson, and Frere were among those who argued for the retention of Kandahar. See Rawlinson, *England and Russia*, p. 278; *Parliamentary Papers*, LXX (1881), 63; Frere's letter to *The Times* of March 3, 1881; and Martineau, II, 439.

101. See Lord Lytton's letter to Lord Cranbrock, in Lady Balfour, pp. 246–47.

102. Public Record Office, F.O. 60 (Persia), 419: Salisbury to Thomson, October 22, 1879. Salisbury expressed the same view in a letter to Sir Stafford Northcote: "To which then shall we confide Herat? The Shah may sell it; the Amir will certainly lose it. We have a certain hold over both.... I lean therefore to the belief that the Shah will serve us better in Herat than the Amir" (as quoted in Cecil, II, 375–76).

103. Public Record Office, F.O. 60 (Persia), 423, and F.O. 65 (Russia), 1097; J. Allen, "British Policy," p. 610.

104. Salisbury to the Queen, December 30, 1879, as quoted in Greaves, p. 51; J. Allen, "British Policy," p. 611.

105. J. Allen, "British Policy," p. 612. See also Buckle, 2d series, III, 56ff.

106. V. Smith, *Oxford History* (1958 ed.), p. 697.

107. Public Record Office, F.O. 65 (Russia), 1104: Dispatch of the Government of India, Foreign Department (Secret), No. 139, June 22, 1880. General Roberts wrote: "I feel sure that I am right when I say that the less Afghans see of us, the less they will dislike us." See Daniel, p. 376.

108. Public Record Office, F.O. 65 (Russia), 1097, 1099: Lord Dufferin to British Ambassador at St. Petersburg, January 16, 1880. For details about the British negotiations with Abdur Rahman, see *ibid.*, 1104: "Papers, Printed for the Use of the Cabinet, Relative to the Recognition of Sirdar Abdul Rahman Khan as Amir of Kabul." See also *ibid.*, 1173; and *Parliamentary Papers*, LXXXVII (1884). Among the secondary works, see Gopal, *Lord Ripon*, Chaps. 2, 3; Singhal, Chap. 5; and Rastogi, Chap. 2.

109. Great Britain, British Museum, Add. MSS. 43610, No. 1: Memo to Hartington, May 9, 1880.

110. *Parliamentary Papers*, LXX (1881), 330ff.

111. Great Britain, British Museum, Add. MSS. 43599, No. 23: Ripon to Northbrook, March 31, 1884; see also Habberton, p. 63.

112. For accounts of the events leading to the border dispute, see Langer, *European Alliances*, pp. 310–15; Kazemzadeh, "Russia and the Middle East," pp. 505–17; A. Meyendorff, I, 155–262; and Alder, pp. 195–203. For a detailed study of the Panjdeh crisis, see Greaves, Chap. 5; Rastogi, Chap. 3; Singhal, pp. 122–26; Ghose; and Anwar Khan. For a Soviet interpretation of those events, see Khalfin, *Proval britanskoi agressii*, pp. 136ff; and Masson and Romodin, II, 283–90. In the 1920's and 1930's, Soviet historians blamed the crisis on both imperialist camps, but especially on the Russians. See Reysner, *Afgan-*

istan, p. 85. The post–World War II historians, however, place the blame on the British, contending that Great Britain, in order to divert Afghan attention from the northwest frontier of India, armed, financed, and encouraged the Afghans to commit an act of aggression in the north. See *BSE*, 2d ed., III; and Iskanderov, pp. 86ff.

113. Great Britain, *British Documents*, I, 306–7, 376ff; Habberton, pp. 68–74; Langer, *Diplomacy of Imperialism*, pp. 668–69; Pokrovskii and Popov, pp. 3–29; Reysner, "Anglo-Russkaiia konventsia," pp. 54–66. For material on the Anglo-Russian understandings and Russian assurances about Afghanistan, see Great Britain, *British Documents*, IV, 512–14, 532; and Habberton, pp. 9–37, 69.

114. Great Britain, *British Documents*, IV, 541–44, 549, 612–14; and Reysner, "Anglo-Russkaiia konventsia." For a detailed study of the convention and its reception, see Churchill; and Adamec, Chap. 4. For the text of the treaty, see Great Britain, *British Documents*, IV, 618–20; and Hurewitz, I, 219ff. On Soviet views of the convention, see Reysner, *Nezavisimyi Afganistan*, pp. 97–110; M. S. Ivanov, pp. 219–22; Efremov, Chaps. 2 and 3; Bovykin; and Bestuzhev.

115. Great Britain, *British Documents*, IV, 577. See also Habberton, p. 81.

116. For details, see Reysner, "Anglo-Russkaiia konventsia," pp. 64–66; Churchill, p. 344; and Temperley, *History of the Peace Conference*, pp. 208–9.

117. Elphinstone, pp. 203–5; "Itinerary from Yezd to Herat," p. 14. See also C. Masson, "Journals," pp. 138f; Holdich, *Gates of India*, p. 337; and Vambery, *Sketches*, p. 432.

118. C. Masson, *Narrative*, II, 244. See also *ibid.*, pp. 45, 79, 82, 86ff, 109, 112, 127, 174, 178, 275; A. Conolly, II, 77–78; Wilson (British Resident in the Persian Gulf) to Norris (chief secretary to the government of Bombay), September 11, 1830, in Forrest, *Selections from Travels and Journals*, pp. 103–4.

119. Gail, p. 115. Burnes also wrote (*Travels*, II, 106): "The Afghan Mohammedans seem to pay respect to Christians which they deny to their Hindoo fellow citizens. Us they call People of the Book." Even as late as 1845, Ferrier reported (*Caravan Journeys*, p. 126n) that in regions not directly affected by the Anglo-Afghan War, such as Herat, Christians were not only considered People of the Book, but "were freely admitted to eat with Mussulmans so long as they abstained from the forbidden food."

120. C. Masson, *Narrative*, I, 150–54; Holdich, *Gates of India*, p. 351.

121. See, for example, G. Rawlinson, p. 72; Kaye, *History of the War*, I, 368; Bellew, "Our Relations with Afghanistan," pp. 33, 37.

122. Fraser-Tytler, *Afghanistan*, p. 113.

123. Kennedy, I, 263, and II, 39; Kaye, *History of the War*, I, 426; Henry Marion Durand, p. 191; P. Sykes, *Afghanistan*, II, 17. The same conclusion is reached in Dodwell, V, 505: "The English retained their hold by force and by the distribution of money among the chiefs."

124. Kaye, *History of the War*, I, 371n.

125. Henry Marion Durand, p. 209.

126. An infantry regiment raised and commanded by a British officer, which was to be the nucleus of an Afghan national royal army, witnessed mass desertions and eventually joined Dost Muhammed's forces. See Kaye, *History of the*

War, I, 548–49. The military reforms that were proposed by Burnes completely ignored tribal and social hierarchies, and aroused both religious and tribal opposition. See Lal, *Amir Dost Mohammed*, II, 371f; and Gupta, "Mohan Lal's Observations," pp. 1388–1401.

127. Kaye, *History of the War*, I, 555. See also Reshtiya, *Afghanestan*, p. 84; G. Rawlinson, pp. 77–78.

128. Kaye, *History of the War*, I, 480–81. See also G. Rawlinson, p. 82.

129. Kaye, *History of the War*, I, 480–81. See also Lal, *Amir Dost Mohammed*, II, 271f; and Outram, p. 69.

130. G. Rawlinson, p. 88; Kennedy, II, 126–27, 141; Sale, p. 20; Kaye, *History of the War*, II, 15–16, and I, 437, 592f, 626n; Lal, *Amir Dost Mohammed*, II, 220–303, 314f; Forrest, *Neville Chamberlain*, pp. 49f; and Reshtiya, *Afghanestan*, pp. 85f.

131. Kaye, *History of the War*, I, 598–99. Mohan Lal even tried to stir up Sunni-Shi'ah antagonism as a diversionary move. See Henry Marion Durand, p. 364.

132. P. Sykes, *Afghanistan*, II, 15.

133. "The Outbreak in Kabul," p. 311; Wolff, *Narrative*, pp. 309–10; Lal, *Amir Dost Mohammed*, II, 393–98; Kaye, *History of the War*, I, 624, and II, 143; Henry Marion Durand, pp. 211–12; and Taylor, pp. 137–38.

134. Kaye, *History of the War*, I, 480. See also C. Masson, *Narrative*, II, 271; Lal, *Amir Dost Mohammed*, II, 314ff; A. Abbott, pp. 77, 84; and Reshtiya, *Afghanestan*, p. 85.

135. Lal, *Amir Dost Mohammed*, II, 319–21. For a selection of anti-Commissariat songs, see Darmesteter, *Chants populaires*, pp. 66–67.

136. See Outram, pp. 92–93.

137. Sale, p. 6; Henry Marion Durand, p. 211.

138. Lal, *Amir Dost Mohammed*, II, 313. Kaye noted that the British officers had no respect for Shah Shuja and resented him. See *History of the War*, I, 532n. This is corroborated by Kennedy (see II, 11). Augustus Abbott wrote (p. 82): "Everyone is surprised at the misinformation given us regarding the roads, and the resources of this country, and the *disposition of its inhabitants towards Shah Shuja.*"

139. Forrest, *Neville Chamberlain*, p. 49; Stocqueler, *William Nott*, I, 395; Kaye, *History of the War*, II, 189f, 218, 224n, 227. On Afghan national unity and the concord between religious leaders and most of the important tribes, see Kaye, *History of the War*, II, 4–5; and Sale, p. 10. For recent analyses of the uprising in Kabul, see Yapp, "Revolution of 1841–42"; and Norris, Chap. 15.

140. Dodwell, V, 513. See also *Parliamentary Papers*, XXXVII (1843): Accounts and Papers, Afghanistan, No. 69.

141. Kaye, *History of the War*, II, 638–39; Lal, *Amir Dost Mohammed*, II, 487–89; Forrest, *Neville Chamberlain*, p. 151; Stocqueler, *Memorials*, p. 289; Kennedy, II, 320–21; P. Sykes, *Afghanistan*, II, 56–57. Ferrier sets the number of those left homeless in Kabul at 100,000 (*History*, pp. 377–78), but this is clearly exaggerated, since the population of Kabul at that time was no more than 50,000–60,000.

142. Kaye, *History of the War*, II, 607n. See also Bellew, *Journal*, p. 184; G. Rawlinson, p. 132; Kennedy, II, 277; and Forrest, *Neville Chamberlain*, p. 135.

Earlier, in 1831 the Sikh ruler had demanded the same gates (alleged to be the gates of Somnath) ; at that time Shah Shuja had replied that to comply would be an act of eternal disgrace for him. See Kaye, *History of the War*, I, 123n.

143. P. Sykes, *Afghanistan*, II, 40; Ferrier, *History*, p. 378; G. Rawlinson, p. 104.

144. Kennedy, II, 317, 344, 346; Kaye, *History of the War*, II, 404, 632–35, 659f; A. Abbott, pp. 107, 318–22; Ferrier, *History*, pp. 375–79; G. Rawlinson, p. 94; Forrest, *Neville Chamberlain*, pp. 61, 85, 135, 144ff, 149. On the vengeance on Ghazni, see Sale, pp. 81–82; and Norris, p. 413. For a survey of the actions of the "Army of Retribution," see Norris, Chap. 16.

145. Kaye, *History of the War*, II, 669.

146. See Martineau, I, pp. 363–64. The principle of punitive expeditions was also criticized by Lord Lytton, who considered it a "perpetuation of a system of semi-barbarous reprisal" and "animosity." See *Parliamentary Papers*, LVIII (1878), 142. For some texts of the anti-British literature and transcripts of some of the oral traditions of the period, see Darmesteter, *Chants populaires*, pp. 48–82. For a full treatment of the British policies toward the frontier tribes, see Davies, *Problem of the NW Frontier*; Spain, *Pathan Borderland*, Chap. 7; and Fraser-Tytler, *Afghanistan*, Chap. 10.

147. Reshtiya, *Afghanestan*, pp. 245–48; Roberts, pp. 412, 416.

148. Soviet Embassy, *News Bulletin* (Kabul), No. 97, May 24, 1959. See also Daud's declaration in the United States on the same subject, in Mohammed Ali, *The Mohammedzai Period*, pp. 304–5. On a similar theme, see the speech of M. Naurozi (president of the Afghan National Assembly in 1959) on the occasion of the opening of Afghan independence day celebrations, in *Anis*, August 25, 1959, or in Mohammed Ali, *New Guide to Afghanistan*, p. 7.

149. Safarov, pp. 286, 290. See "On Soviet Interpretations of Relations Between Britain, Russia and Afghanistan: 1872–1880," along with the comments of Caroe, in *Central Asian Review*, VI (1958), 2, 205–28; see also C. Black, *Rewriting Russian History*.

150. A typical exponent of this view was Col. G. B. Malleson. See his book *Herat*, pp. 8f, 13. See also Bellew, *Races*, p. 55. Even Kaye, a most sympathetic writer, asserted that the Afghans "knew no happiness in anything but strife," and that "it was their delight to live in a state of chronic warfare" (*History of the War*, I, 11ff).

151. Habberton, p. 86; Howland, "Afghanistan," pp. 633ff. See also Cumming *et al.*, p. 370; P. Sykes, *Afghanistan*, Conclusion; and Fraser-Tytler, *Afghanistan*, Conclusion.

152. Pannikar, *Afro-Asian States*, p. 79.

153. On the deterioration of Kandahar and Kabul, see Ferrier, *History*, p. 378; Stocqueler, *Memorials*, p. 111; Atkinson, pp. 319, 321; Roberts, p. 410; *Parliamentary Papers*, LXX (1880) : "Correspondence Relating to the Affairs of Afghanistan," No. 1, pp. 19, 25. See also Kaye, *History of the War*, I, 259f.

154. Roberts, pp. 388–89.

155. "Wahabis in India," p. 189; Forrest, *Neville Chamberlain*, p. 35; Hellwald, p. 217.

156. C. Masson, *Narrative*, I, 391; MacMunn, *Martial Races*, pp. 180, 227, 242.

157. Hellwald, pp. 236–39; Ghose, pp. 19, 59.
158. Bonvalot, pp. 133–34. See also Marsh, p. 60.

CHAPTER FIVE

1. Angus Hamilton, *Afghanistan*, pp. 223–25.
2. Munshi, *Life of Abdur Rahman*, II, 80. According to T. E. Gordon (p. 121), Sher Ali also believed in the divine right of kings and spoke of his "God-granted government," a divine duty that required of him the highest self-sacrifice and the complete subordination of all personal feeling.
3. Munshi, *Life of Abdur Rahman*, II, 2, 15, 50, 198, 220.
4. Angus Hamilton, *Afghanistan*, p. 298.
5. For the text of this proclamation, see S. Wheeler, pp. 248–50.
6. Singhal, pp. 72, 149n; S. Wheeler, p. 122. According to Wheeler, the exact amount the Amir received in subsidies is not recorded in any trustworthy publication. Stating that his account of the sums paid to Abdur Rahman down to the middle of 1881 "may be taken as correct," Wheeler lists dates, locations, and even the agents through whom material aid was transferred to the Amir. See Ripon's letter of June 16, 1883, to the Amir and his grateful reply, in Wheeler, pp. 125–26. On British aid and understandings with Abdur Rahman upon his assumption of power, see *Parliamentary Papers*, LXXXVII (1884); Public Record Office, F.O. 65 (Russia), 1104, 1173; Griffin, pp. 241–69; S. Gopal, *Lord Ripon*, pp. 12–14, 46–47; on Anglo-Afghan relations during his reign, see Adamec, Chap. 1.
7. Curzon, *Tales of Travel*, pp. 69–72.
8. H. Mortimer Durand, pp. 18–19; Enriquez, p. 72.
9. Munshi, *Life of Abdur Rahman*, II, 12–13.
10. P. Sykes, *Afghanistan*, II, 190; Munshi, *Life of Abdur Rahman*, I, 256. One of the chiefs of the Ghilzai tribe was ignobly killed by stoning.
11. Munshi, *Life of Abdur Rahman*, I, 276–84; P. Sykes, *Afghanistan*, II, 192–93. Fletcher (*Afghanistan*, p. 147) speaks of the possibility that Abdur Rahman engineered the Hazara rebellion as a means of stimulating Pathan solidarity, but there are no sources that bear this out. C. E. Stewart (p. 293) reported that the Hazaras of Kandahar later paid for their friendliness toward the British during the occupation of Kandahar in the Second Anglo-Afghan War.
12. According to Soviet historiography, Abdur Rahman's rule placed the Uzbeks, Tajiks, and Hazaras under a double yoke, adding the burden of Afghan ethnic rule to the burden of feudalism. See Akhramovich, in Dvoriankov, pp. 254–55. For a full treatment of this subject, see Iskanderov, pp. 86ff. Iskanderov and Khalfin (*Proval britanskoi agressii*, pp. 136–38) reflect the current interpretations of Soviet historiography. The Soviet historians hold that the British sponsored Afghan expansionism in the north to divert Afghan attention from the Indian frontier. In 1885 the people of Roshan sent a delegation to the Russian Pamir Expedition requesting assistance against the Afghan monarchy. In return they offered to submit Shugnan and Roshan to Russian rule. However, the Russians were unable and unwilling to lend such help. Bukhara, too, attempted to procure Russia's aid, also in vain. See *Parliamentary Papers*,

LXXXVIII (1885), "Central Asia, No. 2," pp. 2–3: "Vlangali Memorandum."
For details, see Becker, pp. 180–81.

13. Gray, pp. 379–80.

14. "Summary of Events," *The Asiatic Quarterly Review*, October 1888,
p. 213.

15. H. Mortimer Durand, pp. 18–19. For a survey of the Amir's centralization policies, see Fletcher, *Afghanistan*, pp. 145–48.

16. Pensa, p. 4.

17. For details on the administrative divisions, reorganization, and legal
framework of the Afghan monarchy under Abdur Rahman, see Munshi, *Life
of Abdur Rahman*, II, 188–89; and Sultan Muhammed Khan, *Laws and Constitution of Afghanistan* (London, 1900). See also Angus Hamilton, *Afghanistan*, pp. 226f; and Fazli, p. 65.

18. Munshi, *Life of Abdur Rahman*, II, 204f.

19. *Ibid.*, I, 218, 251n.

20. *Ibid.*, II, 51.

21. Some of these tracts are available in the Oriental Room of the British
Museum. See Abdur Rahman Khan, *Kalimat*, for the Amir's views on his responsibilities in connection with a jihad. Some of his speeches on this same
subject are translated in the December 1887 issue of *Pioneer*, and a summary
appears in S. Wheeler, pp. 227–28.

22. The Amir estimated that, before his rule, nearly half the revenues of the
kingdom went to the mullahs and other religious luminaries (see Munshi, *Life
of Abdur Rahman*, I, 252), but this seems to be an exaggeration. There are no
studies dealing specifically with either the waqfs in Afghanistan or the Amir's
measures in that domain. There are only passing references to them in Angus
Hamilton, *Afghanistan*, pp. 224–25; Janssens, pp. 13–14; and Wilber, "Islam
in Afghanistan," p. 44.

23. Munshi, *Life of Abdur Rahman*, I, 253. "Clergymen and priests, who
used to look upon themselves as equal to prophets, cannot be appointed to any
post, or admitted to perform the duties of the Church, without first passing an
examination and obtaining a certificate from the Council of Examiners" (*ibid.*,
II, 74).

24. P. Sykes, *Afghanistan*, II, 190.

25. Munshi, *Life of Abdur Rahman*, II, 32. For literary works written on the
conquest of Kafiristan, see Darmesteter, *Chants populaires*. For a Soviet account of that conquest, see Masson and Romodin, II, 303–4.

26. Angus Hamilton, *Afghanistan*, pp. 231–32; Munshi, *Life of Abdur Rahman*, I, 209.

27. E. and A. Thornton, pp. 110, 111; Munshi, *Life of Abdur Rahman*, II,
52–53; Fazli, p. 65; Angus Hamilton, *Afghanistan*, pp. 239, 241.

28. Angus Hamilton, *Afghanistan*, p. 241.

29. *Ibid.*, p. 232; Munshi, *Life of Abdur Rahman*, II, 7, 66, 205; Gray, p. 408.

30. Gray, p. 27; E. and A. Thornton, pp. 182, 196–97; Curzon, *Tales of
Travel*, p. 65.

31. According to Abdur Rahman, the sum was 50 rupees (Munshi, *Life of
Abdur Rahman*, I, 224); however, in the second volume of his autobiography,
the figure was 300 rupees (*ibid.*, II, 66). P. Sykes (*Afghanistan*, II, 197) gives

an erroneous figure of 400 rupees. On the basis of a 50-rupee fine for each murder and a total of 50,000 rupees in fines, the Amir concluded that 1,000 murders had been committed in the small province of Najrab (which had 20,000 families) under the rule of Sher Ali. However, he forgot to take into account the possibility that fines for other offenses were included in that total.

32. Munshi, *Life of Abdur Rahman*, II, 66; P. Sykes, *Afghanistan*, II, 197. Most families would have been ruined financially by this fine. See Gray, p. 55. Later, under Habibullah Khan (1901–19), the fine was increased to 10,000–12,000 rupees. See Jewett, *An American Engineer*, p. 175.

33. F. A. Martin, p. 28.

34. Munshi, *Life of Abdur Rahman*, II, 66–67. According to some accounts, the practice of widows marrying their husbands' next of kin became prevalent during Ahmad Shah's rule. He sanctioned the practice of arranging such a marriage (except to the father, son, or full brother of her dead husband). When there were no relatives, the widow was to continue to reside in her husband's house and live on the income of his property until her death. Ahmad Shah also instituted a very important change in the Afghan laws of inheritance, decreeing that only sons could succeed their fathers. Women were thus deprived not only of financial power but also of the right to pass on family wealth to their husbands. This was significant in that it denied non-Afghans the possibility of inheriting from Afghan in-laws. See Sultan Muhammad Durrani, p. 147; and Ferrier, *History*, p. 93.

35. Munshi, *Life of Abdur Rahman*, II, 67; P. Sykes, *Afghanistan*, II, 197.

36. C. E. Stewart reported (p. 430) that there were about 100,000 slaves in Bukhara, Khiva, and the Turkoman country in the 1870's.

37. Munshi, *Life of Abdur Rahman*, I, 236, and II, 92–93, 110; Angus Hamilton, *Afghanistan*, pp. 168–69. For details about slavery in Kabul and northern Afghanistan on the eve of Abdur Rahman's edict banning the practice, see Gray, pp. 193, 212–13, 323; and Holdich, *Gates of India*, p. 253.

38. Angus Hamilton, *Afghanistan*, pp. 262–68 *passim*.

39. S. Wheeler, p. 217.

40. Munshi, *Life of Abdur Rahman*, I, 7, and II, 52–53; Lyons, p. 171. I. A. Shah (*Tragedy of Amanullah*, p. 182) erroneously asserts that Abdur Rahman adhered to the qomi system. *Stateman's Yearbook: 1901*, p. 363, states that in 1896 the Amir ordered a conscription of one man in every seven (sic), but that the order met with much opposition.

41. C. E. Stewart, pp. 367f.

42. See Angus Hamilton, *Afghanistan*, pp. 271ff; *EB* (11th ed.), p. 312; and Munshi, *Life of Abdur Rahman*, II, 43, 52.

43. Munshi, *Life of Abdur Rahman*, II, 47–48; Angus Hamilton, *Afghanistan*, p. 293.

44. Angus Hamilton, *Afghanistan*, p. 272; and Munshi, *Life of Abdur Rahman*, I, 203.

45. The estimate of the manpower is S. Wheeler's (p. 217). According to him, the army had 58,740 men and 182 guns in 1882. This included about 50,000 infantrymen, 5,000 cavalrymen, and 1,000 artillerymen. By 1890, the Amir's army had some 200 guns. See Lyons, p. 171; Pensa, p. 6; and *Statesman's Yearbook: 1901*, p. 363.

46. Angus Hamilton, *Afghanistan*, p. 274. For mention of the Amir's high hopes, see Munshi, *Life of Abdur Rahman*, II, 190; S. Wheeler, p. 217.

47. Munshi, *Life of Abdur Rahman*, II, 196. In 1885, in a meeting at Rawalpindi with Dufferin, the viceroy of India, Abdur Rahman even refused to allow British officers to assist in the fortification of Herat, "lest complications arise from their presence among his troops." However, in case of war with Russia, he agreed to admit two British officers. See Singhal, pp. 119–20.

48. Holdich, *Indian Borderland*, pp. 167–68.

49. Munshi, *Life of Abdur Rahman*, I, 203; H. Mortimer Durand, p. 19.

50. Angus Hamilton, *Afghanistan*, pp. 242, 246.

51. Mohammed Ali, *The Mohammedzai Period*, pp. 141–42.

52. Munshi, *Life of Abdur Rahman*, II, 22f; S. Wheeler, pp. 218–19, 221.

53. S. Wheeler, p. 222; Munshi, *Life of Abdur Rahman*, II, 27, 47–48; Gray, pp. 19, 32, 263. Pensa estimates (p. 6) that 20,000 cartridges and 15 rifles a day were produced, as do Lyons (pp. 176–77), *Statesman's Yearbook: 1901* (p. 363), and Angus Hamilton (*Afghanistan*, p. 274).

54. Munshi, *Life of Abdur Rahman*, II, 27, 47; H. Mortimer Durand, p. 19. See also M. Qadir, "Karkhaneha," pp. 144–45; and Kohzad, "Maskukat," p. 248.

55. The distilling machinery the Amir imported could produce about 1,500 bottles every eight hours. See Gray, pp. 372–73; and Munshi, *Life of Abdur Rahman*, II, 57.

56. Munshi, *Life of Abdur Rahman*, II, 34–35, 39; Angus Hamilton, *Afghanistan*, p. 244; E. and A. Thornton, pp. 20–28; S. Wheeler, pp. 222, 224; Gray, pp. 12, 476.

57. Munshi, *Life of Abdur Rahman*, II, 68–69; *Statesman's Yearbook: 1901*, p. 365.

58. Angus Hamilton, *Afghanistan*, pp. 225, 238.

59. Warburton, p. 136; Munshi, *Life of Abdur Rahman*, II, 78.

60. Munshi, *Life of Abdur Rahman*, I, 209; Angus Hamilton, *Afghanistan*, pp. 242, 247–48.

61. My figures for the trade of northern and eastern Afghanistan (Kabul) with India are drawn from *Statesman's Yearbook*. See p. 315 in all the volumes from 1892 through 1895, and p. 363 in the volume for 1901.

62. *Statesman's Yearbook: 1901*, p. 364. Here are the figures on the trade of western and southern Afghanistan (Kandahar) with India (in rupees). 1891–92: imports 5,121,750, exports 4,604,840; 1893–94: imports 2,976,570, exports 2,344,280; 1894–95: imports 3,282,000, exports 3,358,000. By 1899–1900, this trade, including both exports and imports, amounted to 7,143,180 rupees. These statistics are based on *Statesman's Yearbook*; see note 61 above.

63. On Russian measures against the Anglo-Indian trade with Central Asia, see Curzon, *Russia in Central Asia*, p. 284.

64. My figures on Russian-Afghan trade for 1888–89 are drawn from Pensa, p. 9; and *Statesman's Yearbook: 1892*, p. 315. Those for 1889–1900 are from M. A. Babakhodzhaev, *Russko-Afganskie torgovo-ekonomicheskie otnosheniia* (Tashkent, 1965), pp. 61–66. According to Drage (p. 521) and Strickland (p. 721), by 1895 the value of Afghan imports from Russia had fallen to 21,000 rubles and that of the exports to Russia to 209,000 rubles. They maintain further that by 1896 this last figure had dwindled to a mere 83,000 rubles, that by

the end of the year trade between the two countries was virtually at a standstill, and that trade was not resumed until 1901. These observations are wrong. Russian-Afghan trade, though it was subject to great fluctuations, did not cease in the 1890's, nor even reach such a low ebb as indicated.

65. Gray, p. 18.

66. Munshi, *Life of Abdur Rahman*, II, 75, 77.

67. *Ibid.*, II, 76; Strickland, p. 718.

68. On Abdur Rahman's prohibitive tariffs, see Pensa, p. 8; Drage, p. 522; *Statesman's Yearbook: 1901*, p. 364; and Singhal, p. 137.

69. Gray, p. 5. The net amount of British subsidies to the tribes of the Pass was some 150–200 thousand rupees. See Warburton, p. 330.

70. S. Wheeler, pp. 199–200; A. C. Yate, "Visit to India," pp. 32–33; P. Sykes, *Afghanistan*, II, 172.

71. Munshi, *Life of Abdur Rahman*, II, 68f; Gray, pp. 32, 261.

72. Holdich, *Indian Borderland*, p. 166. See also Warburton, p. 153; and Gray, p. 69.

73. F. A. Martin, p. 277; E. and A. Thornton, p. 43.

74. *GLE*, p. 709. See also India, *Imperial Gazetteer*, XIV, 13, 242ff, 375, and XIII, 114.

75. My information on improvements in health standards is drawn mainly from Gray, p. 43; S. Wheeler, pp. 219–24 *passim*; Munshi, *Life of Abdur Rahman*, I, 204, and II, 7, 25–26, 70–74 *passim*; and F. A. Martin, p. 45.

76. Gray, pp. 109–10, 119, 165ff.

77. *Ibid.*, pp. 121–22, 127.

78. *Ibid.*, pp. 467, 471; F. A. Martin, pp. 44–45.

79. Munshi, *Life of Abdur Rahman*, II, 46.

80. Gray, p. 321.

81. Munshi, *Life of Abdur Rahman*, I, 46, 74, 204. The students in the "model" school attached to the court were between 12 and 20 years of age. Their curriculum included some science, history, and geography, but religion was the main subject. See Karimi, "Maaref," p. 396.

82. Stolz, "Langues étrangères," p. 27.

83. Munshi, *Life of Abdur Rahman*, II, 18, 46–47, 76; Mohammed Ali, *The Mohammedzai Period*, p. 142; Karimi, "Maaref," p. 396. During this period, a Pashto translation of the Persian literary classic *Yusef va Zoleikha* was printed; so were one or two Pashto textbooks. See Zumeryali, "Pashto," p. 335. The introduction of the Kabul printing press is also reported in M. Qadir, "Karkhaneha," p. 150.

84. Munshi, *Life of Abdur Rahman*, II, 46, 107.

85. Gray, pp. 70, 73, 75, 84f.

86. *Ibid.*, pp. 57, 73, 88f, 476; Munshi, *Life of Abdur Rahman*, II, 44, 47.

87. Munshi, *Life of Abdur Rahman*, II, 44; Gray, pp. 108, 476.

88. H. Mortimer Durand, p. 13. The Amir introduced some of these innovations after his official visit to India, where, among other gifts, he received watches, clocks, cabinets, and music boxes. See Marchioness of Dufferin and Ava, I, 113–14.

89. Gray, p. 321. Gray lists many of the European innovations adopted by

the Amir. See especially pp. 33–43 *passim*, 57, 258, 364. See also Munshi, *Life of Abdur Rahman*, I, 142. In 1878–79, Yakub Khan also posed for British photographers.

90. Marvin, p. 174. See especially the account of A. Stuart, an engineer in the employ of De Lesseps, in Marvin, pp. 396–99, 417ff, 445ff, 476ff, 496ff; and Radau, pp. 386–421.

91. Sir Thomas Holdich, *Morning Post*, November 5, 1907.

92. W. E. Wheeler, p. 585. See also George Dobson, *Russia's Railway Advance into Central Asia* (London, 1890); and Negri.

93. Marvin, p. 174.

94. *Ibid.*, p. 179; Lobanov-Rostovsky, *Russia and Asia*, pp. 174–75; Lyons, p. 147.

95. For details about Russian intentions, see Kazemzadeh, "Russian Imperialism," pp. 355–73, especially pp. 356–66.

96. Salisbury to the Queen (private), December 30, 1879, as quoted by Greaves, p. 51. See also Lyons, p. 21; and British Museum, Kimberly to Ripon, February 22, 1884, and Northbrook to Ripon, February 22, 1884, Add. MSS. 43575 and 43576, respectively. On the importance of extending the railway to Kandahar, see also Salisbury to Bismarck, July 2, 1885, in Greaves, p. 92; and Bruce, pp. 18–22, 35.

97. Letter of J. M. Maclean, former publisher of *The Bombay Gazette*, to *The Times*, April 12, 1900.

98. C. E. Yate, *Khurassan*, p. 14; *The Times*, March 12, 1901, and October 20, November 20, and December 2, 1902.

99. Munshi, *Life of Abdur Rahman*, II, 154; S. Wheeler, pp. 199–200. On the strategic and economic advantages of such a line, see Holdich, *Indian Borderland*, pp. 172–78 *passim*.

100. Munshi, *Life of Abdur Rahman*, II, 77; S. Wheeler, p. 199.

101. Munshi, *Life of Abdur Rahman*, II, 60, 77, 208–9.

102. Lyons, pp. 172–73.

103. Munshi, *Life of Abdur Rahman*, II, 150.

104. *Ibid.*, pp. 72–73, 171, 210. See also A. C. Yate, "Trans-Persian Railway," p. 7; and Panikkar, *Afro-Asian States*, p. 79.

105. Munshi, *Life of Abdur Rahman*, II, 18, 196.

106. *Ibid.*, pp. 124, 168, 171, 260ff, 270ff, 280.

107. Abdur Rahman Khan, *Sar reshte-ye Islami-ye*; Munshi, *Life of Abdur Rahman*, II, 293.

108. Munshi, *Life of Abdur Rahman*, II, 172, 205.

109. *Ibid.*, p. 211.

110. *Ibid.*, pp. 133, 138, 142f, 244.

111. For the text of the Durand Agreement, see India, *Treaties*, XIII, No. 12 (Afghanistan), pp. 255–58.

112. Caroe, *The Pathans*, p. 383; Davies, *Problem of the NW Frontier*, pp. 161–62; Fraser-Tytler, *Afghanistan*, p. 188; Holdich, *Indian Borderland*, pp. 54f. The Amir suggested to the British that the best way of dealing with the tribes was to leave them under the dominion of Afghanistan. He claimed that, if this were done, he would be able to make the tribesmen fight against any

enemy of England (as well as his own), by appealing to their sense of brotherhood and by bringing them under the banner of a Muslim ruler. See Rastogi, p. 159.

113. See Raverty, "Independent Tribes," pp. 312–26.

114. Barton, *India's NW Frontier,* pp. 19, 23.

115. For a discusion of various expeditions, see Davies' excellent study *Problem of the NW Frontier,* Chap. 5 and Appendix B; Singhal, pp. 157–63; and Spain, *Pathan Borderland,* pp. 174ff. For folklore reflecting the Afghans' sympathies for the Pathans in their struggles against the British, see Darmesteter, *Chants populaires.*

116. Curzon, *Tales of Travel,* p. 75.

117. *Ibid.,* pp. 83–84. On the deterioration in the relations between India and Afghanistan in 1892–98, see Rastogi, p. 165; Bellew, "Our Relations with Afghanistan"; Leitner, "Amir of Afghanistan" and "Amir Abdurrahman"; and Abdur Rahman Khan, "A Letter."

118. Holdich, *Indian Borderland,* pp. 140, 171; C. E. Stewart, p. 369.

119. For data on the condition of the peasantry and the rural economy under Abdur Rahman, see *Statesman's Yearbook: 1901,* p. 363; India, *Imperial Gazetteer,* V, 51–54; Efimov, p. 474.

120. Munshi, *Life of Abdur Rahman,* II, 173, 212–13.

CHAPTER SIX

1. Until recently, the study of Tarzi's career and ideas was discouraged in Afghanistan, apparently because of his close family ties and political association with King Amanullah. Until the late 1950's, Afghan official sources omitted any mention of the name "Tarzi." See, for instance, Reshtiya, "Journalism in Afghanistan," and the Afghan government publication *The 40th Anniversary of the Independence of Afghanistan.* Currently, however, Tarzi and his many contributions to the Afghan nationalist-modernist movement are being recognized by Afghan historians. See, for example, Zhobal, "Mahmud Tarzi" and *Adabiyat-e Afghanestan.* There are no monographic or general Afghan studies on Tarzi in either Persian or Pashto. The overwhelming majority of European and American studies on modern Islam and Asian nationalism fail to mention Tarzi, *Siraj al-Akhbar,* or, for that matter, even Afghan nationalism and modernism. A few works make casual reference to Tarzi, his periodical, and the Young Afghans. They are Browne, *Press and Poetry,* pp. 24, 102; Kohn, *Nationalism in the East,* p. 344; Nariman, pp. 252–58; Bogdanov, "Notes," pp. 126–52 *passim;* and P. Sykes, *Afghanistan,* II, 264–65. Among the post–World War II studies, Fraser-Tytler, *Afghanistan,* ignores both *Siraj al-Akhbar* and Tarzi, and Wilber, *Afghanistan* (2d ed.), p. 168, gives them only a few lines. Most surprising of all, both the old and the new editions of the *Encyclopedia of Islam* ignore not only Tarzi and his periodical, but the entire Afghan modernist-nationalist movement. The only meaningful biographical sketch on Tarzi in English is the recent article by Dupree, "Tarzi." In French, Dianous' article "Littérature afghane," Part 2, pp. 138–44, remains the sole attempt to analyze Tarzi's work and role. Adamec, in his recent study, discusses the impact of

Tarzi's periodical and its role in Anglo-Afghan relations (pp. 101–3). The Soviet Afghanists, despite their numerous studies and their constant acknowledgment of the historical importance of Tarzi, *Siraj al-Akhbar*, and the Young Afghans, have as yet produced no monographic studies on the subject. To the best of my knowledge, until 1963 the only published article on Tarzi in Russian was a sketchy translation of a work by the Afghan poet Khalili, "Makhmud-bek Tarzi," pp. 156–57. For a biographical sketch of Tarzi in Russian, see Masson and Romodin, II, 346–51. According to Masson and Romodin (II, 346 fn98, 485), there is an unpublished dissertation on Tarzi by Mirzoev.

2. *SA*, 1st year, No. 5, p. 12; Khalili, "Makhmud-bek Tarzi," p. 156. In Wilber, *Afghanistan* (2d ed.), p. 178, the authors have inadvertently confused Sardar Ghulam Muhammed Khan with his son Mahmud. On the Sardar's life and poetry, see *SA*, 2d year, No. 7, p. 11. See also Behruz, p. 364; Dupree, "Tarzi," pp. 2–4; Dianous, "Littérature afghane," Part 1, p. 143, and Part 2, pp. 138–39; and Masson and Romodin, II, 347.

3. Kātrak, p. xiv.

4. A. W. Tarzi, p. 169; Masson and Romodin, II, 347. Dianous ("Littérature afghane," Part 2, p. 139) asserts that Tarzi was born in Damascus in 1867, but he is wrong: Tarzi was born in Ghazni.

5. Tarzi's father greatly revered al-Afghānī. See A. W. Tarzi, pp. 169–70; and the Sardar's Qasida (laudatory poem) on al-Afghānī in Dianous, "Littérature afghane," Part 2, p. 138.

6. Dupree, "Tarzi," p. 5.

7. Kātrak, p. xiv. In *Raudat-i-hikam* (pp. 139, 144), Mahmud Tarzi speaks of his "heart-breaking nostalgia" for the Afghan fatherland.

8. A. W. Tarzi, p. 170.

9. Browne, *Press and Poetry*, p. 102; Bertels, pp. 10–11. Excluding copies of the Quran and some important standard religious texts, there were no more than ten books published in Afghanistan, including classical Persian literary anthologies, at the time *SA* began publication. See Behruz, p. 369. Dianous, ("Littérature afghane," Part 2, p. 140) sets the number at two, but he seems not to have included the few works that were printed during Abdur Rahman's reign.

10. *SA*, 1st year, Nos. 21, p. 15, and 2, p. 9.

11. *Ibid.*, 7th year, No. 16, p. 6.

12. M. Tarzi, *Raudat-i-hikam*, pp. 140–42. See also *SA*, 7th year, Nos. 14, p. 4, and 18, pp. 4–6; and 3d year, No. 16, pp. 10–12.

13. M. Tarzi, *Raudat-i-hikam*, pp. 146–47, 149.

14. *SA*, 3d year, Nos. 13, p. 13, and 19, p. 7.

15. *Ibid.*, 7th year, No. 18, p. 7.

16. *Ibid.*, 2d year, Nos. 13, p. 3, and 18, p. 15. See also 2d year, Nos. 14, p. 23, and 21, p. 9.

17. *Ibid.*, 6th year, No. 14, p. 2; and 1st year, No. 10, p. 13. See also 2d year, No. 16, p. 3.

18. *Ibid.*, 3d year, No. 16, pp. 10–12.

19. *Ibid.*, 1st year, No. 16, p. 1; and 2d year, No. 12. See also 3d year, No. 17, pp. 5–8.

20. *Ibid.*, 1st year, No. 16, p. 1; 3d year, Nos. 2, p. 8, and 8, pp. 5–8. See also 5th year, No. 17, p. 8, and 7th year, No. 19, p. 8.

21. See the letter of Muhammed Barakatullah, an Indian revolutionary and a contributor to *SA*, in *ibid.*, 3d year, No. 2, p. 8.

22. *Ibid.*, 4th year, No. 8, p. 5; and 5th year, No. 19, p. 2.

23. *Ibid.*, 2d year, No. 1, p. 16.

24. *Ibid.*, No. 16, p. 8.

25. *Ibid.*, 4th year, No. 15, pp. 6–7, 8.

26. M. Tarzi, *Raudat-i-hikam*, p. 156.

27. *SA*, 2d year, No. 14, pp. 14–15; and 5th year, No. 17, pp. 10–11. See also Abdur Rahman's article, 3d year, No. 17, pp. 5–8.

28. *Ibid.*, 3d year, No. 2, pp. 2–3; and 1st year, No. 10, p. 13.

29. *Ibid.*, 3d year, No. 17, pp. 5–8. See also the article by Mullah Tuti, 3d year, No. 8.

30. M. Tarzi, *Raudat-i-hikam*, pp. 9, 11–12, 14ff, 38.

31. *SA*, 6th year, No. 14, pp. 2–3; and 1st year, No. 4, p. 9. See also 3d year, No. 17, p. 4; and 5th year, No. 17, p. 5.

32. *Ibid.*, 1st year, No. 12, pp. 1–2; and 3d year, Nos. 8, p. 5, and 17, p. 4.

33. *Ibid.*, 5th year, No. 23-24, pp. 8–10.

34. *Ibid.*, 3d year, No. 6, p. 4; M. Tarzi, *Raudat-i-hikam*, p. 6.

35. *SA*, 4th year, No. 21, p. 6; and 5th year, No. 17, p. 9. See also 3d year, No. 2, p. 7.

36. *Ibid.*, 5th year, No. 17, p. 7.

37. *Ibid.*, 2d year, No. 13, pp. 3–4; and 3d year, No. 2, p. 8. See also 5th year, No. 17, p. 8; M. Tarzi, *Raudat-i-hikam*, pp. 153–54.

38. On the use of English, see *SA*, 4th year, No. 22, p. 7. On tourism, see M. Tarzi, *Raudat-i-hikam*, pp. 45–47, 49.

39. *SA*, 7th year, No. 19, p. 9; and 2d year, No. 24, p. 3.

40. *Ibid.*, 5th year, No. 6, p. 9.

41. *Ibid.*, No. 17, pp. 1–2; and M. Tarzi, *Raudat-i-hikam*, pp. 151–52, 153.

42. *Siraj al-Atfal*, 1st year, No. 4, p. 4.

43. *SA*, 1st year, No. 12, pp. 14–15; and M. Tarzi, *Raudat-i-hikam*, p. 5.

44. *SA*, 1st year, No. 4, pp. 7–8; and 2d year, No. 16, pp. 11–12.

45. *Ibid.*, 4th year, No. 15, pp. 6–7; 7th year, No. 16, p. 6; and 2d year, No. 16, pp. 11–12. See also M. Fazli's article "On the Need for Public Libraries," 1st year, No. 17, p. 12.

46. Wilber (*Annotated Bibliography*, p. 81) erroneously attributes *Siraj-ul-Tawarikh*, a two-volume history of Afghanistan by Faiz Muhammed Kateb, to Tarzi.

47. *SA*, 2d year, Nos. 8, p. 13, 2, p. 3, and 7, p. 15.

48. *Ibid.*, No. 3, p. 12; and 1st year, No. 3, p. 8.

49. *Ibid.*, 2d year, No. 3, p. 10.

50. *Ibid.*, 1st year, No. 3, pp. 7ff. See also 3d year, No. 7, pp. 10–11. A. A. Jafarova, writing on the position of women in Afghanistan in *KSINA*, No. 73, 1963, says that Tarzi held that secular schools for girls were necessary, but I could not find any categorical statement by Tarzi to this effect. I believe that Tarzi was deliberately ambiguous on this subject because of its controversial nature.

51. *SA*, 1st year, No. 3, p. 3. According to Dupree ("Tarzi," pp. 5, 21), Tarzi had 20 children, 10 of whom are living.

52. *SA*, 3d year, No. 7, pp. 7–8.

53. M. Tarzi, *Raudat-i-hikam*, p. 151. See also *SA*, 1st year, Nos. 5, p. 5, 7, pp. 1–2, 11, p. 10, and 20, p. 2.

54. *SA*, 1st year, No. 24, pp. 10ff; and 5th year, No. 7, p. 8.

55. *SA*, 5th year, No. 7, p. 8.

56. *SA*, 1st year, No. 7, pp. 6–7. On this same theme, see also 4th year, No. 17, pp. 3–4; 3d year, No. 16, pp. 14–15. For poems on the subject of the fatherland (*watan*), see 4th year, No. 10, p. 7; 6th year, No. 24, pp. 1–3.

57. *Ibid.*, 4th year, Nos. 20, pp. 4–5, and 21, p. 6; 1st year, Nos. 18, p. 1, and 8, p. 4.

58. *Ibid.*, 1st year, No. 7, pp. 6–7; 4th year, No. 20, p. 6. Tarzi also compared the ruler to a tree and the nation to its roots. See *SA*, 1st year, No. 10, p. 7.

59. *Ibid.*, 4th year, No. 20, p. 6.

60. M. Tarzi, *Raudat-i-hikam*, p. 151.

61. *SA*, 2d year, Nos. 7, p. 14, and 8, p. 12. See also 5th year, No. 17, pp. 1–2; M. Tarzi, *Raudat-i-hikam*, p. 145.

62. *SA*, 3d year, Nos. 16, p. 13, and 22, p. 1. See also 2d year, Nos. 8, p. 12, and 21, p. 2.

63. *Ibid.*, 1st year, No. 11, p. 8; 6th year, Nos. 6, p. 6, and 13, pp. 4–5. See also 4th year, Nos. 7, pp. 4–5, and 16, pp. 8–10.

64. *Ibid.*, 1st year, No. 6, pp. 3–4. For al-Afghānī's view on British political and cultural strategy toward Muslim societies, see al-Afghānī and 'Abduh, I, 13, and II, 138ff.

65. *SA*, 1st year, Nos. 13, p. 15, and 7, pp. 5–6.

66. *Ibid.*, 4th year, No. 23, pp. 1–3. For a poem on the subject of closer ties with Persia, see *ibid.*, p. 4.

67. For details, see Lockhart, *Nadir Shah*; see also Browne, *A Literary History*, IV, 137; and H. Gibb, *Muhammedanism*, p. 125.

68. Mīrzā Lūtfallāh Khan, pp. 98ff.

69. *SA*, 1st year, Nos. 13, pp. 10–12, 15, and 2, p. 3. See also 4th year, No. 21, p. 6.

70. *Ibid.*, 4th year, No. 7, p. 2; and 2d year, Nos. 20, p. 12, and 22, p. 6. See also 4th year, No. 8, pp. 5–6; and 5th year, No. 17, p. 11.

71. *Ibid.*, 1st year, No. 20, pp. 7, 13.

72. *Ibid.*, 3d year, No. 6, p. 4; and 6th year, No. 12, p. 12.

73. *Ibid.*, 3d year, No. 3, p. 3; 2d year, Nos. 18, p. 15, and 24, p. 12; 5th year, No. 17, pp. 10–11.

74. M. Tarzi, *Raudat-i-hikam*, pp. 144f.

75. *SA*, 2d year, Nos. 16, pp. 13–14, and 17, pp. 7–8.

76. *Ibid.*, 3d year, No. 2, p. 8.

77. *Ibid.*, No. 11. p. 11.

78. *Ibid.*, 7th year, No. 13, pp. 2–4.

79. On official British reaction to Tarzi's periodical and British representations to the Amir, see Adamec, pp. 101–3. The Russians banned the circulation of *SA* in Central Asia. See K. M. Troyanovski, ed., *Siniaiia Kniga* (Moscow, 1918), p. 115.

CHAPTER SEVEN

1. F. A. Martin, pp. 133–34.
2. Mohammed Ali, *The Mohammedzai Period*, p. 153.
3. *EB* (11th ed.), I, 318–19; Mohammed Ali, *The Mohammedzai Period*, pp. 152–53.
4. *SA*, 1st year, No. 20, p. 6.   5. F. A. Martin, pp. 133–34.
6. *SA*, 2d year, No. 4, p. 2.   7. *Ibid.*, 7th year, No. 15, pp. 2–4.
8. *Ibid.*, 2d year, No. 1, pp. 13–14.   9. F. A. Martin, pp. 135, 270–71.
10. *SA*, 3d year, No. 15, p. 5; and I. A. Shah, *Tragedy of Amanullah*, p. 40.
11. India, *Imperial Gazetteer*, V, 59–60.
12. *SA*, 2d year, No. 11, pp. 2–3.
13. On the original school, see Zahir, p. 58; Karimi, "Maaref," p. 396; and Fazli, pp. 52, 73, 82–83. For a unique picture of the military school and its cadets, see Fazli, p. 105.
14. Saise, p. 11; Mohammed Ali, *The Mohammedzai Period*, pp. 152–53; Karimi, "Maaref," p. 396.
15. E. and A. Thornton, p. 161. See also Sami; Fazli, pp. 73, 82–83; and Keppel, p. xiii.
16. F. A. Martin, p. 136; Jewett, "Off the Map," p. 27; and Sir G. S. Robertson's account in *EB* (11th ed.), XV, 634. See also Saise, pp. 13–15; and Keppel, p. 41.
17. India, *Imperial Gazetteer*, XIII, 85.
18. F. A. Martin, p. 136; E. and A. Thornton, pp. 36, 50; Saise, pp. 9, 13.
19. E. and A. Thornton, p. 12.
20. There is some confusion on the year Habibiya was founded. *SA* (2d year, No. 9, p. 2), Ziai ("Fondements du développement," p. 226), Mohammed Ali (*The Mohammedzai Period*, p. 152), and Reshtiya ("Education," p. 20) all agree on the year 1904. E. and A. Thornton (p. 11), a contemporary source, state the college was founded in the autumn of 1906. Wilber (*Afghanistan*, 2d ed., p. 84) asserts that after Habibullah visited India in 1907, "impressed by the training in modern common law and similar subjects being given Moslem youth at Aligarh College near Delhi," he established a secondary school in Kabul. I could not corroborate Wilber's statement, nor that of Stolz ("Langues étrangères," p. 27), who states that Habibiya was founded in 1901.
21. E. and A. Thornton, p. 11; *SA*, 3d year, Nos. 5, p. 11, and 13, pp. 3–4; Zahir, p. 58; Stolz, "Langues étrangères," p. 27; Karimi, "Maaref," p. 396.
22. *SA*, 7th year, No. 7, pp. 4–5.
23. Zahir, p. 58.
24. Ziai, "Challenge of Ideas," p. 89, and "Fondements du développement," p. 226.
25. Ziai, "Fondements du développement," p. 226.
26. *SA*, 3d year, No. 13, pp. 3–4. For the curriculum of the Habibiya elementary school (four years) and secondary school (three years), see *SA*, 7th year, No. 7, pp. 4–5; and Fazli, p. 72.

27. My information on Habibiya is based on *SA*, 3d year, Nos. 1, p. 6, and 18, pp. 4–7; 7th year, No. 16, p. 6; Saise, p. 12; E. and A. Thornton, p. 11; Jewett, *An American Engineer*, p. 112; Furon, *L'Afghanistan*, p. 82; Reshtiya, "Education," p. 20.

28. Ziai, "Challenge of Ideas," pp. 88–90.

29. *SA*, 5th year, No. 10, p. 3; and 7th year, No. 7, pp. 6–16.

30. *Ibid.*, 7th year, No. 7, pp. 4–5. Ali Muhammad, in an article on "Progress Under Habibullah" (*SA*, 6th year, No. 11, p. 3), asserts that there were thousands of students attending Habibiya and "other schools of the realm." The few statistics available do not bear this out.

31. *SA*, 3d year, No. 18, pp. 4–7. On the hafiz, see *SA*, 7th year, No. 2, p. 2.

32. For the by-laws of the Department of Education, the nucleus of the present Ministry of Education, see *SA*, 3d year, Nos. 19, pp. 2–4, 20, pp. 3–5, and 21, pp. 3–7.

33. *Ibid.*, 3d year, No. 14, p. 3.

34. *Ibid.*, 2d year, Nos. 1, p. 7, and 9, p. 2; 3d year, No. 13, p. 4.

35. See the list of advertised books in *ibid.*, 2d year, No. 13. See also No. 9, p. 2.

36. See E. and A. Thornton, p. 11. T. L. Pennell (pp. 140–42) recorded the religious grounds on which the Afghan mullahs based their opposition to Afghans learning the English language.

37. See Habibullah's views on Islam in *SA*, 1st year, No. 14, pp. 1–2.

38. A. C. Yate, "Visit to India," pp. 34–35; and Le Chatelier, pp. 35–49.

39. P. Sykes, *Afghanistan*, II, 228. Another version of the Amir's stand is reported by E. and A. Thornton, who wrote (pp. 10–11) that the Amir's dictum was: "First learn the Quran, and keeping one foot firmly planted upon it, with your other foot stray where you will. Knowing the Quran you may learn what else you choose." See also Jewett, *An American Engineer*, p. 219.

40. B. K. Roy, p. 560.

41. For Inayatullah's speech, see *SA*, 2d year, No. 22, pp. 8–9.

42. *Ibid.*, 1st year, No. 21, p. 1; "Progress," cited in note 30 above, p. 2; and B. K. Roy, p. 560.

43. *SA*, 1st year, No. 2, p. 3; Mohammed Ali, *The Mohammedzai Period*, p. 154.

44. F. A. Martin, p. 45; and Jewett, *An American Engineer*, p. 263.

45. Jewett, *An American Engineer*, p. 16, and "Off the Map," p. 29.

46. E. and A. Thornton, p. 103.

47. For information on the hospital, see *SA*, 3d year, No. 17, pp. 1–2; 4th year, Nos. 10, pp. 1–2, and 16, pp. 2–3; 6th year, No. 11, p. 4.

48. Berke, p. 7.

49. E. and A. Thornton, p. 169.

50. Lyons, p. 175; Jewett, *An American Engineer*, p. 295. In 1904, for instance, Major Bird, the personal physician of the viceroy of India, was sent to Kabul to treat the Amir. See Lyons, p. 173.

51. *SA*, 3d year, No. 17, pp. 1–2. Gray reported (p. 127) in 1896 that those who had been educated in traditional schools were far more rigid in their attitude toward European medicine than the illiterate masses.

52. *SA*, 3d year, No. 17, pp. 1–2; 4th year, No. 16, pp. 2–3.

53. India, *Imperial Gazetteer*, V, 51.

54. T. L. Pennell, pp. 38–41. See also Jewett, "An Engineer," p. 501.

55. T. L. Pennell, pp. 40–41.

56. E. and A. Thornton, p. 111.

57. Gray, pp. 521–22; India, *Imperial Gazetteer*, XIV, 246.

58. India, *Imperial Gazetteer*, XIV, 245; F. A. Martin, pp. 234–35.

59. Lyons, pp. 176–77; Saise, p. 13; Fazli, pp. 75–76.

60. E. and A. Thornton, pp. 33–35, 36; *SA*, 3d year, No. 18, p. 12; 4th year, No. 15, pp. 1–2; 6th year, No. 11, p. 3; Fazli, p. 76.

61. Saise, p. 10; Jewett, *An American Engineer*, p. 221. See also *SA*, 1st year, No. 16, p. 4. An article in *SA* (4th year, No. 22, pp. 1–6) gives a general account of the variety of machinery and workshops in Afghanistan, as does M. Qadir, "Karkhaneha," pp. 145–47. For a report on the textile industries, see *SA*, 3d year, Nos. 10, pp. 1–2, and 18, pp. 1–2. Qadir exaggerates considerably in declaring that the textile mill "was one of the best and most modern ones in the world."

62. Fazli, p. 77.

63. For details, see Mohammed Ali, *The Mohammedzai Period*, p. 154; Saise, p. 10; *SA*, 2d year, No. 1, p. 4; 4th year, No. 9, pp. 1–4; and M. Qadir, "Karkhaneha," pp. 147–48.

64. F. A. Martin, pp. 234–35; Jewett, *An American Engineer*, pp. v, 19, 22; M. Qadir, "Karkhaneha," p. 147.

65. F. A. Martin, pp. 238f; E. and A. Thornton, p. 50; Saise, p. 8.

66. F. A. Martin, pp. 194, 197, 199, 230, 235, 237. According to Gray (p. 522), one of the most popular songs in Kabul in the 1890's was the sad tale of a young man employed in the government workshops who had been caught in the machinery and killed.

67. E. and A. Thornton, pp. 54f; and F. A. Martin, p. 265.

68. F. A. Martin, p. 265.

69. Keppel, pp. 42–43, 45. See the account of Dr. Winter, the court physician, as reported by Lyons, pp. 175–76; and E. and A. Thornton, pp. 11, 40–41; Angus Hamilton, *Problems*, p. 251; Fraser-Tytler, *Afghanistan*, pp. 177–78; Jewett, *An American Engineer*, p. 257.

70. Jewett, *An American Engineer*, p. 8; F. A. Martin, p. 130; E. and A. Thornton, p. 32. See also Angus Hamilton, *Afghanistan* (London, 1906), pp. 391–95.

71. E. and A. Thornton, pp. 33–36, 127, 169, 186; Jewett, *An American Engineer*, pp. 127, 170; Lyons, pp. 175–76.

72. Jewett, *An American Engineer*, pp. 25, 76, 189.

73. E. and A. Thornton, pp. 56, 60–62, 131–32.

74. Jewett, *An American Engineer*, pp. 229f, 253–55.

75. *SA*, 1st year, No. 20, p. 2.

76. Saise, p. 5; *SA*, 1st year, No. 10, pp. 1–4; 2d year, Nos. 1, pp. 3–7, and 7, pp. 3–4; 7th year, No. 6, p. 2; Jewett, *An American Engineer*, pp. 19, 225–26, and "Off the Map," p. 27.

77. Saise, p. 7; Fazli, pp. 79–80.

78. Fazli, p. 85.
79. Saise, p. 8; Jewett, *An American Engineer*, pp. 226–27, and "Off the Map," p. 28.
80. *SA*, 1st year, No. 2, p. 10; Saise, p. 8.
81. Jewett, "Off the Map," p. 30.
82. *SA*, 1st year, Nos. 5, p. 5, and 20, p. 2; 2d year, No. 15, p. 6; Jewett, *An American Engineer*, p. 220.
83. Jewett, "Off the Map," p. 30. According to Taillardat ("Amanullah en Angleterre," p. 186), there were 12 automobiles in 1913.
84. Jewett, *An American Engineer*, p. 196; E. and A. Thornton, p. 36.
85. Fazli, p. 82; Jewett, *An American Engineer*, p. 1.
86. India, *Imperial Gazetteer*, V, 58; *Statesman's Yearbook: 1915*, p. 654; Jewett, *An American Engineer*, pp. 67f; Fazli, pp. 43–50, 82.
87. Jewett, *An American Engineer*, p. 41; Fazli, p. 83; Angus Hamilton, *Problems*, p. 255; Mohammed Ali, *The Mohammedzai Period*, p. 188. According to Keppel (p. 46), telephonic communication was established between Kabul and the principal provincial capitals as early as 1906. No other source corroborates this.
88. Angus Hamilton, *Problems*, p. 212, and *Afghanistan*, p. 249; Lyons, p. 174.
89. For official estimates, see Angus Hamilton, *Afghanistan*, pp. 250–52; *Statesman's Yearbook: 1900–1907*; India, *Trade of India*, and *Imperial Gazetteer*, XIV, 246, 375; and Gurevich, *Vneshniaia torgovlia*, pp. 16–18.
90. Angus Hamilton, *Problems*, pp. 212f, and *Afghanistan*, pp. 253–54.
91. Gurevich, *Vneshniaia torgovlia*, pp. 18, 95, 135; and M. A. Babakhod-zhaev, *Russko-Afganskie*, pp. 76–85. According to Angus Hamilton (*Problems*, p. 213), in 1902 the value of the goods passing through the Russo-Afghan posts was 450,000 pounds. Woeikof, on the other hand, reported (p. 292) that in 1908 the Afghan import-export trade with Turkestan alone exceeded this figure, amounting to some 7.7 million francs in Afghan imports and 8 million francs in exports (about 713,637 pounds sterling).
92. Gurevich, *Vneshniaia torgovlia*, pp. 18, 20ff, 109. The author attributes Russia's small share of the Afghan market largely to the political advantages that Britain enjoyed in Afghanistan. However, there were other factors that favored the Anglo-Indian trade. Among these were: the lack of adequate roads and means of transportation between northern Afghanistan and the Kabul-Ghazni-Kandahar region; the interregional trade between the Pathan tribes of the tribal belt; a similarity in weights and measures; the geographic proximity of the two major provinces, Kabul and Kandahar, to India; and the fact that the perishable fruits and vegetables that made up the largest part of the Afghan export trade could find a ready, close, and competitive market only in India. (In 1900, for instance, fruits constituted almost half of the Afghan exports. See *Statesman's Yearbook: 1901*, p. 364.)
93. On the economic implications of the Anglo-Russian Convention, see Mannanov, pp. 119–24. The author shows that (except for the years 1911 and 1912) Afghanistan had a favorable trade balance with Russia and an unfavorable one with India (pp. 127–28). He does not make very clear whether this

should be attributed solely to wartime conditions or whether he believes that Russian imperialism was less aggressive than British imperialism, and this was a factor.

94. Gurevich, *Vneshniaia torgovlia*, pp. 23, 95; and M. A. Babakhodzhaev, *Russko-Afganskie*, pp. 85, 96. For 1913 statistics, see B. Nikitine, "L'Asie Russe," p. 197.

95. Gurevich, *Vneshniaia torgovlia*, p. 45; Angus Hamilton, *Afghanistan*, p. 254, and *Problems*, pp. 213–14. For an itemization of the Russian exports in the 1870's, see Schuyler, II, 96–97.

96. *Statesman's Yearbook: 1912*, p. 584; *1915*, p. 653; and *1919*, p. 642.

97. According to *SA*, 3d year, No. 3, p. 12, in 1910–14, Afghanistan imported some 33 lakhs of Afghan rupees worth of tea. See also Angus Hamilton, *Afghanistan*, p. 250. For a list of the items of Afghan-Indian trade in the years 1896–1901, see *Statesman's Yearbook: 1901*, p. 364; and Angus Hamilton, *Afghanistan*, pp. 165–67, 251–52. Other goods imported from India in the 1900's included Swedish matches, American kerosene (Standard Oil Co.), and German, Austrian, and Japanese products. See also Jewett, *An American Engineer*, pp. 4, 48.

98. F. A. Martin, p. 60. See also Angus Hamilton, *Afghanistan*, pp. 112, 268; E. and A. Thornton, p. 51; and Saise, p. 13.

99. Saise, p. 10.

100. According to Fazli (p. 45), Herat's sheepskin industry was the only viable enterprise. The city had become mainly a transit center for Kabuli, Kandahari, Indian, and Russian goods on their way to Persia (Meshed, Yezd, and Tehran). See Angus Hamilton, *Afghanistan*, pp. 148–49; and India, *Imperial Gazetteer*, V, 56–57.

101. No Westerner could enter Afghanistan without an invitation, which had to be sealed by the Amir himself. See E. and A. Thornton, p. 190. Even then, the government of India sometimes refused passage to Europeans, if their visits to Afghanistan were considered not to be in the best interest of Britain. See Adamec, p. 218, 58n. When a visitor was issued a pass at the Indian border, he had to sign a paper discharging the British government in India of any responsibility for his personal safety or for his business. See Jewett, *An American Engineer*, p. 7.

102. Merchants taking goods to sell in India were not only charged export duty at Dakka, but also had to pay 5 per cent on any cash they had in hand for trading. See E. and A. Thornton, p. 108. On various taxes, see Angus Hamilton, *Afghanistan*, pp. 167, 217, and *Problems*, p. 212. See also *Statesman's Yearbook: 1915*, p. 653.

103. *SA*, 2d year, No. 1, p. 7.

104. F. A. Martin, p. 97; *SA*, 2d year, No. 17, p. 3; 3d year, No. 1, pp. 5–6.

105. India, *Imperial Gazetteer*, V, 50; Jewett, "Habibullah Khan," p. 278.

106. *SA*, 2d year, No. 17, p. 3.

107. *Ibid.*, 3d year, No. 1, p. 4.

108. *Ibid.*, 2d year, No. 17, p. 3; Jewett, *An American Engineer*, p. 175, and "Habibullah Khan," p. 282.

109. E. and A. Thornton, pp. 100, 183, 198. F. A. Martin writes (p. 170) that the nailing of a butcher to the door of his shop was a punishment that had been prescribed in Sher Ali's days.

110. Jewett, *An American Engineer*, p. 174.

111. *SA*, 3d year, No. 1, pp. 4–5.

112. Jewett, "Habibullah Khan," p. 282.

113. F. A. Martin, p. 59; Jewett, "Habibullah Khan," p. 277; Saise, p. 13.

114. E. and A. Thornton, p. 70.

115. Munshi, *Life of Abdur Rahman*, II, 43.

116. See the speech cited in note 41 above.

117. *SA*, 2d year, Nos. 3, p. 4, and 20, p. 3, respectively.

118. *Ibid.*, 1st year, No. 11, p. 1; F. A. Martin, pp. 91–92.

119. F. A. Martin, p. 141; Jewett, *An American Engineer*, pp. 122–23, 303; *SA*, 1st year, No. 5, p. 5. The cameras and the automobile were gifts of the Indian government, sent during the negotiations for a political settlement in 1905. See Angus Hamilton, *Problems*, p. 26. During the Amir's 1907 visit to India, the British made him a gift of two cars. See Jewett, "Off the Map," p. 27.

120. On Habibullah's interest in photography, see *SA*, 1st year, No. 4, pp. 1–2; and 2d year, Nos. 15, p. 2, and 20, p. 3.

121. E. and A. Thornton, pp. 57–58, 98.

122. Jewett, "Habibullah Khan," p. 280; E. and A. Thornton, pp. 79–87 *passim*.

123. E. and A. Thornton, pp. 125, 158–61; *SA*, 2d year, No. 24, p. 4; Jewett, "Habibullah Khan," p. 281, and *An American Engineer*, p. 222. See also Mohammed Ali, *The Mohammedzai Period*, p. 154.

124. Jewett, *An American Engineer*, pp. 65, 264, 273.

125. See *Statesman's Yearbook: 1912*, p. 582; and Angus Hamilton, *Problems*, p. 230.

126. Efimov, pp. 476–77.

127. Ward and Gooch, pp. 329–30.

128. Lynch, "Railways" (March 1911), pp. 14–17. The British opponents of a trans-Afghanistan railway argued that such a step would be a disastrous, "weak and suicidal policy," since extending the railway to Herat would help Russia bridge a crucial strategic gap. These same men opposed a Russian extension of the Merv-Kushk railway into Afghanistan as well. Those who favored an Anglo-Russian alliance also opposed the projected railways, fearing that these projects might lead to strained Anglo-Russian relations. See, respectively, Lyons, p. 157, and A. C. Yate, "Trans-Persian Railway," p. 30.

129. A. C. Yate, "Trans-Persian Railway," p. 7.

130. *The Times*, November 21–22, 1910, and January 29, 1911; A. C. Yate, "Trans-Persian Railway," p. 21. For details about previous Anglo-Russian political and economic rivalries, and ensuing diplomatic moves and countermoves over the question of the Persian railways, see Kazemzadeh, "Russian Imperialism," pp. 356–73. See also Pavlovitch, pp. 19–22.

131. A. C. Yate, "Trans-Persian Railway," p. 26.

132. *Ibid.*, pp. 25–26.

133. Saise, p. 10.
134. P. Sykes, *Afghanistan*, II, 219–20. See also Mohammed Ali, *The Mohammedzai Period*, p. 148.
135. See Angus Hamilton, *Problems*, p. 263.
136. *Ibid.*, p. 255; Mohammed Ali, *The Mohammedzai Period*, p. 188.
137. F. A. Martin, p. 306.

CHAPTER EIGHT

1. Mohammed Ali, *War of Independence*, pp. 23–24.
2. Gooch and Temperley, I, 306–7; IV, 187, 512–14, 519, 621; Angus Hamilton, *Problems*, pp. 206–7; Langer, *Diplomacy of Imperialism*, p. 669; Singhal, pp. 168–69; Adamec, pp. 34f.
3. I. A. Shah, "The German Threat," pp. 69–70.
4. Ward and Gooch, p. 329; Davies, *Problem of the NW Frontier*, pp. 140, 164, 166–67; Keppel, pp. 20–23; Adamec, pp. 40, 42, 47, 50.
5. Von Quadt to Von Bülow, October 26, 1904, in Dugdale, III, 186; Singhal, pp. 171–72.
6. Bullard, p. 56.
7. Ward and Gooch, p. 329; "Sir Henry C. Dobbs," pp. 708–9; Grant, "At the Court of an Absolute Monarch." For a detailed study of the Dane Mission see Singhal, Chap. 11; and Adamec, Chap. 3. For a Soviet interpretation of the mission and the Anglo-Afghan treaty of 1905, see Reysner, *Nezavisimyi Afganistan*, pp. 95ff; and Masson and Romodin, II, 313–15. For the text of the treaty, see India, *Treaties*, XIII, No. XXI; *Parliamentary Papers* (1905) LVII; and Angus Hamilton, *Problems*, pp. 267–68.
8. "Sir Henry Dobbs," p. 709; Angus Hamilton, *Problems*, p. 268.
9. Ward and Gooch, p. 360.
10. Angus Hamilton, *Problems*, pp. 256–57, 268; P. Sykes, *Afghanistan*, II, 222; Mohammed Ali, *The Mohammedzai Period*, p. 148, and *War of Independence*, pp. 23–24; Singhal, p. 172.
11. Davies, *Problem of the NW Frontier*, p. 167.
12. Angus Hamilton, *Problems*, p. 257; Adamec, p. 62.
13. Fraser-Tytler, *Afghanistan*, p. 179; P. Sykes, *Afghanistan*, II, 224; "Sir Henry C. Dobbs," p. 710.
14. Keddie, "Religion and Irreligion," p. 265. Stoddard, p. 126; Kohn, *Nationalism in the East*, pp. 128–30; P. Sykes, *Afghanistan*, II, 264; V. Smith, *Oxford History* (1958 ed.), pp. 762–63; Pavlovich, pp. 21–35 *passim*; and Ball, p. 15, among others, refer in a general way to the impact Japan had on the increasingly nationalistic Middle East, but unfortunately there are no monographic studies on the subject.
15. See Brown, pp. 8–9, 72, 86; and R. P. Dua, *The Impact of the Russo-Japanese (1905) War on Indian Politics*, New Delhi, 1966, pp. 23, 26.
16. Berkes, pp. 342, 349, 359ff; F. Ahmad, pp. 306, 309.
17. Hourani, p. 205.
18. Kamshad, p. 19; Ishaque, pp. 2, 4.
19. Carrère d'Encausse, "Politique culturelle tsariste," p. 394; Bennigsen, *Presse et mouvement national*, pp. 34, 70, 136, 157; Ishaque, p. 144.

20. *SA*, 4th year, No. 8, p. 6; 1st year, Nos. 16, pp. 1–2, and 24, p. 11; 7th year, No. 18, p. 8.

21. *Ibid.*, 3d year, No. 2, p. 6.   22. *Ibid.*, p. 8.

23. *Ibid.*, 1st year, No. 21.   24. *Ibid.*, 2d year, No. 9, p. 2.

25. Saise, p. 11.

26. Efimov, p. 477; Dvoriankov, pp. 256–57; and Reysner, "Russkaia Revoliutsiia," and "Pervaia Russkaia Revoliutsiia." For a survey of some of the Soviet writings on the topic, see *CAR*, IV, 3 (1956), 218–25.

27. Pavlovich, "SSSR i Vostok," p. 22. See also Kohn, *Nationalism in the East*, p. 130.

28. Pavlovich, "SSSR i Vostok," p. 34. See also Skalov, p. 244.

29. The historians who have written on the subject do not go beyond generalities to give specific instances of any direct or major impact on Afghanistan. Unfortunately, Spector's study, *The First Russian Revolution*, does not add much, since it does not go beyond the major tenets of Soviet historiography and the above study of Pavlovich.

30. For the details of the Convention and Anglo-Russian understandings concerning Afghanistan, see Gooch and Temperley, IV, No. 521, Enclosure, p. 581, No. 518, p. 578, and No. 524, pp. 584–85; Hansard's *Parliamentary Debates*, 4th series, CLXXXIV, 557; and Reysner, "Anglo-Russkaiia Konventsia," pp. 54–66.

31. On the Afghan government's reaction to the Convention, see P. Sykes, "The Present Position," pp. 146–47; and Adamec, pp. 67–76.

32. *SA*, 4th year, No. 6, pp. 4–5; P. Sykes, "The Present Position," p. 147.

33. Hansard's *Parliamentary Debates*, 4th series, CLXXXIV, 548; Shuster, p. xxiv; Kasravi, I, 95ff; Cottam, p. 164.

34. Browne, *Press and Poetry*, pp. 255–56.

35. Ishaque, p. 128.

36. *Habl-ul-Matin*, September 11, 1907, as quoted by Cottam, p. 165. For details about public and press reaction to the Convention, see Browne, *Mouvement constitutionel*, p. 25, and *Persian Revolution*, pp. 172–96. On the impact of the Convention on the Persian and Afghan nationalist movements, see "La révolution persane"; Browne, "Present Situation"; Stoddard, pp. 189–90; Bullard, p. 58; Cottam, pp. 166, 172–75, 177; P. Sykes, *Afghanistan*, II, 251; and Kohn, *Nationalism in the East*, p. 329.

37. Ward and Gooch, p. 365.

38. Saise, p. 12.

39. Among those detained was Dr. Abdul Ghani, an Indian Muslim who served as the government's education officer. See Jewett, *An American Engineer*, p. 223. For an interesting account of the Young Afghan movement and political developments in Afghanistan, see Abdul Ghani's *A Review of the Political Situation in Central Asia*.

40. For details, see Bahadur, pp. 97–100; and W. Smith, *Modern Islam*, pp. 235–36. See also Maulana Mohammed Ali, pp. 37–40. In general, even the Muslim press in Russia expressed pro-Turkish sentiments. *Bayan ul-Haq, Yilduz, Yalt-Yult*, in Kazan, *Vaqt*, in Orenburg, and the *Musulmanskaiia Gazeta*, all displayed pro-Turkish sympathies. See Bennigsen, *Presse et mouvement national*, pp. 69f, 73, 91f, 173.

41. *Histoire de la guerre italo-turque*, p. 90.

42. *SA*, 2d year, Nos. 7, pp. 5 and 9, 8, p. 5, and 10, p. 7; 4th year, No. 19, p. 15.

43. *Ibid.*, 2d year, Nos. 20, p. 15, and 16, pp. 13–14.

44. *Ibid.*, 3d year, Nos. 13, p. 12, and 17, p. 12.

45. *Ibid.*, No. 3, p. 3.

46. On the Pan-Islamism of the Ottoman Sultan Abdul Hamid II, see Berkes, pp. 267–70; see also Samné, pp. 14ff; Keddie, "Pan-Islamic Appeal"; Landau, pp. 50–54; and Kohn, *Nationalism in the East*, Chap. 3.

47. See Mullah Tuti's poem on Enver Bey in *SA*, 2d year, No. 16, p. 5.

48. In espousing Pan-Islamism, Al-Afghānī had not rejected the idea of individual nations developing their own forms of nationalism within the greater Muslim community. See Hourani, pp. 115–20. See also Keddie, "Pan-Islam as Proto-Nationalism," pp. 2–3; and Haim, "Islam," and *Arab Nationalism*, pp. 13–15.

49. *SA*, 3d year, No. 21, pp. 55–64. This is the only issue of *SA* reviewed by *RMM* (XXX, 1915).

50. *Ibid.*, 4th year, No. 6, p. 8.

51. Sir E. Denison Ross, in a speech at the Royal United Service Institute entitled "The Situation in the Middle East," attributed the awakening of the East to the war—to the self-destruction of the Great Powers and the changing attitudes of Eastern nations and states to the glorified West and its "so-called civilization." See *The Times*, December 12, 1929.

52. *SA*, 4th year, No. 9, pp. 12–13.

53. Afghan Foreign Minister Faiz Muhammad Khan's statement to the correspondent of *Iran* (Tehran), April 22, 1936.

54. *SA*, 4th year, No. 4, p. 1. See also the letter of Lord Hardinge, the viceroy of India, to Habibullah and the reply to that letter in *ibid.*, No. 1, p. 3.

55. *Ibid.*, No. 6, p. 10.

56. *Ibid.*, No. 16, p. 13.

57. *Ibid.*, 5th year, No. 16, p. 12; 4th year, Nos. 6, p. 9, 7, p. 13, and 2, p. 7.

58. *Ibid.*, 4th year, No. 4, p. 1.

59. *Ibid.*, Nos. 1, p. 6, 2, pp. 1–3, and 4, p. 1.

60. *Ibid.*, No. 13, p. 14.

61. *Ibid.*, No. 3, p. 2.

62. *Ibid.*, No. 6, pp. 4–5.

63. *Ibid.*, 6th year, No. 2, pp. 9–10.

64. *Ibid.*, 3d year, Nos. 21 and 26. For the text of the Sultan's call to jihad, see *Welt des Islams*, March 15, 1915. The Hoover Institution, at Stanford University, has an original copy of that proclamation.

65. *SA*, 1st year, No. 8, pp. 10–11.

66. Ishaque, p. 137.

67. Mahmud Syed, pp. 11ff.

68. W. Smith, *Modern Islam*, pp. 235–36; Guimbretière, Part 2, pp. 50–52.

69. India, Sedition Committee, p. 169; and "Pan-Islamism."

70. Bahadur, p. 10; W. Smith, *Modern Islam*, p. 295.

71. Bahadur, pp. 10–12; W. Smith, *Modern Islam*, pp. 49ff; Guimbretière.

72. Bahadur, p. 11. For a discussion of Barelvi's theories, see A. Ahmad, "Mouvement des mujahidin," pp. 105–16.

73. A. Ahmad, "Mouvement des mujahidin," pp. 105–16; and "Wahabis in India," p. 189.

74. Binder, *Religion and Politics*, pp. 16, 31ff.

75. Guimbretière, Part 2, pp. 50–55.

76. Griffiths, *British Impact*, pp. 309–10.

77. Vernier, p. 9.

78. Cottam, p. 179, and Démorgny, pp. 251, 277, 279.

79. Fletcher, *Afghanistan*, pp. 176–77.

80. P. Sykes, *Afghanistan*, II, 246, and "The Present Position," pp. 148–49. On the activities of the pro-Turkish factions in Afghanistan, see I. A. Shah, "The German Threat," pp. 60–61; Molesworth, p. 21; and Adamec, pp. 85–86, 90, and *passim*.

81. Pratap presents a very interesting case study, both for his intellectual confusion and his numerous revolutionary activities. When World War I broke out, Pratap left India for Europe. In 1915 he went from Switzerland to Berlin, where he assumed the role of a major Indian prince and was received by the Kaiser. From Germany he proceeded to Constantinople, where he was welcomed by such notables as the Sultan, Enver Pasha, and Shaikh-ul-Islam (the highest official religious authority in the empire). While in Kabul, Pratap proclaimed himself "life president" of the Provisional Government of India, appointed Barakatullah as his prime minister, and gave 'Obaid-ullah (Ubai-dullah) the "portfolio of the home ministry." Forced to leave Afghanistan in 1917, he went to Soviet Russia and was received by Trotsky and later by Lenin. On his second meeting with the Kaiser and Enver Pasha in 1918, he proposed the formation of an "International Socialist Army," consisting of German, Austrian, Bulgarian, Turkish, and Russian socialists, that was to cross Soviet Russia and help liberate India. This idea was rejected by the Germans, and the Turks showed only a polite interest. After dedicating himself to German, Turkish, Pan-Islamic, and later (1919) Bolshevik causes, Pratap gradually drifted from politics to religion. As "a Friend of Humanity and Christians, Hindus, and Muslims," and a "fighter for Peace and Freedom," he attempted to promote a religion of love in Hungary and Japan. He later came to the United States on the same mission. See his *My Life*, pp. 41–66, and "My German Mission." For some of his views, see also *SA*, 5th year, No. 17, p. 11.

82. On the aims and activities of the mission, see P. Sykes, *Afghanistan*, II, 246–64, especially p. 252, and *Persia*, II, 431–56, 541–45. Sykes directed the British operations in southern Persia against pro-German and Turkish agents and their sympathizers. See also A. W. Tarzi, p. 170; Tod, pp. 45–67; Great Britain, *Official History of the War*, IV; Druhe, pp. 21–23; Vernier, pp. 14f; Adamec, Chap. 5; Griesinger, pp. 6, 30, 36, 38 (this work is a diary that was confiscated); Hentig; Niedermayer, *Im Weltkrieg*; Pratap, "My German Mission," and *My Life*, especially pp. 45–52; and Siddiqi, pp. 380ff. For Soviet accounts of the mission, see M. A. Babakhodzhaev, "Missia Nidermaiera," pp. 22–26; and Masson and Romodin, II, 351–56.

83. *SA*, 5th year, No. 11, p. 3.

84. I. A. Shah, "Afghanistan and the War," p. 135.

85. See P. Sykes, "The Present Position," p. 148, and *Afghanistan*, II, 256. To forestall the complete failure of the mission there was even talk of staging a palace coup. See Vernier, p. 14; and Adamec, p. 95.

86. MacMunn, *From Darius to Amanullah*, pp. 254–55; P. Sykes, *Afghanistan*, II, 257–58; Barton, *India's NW Frontier*, p. 141. According to I. A. Shah (*Tragedy of Amanullah*, p. 92), the treaty provided for assistance in the amount of 20 million pounds in gold, as well as 50,000 artillery pieces, 100,000 rifles, and an enormous amount of ammunition. Adamec (p. 179) supplies more accurate figures; the treaty called for 10 million pounds sterling, 100,000 rifles, and 300 guns. For the text of a letter from Nasrullah to Von Bethmann-Hollweg, the German chancellor, as well as the text of the proposed German-Afghan treaty of friendship, see Adamec, pp. 200–204.

87. Fletcher, *Afghanistan*, pp. 179, 182; Vernier, pp. 14f. The Germans and the Turks also made an attempt to win over the Pathan, Baluchi, and Sikh troops of the Indian army, who were active in Mesopotamia, Gallipoli, Palestine, Aden, Egypt, East Africa, Burma, Singapore, and France. They tried to influence the Pathans and the Baluchis through Pan-Islamism and the Sikhs through the Ghadr party, but they had only limited success. See Bury, p. 28; MacMunn, *Martial Races*, p. 245. See also A. R. Desai, pp. 312–13.

88. *SA*, 6th year, No. 17, pp. 14–15.

89. *Ibid.*, 7th year, Nos. 3, p. 11, and 5, pp. 12, 14.

90. *Ibid.*, No. 6, pp. 13–14. For the Russian text, see *Pravda* and *Izvestia* of November 17, 1918. On the Muslim movements in Russia during the rule of the Provisional Government, see Browder and Kerensky, I, 408–28; and Bennigsen and Quelquejay, pp. 66–80 *passim*.

91. Fatemi, p. 7. For the texts of these decrees, see Browder and Kerensky, I, 210–12, 318.

92. For the text of the appeal, see Kluchnikov and Sabanin, II, 94–96; Degras, *Soviet Documents*, I, 15–17; Boersner, pp. 64ff; and Bunyan and Fisher, pp. 467–69.

93. K. M. Troyanovski, ed., *Siniaiia Kniga* (Moscow, 1918), pp. 36–114 *passim*. Aside from the existing Anglo-Russian agreements and understandings, during the war there were expressions both in India and in Russia of intentions to consolidate the military, political, and economic interests of the respective parties. One such proposal was advanced in Russia by General A. N. Kuropatkin, who, among other things, urged the Tsar to conclude an agreement with Great Britain that would lead to the establishment of a Russian protectorate in northern Persia, an extension of Russian control over the headwaters of the Amu Daria and the Murghab, and the opening of Afghanistan to Russian trade and to a rail link between Russian Central Asia and India.

94. For details see Boersner, p. 64; Teplinskii, pp. 6ff; Akhramovich, "Velikaia oktiabrskaia revoliutsiia," pp. 215ff.

95. *SA*, 7th year, Nos. 10, pp. 15–16, and 11, pp. 14–15.

96. Roome, p. 209.

97. *SA*, 7th year, No. 13, pp. 2–7.

98. *Ibid.*, Nos. 22, pp. 15–16, and 23, pp. 15–16.

99. V. Smith, *Oxford History* (1958 ed.), p. 763.

100. Hansard's *Parliamentary Debates*, XLII, 282; Dickson, pp. 56–57.

101. I. A. Shah, "The German Threat," p. 71.

102. I. A. Shah, "Future of Afghanistan," p. 434.

103. A. C. Yate, "Afghans at Merv," pp. 635f; Adamec, p. 106. I. A. Shah argued at the time ("Future of Afghanistan") that such a confederation, with Kabul as its center, would have helped ensure the defense of India against the "Russian menace," and therefore deserved British support.

104. Mohammed Ali, *War of Independence*, p. 25; Adamec, p. 105.

105. A. C. Yate, "Afghans at Merv," pp. 635–36; Adamec, pp. 103–6. Roome wrote: "In Afghanistan more than anywhere else the sword and the gun should yield to the plough and the mill. Protected against foreign aggression, the Afghans will prove themselves as efficient as workers as they have proved themselves as soldiers" (p. 209).

106. P. Sykes, *Afghanistan*, II, 265. See also Adamec, p. 104.

CHAPTER NINE

1. P. Sykes, *Afghanistan*, II, 267, and "The Present Position," p. 150. Amanullah's mother was the daughter of Muhammed Sarwar, one of the most powerful tribal leaders in the country. See Fletcher, *Afghanistan*, p. 185.

2. P. Sykes, "The Present Position," p. 149; Mohammed Ali, *War of Independence*, p. 26.

3. I. A. Shah, *Modern Afghanistan*, p. 94; P. Sykes, *Afghanistan*, II, 274, "The Present Position," p. 150, and "Afghanistan," p. 189. I. A. Shah (*Afghanistan*, p. 197) ascribes Amanullah's success to the fact that he had perceived that the Afghans "were fretting under the yoke of the nobles," and had therefore emphasized that "he was representative of the masses, a King risen out of the humble ranks of his kinsmen." However, I could find no specific instances of Amanullah appealing to the Afghans' class consciousness. Maybe Shah is referring to Amanullah's promise to abolish the system of *begar* (impressed labor).

4. P. Sykes, *Afghanistan*, II, 267.

5. The up-to-date Afghan versions are Ghazi, p. 5; Mohammed Ali, *War of Independence*, p. 28; the Afghan government publication *40th Anniversary*, p. 21. Najib Ullah ("Afghanistan," p. 13) is the only source stating explicitly that Amanullah declared war on Britain.

6. Ghazi, pp. 22–23, 25–27; Mohammed Ali, *War of Independence*, p. 5.

7. Great Britain, British White Paper: *Hostilities with Afghanistan*; India, *Third Afghan War*.

8. Molesworth, p. 23.

9. P. Sykes, *Afghanistan*, II, 268–70, and "Afghanistan," p. 189; Fraser-Tytler, *Afghanistan*, p. 195. On this, as well as the causes of the Third Anglo-Afghan War, see Toynbee, *Survey, 1920–1923*, pp. 377–80; and Nicolson, *Curzon*, pp 159–60.

10. Molesworth, p. 22.

11. Reysner, *Afganistan*, pp. 143–60, and "Desiat let," pp. 67–86. According to L. R. Gordon, the fact that the Pathan tribesmen joined the war on the side of Afghanistan is evidence that an anti-imperialist movement had started in India under the influence of the October Revolution (*Agrarnye otnosheniia,*

pp. 186–97, and "Voina Afganistana za nezavisimost," pp. 245–69). See also A. Kh. Babakhodzhaev, *Afghanistan's War*, p. 4 (for a résumé in Russian, see his "Voina Afganistana," pp. 235–40); Dvoriankov, pp. 259–61; Masson and Romodin, II, 396ff; and Akhramovich, "Velikaia oktiabrskaia revoliutsiia," pp. 217–21.

12. A. Kh. Babakhodzhaev, *Afghanistan's War*, pp. 8–9. The author's interpretation is interesting, but unfortunately some of his sources are either questionable or quoted out of context, and his chronology is sometimes faulty. He does not, for example, even mention that the Turkestan Republic did not give any material aid to the Afghans in 1919 for fear that it might be used against the Soviets. See the declarations of Kazakov, a representative of the Turkestan Central Executive Committee, and the Afghan protests, in *Communist* (Tashkent), September 24, 1919. In this report, the Afghans declared, "We thought that help to us was delayed for technical reasons; it appears, however, that this was contrived and purposeful." On Soviet apprehensions, see also M. V. Frunze, *Izbrannye Proizvedeniia*, Moscow, 1957, I, 230, 237ff, 243, 452. The numerical strength of the British forces in Persia during World War I and Britain's diplomatic position indicate that the British had no plans to open a second front against Afghanistan. Dickson, pp. xii, 228–43.

13. I. A. Shah, *Afghanistan*, p. 197. On February 28, 1919, shortly after his father's murder, Amanullah had issued a proclamation committing himself to the cause of complete independence for the "Afghan nation." For the text, see Reysner, *Nezavisimyi Afganistan*, p. 138. In that same year, on April 13, he proclaimed publicly that the government of Afghanistan would and "should be externally and internally independent and free, that is to say that all rights of Governments that are possessed by other independent powers of the world should be possessed in their entirety by Afghanistan." Great Britain, British White Paper: *Hostilities with Afghanistan*, pp. 4f.

14. P. Sykes, "Afghanistan," p. 189. See also P. Sykes, *Afghanistan*, II, 265; and I. A. Shah, *Afghanistan*, pp. 194–95.

15. Great Britain, British White Paper: *Hostilities with Afghanistan*, p. 5; Adamec, pp. 110–11; Marin, "L'entrée," p. 137; Mohammed Ali, *War of Independence*, p. 27.

16. Ghazi, p. 2.

17. *Ibid.*, pp. 5, 7.

18. *Ibid.*, pp. 8, 10–11.

19. See Nehru's attack against the British use of Indian troops in China, Afghanistan, Tibet, Mesopotamia, and Burma, in B. A. Mirza, p. 559.

20. Nicolson, *Curzon*, p. 159; Toynbee, *Survey, 1920–1923*, pp. 377–78.

21. Nicolson, *Curzon*, p. 159.

22. See the May 28 communiqué of the India Office, *The Near East*, May 30, 1919, p. 501.

23. May 29 communiqué of the India Office, *The Near East*, June 6, 1919, p. 525; Fletcher, *Afghanistan*, p. 192; Adamec, p. 122.

24. For the text of the treaty, see India, *Treaties*, XIII, No. XXIII, pp. 286–88. Amanullah's letter of May 24, 1919, in which he sought an armistice and a negotiated settlement, and attributed the Anglo-Afghan conflict to misunderstanding, is discussed in the May 29 communiqué of the India Office, *The*

Near East, June 6, 1919, p. 525; and Adamec, p. 117. For other communications dealing with the armistice, see *The Near East,* June 27, 1919, p. 613. For a discussion of the British political interests that were at stake during the peace negotiations, see Rushbrook Williams, *India: 1920,* pp. 4–15; and Adamec, pp. 123–35.

25. For various interpretations of the treaty, see Mourey, pp. 262–64. For a Soviet view of The Third Afghan War and the Peace of Rawalpindi, see Reysner, *Afganistan,* pp. 143–60. According to a later work Reysner edited (*Noveishaia istoriia,* p. 175), the Afghan government sought an armistice because it was dominated by landowning interests and feared to unleash a people's liberation war against British imperialism.

26. *Izvestia* (Tashkent), May 21, 1919; *Dokumenty,* II, 175; Teplinskii, pp. 7–10; Masson and Romodin, II, 402–5.

27. *Izvestia* (Tashkent), June 1, 1919; *The Times,* June 13, 1919. Nollau and Wiehe state (pp. 95–96) that in Lenin's reply he declared: "Convinced that the friendship between Russia and Afghanistan will henceforth continue to grow in strength, I take the liberty of expressing to you my sympathetic feeling and my conviction that the independence of the great Afghan state will never be violated either by force or by stratagem." However, the text of Lenin's May 27 letter does not include any such statement. See *Dokumenty,* II, 174–75.

28. *Izvestia,* May 6, 1919; and Eudin and North, p. 83.

29. See the declaration of A. Voznesensky, the chief of the Eastern Department of the People's Commissariat, in *Izvestia,* May 8, 1919, as quoted by Eudin and North, p. 83.

30. Fischer, *The Soviets,* I, 286.

31. Reysner, *Afganistan,* p. 207; Raskolnikov, *Afganistan,* p. 20. See the text of the Soviet-Afghan treaty in *Dokumenty,* III, 550–55; and Degras, *Soviet Documents,* I, 233–37.

32. *The Times,* September 21, 1921.

33. *L'Asie Française,* April 1921, pp. 173–74; Castagné, "La politique extérieure," pp. 1–25.

34. U. S. Department of State, *Papers, 1921,* pp. 258–61: Hughes to Harding, July 18 and 21, 1921, and Harding to Amanullah, July 29, 1921.

35. *L'Asie Française,* November 1921, p. 421; *The Times,* March 17, 1921; Dennis, p. 256. According to a contemporary Soviet source, "Jemal Pasha gave lessons in enlightened statesmanship" to Afghan leaders, "dispelling Afghan suspicions of Moscow." Nikulin, "Afganistan i Angora," *Novii Vostok,* 1922, No. 2, as quoted in a review of Soviet studies in Afghanistan, in *CAR,* IV (1956), 2, 173–74.

36. *L'Asie Française,* November 1921, p. 421. See also Fischer, *The Soviets,* I, 385.

37. See the text in Toynbee, *Survey, 1925,* pp. 385–87; Mears-Grinnell, pp. 643–44; *The Islamic News,* May 12, 1921.

38. See *The Near East,* August 18, 1921, and *Echos de l'Islam,* January 15, 1922. For the text of the treaty and additional provisions, see League of Nations, *Treaty Series,* XXXIII, 295–301.

39. *The Islamic News,* June 16, 1921.

40. For the text of this letter, see Arthur Ranson's article in *The Manchester Guardian*, August 5, 1921, and *L'Asie Française*, November 1921, pp. 420–21.

41. *S. M. R. L'Emir*, pp. 1–4. A copy of the text of his speech is available at the Bibliothèque Nationale in Paris, and appeared also in *L'Asie Française*, June 1920, pp. 207–8.

42. *L'Asie Française*, June 1920, pp. 207–8; *S. M. R. L'Emir*, p. 3.

43. To the Soviets, the Afghan-Bukharan and the Afghan-Basmachi cooperation presented both an actual and a potential political and military threat to the triumph and consolidation of Soviet rule in Turkestan. They were in constant fear of an Anglo-Afghan rapprochement and the possibility that Britain might lend both political and financial support to a confederacy of anti-Soviet nationalist and Pan-Islamic forces. In the aftermath of the Third Anglo-Afghan War, Trotsky had written to the Central Committee of the Communist Party (September 20, 1919) that the truce between Afghanistan and England may "wholly rebound against us," that "England is actively at work uniting Persia, Bukhara, Khiva and Afghanistan against Soviet Turkestan. It would be incredible if she were not to do so." See Jan M. Meijer, ed., *The Trotsky Papers, 1917–1922*, London, 1964, p. 673. The disclosure of Amanullah's correspondence with and assistance to the Emir of Bukhara and of the extensive contacts between the Basmachis and the Afghans heightened Soviet apprehensions. For details see Reysner, *Afganistan*, pp. 205–7; and A. Mashitskii, ed., "Materialy po istorii bukharskoi revoliutsii," in *Vestnik* of Narodnyi Komissariat Inostrannykh del (1922), No. 4–5, pp. 134–35; and *Iz istorii grazhdanskoi voiny v SSSR: Sbornik dokumentov i materialiov, 1918–1922*, Moscow, 1961, III, 556–58; A. I. Ishanov, *Sozdanie Bukharskoi narodnoi sovetskoi Respubliki (1920–1924gg.)*, Tashkent, 1955, pp. 68ff. The recent study of Adamec (pp. 161–62) reveals that some of the Soviet apprehensions were well founded: Amanullah was ready to break away from the Soviets if Britain acceded to the political, military, and economic requests put forth by the Afghans: 40 lakhs of rupees, 20,000 rifles, 200 machine guns, two 18-pound batteries, ammunition, six airplanes, material for a telegraph line between Kabul, Kanahar, and Herat, a say in affairs in the tribal belt, and British assistance in the event of unprovoked Russian aggression.

44. W. Smith, *Modern Islam*, pp. 243–44. On the Pan-Islamic credo and the demands of the Khilafat, see Bahadur, pp. 133–34; and the following publications of the Khilafat delegation to Europe: (1) *Le traité de paix avec la Turquie: l'attitude des musulmans et de l'Inde*, (2) *Le Secrétaire d'Etat pour les Indes et la Délégation de l'Inde pour le Califat*, (3) *M. Lloyd George et la Délégation Indienne pour le Califat*, and (4) *Le verdict de l'Inde*. These pamphlets were published in Paris in 1920–21 and can be found in the library of the Hoover Institution, Stanford, Calif.

45. W. Smith, *Modern Islam*, pp. 243–44; Ram Gopal, pp. 144–46.

46. A. Ahmad, "Les musulmans," p. 82. In 1919 Mahatma Gandhi and the Congress Party had announced their support of the Muslim Khilafat movement. However, unilateral pronouncements like this led to strained relations between the Khilafat and Congress leaders. The Congress leaders continued to believe that passive resistance was the best means of liberating India and achieving the aims of the Khilafat. See Gandhi's declarations on this point

and Muslim reaction to it in the *Islamic News*, July 14, 1921. See also *The Indian Annual Register 1922*, Calcutta, 1923, I, 172.

47. For Amanullah's welcoming speech to the Emir of Bukhara, see *Aman-i-Afghan*, 1st year, No. 45, pp. 4–5. For Soviet-Afghan diplomatic correspondence, see *Dokumenty*, III, 193–94, 199–200, 449–50, 558–61, and V, 489–90, 532. For a good survey, see H. Kapur, *Soviet Russia and Asia, 1917–1927* (Geneva, 1966), Part 3.

48. See Ishaque, p. 145.

49. A. Ahmad, "Sayyid Ahmad Khan," pp. 69–73. For details on the Deoband school, see Faruqi.

50. *Zhizn Natsionalnostei*, June 15, 1919, cited in both Eudin and North, p. 104, and Laqueur, *Soviet Union*, p. 48.

51. Fatemi, pp. 157, 164–65.

52. Harutunian, pp. 52, 60.

53. Comyn-Platt, p. 300; Nollau and Wiehe, p. 102; Agabekov, pp. 47–49, 51.

54. Fatemi, p. 183. Fatemi mentions a revolt by an Afghan garrison on the northern frontier, under the leadership of "soldiers' councils," but no other sources substantiate this information. The official instructions of Raskolnikov, the Soviet envoy to Afghanistan, warned against "the fatal mistake of artificially implanting communism" in that country. See *Dokumenty*, IV, 166.

55. Castagné, "Soviet Imperialism," p. 700.

56. M. N. Roy, pp. 442, 473, 492–93; Druhe, pp. 41–42.

57. For details about the British political measures and military operations in the border area, see Fraser-Tytler, *Afghanistan*, Chap. 13; and Caroe, *Pathans*, pp. 405ff. On British diplomatic notes, see *The Times*, August 20, 1921; and Great Britain, Foreign Office, *A Selection of Papers*, pp. 4–12.

58. *Terjiman* (Istanbul), November 3, 1960; Çebesoy, pp. 292–94. See also Great Britain, Foreign Office, *A Selection of Papers*, pp. 10f.

59. For the text of the treaty, see India, *Treaties*, XIII, 288–96; and *The Times*, November 24, 1921.

60. M. N. Roy, pp. 492–93; Siddiqi, pp. 379–89; and Druhe, p. 43.

61. L. Thomas, *Khyber Pass*, pp. 181–82.

62. Marin, "L'Afghanistan," p. 223; Fouchet, p. 8. See also *Al-Akhbar* (Cairo), March 6, 1922; and *Le Temps* (Paris), March 27, 1922.

63. Zahir, p. 58.

64. Reshtiya, "Education," p. 21; Stolz, "Les langues," p. 28; Furon, *L'Afghanistan*, p. 82; Kātrak, p. 44. Caspani and Cagnacci (p. 136) give 1923 as the date the school opened.

65. Fouchet, p. 176; Furon, *L'Afghanistan*, p. 82; Pernot, *L'inquiétude de l'Orient*, p. 28.

66. Stolz, "Les langues," p. 28; Zahir, p. 58. Contrary to these sources, Wilber, *Afghanistan* (2d ed.), p. 84, Caspani and Cagnacci, p. 136, and Reshtiya, "Education," p. 21, date the founding of Amani in 1924.

67. Furon, *L'Afghanistan*, p. 82.

68. Stolz, "Les langues," pp. 27, 29; Reshtiya, "Education," p. 21.

69. Stolz, "Les langues," p. 29; Zahir, p. 58. See also the *Muslim Standard*, September 15, 1921; and *L'Asie Française*, January 1922, p. 45.

70. Furon, *L'Afghanistan*, p. 83; I. A. Shah, *Afghanistan*, p. 239.

71. Zahir, p. 58; Stolz, "Les langues," p. 30.
72. Zahir, p. 58; Karimi, "Maaref," p. 397.
73. Reshtiya, "Education," p. 21.
74. Taillardat, "Voyage du Roi Amanullah," p. 69.
75. I. A. Shah, *Afghanistan*, p. 239.
76. Kātrak, p. 44; Pernot, *L'inquiétude de l'Orient*, pp. 28f.
77. *L'Asie Française*, January 1922, p. 45; Mohammed Ali, *The Mohammedzai Period*, p. 161.
78. Furon, *L'Afghanistan*, p. 82. Caspani and Cagnacci state (p. 160) that some 200 primary schools were opened during Amanullah's reign, but there is no way to check the accuracy of this figure.
79. Ziai, "Challenge of Ideas," p. 89.   80. L. Thomas, *Khyber Pass*, p. 212.
81. M. Nikitine, p. 7.   82. Fouchet, pp. 176–77.
83. "Amanullah's Reforms," p. 609; I. A. Shah, *Tragedy of Amanullah*, p. 171.
84. Mohammed Ali, *The Mohammedzai Period*, p. 161.
85. Ténèbre, pp. 87ff.
86. Stolz, "Le théâtre," p. 42.
87. Stolz, "Les langues, p. 29.
88. Marin, "L'Afghanistan," p. 222; *The Times*, October 10, 1921; "Visit of King Amanullah, p. 558. Hidayatullah Khan, later enrolled in the Lycée J. de Sailly in preparation for the French military academy of St. Cyr. See Taillardat, "Voyage du Roi Amanullah," pp. 68–69.
89. *Bombay Chronicle*, June 4, 1922; I. A. Shah, *Tragedy of Amanullah*, p. 171.
90. *Aman-i-Afghan*, 1st year, No. 48, p. 1. On Afghan students in England, see Taillardat, "Amanullah en Angleterre," p. 184.
91. Kātrak, p. 44.
92. *Aman-i-Afghan*, 1st year, No. 48, pp. 3–5.
93. *Revue des Etudes Islamiques*, II (1929), p. 191; Caspani and Cagnacci, p. 138.
94. *Aman-i-Afghan*, 1st year, No. 45, pp. 2–4.
95. This is the estimate of Dr. Ténèbre in Taillardat, "Voyage du Roi Amanullah," p. 69; see also "Amanullah's Reforms," p. 557. Amanullah cited a figure of 2,000 female students in Kabul alone (see L. Thomas, *Khyber Pass*, p. 212) as does I. A. Shah (*Afghanistan*, p. 239). In view of the prevailing conditions and attitudes, however, this must be regarded as a very liberal estimate. See also Taillardat, "Révolte afghane," p. 13; and Dr. J. Barthoux, in *L'Europe Nouvelle*, January 5, 1929, p. 16.
96. "Visit of King Amanullah," p. 126. Princess Sultanjan was attending school in Berne. See *L'Asie Française*, March 1928, p. 134.
97. Taillardat, "Amanullah en Angleterre," p. 187; "Amanullah's Reforms," p. 609.
98. For information on the status of Afghan women before, during, and after the fall of Amanullah, see Larissa Reysner, in *Pravda*, May 28, 1922; and *Zaria Vostoka*, March 8, 1929.
99. Pernot, *L'inquiétude de l'Orient*, p. 20. For an analysis of the family code of 1921, see *RMM*, No. 48, pp. 55–58. On the official limitations on wedding expenses (*shir baha*), see Caspani and Cagnacci, p. 178.

100. *Revue des Etudes Islamiques,* II (1929), p. 191; *L'Asie Française,* January 1922, p. 45.

101. *Aïne-ye-Irfan,* 1st year, Nos. 2 and 5-6. For a résumé, see M. Nikitine, pp. 11–12.

102. Wild, p. 68.

103. *Revue des Etudes Islamiques,* II (1929), p. 192.

104. Kātrak, p. xx. On the evils of child marriage, see *Aïne-ye-Irfan,* 1st year, No. 1.

105. "Visit of King Amanullah," p. 126.

106. Morrish, pp. 7–8; *Pravda Vostoka,* October 17, 1928; *Revue des Etudes Islamiques,* II (1929), p. 193; "Amanullah's Reforms," p. 609. Fischer (*The Soviets,* II, 789) reports that Queen Sorayya wrote a pamphlet entitled *Islam and Women* in 1928; I was unable to verify this.

107. M. Nikitine, p. 13.

108. Reshtiya, "Journalism," p. 73. According to Bogdanov ("Notes," pp. 134–35), government officials were expected to subscribe to it and to "pay what they deemed to be convenient according to their liberality." (The official subscription rate was 12 Kabuli rupees a year.) The periodical was "to discuss every kind of scientific and political question and things of interest to the Government and the Nation." According to the editors, *Aman-i-Afghan* was "sent without demand to all good Afghans who are considered worthy of it."

109. The motto of the paper was: "Work hard for Union, O Muslims! The Afghan King of Kings is calling [us] to Union. We are free from waiting for the shadow of the wing of Huma [the Phoenix of Eastern tales], as long as we have over our heads the sun of the banner of unity." See Bogdanov, "Notes," p. 138.

110. Reshtiya, "Journalism," p. 73; Caspani and Cagnacci, p. 162. Dianous ("La presse afghane," p. 178) gives 1925 as the year *Anis* began publication. That is not correct. The first issue appeared on May 5, 1927. See Bogdanov, "Notes," p. 152. For a complete list of Afghan periodicals published during Amanullah's reign, see Dvoriankov, pp. 415–18; and Bogdanov, "Notes." The latter source provides the subscription rates of these periodicals and the names of their editors. M. Qadir ("Karkhaneha," pp. 150–51) gives a list of known printing presses in the kingdom.

111. Reshtiya, "Journalism," p. 73; Bogdanov, "Notes," pp. 145–46; and Dvoriankov, pp. 415–16.

112. Reshtiya, "Journalism," p. 74.

113. A. Qadir, "The Outlook," p. 464. According to Bogdanov ("Notes," p. 152), a majority of these periodicals received government subsidies.

114. See an analysis of the Afghan press by the correspondent of *The Times,* August 3, 1921. It is interesting that he reported to the effect that both *Aman-i-Afghan* and *Ittihad-i-Mashriqi* were of Bolshevik inspiration.

115. See, for instance, the poem "Vatan" (Fatherland) in *Aïne-ye-Irfan,* 1st year, No. 1. For a survey of Afghan poetry of the period, see Puretskii, pp. 141–51.

116. Sher Muhammad, pp. 3–4; and *Aman-i-Afghan,* 1st year, No. 48, pp. 11–12.

117. *Aman-i-Afghan,* 1st year, Nos. 45, p. 12, and 48, p. 12.

118. On Amanullah's public health measures, see Kātrak, pp. 47, 59; Cas-

pani and Cagnacci, p. 135; L. Thomas, *Khyber Pass*, p. 152; Berke, p. 7; and *The Times*, July 14, 1928.

119. I. A. Shah, *Tragedy of Amanullah*, p. 171; Beck, pp. 132–33.

120. Furon, *L'Afghanistan*, p. 101.

121. On Afghan communications under Amanullah and his plans, see *L'Asie Française*, February 1922, p. 93; *The Times*, September 29 and 30, 1922, and December 20, 1922; Fouchet, pp. 22, 58; L. Thomas, *Khyber Pass*, p. 111; Kātrak, p. 43; Nariman, p. 254.

122. Ténèbre, p. 558.

123. Reshtiya, "Kabul Calling," p. 1; see also Bogdanov, "Notes," p. 136.

124. *Pravda*, October 5, 1924.

125. *Izvestia*, June 19, 1928; Pernot, *L'inquiétude de l'Orient*, p. 43.

126. Pernot, *L'inquiétude de l'Orient*, p. 43; *Pravda Vostoka*, November 23, 1926.

127. *Izvestia*, January 15, 1928, and June 27, 1928.

128. *L'Asie Française*, September–October 1928, p. 322.

129. Pernot, *L'inquiétude de l'Orient*, p. 36; Taillardat, "Amanullah en Angleterre," p. 186.

130. Furon, *L'Afghanistan*, p. 99.

131. MacMunn, *From Darius to Amanullah*, p. 307.

132. Wild, p. 89.

133. *Ittifaq-i-Islam*, October 1923; Fouchet, p. 43; Pernot, *L'inquiétude de l'Orient*, pp. 26ff.

134. "Afghan Independence Day," p. 500.

135. Reshtiya, "Education," pp. 20–21.

136. Fouchet, p. 57.   137. Fazli, p. 65.

138. I. A. Shah, *Afghanistan*, p. 249.   139. Beck, p. 95.

140. *Ibid.*, pp. 96, 98.

141. For the provisions of customary law regarding the status and rights of women, see Rose, "Customs." For information on the blood money, or "make up money," prescribed by the customary law and practiced among the Waziri and Mohmand tribes, see Oliver, pp. 109–16. According to Pazhwak ("Taame-lat-e hughughi," pp. 341–58), in cases involving adultery or murder the tribal code as well as Shar'ia law had to be consulted.

142. *The Times*, November 21, 1922.

143. For a summary of the provisions, see Yapp, "Afghanistan," p. 55. There is also a summary available in *Oriente Moderno*, IV (1924), 3, 196–99. For the full text in Arabic, see *Al-Akhbar* (Cairo), January 28, 1924.

144. See Taillardat, "Amanullah en Angleterre," p. 186; I. A. Shah, *Afghanistan*, pp. 248–49; Karimi, "Constitution," p. 3.

145. James, p. 191.

146. Wild, p. 99; MacMunn, *From Darius to Amanullah*, p. 318. The estimated total strength of the Afghan army in 1920 was 98,000, including 18,000 cavalrymen. There were also some 396 guns. In 1928, the strength of the regular army was set at 26,000. See *Statesman's Yearbook: 1920*, p. 657, and *1928*, p. 644.

147. Caspani and Cagnacci, p. 135; Pernot, *L'inquiétude de l'Orient*, p. 41.

148. *L'Asie Française*, September–October 1928, p. 322, and January 1929,

p. 18; *Terjiman-i-Haqiqat* (Istanbul), June 18, 1922; MacMunn, *From Darius to Amanullah*, p. 319.

149. Iybar, p. 99.

150. L. Thomas, *Khyber Pass*, p. 111.

151. I. A. Shah, *Tragedy of Amanullah*, pp. 183–84.

152. MacMunn, *From Darius to Amanullah*, p. 330.

153. Furon, *L'Afghanistan*, pp. 89, 91.

154. Rhein and Ghaussy, p. 21.

155. I. A. Shah, *Tragedy of Amanullah*, p. 162. On Afghan tariffs, see also *The Times*, May 25, 1922; and Abdul Ghani, p. 285.

156. Bogdanov, "The Metric System in Afghanistan," *The Visva-Bharati Quarterly*, July 1928, and "Afghan Weights," pp. 419–35.

157. I. A. Shah, *Tragedy of Amanullah*, pp. 162–63; Kātrak, p. 36.

158. Trinkler, pp. 187–90.

159. I. A. Shah, *Tragedy of Amanullah*, pp. 163–70, especially pp. 164–69, which include the Amir's decree on customs reform.

160. Wild, pp. 51–52.

161. Fouchet, pp. 105–8.

162. I. A. Shah, *Tragedy of Amanullah*, p. 163.

163. See *Statesman's Yearbook: 1921*, p. 664; *1923*, p. 685; *1925*, p. 657. In 1925 the government of India's statistical department ceased to publish the figures on foreign trade over the land frontier.

164. See Violet Conolly, *Soviet Economic Policy in the East*, London, 1933, pp. 82–83; *Ekonomicheskaiia Zhizn*, February 21, 1925; *Izvestia*, January 8, 1928.

165. MacMunn, *From Darius to Amanullah*, p. 312. *Statesman's Yearbook: 1927*, p. 641, estimated the total revenues of Afghanistan in 1927 to be 50 million Afghan rupees.

166. Joseph Potocki, p. 114.

167. See an interview with Mahmud Tarzi in *Izvestia*, October 18, 1924; see also I. A. Shah, *Afghanistan*, p. 238.

168. For a French analysis of the code, see Bouvat, "Notes," pp. 26–54.

169. See *Aman-i-Afghan*, 5th year, No. 1, p. 6, for a speech Amanullah made on the origins of the Khost rebellion. See also the Tarzi interview cited in note 167 above.

170. P. Sykes, *Afghanistan*, II, 298, and "The Present Position," p. 155. See also A. W. Tarzi, p. 173.

171. L. Thomas, *Khyber Pass*, pp. 238–39.

172. P. Sykes, *Afghanistan*, II, 298–99; Mohammed Ali, *The Mohammedzai Period*, p. 161.

173. Fraser-Tytler, *Afghanistan*, p. 205.

174. *Izvestia*, April 20, 1924. The Afghans, too, maintain that the trouble was not purely internal but was instigated by the British government in India. See Fletcher, *Afghanistan*, pp. 206–7.

175. *Izvestia*, March 6, 1925.

176. Rushbrook Williams, *India: 1924–25*, p. 12.

177. P. Sykes, *Afghanistan*, II, 298; Fraser-Tytler, *Afghanistan*, p. 206.

178. MacMunn, *From Darius to Amanullah*, p. 175.

179. For these statements, which were made to the Afghan leaders, see "Les débuts du voyage," p. 53; Ténèbre, p. 556; Fraser-Tytler, *Afghanistan*, p. 207; N. N. Ghosh, p. 177; Das, pp. 567–69.

180. Wild, p. 94.

181. *Muslim Outlook* (Lahore), July 24, 1928; *Indian National Herald*, December 6, 1928.

182. Fraser-Tytler, *Afghanistan*, p. 208; "Les débuts du voyage," p. 54; P. Sykes, "The Present Position," p. 155.

183. For an account of Amanullah's stay in Italy, see Taillardat, "Voyage du Roi Amanullah," p. 67; Fraser-Tytler, *Afghanistan*, p. 208; P. Sykes, *Afghanistan*, II, 304; Wild, p. 102.

184. Taillardat, "Voyage du Roi Amanullah," p. 68. See also *Le Temps* (Paris), January 27, 1928.

185. *L'Asie Française*, March 1928, pp. 134–35; Wild, p. 103.

186. For details about the Amir's visit to England, see Taillardat, "Amanullah en Angleterre," pp. 184–85; P. Sykes, *Afghanistan*, II, 304, and "The Present Position," p. 155; Fraser-Tytler, *Afghanistan*, p. 209; and Wild, pp. 115–19.

187. Ténèbre, p. 558. Fischer writes (*Lenin*, p. 539): "Amanullah fancied himself a Peter the Great of Central Asia ... but he was a weakling ahead of his time." This is indeed unfair, since it was not Amanullah but outside observers, including Fischer himself, who drew the parallel between Amanullah's visit to England and that of Peter the Great.

188. Taillardat, "Fin du Voyage," pp. 320–21.

189. P. Sykes, *Afghanistan*, II, 307; *Daily Telegraph*, May 8, 1928; *Daily Mail*, May 12, 1928.

190. Fischer, *The Soviets*, II, 790. For accounts of the Amir's stay in the Soviet Union, see *Izvestia*, May 5, 1928; *Daily News*, May 4, 1928; *The Times*, May 7, 1928.

191. MacMunn, *From Darius to Amanullah*, p. 328; Fraser-Tytler, *Afghanistan*, p. 211. He also concluded treaties of friendship with Persia (for the text, see *Oriente Moderno*, March 1928, pp. 154–56); Turkey (for the text, see *ibid.*, July 1928, pp. 283–85); and Egypt (for the text, see *La Bourse Egyptienne*, June 8, 1928).

192. On German and Italian commercial activity in Afghanistan before Amanullah's fall, see Pernot, *L'inquiétude de l'Orient*, pp. 40–41.

193. Fraser-Tytler, *Afghanistan*, p. 209; P. Sykes, *Afghanistan*, II, 307–8.

194. Taillardat, "Fin du voyage," p. 322.

195. Wild, p. 99.

196. Jackson Fleming, "The Troubles of an Afghan King," *Asia*, May 1929, pp. 406-7.

197. *Aman-i-Afghan*, August 30 through September 2, 1928.

198. P. Sykes, *Afghanistan*, II, 310.

199. *Pravda* (September 4, 1928) and *The Times* (September 7 and 12, 1928) are the only major foreign sources that give full treatment to the Amir's 1928 proposals.

200. *Pravda*, September 4, 1928; *L'Asie Française*, December 1928, p. 450.

201. P. Sykes, *Afghanistan*, II, 311; *Pravda*, September 4, 1928.

202. P. Sykes, *Afghanistan*, II, 311; *L'Asie Française*, December 1928, p. 450; *Pravda*, September 4, 1928.

203. *Pravda*, September 4, 1928.

204. *L'Asie Française*, December 1928, p. 449; P. Sykes, *Afghanistan*, II, 311.

205. *The Times*, September 7, 1928; P. Sykes, *Afghanistan*, II, 231n, 311.

206. P. Sykes, *Afghanistan*, II, 311, and "The Present Position," p. 156; *The Times*, September 14, 1928; *Daily Telegraph*, September 26, 1928. See also Fraser-Tytler, *Afghanistan*, p. 212; I. A. Shah, *Tragedy of Amanullah*, p. 194; Ahmad and Abd al-Aziz, p. 67; and Rhein and Ghaussy, p. 23.

207. I. A. Shah, *Tragedy of Amanullah*, p. 178.

208. *Ibid.*; "Afghan Independence Day," p. 500; MacMunn, *From Darius to Amanullah*, p. 324.

209. I. A. Shah, *Tragedy of Amanullah*, p. 172.

210. Mohammed Ali, *Progressive Afghanistan*, pp. 13–14; *The Times*, September 7, 1928.

211. Taillardat, "Révolte afghane," p. 17.

212. Pernot, *L'inquiétude de l'Orient*, pp. 32f.

213. Morrish, p. 3.

214. Taillardat, "Révolte afghane," p. 15.

215. Morrish, pp. 7–8.

216. I. A. Shah, *Tragedy of Amanullah*, p. 178.

217. *The Times*, September 15, 1928; Fraser-Tytler, *Afghanistan*, p. 214; P. Sykes, *Afghanistan*, II, 312; Taillardat, "Révolte afghane," p. 15.

218. Fraser-Tytler, *Afghanistan*, p. 214.

219. Fletcher, *Afghanistan*, pp. 215–16.

220. Taillardat, "Révolte afghane," p. 15.

221. For the text of the proclamation in which Amanullah made these concessions, see *Aman-i-Afghan*, January 7, 1929. Some of the main features of it appeared in *The Times*, January 12, 1929; "La guerre civile," p. 267; Morrish, p. 11; and N. N. Ghosh, p. 179. For details about the various tactical moves Amanullah made to save his throne, see I. A. Shah, *Tragedy of Amanullah*, p. 208; and Taillardat, "Révolte afghane," p. 16. On the ruling on clothing, see Toynbee, *Survey, 1929*, p. 205.

222. This information was obtained from an eyewitness who was in the British Legation at the time.

223. Mohammed Ali, *Progressive Afghanistan*, p. 39. See also *Daily Mail*, May 31, 1929. According to Toynbee (*Survey, 1930*, p. 183), Amanullah escaped to Kandahar by air. Fraser-Tytler (*Afghanistan*, p. 216) and Fletcher (*Afghanistan*, p. 218) assert he traveled by road.

224. Jackson Fleming, "The Afghan Tragi-Comedy," *Asia*, June 1929, pp. 508–10. See also Fraser-Tytler, *Afghanistan*, p. 216; and Toynbee, *Survey, 1930*, p. 183. On Inayatullah's concessions and attempt to win over the religious establishment and the Kabulis, see *The Times*, January 16, 1929.

225. See India, Royal Air Force.

226. Taillardat, "Révolte afghane," p. 16. The book *My Life from Brigand to King* by Habib-Allah purports to be Bacha's autobiography. The authenticity of this work (which in describing Bacha's spectacular rise and flamboy-

ant activities presents him as a sort of Robin Hood) is highly questionable. A close study of various passages, as well as the book's English syntax, has convinced me that it is not genuine. It may well be the work of several writers: certain passages resemble a variety of other published works on Afghanistan.

227. "La guerre civile," p. 267. According to Taillardat ("Révolte afghane," p. 16), Amanullah was able to reach all the tribal leaders via radio receiving sets that he had given them upon his return from Europe. I could not substantiate this information.

228. Agabekov, pp. 159–60; Castagné, "Soviet Imperialism," p. 701. According to Agabekov (pp. 159, 164–66), Ghulam Jelami Khan, the foreign minister of Afghanistan (since 1927), urged Moscow to intervene on Amanullah's behalf. Once again Mahendra Pratap offered his services, proposing to go to Badakhshan, organize a "revolutionary army of the people," and march on Kabul against Bacha-i-Saqao. His proposal was not taken seriously. See Pratap, *My Life*, pp. 156f.

229. Fraser-Tytler, *Afghanistan*, p. 217; "La guerre civile," pp. 267ff; Mohammed Ali, *Progressive Afghanistan*, p. 61. Various sources reported that Amanullah took treasure valued at 50 million dollars with him! See "Amanullah in Exile," p. 257.

230. *Pravda* and *Izvestia*, December 20, 1928; Chokaiev, "Bolsheviks and Afghanistan," pp. 506–7. On Soviet reaction to the events in Afghanistan, see Castagné, "Soviet Imperialism," pp. 701–2; "Afghanistan," in *BSE*, 2d ed., Vol. III; Reysner, *Noveishaia istoriia*, pp. 211–34; Akhramovich, "Afghanistan," pp. 766–67; and Masson and Romodin, II, 406–8.

231. For the views of the German and the French press, respectively, see the January 16, 1929, editions of *The Times* and the *Manchester Guardian*.

232. *Hansard's Parliamentary Debates*, January 20 and February 6, 1929; *Daily Herald*, January 5 and 7, 1929; *Daily News*, February 4, 1929. Raskolnikov ("War in Afghanistan," p. 185) states that during Amanullah's Grand Tour, Bacha was in close touch with the British Legation at Kabul. This, of course, the British categorically deny.

233. Comyn-Platt, p. 297; *Daily Mail* and *Sunday Express*, January 20, 1929; Emanuel, p. 202.

234. The statements of Amanullah and Hidayatullah can be found in "La guerre civile," p. 268; and Taillardat, "Révolte afghane," p. 50; Inayatullah's is in Morrish, p. 13. The Afghan envoy to Paris was blunter: he accused Great Britain of inciting the Afghan tribes against Amanullah. See the *Morning Post*, January 17, 1929.

235. See, for instance, Mohammed Ali, *Progressive Afghanistan*, pp. 6f, 11; I. A. Shah, *Tragedy of Amanullah*, p. vii; Karimi, "Maaref," p. 397; and Pazhwak, *Afghanistan*, p. 12.

236. Raskolnikov, "War in Afghanistan," pp. 180, 183.

237. *Pravda Vostoka*, November 2, 1928, as quoted by Chokaiev, "Bolsheviks and Afghanistan," p. 506.

238. *Ibid.*, January 1, 1929, as quoted by Chokaiev, "Bolsheviks and Afghanistan," p. 507. For a Soviet analysis of Amanullah's reforms and the nature of the opposition to them, see Ilinskii, pp. 68–79.

239. B. Nikitine, "L'Asie qui change," p. 15.

240. Wild, p. 69.

241. I. A. Shah, *Tragedy of Amanullah*, pp. 162–63; Kātrak, p. 36; Furon, *L'Afghanistan*, p. 95; Trinkler, p. 189.

242. Wild, p. 70.

243. Taillardat, "Révolte afghane," pp. 18–19; Mohammed Ali, *Progressive Afghanistan*, pp. 8ff. See also Habib-Allah, pp. 50, 110, 112; and Chokaiev, "Bolsheviks and Afghanistan," pp. 507–9.

244. Wild, pp. 86, 143.

245. Morrish, p. 36; Taillardat, "Révolte afghane," pp. 17f.

246. M. Nikitine, p. 13. See Amanullah's statement to the correspondent of *Young India*, October 12, 1922. See also Rhein and Ghaussy, p. 22.

247. Joseph Potocki, p. 113.

248. *Anis*, 1st year, No. 15.

249. For these innovations, see L. Thomas, *Khyber Pass*, pp. 234–55; Wild, pp. 87, 95, 161, 163, 172; MacMunn, *From Darius to Amanullah*, pp. 292, 296; Kātrak, pp. 38f, 50–58 *passim*; James, pp. 122f; and Jackson Fleming, "The Afghan Tragi-Comedy," *Asia*, June 1929, pp. 469ff.

250. Chokaiev, "Situation in Afghanistan," p. 330.

251. Personal interview on October 19, 1960, in London.

CHAPTER TEN

1. For the text of the manifesto Bacha-i-Saqao addressed to the "Afghan Nation and the Muslim World at Large," see *Oriente Moderne*, IX, 3 (March 1929), 134–35.

2. Mohammed Ali, *Progressive Afghanistan*, pp. 43, 46ff; see also Wild, pp. 240f. According to Fletcher (*Afghanistan*, p. 219), Bacha eliminated all potential rivals remaining in Afghanistan: he executed Amanullah's half brothers Hayatullah Khan and Abdul Majid Khan and one of the Amir's cousins, Ali Ahmed Jan.

3. Viollis, pp. 190f. For a firsthand and detailed account of the fall of Kabul and the reign of terror, see Muhieddin, pp. 93–106.

4. *Daily Telegraph*, February 2, 1929.

5. Taillardat, "Révolte afghane," p. 16.

6. "La guerre civile," p. 267. It was the ulama who first pronounced him a ghazi, or defender of the faith, "and went from place to place inciting the people to rally round his standard." See Mohammed Ali, *Progressive Afghanistan*, p. 22.

7. As quoted by N. N. Ghosh, p. 179. See also Bacha's "autobiography" (Habib-Allah, p. 105).

8. Toynbee, *Survey, 1930*, p. 186. For details about the war and the capture of Herat, see *Pravda*, May 10, 1929.

9. Mohammed Ali, *Progressive Afghanistan*, pp. 42–43; Muhieddin, pp. 96ff.

10. Toynbee, *Survey, 1930*, p. 184. The *Daily Telegraph* (February 2, 1929) speculated that the reason foreigners were not hurt was that Bacha realized he needed their friendship so as to be able to invoke their aid, if need be, and save himself.

11. Viollis, pp. 187, 193f.

12. *Ibid.*, pp. 191–92.
13. See Reshtiya, "Journalism," p. 74.
14. Chokaiev, "Situation in Afghanistan," p. 329.
15. Agabekov, pp. 159, 164–66.
16. A. Qadir, "Since the Revolution," p. 332. On the reported Soviet assistance to Nabi, see Agabekov, pp. 166–69; Viollis, p. 186; and Castagné, "Soviet Imperialism," p. 702. On the war between the forces of Nabi and Bacha at Mazar-i-Sharif, see *Pravda*, May 8, 1929. *Habib-ul-Islam*, Bacha's official paper, reported that airplanes of unknown origin had bombarded certain villages in northern Afghanistan. However, the paper later retracted the story. See Viollis, p. 186.
17. *Zaria Vostoka* (Tiflis), February 17, 1929.
18. *Izvestia*, February 26, 1929.
19. *Ibid.*, February 28, 1929.
20. *Pravda*, May 10, 1929; *Izvestia*, May 10, 1929.
21. *Krasnaia Zvezda*, May 9, 1929. On the attitude of the Soviet press toward Bacha and Amanullah during the civil war, see Chokaiev, "Situation in Afghanistan," p. 326, and "Bolsheviks and Afghanistan," p. 510. For a review of Soviet historiography's past and current treatment of Bacha, see *CAR*, IV (1956), 2, 179–81.
22. For the Soviet diplomatic note to Iran, see *Zaria Vostoka* (Tiflis), April 18, 1929. For the reply of the Iranian government reaffirming its policy of non-intervention in the internal affairs of neighboring countries and its friendship toward Afghanistan, see *Pravda*, April 25, 1929.
23. Fraser-Tytler, *Afghanistan*, p. 220.
24. A. Qadir, "The Outlook," p. 466.
25. Ghani Khan, pp. 48–49.
26. Morrish, p. 25.
27. *Ibid.*, pp. 23, 27.
28. *Ibid.*, p. 27.
29. P. Sykes, "The Present Position," pp. 156–57; Strickland, p. 714.
30. Fraser-Tytler, p. 223. Another source gives the date of his birth as 1885 and the place as Amballa, India. See Fazl Ahmad, p. 148.
31. Mohammed Ali, *Progressive Afghanistan*, p. 169; Ahmad and Abd al-Aziz, p. 71. For details, see Fazl Ahmad, pp. 144–45, 148–49.
32. Viollis, pp. 116f.
33. Taillardat, "Nadir Khan," p. 121.
34. Fraser-Tytler, *Afghanistan*, p. 223.
35. *Ibid.*; Molesworth, pp. 114ff; Ghazi; Mohammed Ali, *War of Independence*, pp. 51ff; India, *Third Afghan War*, p. 62.
36. For the nature of the rift and the personality conflicts between Nadir and various members of the Amanullah, Tarzi, and Charki families, see Taillardat, "Nadir Khan," p. 122; and Viollis, pp. 117–18.
37. According to Abdul Aziz Khan, the ex-envoy to Iran, he and Ahmad Shah Khan were sent to France to offer Nadir such a position. See *Ettelaat* (Tehran), May 4–13, 1929. See also Chokaiev, "Situation in Afghanistan," p. 328. Nadir's brother Shah Wali Khan adds that the two delegates returned to Peshawar from France and, speaking for Bacha, promised Nadir "a major post" in the administration. See Ghazi, pp. 38–40.
38. N. N. Ghosh, p. 181.

39. Taillardat, "Nadir Khan," p. 122; Ghazi, p. 40.

40. N. N. Ghosh, p. 181; Viollis, p. 111.

41. Morrish, pp. 23f. See also Fazl Ahmad, pp. 146–47.

42. P. Sykes, "The Present Position," p. 157.

43. Taillardat, "Nadir Khan," p. 123. For details about Nadir's strategy for the tribes of the Kandahar-Jalalabad-Kabul triangle, see Ghazi, pp. 46ff; and Muhieddin, pp. 120–89.

44. Toynbee, *Survey, 1930*, pp. 185–86. According to Taillardat ("Nadir Khan," p. 123), it was Hazrat Sahib who convened the jirga and proclaimed his suport for Nadir. I could not find any corroboration for this assertion; on the contrary, according to Shah Wali Khan (see Ghazi, p. 59), Hazrat Sahib suggested that the Musahiban brothers take their families to India for safety and promised the Musahibans he would intercede with Bacha and obtain suitable stipends for them. For details about the change in allegiance of various tribes, see Muhieddin, pp. 213–59. For the political activities and military operations of Nadir, see *The Times*, September 11, 18, 23, 30, October 10, 14, 16, 17, 19, 1929.

45. Toynbee, *Survey, 1930*, p. 186.

46. Muhieddin, pp. 270ff; Viollis, p. 90.

47. Fraser-Tytler, *Afghanistan*, p. 226.

48. Viollis, pp. 72, 90; *Petit Parisien*, October 20, 1920. In discussing the fall of Kabul, Ghazi (pp. 84ff) does not discuss the plundering and destruction wrought by the tribesmen. Muhieddin, though he notes the destruction of the citadel (pp. 270ff), does not mention any plundering either.

49. Viollis, p. 113.   50. Habib-Allah, p. 270.

51. Viollis, p. 194.   52. Fletcher, *Afghanistan*, p. 221.

53. Fraser-Tytler, *Afghanistan*, p. 226. Ghazi states that Bacha was captured, and that he was executed on public demand (p. 95).

54. Taillardat, "Nadir Khan," p. 124.

55. *Petit Parisien*, October 20, 1929; Viollis, p. 120; P. Sykes, *Afghanistan*, II, 321; Muhieddin, pp. 275–87. See also *The Times*, October 19, 1929.

56. Toynbee, *Survey, 1930*, p. 186. On Amanullah's congratulations to Nadir for his *victory*, see *Le Temps*, October 22, 1929.

57. *Pioneer*, October 18 and 19, 1929.

58. N. N. Ghosh, p. 184.

59. Fletcher, *Afghanistan*, pp. 221–22.

60. N. N. Ghosh, p. 185. See also his statement to the *Daily Mail*, May 31, 1929. Amanullah argued that the choice of Nadir ought not to be construed as a rejection of his own administration. After all, Nadir was *his* commander-in-chief, *his* representative in Paris. See *La Tribuna di Roma*, October 11, 1929.

61. Taillardat, "Nadir Khan," pp. 123–24.

62. *Izvestia*, July 24, 1930.   63. *Islah*, March 21, 1931.

64. Ghazi, pp. 46–47, 50, 52.   65. *Ibid.*, pp. 71–79 *passim*.

66. N. N. Ghosh, p. 181.

67. I. A. Shah, *Tragedy of Amanullah*, pp. 220–27 *passim*.

68. Pazhwak, *Afghanistan*, p. 34.

69. Roashan, p. 108.

CHAPTER ELEVEN

1. Viollis, p. 19; *Hamburger Nachrichten*, November 9, 1929, as quoted by Taillardat, "Nadir Khan," p. 125.

2. Wild, p. 270.

3. *Islah*, August 28, 1930 (speech of Abdul Ahad Khan). See also *Islah*, September 7, 1930 (article by Sher Ahmed).

4. Ahmad and Abd al-Aziz, p. viii.

5. Taillardat, "Nadir Khan," p. 125; Fletcher, *Afghanistan*, p. 227.

6. Mohammed Ali, *Progressive Afghanistan*, p. 209.

7. For the text, see *ibid.*, pp. 169–70.   8. *Pravda*, September 27, 1930.

9. *Islah*, October 21, 1930.   10. A. Qadir, "The Outlook," p. 467.

11. *Al-Falah* (Kabul), 7th year, No. 7, p. 43. This journal was published by the Society of the Afghan Ulama.

12. Woodsmall, pp. 152ff. On the decree reestablishing purda, see Mohammed Ali, *Progressive Afghanistan*, pp. 171–72.

13. Wild, pp. 240–41; *Pioneer Mail*, February 7, 1930.

14. *Pravda*, September 27, 1930.

15. Mohammed Ali, *Progressive Afghanistan,* pp. 171–72.

16. *Islah*, October 21, 1930.

17. For the text of the royal proclamation, see Mohammed Ali, *Progressive Afghanistan*, pp. 172–73.

18. *Islah*, July 23, 1930.

19. Ahmad and Abd al-Aziz, p. 110; Muhammed Khan, "Progress in Afghanistan," p. 864.

20. Mohammed Ali, *Progressive Afghanistan*, p. 184.

21. Morrison, "Nadir Shah," p. 173.

22. Ahmad and Abd al-Aziz, p. 111; Mohammed Ali, *Progressive Afghanistan*, p. 184.

23. Taillardat, "Nadir Khan," p. 125.

24. Twiss (p. 450) estimates 40,000; Ahmad and Abd al-Aziz (p. 110), Morrison ("Nadir Shah," p. 173), and *Statesman's Yearbook: 1934* (p. 654) estimate 70,000.

25. A. Qadir, "The Outlook," p. 470.

26. Mohammed Ali, *Progressive Afghanistan*, pp. 212, 214.

27. Taillardat, "Nadir Khan," p. 125.

28. *Islah*, December 2, 1930.

29. *Kaboul Almanach: 1934–35,* p. 17.

30. For the organization of the administrative divisions and the functions of various Afghan ministries, see *ibid.*, pp. 17–32, 35–80. For a brief summary, see Ahmad and Abd al-Aziz, pp. 105–6.

31. Muhammed Khan, "Progress in Afghanistan," p. 864; Ahmad and Abd al-Aziz, p. 109.

32. On the juridical structure in Nadir's reign, see *Kaboul Almanach: 1934–35*, pp. 35–80; Ahmad and Abd al-Aziz, p. 108; Muhammed Khan, "Progress in Afghanistan," p. 864.

33. A. Qadir, "Afghanistan in 1934," p. 212.

34. Mohammed Ali, *Progressive Afghanistan*, p. 190.

35. *Pioneer Mail*, July 2, 1930.

36. Mohammed Ali, *Progressive Afghanistan*, p. 189.

37. For a Persian text of the Afghan constitution, see *Islah*, November 2, 1931; *Kaboul Almanach: 1934–35*, pp. 3–16. For an English text, see Ahmad and Abd al-Aziz, pp. 97–101; Helen Davis, pp. 4–13; Peaslee, pp. 17–21. For texts in French and Italian, see, respectively, Godchot, pp. 6–21; and Giannini, *Le costituzioni degli stati*, or "La costituzione afgana." For a German text and commentary, see Schwager.

38. Yapp, "Afghanistan," p. 55; Godchot, p. 9.

39. *Islah*, July 8, 1931. A French translation of the Afghan monarch's speech is in *Revue des Etudes Islamiques*, 1932, pp. 553–57.

40. For the rules and duties of the National Consultative Assembly, see "Usul-e asasi-ye," pp. 37–49; and Fazl Ahmad, pp. 132–36.

41. Mohammed Ali, *Progressive Afghanistan*, p. 191.

42. Wilber, *Afghanistan* (2d ed.), p. 158.

43. *Islah*, February 22, 1933; Godchot, p. 21; Rossi, "La costituzione," pp. 1–6; Helen Davis, pp. 4–13. For various interpretations of the constitution, see Karimi, "Constitution," pp. 3–8; Fazl Ahmad, pp. 127–42; Wilber, *Afghanistan* (2d ed.), pp. 155–64; Akhramovich, *Outline History*, pp. 29–32. For the immediate Soviet reaction to various clauses, see *Zariya Vostoka* (Tiflis), March 24, 1932.

44. On the laws dealing with citizenship, consult Morrison, "Nadir Shah," pp. 171–73.

45. James, p. 262.

46. *Ibid.*, p. 267.

47. Viollis, p. 199.

48. James, p. 268.

49. Ahmad and Abd al-Aziz, pp. 111–12.

50. Sassani, p. 7. See also Fazl Ahmad, pp. 162–64.

51. I. A. Shah, *Modern Afghanistan*, p. 267.

52. Sassani, p. 7.

53. Ahmad and Abd al Aziz, p. 112; Fazl Ahmad, pp. 164–66.

54. A. Qadir, "Afghanistan in 1934," p. 213; Mohammed Ali, *Progressive Afghanistan*, p. 187; I. A. Shah, *Modern Afghanistan*, p. 270; Metta, "Changing Afghanistan," p. 1107.

55. I. A. Shah, *Modern Afghanistan*, p. 265.

56. *Ibid.*, pp. 265–66.

57. Muhammed Khan, "Progress in Afghanistan," p. 865; Ziai, "Challenge of Ideas."

58. I. A. Shah, *Modern Afghanistan*, p. 268.

59. Woodsmall, p. 159.

60. Sassani, p. 33; Fazl Ahmad, pp. 167–68.

61. I. A. Shah, *Modern Afghanistan*, p. 270.

62. Reshtiya, "Education," p. 22; Sassani, p. 40; Fazl Ahmad, pp. 169–70.

63. Mohammed Ali, *Progressive Afghanistan*, p. 186.

64. Reshtiya, "Education," p. 22.

65. *Ibid.*

66. Ahmad and Abd al-Aziz, p. 112.

67. Ziai, "Challenge of Ideas," p. 90.

68. Wilber, *Afghanistan* (2d ed.), p. 84.

69. Ahmad and Abd al-Aziz, p. 114.

70. *Ibid.*, p. 113; Karimi, "Maaref," p. 398.

71. Reshtiya, "L'Afghanistan moderne," p. 7.

72. For the press under Nadir, see Reshtiya, "Journalism," pp. 74–76; Karimi, "Maaref," p. 404; Roashan, pp. 42–43; Dvoriankov, pp. 322–23; Ahmad and Abd al-Aziz, p. 142; and Fazl Ahmad, pp. 340–42.

73. Ahmad and Abd al-Aziz, p. 123; Strickland, p. 715; Mohammed Ali, *The Mohammedzai Period*, p. 188.

74. Peaslee, p. 18.

75. See Emanuel, p. 205. See also Rhein and Ghaussy, p. 24; Strickland, p. 716; Mohammed Ali, *Progressive Afghanistan*, p. 221; A. Qadir, "Afghanistan in 1934," p. 212.

76. Mohammed Ali, *The Mohammedzai Period*, p. 188.

77. Ahmad and Abd al-Aziz, p. 124.

78. Reshtiya, "Kabul Calling," p. 1; Dvoriankov, p. 332.

79. James, pp. 147, 160.

80. Ahmad and Abd al-Aziz, p. 114.

81. Berke, p. 2.

82. Muhammed Khan, "Progress in Afghanistan," p. 866; Ahmad and Abd al-Aziz, pp. 114–15.

83. Berke, p. 1.

84. Roashan, p. 21.

85. Reshtiya, "L'Afghanistan moderne," p. 9.

86. Berke, p. 2; Ahmad and Abd al-Aziz, p. 115; Roashan, p. 21.

87. Berke, pp. 3ff.

88. See, for example, *MH*, 2d year, Nos. 2, p. 101, and 3, pp. 173–74.

89. Ahmad and Abd al-Aziz, p. 115; Muhammed Khan, "Progress in Afghanistan," p. 866; Fazl Ahmad, p. 215.

90. A. Qadir, "Afghanistan in 1934," p. 214.

91. Gurevich, *Voprosy ekonomiki*, p. 127. On the factories in these years, see Ahmad and Abd al-Aziz, p. 120; Strickland, p. 720; and M. Qadir, "Karkhaneha," pp. 148–50.

92. A. Qadir, "Afghanistan in 1934," p. 217.

93. Caspani and Cagnacci, p. 166; Sadigh Khan, p. 227; Hakimi, pp. 49f.

94. Ahmad and Abd al-Aziz, pp. 124–25; A. Qadir, "Afghanistan in 1934," p. 214.

95. Metta, "Changing Afghanistan," p. 1105.

96. A. Qadir, "Afghanistan in 1934," p. 213; Ahmad and Abd al-Aziz, p. 124. On the parochial financial transactions and credit system, see Strickland, p. 722.

97. Sadigh Khan, p. 228; Reshtiya, "L'Afghanistan moderne," p. 12. Fletcher (*Afghanistan*, p. 230) states that the bank was capitalized at 120 million afghanis. I could not corroborate this.

98. Wilber, *Afghanistan* (2d ed.), p. 217; Rhein and Ghaussy, p. 24.

99. A. Qadir, "Afghanistan in 1934," pp. 213–14.

100. Cervinka, pp. 39–40. For details about the structure and activities of the bank, see Sadigh Khan, pp. 226–30.

101. Abdul Majid Zabuli, *General Economic Information About Afghanistan*, Kabul, 1948, p. 1. Unpublished manuscript; as quoted by Hakimi, p. 47.

102. *Kaboul Almanach: 1935–36*, pp. 108f, 110–12. See also Sadigh Khan, pp. 234, 239; Reshtiya, "L'Afghanistan moderne," p. 13; and Fazl Ahmad, pp. 350–54.

103. Rhein and Ghaussy, p. 23.

104. Gurevich, *Voprosy ekonomiki*, p. 127; Rhein and Ghaussy, p. 24; Strickland, p. 720.

105. Kukhtina, "K voprosy," pp. 133–34.

106. Strickland, pp. 720–21; Morrison, "Nadir Shah," p. 174.

107. I. A. Shah, *Modern Afghanistan*, p. 311.

108. Ahmad and Abd al-Aziz, p. 147. For the provisions of this customs code, see I. A. Shah, *Modern Afghanistan*, pp. 303–36.

109. Akhramovich, *Outline History*, pp. 20ff.

110. Ahmad and Abd al-Aziz, p. 116.

111. *Ettelaat* (Tehran), January 1, 1931.

112. Strickland, p. 721.   113. Morrison, "Nadir Shah."

114. Beloff, pp. 208, 210.   115. Morrison, "Nadir Shah," p. 174.

116. Akhramovich, *Outline History*, p. 37, n12.

117. Mohammed Ali, *Progressive Afghanistan*, p. 221.

118. Ahmad and Abd al-Aziz, p. 118; Strickland, pp. 717f.

119. Rhein and Ghaussy, p. 24.

120. For details, see Akram, "L'agriculture," pp. 26–29.

121. Cervinka, pp. 37–38.

122. Akhramovich, *Outline History*, pp. 8–9; Poliak, "Sel'skoe Khoziaistvo," pp. 126–31; Gurevich, *Voprosy ekonomiki*, pp. 57–124.

CHAPTER TWELVE

1. *Islah*, July 8, 1931.

2. Fraser-Tytler, *Afghanistan*, pp. 231, 236.

3. *Islah*, July 8, 1931.

4. *Ibid.* Fletcher (*Afghanistan*, p. 232) states that "the British had given nothing to the hard-pressed Amanullah," but this is not the case.

5. Ghazi, pp. 34, 39, 43. The British government in India had refused to permit the Orakzais and the Waziris to participate in the struggle for Kabul. See *Islah*, July 8, 1931.

6. Caroe, *Pathans*, Appendix B, Section V; Strickland, p. 721.

7. Fraser-Tytler, *Afghanistan*, pp. 236f.

8. Benawa, "Les leaders," p. 14.

9. S. Gopal, *Lord Irwin*, pp. 67–68; H. R. S., "Unrest," pp. 627, 631; Caspani and Cagnacci, pp. 133–34.

10. Shridharani, p. 470.

11. M. Desai, p. 18.

12. Benawa, "Les leaders," p. 14.

13. M. Yunus, p. 142; Shridharani, p. 469; M. Desai, pp. 27, 47.

14. H. R. S., "Unrest." See also Ghani Khan, *The Pathans, A Sketch* (Bombay, 1947), p. 51. The author is the son of Abdul Ghaffar Khan.

15. Benawa, "Les leaders," p. 15; Shridharani, p. 468. The party also adopted an anthem. For the text, see M. Yunus, pp. 149–50.

16. *The Pukhtun*, April 1930, as quoted by S. Gopal, *Lord Irwin*, p. 68.

17. *Young India*, June 11, 1931, as quoted by M. Desai, p. 68.

18. Shridharani, p. 467. 19. M. Desai, pp. 31, 35ff.

20. Benawa, "Les leaders," p. 18. 21. Shridharani, p. 468.

22. M. Desai, p. 45. 23. Benawa, "Les leaders," pp. 18–19.

24. M. Desai, p. 45. 25. Benawa, "Les leaders," p. 19.

26. M. Yunus, p. 166.

27. M. Desai, p. 48; H. R. S., "Unrest," pp. 627–28. Originally, the Servants of God wore uniforms of khaddar, a native white cloth.

28. *Zaria Vostoka* (Tiflis), July 16, 1930. S. Gopal also reported (*Lord Irwin*, p. 68) that the emblem included a hammer and sickle. However, I could not corroborate this.

29. *Pravda*, July 4, 1931.

30. *Zaria Vostoka* (Tiflis), September 10, 1931. In the post-Stalinist Soviet interpretation, the Red Shirt movement was a movement led by bourgeois land-owner nationalists, whose aim was to eject the British imperialists from the local market. L. R. Gordon, *Agrarnye otnosheniia*, pp. 156–79. For a review of the Soviet historical literature on the North-West Frontier Province, see *CAR*, V (1957), 3, 295–328.

31. *Pioneer*, July 13, 1931.

32. M. Desai, pp. 51–58 *passim*.

33. *Ibid.*, p. 56. See also H. R. S., "Unrest," p. 628; S. Gopal, *Lord Irwin*, p. 68.

34. P. Sykes, "The Present Position," p. 158.

35. M. Yunus, pp. 141–42. 36. Shridharani, p. 469.

37. *Pioneer Mail*, July 4, 1930. 38. H. R. S., "Unrest," pp. 628–29.

39. Thomson, p. 478.

40. See the comments of Sir Michael O'Dwyer in Barton, "Law and Order," p. 19. See also A. Qadir, "The Outlook," p. 471; Fraser-Tytler, "Afghanistan," pp. 237–38; and P. Sykes, *Afghanistan*, II, 323.

41. Barton, "Law and Order," pp. 6, 8–10.

42. S. Gopal, *Lord Irwin*, p. 73.

43. Brock.

44. On the Pathan renaissance, see Caroe, *Pathans*, Chap. 26; and Barton, "Law and Order," pp. 11–12.

45. S. Gopal, *Lord Irwin*, pp. 73–74.

46. *Ibid.*, pp. 75–76, 82.

47. *Islah*, July 7, 1932, as quoted by Fletcher, *Afghanistan*, p. 232.

48. Fraser-Tytler, *Afghanistan*, p. 238.

49. P. Sykes, "The Present Position," p. 160.

50. Fischer, *The Soviets*, II, 793–94.

51. *Zaria Vostoka* (Tiflis), July 21, September 14, and September 21, 1930; and *Pravda Vostoka*, August 8, 1930. According to an unconfirmed report of Agabekov (pp. 169–70), Nadir had applied to the Soviets for a visa in order to enter Afghanistan through Soviet territory. Agabekov asserts that the Soviets, after delaying their response, agreed, on the condition that Nadir undertake an anti-British campaign.

52. Cachin, pp. 13–14. Similar charges were leveled against the Afghan

monarchy by the Soviet press, which saw in French and British military assistance and financial credits the shadows of anti-Soviet designs. See, for example, *Zaria Vostoka* (Tiflis), December 27, 1931.

53. *Izvestia*, October 20, 1929; Degras, *Soviet Documents*, II, 400–401.

54. *Ibid.*, 430–31.

55. Castagné, "Soviet Imperialism," p. 703.

56. For the text of the non-aggression pact, see Litvinov, pp. 144–47; *Izvestia*, July 11, 1931. For an article written on this occasion that clearly illustrates the nature of the Soviet interests and peace offensive, see *Izvestia*, November 29, 1932.

57. Castagné, "Soviet Imperialism," p. 703.

58. Beloff, p. 209; Strickland, p. 714; Fraser-Tytler, *Afghanistan*, p. 230. On this Soviet-Afghan agreement, see *Islah*, July 13, 1933.

59. Viollis, pp. 225–26. According to the Soviets, a threat to Afghan independence could come only from the British, not the Soviets. They maintained that the possibility of Soviet aggression against Afghanistan was a phony issue, designed to permit the British to bring Afghanistan under their control in the name of defense. *Zaria Vostoka* (Tiflis), January 28, 1931.

60. A. Qadir, "The Outlook," pp. 470–71.

61. *Ibid.*; French.

62. Strickland, p. 721.

63. *Islah*, April 25, 1932; Mohammed Ali, *Progressive Afghanistan*, pp. 214–15.

64. *Islah*, July 2, 1930.

65. *Ettelaat*, August 18, 1930.

66. *Um-el-Kora* (Mecca), March 25, 1932, as quoted by Rondot, "L'évolution sociale," p. 286.

67. Mohammed Ali, *The Mohammedzai Period*, p. 174.

68. Ahmad and Abd al-Aziz, p. 126; *Islah*, January 20, 1931.

69. Viollis, pp. 201–2.

70. *Islah*, March 24, 1931.

71. Caspani and Cagnacci, pp. 105, 157.

72. See U.S. Department of State, *Papers, 1934*, pp. 748–49: Phillips to Roosevelt, August 21, 1934. Other sources confirm that the United States did not establish diplomatic relations with and a mission in Afghanistan because American interests there were insignificant. See U. S. Department of State, *Foreign Relations*, p. 256: Murray to Dreyfus. An American visitor remarked that there was "not enough business in Afghanistan to warrant the expense [of establishing a diplomatic mission]. It might be done as a measure of good will but times are too hard to indulge in fancy gestures" (James, p. 269).

73. *Islah*, July 1, 1931.

74. James, p. 269.

75. U. S. Department of State, *Foreign Relations*, pp. 256–58.

76. *Islah*, December 31, 1930; *Ettelaat*, January 1, 1931.

77. Morrison, "Nadir Shah," p. 174.

78. Fraser-Tytler, *Afghanistan*, p. 235. *Krasnaiia Zvezda*, August 30, 1933, carried a report on the Soviet trade exhibition in Kabul.

79. P. Sykes, *Afghanistan*, II, 324.

80. *Islah*, July 8, 1931; Mohammed Ali, *Progressive Afghanistan*, p. 214.

81. *Pioneer*, April 3, 1932.

82. *Pravda*, June 10, 1930; *Zaria Vostoka* (Tiflis), June 9, 1930.

83. Morrish, p. 37. In Nadir's attempt to embark on a large-scale modernization program without adequate financial resources, the Soviet authorities saw a means by which the British could exploit the financial needs of the Afghans to obtain a variety of concessions. See *Zaria Vostoka* (Tiflis), February 11, 1930.

84. Fraser-Tytler, *Afghanistan*, p. 24. According to I. A. Shah (*Modern Afghanistan*, p. 249), Ghulam Nabi confessed his guilt and was blown from a gun. No other source confirms this gruesome story.

85. Fraser-Tytler, *Afghanistan*, p. 240; Fletcher, *Afghanistan*, p. 233; P. Sykes, "The Present Position," p. 159.

86. Fletcher, *Afghanistan*, p. 233; P. Sykes, "The Present Position," p. 159.

87. For this declaration and that of Shah Wali below, see *Izvestia*, November 12, 1933.

88. Rhein and Ghaussy, p. 24; *Pioneer*, December 21, 1931.

CHAPTER THIRTEEN

1. Afghanistan, Department of Press, *Afghanistan*, pp. 1–2.

2. For a sympathetic characterization of Hashim Khan, see Fraser-Tytler, *Afghanistan*, pp. 243–45.

3. Gulbedin Khan, pp. 136–37. See also Abdul Ali Khan, "Maghalat-e elmi," p. 182.

4. Azmi, "Madaniyat," p. 6; Abdul Ali Khan Habibi, p. 157. One of the post–World War II writers who singles out the Mongol invasion as the basic cause of the decline of civilization in Afghanistan is Muhammed Osman Khan Sedqi. See his "Un aperçu," p. 56.

5. Azmi "Pand-e pedar," pp. 16–17, and "Rmuz-e Taraghi," pp. 1, 5–6. On the same theme, see Bahré, "Ahamiyat-e vazife-shenasi," p. 24; and the poems in *MH*, 2d year, No. 1, pp. 30, 32, 34, 36; and No. 2, p. 85.

6. Mostaghni, "Elm," pp. 18–27. On the importance of industries, applied science, and technology, see also Abdul Ali Khan, "Maghalat-e elmi," pp. 66–68; Mostaghni, "Tashvigh," pp. 10–15; Azmi, "Maaref," p. 23.

7. See *MH*, 2d year, No. 2, pp. 19–20, 83–85. See also Munshizadeh, pp. 1–3, 5, 7.

8. Ahrari, pp. 56f.

9. Mostaghni, "Ehtiajat," pp. 15–19; Kazizadeh, "Vazife shenasi," pp. 1, 3–4.

10. Abdul Ali Khan, "Hayat-e ejtemaii," pp. 75–78.

11. Bahré, "Jashn-e esteghlal," p. 266. See also *MH*, 2d year, No. 5, p. 268; Pardis, pp. 49–52; Padshah Khan, pp. 57ff; and Azmi, "Din," p. 6.

12. Abdul Ali Khan, "Elm," p. 302; Ghulam Haidar Khan, pp. 361–63.

13. "Iman bilal amal," p. 76.

14. Tulimsher, pp. 62–63, 64f.

15. Azmi, "Din," pp. 5–6.

16. Abdul Ali Khan, "Maghalat-e elmi," pp. 62, 64.

17. Shahzadeh Durrani, "Mozaia-ye Islam," pp. 31, 35, 36–37. On Islam as a source of spiritual and ethical values, see Kazizadeh, "Dianat," pp. 37–43.

18. Abdul Ali Khan, "Favayed-e emumi," pp. 357ff; Huseini, pp. 308–19.

19. Ahrari, pp. 57, 58.

20. *Ibid.*, pp. 55–56; Abdul Ali Khan, "Ghomiyat," p. 369.

21. See Barthoux, "Les fouilles de Hadda" (1933), pp. 121–32; Hackin, "Les travaux," pp. 2–11, *L'oeuvre*, and "The 1939 Dig," pp. 525–28, 608–12; Godard *et al.*; Hackin and Carl, *Nouvelles recherches*; Auboyer, pp. 213–22; Kohzad, "Recherches," pp. 1–11; Schlumberger, pp. 11–16; and Ghirshman, "Bégram." See also Barger, "Exploration of Ancient Cities," pp. 377–98, and "Problems of Central Asian Exploration," pp. 1–18; Barger and Wright; R. E. M. Wheeler, pp. 57–65; and Stein, *Archaeological Reconnaissance*.

22. Kohzad, "Emperatouri-ye Kushan," pp. 151–203. See also Kohzad, "Aryana," pp. 12–13, and "Tahghighat-e arkialojy," pp. 13–18; and Hassan Khan, "Negahi," pp. 137–72. For a list of translations into Persian of various works by Western writers on ancient Afghanistan, see Anjoman-e Adabi, pp. 485–94.

23. Ghubar, "Role of Afghanistan," pp. 26–32. Some of the other great Afghan learned men the Afghan nationalists listed were Abu Hanifa, al-Bīrunī, Sinaï, Farabi, Sistani, Jalal-ad-Din Rumi, Daqiqi, Masud-Saad-e Salman. See Karimi, "Maaref," pp. 391–95. Naimi ("Calligraphy," p. 37) considered Shah Rukh a King of Afghanistan.

24. Ghubar, "Afghanestan," p. 43; Kohzad, "Aryana," p. 12; Hassan Khan, "Negahi," pp. 137–72. Among the contemporary works, see Afghanistan, Department of Press, *Afghanistan*, p. 16; Roashan, p. 100; and Pazhwak, *Afghanistan*, pp. 4–5.

25. Kohzad, in Anjoman-e Aryana, p. 17; Ahrari, pp. 55–56; Latifi, p. 11. See also Afghanistan, Department of Press, *Afghanistan*, p. 24; and Pazhwak, *Afghanistan*, p. 59.

26. See Zumeryali, "Pashtun," pp. 239ff.

27. *Ibid.*, p. 238.

28. Abdul Ali Khan Habibi, pp. 157ff; Abdulhayy Khan Habibi, "Kotob-e Pashto," pp. 301–10.

29. Zumeryali, "Pashto," pp. 286–300.

30. Hassan Khan, "Zabanha," pp. 134, 138.

31. *Ibid.*, p. 140; Karim Khan, p. 198.

32. Anjoman-e Adabi. On the publication of textbooks on the Pashto language, and on collections of Afghan folklore, see *ibid.*, pp. 490–91. On the study of Pashto poetry, see Abdulhayy Khan Habibi, "Tarikhcha," pp. 161–228. For a list of the publications of the Ministry of Instruction on Pashto folklore and literature, see *Kaboul Almanach: 1940–41*, pp. 72, 74–76.

33. See *MH*, 2d year, No. 5, pp. 271–78; and especially Abdul Ali Khan, "Favayed-e emumi," pp. 357–59. For a Muslim apologist view on the same theme, see Huseini, pp. 311–18; and Haydar Khan, pp. 361–63. See also *MH*, 2d year, Nos. 3, p. 53; 5, pp. 269–71; 7, pp. 378–79; 8, pp. 446–51; Taleb, p. 62; Shayegh, "Nefagh," pp. 46–49; Sepahi, pp. 254–55, 257f; and Bahré, "Jashn-e esteghlal," p. 266.

34. Abdul Ali Khan, "Bahar," pp. 92ff; Rejaii, "Ghazal," pp. 44f; Salem, p. 51; Seljuki, "Vatan," p. 54, "Ghazal," pp. 58–59, and "Naleh," pp. 55–56; Mona'am, p. 55; Shayegh, "Moshaer," p. 77; *MH*, 7th year, Nos. 4–5, p. 80, and 6, pp. 36, 60; and Munshi, "Andarz," pp. 44–47.

35. Rejaii, "Adabiyat," pp. 42f. See also *Islah*, April 28, 1937.

36. *Iqtisad*, 9th year, Nos. 209, p. 824; 210, pp. 838–39, 840; and 213, p. 1003. On the importance of agriculture, see Shayegh, "Zera'at," p. 29. On the benefits of trade and the need to exploit the country's mineral resources, see M. Qadir, "Taraghiat-e eghtesadi," p. 382. On the benetfis of technology, see also G. H. Shayegh, p. 16.

37. See, respectively, Sadighi, pp. 69–74; and Naimi, "Ekhteraat-e jadid," pp. 366–83.

38. *Iqtisad*, 9th year, No. 209, pp. 790–91, 820.

39. See *Kabul* (the literary journal), 1st year, Nos. 6, pp. 22–26, 40–47; and 2d year, No. 14, pp. 9–22 *passim*. See also *MH*, 7th year, Nos. 6, pp. 23–28, and 7-8, pp. 19–20.

40. See *Kabul*, 1st year, No. 12, pp. 39–41; 2d year, No. 13, pp. 21–27; and *MH*, 7th year, No. 11-12, pp. 20–28.

41. On this point, for example, see Shahzadeh Durrani's very interesting article "Ahamiyat-e tarjoma," pp. 31–44.

42. Abdul Ali Khan, "Adabiyat," pp. 13–16. See also Rejaii, "Taasir," p. 18, and "Adabiyat," p. 42; Kazizadeh, "Integhad," pp. 37ff.

43. Zubeyullah, pp. 236f.

44. Seljuki, "Ghazal," p. 58. See also his "Ghazal-e digar," p. 40.

45. Rejaii, "Avalem," pp. 70ff. Mahjuba Herati made a direct plea (pp. 61–62), arguing that nobody could equitably love and protect four wives, and that therefore only monogamy conformed to the spirit of Islam.

46. Shayegh, "Ezdevaj," and "Lezum-e ezdevaj," pp. 68–69.

47. See his article in *MH*, 7th year, No. 11-12, pp. 29–39.

48. *Islah*, June 19, 1937.

49. *Al-Falah*, 7th year, No. 10, pp. 59–60. For another of the King's speeches on the compatibility of Islam and progress, see *ibid.*, pp. 64–66.

50. *Ibid.*, No. 12, pp. 61, 65–66. See also *MH*, 7th year, No. 9-10, pp. 98–100.

51. *MH*, 7th year, No. 3, pp. 34–36.

52. Maillart, p. 224.

53. *Ibid.*

54. *Kaboul Almanach: 1934–35*, p. 67.

55. Hudson and Bacon, p. 121.

56. Maillart, p. 227.

57. *Habl-ul-Matin*, October 21, 1930.

58. Humlum, p. 89. See also *Islah*, March 3, 1937.

59. Hudson and Bacon, p. 121; *Islah*, July 5, 1937. On Pashto textbooks and translated works, see *Kaboul Almanach: 1939–40*, pp. 85–86, and *1941–42*, pp. 182–87. On the activities and objectives of the Pashto Tulana, see *ibid.*, *1939–40*, pp. 121–22. On the Ministry of Education's activities and policies in connection with the teaching of Pashto, see *ibid.*, *1940–41*, pp. 81–82, 306–22; and *1942–43*, pp. 60–61.

60. See, for example, Lentz.

61. Humlum, pp. 89f. As late as 1965 the Afghan government was still preoccupied with the problem of making Pashto an effective official and national language. See *Kabul Times*, November 4, 1965. The new Afghan constitution, however, recognizes the co-equality of Persian and Pashto.

62. Pazhwak (*Afghanistan*, p. 113) estimates the number of nomads at two million; Prince Peter of Greece asserts that two-thirds of the population are "practically nomads." On the adherence of the Hashim Khan government to the principle of free and compulsory elementary education, see Karimi, "Maaref," p. 401.

63. See Afghanistan, Ministry of Education, *Manual of Primary Education* and *Education in Afghanistan*, p. 11 (also quoted by Sassani, p. 11).

64. Sassani, p. 14. According to Mohammed Ali (*The Mohammedzai Period*, p. 179), there were only 453 village schools for boys and four for girls in 1958. According to the Ministry of Education (*Education in Afghanistan*, p. 91), in 1954 there were 338 village schools.

65. Wilber, "Islam in Afghanistan," p. 11.

66. Kukhtina, "K voprosy," p. 135. According to the Ministry of Education (*Education in Afghanistan*, p. 91) there were only 240 primary schools in 1954.

67. Sassani, p. 12.

68. Karimi, "Maaref," p. 401.

69. *Kaboul Almanach: 1942–43*, p. 62; and Kukhtina, "K voprosy," pp. 137–38.

70. Sassani, p. 18.

71. Afghanistan, Ministry of Education, *Education in Afghanistan*, pp. 20, 22.

72. *Ibid.*, p. 24; Karimi, "Maaref," pp. 398, 401f; Sassani, pp. 23–35; Mohammed Ali, *The Mohammedzai Period*, p. 179; Reshtiya, "L'Afghanistan moderne," p. 5.

73. Karimi, "Maaref," p. 402.

74. Kukhtina, "K voprosy," p. 144; Karimi, "Maaref," p. 402; Maillart, p. 226.

75. *Kaboul Almanach: 1940–41*, pp. 77, 79; Kukhtina, "K voprosy," p. 136; Sassani, p. 18.

76. Afghanistan, Ministry of Education, *Education in Afghanistan*, p. 21; Sassani, p. 18.

77. Sassani, p. 19; Afghanistan, Ministry of Education, *Education in Afghanistan*, p. 22.

78. Kukhtina, "K voprosy," p. 138. UNESCO's *Basic Facts and Figures* (pp. 18, 22) estimates the number of primary school children in 1950 at 79,000 and the number of teachers at 2,622.

79. Stolz, "Langues étrangères," pp. 30–32.

80. Maillart, p. 226; Bacon and Hudson, p. 35.

81. Stolz, "Langues étrangères," pp. 28f.

82. Maillart; Kukhtina, "K voprosy," pp. 145–46; *Kaboul Almanach: 1938–39*, p. 78, and *1939–40*, p. 91.

83. *Kaboul Almanach: 1939–40*, pp. 85–86, *1940–41*, pp. 72–73, *1934–35*, pp. 93f, *1935–36*, pp. 74–81.

84. Reshtiya, "L'Afghanistan moderne," pp. 6–7. See also *Kaboul Almanach: 1938–39*, pp. 79–80, and *1939–40*, p. 86.

85. *Kaboul Almanach: 1938–39*, pp. 80f, *1939–40*, p. 90, *1942–43*, p. 69.

86. *Ibid.*, *1942–43*, p. 70.

87. *Ibid.*, *1939–40*, p. 89, *1942–43*, pp. 68–69, *1938–39*, p. 402.

88. Ayeen, p. 2. See also UNESCO, *Basic Facts and Figures*, p. 27.

89. UNESCO, *Report*, p. 21. See also Kukhtina, "K voprosy," p. 138; and UNESCO, *Basic Facts and Figures*, pp. 18, 22.

90. Afghanistan, Ministry of Education, *Education in Afghanistan*, p. 91.

91. *Ibid.*; see also Woodsmall, p. 158.

92. Woodsmall, p. 159. According to Stolz ("Langues étrangères," p. 32), the students at Malalai later were given a choice of French, German, or English to study.

93. Eberhard, *Young Elite*.

94. *Ibid.*, p. 10. For details, see Spencer.

95. Kukhtina, "K voprosy," p. 130.

96. Ayeen, p. 1.

97. Rejaii, "Tiatr," *MH*, 7th year, No. 3, pp. 37, 43.

98. Stolz, "Théâtre afghan," p. 38, 42–43; Dvoriankov, pp. 360–62.

99. *UN Statistical Yearbook: 1959*, p. 584; UNESCO, *Basic Facts and Figures*, p. 73. My information on Radio Kabul and the Afghan news agency is based mainly on Metta, "Changing Afghanistan," p. 1106; Reshtiya, "Kabul Calling," pp. 1–3; Feroz, pp. 20–21; *Kaboul Almanach: 1939–40*, p. 120; Roashan, pp. 40–41; Maillart, p. 226; Dvoriankov, pp. 332–33; and Hudson, "Inside Afghanistan," p. 121.

100. My information on the Afghan press is based on *The Middle East*, pp. 17–26; Dvoriankov, pp. 322–24, 415–29; Caspani and Cagnacci, p. 163; Ahmad and Abd al-Aziz, p. 142; *Kaboul Almanach: 1934–35*, pp. 108–9, and *1939–40*, pp. 118–20; Roashan, pp. 42–43; Karimi, "Maaref," p. 404; Reshtiya, "Journalism," pp. 74–77; and Fazl Ahmad, pp. 340–42.

101. *UN Statistical Yearbook: 1958*, p. 581. For information on Afghan movie houses, see Emanuel, p. 203; and Karimi, "Maaref," p. 406.

102. On the museums, see Ahmad and Abd al-Aziz, p. 113; *Kaboul Almanach: 1934–35*, p. 96, and *1940–41*, pp. 91–92, 95–96, 99; and Dvoriankov, pp. 317–20. The establishment of a Directorate of Press is reported in *Iqtisad*, 9th year, No. 211, p. 935.

103. On the libraries, see *World of Learning: 1959–60*, p. 33, and *1961–62*, p. 45; Ahmad and Abd al-Aziz, p. 113; Dvoriankov, pp. 314–16; *The Middle East*, pp. 17–26 *passim*.

104. Pikulin, *Razvitie*, fn49.

105. *Iqtisad*, 9th year, No. 210, pp. 838–40. See also M. Qadir, "Taraghiat-e eghtesadi," p. 382.

106. Dastgir Khan, pp. 605f.

107. M. Qadir, "Karkhaneha," p. 154.

108. For details on the two Afghan banks, see Younossi, pp. 78–81; H. H. Tarzi, p. 48; A. K. Hakimi, pp. 49–52; Alizo, pp. 110–12; Cervinka, pp. 31–40; Cervin, pp. 411–12; Dvoriankov, pp. 197–209; Sadigh Khan, pp. 226–30.

109. On the establishment of the first Afghan bank and the industrial development of the country, see D. and F. Kuhn, pp. 255–58; Rhein and Ghaussy, p. 25; and A. K. Hakimi, p. 47.

110. My information on the cotton and silk industry is based on *Iqtisad*, 9th year, Nos. 206, pp. 662–63, 668, and 207, p. 736; Sadigh Khan, p. 164; Ahmad and Abd al-Aziz, pp. 118, 120; Mohammed Ali, *New Guide to Afghanistan*,

pp. 40, 67, 70–72; Roashan, pp. 52–54; Reshtiya, "L'Afghanistan moderne," pp. 9–10; *Kaboul Almanach*: *1938–39*, pp. 132, 135, and *1939–40*, pp. 69, 78–79, 108f; O. R. Ginnever, "Cotton in Afghanistan," *Geographical Journal*, November 1944; and Humlum, pp. 178–79.

111. For details on the new workshops, see *Kaboul Almanach: 1938–39*, p. 132, *1939–40*, pp. 68, 78–79, and *1941–42*, pp. 155f; *Iqtisad*, 9th year, No. 207, pp. 738–39; M. Qadir, "Karkhaneha," pp. 148–50; Mohammed Ali, *New Guide to Afghanistan*, p. 72; Ahmad and Abd al-Aziz, p. 120; Roashan, pp. 54–55; Pazhwak, *Afghanistan*, p. 51; and Hudson, "Inside Afghanistan," p. 122.

112. Roashan, p. 59. On the Ministry of Mines, see *Iqtisad*, 9th year, Nos. 208, p. 785, and 209, p. 834; *Kaboul Almanach: 1939–40*, pp. 99–107; and Metta, "Changing Afghanistan," p. 1105. For a survey of the mineral resources of Afghanistan, see U.S. Department of Commerce, *Basic Data on the Economy of Afghanistan*, Washington, D.C., World Trade Information Service, Economic Reports, Part 1, No. 62–77, pp. 5–6; and Afghanistan, Department of Press, *Afghanistan*, pp. 37–38.

113. Emanuel, p. 209.

114. Cervinka, pp. 32–34; Rhein and Ghaussy, p. 24; Hudson, "Inside Afghanistan," p. 120; A. Qadir, "Afghanistan in 1934," p. 212; Reshtiya, "L'Afghanistan moderne," p. 11.

115. *Iqtisad*, 9th year, Nos. 207, p. 699, and 208, pp. 777, 783; *Kaboul Almanach: 1938–39*, p. 131, and *1939–40*, pp. 71–76. See also Bloch-Favier, p. 1–11; Mohammed Ali, *New Guide to Afghanistan*, pp. 45, 63–65; and Roashan, pp. 55–56. For the number of trucks in the country, see Afghan Ministry of Transportation and Communications, Department of Transportation, Report No. 117/156. Kabul, n.d.

116. James, pp. 59, 164; Cervinka, p. 71; *Iqtisad*, 9th year, Nos. 205, p. 641, and 206, p. 686.

117. Akhramovich, *Outline History*, p. 11.

118. Cervin, pp. 412–13.

119. *Kaboul Almanach: 1939–40*, pp. 66–67. On the assets of these companies, see *Kaboul Almanach: 1935–36*, pp. 110–12. See also Dvoriankov, p. 176; and Roashan, p. 65.

120. The estimates of the karakul trade in the years 1935–45 vary. See Mohammed Ali, "Karakul," pp. 49–50; Mohammed Ali, *New Guide to Afghanistan*, p. 72; P. Sykes, *Afghanistan*, II, 329–30; Sadigh Khan; and Reshtiya, "L'Afghanistan moderne," p. 13. According to Hashim Khan, karakul made up 50 per cent of the kingdom's exports (see Maillart, p. 225). In 1938 the capital of the Karakul Company reached some 70 million afghanis. See *Kaboul Almanach: 1938–39*, p. 83.

121. On the companies that traded in commodities other than karakul, see *Kaboul Almanach: 1934–35*, pp. 109, 234–35; *1935–36*, pp. 83, 110–12; *1936–37*, p. 512; *1939–40*, pp. 68–69; and *1941–42*, p. 156. See also *Iqtisad*, 9th year, No. 210, p. 865; and Humlum, pp. 175, 182.

122. Fazl Ahmad, pp. 107–16. Both Peter Franck ("Problems of Development," Part 1, p. 299) and Alizo (p. 16) provide the following dollar figures for the Afghan import-export trade in the years 1939–47. The figures are in millions:

Year	Afghan Imports	Afghan Exports
1939–40	27.7	34.2
1940–41	32.8	41.0
1941–42	42.7	37.0
1942–43	26.5	17.4
1943–44	23.7	35.5
1944–45	25.6	44.2
1945–46	48.2	56.5
1946–47	53.0	60.0

123. Beloff, pp. 208, 210; Fazl Ahmad, p. 106.

124. P. Franck, "Problems of Development," Part 1, pp. 297–98.

125. A. K. Hakimi, p. 60. See also the statement of the Afghan foreign minister to the newspaper *Iran* (Tehran), April 22, 1936.

126. For the text of King Zahir's speech to the Afghan National Assembly in 1934, see *Kaboul Almanach: 1934–35*, pp. 66–67.

127. *Ibid., 1935–36*, p. 52, and *1939–40*, p. 37.

128. R. Forbes, *Forbidden Road*, p. 38. On the improvements in the Afghan army, see *Kaboul Almanach: 1934–35*, pp. 81–84; *1938–39*, p. 54; *1939–40*, pp. 37–42, 44ff; and *1940–41*, pp. 42–43. See also Hudson and Bacon, p. 121; Maillart, p. 226; Metta, "Changing Afghanistan," p. 1109; and Ahmad and Abd al-Aziz, p. 111.

129. R. Forbes, *Forbidden Road*, pp. 37f, 60; Ali Mohammed Khan, "Progress," p. 864; Ahmad and Abd al-Aziz, p. 110.

130. *Statesman's Yearbook: 1934*, p. 654, *1938*, p. 682, and *1942*, p. 686; *Iran* (Tehran), April 22, 1936. See also Howland, "Afghanistan," p. 635; and P. Sykes, "The Present Position," p. 161.

131. *Kaboul Almanach: 1939–40*, pp. 55–57, and *1940–41*, pp. 59, 62–63.

132. Ali Mohammed Khan, "Progress," p. 864; *Kaboul Almanach: 1934–35*, p. 90, and *1939–40*, p. 60; Reshtiya, "L'Afghanistan moderne," p. 15; Ahmad and Abd al-Aziz, p. 108.

133. For the text of the decree, see *Kaboul Almanach: 1935–36*, pp. 68–69.

134. *Ibid., 1940–41*, p. 61. See also Ahmad and Abd al-Aziz, p. 109–11.

135. My information on health conditions in Afghanistan is based chiefly on Berke, pp. 1–7; Fazl Ahmad, pp. 345–46; *Islah*, January 5, 1937, and July 4, 1939; *Kaboul Almanach: 1935–36*, p. 96, *1938–39*, p. 9, and *1939–40*, pp. 81–83, 89–90; Mohammed Ali, *The Mohammedzai Period*, p. 184; Ahmad and Abd al-Aziz, pp. 114–15; and Zuhdi Berke, "Inoculation Experiments Against Typhus in Afghanistan," *British Medical Journal*, 1946, No. 2.

CHAPTER FOURTEEN

1. See King Zahir's speech to the Afghan parliament in *Kaboul Almanach: 1934–35*, p. 67.

2. Castagné, "Soviet Imperialism," p. 703.

3. P. Sykes, "The Present Position," p. 161.

4. *Pravda*, March 30, 1936; *Izvestia*, September 6, 1936. For sources on the text and the protocols of the treaty, see Degras, *Calendar of Soviet Documents*, p. 152.

5. For the full text of this agreement, see *Islah*, May 23, 1936.

6. *Pravda*, February 7, 1937.

7. *Islah*, April 25, 1938.

8. For the text of the pact, see League of Nations, pp. 21–27; *Ettelaat*, March 21, 1938; *Izvestia*, July 12, 1937; Hurewitz, II, Document No. 63; Sutton, Appendix IV; and Heald, pp. 530–33. See also D. C. Watt, "The Sa'dabad Pact of July 8, 1937," *JRCAS*, July–October 1962.

9. See *Ettelaat*, July 1 and July 9, 1937, and March 21, 1938; and *Islah*, January 30, 1938. See also B. Lewis, *Turkey Today*, pp. 67–68.

10. Kirk, *Survey*, pp. 489–90. See also B. Lewis, *Turkey Today*, pp. 77–78. For an Iranian commentary, see Abbas Khalatbary, *L'Iran et le Pacte Orientale*, Paris, 1938, Part 3.

11. *Izvestia*, July 10, 1937. For a British commentary, see *The Times*, July 19, 1939.

12. B. Lewis, *Turkey Today*, pp. 68, 77.

13. P. Sykes, *Afghanistan*, II, 334.

14. *La Tribuna di Roma*, May 8, 1940; *Rassegna Italiana*, April 1940. See also B. Lewis, *Turkey Today*, p. 67; Kirk, *Survey*, p. 490; and Vernier, pp. 96f.

15. For the text of the postal convention, see *Islah*, August 2, 1938. For the agreement on the telegraph link, see *Ettelaat*, January 1, 1939, and *Islah*, January 22, 1939.

16. *Ettelaat*, July 1, 1939. On the settlement of the Helmand issue, see *Islah*, January 28, 1939.

17. *Islah*, February 1, 1938.

18. *Ibid.*, August 8, 1939. For a list of the Afghan friendship treaties with European powers, see Ahmad and Abd al-Aziz, p. 126.

19. *Islah*, January 12, 1935.

20. For the text, see U.S. Department of State, *Agreement Between U.S. and Afghanistan*.

21. U.S. Department of State, *Foreign Relations*, p. 256: Murray to Dreyfus, January 28, 1941.

22. *Ibid.*, p. 258: Dreyfus to Secretary of State, June 27, 1941.

23. Vernier, p. 97. See also *Pravda*, May 24, 1938; and Fox, p. 18.

24. P. Sykes, "The Present Position," p. 168; Maillart, p. 227. See also Vernier, p. 102; Bacon and Hudson, p. 35; and *Pioneer* (Lucknow), October 21, 1937.

25. Fox, p. 18.

26. Kirk, *Survey*, p. 142. My information on German economic activities and technical assistance is based on *Pravda*, June 5, 1938; *Pioneer* (Lucknow), August 19, 1939; JRCAS, January 1940, Part 1, p. 126; R. Forbes, *Forbidden Road*, pp. 38, 59; Vernier, pp. 55, 102; Bacon and Hudson, p. 35; Byron, *Road to Oxiana*, p. 285; Barton, "NW Frontier and the War," p. 1103; P. Sykes, *Afghanistan*, II, 331; Metta, "Changing Afghanistan," p. 1109; and Emanuel, p. 216.

27. Maillart, p. 226.

28. *Ibid.*; Bacon and Hudson, pp. 32, 35; Wild, p. 289; Metta, "Changing Afghanistan," p. 1109; *Kaboul Almanach: 1935–36*, pp. 105–6.

29. *Kaboul Almanach: 1935–36*, pp. 105–6; Maillart, p. 226; Bacon and

Hudson, p. 35; Wild, p. 289; Metta, "Changing Afghanistan," p. 1109; Emanuel, p. 216; Barton, "NW Frontier and the War," p. 1103.

30. For the text of the agreement, see *Islah*, May 3, 1937.

31. Fox, pp. xvii–xviii, 23, 65. See also Maillart, p. 226; Bacon and Hudson, p. 35; P. Sykes, "The Present Position," p. 160; and Howland, "Afghanistan," p. 636.

32. See Metta, "Changing Afghanistan," p. 1109; and Bacon and Hudson, p. 32.

33. Barton, "NW Frontier and the War," pp. 1103.

34. Kirk, *Survey*, p. 142.

35. Spain, *Pathan Borderland*, p. 235, and *People of the Khyber*, pp. 134–35; Fletcher, *Afghanistan*, p. 239.

36. Fraser-Tytler, *Afghanistan*, pp. 253, 267. For information about the Fakir of Ipi, see Quaroni; Caspani and Cagnacci, p. 145; Fletcher, *Afghanistan*, p. 238; and Spain, *People of the Khyber*, pp. 131–32.

37. Mussolini's conversation with Ribbentrop, May 13, 1941, as quoted in Kirk, *Survey*, p. 143. See also *Ibid.*, p. 144; and W. B. Smith, *Trois années à Moscou* (Paris, 1951), p. 100.

38. Hirszowicz, pp. 70–71.

39. See U.S. Department of State, *Documents on German Foreign Policy*, XIII, 463–64.

40. Kirk, *Survey*, p. 143.

41. Hirszowicz, pp. 116, 148. For Faiz Muhammed Khan's statements on Rashid Ali al-Gailani, see the *New York Times*, May 16 and 18, 1941; and Kirk, *Survey*, p. 144.

42. For the text of the Afghan neutrality act, see *Kaboul Almanach: 1939–40*, pp. 432–33; its approval by the Afghan parliament was reported in *ibid.*, p. 47, and its reaffirmation was carried in *The Times*, July 3, 1942.

43. U.S. Department of State, *Foreign Relations*, p. 508: MacMurray (U.S. ambassador to Turkey) to Secretary of State, May 13, 1941.

44. Fraser-Tytler, *Afghanistan*, p. 253.

45. See U.S. Department of State, *Documents on German Foreign Policy*, XIII, 51: June 29, 1941, instructions of Ribbentrop.

46. *Ibid.*, XII, 971.

47. *The Times*, October 21, 1941; Kirk, *Survey*, pp. 145–46; Fraser-Tytler, *Afghanistan*, pp. 254–55.

48. For the proceedings of the Loe Jirga of 1941, see *Kaboul Almanach: 1941–42*, pp. 280–85. For details about the exodus of Axis nationals, see U.S. Department of State, *Documents on German Foreign Policy*, XIII, 640–41.

49. *Britannica Book of the Year: 1941*, p. 21.

50. See *Statesman's Yearbook: 1944*, p. 692, and *1946*, p. 688; *Britannica Book of the Year: 1940*, p. 23.

51. On the problem of inflation in Afghanistan, see Fazl Ahmad, pp. 117f; *Kaboul Almanach: 1942–43*, pp. 49–128 passim, 311–22; *Anis*, October 31, 1945, and March 17, 1946; and *Iqtisad*, 9th year, No. 205, pp. 598–99. "It seems clear from our study," a UN mission to Afghanistan reported in 1949, "that in 1938 a family of four could live reasonably well on 300 afghanis per month. At present the same family would need about 1,600 afghanis per month. Teaching

salaries vary between 150 and 712 afghanis per month, the higher figure being the salary of a university professor." See UNESCO, *Report*, pp. 60f.

52. See A. K. Hakimi, pp. 51–52; and *Statesman's Yearbook: 1939*, p. 685, *1942*, p. 687, and *1946*, p. 690.

53. Mohammed Ali, "Karakul," p. 51; *Kaboul Almanach: 1938–39*, p. 13; *Iqtisad*, 9th year, Nos. 205, p. 640, and 206, p. 683.

54. U.S. Department of State, *Foreign Relations*, pp. 259–63: Dreyfus to Secretary of State, June 27, 1941.

55. A. K. Hakimi, p. 61.

56. See *Islah*, January 3, 7, and 19, February 2, 7, and 13, 1946.

57. *Ibid.*, July 15 and 16, and November 13, 1945.

58. *Forugh* (Tehran), January 22, 1946.

59. C. Black, *Dynamics of Modernization*, pp. 121f.

60. Rupert Emerson, "The Progress of Nationalism," in P. W. Thayer, *Tensions in the Middle East*, Baltimore, 1958, pp. 73f.

61. See Rupert Emerson, "Nationalism and Political Development," *Journal of Politics*, February 1960; Hoselitz, "Agrarian Societies," pp. 1, 8; Bottomore, p. 97; Deutsch, *Nationalism*; Binder, *Ideological Revolution*, pp. 1–2, 5. See also D. E. Apter, ed., *Ideology and Discontent*, New York, 1964; and Silvert.

62. C. Black, *Dynamics of Modernization*, p. 122.

63. Edward Shils, "The Intellectuals in the Political Development of the New States," *World Politics*, April 1960, p. 342.

64. Eisenstadt, *Modernization*, p. 4.

65. Huntington, p. 779. See also Bottomore, p. 90.

Bibliography

The Bibliography is divided into four sections: a list of bibliographies; a list of all primary and secondary works and articles consulted, including official documents and manuscript sources; a list of reference works, such as encyclopedias and yearbooks; and a partial list of newspapers and journals used. The entries within each section are in alphabetical order. For a list of the abbreviations used here and in the Notes, see p. 409.

A. BIBLIOGRAPHIES

Akademiia Nauk SSSR. Institut Vostokovedeniia. Sovremennyi Afganistan. Moscow, 1960. Edited by N. A. Dvoriankov.

Akram, Mohammed. Bibliographie analytique de l'Afghanistan. Paris, 1947.

American Universities Field Staff. A Select Bibliography: Asia, Africa, Eastern Europe, Latin America. New York, 1960.

Arberry, A. J. British Contributions to Persian Studies. London, 1942.

———. "Persian Books," in Vol. II, Part 4, Catalogue of the Library of India Office. Oxford, 1937.

———. A Second Supplementary Hand-List of the Muhammadan Manuscripts in the University and Colleges of Cambridge. Cambridge, Eng., 1952.

Backer, A. Bibliothèque des écrivains de la Compagnie de Jésus, ou notices bibliographiques. Série 1–7. Liège, 1853–61. 7 vols.

Beaurecueil, S. de Laugier de. "Manuscrits d'Afghanistan," in Vol. III, Mélanges de l'Institut Dominicain d'Etudes Orientales. Cairo, 1956.

Blumhardt, J. F. Catalogues of Hindi, Punjabi and Hindustani Manuscripts in the Library of the British Museum. London, 1899.

———. Catalogues of the Hindi, Punjabi, Sindhi and Pushtu Printed Books in the Library of the British Museum. London, 1893.

Browne, E. G. A Hand List of the Muhammadan Manuscripts, Including All Those Written in Arabic Character, Preserved in the Library of the University of Cambridge. Cambridge, Eng., 1900.

Central Asian Research Centre. Bibliography of Russian Works on Afghanistan. London, 1956.

Council on Foreign Relations. Foreign Affairs Bibliography 1919–1962. New York, 1933–64. 4 vols.

Degras, Jane, ed. Calendar of Soviet Documents on Foreign Policy. London, 1948.

Dianous, Hugues Jean de. "La contribution récente de l'orientalisme soviétique à l'étude de l'histoire et du développement économique de l'Afghanistan," *Cahiers du Monde Russe et Soviétique*, II (1961), 4.

Edwards, E. A. Catalogue of the Persian Printed Books in the British Museum. London, 1922.

Elwell-Sutton, L. P. "The Iranian Press, 1941–1947," *Iran: Journal of the British Institute of Persian Studies*, VI (1968).

Engert, Cornelius van H. A Report on Afghanistan. Department of State, Division of Publications, Series C, No. 53: Afghanistan, No. 1. Washington, D.C., 1942.

Ethe, Hermann. Catalogue of the Persian Manuscripts in the Library of India Office. Oxford, 1903, 1937. Vols. I, II.

Ettinghausen, Richard. A Selected and Annotated Bibliography of Books and Periodicals in Western Languages Dealing With the Near and Middle East. Washington, D.C., 1952.

Farid, Ahmad. Bibliografi. Kabul, 1965.

Fernandes, B. A. Bibliography of Indian History and Oriental Research. Bombay, 1938–42.

Ghani, A. R. Pakistan: A Select Bibliography. Lahore, 1951.

Glazer, Sydney S. Bibliography of Periodical Literature on the Near East and Middle East. Washington, D.C., 1947.

Heravi, Ghulam Reza "Mayel." Fehrest-e Kotob-e matbu-e Afghanestan az sal-e 1330 ila 1344. Kabul, 1965.

————. Moarefi-ye ruznameha, jarayed va majallat-e Afghanestan. Kabul, 1962.

India Office. Guide to the India Office Records, 1600–1858. London, 1919.

Jafar, S. M., comp. A Guide to the Archives of the Central Record Office of the North-West Frontier Province. Peshawar, 1948.

Khan, S. A. Sources for the History of British India in the XVIIth Century. Oxford, 1926.

Kieffer, Charles M. "Les problèmes d'une bibliographie exhaustive de l'Afghanistan," *Afghanistan*, April-June and July-September 1958. 2 parts.

Kohzad, Ahmad Ali. "Les manuscrits relatifs à l'histoire de l'Afghanistan au XIXᵉ siècle," in Vol. II, *TDPMKV*. Moscow, 1963.

Kukhtina, T. I., ed. Bibliografiia Afganistana: Literatura na russkom iazyke. A. N. SSSR. Moscow, 1965.

Lewis, B., and P. M. Holt, eds. Historians of the Middle East. Oxford, 1962.

Löewenthal, Rudolf. The Turkic Languages and Literatures of Central Asia: A Bibliography. Gravenhage, 1957.

Maslovskii, S. D., comp. Bibliografiia Avganistana. St. Petersburg, 1908.

Masson, V. M., and V. A. Romodin. Istoriia Afganistana. Moscow, 1964–65. 2 vols.

Mezhov, V. I. Bibliografiia Azii. St. Petersburg, 1891–94. Vol. I.

North, Roger E. The Literature of the North West Frontier of India: A Select Bibliography. Peshawar, 1946.

Pearson, J. D. Index Islamicus 1906–1955. A Catalogue of Articles on Islamic

Subjects in Periodicals and Other Collective Publications. Cambridge, Eng., 1958.

————. Index Islamicus Supplement: 1956–1960. Cambridge, Eng., 1962.

Phillips, C. H., ed. Historians of India, Pakistan, and Ceylon. Oxford, 1961.

Pierce, Richard A. Soviet Central Asia: A Bibliography. Berkeley, Calif., 1966.

Press Lists of Ancient Documents Preserved in the Bombay Record Office 1646–1760. Bombay, n.d. 4 vols.

Rieu, C. Catalogue of the Persian Manuscripts in the British Museum. London, 1879–95. 3 vols.

Romodin, V. A. Afghan Studies. Moscow, 1967. Part of Fifty Years of Soviet Oriental Studies. Brief Reviews: 1917–1967.

Rubinstein, A. Z. "Selected Bibliography of Soviet Works on Southern Asia, 1954–56: Afghanistan," *Journal of Asian Studies*, November 1957.

Saba, Mohsen. Bibliographie française de l'Iran. Tehran, 1951.

Sachau, E., and H. Ethe. Catalogue of the Persian, Turkish, Hindustani and Pushtu Manuscripts in the Bodleian Library. Oxford, 1889–1920.

Sauvaget, J. Introduction à l'histoire de l'Orient musulman. C. Cahen, ed. Paris, 1961.

————. Introduction to the History of the Muslim East. A Bibliographical Guide. Berkeley, Calif., 1963.

Shapiro, Leonard, ed. Soviet Treaty Series. Washington, D.C., 1950. Vol. I.

Sharma, Sri Ram. A Bibliography of Mughal India (A.D. 1526–1707). Bombay, n.d.

Snessarev, A. E. Avganistan. Moscow, 1921. Bibliographical essay, pp. 20–39.

Storey, Charles A. Persian Literature. A Bio-Bibliographical Survey. London, 1927–58. Section II, Fasciculus 2. London, 1936.

Sykes, Sir Percy M. A History of Afghanistan. London, 1940. 2 vols.

UNESCO. Middle East Social Science Bibliography, 1955–1960. Cairo, 1961.

United States. Department of State, Division of Library and Reference. A Selected Bibliography of Published Material on the Area Where Pashtu Is Spoken. Washington, D.C., 1951.

————. Point Four. Near East and Africa. A Selected Bibliography of Studies on Economically Underdeveloped Countries. Washington, D.C., 1951.

Wilber, Donald N. Annotated Bibliography of Afghanistan. 1st and 2d eds. New Haven, Conn., 1956, 1963.

————. "Matbu'at-e Afghanestan," *Danesh* (Tehran), III (1951).

Wilson, Sir Arnold T. A Bibliography of Persia. Oxford, 1930.

B. PRIMARY AND SECONDARY WORKS AND ARTICLES

Abawi, Mohammed Jahja. Die Wirtschaftsstruktur, insbesondere die Agrarstruktur in Afganistan und die Möglichkeiten genossenschaftlicher Betätigung in der Landwirtschaft. Münster, 1964.

Abbot, Augustus. The Afghan War: 1838–1842. Journal and Correspondence. London, 1879.

Abbott, James. Narrative of a Journey from Heraut to Khiva, Moscow, and St. Petersburg. London, 1843. 2 vols.

Abd al-Ghaffār, Qāzī Muhammad. Asār-i Jamāl al-dīn Afghānī. Delhi, 1940.

Abdul Ali Khan, Mir. "Adabiyat va asarat-e an dar jam'aa, *MH*, 2d year, No. 1.
———. "Bahar va esteghlal," *MH*, 7th year, Nos. 1–2.
———. "Elm va barkhi az fazael-e an," *MH*, 2d year, No. 6.
———. "Favayed-e emumi," *MH*, 2d year, No. 6.
———. "Ghomiyat," *MH*, 2d year, No. 7.
———. "Hayat-e ejtemaii," *MH*, 2d year, No. 2.
———. "Maghalat-e elmi," *MH*, 2d year, No. 3.
Abdul Kerim Munshi, Mohammed. "Itinéraires de Pichaver à Kaboul, de Kaboul à Qandahar, de Qandahar à Herat," in Schérzer and Léger, listed below.
Abdullah, Sheikh Ahmed. "Asia and the War," *Harper's Weekly*, December 11, 1915.
Abdur Rahman Khan, Amir. Halat-e Amir Abd al-Rahman Khan. Tehran, 1903. A translation into Persian of Mir Munshi Sultan Mahomed Khan's two-volume biography of the Afghan ruler by Ghulam Murteza Khan Kandahari. For the English version, see entry under Munshi.
———. Kalimāt amīr al-bilād, fī al-tārghīb ilā al-jihād. Kabul, 1887.
———. "A Letter from His Highness the Amir Abdur Rahman on His Past and Present Relations to England," *The Imperial and Asiatic Quarterly Review*, October 1894.
———. Sar reshte-ye Islami-ye Rum. Kabul, 1887.
Abrahamian, Ashot G. Hamarot Urvagidts Hai Gaghtavayreri Patmutian. Erivan, 1964. In Armenian.
Abu al-Fazl 'Allāmī. A'in-i Akbarī. 3 vols. English trans.: Vol. I (H. Blochmann), Calcutta, 1927; Vol. II (H. S. Jarrett), Calcutta, 1891; Vol. III (H. S. Jarrett and J. Sarkar), Calcutta, 1948.
Adamec, Ludwig W. Afghanistan, 1900–1923: A Diplomatic History. Berkeley, Calif., 1967.
Adams, Charles C. Islam and Modernism in Egypt. A Study of the Modern Reform Movement Inaugurated by Muhammad 'Abduh. London, 1933.
Adivar, Abdulhak Adnan. "Interaction of Islamic and Western Thought in Turkey," in Young, listed below.
Adye, J. M. Indian Frontier Policy. An Historical Sketch. London, 1897.
Afghan Committee. Causes of the Afghan War—Being a Selection of the Papers Laid Before Parliament with a Connecting Narrative and Comment. London, 1879.
"The Afghan Conquest of Persia: Unpublished Contemporary Correspondence," *The Asiatic Quarterly Review*, July-October 1886.
"Afghan Independence Day," *The Modern Review*, October 1928.
"Afghan Mission 'Spent Busy Time in Japan,'" *China Weekly Review* (Shanghai), May 31, 1941.
"The Afghan Trouble," *The Near East*, May 30, 1919.
Afghanistan. Afghan Royal Embassy. General Information on Modern Afghanistan. Washington, D.C., 1953.
———. Da Afghanistan Bank. Statutes of Da Afghanistan Bank. Bombay, 1942.
———. Department of Press and Information. Afghanistan, Present and Past. Kabul, 1958.

——, ——. Fortieth Anniversary of the Independence of Afghanistan. Kabul, 1959.

——. Ministry of Education and the Afghan Cultural Board. Education in Afghanistan During the Last Half Century. Munich, 1956.

——, ——. Manual of Primary Education in Afghanistan. Kabul, 1953.

——. Nizamnama-ye tashkilat-e asasi-ye Afghanestan. Kabul, 1921.

"Afghanistan and the Destiny of the Afghans Beyond the Frontier," *Afghanistan*, July-September 1947.

"Afghanistan and Great Britain," *The Modern Review*, March 1929.

"Afghanistan: King Nadir and the Afghans: Two Years Rule," *The Times* (London), August 22, 1931.

"Afghanistan: Neutral in a Hurry," *The Times* (London), March 15, 1961.

L'Afghanistan Nouveau. Paris, 1924.

"Afghanistan Today," *The Times* (London), April 16, 1932.

"Afghanistan's Economic Position," *Great Britain and the East*, September 28, 1940.

"Afghanistan's 'Modern' Ruler," *Current History*, April 1927.

Afghannevis, Abdullah Khan. "Fozala-ye faramush shodeh," *Kabul*, 1st year, Nos. 8, 9, and 11. 3 parts.

Afschar, Mahmoud. La politique européenne en Perse. Berlin, 1921.

Aga Khan (Sultan Muhammed Shah). Memoirs. London, 1954.

Agabekov, George. O. G. P. U.: The Russian Secret Terror. New York, 1931.

Agha Abbas of Shiraz. "Journal of a Tour Through Parts of the Panjab and Afghanistan in the Year 1837," *JASB*, January 1843.

Aghanian, Rev. Gut. Divan Hayotz Patmoutian. Tiflis, 1904. Vols. III, VIII. In Armenian.

Ahmad, Aziz. Islamic Modernism in India and Pakistan, 1857–1964. Oxford, 1967.

——. "Le mouvement des Mujahidin dans l'Inde au XIXᵉ siècle," *Orient*, No. 15 (1960).

——. "Les musulmans et le nationalisme indien," *Orient*, No. 22 (1962).

——. "Sayyid Ahmad Khān, Jamāl al-dīn al-Afghānī and Muslim India," *Studia Islamica*, XIII (1960).

——. Studies in Islamic Culture in the Indian Environment. Oxford, 1964.

Ahmad, Fazl, ed. Rahnema-ye Afghanestan. Kabul, 1949.

Ahmad, Feroz. "Great Britain's Relations with the Young Turks: 1908–1914," *MES*, July 1966.

Ahmad, Jamal-ad-Din, and Muhammed Abd-al-Aziz. Afghanistan—A Brief Survey. London, 1936.

Ahmad, Rafiuddin. "The Future of the Anglo-Afghan Alliance," *The Nineteenth Century*, February 1898.

Ahmed, S. M. Islam in India and the Middle East. Allahabad, 1949.

Ahrari, Abdul Karim Khan. "Masael-e tarikhi," *MH*, 2d year, No. 1.

Akademiia Nauk SSR. See Dvoriankov.

Akhramovich, R. T. "Afganistan," in Vol. IV, Ocherki istorii istoricheskoi nauki v SSSR. Moscow, 1966.

——. "K kharakteristike vneshnei politiki Afganistana v nachal'nyi period vtoroi mirovoi voyny (1939–1941 gg.)," *KSIV*, XXXVII (1960).

——, ed. Nezavisimyi Afganistan, 40 let nezravisimosti. Moscow, 1958.

——. Outline History of Afghanistan After the Second World War. Moscow, 1966.

——. "Velikaia Oktiabrskaia revoliutsiia i utverzhdenie natsionalnoi nezavisimosti Afganistana," in Velikii Oktiabr i narody Vostoka 1917–1957. Moscow, 1957.

Akram, Mohammed. "L'agriculture en Afghanistan," *Afghanistan*, October-December 1948 and January-March 1949. 2 parts.

——. Bibliographie analytique de l'Afghanistan. Paris, 1947.

Aitchison. See India.

al-Afghānī, Jamāl ad-Dīn. "La nationalité (*djinsiya*) et la religion musulmane" (translated into French by Marcel Colombe), *Orient*, No. 22 (1962).

——. Réfutation des matérialistes. Translated into French by A. M. Goichon. Paris, 1942.

——. Tatimmat al-bayan fi tarikh al-Afghan. Edited by Ali Yusuf al-Kurdili. Cairo, 1901.

——. "Unité et souveraineté ou concorde et victoire: pages choisies de Djamal al-din al-Afghani" (translated into French by Marcel Colombe), *Orient*, No. 24 (1962).

al-Afghānī, Jamāl al-Dīn, and Muhammad 'Abduh, eds. Al-'Urwah al-wuthqā. Beirut, 1910. 2 vols.

Alami, 'Abd al-Karim. Tarikh-i-Ahmad. Lucknow, 1850.

al-Balādhuri, Abu'l Hasan Ahmad Ibn Yahyā. Futuh al-buldan. Cairo, 1932.

Albertini, Luigi. The Origins of the War of 1914. Oxford, 1952. 2 vols.

al-Bīrūnī, Abū Rayhān. Tarikh al-Hind. Translated into English by E. C. Sachau. London, 1910. 2 vols.

Albuquerque, Alfonso d'. The Commentaries of the Great Alfonso d'Alboquerque. Translated into English from the Portuguese edition of 1774, published in Lisbon by Walter de Gray Birch. Hakluyt Society, London, 1875–77. 4 vols.

Alder, G. J. British India's Northern Frontier, 1865–95. A Study in Imperial Policy. London, 1963.

al-Ghazālī, Abu Hamid. Ihyā' 'ulūm al-din. Cairo, 1927. 2 vols.

al-Harāwī, Khwājah Ni'mat Allah ibn Habib Allah (Nematullah). Tarikh-i Khān Jahānī u Makhzān-i Afghānī. (?1612). For a recent English rendition on the basis of "its earliest and six other MSS," see the translation of S. M. Imamal-Din (Decca, 1960). For the standard English translation of this work, see Dorn, below.

Ali, Maulana Mohammed. My Life: A Fragment. Edited by Afzal Iqbal. Lahore, 1942.

Ali, Mohammed. Afghanistan (The Mohammedzai Period). Kabul, 1959.

——. Afghanistan: The War of Independence, 1919. Kabul, 1960.

——. A Cultural History of Afghanistan. Lahore, 1964.

——. "Karakul as the Most Important Article of Afghan Trade," *Afghanistan*, October-December 1949.

——. Manners and Customs of the Afghans. Lahore, 1958.

——. National Awakening. Lahore, 1958.

——. A New Guide to Afghanistan. 3d ed. Kabul, 1959.

————. Progressive Afghanistan. Lahore, 1933.

————. "Sayid Jamal ud-Din Afghani," *Afghanistan*, January-March 1962.

Ali Mohammed Khan. See Muhammed Khan, Ali.

Ali, Sayyid Ameer. "England and Russia in Afghanistan," *The Nineteenth Century*, May 1905.

————. The Spirit of Islam. London, 1922.

Alizo, Mohammed Ghaus. "The Agricultural Economy of Afghanistan and the Problems Confronting the Development of a Commercialized Agriculture," M.A. Thesis, University of Texas, 1954.

Allen, Isaac N. Diary of a March Through Sinde and Afghanistan, with the Troops Under Command of General Sir William Nott. London, 1843.

Allen, James G. "British Policy Towards Persia in 1879," *JRCAS*, October 1935.

————. "Strategic Principles of Lord Lytton's Afghan Policy," *JRCAS*, July 1937.

al-Makhzūmī, Muhammad. Khātirāt Jamāl al-Dīn al-Afghānī. Beirut, 1931.

Almond, Gabriel A., and James S. Coleman, eds. The Politics of the Developing Areas. Princeton, N.J., 1960.

Altheim, Franz. Alexandre et l'Asie: histoire d'un legs spirituel. Paris, 1954.

al-Utbī, Abū Nasr M. b. 'Abd al-Jabbar. Tarikh al-Yamini. Translated into English by J. Reynolds. London, 1858. See also Tarikh-i-Yamini, in Elliot and Dawson, eds., *The History of India*, 2d ed., listed below.

"Amanoullah dit pourquoi il abandonna son trône," *Journal des Débats*, June 28, 1929.

"Amanullah in Exile," *The Modern Review*, February 1935.

Amanullah Khan, Amir. Discours prononcé par S.M.R. l'Emir. Paris, 1920–21.

"Amanullah's Reforms," *The Modern Review*, November 1928.

Amin, Muhammed. "Hayat-e Sayyid Jamal ad-Din-e Afghan," *Iqtisad*, 9th year, No. 211.

Anderson, M. S. The Eastern Question. New York, 1966.

André, P. J. L'Islam et les races. Paris, 1922. 2 vols.

Andrew, Sir W. P. Our Scientific Frontier. London, 1880.

"The Anglo-Russian Agreement," *Fortnightly Review*, October 1907.

"The Anglo-Russian Convention," *Spectator*, September 28, 1907.

Anjoman-e Adabi. "Raport-e salane: 1317," *Kaboul Almanach: 1938–39*.

Anjoman-e Aryana. Afghanestan. Kabul, 1955.

Antermony, John Bell. "Travels from St. Petersburg in Russia to Various Parts of Asia in 1716, 1719, 1722, etc.," in Vol. VII, Pinkerton, listed below.

Anwar Khan. See Khan, Mohammad Anwar.

Arberry, A. J. British Contributions to Persian Studies. London, 1942.

————. British Orientalists. London, 1943.

————, ed. The Legacy of Persia. Oxford, 1953.

————. Oriental Essays. Portraits of Seven Scholars. London, 1960.

Arberry, A. J., and R. and M. Landau, eds. Islam Today. London, 1943.

Argyll, George D. C. The Afghan Question from 1841 to 1878. London, 1879.

Arin, M. F. "Essai sur le démembrement de la proprieté foncière en droit musulman," *RMM*, No. 26 (1914).

Arnold, Thomas W. The Caliphate. London, 1924.

————. "Khalifa," in A. Wensinck and J. H. Kramers, eds., Handworterbuch des Islam. Leiden, 1941.

————. The Preaching of Islam. London, 1896.

Arnold, Thomas W., and A. Guillaume, eds. The Legacy of Islam. Oxford, 1936.

Arthur, Sir George. Life of Lord Kitchener. London, 1920. 3 vols.

Arthur, William. Afghanistan in Relation to Past Conquests of India. London, 1879.

Arunova, M. R. "Geratskoe vosstanie 1716–1732 gg.," in Akhramovich, Nezavisimyi Afganistan, 40 let nezavisimosti. Moscow, 1958.

Asadabadi, Mirza Lutfallah. Sharh-e hal va asar-e Sayyid Jamal ad-Din Asadabadi, ma'ruf be "Afghani." Tabriz, 1947. For an Arabic translation of this work, see Mīrzā Lutfallāh Khān.

Ashe, W. Personal Records of the Kandahar Campaign. London, 1881.

Ashley, A. Evelyn. Life of Lord Palmerston. London, 1876. 2 vols.

Ashraf, Khalid. Tribal People of West Pakistan: A Demographic Study of a Selected Population. Peshawar, 1962.

The Asiatic Annual Register, or a View of the History of Hindustan and of the Politics, Commerce and Literature of Asia for the Year 1799. London, 1801.

"Asiatic Intelligence: Afghanistan," The Asiatic and Colonial Quarterly Journal (London), I (1846–47).

Aslanov, M. G. "Narodnoe dvizhenie roshani i ego otrazhenie v afganskoi literature XVI–XVII, vv.," SV, 1955, No. 5.

————. "Roushanity," in Vol. XXXVII, BSE, 2d ed.

Astarabadi, Muhammed Mahdi bin Muhammed Nasir. Tarikh-i Jahan Kushā-ī Nādiri. Bombay, 1876.

Atkinson, James. The Expedition into Afghanistan—Notes and Sketches Descriptive of the Country. London, 1842.

Aubin, Eugène. La Perse d'aujourd'hui. Paris, 1908.

Aubin, Jean. "Le mécénat Timourid à Chiraz," Studia Islamica, VIII (1957).

Auboyer, Jeannine. "French Excavations in Indo-China and Afghanistan (1935–37)," Harvard Journal of Asiatic Studies, III (1938).

Avery, Peter. Modern Iran. London, 1965.

Ayeen, Ghulam Ali. "Teacher Training in Afghanistan," Asia Foundation. Program Bulletin, December 1959.

Ayscoyhe, Floyer E. Unexplored Baluchistan. London, 1882.

Ayvazian, Abraham. Shar Hay Kensagroutianz. Constantinople, 1893. 3 vols. In Armenian.

Azmi, Ghulam Jailani Khan. "Adabiyat dar Afghanestan," Kabul, 1st year, No. 1.

————. "Akhlagh," Kabul, 1st year, No. 7.

————. "Az moshahir-e rajal-e vatan; Jamal ad-Din al-Afghani," Kabul, 1st year, No. 2.

————. "Din-e fetriat," Kabul, 1st year, No. 11.

————. "Elm va tarbiyat," Kabul, 1st year, No. 9.

————. "Ma va madaniyat," Kabul, 1st year, No. 12.

————. "Maaref va maaref-parvari," Kabul, 1st year, No. 12.

————. "Pand-e pedar," *Kabul*, 1st year, No. 5.

————. "Rmuz-e taraghi," *Kabul*, 1st year, No. 4.

Babakhodzhaev, A. Kh. Afghanistan's War for Independence in 1919. Moscow, 1960.

————. Proval angliiskoi politiki v Srednei Azii na Srednem Vostoke (1918–1924). Moscow, 1962.

————. "Voina Afganistana za nezavisimost v 1919g.," in Vol. I, *TDPMKV*. Moscow, 1961.

Babakhodzhaev, M. A. "Angliiskaia agressivnaia politika v Afganistane i borba afganskogo naroda za nezavisimost v 70-e gody XIX veka," in Akhramovich, *Nezavisimyi Afganistan*, listed above.

————. Borba Afganistana za nezavisimost (1838–1842). Moscow, 1960.

————. "Missia Nidermaiera-Gentiga v Afganistane (1915–1916)," *KSIV*, XXXVII (1960).

————. Russko-Afganskie torgovo-ekonomicheskie otnosheniia. Tashkent, 1965.

Bābur, Zahiru'd din Muhammad Babur Padshah. The Babur Nama in English (Memoirs of Babur). Translated by Annette S. Beveridge. London, 1921. 2 vols.

Bacon, Elizabeth E. Central Asians Under Russian Rule: A Study in Culture Change. Ithaca, N.Y., 1966.

————. "An Inquiry into the History of the Hazara Mongols of Afghanistan," *Southwestern Journal of Anthropology*, VII (1951), 3.

Bacon, Elizabeth E., and Alfred E. Hudson. "Afghanistan Waits," *Asia*, January 1941.

Badakhshi, Shah Abdullah. "Les langues du Pamir," *Afghanistan*, July-September 1953.

Badger, George O., ed. The Travels of Ludovico di Varthema in Egypt, Syria, Arabia Deserta, and Arabia Felix, in Persia, India, and Ethiopia, A.D. 1503–1508. Translated by John W. Jones. Hakluyt Society Series, London, 1863. Vol. XXXII.

Ba'hadour Khan, Abou'l Ghazi. Histoire des Mongols et des Tartares. Translated into French by Baron J. J. P. Desmaisons. St. Petersburg, 1871.

Bahadur, Lal. The Muslim League: Its History, Activities, and Achievements. Agra, 1954.

Bahré, Abdulwahed. "Ahamiyat-e vazife-shenasi dar jam'aa," *MH*, 2d year, No. 1.

————. "Bemenasebat-e jashn-e esteghlal," *MH*, 2d year, No. 5.

Bailey, F. M. Mission to Tashkent. London, 1946.

Baker, J. N. L. A History of Geographical Discovery and Exploration. London, 1948.

Balfour, Lady Betty. The History of Lord Lytton's Indian Administration of 1876–1880. London, 1899.

Balfour, Patrick. "Through Afghanistan by Car," *Field*, August 1935.

Baljon, J. M. S. Modern Muslim Koran Interpretation: 1880–1960. Leiden, 1961.

————. The Reforms and Religious Ideas of Sir Sayyid Ahmad Khān. Leiden, 1949.

Ball, W. MacMahon. Nationalism and Communism in East Asia. Melbourne, 1952.

Balsan, François. Inquisitions de Kaboul au Golfe Persique. Paris, 1949.

Banani, Amin. Modernization of Iran. Stanford, Calif., 1961.

Banerjee, Anil Chandra. "British Policy Towards the Afghan War of Succession 1863–1868," *Indian Historical Quarterly*, No. 20 (1944).

——. "Neutralization of Afghanistan: 1869," *Proceedings of the Seventh Indian Historical Congress* (1944).

Barbosa, Duarte. The Book of Duarte Barbosa, 1518 A.D. Translated by M. Longworth-Dames. London, 1918–21. 2 vols.

Barckhausen, Joachim. L'Empire jaune de Genghis Khan. Paris, 1942.

Barclay, T. The Turko-Italian War and Its Problems. With appendixes containing chief state papers bearing on the subject and an additional chapter on Muslim feeling by A. Ali. London, 1912.

Barger, Evert. "Exploration of Ancient Cities in Northern Afghanistan," *The Geographical Journal*, May 1939.

——. "Some Problems of Central Asian Exploration into Northern Afghanistan and Explorations of the Ancient Sites in Bactria, with Discussion," *The Geographical Journal*, January 1944.

Barger, Evert, and Philip Wright. "Excavations in Swat and Explorations in the Oxus Territories of Afghanistan: A Detailed Report of the 1938 Expedition," *Memoirs of the Archaeological Survey of India* (Delhi), No. 64 (1941).

Baron, Salo W. A Social and Religious History of the Jews. 2d ed. New York, 1957. Vol. III.

Barr, William. Journal of a March from Delhi to . . . Cabul with the Mission of Sir C. M. Wade. Calcutta, 1844.

Barth, F. Political Leadership Among Swat Pathans. (London School of Economics: Monographs on Social Anthropology, No. 19.) London, 1959.

Barthold, V. V. La découverte de l'Asie. Translated into French by B. Nikitine. Paris, 1947.

——. Four Studies on the History of Central Asia. Edited and translated by V. and I. Minorsky. Leiden, 1958. 2 vols.

——. Histoire des Turcs d'Asie Centrale. Translated into French by M. Donskis. Paris, 1945.

—— (Bartold, V. V.). Istoriia izucheniia Vostoka v Evrope i Rossii. 2d ed. Leningrad, 1925.

——. Istoriia kulturnoi zhizni Turkestana. Leningrad, 1927.

——. O khristianstve v Turkestane v do-mongolskii period. St. Petersburg, 1894.

——. Turkestan Down to the Mongol Invasion. Translated by H. A. R. Gibb. 2d ed. London, 1928.

Barthold, V. V., and R. N. Frye. "Bukhara," in Vol. I, *EI*, 2d ed.

Barthoux, Jules. "Les fouilles de Hadda (Afghanistan)," *Gazette de beaux-arts* (Paris), I (1929).

——. "Les fouilles de Hadda," in Vol. I, Mémoires de la délégation archéologique française en Afghanistan. Paris, 1933.

Barton, Sir William. India's North-West Frontier. London, 1939.

———. "India's North-West Frontier and the War," *United Empire*, November 1939.

———. "The Problems of Law and Order in the North-West Frontier Province," *JRCAS*, January 1932.

"The Basmachis—The Central Asian Resistance Movement: 1918–1924," *CAR*, VII (1959).

Baster, A. S. J. The Introduction of Western Economic Institutions into the Middle East. Oxford, 1960.

Baudet, Roger. "Aérophilatélie," *Afghanistan*, January-March 1954.

———. "Les émissions commémoratives afghanes," *Afghanistan*, October-December 1953.

———. "La philatélie en Afghanistan," *Afghanistan*, July-September 1950.

Bayani, K. Les relations de l'Iran avec l'Europe Occidentale à l'époque Safavide. Paris, 1937.

Bayur, Y. Hikmet. "Maysor Sultani Tipu ile Osmanli Pâdisahlarindan I Abdul Hamid ve III Selim arasindaki Mektuplasma," *Belletin*, XLVII (1948).

Beaurecueil, S. de Laugier de. "Manuscrits d'Afghanistan," in Vol. III, *Mélanges de l'Institut Dominicain d'Etudes Orientales*. Cairo, 1956.

Beazley, Charles B. Dawn of Modern Geography. Oxford, 1897–1906. 3 vols.

Beck, S. "Das afganische Strafgesetzbuch vom Jahre 1924 mit dem Zusatz vom Jahre 1925," *Die Welt Des Islams*, II (1928).

Becker, Seymour. "Russia's Central Asian Protectorates: Bukhara and Khiva, 1865–1917," Ph.D. Dissertation, Harvard University, 1963.

Behruz, Muhammed Hussein. "Adabiyat az Abulfaraj be bad," in Anjoman-e Aryana, *Afghanestan*, listed above.

Belenitskii, A. M. "Les Mongols et l'Asie Centrale," *JWH*, V (1960), 3.

———. "K voprosu o sotsialnykh otnosheniiakh Irana v Khulaguidskuiu epokhu," *SV*, 1948, No. 5.

Beliaev, V. M. Afganskaia narodnaia muzyka. Moscow, 1960.

Bell, H. C. F. Lord Palmerston. London, 1936. 2 vols.

Bellew, H. W. Afghanistan and the Afghans. London, 1879.

———. A Dictionary of the Pukkhto or Pukshto Language in Which the Words Are Traced to Their Sources in the Indian and Persian Languages. Lahore, 1901.

———. From the Indus to the Tigris. A Narrative of a Journey Through Balochistan, Afghanistan, Khorassan and Iran in 1872. London, 1873.

———. A General Report on the Yusufzais. Calcutta, 1864.

———. A Grammar of the Pukkhto or Pukshto Language. London, 1867.

———. An Inquiry into the Ethnography of Afghanistan. (Prepared for and presented to the Ninth International Congress of Orientalists.) London, 1891.

———. "Introductory Remarks to an Inquiry into the Ethnography of Afghanistan," *The Imperial and Asiatic Quarterly Review*, January 1891.

———. Journal of a Political Mission to Afghanistan in 1857 with an Account of the Country and People. London, 1862.

———. A New Afghan Question, or, Are the Afghans Israelites, and Who Are the Afghans? Simla, 1881.

———. "Our Relations with Afghanistan Past and Present," *The Imperial and Asiatic Quarterly Review*, January 1891.

514   *Bibliography*

————. The Races of Afghanistan. Calcutta and London, 1880.

Beloff, Max. The Foreign Policy of the Soviet Union: 1921–1941. 3d ed. Oxford, 1952. 2 vols. Vol. I.

Benawa, Abdul Rauf. Hotakiha. Kabul, 1951.

————. Khushhal Khattak tseh wayi. Kabul, 1950.

————. "Les leaders actuels du Pashtoonistan," *Afghanistan*, July-September 1952.

————. Mir Waïs nikeh. Kabul, 1946.

————. "Pashtoonistan," *Afghanistan*, January-March 1950.

Benjamin, J. J., II. Eight Years in Asia and Africa from 1846 to 1855. Hanover, 1859.

Bennigsen, Alexandre. "The Muslim Peoples of Soviet Russia and the Soviets," *The Islamic Review*, April-July 1955.

————. La presse et le mouvement national chez les musulmans de Russie avant 1920. The Hague, 1964.

Bennigsen, Alexandre, and Chantal Quelquejay. Islam in the Soviet Union. London, 1967.

————. Les mouvements nationaux chez les musulmans de Russie. Paris, 1960.

————. "Le problème linguistique et l'évolution des nationalités musulmanes en U.R.S.S.," *Cahiers du Monde Russe et Soviétique*, April-June 1960.

Benoit, F. "Modernisation in Afghanistan under King Amanullah," *Visva-Bharati Quarterly*, VII (1929–30).

Berke, Zuhdi. "Public Health and Hygiene in Afghanistan," *Afghanistan*, July-September 1946.

Berkes, Niyazi. The Development of Secularism in Turkey. Montreal, 1964.

Berliner, Joseph S. Soviet Economic Aid: The New Aid and Trade Policy in Underdeveloped Countries. New York, 1958.

Bernier, F. Travels in the Mogul Empire A.D. 1656–1668. Edited by A. Constable. Westminster, 1891. 2d ed. Edited by V. A. Smith. Oxford, 1914.

————. "Voyage to the East Indies Containing the History of the Late Revolution of the Empire of the Great Moghul," in Vol. VIII, Pinkerton, listed below.

Bertels, E. E. "Afganskaia pressa," in Bibliografiia Vostoka. Leningrad, 1934.

Besant, Annie. England, India and Afghanistan and the Story of Afghanistan. Madras, 1931.

Besson, Maurice. "L'éveil du monde afghan,"*Action Nationale* (Paris), n.s. XXIII (1924).

Bestuzhev, I. V. Borba v Rossii po voprosam vneshnei politiki 1906–1910. Moscow, 1961.

Biddulph, C. E. "Afghan Poetry of the Seventeenth Century," *The Asiatic Quarterly Review*, January 1890.

————. Afghan Poetry of the Seventeenth Century. London, 1890.

————. Tribes of the Hindu Kush. Calcutta, 1880.

Biggerstaff, Knight. "Modernization—and Early Modern China," *The Journal of Asian Studies*, August 1966.

Bina, Ali Akbar. La question iranienne au début du XIX siècle. Paris, 1939.

Binder, Leonard. The Ideological Revolution in the Middle East. New York, 1964.

——. "Pakistan and Modern Islamic Nationalist Theory," *MEJ*, Fall 1957, Winter 1958. 2 parts.

——. Religion and Politics in Pakistan. Berkeley, Calif., 1961.

Birdwood, Sir George, and William Foster, eds. The First Letter Book of the East India Company, 1600–1619. London, 1893.

Black, Cyril E. The Dynamics of Modernization: A Study in Comparative History. New York, 1967. Paperback.

——, ed. Rewriting Russian History; Soviet Interpretations of Russia's Past. New York, 1956.

——, ed. The Transformation of Russian Society. Cambridge, Mass., 1960.

Black, J. B., ed. The Oxford History of England. Oxford, 1959. Vol. VIII.

Bloch-Favier, Y. "Les centrales hydroéléctriques alimentant Kaboul," *Afghanistan*, January-March 1948.

Bochkarev, P. S. Afganistan. Moscow, 1953.

Boeke, I. H. "The Recoil of Westernization in the East," *Pacific Affairs*, September 1936.

Boersner, Demetrius. The Bolsheviks and the National and Colonial Question (1917–1928). Geneva, 1957.

Bogdanov, L. "The Afghan Weights and Measures," *JASB*, n.s. XXIV (1928).

——. "The Metric System in Afghanistan," *Visva-Bharati Quarterly*, July 1928.

——. "Notes on the Afghan Periodical Press," *Islamic Culture*, January 1929.

Boinet, R. "Une révolution raconté par un témoin," *Les Annales Politiques et Littéraires*, No. 93 (1929).

Bolsover, G. H. "David Urquhart and the Eastern Question, 1833–37: A Study in Publicity and Diplomacy," *The Journal of Modern History*, VIII (December 1936).

Bolton, H. N. Summary of the Tribal Customs of the Dera Ismail Khan District. Peshawar, 1907.

Bonné, Alfred. State and Economics in the Middle East: A Society in Transition. London, 1948.

——. Studies in Economic Development. London, 1957.

Bonvalot, Gabriel. En Asie Centrale, de Moscou en Bactriane. Paris, 1884.

Bornford, Henry. The English Factories in India, 1637–1641. Oxford, 1912.

Bosworth, C. E. "The Development of Persian Culture Under the Early Ghaznawids," *Iran: Journal of the British Institute of Persian Studies*, VI (1968).

——. "Early Sources for the History of the First Four Ghaznawid Sultans: 977-1041," *The Islamic Quarterly*, VII, 1–2 (January, June 1963). 2 parts.

——. "Ghazna," in Vol. II, *EI*, 2d ed.

——. The Ghaznawids: Their Empire in Afghanistan and Eastern Iran, 994–1040. Edinburgh, 1963.

Bottomore, T. B. Elites and Society. London, 1964.

Boukhary, Mir Abdoul Kerim. Histoire de l'Asie Centrale. Translated into French by C. Schéfer. Paris, 1876.

Boulger, Demetrius C. "Cabul and Herat," *Contemporary Review*, January 1900.

————. Central Asian Questions. Essays on Afghanistan, China and Central Asia. London, 1885.

————. England and Russia in Central Asia. London, 1879. 2 vols.

————. The Life of Yakoob Beg, Ameer of Kashgar. London, 1878.

————. "Our Relations with Afghanistan," *Contemporary Review*, July 1919.

Boulnois, C., and W. H. Rattigan. Notes on Customary Law as Administered in the Courts of the Punjab. London, 1878.

Bouvat, Lucien. "Essai sur la civilisation timouride," *Journal Asiatique*, CCVIII (1926).

————. "Notes sur la politique extérieure de l'Afghanistan depuis 1919," *RMM*, December 1921.

Bovykin, V. I. Ocherki istorii vneshnei politiki Rossii, konets XIX veka-1917 god; posobie dlia uchitelia. Moscow, 1960.

Bowrey, Thomas. A Geographical Account of the Countries Around the Bay of Bengal. Cambridge, Eng., 1903.

Bowring, Lewin B. Haidar Ali and Tipu Sultan. Oxford, 1899.

Braibanti, Ralph, and Joseph J. Spengler, eds. Tradition, Values and Socio-Economic Development. Durham, N.C., 1961.

Brauer, E. "The Jews of Afghanistan," *Jewish Social Studies*, IV (1942).

Breeze, Lawrence E. "British Opinion of Russian Foreign Policy. 1841–1871," Ph.D. Dissertation, University of Missouri, 1960.

"Britain's Hand in Afghanistan," *Literary Digest*, March 30, 1929.

Broadfoot, James A. "Report on Parts of the Ghilzai Country and on Some of the Tribes in the Neighbourhood of Ghazni," *Royal Geographical Society*, 1886. Supplementary Papers No. 1.

Brock, H. Le M. "Air Operations on the N. W. Frontier," *JRCAS*, January 1932.

Brockelmann, C. History of Islamic Peoples. Translated by Joel Carmichael and Moshe Perlmann. New York, 1960. Paperback.

Brockway, Thomas. "Britain and the Persian Bubble, 1888–1892," *The Journal of Modern History*, XIII (March 1941).

Brosset, Marie-Félicité. Histoire de la Géorgie. St. Petersburg, 1856–57. Vol. II.

Browder, Robert P., and Alexander F. Kerensky, eds. *The Russian Provisional Government*. Stanford, Calif., 1961. 3 vols.

Brown, D. Mackenzie. Indian Political Thought: From Ranade to Bhave. Berkeley, Calif., 1961.

Browne, Edward G. A Literary History of Persia. 2d ed. Cambridge, Eng., 1956–59. 4 vols.

————. Le mouvement constitutionel persan. Paris, 1919.

————. The Persian Revolution of 1905–1909. Cambridge, Eng., 1910.

————. "The Present Situation in Persia," *Contemporary Review*, November 1912.

————. The Press and Poetry of Modern Persia. Cambridge, Eng., 1914.

Bruce, R. I. The Forward Policy and Its Results or Thirty-Five Years Work Amongst the Tribes of Our N. W. Frontier. London, 1900.

Brunn, P., ed. The Bondage and Travels of Johann Schiltberger, a Native of

Bavaria, in Europe, Asia, and Africa, 1396–1427. Translated by J. Buchan Telfer. London, 1871.

Brunschvig, R. "Perspectives," *Studia Islamica*, I (1953).

Brunschvig, R., and G. E. von Grunebaum, eds. Classicisme et déclin culturel dans l'histoire de l'Islam. Paris, 1957.

Brusasca, Giuseppe. Il Ministero degli affari esteri al servizio del popolo Italiano (1943–1949). 2d ed. Rome, 1949.

Brydges, Sir Harford Jones. An Account of the Transactions of H.M.'s Mission to the Court of Persia in the Years 1807–1811. London, 1834. 2 vols.

Buchner, V. F. "Samanids," in Vol. IV, *EI*, 1st ed.

Buckle, G. E., ed. The Letters of Queen Victoria. 2d series (1862–85). New York, 1926–28. 3 vols. 3d series (1886–1901). New York, 1930–32. 3 vols.

Bukhsh, S. Khuda. Essays: Indian and Islamic. London, 1912.

Bullard, Sir Reader. Britain and the Middle East from the Earliest Times to 1950. London, 1951.

Bunyan, James, and Harold H. Fisher, eds. The Bolshevik Revolution: 1917–1918. Documents and Materials. 2d ed. Stanford, Calif., 1961.

Burkes, Ardath W. "Modernization" (Report: International Conference on the Problems of Modernization in Asia, June 28–July 7, 1965. Seoul, Korea), *The Journal of Asian Studies*, May 1968.

Burnaby, Fred. A Ride to Khiva. Travels and Adventures in Central Asia. 8th ed. London, 1877.

Burnes, Sir Alexander. Cabool: Being a Personal Narrative of a Journey to and Residence in That City in the Years 1836–7, and 8. London, 1842.

———. "Description of Bokhara," *JASB*, May 1833.

———. Travels into Bokhara, a Journey from India to Cabool, Tartary, and Persia in 1831–33. 2d ed. London, 1835. 3 vols.

Burnes, Alexander, R. Leech, P. Lord, and J. Wood. Reports and Papers. Calcutta, 1839.

Bury, G. Wyman. Pan-Islam. London, 1919.

Bushev, P. P. Gerat i anglo-iranskaia voina 1856–57 gg. Moscow, 1959.

Buxton, Noel. Travel and Politics in Armenia. London, 1914.

Byron, Robert. "From Herat to Kabul," *JRCAS*, April 1935.

———. The Road to Oxiana. London, 1937.

Cachin, Marcel. "Preparation for War Against the Soviet Union" (speech delivered at the 19th session of the XI Plenum of the ECCI on April 8, 1931), in War Preparations Against the Soviet Union. London, 1931.

Cahen, C. "The Body Politic," in G. E. von Grunebaum, *Unity and Variety*, listed below.

———. "L'évolution de l'*iqta* du IXe au XIIIe siècles," *Annales*, VIII (1953).

———. "Histoire de l'Orient Musulman médieval," *Studia Islamica*, III (1955).

Calverley, Edwin E. "The Fundamental Structure of Islam," *JRCAS*, April 1939.

Camp, Isaac N. "The Turkish Races and Missionary Endeavor," *The Moslem World*, April 1918.

Campbell, Sir George. The Afghan Frontier. London, 1879.

Caroe, Sir Olaf. "On Soviet Interpretations of Relations Between Britain, Russia, and Afghanistan 1872–80," *CAR*, VI (1958).
——. The Pathans, 550 B.C. to A.D. 1957. London, 1958.
——. Soviet Empire: The Turks of Central Asia and Stalinism. London, 1953.
Carrère d'Encausse, Hélène. "La politique culturelle du pouvoir tsariste au Turkestan (1867–1917)," *Cahiers du Monde Russe et Soviétique*, July-September 1962.
——. Réforme et révolution chez les Musulmans de l'empire Russe: Bukhara 1867–1927. Paris, 1966.
——. "Tsarist Educational Policy in Turkestan, 1867–1917," *CAR*, XI (1963).
Caspani, P. E. "The First American in Afghanistan," *Afghanistan*, July-September 1947.
Caspani, P. E., and E. Cagnacci. Afghanistan Crocevia Dell'Asia. Milan, 1951.
Castagné, Joseph. Les Basmatchis: le mouvement national des indigènes d'Asie Centrale depuis la révolution d'Octobre 1917 jusqu'en Octobre 1924. Paris, 1925.
——. "Le Bolshevism et l'Islam," *RMM*, October-December 1922.
——. "Le mouvement d'émancipation de la femme musulmane en Orient," *Revue des Etudes Islamiques*, 1929.
——. "Notes sur la politique extérieure de l'Afghanistan depuis 1919," *RMM*, December 1921.
——. "Russie slave et Russie turque," *RMM*, December 1923.
——. "Soviet Imperialism in Afghanistan," *Foreign Affairs*, July 1935.
——. "Le Turkestan depuis la révolution russe (1917–1921)," *RMM*, June 1922.
Çebesoy, Ali Fuat. Moskva Hatiralari. Istanbul, 1955.
Cecil, Lady Gwendolen. Life of Robert, Marquis of Salisbury. London, 1922–32. 4 vols.
Çemal Pasha. Hatiralar. Istanbul, 1959.
Cervin, V. "Problems in the Integration of the Afghan Nation," *MEJ*, Autumn 1952.
Cervinka, Vladimir. Afghanistan: structure économique et sociale, commerce extérieure. Lausanne, 1950.
Chahardehi, Murtaza Mudarrissi. Zendagani va falsafa-ye ejtemaii va siasi-ye Sayyid Jamal ad-Din al-Afghani. Tehran, 1955.
Chandhuri, N. C. "Military Background of the Third Afghan War: 1919," *The Modern Review*, October 1932.
Charles-Roux, F. L'Angleterre et l'expédition française en Egypte. Cairo, 1925. 2 vols.
——. Autour d'une route: l'Angleterre, l'isthme de Suez et l'Egypte au 18e siècle. Cairo, 1922.
——. Les échelles de Syrie et de Palestine au XVIII siècle. Paris, 1928.
——. Les origines de l'expédition d'Egypte. Paris, 1910.
——. "Un projet français de commerce avec l'Inde par Suez sous le règne de Louis XVI," *Revue de l'Histoire des Colonies Françaises*, 1925.
Chestakov, A. Précis d'histoire de l'U.R.S.S. Moscow, 1938. 3 vols.

Chirol, Sir Valentine. India. London, 1930.

———. "Indian Borderland: the Russian and German Pressures Before the War," *Asia*, April 1919.

———. The Middle Eastern Question, or Some Political Problems of Indian Defence. London, 1903.

———. The Occident and the Orient. Chicago, 1925.

Chokaiev, Mustapha. "The Bolsheviks and Afghanistan," *The Asiatic Review*, July 1929.

———. "The Situation in Afghanistan," *The Asiatic Review*, April 1930.

Chopra, Janki. "Dost Muhammed Khan in India," *IHRC*, XIX (1943).

Chorpa, P. N. "Rencontre de l'Inde et de l'Islam," *JWH*, VI (1960), 2.

Christensen, J. "The New Afghanistan," *The Muslim World*, October 1926.

Churchill, Rogers P. The Anglo-Russian Convention of 1907. Cedar Rapids, Iowa, 1939.

Clavijo, Ruy Gonzales di. Narrative of the Embassy to the Court of Tamerlane of Samarkand, A.D. 1403–1406. Translated by Guy Le Strange. London, 1928.

Clifford, Mary L. The Land and People of Afghanistan. New York, 1962.

Codrington, K. D. "Geographical Introduction to the History of Central Asia," *The Geographical Journal*, July-September 1944.

Collins, J. Walter. "Modern Turkey," *JRCAS*, April 1932.

"Colonel Lawrence and the Afghan Revolt," *China Weekly Review* (Shanghai), February 23, 1929.

Colvin, Sir Auckland. John Russell Colvin, the Last Lieut.-Governor of North-West Under the Company. Oxford, 1911.

Comyn-Platt, Sir Thomas. "Afghanistan and the Soviets," *The Nineteenth Century and After*, March 1929.

Connell, B. Regina versus Palmerston: 1837–65. London, 1962.

Conolly, Arthur. Journey to the North of India, Overland from England, Through Russia, Persia and Afghanistan. London, 1834. 2 vols.

Conolly, Edward. "Journal Kept While Travelling in Seistan," *JASB*, April 1841.

"Considerations on the Invasion of India and Defence of the N.W. Frontier," *The Asiatic Journal*, September-December 1837.

Cooke, Hedly V. Challenge and Response in the Middle East: The Quest for Prosperity 1919–1951. New York, 1952.

Cordier, Henri. Le Christianisme en Chine et en Asie sous les Mongols. Paris, 1918.

Cotard, C. Le chemin de fer Central Asiatique. Paris, 1875.

Cottam, Richard W. Nationalism in Iran. Pittsburgh, Pa., 1964.

Cotton, J. S. Mountstuart Elphinstone. Oxford, 1896.

Cowling, M. "Lytton, the Cabinet and the Russians, August to November, 1878," *The English Historical Review*, January 1961.

Cox, Sir Percy. "Wassamus," *JRCAS*, January 1932.

Cragg, Kenneth. "Religious Development in Islam in the 20th Century," *JWH*, III (1956), 2.

Crawley, C. S. "Anglo-Russian Relations: 1815–1840," *Cambridge Historical Journal*, III (1929), 1.

Cressey, George B. Crossroads: Land and Life in Southwest Asia. Chicago. 1960.

Crocker, H. E. "Afghanistan a Buffer State [between Russia and Pakistan]," *Contemporary Review*, June 1953.

Cumming, Sir John. Political India: 1832–1932. Oxford, 1932.

Cumming, Sir John, Sir Richard Dane, Sir Patrick Fagan, and Sir George MacMunn. "Some Features of the Afghan Problem," *The Asiatic Review*, July 1929.

Cunningham, Joseph D. A History of the Sikhs, from the Origin of the Nation to the Battles of the Sutlej. Edited by H. L. O. Garrett and R. R. Sethi. New Delhi, 1955.

Curzon, George N. Frontiers. (Romanes lecture delivered at Oxford, November 2, 1907.) Oxford, 1907.

———. Leaves from a Viceroy's Notebook and Other Papers. London, 1926.

———. Persia and the Persian Question. London, 1892. 2 vols.

———. A Recent Journey to Afghanistan. London, 1895.

———. Russia in Central Asia. London, 1889.

———. Speeches as Viceroy and Governor General of India. London, 1906.

———. Tales of Travel. New York, 1923.

Daalder, H. The Role of the Military in the Emerging Countries. Gravenhage, 1962.

Dalhousie, James A. B. Ramsay, First Marquess of. Private Letters of Marquess Dalhousie. Edited by J. G. A. Baird. Edinburgh, 1911.

Dallin, David J. The Big Three: the U.S., Britain, Russia. New Haven, Conn., 1945.

———. The Rise of Russia in Asia. 2d ed. London, 1950.

Daniel, Norman. Islam, Europe and Empire. Edinburgh, 1966.

Danvers, Frederick C., ed. Letters Received by the East India Company from Its Servants in the East. London, 1896. Vol. I.

———. The Portuguese in India. London, 1894. 2 vols.

Darmesteter, James. A la frontière afghane. Paris, 1888.

———. Chants populaires des Afghans. Paris, 1888–90.

Das, Taraknath. "Afghanistan in World Politics," *The Modern Review*, May 1928.

Dastgir Khan, Ghulam. "Hemayat az sanaya-ye melli," *Iqtisad*, 9th year, No. 205.

Dashxurançi, Movsēs. The History of the Caucasian Albanians. Translated by C. J. F. Dowsett. London, 1962.

Dauvillier, Jean. Le droit chaldéen. Paris, 1939.

David, W. D. European Diplomacy in the Near Eastern Question 1906–1909. Urbana, Ill., 1940.

Davidson, Flora M. "A Christian at Kabul," *The Moslem World*, January 1919.

Davies, C. Collin. "Afridi," in Vol. I, *EI*, 2d ed.

———. "The Amir and the Frontier Tribesmen of India," *Army Quarterly*, April 1926.

———. The Problem of the North-West Frontier. Cambridge, Eng., 1932.

Davis, H. W. C. "The Great Game in Asia, 1800–1844," in Proceedings of the British Academy. Oxford, 1926.

Davis, Helen M., ed. Constitutions, Electoral Laws, Treaties of States in the Near and Middle East. 2d ed. Durham, N.C., 1953.

Davison, Roderic H. "Where Is the Middle East?" in Richard H. Nolte, ed., The Modern Middle East. New York, 1963.

Davydov, A. D. "Imeniia medrese Subkhan-kuli-khana v Balkhe," *KSIV*, XXXVII (1960).

Dawson, William H. "The 'Forward' Policy in Central Asia 1874–1880," in Vol. II, Ward and Gooch, eds., listed below.

"Les débuts du voyage du Roi en Europe," *L'Asie Française*, January 1928.

DeColyar, H. A. Candahar: Our Right To Retain It. London, 1881.

Defrémery, M. C., ed. and trans. Histoire des Samanides par Mirkhond. Paris, 1845.

――――. "Histoire des Sultans Ghourides, extraits de l'histoire universelle de Mirkhond," *Journal Asiatique*, July-December 1843 and January-June 1844. 2 parts.

Degras, Jane, ed. Calendar of Soviet Documents on Foreign Policy. London, 1948.

――――, ed. The Communist International 1919–1943. Oxford, 1956. Vol. I.

――――, ed. Soviet Documents on Foreign Policy. Oxford, 1951–52. 2 vols.

Démorgny, G. La question persane et la guerre. Paris, 1916.

Dennie, William H. Personal Narrative of the Campaigns in Afghanistan. Dublin, 1843.

Dennis, Alfred L. P. The Foreign Policies of Soviet Russia. New York, 1924.

Desai, A. R. Social Background of Indian Nationalism. Oxford, 1948.

Desai, Māhādeva. Two Servants of God. Delhi, 1935.

Deutsch, Karl W. Nationalism and Social Communications. New York, 1953.

――――. "Social Mobilization and Political Development," *American Political Science Review*, September 1961.

Deyder, H. Contribution à l'étude de l'art du Gandhara. Paris, 1950.

Dianous, Hugues Jean de. "La contribution récente de l'orientalisme soviétique à l'étude de l'histoire et du développement économique de l'Afghanistan," *Cahiers du Monde Russe et Soviétique*, October-December 1961.

――――. "Hazaras et Mongols en Afghanistan," *Orient*, Nos. 19 and 20 (1961). 2 parts.

――――. "La littérature afghane de langue persane," *Orient*, No. 27 (1963).

――――. "Notes sur la presse afghane," *Orient*, No. 15 (1960).

Dickson, W. E. R. East Persia, a Backwater of the Great War. London, 1924.

Dinshoon, Pack. "The Revolutionary East and the Next Task of the Communist International," *The Communist International*, Nos. 11 and 12 (June and July 1920). 2 parts.

Disraeli, Benjamin. Selected Speeches of the Earl of Beaconsfield. Edited by T. E. Kelbel. London, 1882. 2 vols.

Diver, M. The Hero of Herat: Major Eldred Pottinger. London, 1924.

Dobson, George. Russia's Railway Advance into Central Asia. London, 1890.

Dodwell, H. H., ed. The Cambridge History of India. Cambridge, Eng., 1929. Vols. II, IV, V.

D'Ohsson, Baron A. C. M. Histoire des Mongols depuis Tchinguiz Khan jusqu'à Timour Bey ou Tamerlan. Paris, 1834–35. 4 vols.

Dokumenty vneshnei politiki SSSR. Moscow, 1958–60. Vols. II–V.

Dollot, R. L'Afghanistan: histoire, description, moeurs, et coutumes: folklore, fouilles. Paris, 1937.

Dorn, Bernard A. A Chrestomathy of the Pushtu or Afghan Language, to Which Is Subjoined a Glossary in Afghan and English. St. Petersburg, 1847.

———. History of the Afghans. A translation of al-Harāwī, *Tarikh-i Khān*, listed above. London, 1829. 2d ed. London, 1965.

Dovlatabadi, Yahya. Hayat-e Yahya. Tehran, 1949.

Drage, Geoffrey. Russian Affairs. London, 1904.

Driault, E. La politique orientale de Napoléon: Sébastiani et Gardane, 1806–1808. Paris, 1904.

———. La question d'Orient. 8th ed. Paris, 1921.

Druhe, David N. Soviet Russia and Indian Communism, 1917–1947. New York, 1959.

D. S. M. "Pan-Islamism," in Vol. XXXII, *EB*, 1922 ed.

Dua, R. P. The Impact of the Russo-Japanese (1905) War on Indian Politics. New Delhi, 1966.

Dubeux, M. L., and M. V. Valmont. L'univers, ou histoire et description de tous les peuples ... Tartarie, Belouchistan, ... Afghanistan. Paris, 1848.

Dubler, Cesar E. "Survivances de l'ancien Orient dans l'Islam," *Studia Islamica*, VII (1957).

Dubois, Marcel, and Auguste Terrier. Les colonies françaises. Paris, 1902.

Ducrocq, Georges. "Les Allemands en Perse," *RMM*, June 1923.

Dugdale, E. T. S., ed. German Diplomatic Documents, 1871–1914. London, 1930. 4 vols.

Dupree, Louis. "Afghanistan's Big Gamble: Historical Background of Afghan-Russian Relations," *American Universities Field Staff Reports*, South Asia Series, IV (1960), 3.

———. "Afghanistan's Slow March to Democracy," *American Universities Field Staff Reports*, South Asia Series, VII (1963), 1.

———. "The Afghans Honor a Muslim Saint," *American Universities Field Staff Reports*, South Asia Series, VII (1963), 2.

———. "Democracy and the Military Base of Power," *MEJ*, Winter 1968.

———. "The Durand Line of 1893: A Case Study in Artificial Political Boundaries and Culture Areas," in Princeton University Conference, *Current Problems*, listed below.

———. "An Informal Talk with King Mohammad Zahir of Afghanistan," *American Universities Field Staff Reports*, South Asia Series, VII (1963), 9.

———. "Mahmud Tarzi: Forgotten Nationalist," *American Universities Field Staff Reports*, South Asia Series, VIII (1964), 1.

———. "A Suggested Pakistan-Afghanistan-Iran Federation," *MEJ*, Autumn 1963.

Durand, Sir H. Mortimer. "The Amir Abdur Rahman Khan," *Proceedings of the Central Asian Society* (London), November 6, 1907.

Durand, Sir Henry Marion. The First Afghan War and Its Causes. London, 1879.

Durrani, Shahzadeh Ahmad Ali Khan. "Ahamiyat-e tarjoma," *Kabul*, 1st year, No. 4.

―――. "Moazaiia-ye Islam," *Kabul*, 1st year, No. 12.

―――. "Yadi az fozala-ye Ghazni," *Kabul*, 1st year, No. 5.

Durrani, Sultan Muhammad Ibn Musa Khan. Tarikh-e Sultani. Bombay, 1881.

Dutt, Romsesh. The Economic History of India in the Victorian Age. 7th ed. London, 1950.

Dvoriankov, N. A., ed. Sovremennyi Afganistan. Moscow, 1960.

East, Gordon W., and O. H. K. Spate, eds. The Changing Map of Asia. London, 1958.

East India Committee. See India.

Eastwick, E. B. Journal of a Diplomat's Three Years' Residence in Persia. London, 1864. 2 vols.

Eberhard, Wolfram. Afghanistan's Young Elite. Berkeley, Calif., 1962. Mimeographed. Also published in *Asian Survey*, February 1962.

Edwardes, Herbert B. Memorials of the Life and Letters of Major General Sir Herbert B. Edwardes. London, 1886. 2 vols.

―――. A Year on the Punjab Frontier, 1848–49. London, 1851.

Edwardes, Herbert B., and Herman Merivale. Life of Sir Henry Lawrence. London, 1872. 2 vols.

Edwards, H. Sutherland. Russian Projects Against India from the Czar Peter to General Skobeleff. London, 1885.

Efimov, G. V., ed. Novaia istoriia stran zarubezhnoi Azii i Afriki. Leningrad, 1959.

Efremov, P. N. Vneshniaia politika Rossii 1907–1914 gg. Moscow, 1961.

Egypt. Treaty of Amity Between Egypt and Afghanistan: Cairo, May 30, 1928. English and Arabic text. Cairo, 1928.

Eisenstadt, S. N. Essays on Sociological Aspects of Political and Economic Development. The Hague, 1961.

―――. Modernization: Protest and Change. Englewood, N.J., 1966.

El Hashimi, Sayed. "Afghanistan on the Tightrope," *Contemporary Review*, February 1958.

―――. "Afghanistan Revisited," *Contemporary Review*, July 1952.

Elliot, Sir Henry M. "Afghan Dynasties," in Elliot and Dawson, 2d ed., listed below.

Elliot, Sir Henry M., and J. Dawson, eds. The History of India as Told by Its Own Historians. London, 1866–67. 2d ed. Calcutta, 1953–55.

Ellis, C. H. The British "Intervention" in Transcaspia, 1918–1919. Berkeley, Calif., 1963.

―――. "Operations in Transcaspia 1918–1919 and the 26 Commissars Case," St. Anthony's Papers: Soviet Affairs No. 2. London, 1952.

Elphinstone, Mountstuart. An Account of the Kingdom of Caubul and Its Dependencies in Persia, Tartary and India. London, 1815.

Eltezam, Z. A. "Afghanistan's Foreign Trade," *MEJ*, Winter 1966.

Emanuel, W. V. "Some Impressions of Swat and Afghanistan," *JRCAS*, April 1939.

Emerson, Rupert. From Empire to Nation: The Rise of Self-Assertion of Asian and African Peoples. Cambridge, Mass., 1960.

Enriquez, C. M. The Pathan Borderland. Calcutta and Simla, 1910.

Entner, Marvin L. Russo-Persian Commercial Relations 1828–1914. (University of Florida Monographs: Social Sciences No. 28.) Gainesville, Fla., 1965.

Erskine, W. A History of India Under the Two First Sovereigns of the House of Taimur: Baber and Humayun. London, 1854. Vol. I.

Eshak Khan, Seyyed. "Sport dar Afghanestan," *Kaboul Almanach: 1934–35.*

Etherton, Percy T. In the Heart of Asia. Boston, 1926.

Eudin, Xenia J., and Robert C. North, eds. Soviet Russia and the East, 1920–1927. A Documentary Survey. Stanford, Calif., 1957.

Evans, DeLacy. The Designs of Russia. London, 1828.

———. On the Practicability of an Invasion of British India. London, 1829.

"Extracts of a Letter from Lieut. Alexander Burnes, Dated Balkh, 11th June, 1832," *JASB*, October 1832.

Eyre, Sir Vincent. The Kabul Insurrection of 1841–42. Edited by G. B. Malleson. London, 1879.

———. The Military Operations at Cabul which Ended in the Retreat and Destruction of the British Army, January, 1842. 4th ed. London, 1843.

———. A Retrospect of the Afghan War with Reference to Passing Events in Central Asia. London, 1869.

Fairbank, J. K. "China's Response to the West: Problems and Suggestions," *JWH*, III (1956), 2.

Farid, F. R. "The Modernisation of Afghanistan," *Afghanistan,* July-September 1962.

Faruqi, Ziya ul-Hasan. The Deoband School and the Demand for Pakistan. London, 1963.

Fatemi, Nasrollah S. Diplomatic History of Persia, 1917–1923: Anglo-Russian Power Politics in Iran. New York, 1952.

Fazli, Mehmed. Resimli Afghan Siahati. Istanbul, 1909.

Federbush, S., ed. World Jewry Today. Jerusalem, 1959.

Ferdinand, Klaus. Preliminary Notes on Hazāra Culture. Copenhagen, 1959.

Ferishta, Muhammad Abu'l Qāsim. See Jonathan Scott.

———. Tarikh-i Ferishta or History of the Rise of the Mahomedan Power in India. Translated and edited by J. Briggs. London, 1829–32. 4 vols.

Fernau, F. W. Moslems on the March: People and Politics in the World of Islam. Translated by E. W. Dikes. New York, 1954.

Feroz, M. "Bakhtar News Agency," *Afghanistan,* July-September 1948.

Ferrier, J. P. Caravan Journey and Wanderings in Persia, Afghanistan, Turkistan, and Beloochistan. Translated by William Jesse. London, 1857.

———. History of the Afghans. Translated by William Jesse. London, 1858.

Field, Claude H. A. With the Afghans. London, 1908.

Fischel, Walter J. "Israel in Iran (A Survey of Judeo-Persian Literature)," in Louis Finkelstein, ed., The Jews: Their History, Culture and Religion. 3d ed. New York, 1960.

———. "The Jews in Central Asia (Khorasan) in Medieval Hebrew and Islamic Literature," *Historia Judaica,* VII.

———. "The Leaders of the Jews of Bokhara," in Leo Jung, ed., Jewish Leaders (1750–1940). New York, 1953.

———. "Rediscovery of the Medieval Jewish Community at Firūzkūh in Central Afghanistan," *Journal of the American Oriental Society,* April 1965.

Fischer, Louis. The Life of Lenin. New York, 1964.

————. The Soviets in World Affairs. London, 1930. 2 vols.

Fleming, J. "Afghan Tragi-Comedy," *Asia*, June 1929.

————. "Kabul to Herat in a Junkers Plane," *Asia*, July 1929.

Fletcher, Arnold. "Afghanistan: Highway of Conquest," *Current History*, January 1950.

————. Afghanistan: Highway of Conquest. Ithaca, N.Y., 1965.

Florinsky, Michael T. World Revolution and the U.S.S.R. London, 1933.

Fofalzai, Aziz al-Din (Popalzai, Azizuddin). Dorrat-ul-Zaman: Tarikh-e Shah Zaman. Kabul, 1959.

————. Timur Shah Durrani. Kabul, 1953.

Forbes, Archibald. The Afghan Wars, 1839–42 and 1878–80. 4th ed. London, 1906.

Forbes, Rosita. Conflict: Angora to Afghanistan. New York, 1931.

————. Forbidden Road: Kabul to Samarkand. London, 1937.

————. Russian Road to India—by Kabul and Samarkand. London, 1940.

Forrest, George W. Life of Field Marshal Sir Neville Chamberlain. London, 1909.

————. The Life of Lord Roberts. London, 1914.

————, ed. Selections from the State Papers Preserved in the Bombay Secretariat. Bombay, 1885, 1887. 2 vols.

————, ed. Selections from the Travels and Journals Preserved in the Bombay Secretariat. Bombay, 1906.

Forster, George. "Extracts from Forster's Travels," in Vol. IX, Pinkerton, listed below.

————. A Journey from Bengal to England Through the Northern Parts of India, Kashmir, Afghanistan and Persia and into Russia by the Caspian Sea. London, 1798, 1808. 2 vols.

Fortescue, Sir John. A History of the British Army. London, 1927. Vol. XII.

Foster, William, ed. Early Travels in India, 1583–1619. London, 1921.

————, ed. The English Factories in India 1618–1669. Oxford, 1906–27. 16 vols. Supplementary volume covering 1600–1640. London, 1928.

————, ed. Letters Received by the East India Company (1613–1617). London, 1897–1902. Vols. II–VI.

Foucher, Alfred C. L'art gréco-bouddhique du Gandhara. Paris, 1905, 1918–22. 2 vols.

————. "Notes sur l'itinéraire de Hiuan-Tsang en Afghanistan," *Etudes Asiatiques*, 1925.

————. La vieille route de l'Inde de Bactres à Taxila. Paris, 1942–47. 2 vols.

Fouchet, Maurice. Notes sur l'Afghanistan. Paris, 1931.

Fougeyrollas, Pierre. Modernisation des hommes: l'exemple du Sénégal. Paris, 1967.

Fox, Ernst F. Travels in Afghanistan. New York, 1943.

Franck, Dorothea S., ed. The New International Yearbook: 1955. New York, 1955.

————. "Pakhtunistan—Disputed Disposition of a Tribal Land," *MEJ*, Winter 1952.

Franck, Dorothea S., and Peter G. "The Middle East Economy in 1948," *MEJ*, April 1949.

———. "The Middle East Economy in 1949," *MEJ*, April 1950.

Franck, Peter G. Afghanistan Between East and West. Washington, D.C., 1956.

———. "Economic Progress in an Encircled Land," *MEJ*, Winter 1956.

———. "Problems of Economic Development in Afghanistan," July and October 1949. 2 parts.

Francklin, William. "Observations Made on a Tour from Bengal to Persia in the Years 1786–1787," in Vol. IX, Pinkerton, listed below.

Fraser, David. Persia and Turkey in Revolt. Edinburgh, 1910.

———. "The Strategic Position of Russia in Central Asia," *Proceedings of the Central Asian Society* (London), June 12, 1907.

Fraser, James B. An Historical and Descriptive Account of Persia from the Earliest Ages to the Present Time Including a Description of Afghanistan and Beloochistan. Edinburgh, 1834.

———. Narrative of a Journey into Khorasan in the Year 1821 and 1822. London, 1825.

Fraser, Lovat. India Under Curzon and After. London, 1911.

Fraser-Tytler, Sir W. Kerr. "Afghanistan: A Brief Description," *JRCAS*, July-October 1942.

———. Afghanistan: A Study of Political Developments in Central and Southern Asia. Oxford, 1953.

———. "A Great North Road: Kabul-Andkuhi," *JRCAS*, April 1942.

Frechtling, Louis E. "Anglo-Russian Rivalry in Eastern Turkestan 1863–1881," *JRCAS*, July 1939.

French, J. G. "Changes Under Nadir Shah," *The Times* (London), November 11, 1933.

———. "A Tour Through Afghanistan," *JRCAS*, January 1933.

Frey, Frederick W. "Political Development, Power and Communications in Turkey," in Lucian W. Pye, ed., Communications and Political Development. Princeton, N.J., 1963.

———. The Turkish Political Elite. Cambridge, Mass., 1965.

Frye, Richard N. "Balkh," in Vol. I, *EI*, 2d ed.

———. "Harat," in Vol. III, *EI*, 2d ed.

———, ed. Islam and the West. The Hague, 1957.

———. "Oriental Studies in Afghanistan," *Journal of the American Oriental Society*, July 1944.

Fryer, John. A New Account of East India and Persia 1672–1681. Edited by William Crooke. London, 1909–15. 3 vols.

Furon, Raymond. L'Afghanistan, géographie, histoire, ethnographie, voyages. Paris, 1926.

———. L'Iran, Perse et Afghanistan. Paris, 1951.

"The Future of Afghanistan," *The Near East*, November 21, 1919.

Fyzee, Asaf A. A. "Muhammadan Law in India," *Comparative Studies in Society and History*, July 1963.

Gafferberg, E. G. "Narody Afganistana, Khazara, Dzemshidy, Kafiry," in Narody Perednei Azii. Moscow, 1957.

———. "Zhilish dzhemshidov kushkinskogo rayona," *Sovetskaia Etnografia*, 1948, No. 4.

Gafurov, B. G. Istoriia tadzhikskogo naroda. 2d ed. Moscow, 1951. 2 vols.

Gail, Marzieh. Persia and the Victorians. London, 1951.

Gankovskii, Yu. V. "Armiia i voennaia sistema shakhov Durrani (1747–1819)," in Indiia i Afganistan. Ocherki istorii i ekonomiki. Moscow, 1958.

———. Imperiia Durrani. Ocherki administrativnoi i voennoi sistemy. Moscow, 1958.

———. "Iz istorii osady Kandagara Nadir-shakhom Afsharom v 1737–1738 gg.," *KSIV*, XXXVII (1960).

———. "Missiia Bogdana Aslanova v Afganistan v 1764 g.," *SV*, 1958, No. 2.

———. "Nezavisimoe afganskoe gosudarstvo Akhmad-shakha Durrani i ego preemnikov (1747–1819)," in Akhramovich, *Nezavisimyi Afganistan*, listed above.

Gardane, Comte Alfred de. Mission du General Gardane en Perse sous le Premier Empire. Paris, 1865.

Garnett, David, ed. The Letters of T. E. Lawrence. London, 1938.

Gauthiot, R. "Notes sur le Yazgoulami, dialecte iranien des confins du Pamir," *Journal Asiatique*, 1916, No. 1.

Gehrke, Ulrich. Persien in der Deutschen Orientpolitik während des Ersten Weltkrieges. Stuttgart, 1960. 2 vols.

Georges-Gaulis, Berthe. Angora, Constantinople, Londres. Paris, 1922.

Gerard, James G. "Continuation of the Route of Lieut. A. Burnes and Dr. Gerard from Peshawar to Bokhara" (Dr. Gerard's letter to his brother Capt. A. Gerard), *JASB*, January and March 1833. 2 parts.

———. "Journey from Peshawar to Bokhara," *JASB*, March 1838.

———. "Memoir on the Topes and Antiquities of Afghanistan," *JASB*, July 1834.

Gerasimova, A., and G. Girs. Literatura Afganistana. Kratkii ocherk. Moscow, 1963.

Gerth, H. H., and C. Wright Mills, trans. "The Sociology of Charismatic Authority," in From Max Weber. Essays in Sociology. New York, 1958.

Ghani, Abdul. A Review of the Political Situation in Central Asia. Lahore, 1921.

Ghani Khan. The Pathans: A Sketch. Bombay, 1947.

Ghazi, Marshal Shah Vali Khan. Yaddashta-ye man. 5th ed. Kabul, 1959.

Ghirshman, R. "Bégram, recherches archéologiques et historiques sur les Kouchans," in Vol. XII, Memoires de la délégation archéologique française en Afghanistan. Cairo, 1946.

———. "Les Chionites-Héphtalites," in Vol. XIII, Memoires de la délégation archéologiques française en Afghanistan. Cairo, 1948.

———. Iran. London, 1954. Paperback.

Ghose, Dilip Kumar. England and Afghanistan: A Phase in Their Relations. Calcutta, 1960.

Ghosh, N. N. "The Afghan Civil War 1928–29," *The Modern Review*, February 1930.

Ghosh, Ramesh Chandra. Constitutional Documents of the Major Islamic States. Lahore, 1947.

Ghoshal, Upendranātha. Ancient Indian Culture in Afghanistan. Calcutta, 1928.

Ghubar, Mir Ghulam Muhammad. "Adabiyat dar Afghanestan," *Kabul*, 1st year, No. 1.

―――. "Afghanestan va negahi betarikhe an," *Kabul,* 1st year, No. 9.

―――. Ahmed Shah Baba. Kabul, 1943.

―――. Akhmad shakh—osnovatel Afganskogo gosudarstva. Translated into Russian by I. M. Reysner and E. M. Riks. Moscow, 1959.

―――. "The Role of Afghanistan in the Civilization of Islam," *Afghanistan,* January-March 1946.

Ghulam Haidar Khan, Mir. "Ayat-e Qurani, ke shavahedand bar fazayat-e elm," *MH,* 2d year, No. 7.

Giannini, Amedeo. "La constituzione afgana," *Oriento Moderno,* XI (1931).

―――. Le constituzioni degli stati de vicino Oriente. Rome, 1931.

Gibb, E. J. W. A History of Ottoman Poetry. London, 1900–1909. 6 vols.

Gibb, Hamilton A. R. "Constitutional Organization," in Khadduri and Liebesny, listed below.

―――. "An Interpretation of Islamic History," *JWH,* I (1953), 1.

―――. Islamic Society and the West. London, 1950.

―――. Modern Trends in Islam. Chicago, 1947.

―――. Mohammedanism. Oxford, 1962. Paperback.

―――. "Problems of Middle Eastern History," *Middle East Studies* (New York), IV (1963), 2.

―――. "Problems of Modern Middle Eastern History," in Anne W. Noyes, ed., Report on Current Research: Survey of Current Research on the Middle East. Washington, D.C., 1956.

―――. "Social Change in the Near East," in P. Ireland, ed., The Near East. Chicago, 1942.

―――. Studies on the Civilization of Islam. Boston, 1962.

―――. Whither Islam? London, 1932.

Gibb, H. A. R., and Harold Bowen. Islamic Society in the XVIII Century. Oxford, 1950. Vol. I.

Gladstone, W. E. Sudan and Afghanistan: The Vote of Credit (speech). London, 1885.

Gleason, J. H. The Genesis of Russophobia in Great Britain: A Study of the Interaction of Policy and Opinion. Cambridge, Mass., 1950.

Gleig, G. R. Sale's Brigade in Afghanistan with an Account of the Seizure and Defense of Jellalabad. London, 1846.

Godard, A. and Y., J. Hackin, and J. Carl. Les antiquités bouddhiques de Bamiyan. Paris and Brussels, 1928.

Godchot, J. E. Les constitutions de Proche et du Moyen Orient. Paris, 1957.

Goëz, Benedict. "Travels of Benedict Goëz," in Vol. VIII, Pinkerton, listed below.

Goitein, S. D. "The Rise of the Near Eastern Bourgeoisie in Early Islamic Times," *JWH,* III (1957), 3.

―――. Studies in Islamic History and Institutions. Leiden, 1966.

Goldsmid, Sir F. J. Central Asia and Its Question. London, 1873.

Golovin, Iu. M. Afganistan: Ekonomika i vneshniaia torgovlia. Moscow, 1962.

Gooch and Temperley. See Great Britain, British Documents.

Goodrich, Leland M., and Marie J. Carroll, eds. Documents on American Foreign Relations. Boston and Princeton, N.J., 1944, 1947. Vols. V, VII.

Gopal, Ram. Indian Muslims: A Political History (1858–1947). New York, 1959.

Gopal, S. The Viceroyalty of Lord Irwin. Oxford, 1957.

——. The Viceroyalty of Lord Ripon: 1880–1884. Oxford, 1953.

Gordon, Leonard A. "Portrait of a Bengal Revolutionary," *Journal of Asian Studies*, February 1968.

Gordon, L. R. Agrarnye otnosheniia v Severo-zapadnoi pogranichnoi provintsii Indii (1914–1947 gg.). Moscow, 1953.

——. "Voina Afganistana za nezavisimost i uchastie v nei pushtunskikh plemen (1919–1921 gg.)," in Akhramovich, *Nezavisimyi Afganistan*, listed above.

Gordon, Sir Thomas E. A Varied Life. A Record of Military and Civil Service, of Sport and of Travel in India, Central Asia and Persia, 1849–1902. London, 1906.

Goriainov, S. La question d'Orient à la veille du traité de Berlin (1870–1876). Paris, 1948.

Gowen, Herbert H. Asia. Boston, 1927.

Goya, Sarvar Khan. "Baazi az noskhaha-ye nayab," *Kaboul Almanach: 1935–36*.

Graham, G. F. I. Syed Ahmad Khan. London, 1885.

Grant, Sir Hamilton. "Afghanistan and the Pathan Border," *United Empire*, February 1930.

——. "A Winter at the Court of an Absolute Monarch," *Blackwood's Magazine*, November 1906.

Gray, John A. At the Court of the Amir. A Narrative. London 1895.

Great Britain. British and Foreign State Papers, 1812–1960. H.M. Stationery Office, London, 1841–1967. 164 vols. Vols. I, XXIII, XXV, XXVII, LXIII, LXV, LXVI, LXVII, LXVIII, LXIX, LXX, LXXII, LXXV, LXXVI, LXXVII, LXXVIII, LXXIX, LXXXVII, XCV, XCVIII.

——. British Documents on the Origins of the War, 1898–1914. Edited by G. P. Gooch and H. Temperley. London, 1926–38. 11 vols. Vols. I–IV.

——. British Museum. The Papers of Lord Ripon. 1880–84. B.M. Add. MSS. 43575; B.M. Add. MSS. 43576; B.M. Add. MSS. 43599, No. 23; B.M. Add. MSS. 43610, No. 1.

——. British White Paper: Papers Regarding Hostilities with Afghanistan, 1919. Cmd. 324, No. 2. London, 1919.

——. British White Paper: Papers Relating to Military Operations in Afghanistan. Presented to Both Houses of Parliament by Command of Her Majesty, 1843. London, 1843.

——. Foreign Office. Anglo-Afghan Trade Convention. Treaty Series, No. 21. London, 1923.

——, ——. Correspondence Between His Majesty's Government and the Soviet Government Respecting the Relations Between the Two Governments. Cmd. 1869 (Russia No. 2). London, 1923.

——, ——. Correspondence Relating to Persia and Afghanistan. London, 1939.

——, ——. Documents Illustrating Hostile Activities of the Soviet Government and Third International Against Great Britain. Cmd. 2874. London, 1927.

——, ——. Further Correspondence Between His Majesty's Government and the Soviet Government Respecting Relations Between the Two Governments. Cmd. 1890 (Russia No. 4). London, 1923.

——, ——. Note from His Majesty's Government to the Government of the USSR Respecting Relations Existing Between the Two Governments and Note in Reply. Cmd. 2822 (Russia No. 1). London, 1927.

——, ——. Reply of the Soviet Government to His Majesty's Government Respecting the Relations Between the Two Governments. Cmd. 1874 (Russia No. 3). London, 1923.

——, ——. A Selection of Papers Dealing with Relations Between His Majesty's Government and the Soviet Government, 1921–27. Cmd. 2895. London, 1927.

——, ——. Treaty Between the British and Afghan Governments, November 22, 1921. Cmd. 1786. Treaty Series, No. 19. London, 1922.

——. General Staff, War Office. Daily Review of the Foreign Press: Confidential Supplement, June 1916. London, 1916.

——. Official History of the War, 1914–1918. London, 1924. Vol. IV.

——. Parliamentary Papers. H.M. Stationery Office, London.
  1839, XL: *Afghanistan*; 1840, XXXVII: *Afghanistan*; 1842, XLV: *Afghanistan*; 1843, XXXVII: *Afghanistan*; 1859, XXV: *Afghanistan*, Nos. 1 and 2; 1873, LXXV: *Central Asia*, No. 1; 1878, LXXX: *Central Asia*, No. 1; 1878, LVIII: *Central Asia*, No. 1; 1878–79, LVI: *Afghanistan*, Nos. 1 and 6; 1880–81, XCVIII: *Central Asia*; 1881, LXX: *Afghanistan*, No. 4; 1884, LXXXVII: *Central Asia*; 1884–85, LXXXVIII: *Central Asia*, No. 2; 1887, LXIII: *Central Asia*, No. 1; 1888, LXXVII: *Central Asia*; 1895, CIX: *Pamir Boundary*; 1898, LXIII: *North West Frontier*; 1901, XLIX: *North West Frontier*; 1905, LVII: *Afghanistan*; 1908, LXXIV: *North West Frontier*; 1908, CXXV: *Afghanistan*.

——. Public Record Office, Foreign Office Archives. F.O. 60 (Persia), 42, 44, 47, 55, 419, 423; F.O. 65 (Russia), 258, 259, 273, 1097, 1099, 1104, 1202; F.O. 181/488.

Greaves, Rose L. Persia and the Defense of India, 1884–1892. London, 1959.

Green, Sir W. H. R. The Retention of Candahar. London, 1881.

Gregorian, Vartan. "The Emergence of Modern Afghanistan, Politics of Modernization 1880–1930," Ph.D. Dissertation, Stanford University, 1964.

Grekov, Boris D., and Aleksandr Y. Yakubovskii. Zolotaia orda i eë padenie. Moscow and Leningrad, 1950.

Grierson, George A., ed. Linguistic Survey of India. Calcutta, 1904–21. Vols. VI, IX, X.

Griesinger, W. German Intrigues in Persia: The Niedermayer Expedition Through Persia to Afghanistan and India. London, 1918.

Griffin, Lepel. "A Page of Afghan History," *The Asiatic Quarterly Review*, October 1888.

Griffith, William. Posthumous Papers Bequeathed to the Honorable The East India Company and Printed by Order of the Government of Bengal. Calcutta, 1847–48. 2 vols.

Griffiths, John C. Afghanistan. New York, 1967.

Griffiths, Sir Percival J. British Impact on India. London, 1952.

Grodekov, N. L. Colonel Grodekoff's Ride from Samarcand to Herat in 1878. Translated by Charles Marvin. London, 1880.

Grousset, René. L'empire des steppes. Paris, 1939.

———. L'empire mongol. Paris, 1941.

———. Histoire de l'Asie. Paris, 1922. Vol. III.

———. Le réveil de l'Asie. Paris, 1924.

Grousset, R., J. Auboyer, and J. Buhot. Histoire du Moyen Age: L'Asie Centrale des origines au XVe siècle. Paris, 1941.

Grunebaum, G. E. von. "Arabic Literature," in Young, listed below.

———. Islam: Essays in the Nature and Growth of a Cultural Tradition. London, 1961.

———. Medieval Islam. Chicago, 1946.

———, ed. "Studies in Islamic Cultural History," *The American Anthropologist*, April 1954.

———, ed. Unity and Variety in Islamic Civilization. Chicago, 1955.

Guedalla, Philip. Palmerston. New York, 1927.

"La guerre civile et ses conséquences," *L'Asie Française*, July-August 1929.

Guilbeaux, Henri. "L'Orient, libérateur de l'Europe," *Bulletin Communiste*, January 13, 1921.

Guimbrétière, André. "Le réformisme musulman en Inde," *Orient*, No. 16 (1960) and No. 18 (1961). 2 parts.

Gulbedin Khan. "Din-e mobin-e Islam," *MH*, 2d year, No. 3.

Gupta, Hari Ram. "Afghanistan at Shah Zaman's Accession, 1793," *IHRC*, No. 18 (1942).

———. "Mohan Lal's Observations on the Causes of Insurrection in Kabul, 1841–1842," in Proceedings of the Third Indian Historical Congress (1939).

———. "Timur Shah's Army in 1793," *Journal of Indian History*, No. 20 (1940).

Gurevich, Naum M. Ocherki istorii torgovogo kapitala v Afganistane. Moscow, 1967.

———. Vneshniaia torgovlia Afganistana do vtoroi mirovoi voiny. Moscow, 1959.

———. Voprosy ekonomiki Afganistana. Moscow, 1963.

Habberton, William. Anglo-Russian Relations Concerning Afghanistan: 1837–1907. Urbana, Ill., 1937.

Habib, Irfan. "Usury in Medieval India," *Comparative Studies in Society and History*, July 1964.

Habib-Allah, Amir of Afghanistan. My Life from Brigand to King. London, n.d. [?1930].

Habibi, Abdul Ali Khan. "Asar-e barjaste-ye san'aat va adab-e Pashto," *Kaboul Almanach: 1939–40*.

Habibi, Abdulhayy Khan. Da Pushtu adabiyatu tarikh. Kabul, 1946.

———. "Geranbahatarin Kotob-e Pashto," *Kaboul Almanach: 1940–41*.

———. Tarikh-e Afghanestan dar asr-e Gurgani-ye Hind. Kabul, 1962.

———. "Tarikhche-ye Sabakha-ye ashaar-e Pashto," *Kaboul Almanach: 1942–43*.

Habibullah Khan, Amir. Ghavaid-e Siraj-ul-Millat dar kharidari-ye mal az doval-e kharija. Kabul, 1904.

Hackin, Joseph. "L'art bouddhique de la Bactriane et les origines de l'art gréco-bouddhique, *Afghanistan*, January-March 1950.

——, ed. Diverses recherches archéologiques en Afghanistan (1933–1940). (Par J. Hackin, J. Carl, et J. Meunié, avec des études de R. Ghirshman et J.-C. Gardin.) Paris, 1959.

——. "Les idoles du Kafiristan," *Artibus Asiae*, 1926, No. 4.

——. "In Persia and Afghanistan with the Citroen Trans-Asiatic Expedition," *The Geographical Journal*, May 1934.

——. "The 1939 Dig at Begram," *Asia*, October-November 1940.

——. L'oeuvre de la délégation archéologique française en Afghanistan. Tokyo, 1933. Vol. I.

——. "Les travaux de la délégation archéologique française en Afghanistan," *Revue des Arts Asiatiques*, XII (1938), 1.

Haddad, George M. Revolutions and Military Rule in the Middle East: The Northern Tier. New York, 1965.

Haim, Sylvia G., ed. Arab Nationalism. Berkeley, Calif., 1962.

——. "Islam and the Theory of Arab Nationalism," in Walter Z. Laqueur, ed., The Middle East in Transition. New York, 1958.

Hakim, Abdul. "L'organisation de l'instruction publique et des écoles en Afghanistan," *Afghanistan*, January-March 1949.

Hakim, Khalifa Abdul. Islamic Ideology. Lahore, 1953.

Hakimi, Abdul Karim. "Economic Development in Afghanistan," M.A. Thesis, University of Texas, 1953.

Hallgarten, George W. F. "General Hans von Seeckt and Russia, 1920–1922," *Journal of Modern History*, March 1949.

Halpern, Manfred. "Middle Eastern Armies and the New Middle Class," in John J. Johnson, ed., The Role of the Military in Underdeveloped Countries. Princeton, N.J., 1962.

——. The Politics of Social Change in the Middle East and North Africa. Princeton, N.J., 1963.

Hamilton, Alexander. "A New Account of the East Indies," in Vol. VIII, Pinkerton, listed below.

Hamilton, Angus. Afghanistan. Boston, 1910.

——. "The Anglo-Russian Agreement: The Question of Persia," *Fortnightly Review*, November 1907.

——. "Indo-Afghan Relations Under Lord Curzon," *Fortnightly Review*, December 1906.

——. Problems of the Middle East. London, 1909.

Hamilton, Charles. An Historical Relation of the Origin . . . of the . . . Rohilla Afghans. 2d ed. London, 1783.

Hamilton, Walter. A Geographical, Statistical and Historical Description of Hindostan and the Adjacent Countries. London, 1820. 2 vols.

Hanna, H. B. The Second Afghan War, 1878–79–80. Its Causes, Its Conduct and Its Consequences. Westminster and London, 1899–1910. 3 vols.

Hans, Hugh, ed. The Jewish Yearbook. London, 1960.

Hansard's Parliamentary Debates. London. 3d series: 1880, CCLI–CCLV;

1881, CCLVI–CCLXII; 1882, CCLXVI–CCLXXV; 1884–85, CCXCIV–CCCI; 1886, CCCII–CCCIV; 1887, CCCV–CCCXXI; 1888–90, CCCXXII–CCCXLVIII; 1891, CCCXLIX–CCCLVI; 1892–1900, I–LXXXVIII. 4th series: XLII, CLXXXIV.

Hanway, Jonas. The Revolutions in Persia. London, 1753. 4 vols.

Harlan, Josiah. Central Asia. Personal Narrative of General Josiah Harlan, 1832-1841. Edited by Frank E. Ross. London, 1939.

———. A Memoir of India and Avghanistaun, with Observations on the Present Exciting and Critical State and Future Prospects of Those Countries. Comprising Remarks on the Massacre of the British Army in Cabul, British Policy in India … With an Appendix on the Present Prophetic Condition of Mahomedan Nations Throughout the World, and the Speedy Dissolution of the Ottoman Empire. Philadelphia, 1842.

Harris, Audrey. "From Kabul to the Oxus," *The Times* (London), April 5–7, 1937.

Harutunian, A. B. Arevelki joghovrdneri aradjin hamagumare. Erevan, 1960. In Armenian.

Hashmat, A. "Notes of a Journey," *Afghanistan*, October-December 1948.

Hassan Khan, Yakub. "Negahi betarikh-e ghadim-e Afghanestan," *Kaboul Almanach: 1935–36.*

———. "Zabanha dar Afghanestan," *Kaboul Almanach: 1934–35.*

Havelock, Sir Henry. Narrative of the War in Afghanistan in 1838 and 1839. London, 1840. 2 vols.

Hayat, Baymirza. Turkestan im XX Jahrhundert. Darmstadt, 1956.

Hayat Khan, Muhammad. Hayat-i-Afghan. Lahore, 1867. Translated by Henri Priestly as Afghanistan and Its Inhabitants. Lahore, 1874.

Haydar Khan, Mir Ghulam. "Ayat-e Qurani ke shavahedand bar fazaiate elm," *MH*, 2d year, No. 7.

Haye, K. A. "Amir Dost Muhammed Khan Barakzai," *Proceedings of Pakistan Historical Conference*, No. 2, 1952.

———. "The First Afghan War—A Review," *Indian Historical Quarterly*, No. 23 (1947).

Hayes, R. S. Unmasterly Inactivity in Central Asia. London, 1873.

Heald, Stephen, ed. Documents on International Affairs, 1937. Oxford, 1939.

Hellwald, Frederick von. The Russians in Central Asia. Translated by T. Wirgman. London, 1874.

Hentig, Werner Otto von. Mein Leben eine Dienstreise. Göttingen, 1963.

Herati, Mahjuba. "Ezdevaj," *MH*, 7th year, No. 9-10.

Herati, Muhammed Hussein, and Shah Shujah. Vagheat-e Shah Shujah. Kabul, 1953.

Herbert, Sir Thomas. Some Years Travel into Africa and Asia the Great. London, 1677.

———. Travels in Persia. Edited by W. Foster. London, 1928.

Hermann, J. A., and C. R. Borg. Retracing Genghis Khan: A Record of a Journey Through Afghanistan and Persia. Boston, 1937.

Hertslet, Sir Edward, ed. Hertslet's Commercial Treaties. 1827–1925. London, 1840-1925. 31 vols. Vol. VIII.

Hirszowicz, Lukasz. The Third Reich and the Arab East. London, 1966.

Histoire de la guerre Italo-Turque, 1911–1912. Paris, 1912. Signed Un Témoin.

Hitti, Philip K. Islam and the West. New York, 1963. Paperback.

Hodgson, Marshall G. S. "The Unity of Later Islamic History," *JWH*, V (1960), 4.

Holdich, Sir Thomas H. "The Afghan Claim of Descent from Israel," *The Nineteenth Century and After*, July 1919.

———. "The Beni-Israel of Afghanistan," *The Moslem World*, April 1918.

———. The Gates of India; Being a Historical Narrative. London, 1910.

———. The Indian Borderland: 1880–1900. London, 1901.

———. "The Influence of Bolshevism in Afghanistan," *New Europa*, December 4, 1919.

———. "The Origins of the Kafir of the Hindu-Kush," *Journal of the Royal Geographical Society*, January 1896.

———. "The Perso-Baluch Boundary," *Geographical Journal*, April 1897.

———. Political Frontiers and Boundary Making. London, 1916.

Holdsworth, Mary. Turkestan in the Nineteenth Century. London, 1959.

Holland, William L., ed. Asian Nationalism and the West: A Symposium Based on Documents and Reports of the Eleventh Conference of the Institute of Pacific Relations. New York, 1953.

Honigberger, Martin. "Journal of a Route from Dera Ghazi Khan Through the Veziri country to Kabul (a letter to Captain C. M. Wade)," *JASB*, April 1834.

Horniker, Arthur L. "William Harborne and the Beginning of Anglo-Turkish Commerce," *The Journal of Modern History*, September 1942.

Hoselitz, Bert F., ed. "Agrarian Societies in Transition," *Annals of the American Academy of Political and Social Science*, May 1956.

———, ed. The Progress of Underdeveloped Areas. Chicago, 1952.

———. "Small Industry in Underdeveloped Countries," *Journal of Economic History*, December 1959.

Hoselitz, Bert F., and Wilbert E. Moore, eds. Industrialization and Society. Proceedings of the Chicago Conference on Social Implications of Industrialization and Technical Change, September 15–22, 1960. The Hague, 1963.

———, eds. Industrialization and Technical Change. New York, 1963.

Hoskins, Halford L. British Routes to India. Philadelphia, 1928.

Hösten, Father H., S.J. "Extracts of Jesuit Annual Letters from Goa and Cochin," *The Examiner* (Bombay), February 17, March 9, and April 6, 1912.

Hostler, Charles W. Turkism and the Soviets. London, 1957.

Hough, William. A Narrative of the March and Operations of the Army of the Indus, in the Expedition into Afghanistan in the Years 1838–1839 under the Command of H.E. Lt.-Gen. Sir John Keane. Calcutta, 1840.

Hourani, Albert. Arabic Thought in the Liberal Age: 1798–1939. Oxford, 1962.

Howard, J. F., ed. Letters and Documents of Napoleon. London, 1961. Vol. I.

Howland, Felix. "Afghanistan Has No Frontiers," *Asia*, December 1940.

———. "Crossing the Hindu Kush," *Geographical Review*, XXX (1940).

Howorth, Sir Henry. History of the Mongols from the Ninth to the Nineteenth Century. London, 1876–88. 4 vols. Supplement and indices. London, 1927.

H. R. S. "Unrest in the Peshawar District 1930–1932," *JRCAS*, October 1932.

Hsü, Immanuel C. Y. "British Mediation of China's War with Yakub Beg, 1877," *Central Asiatic Journal* (The Hague), June 1964.

Huart, C. "Kizilbash," in Vol. II, *EI*, 1st ed.

Huddleston, S. "Europe and Afghanistan," *The New Statesman*, January 28, 1928.

Hudson, Alfred E., and Elizabeth Bacon. "Inside Afghanistan Today," *Asia*, March 1940.

Hūdūd al-'Alam (The Regions of the World). Translated by V. Minorsky. Oxford, 1937.

Huffman, Arthur V. "The Administrative and Social Structure of Afghan Life," *JRCAS*, January 1951.

Hughes, A. W. The Country of Balochistan, Its Geography, Topography, Ethnology, and History. London, 1877.

Humlum, J. La géographie de l'Afghanistan. Etude d'un pays aride. Copenhagen, 1959.

Hunter, Edward. The Past Present: A Year in Afghanistan. London, 1959.

Hunter, Sir William W. A History of British India. London, 1899. 2 vols.

———, ed. The Imperial Gazetteer of India, 2d ed. London, 1885–87. 14 vols.

———. Life of the Earl of Mayo. Oxford, 1892. 2 vols.

Huntington, Samuel P. "The Political Modernization of Traditional Monarchies," *Daedalus*, Summer 1966.

Hurewitz, J. C. Diplomacy in the Near and Middle East: A Documentary Record, 1535–1914. New York, 1956. 2 vols.

Husain, Mahmud, ed. A History of the Freedom Movement: Being the Story of the Muslim Struggle for the Freedom of Hind-Pakistan 1707–1947. Karachi, 1957–61. 3 vols.

Huseini, Mullah Sayyid Ahmad Khan. "Tarz-e hayat dar alem-e taavon va ejtema," *MH*, 2d year, No. 6.

Hutton, W. H. The Marquess of Wellesley. Oxford, 1897.

Hyder Khan, Gholaum. "Mr. Moorcraft's Journey to Balkh and Bokhara" (journal of Gholaum Hyder Khan, edited by Major Hearsey), *The Asiatic Journal*, September-December 1835 and January-April 1836. 2 parts.

Iavorskii, I. L. Russkie v Avganistane. Puteshestvie russkogo posolstva po Avganistanu i Bukharskomu Khanstvu v 1878–1879. St. Petersburg, 1882–83. 2 vols.

Ibn' Arab Shah, Ahmad. 'Aja'ibul-maqdur fī Akhbari Timur. Cairo, 1906.

Ibn Battúta. Travels in Asia and Africa 1325–1354. Translated by H. A. R. Gibb. London, 1953.

Ibn Khaldūn. Muqaddimah. Translated by F. Rosenthal. London, 1958. 3 vols.

Iftikhar-ud-din, Faqir Saiyid. Report on the Tour in Afghanistan of H.M. Amir Habibullah, 1907. Simla, 1908.

Ilinskii, G. "Reformy i rodovye perezhitki v Afganistane," *Mirovoe khoziaistvo i mirovaia politika* (Moscow), 1929, No. 1.

Imamuddin, S. M. "The Nature of Afghan Monarchy in India," *Islamic Culture*, October 1958. Also appears in 2 parts in *Afghanistan*, October-December 1958 and January-March 1959.

"Iman bilal amal," *Al-Falah*, 7th year, No. 9. Reprinted from *Islah*.

India. Army Intelligence Branch. The Second Afghan War. Calcutta, 1908.

————. A Collection of Treaties, Engagements and Sanads Relating to India and Neighbouring Countries. Compiled by Charles U. Aitchison. 5th ed. Calcutta, 1929–33. 14 vols. Vols. XI–XIII.

————. East India Committee of the Colonial Society. Report on the Causes and Consequences of the Afghan War. 2d ed. London, 1842.

————. Review of the Trade of India in 1906–07. London, 1907.

————. Royal Air Force. East India (military) Report on the Air Operations in Afghanistan Between December 12th, 1928, and February 25th, 1929: Presented by the Secretary of State for India to Parliament, by Command of His Majesty. London, 1929.

————. Secretary of State for India in Council. The Imperial Gazetteer of India. Oxford, 1907–9. 26 vols.

————. Sedition Committee. Report. Calcutta, 1918.

————. Selections from the Records of the Bombay Government. n.s. Bombay. 1856. Vol. XXIV.

————. The Third Afghan War, 1919: Official Account. Calcutta, 1926.

Iqbal, Muhammad. Le message de l'Orient. Translated into French by Eva Meyerovitch and Muhammed Ashena. Paris, 1956.

————. Selected Speeches and Writings. Lahore, 1944.

Irvine, William. The Later Mughals. Edited by J. Sarkar. Calcutta, 1921–22. 2 vols.

Irwin, Lt. "Memoir on the Climate, Soil, Produce and Husbandry of Afghanistan and the Neighbouring Countries, *JASB*, September 1839–February 1840. 6 parts.

Ishaque, M. Modern Persian Poetry. Calcutta, 1943.

Iskanderov, B. I. Iz istorii Bukharskogo emirata. Moscow, 1958.

"Itinerary from Yezd to Herat and Herat to Kabul via Kandahar," in Forrest, Selections from Travels, listed above.

Iuldashbaeva, Fatima Kh. Iz istorii angliiskoi kolonialnoi politiki v Afganistane i Srednei Azii. Tashkent, 1963.

Ivanin, Mikhail I. O voennom iskusstve i zavoevaniiakh mongolo-tatar i sredneaziatskikh narodov pri Chingis-khane i Tamerlane. St. Petersburg, 1875.

Ivanov, M. S. Ocherk istorii Irana. Moscow, 1952.

Ivanov, W. "Notes on the Ethnology of Khurasan," *The Geographical Journal*, January 1926.

Iybar, Tahsin. Sibiryadan Serendibé. Ankara, 1950.

Izzet Ullah, Mir. Travels in Central Asia by Meer Izzut Oollah in the Year 1812–1813. Translated by Captain Henderson. Calcutta, 1872.

Jacob, John. The Views and Opinions of Brigadier-General John Jacob. London, 1858.

Jalalabadi, Mirza Sher Ahmad. Fathname-ye Kafiristan. Lahore, 1896.

James, Ben. Afghan Journey. London, 1935.

Janowitz, Morris. The Military in the Political Development of New Nations: An Essay in Comparative Analysis. Chicago, 1965. Paperback.

Jansen, Marius B., ed. Changing Japanese Attitudes Toward Modernization. Princeton, N.J., 1965.

————. "On Studying the Modernization of Japan," *Asian Cultural Studies* (Tokyo), October 1962.

Janssens, G. Busson de. "Les *waqfs* dans l'Islam contemporain," *Revue des Etudes Islamiques*, 1951.

Japanese National Commission for UNESCO. The Modernization of Japan. A Special Edition in the Philosophical Studies of Japan. Tokyo, 1966.

Jarric, Father Pierre du, S.J. Akbar and the Jesuits: An Account of the Jesuit Missions to the Court of Akbar. Edited by Sir E. Denison Ross and Eileen Power. New York, 1926.

Jarring, Gunnar. On the Distribution of Turkic Tribes in Afghanistan. Lund, 1939.

Jewett, A. C. An American Engineer in Afghanistan. Minneapolis, 1948.

——. "An Engineer in Afghanistan," *Asia*, June 1920.

——. "Off the Map in Afghanistan," *Asia*, January 1920.

——. "Sum of All Wisdom: Habibullah Khan," *Asia*, April 1920.

Jomier, J. Le commentaire coranique de Manār. Paris, 1954.

Jonveaux, Emile. "Les Russes dans l'Asie Centrale," *Revue des Deux Mondes*, February 15, 1867.

Joshi, V. V. Clash of Three Empires. Allahabad, 1941.

Juvainī, 'Alā Al-Dīn 'Atā' Malik. The History of the World Conqueror. Edited by Mirza Muhammad Qazvini; translated by John A. Boyle. Manchester, Eng., 1958. 2 vols.

Juzjānī, Minhāj Al-Sīrāj. Tabakāt-i-Nāsirī, in Elliot and Dawson, listed above.

Kaliprasana, D. Life of Sir L. Cavagnari, with an Outline of the Second Afghan War. Calcutta, 1881.

Kamrany, Nake M. "The First Five-Year Plan of Afghanistan 1956–1962: An Economic Evaluation," Ph.D. Dissertation, University of Southern California, 1963.

Kamshad, Hassan. Modern Persian Literature. Cambridge, Eng., 1966.

Kapadia, E. R. "Alexander Burnes: Mission to Kabul," *Journal of Indian History*, August 1944.

Kapur, Anup Chand. "Disraeli's Forward Policy in the Northwest Frontier of India, 1874–1877," *The Research Bulletin of the University of Punjab* (Lahore), 1951, No. 1.

Karim Khan, Muhammed. "Tarikhche-ye adabiyat-e Afghanestan," *Kaboul Almanach: 1935–36.*

Karimi, Ahmadullah Khan. "The Constitution of Afghanistan," *Afghanistan*, January–March 1946.

——. "Maaref dar Afghanestan," *Kaboul Almanach: 1938–39.*

Kasravi, Ahmad. Tarikh-e hejdah sale-ye Azerbaijan. Tehran, 1939–41. 6 vols.

Kateb, Fayz Muhammad. Siraj ul Tawarikh. Kabul, 1913–15. 2 vols.

Kātrak, Sohrab K. H. Through Amanullah's Afghanistan. Karachi, 1929.

Kautsky, John H., ed. Political Change in Underdeveloped Countries: Nationalism and Communism. 4th ed. New York, 1965.

Kaye, John William. History of the War in Afghanistan. London, 1851–57. 3 vols.

——. The Life and Correspendence of Major-General Sir John Malcolm. London, 1856. 2 vols.

Kazem Zadeh, H. Relations d'un pélérinage à la Mecque en 1910–1911. Paris, 1912.

Kazemzadeh, Firuz. "Russia and the Middle East," in I. J. Lederer, ed., Russian Foreign Policy. New Haven, Conn., 1962.

———. "Russian Imperialism and Persian Railways," *Harvard Slavic Studies* (The Hague), IV (1957).

Kazizadeh, Muhammad Karim. "Dianat va tahzib-e akhlagh," *Kabul*, 1st year, No. 11.

———. "Integhad va musikeh," *Kabul*, 1st year, No. 10.

———. "Vazife shenasi," *Kabul*, 1st year, No. 5.

Keane, A. H. Asia. 2d ed. London, 1906–9. 2 vols.

Keddie, Nikki R. "Afghanī in Afghanistan," *MES*, July 1965.

———. "Biographical Review. Sayyid Jamāl al-Dīn al-Afghānī's First Twenty-Seven Years: The Darkest Period," *MEJ*, Autumn 1966.

———. "Pan-Islam as Proto-Nationalism." (Paper delivered at the annual convention of the American Historical Association.) New York, 1966.

———. "The Pan-Islamic Appeal: Afghānī and Abdul Hamid II," *MES*, October 1966.

———. "Religion and Irreligion in Early Iranian Nationalism," *Comparative Studies in Society and History*, April 1962.

Kedourie, Elie. Afghānī and 'Abduh: An Essay on Religious Unbelief and Political Activism in Modern Islam. London, 1966.

———. "Nouvelle lumière sur Afghānī et 'Abduh," *Orient*, Nos. 30 and 31 (1964). 2 parts.

Kemp, E. G. The Face of Manchuria, Korea and Russian Turkestan. London, 1910.

Kennedy, Richard H. Narrative of the Campaign of the Army of the Indus in Sind and Kaubool in 1838–1839. London, 1840. 2 vols.

Keppel, Arnold. Gun-Running and the Indian North-West Frontier. London, 1911.

Kerr, Malcolm H. Islamic Reform: The Political and Legal Theories of Muhammad 'Abduh and Rashid Rida. Berkeley, Calif., 1966.

Khadduri, Majid. Islamic Jurisprudence: Shafii's Risālā. Baltimore, 1961.

———. War and Peace in the Law of Islam. Baltimore, 1955.

Khadduri, Majid, and Herbert Liebesny, eds. Law in the Middle East. Washington, D.C., 1955.

Khadem, Qiyam al-Din. Bayazid Roshan. Kabul, 1945.

———. Pushtunwali. Kabul, 1952.

Khafi, Mirza Yakub Ali. Padshahan-e motaakher. Kabul, 1956–57. 2 vols.

Khalfin, N. A. "Angliiskaia ekspantsiia v Afganistan i osvoboditelnaia borba afganskogo naroda v pervoi polovine XIX veka," in Akhramovich, *Nezavisimyi Afganistan*, listed above.

———. Politika Rossii v Srednei Azii (1857–1868). Moscow, 1960.

———. Proval britanskoi agressii v Afganistane. (XIX v.–nachalo XX v.) Moscow, 1959.

———. Soviet Historiography on the Development of the Afghan State in the XVIII–XX Centuries. Moscow, 1960.

Khalili, Kh. "Makhmud-bek Tarzi," *Problemy vostokovedeniia* (Moscow), 1959, No. 2.

———. Saltanat-e Ghaznaviyan. Kabul, 1954.

Khan, Mohammad Anwar. England, Russia and Central Asia (A Study in Diplomacy) 1857–1878. Peshawar, 1963.

Khan, Shafaat Ahmad. The East India Trade in the XVIIth Century. Oxford, 1923.

Khanykov, N. V. (Khanikoff, Nicholas). Bokhara; Its Amir and Its People. Translated by Baron C. A. de Bode. London, 1845.

Kiazim, Omer. Angora et Berlin. Paris, 1922.

King, David W. Living East. New York, 1929.

King, L. See White-King.

"King of Afghanistan's Policy," *The Near East*, August 20, 1931.

King, Peter M. Afghanistan: Cockpit in High Asia. London, 1966.

Kingsbury, Patricia and Robert. Afghanistan and the Himalayan States. New York, 1960.

Kirk, George E. A Short History of the Middle East. 3d ed. London, 1955.

———, ed. Survey of International Affairs: The Middle East in the War— 1939–1946. Oxford, 1952.

Kishimoto, Hideo. "Modernization versus Westernization in the East," *JWH*, VII (1963), 4.

Klass, Rosanne. Land of the High Flags: A Travel Memoir of Afghanistan. New York, 1964.

Klimburg, Max. Afghanistan. Vienna, 1966.

Kluchnikov, I. V., and A. Sabanin, eds. Mezhdunarodnaiia politika noveishego vremeni v dogovorakh, notakh i deklaratsiakh. Moscow, 1925. Vol. II.

Kohn, Hans. A History of Nationalism in the East. New York, 1929.

———. Nationalism and Imperialism in the Hither East. London, 1932.

———. Western Civilization in the Near East. London, 1936.

Kohzad, Ahmad Ali. "Arms of the Arians: Heroes in Avesta Period," *Afghanistan*, July-September 1953.

———. "Aryana ya Afghanestan-e ghabl al-Islam," in Latifi, Afghanestan, listed below.

———. "Un court aperçu sur l'évolution de l'art en Afghanistan," *Afghanistan*, January-March 1957.

———. "Emir Cher Ali en face de la diplomatie anglaise: la fidélité des tribus," *Afghanistan*, October-December 1952.

———. "Emperatouri-ye Kushan," *Kaboul Almanach: 1938–39.*

———. "Frontier Discord Between Afghanistan and Pakistan," *Afghanistan*, January-March 1951.

———. In the Highlight of Modern Afghanistan. Historical Society of Afghanistan, Publication No. 56. Kabul, n.d.

———. "Maskukat-e Afghanestan dar asr-e Islam," *Kaboul Almanach: 1940–41.*

———. "Les manuscrits relatifs à l'histoire de l'Afghanistan au XIX siècle," in Vol. III, *TDPMKV*. Moscow, 1963. Also appears in *Afghanistan*, October-December 1960.

———. Men and Events Through 18th- and 19th-Century Afghanistan. Historical Society of Afghanistan, Publication No. 44. Kabul, n.d.

———. "The Nuristanis Are Aryans and Not Greek Remnants," *Afghanistan*, April-June 1954.

————. "Recherches archéologiques en Afghanistan," *Afghanistan*, April-June 1953.

————. "Tahghighat-e arkialojy dar Afghanestan," in Latifi, Afghanestan, listed below.

————. Tarikh-e Afghanestan. Kabul, 1946.

————. "Two Coronations," *Afghanistan*, July-September 1950.

————. "Zaman Shah et l'activité des puissances coloniales," *Afghanistan*, October-December 1953.

Komroff, Manuel. Contemporaries of Marco Polo . . . John of Pian de Carpini . . . Friar Odoric, etc. New York, 1928.

Krausse, Alexis. Russia in Asia, a Record and a Study, 1558–1899. London, 1899.

Kudsi-Zadeh, A. Albert. "Jamāl al-Dīn al-Afghānī; A Select List of Articles," *MES*, January 1965.

Kuhn, Delia and Ferdinand. Borderlands. New York, 1962.

Kukhtina, T. I., comp. Bibliografiia Afganistana Literatura na russkom iazyke. Moscow, 1965.

————. "K voprosy o podgotovke natsionalnykh tekhnicheskikh kadrov v Afganistane (1919–1961)," in Gurevich, *Voprosy*, listed above.

Kuliyev, Nadir. Antinauchnaia sushchnost Islama i zadachi ateisticheskogo vospitaniia trudiashchiksia v usloviiakh Sovetskogo Turkmenistana. Ashkabad, 1960.

Kumar, Ravinder. "Kuwait and the Problems of British Routes to India," *IHRC*, XXXV (1960).

Kuropatkin, A. N. Kashgaria. Translated by Walter E. Gowan. Calcutta, 1882.

Kushkaki, Burhan-al-Din. Rahnemay-e Ghataghan va Badakshan. Kabul, 1924.

Labonne, Roger. "La révolution afghane," *Correspondent* (Paris), No. 283 (1930).

"Labour Legislation in Afghanistan," *International Labour Review*, January 1948.

Lacoste, DeBouillance de. Autour de l'Afghanistan. Paris, 1908.

Lacour-Gayet, Jacques, ed. Histoire du Commerce. Paris, 1950. 4 vols.

Lal, Munshi Mohan. "A Brief Description of Herat," *JASB*, January 1834.

————. "Further Information Regarding Siah Posh Tribe or Reported Descendants of the Macedonians," *JASB*, January 1834.

————. Journal of a Tour Through the Panjab, Afghanistan, Turkistan, Khorassan and a Part of Persia in Company with Lieut. Burnes and Dr. Gerard. Calcutta and London, 1834–35.

————. Life of the Amir Dost Mohammed Khan of Kabul: and His Political Proceedings Towards the English, Russian and Persian Governments, Including the Victory and Disasters of the British Army in Afghanistan. London, 1846. 2 vols.

————. Travels in Panjab, Afghanistan and Turkistan, to Balkh, Bokhara and Herat: and a Visit to Great Britain and Germany. London, 1846.

Lambrick, H. T. John Jacob of Jacobabad. London, 1960.

Lambton, Ann K. Landlord and Peasant in Persia: A Study of Land Tenure. London, 1953.

———. "The Problem of the Unrighteous Ruler," in International Islamic Colloquium. Lahore, 1960.

———. "Quis Custodiet Custodes: Some Reflections on the Persian Theory of Government," *Studia Islamica,* V and VI (1956). 2 parts.

———. "Secret Societies and the Persian Revolution of 1905–6," *St. Anthony's Papers: Middle Eastern Affairs* (London), No. 4. 1958.

———. "The Theory of Kingship in the *Nāsihat ul-Mulūk* of Ghāzālī," *The Islamic Quarterly,* I (1954), 1.

Landau, Jacob M. "Al-Afghani's Pan-Islamic Project," *Islamic Culture,* July 1952.

Lane-Poole, Stanley. Medieval India Under Muhammedan Rule. London, 1903.

———. Muhammedan Dynasties. London, 1894.

Langer, William L. The Diplomacy of Imperialism, 1890–1902. 2d ed. New York, 1951.

———. European Alliances and Alignments, 1871–1890. New York, 1931.

Lansdell, Henry. Russian Central Asia, Including Kuldja, Bokhara, Khiva and Merv. Boston, 1885. 2 vols.

———. Through Central Asia: with an Appendix on the Russo-Afghan Frontier. London, 1887.

Laoust, H. "Le réformisme orthodoxe des Salafiyya et les caractères généraux de son orientation actuelle," *Revue des Etudes Islamiques,* 1932.

Laqueur, Walter Z., ed. The Middle East in Transition. New York, 1958.

———, ed. The Soviet Union and the Middle East. London, 1959.

Latifi, Abdul Baghi, ed. Afghanestan. Kabul, 1946.

Latourette, Kenneth S. A History of the Expansion of Christianity. London, 1945. Vols. VI, VII.

Lawrence, Sir George. Forty-Three Years in India. London, 1874.

League of Nations. Treaty Series; Publication of Treaties and International Engagements Registered with the Secretariat of the League. September 1920–July 31, 1946. London, 1920–46. 205 vols.

Lebedev, K. Afganskie skazki. Moscow, 1955.

Lebrun, Renaud. La Perse politique et militaire au XIXᵉ siècle: histoire de la dynastie des Kajars (1794–1894). Paris, 1894.

Le Chatelier, A. L'Emir d'Afghanistan aux Indes, *RMM,* II (1907).

Lee, Dwight E. Great Britain and the Cyprus Convention Policy of 1878. Cambridge, Eng., 1934.

———. "The Origins of Pan-Islamism," *The American Historical Review,* October 1941 and July 1942. 2 parts.

———. "A Turkish Mission to Afghanistan in 1877," *The Journal of Modern History,* September 1941.

Leech, Robert. "An Account of the Early Abdalees," *JASB,* February 1845.

———. "A Description of the Country of Seisthan," *JASB,* February 1845.

———. "Grammar of the Brahuiky Language," *JASB,* June–September 1838. 4 parts.

———. "A Vocabulary of the Language of the Moghal Aimako," *JASB,* November 1838.

Lefevbre, Georges. Napoléon. Paris, 1935.

Legrand, M. Les routes de l'Inde. Paris, 1880.

Leibnitz, G. W. von. Mémoire de Leibnitz à Louis XIV sur la conquête de l'Egypt. (Preface and notes by N. de Hoffmans.) Paris, 1840.

Leitner, G. W. "The Amir Abdurrahman and the Press," *The Imperial and Asiatic Quarterly Review*, April 1893. Signed "an ex-Panjab official."

———. "The Amir of Afghanistan and Great Britain," *The Imperial and Asiatic Quarterly Review*, April 1894.

Lejean, Guillaume. "La Russie et l'Angleterre dans l'Asie Centrale," *Revue des Deux Mondes*, June 1 and August 1, 1867. 2 parts.

Lenczowski, George. Russia and the West in Iran: 1913–1948. Ithaca, N.Y., 1949.

Lenin, V. I. The National Liberation Movement in the East. Moscow, 1962.

Lentz, Wolfgang. Ein Lateinalphabet für das Paschto. Berlin, 1937.

Lerner, Daniel. The Passing of Traditional Society. 1st ed. Glencoe, Ill., 1958. Paperback ed. New York, 1964.

Le Strange, G. The Lands of the Eastern Caliphate. Cambridge, Eng., 1905.

Lewin, Evans. The German Road to the East. London, 1916.

Lewis, Arthur. George Maxwell Gordon: The Pilgrim Missionary of the Punjab. A History of His Life and Work, 1839–1880. London, 1889.

Lewis, Bernard. The Arabs in History. 3d ed. London, 1956.

———. The Emergence of Modern Turkey. Oxford, 1961.

———. "The Muslim Discovery of Europe," *BSOAS*, XX (1957).

———. "Some Observations on the Significance of Heresy in the History of Islam," *Studia Islamica*, I (1953).

———. Turkey Today. London, 1940.

Lewis, Bernard, and P. M. Holt, eds. Historians of the Middle East. Oxford, 1962.

Lichtenstadter, Ilse. Islam and the Modern Age: An Analysis and an Appraisal. New York, 1958.

"Life of Ahmed Shah, King of the Abdalees," in *The Asiatic Annual Register*, listed above. Translated by Henri Vansittart.

Litvinov, Maxim. Against Aggression. New York, 1939.

Lobanov-Rostovsky, Prince André. Russia and Asia. New York, 1933.

———. "Soviet Russia and Afghanistan," *Asiatic Review*, July 1926.

Lockhart, Lawrence. The Fall of the Safavi Dynasty and the Afghan Occupation of Persia. Cambridge, Eng., 1958.

———. "Nadir Shah," *JRCAS*, April 1939.

———. Nadir Shah. Critical Study Based Mainly Upon Contemporary Sources. London, 1938.

———. Persian Cities. London, 1960.

———. "The Political Testament of Peter the Great," *Slavonic Review*, XIV (1936).

Löewenthal, Rudolf. The Judeo-Muslim Marranos of Bukhara. Central Asian Collectanea, No. 1. Washington, D.C., 1958.

———. "Les Juifs de Boukhara," *Cahiers du Monde Russe et Soviétique*, January-March 1961.

———. The Turkic Languages and Literatures of Central Asia: Bibliography. The Hague, 1957.

Logofet, D. N. Bukharskoe khanstvo pod russkim protektoratom. St. Petersburg, 1911. 2 vols.

Longrigg, S. H. Four Centuries of Modern Iraq. Oxford, 1925.

Longworth-Dames, M. "Afghanistan," in Vol. I, *EI*, 1st ed.

———. The Baloch Race, a Historical and Ethnographical Sketch. London, 1904.

———. "Ghāznāwids," in Vol. II, *EI*, 1st ed.

———. "Hazara," in Vol. II, *EI*, 1st ed.

———. "The Portuguese and the Turks in the Indian Ocean in the Sixteenth Century," *Journal of the Royal Asian Society*, 1921.

Lopez, R. "Les influences orientales et l'éveil économique de l'Occident," *JWH*, I (1954), 3.

Lord, Percival B. "Some Account of a Visit to the Palin of Koh-i-Daman, the Mining District of Ghorband, and the Pass of Hindu Kush," *JASB*, June 1838.

Lorimer, J. G. Customary Law of the Main Tribes in the Peshawar District. 2d ed. Revised by J. G. Acheson. Peshawar, 1934.

———. Grammar and Vocabulary of Waziri Pashto. Calcutta, 1902.

Low, C. R., ed. Life and Correspondence of Field Marshal Sir G. Pollock. London, 1873.

Lowe, C. J. Salisbury and the Mediterranean, 1886–1896. Toronto, 1965.

Ludovico di Varthema. The Travels of Ludovico di Varthema in Egypt, Syria, Arabia, Persia and India. Translated by John W. Jones. London, 1863.

Lumsden, H. B. "Report on the Yusufzai District," in Vol. I, Selections from the Public Correspondence of the Administration for the Affairs of Punjab, 1853. Lahore, 1857.

Lumsden, Peter. "Countries and Tribes Bordering on the Kohi-Baba Range," *Proceedings of the Royal Geographical Society*, VII (1885).

Lumsden, Peter S., and George R. Elsmie. Lumsden of the Guides: A Sketch of the Life of Lieut.-General Sir Harry Burnett Lumsden. 2d ed. London, 1890.

Lyall, Sir Alfred. Life of Marquis of Dufferin and Ava. London, 1905. 2 vols.

Lybyer, A. H. "Afghan Constitution," *Current History*, May 1932.

———. "Afghan Revolt Against Westernization," *Current History*, March 1929.

Lybyer, Albert. "The Influence of the Rise of the Ottoman Turks Upon the Routes of Oriental Trade," *Annual Report*, American Historical Association, I (1916).

Lynch, H. F. B. "Railways in the Middle East," *Proceedings of the Central Asian Society* (London), March 1911.

———. "Railways in the Middle East," *The Asiatic Quarterly Review*, April 1911.

Lyons, James Gervais. Afghanistan: The Buffer State. London, 1910.

MacGregor, C. M., ed. Central Asia: A Contribution Toward the Better Knowledge of the Topography, Ethnography, Statistics, and History of the North-West Frontier of British India. Calcutta, 1871–73. 3 parts.

MacGregor, G. H. "A Geographical Notice of the Valley of Jalalabad," *JASB*, May 1844.

MacKenzie, D. N. "Pashto Verse," *BSOAS*, XXI (1958).

——, trans. Poems from the Divan of Khushhal Khan Khattak. London, 1965.

Maclagan, Sir Edward. "Jesuit Missions to the Emperor Akbar," *JASB*, May 1896.

Maclean, Sir Fitzroy. A Person from England and Other Travelers. New York, 1958.

MacMunn, Sir George. "Afghanistan and India," *The Asiatic Review*, April 1928.

——. "Afghanistan and the Outer World," *The Nineteenth Century and After*, March 1928.

——. Afghanistan from Darius to Amanullah. London, 1929.

——. "The Centenary of the Tripartite Treaty and the British First Entry into Afghanistan," *Army Quarterly*, April 1939.

——. The Martial Races of India. London, 1933.

——. "Real British Attitude Towards Afghanistan," *Journal of Royal Artillery*, January 1929.

——. "Reviving the Russian Menace to India: Dangerous Situation in Afghan Turkestan," *World Today* (London), July 1929.

——. "Strategic Position of Afghanistan," *Great Britain and the East*, February 11, 1937.

——. "The Tragedy of the Afghan Throne," *The Nineteenth Century and After*, December 1933.

MacPherson, D. Annals of Commerce, Manufactures, Fisheries, and Navigations. London, 1805. 4 vols.

Macrory, Patrick. Signal Catastrophe: The Story of the Disastrous Retreat from Kabul, 1842. London, 1966.

Mahfouz, Imza. "En Asie. II: Afghanistan," *Revue des Etudes Islamiques*, 1937.

Mahmoud, Shah. "The Balance of Payments Problem in Underdeveloped Nations: A Case Study of Afghanistan," Ph.D. Dissertation, Columbia University, 1964.

Mahmud, Syed. The Khilafat and England. Patna, 1921.

Maillart, E. "Afghanistan's Rebirth," *JRCAS*, April 1940. Interview with H.R.H. Hashim Khan in 1937.

Maiskii, I. Vneshniaia politika RSFSR 1917–1922. Moscow, 1922.

Majrouh, S. B. "Etude du Destar-Nama de Khoshhal Khan Khatak," in Vol. II, *TDPMKV*. Moscow, 1962.

Malcolm, Sir John. The History of Persia from the Most Early Period to the Present Time. London, 1815. 2 vols.

Malleson, G. B. Herat: The Granary and the Garden of Central Asia. London, 1880.

——. History of Afghanistan from the Earliest Period to the Outbreak of the War of 1878. London, 1879.

——. The Russo-Afghan Question and the Invasion of India. 2d ed. London, 1885.

Mamayev, I. I. Economic Geography of Foreign Countries. Leningrad, 1957.

Mannanov, B. Iz istorii russko-iranskikh otnoshenii v kontse XIX-nachale XX veka. Tashkent, 1964.

Manrique, Fray Sebastien. Travels of Fray Sebastien Manrique, 1629–1643. Translated by C. Eckford Luard and H. Hösten, S.J. Oxford, 1927. 2 vols.

Manucci, N. Storia do Mogor or Mogul India. Edited by W. Irvine. London, 1907–8. 4 vols.

Marchioness of Dufferin and Ava. Our Viceregal Life in India. London, 1890. 2 vols.

Marco Polo. La description du monde. Translated into French by Louis Hambis. Paris, 1955.

Marin, Louis. "L'Afghanistan et la France," *L'Asie Française,* July 1923.

——. "L'entrée en relations independantes de l'Afghanistan avec les puissances," *L'Asie Française,* May 1923.

Marriott, J. A. R. The Eastern Question: An Historical Study in European Diplomacy. 4th ed. Oxford, 1951.

Marsh, H. C. A Ride Through Islam, Being an Overland Journey to India via Khorassan, Herat, and Afghanistan in the Year 1872. Allahabad, 1874.

Marshall, G. S. Hodgson. "The Unity of Later Islamic History," *JWH,* V (1960), 2.

Marshall, Sir John. The Buddhist Art of Gandhara. Cambridge, Eng., 1960.

——. Taxila. Cambridge, Eng., 1951. 3 vols.

Martens, F., ed. Recueil des traités et conventions conclus par la Russie avec les puissances étrangères. St. Petersburg, 1874–1906. 15 vols. Vol. XII.

Martens, M. F. de. La Russie et l'Angleterre dans l'Asie Centrale. Gand, 1879.

Martin, B. G. German-Persian Diplomatic Relations 1873–1912. The Hague, 1959.

Martin, Frank A. Under the Absolute Amir. New York, 1907.

Martin, Montgomery, ed. Despatches, Minutes and Correspondence of the Marquess Wellesley. London, 1836–37. 5 vols.

Martineau, John. The Life and Correspondence of Sir Bartle Frere. London, 1895. 2 vols.

Marvin, Charles T. The Russian Advance Toward India; Conversations with Skobeleff, Ignatieff, and Other Distinguished Russian Generals and Statesmen on the Central Asian Question. London, 1882.

Massé, Henri. "L'Académie afghane et ses publications. Appendice: la presse en Afghanistan," *Revue des Etudes Islamiques,* 1939.

Massignon, Louis. Annuaire du monde musulman: 1954. Paris, 1955.

——. "Etudes sur les corporations musulmanes indo-persanes," *Revue des Etudes Islamiques,* 1927.

——. "Guilds," in E. R. A. Seligman and A. Johnson, eds., Encyclopedia of the Social Sciences. New York, 1937.

——, ed. L'Islam et l'Occident. Special Issue of *Cahiers du Sud,* 1947.

Masson, Charles. "Journals," in Forrest, *Selections from Travels,* listed above.

——. "Memoir on the Ancient Coins Found at Beghram, in the Kohistan of Kabul," *JASB,* April 1834.

——. Narrative of Various Journeys in Baloochistan, Afghanistan, the Panjab and Kalat, Including a Residence in Those Countries from 1826 to 1838. London, 1842. 3 vols.

——. "Notes on the Antiquities of Bamian," *JASB,* November 1836.

Masson, P. Histoire du commerce français dans le Levant au XVIIIᵉ siècle. Paris, 1911.

Masson, V. M., and V. A. Romodin. Istoriia Afganistana. Moscow, 1964–65. 2 vols.

Maunier, René. The Sociology of Colonies: An Introduction to the Study of Race Contact. London, 1949. 2 vols.

Mayer, T. J. L., trans. The New Testament in Pashtu. London, 1890.

McCrindle, J. W. The Invasion of India by Alexander the Great. Westminster, 1896.

McNeill, John. Progress and Present Position of Russia in the East. London, 1836.

Mead, Margaret, ed. Culture Patterns and Technical Change. Paris, 1953.

Meakin, Annette M. B. In Russian Turkestan: A Garden of Asia and Its People. London, 1903.

Mears-Grinnell, Eliot. Modern Turkey. New York, 1924.

Mércère, E. de. Une ambassade à Constantinople: la politique orientale de la Révolution Française. Paris, 1927. 2 vols.

Merritt, Abrash. "Personalities Behind Policies: Studies of Seven Leading Figures in Anglo-Russian Relations, 1855–1895," Ph.D. Dissertation, Columbia University, 1961.

Metta, Vasudeo B. "Afghanistan Under a Modern Ruler," *Current History*, April 1927.

———. "Changing Afghanistan," *United Empire*, November 1939.

Meyendorf, Baron G. von. A Journey from Orenburg to Bokhara in the Year 1820. Jena, 1826.

Meyendorff, Baron A., ed. Correspondence diplomatique de M. de Staal 1884–1900. Paris, 1929. 2 vols.

Micaud, Charles A. Tunisia: The Politics of Modernization. New York, 1964.

Michel, Aloys A. "Foreign Trade and Foreign Policy in Afghanistan," *Middle Eastern Affairs*, January 1961.

———. The Kabul, Kunduz and Helmand Valleys and the National Economy of Afghanistan: A Study of Regional Resources and the Comparative Advantages of Development. (National Academy of Sciences.) Washington, D.C., 1959.

———. "On Writing the Geography of Strange Lands and Faraway Places— Afghanistan for Example. A Review Article," *Economic Geography*, No. 36 (1960).

Middleton, K. W. B. Britain and Russia. London, 1947.

Milburn, William. Oriental Commerce. London, 1813. 2 vols.

Mill, James. The History of British India. 4th ed. London, 1898. Vol. I.

Minorsky, V. "Iran: Opposition, Martyrdom and Revolt," in G. E. von Grunebaum, *Unity and Variety*, listed above.

———. "The Turkish Dialect of the Khalaj," *BSOAS*, X (1940–42).

Mīr Khwānd (Mohammed b. Khāwand-Shah b. Mahmud). Raudat-al Safā fi sīrat al anbiyā, wa'l muluk w'al Khulāfā. (Partially translated into French; see Defrémery, *Histoire des Samanides*, listed above.)

Mirza, Bakar Ali. "Congress Against Imperialism," *The Modern Review*, January-June 1927.

Mīrzā Lūtfallāh Khān. Jamāl al-Dīn al-Asadabadi. Translated into Arabic by S. Nash'at and A. Hasanayn. Cairo, 1957.

Mitford, R. C. W. To Cabul with the Cavalry Brigade. London, 1881.

Mohendis, L. "L'Afghanistan et son Padischah," *Journal des Débats*, January 27, 1928.

Molesworth, G. N. Afghanistan, 1919. An Account of Operations in the Third Afghan War. New York, 1962.

Mona'am, Abdul Majid Khan. "Andarz," *MH*, 7th year, No. 4-5.

Monserrate, Father. The Commentary of Father Monserrate, S.J., on His Journey to the Court of Akbar. Translated by J. S. Hoyland and S. W. Banerjee. Oxford, 1922.

Monypenny, W. F., and G. E. Buckle. The Life of Benjamin Disraeli, Earl of Beaconsfield. London, 1913–20. 6 vols.

Moorcroft, William, and George Trebeck. Travels in the Himalayan Provinces of Hindostan and the Punjab; in Ladakh and Kashmir; in Peshawar, Kabul, Kunduz and Bokhara from 1819 to 1825. London, 1841. 2 vols.

Morgan, E. D., and C. H. Coote, eds. Early Voyages and Travels to Russia and Persia by Anthony Jenkinson and Other Englishmen. London, 1886. 2 vols.

Morgenstierne, G. "Afghān," in Vol. I, *EI*, 2d ed.

――――. "Afghanistan" (portions dealing with ethnography, languages, religion), in Vol. I, *EI*, 2d ed.

――――. An Etymological Vocabulary of Pashto. Oslo, 1927.

――――. The Indo-Iranian Frontier Languages. Oslo, 1929–56. 4 vols.

――――. "Khushhal Khan—The National Poet of the Afghans," *JRCAS*, January 1960.

――――. Report on Linguistic Mission to Afghanistan. Oslo, 1926.

Morison, J. L. "From Alexander Burnes to Frederick Roberts: A Survey of Imperial Frontier Policy," *Proceedings of the British Academy*, XXII (1936).

Morrish, C. Afghanistan in the Melting Pot. Lahore, 1930.

Morrison, Ronald M. S. "Afghanistan Today," *The Near East*, February 28, 1935.

――――. "H.M. King Mohammed Nadir Shah-i-Ghazi of Afghanistan" (obituary), *JRCAS*, January 1934.

――――. "Military Efficiency in Afghanistan," *The Near East*, July 11, 1935.

Mosely, Philip E. Russian Diplomacy and the Opening of the Eastern Question: 1838–9. Cambridge, Mass., 1934.

――――. "Russian Policy in Asia: 1838–39," *Slavonic Review*, April 1936.

――――. "Russian Policy in 1911–12" (review), *The Journal of Modern History*, March 1940.

Moser, Henri. A travers l'Asie Centrale: la steppe Kirghize, le Turkestan Russe, Boukhara, Khiva, le pays des Turcomans et la Perse. Impression de voyage. Paris, 1886.

Mostaghni. "Ehtiajat-e asri," *Kabul*, 1st year, No. 11.

――――. "Elm va amal," *Kabul*, 1st year, No. 9.

――――. "Mobareze dar hayat," *Kabul*, 1st year, No. 7.

――――. "Tashvigh be elm va fann," *Kabul*, 1st year, No. 6.

Mouraviev (Mouravieff), M. N. Voyage en Turcomanie et à Khiva fait en

1819 et 1820. Translated into French by M. G. Lacointe de Laveau. Paris, 1823.

Mourey, Charles. "Affaires d'Afghanistan: la traité de paix du 8 août," *L'Asie Française*, August-November 1919.

Muhammad, Sher. Asr-e Saadat. Kabul, n.d. [?1925].

Muhammad Khan, Shir. Tawārikh-i Khwurshid-i Jahan. Lahore, 1894.

Muhammed Khan, Ali. "Progress in Afghanistan," *The Asiatic Review*, October 1936.

Muhieddin (Muhyi al-Din). Bohran va najat-e vatan. Kabul, 1931.

Munawwar Khan. Anglo-Afghan Relations: 1798–1878. A Chapter in the Great Game in Central Asia. Peshawar, 1963.

Mundy, Peter. The Travels of Peter Mundy in Europe and Asia, 1608–1667. London, 1914. Vol. II.

Munshi. "Andarz," *MH*, 7th year, No. 6.

Munshi, Mir Sultan Mahomed Khan, ed. The Life of Abdur Rahman: Amir of Afghanistan. London, 1900. 2 vols.

Munshizadeh, Muhammed Beshir Khan. "Zendegani va gharn-e hazer," *Kabul*, 1st year, No. 8.

Mury, Francis. "L'Inde anglaise réclame des libertés," *A Travers le Monde*, May 30, 1908.

Nafisi, Saïd. Tarikh-e ejtemaii va siyasi-ye Iran. Tehran, 1956–57. 2 vols.

Naimi, Ali Ahmad Khan. "Afghan Calligraphy," *Afghanistan*, January-March 1946.

———. "Baazi az ekhteraat-e jadid," *Kaboul Almanach: 1939–40*.

Najib Ullah. "Afghanistan in Historical Perspective," in Princeton University Conference, *Current Problems*, listed below.

———. "Pakhtoonistan," *Afghanistan*, April-June 1948.

Nakhaii, M. L'évolution politique de l'Iran. Brussels, 1938.

Napier, W. F. P. The Conquest of Scinde. 2d ed. London, 1845.

Nariman, G. K. "Afghanistan Today," *Islamic Culture*, April 1927.

Nash, Charles. History of War in Afghanistan. London, 1843.

Nazim, Muhammad. The Life and Times of the Sūltān Mahmūd of Ghazna. Cambridge, Eng., 1931.

Nebel, H. C. "Japan Enters Afghanistan," *Living Age*, March 1935.

Nechkina, M. V., ed. Istoriia S.S.S.R. Moscow, 1941. Vol. II.

Negri, C. Rifessioni geografiche e politiche sur progetti inglesi e russi di nuove communicazioni ferroviarie fra l'Europa e l'Asia. Milan, 1878.

Nessawī. Sirāt-al-Sultān Djelal-ed-Din Mankobirti. Translated into French by O. Houdas. Paris, 1895.

Nesterevich, S. "Russkie puteshestvenniki v Afganistane," *Zvezda Vostoka* (Tashkent), 1958, No. 3.

"New Rulers in Kabul: Order Out of Chaos," *The Times* (London), July 13, 1936.

Nicolson, Harold. Curzon: The Last Phase 1919–1925. A Study in Post-War Diplomacy. London, 1934.

———. Sir Arthur Nicolson, First Lord Carnock: A Study in the Old Diplomacy. London, 1930.

Niedermayer, Oskar von. Afghanistan. Leipzig, 1924.

————. Im Weltkrieg von Indiens Toren. Hamburg, 1942.

Niedermayer, Oskar von, and E. Diez. Unter der Glutsonne Irans. Dachau, 1925.

Nikitine, B. "L'Afghanistan dans la politique internationale," *Revue des Sciences Politiques*, March 1927.

————. "L'Asie qui change," *L'Asie Française*, January 1930.

————. "L'Asie Russe économique," *L'Asie Française*, May 1928.

————. "Orientalisme révolutionnaire: étude des methodes bolchevistes," *L'Asie Française*, February and March 1931. 2 parts.

Nikitine, M. La mentalité afghane moderne. Extract from the *Bulletin de la Société d'Ethnographie*. Paris, 1929.

Nikulin, L. V. Zapiski sputnika. Leningrad, 1932.

Nizām ul-Mūlk. Siyaset Nāmeh. Translated into French by C. Schéfer. Paris, 1893.

Nollau, Günther, and Hans Jürgen Wiehe. Russia's South Flank. Translated by V. Andersen. New York, 1963.

Norris, J. A. The First Afghan War, 1838–1842. Cambridge, Eng., 1967.

"Notice of the Peculiar Tenets Held by the Followers of Syed Ahmed, Taken Chiefly from the '*Sirāt ul Mūstaqīm*; a Principal Treatise of the Sect Written by Moulavi Mahommed Ismail," *JASB*, November 1832.

Notovitch, Nicolas. La Russie et l'alliance anglaise. Paris, 1906.

Noyce, F. England, India and Afghanistan. London, 1902.

Nubee, Haji Abdun (of Kabul). "Notes Taken on a Tour Through Parts of Baloochistan in 1838 and 1839," *JASB*, March and April 1844. 2 parts.

Nusraty, Mohammad Karim. "Some Economic Institutions and Problems in Afghanistan," M.A. Thesis, Stanford University, 1955.

O'Donovan, Edmond. The Merv Oasis: Travels and Adventures East of the Caspian During the Years 1879–80–81, Including Five Months Residence Among the Tekké's of Merv. London, 1882. 2 vols.

O'Dwyer, Sir Michael. India As I Knew It, 1885–1925. London, 1925.

Oliver, E. E. Across the Border, or Pathan and Biloch. London, 1890.

O'Malley, Lewis S. S., ed. Modern India and the West: A Study of the Interaction of Their Civilizations. Oxford, 1941.

"The Outbreak in Kabul and Its Causes," *Calcutta Review*, December 1850.

Outram, James. Rough Notes of the Campaign in Sinde and Afghanistan in 1838–9, Being Extracts from a Personal Journal. London, 1840.

Owen, S. J. A Selection from the Despatches, Treaties and Other Papers of Marquess Wellesley. Oxford, 1877.

Padshah Khan, Gul. "Shariat ya rahbar-e saadat," *Al-Falah*, 7th year, No. 7.

Panikkar, K. M. The Afro-Asian States and Their Problems. New York, 1959.

————. India and the Indian Ocean: An Essay on the Influence of Sea Power on Indian History. New York, 1945.

"Le Pan-Islamisme et le Pan-Turquisme," *RMM*, March 1913. Signed "X."

Pankratova, A. M. Razvitie kapitalizma v Rossii i vozniknovenie rabochego dvizheniia. Moscow, 1947.

Pardis, Muhammed Ibrahim Khan. "Islam," *Al-Falah*, 7th year, No. 11.

Park, Alexander G. Bolshevism in Turkestan, 1917–1927. New York, 1957.

Parkyn, S. S. Transport in Southern Afghanistan, 1878–1880. London, 1882.

Paul, Arthur. "Role of Trade in Afghanistan's Development," *Asia Foundation Program Bulletin*, December 1963.

Pavlovich, M. "SSSR i vostok," in Vol. I, Revoliutsionnyi Vostok. Moscow and Leningrad, 1927.

Pavlovitch, Michel. "La Russie et le problème des chemins de fer en Perse," *L'Asie Française*, January 1912.

Pazhwak, Abdur Rahman Khan. Afghanistan, Ancient Aryana. London, 1958.

——. "Taamelat-e hughughi va jazaye-ye melli, *Kaboul Almanach: 1939–40*.

Pearce, R. R. Memoirs and Correspondence of Marquess Wellesley. London, 1846. 3 vols.

Peaslee, Amos J., ed. Constitutions of Nations. 2d ed. London, 1956. Vol. I.

Pedersen, J. "Māsjid," in Wensinck and Kramers, eds., Handworterbuch des Islam. Leiden, 1941.

Pelliot, Paul. Chrétiens d'Asie Centrale et d'Extrême Orient. T'Oung-Pao, 1914.

——. "Christianity in Central Asia in the Middle Ages," *JCAS*, July 1930.

——. "Les Mongols et la Papauté," *La Revue de l'Orient Chrétien*, XXIII (1922–23), XXIV (1924), and XXVIII (1931–32). 3 parts.

Pelly, Lewis, ed. Views and Opinions of General John Jacob. London, 1858.

Pennell, A. M. "The Afghans of Thal," *Church Missionary Review*, March 1920.

Pennell, T. L. Among the Wild Tribes of the Afghan Frontier. London, 1909.

Pensa, Henri. Les Russes et les Anglais en Afghanistan. Paris, n.d.

Penzl, Herbert. A Grammar of Pashto; A Descriptive Study of the Dialect of Kandahar, Afghanistan. Washington, D.C., 1955.

Pernot, Maurice. "Awakening of Afghanistan," *Living Age*, July 1925.

——. "La défaite d'Amanoullah," *Journal des Débats*, January 18, 1929.

——. L'inquiétude de l'Orient. En Asie musulmane. Paris, 1927.

——. "L'inquiétude de l'Orient," *Revue des Deux Mondes*, January 1927.

——. "L'oeuvre de la France en Afghanistan," *Journal des Débats*, July 17, 1925.

——. "Les réformes en Afghanistan," *Journal des Débats*, July 10, 1925.

——. "Les troubles d'Afghanistan," *Journal des Débats*, January 4, 1929.

Perrin, N. L'Afghanistan. Paris, 1842.

Peter, H.R.H., the Prince of Greece and Denmark. "The Post-War Developments in Afghanistan," *JRCAS*, July-October 1951.

Peterson, F. G. R. "Through the Khyber to Kabul," *The Listener* (London), 1932.

Petrushevskii, I. P. Zemledelie i agrarnye otnosheniia v Irane XIII–XIV vekov. Moscow, 1960.

Phillips, C. H., ed. The Correspondence of David Scott Relating to Indian Affairs, 1787–1805. London, 1951. 2 vols.

Phillips, Paul A. M. Van. Public Finance and Less Developed Economy. The Hague, 1957.

Pichon, Jean. Les origines orientales de la guerre mondiale. Paris, 1937.

——. Le partage du Proche-Orient. Paris, 1938.

Pierce, Richard A. Russian Central Asia, 1867–1917. Berkeley, Calif., 1960.

Pikulin, M. G. Afganistan (ekonomicheskii ocherk). Tashkent, 1956.

————. Razvitie natsionalnoi ekonomiki i kulturi Afganistana, 1955–1960. Tashkent, 1961.

Pinkerton, J., ed. A General Collection of the Best and Most Interesting Voyages and Travels. London, 1811. 17 vols.

Pipes, Richard E. "Russian Muslims Before and After the Revolution," in Waldemar Gurian, ed., Soviet Imperialism: Its Origins and Tactics. Notre Dame, Ind., 1953.

Plaisted, Bartholomew. A Journal from Calcutta in Bengal by Sea to Bussrah, From Thence Across the Great Desert to Aleppo in 1750. London, 1758.

Pokrovskii, M. N., and A. L. Popov. "Tsarskaia diplomatiia o zadachakh Rossii na Vostoke v 1900 g.," *Krasnyi Arkhiv*, V, 18 (1926).

Poliak, Aleksandr A. Ekonomicheskii stroi Afganistana (ocherki). Moscow, 1964.

————. "Sel'skoe Khoziaistvo," in Dvoriankov, listed above.

Polk, W. R. "The Nature of Modernization," *Foreign Affairs*, October 1965.

Polovtsoff, A. The Land of Timur. Recollections of Russian Turkestan. London, 1932.

Popov, A. L. "Angliskaiia politika v Indii: Russko-Indiiskii otnocheniia v 1897–1905 gg.," *Krasnyi Arkhiv*, VI, 19 (1926).

————. "Iz istorii zavoevaniia Srednei Azii," *Istoricheskie Zapiski*, IX (1940).

Popowski, Josef. The Rival Powers in Central Asia: The Struggle Between England and Russia in the East. Translated by C. E. D. Black. Westminster, 1893.

Potemkin, Vladimir P., ed. Histoire de la diplomatie. Translated into French by Xenia Pamphilova and Michel Eristov. Paris, 1946–47. 3 vols.

Potocki, Jean. Voyages dans les steppes d'Astrakhan et du Caucase. Paris, 1829. 2 vols.

Potocki, Joseph. "Afghanistan Looks Abroad," *Foreign Affairs*, October 1928.

Pottinger, Henry. Travels in Beloochistan and Sinde. London, 1816.

Poulada, Leon B. "Problems of Social Development in Afghanistan," *JRCAS*, January 1962. Also appears in Princeton University Conference, *Current Problems*, listed below.

Power, Eileen. "The Opening of the Land Routes to Cathay," in Arthur P. Newton, ed., Travel and Travellers of the Middle Ages. London, 1926.

Prasad, Bisheshwar. The Foundations of India's Foreign Policy. Calcutta, 1955. Vol. I.

Prasad, M. Ishwari. L'Inde du VIIᵉ au XVIᵉ siècle. Paris, 1937.

Pratap, Mahendra. Afghanistan, the Heart of Aryan. (Publication of the World Federation.) Peiping, n.d. [?1929].

————. "My German Mission to High Asia," *Asia*, May 1925.

————. My Life Story of Fifty-Five Years. Delhi, 1947.

Prawdin, Michael. L'empire mongol et Tamerlan. Paris, 1937.

Prentout, H. L'Ile de France sous Décaen, 1803–1810. Paris, 1901.

Price, M. Philips. "Impressions of Afghanistan and the N.W. Frontier," *The Islamic Review*, June 1949.

————. "The Present Situation in Persia," *JRCAS*, April-July 1951.

————. "A Visit to Afghanistan," *JRCAS*, April 1949.

Princeton University Conference. Current Problems in Afghanistan. Princeton, N.J., 1961.

"Problems of Afghanistan," *The Near East*, March 18, 1926.

Prothero, G. W. Mohammedan History. London, 1920.

Puliarkin, V. A. Afganistan. Ekonomicheskaia geografiia. Moscow, 1964.

Purchas, Samuel, the Elder. Hakluytus Posthumus, or Purchas his Pilgrimes. Edited by James MacLehose. Glasgow, 1905–7. 20 vols.

Puretskii, B. "Poeticheskoe tvorchestvo afgantsev," *Novyi Mir* (Moscow), 1927, No. 3.

Puryear, Vernon J. England, Russia, and the Straits Question, 1844–1856. Berkeley, Calif., 1931.

———. International Economics and Diplomacy in the Near East. Stanford. Calif., 1935.

Pyarelal, Nair. A Pilgrimage for Peace. Gandhi and Frontier Gandhi. Ahmedabad, 1950.

Qadir Khan, Abdul. "Afghanistan in 1934," *JRCAS*, April 1935.

———. "Afghanistan Since the Revolution," *JRCAS*, July 1930.

———. "Economic Reconstruction of Afghanistan," *Great Britain and the East*, February 27, 1936.

———. "Modern Afghanistan; Summary," *The Near East*, January 31, 1935.

———. "The Outlook in Afghanistan," *JRCAS*, July 1932.

Qadir Khan, Muhammad. "Karkhaneha dar Afghanestan," *Kaboul Almanach: 1941–42.*

———. "Mokhtasari az taraghiat-e eghtesadi," *Kaboul Almanach: 1941–42.*

Qaiyum, Abdul. Gold and Guns on the Pathan Frontier. Bombay, 1945.

Quaroni, Pietro. Il mondo di un ambasciatore. Milan, 1965.

Qāzwinī, Hamd Allāh. Tarikh-i-Guzida. Abridged and translated by E. G. Browne. London, 1913.

Qureshi, Anwar Iqbal. Islam and the Theory of Interest. Lahore, 1945.

Qureshi, S. M. M. "Pakhtunistan: the Frontier Dispute Between Afghanistan and Pakistan," *Pacific Affairs*, Spring-Summer 1966.

Radau, R. "Les routes de l'avenir à travers l'Asie," *Revue des Deux Mondes*, July 15, 1876.

Radolff, T. "Itinéraire de la vallée du moyen Zéréfchan," in Schérzer and Léger, listed below.

Rahim, M. A. History of the Afghans in India: A.D. 1545–1631, with Especial Reference to Their Relations with Mughals. Karachi, 1961.

———. "The Nature of the Afghan Monarchy and the Position of the Afghan Chiefs," *Journal of Pakistan Historical Society*, 1956, No. 4.

Rahman, F. "Internal Religious Developments in Present Century Islam," *JWH*, II (1955), 4.

———. "Modern Muslim Thought," *Muslim World*, January 1955.

———. "Muslim Modernism (Religious Reform Movement) in the Indo-Pakistan Subcontinent," *BSOAS*, XXI (1958), 1.

Rahmany, Magdaline. "Deux poétesses afghanes du XIII siècle," *Afghanistan*, January-March 1952.

———. "La société féminine de bienfaisance," *Afghanistan*, October-December 1954.

Ramazani, Rouholla K. "Afghanistan and the U.S.S.R.," *MEJ*, Spring 1958. For a reply by S. M. Haq, see *MEJ*, Winter 1959.

———. "Cultural Change and Intellectual Response in Algeria, Tunisia and Iran," *Comparative Studies in Society and History*, January 1964.

———. The Foreign Policy of Iran, 1500–1941. Charlottesville, Va., 1966.

———. The Northern Tier: Afghanistan, Iran and Turkey. Princeton, N.J., 1966.

Rao, M. V. Krishna. The Growth of Indian Liberalism in the XIX Century. Mysore, 1951.

Raskolnikov, F. F. Afganistan i angliiskii ultimatum. Moscow, 1924.

———. "Rossiia i Afganistan," *Novyi Vostok* (Moscow), 1923, No. 4.

———. "The War in Afghanistan," *The Labour Monthly* (London), March 1929.

Rastogi, Ram Sagar. Indo-Afghan Relations: 1880–1900. Lucknow, 1965.

Raverty, Henry G., ed. The Gulshan-i-Roh, Being Selections, Prose, and Poetical in the Pushto or Afghan Language. London, 1860.

Raverty, Henry G. "The Independent Afghan or Pathan Tribes," *The Imperial and Asiatic Quarterly Review*, April 1894.

———. Muscovite Proceedings on the Afghan Frontier. London, 1885.

———. Notes on Afghanistan and Part of Baloochistan, Geographical, Ethnographical and Historical, Extracted from the Writings of Little-Known Afghan and Tajzzik Historians, Geographers and Genealogists, the Histories of the Ghuris, the Turk Sovereigns of the House of Timur and Other Muhammedan Chronicles; and from Personal Observations. London, 1881.

———. "Notes on Kaffiristan," *JASB*, April 1859.

———. "Notes on Kokand, Kashgar, Yarkand and Other Places in Central Asia," *JASB*, April 1857.

———. Pukhto Grammar. London, 1867.

———. Selections from the Poetry of the Afghans. London, 1890.

Rawlinson, George. A Memoir of Major-General Sir Henry C. Rawlinson. London, 1898.

Rawlinson, Sir Henry C. England and Russia in the East. London, 1875.

———. "Report on the Dooranee Tribes dated 19th April 1841," in Part 2 of C. M. MacGregor, *Central Asia*, listed above.

———. "The Results of the Afghan War," *The Nineteenth Century*, August 1879.

———. "The Situation in Afghanistan," *The Nineteenth Century*, February 1880.

Ray, Sibnarayan, ed. M. N. Roy, Philosopher-Revolutionary. Calcutta, 1959.

Reclus, Elisée, ed. Nouvelle géographie universelle. Paris, 1884. Vol. IX.

Rejaii, Muhammad Ibrahim Khan. "Adabiyat dar asr-e tajaddod," *MH*, 7th year, No. 7-8.

———. "Avalem-e ezdevaj," *MH*, 7th year, No. 7-8.

———. "Ejtemiyat," *MH*, 7th year, No. 3.

———. "Ghazal," *MH*, 7th year, No. 3.

———. "Taasir-e mohit bar adabiyat," *MH*, 7th year, No. 6.

Repington, C. A. La première guerre mondiale. Paris, 1924.

Resai, Mohammed Ismail. Struktur und Entwicklungs-möglichkeiten der Wirtschaft von Afganistan. Bonn, 1958.

Reshtiya (Rushtiya), Qasim. Afghanestan dar gharn-e nouzdah. Kabul, 1950. For a Russian translation of this work, see Iu. V. Gankovskii, Afganistan v XIX veke. Moscow, 1958.

————. "L'Afghanistan au point de vue géographique," *Afghanistan*, January-March 1947.

————. "L'Afghanistan moderne," *Kaboul Almanach: 1938–39*.

————. "Education in Afghanistan," *Afghanistan*, January-March 1946.

————. "Journalism in Afghanistan," *Afghanistan*, April-June 1948.

————. "Kabul Calling," *Afghanistan*, April-June 1946.

————. "The Rivers of Afghanistan,' *Afghanistan*, April-June 1947.

"The Revolt in Transcaspia 1918–1919," *CAR*, VII (1959).

"La révolution persane et l'accord anglo-russe," *Revue des Deux Mondes*, April 1, 1908.

Reyser, M. G. Afganistan, ekonomiko-geograficheskaia kharakteristika. Moscow, 1946.

Reysner (Reisner), I. M. Afghanistan. Moscow, 1929.

————. "Anglo-russkaiia konventsia 1907 goda i razdel Afganistana," *Krasnyi Arkhiv*, III, 10 (1925).

————. "Desiat let vneshnei politiki Afganistana," *Novyi Vostok* (Moscow), 1928, No. 22.

————. Nezavisimyi Afganistan. Moscow, 1928.

————, ed. Noveishaia istoriia stran zarubezhnogo vostoka. Moscow, 1954. Vol. I.

————. "Padenie derzhavy Sefevidov i nashestvie afgantsev na Iran (1722–1729 gg.)," *Doklady i soobshcheniia M.G.U.*, X, 1950.

————. "Pervaia russkaia revoliutsiia i probuzhdenie Azii," *Prepodavanie istorii v shkole*, 1955, No. 5.

————. Razvitie feodalizma i obrazovanie gosudarstva u afgantsev. Moscow, 1954.

————. "Reaktsionnye idei v sovremennoi istoriografii Afganistana," *Vestnik Akademii Nauk SSR*, 1948, No. 5.

————. "Russkaia revoliutsiia 1905–1907 gg. i probuzhdenie Azii," *SV*, 1955, No. 2.

————. Strany Vostoka. Moscow, 1936.

Reysner, I. M., and B. K. Rubtsov. Novaiia istoriia stran zarubezhnogo vostoka. Moscow, 1952. 2 vols.

Rhein, Eberhard, and A. Ghanie Ghaussy. Die Wirtschaftliche Entwiklung Afghanistans 1880–1965. Opladen, 1966.

Ridgeway, R. T. I. Pathans. Calcutta, 1918.

Riza Qouly Khan. Relation de l'ambassade au Kharezm de R. Q. Khan. Translated by C. Schéfer. Paris, 1876–79.

Roashan, Mohammed Khalid. Afghanistan: Development in Brief. London, 1958.

Roberts, F. S., Field Marshal Lord. Forty-One Years in India. London, 1898.

Robertson, Sir George. Kafirs of the Hindu-Kush. 2d ed. London, 1900.

————. Kurum, Kabul, and Kandahar: Three Campaigns Under General Roberts. London, 1881.

Robinson, Nehemiah. Persia and Afghanistan and Their Jewish Communities. New York, 1953.

Rodenbough, T. F. Afghanistan and the Anglo-Russian Dispute. New York and London, 1885.

Roe, Sir Thomas. The Embassy of Sir Thomas Roe to India, 1615–1619. Edited by Sir William Foster. Oxford, 1926.

Romodin, V. A. Afghan Studies. Moscow, 1967. Part of Fifty Years of Soviet Oriental Studies; Brief Reviews 1917–1967.

Rondot, Pierre. "L'évolution sociale de l'Islam contemporain en Orient," *L'Asie Française*, November 1938.

————. "Parliamentary Regimes in the Middle East," *Middle Eastern Affairs*, August-September 1953.

Roome, J. Clive. "The Future of Afghanistan," *The Near East*, March 7, 1919.

Rose, Horace A. "Customs in the Trans-Border Territories of the North-West Frontier Province," *JASB*, Supplement to Vol. LXXIII (1904).

————. A Glossary of the Tribes and Castes of the Punjab and North-West Frontier Province. Lahore, 1919. 3 vols.

Rosenthal, Erwin I. J. Islam in the Modern National State. Cambridge, Eng., 1965.

————. Political Thought in Medieval Islam. Cambridge, Eng., 1958.

Ross, Sir E. Denison. "The Portuguese in India and Arabia Between 1507 and 1517," *Journal of the Royal Asian Society*, 1921.

Ross, Frank E. "An American Adventurer in Central Asia," *Journal of Indian History*, December 1933.

Rossi, E. "Il centenario della nascita di Gemal ud-Din el-Afghani celebrato à Kabul," *Oriente Moderno*, XX (1940).

————. "La costituzione afghāna del 31 ottobre, 1931," *Oriente Moderno*, XIII (1933).

Roueck, Joseph S. "Afghanistan in Geopolitics," *Eastern World*, December 1963.

Roy, B. K. "Angling for Afghanistan," *Asia*, July 1918.

Roy, M. N. Memoirs. New Delhi, 1964. Also published in Amrita Bazar Patrika. Calcutta, 1952– .

Russell, R. India's Danger and Russia's Advance into Afghanistan. The History of the Russian Advance Upon Afghanistan. London, 1885.

Russia. Ministry of Foreign Affairs. Afganskoe razgranichenie; peregovory mezhdu Rossiei i Velikobritanei 1872–1885. St. Petersburg, 1886.

Rustow, Dankwart A. Politics and Westernization in the Near East. Princeton, N.J., 1956.

Rybitschka, Emil. Im Gottgegebenen Afghanistan. Leipzig, 1927.

Rywkin, Michael. Russia in Central Asia. New York, 1963. Paperback.

Saba, Muhammed Sarvar Khan. "Kushesh," *Kabul*, 1st year, No. 8.

Sadigh Khan, Mir Muhammad. "Geografia-ye eghtesadi-ye Afghanestan," *Kaboul Almanach: 1939–40*.

Sadighi, Muhammad Karim Khan. "Bakteriolojy, elm-e halat-e maikrob ya elm-e jarayem," *MH*, 2d year, No. 2.

Safarov, G. "L'Orient et la révolution," *Bulletin Communiste*, April 28, 1921.
Said Ali Khan. "Red Propaganda in the Middle East," *Outlook*, April 2, 1927.
Sainsbury, E. B., ed. Court Minutes, etc., of the East India Company 1635–1679. London, 1907–29. 8 vols.
Sainsbury, W. Noël, ed. Calendar of State Papers. East Indies, 1513–1634. London, 1862–92. 5 vols.
Saise, Walter. "A Visit to Afghanistan," *Proceedings of the Central Asian Society*, April 12, 1911.
Sale, Lady Florentia. A Journal of the Disasters in Afghanistan 1841–2. London, 1843.
Salem, Mir Abdul Rauf Khan. "Ghazal," *MH*, 7th year, No. 3.
Sami, Mahmud. Tarbiyeh-e askariyeh. Kabul, 1909.
Samné, Georges. Le Khalifat et le Pan-Islamisme. Paris, 1919.
Sanhoury, A. Le Califat. Paris, 1926.
Sarkar, Jadunath N. The Fall of the Mughal Empire. Calcutta, 1934–50. 3 vols.
Sarkar, Upendra Nath. "The Merchandise of Peshawar and Neighbouring Markets in 1838," *IHRC*, XXII (1945).
Sassani, Abdul H. See United States, Department of Health, Education and Welfare.
Saunders, J. J. "The Problem of Islamic Decadence," *JWH*, VII (1963), 3.
Saxena, Sri Krishna. "Dr. Lord's Interview with Maharaja Ranjit Singh at Amritsar in 1838 on His Mission to Peshawar," *IHRC*, XXII (1945).
Sazonov, S. Fateful Years: 1909–1916. London, 1928.
Schacht, J. "Classicisme, traditionalisme ankylose dans la loi religieuse de l'Islam," in Brunschvig and Grunebaum, Classicisme et déclin culturel dans l'histoire de l'Islam. Paris, 1957.
———. "Islam, in Vols. VII–VIII, Encyclopedia of the Social Sciences. New York, 1937.
———. "Mirāth" and "Shariā," in Wensinck and Kramers, eds., Handworterbuch des Islam. Leiden, 1941.
Schéfer, C., ed. Description topographique et historique du Boukhara par Moh. Nerchakhy. Paris, 1892.
Schérzer, F., and Louis Léger, eds. Recueil d'itinéraires et de voyages dans l'Asie Centrale et l'Extrême Orient. Paris, 1878.
Schlumberger, Daniel. "Archaeology in Afghanistan," *Archaeology* (Cambridge, Eng.), Spring 1949.
Schurmann, H. F. The Mongols of Afghanistan. The Hague, 1962.
Schuyler, Eugene. Notes of a Journey in Russian Turkistan. London, 1876. 2 vols.
Schwager, Joseph. Die Entwicklung Afghanistans als Staat und Seine Zwischhenstaatlichen Beziehunger. Leipzig, 1932.
Schwarzenbach, Annemarie. "Military Importance of Afghanistan," *Living Age*, August 1940.
Scott, George B. Afghan and Pathan, a Sketch. London, 1929.
Scott, Jonathan, ed. and trans. Ferishta's History of Dakkan, from the First Muhammedan Conquests, etc., and the History of Bengal ... to the Year 1780. London, 1794. 2 vols.

Scott, W. R. Constitution and Finance of English, Scottish, and Irish Joint Stock Companies to 1720. Cambridge, Eng., 1910–12.

Sedqi, Muhammed Osman Khan. "Un aperçu d'histoire de l'art afghane," *Afghanistan*, October-December 1948.

———. "Fehrest-e shahrha-ye Afghanestan," *Kaboul Almanach: 1941–42.*

———. "Les villes d'Ariana," *Afghanistan*, January–September 1952. 3 parts.

Seljuki, Fekri. "Ghazal," *MH*, 7th year, No. 4–5.

———. "Ghazal-e digar," *MH*, 7th year, No. 6.

———. "Hobb-e vatan," *MH*, 7th year, No. 4–5.

———. "Nale-ye shaer," *MH*, 7th year, No. 9–10.

Sen, B. R. "Nationalism and the Asian Awakening," *Annals of the American Academy of Political and Social Science*, July 1952.

Sepahi, Mūhammed Ibrāhim Khān. "Mozār-e esārat va mafad-e hurriet," *MH*, 2d year, No. 5.

Seth, Mesrovb J. Armenians in India. From the Earliest Times to the Present Day. Calcutta, 1937.

Seton-Watson, R. W. Disraeli, Gladstone and the Eastern Question. A Study in Diplomacy and Politics. London, 1935.

Shadbolt, Sydney H. The Afghan Campaign of 1878–1880. London, 1882. 2 vols.

Shafaq, Rezazade. "Patriotic Poetry in Modern Iran," *MEJ*, Autumn 1952.

Shafi, Mūhammad. "Bāyazid Ansārī," in Vol. I, *EI*, 2d ed.

Shah, Ikbal Ali. "A Caboul: scènes nocturnes," *L'Asie Française*, April 1928. Originally published as "Kabul Night" in *The New Statesman*, January 15, 1927.

———. "The Afghan Revolt and After," *Asia*, September 1934.

———. "Afghanistan and the German Threat," *Edinburgh Review*, July 1918.

———. "Afghanistan and the War," *The Near East*, February 15, 1918.

———. "Afghanistan in 1919," *JCAS*, VII (1920).

———. Afghanistan of the Afghans. London, 1928.

———. "Amanullah, ex-King of Afghanistan: Controlling Minds of Asia," *Fortnightly Review*, June 1929.

———. "The Claims of Afghanistan for Restoration of Lost Provinces of the North-West and North-East," *Edinburgh Review*, January 1919.

———. "The Federation of the Central Asian States Under the Kabul Government," *JCAS*, VIII (1921).

———. "The Folk-Life and Folk-Lore of Afghanistan," *Folklore*, December 1919.

———. "The Future of Afghanistan," *The Near East*, October 24, 1919.

———. "Kafirs: A Hidden Race Roaming in Kafiristan," *Conquest*, December 1921.

———. Modern Afghanistan. London, 1939.

———. "Nadir Shah and After," *Contemporary Review*, March 1934.

———. "Russia, Afghanistan and India," *United Service Magazine*, August 1919.

———. The Tragedy of Amanullah. London, 1933.

Shah, Muhammed Khan. See Muhammed Khan, Shir.

Shahab, Qudratullah. *Pathans*. The People of Pakistan Series, No. 1. N.p., n.d.

Shakespear, Richmond. "A Personal Narrative of a Journey from Herat to Ourenbourg, on the Caspian in 1840," *Blackwood's Edinburgh Magazine*, June 1842.

Sharabi, Hisham. "Islam and Modernization in the Arab World," in Thompson and Reischauer, *Modernization*, listed below.

Shay, Mary L. The Ottoman Empire from 1720–1734 As Revealed in Despatches of the Venetian Baili. (University of Illinois Studies in Social Sciences, XXVII.) Urbana, Ill., 1944.

Shayegh. "Bela-ye nefagh," *MH*, 7th year, No. 3.

———. "Ezdavaj," *MH*, 7th year, No. 7-8.

———. "Lezum-e ezdavaj," *MH*, 7th year, No. 7-8.

———. "Moshaer," *MH*, 7th year, No. 4-5.

———. "Zera'at," *MH*, 7th year, No. 11-12.

Shayegh, Ghulam Hazrat. "Andarz," *Kabul*, 1st year, No. 2.

Shestakov, A. See Chestakov.

Shils, E. "Intellectuals in the Political Development of the New States," *World Politics*, April 1960.

Shinobu, Iwamura, and H. F. Schurmann. "Mongolian Groups in Afghanistan," in Silver Jubilee Volume of the Zinbu-Kagaku-Kenkyusyo. Kyoto, 1954.

Shinomura, Torataro. "The Modernization of Japan, with Special Reference to Philosophy," in Japanese National Commission for UNESCO, Philosophical Studies of Japan. Tokyo, 1966.

Showers, C. L. The Cossack at the Gate of India. London, 1885.

Shridharani, Krishnalal. "The Frontier Gandhi," *Asia*, September 1941.

Shteinberg, E. L. "Angliiskaia versiia o 'Russkoi ugroze' Indii v XIX–XX vv.," *Istoricheskie Zapiski*, XXXIII (1950).

———. Istoriia britanskoi agressi na Srednem Vostoke. Moscow, 1951.

Shuster, W. Morgan. The Strangling of Persia. New York, 1912.

Siassi, Ali Akbar. "L'Iran au XIXᵉ siècle," *JWH*, II (1955), 3.

Siddiqi, M. Mazheruddin. "Obaid-ulla Sindhi," *The Islamic Literature*, VIII, 7 (July 1956).

Silvert, K. H., ed. Expectant Peoples: Nationalism and Development. New York, 1964.

Simplich, J., and Haji Mirza Hussein. "Everyday Life in Afghanistan," *National Geographic Magazine*, January 1921.

Sinai, Robert. The Challenge of Modernization. The West's Impact on the Non-Western World. New York, 1964. Paperback.

Sinclair, G. Khyber Caravan; Through Kashmir, Waziristan, Afghanistan, Baluchistan, and Northern India. London, 1936.

Singh, Ganda. Ahmad Shah Durrani, Father of Modern Afghanistan. London, 1959.

———. The British Occupation of the Panjab. Amritsar, 1955.

———, ed. The Panjab in 1839–40. Amritsar, 1952.

———, ed. Private Correspondence Relating to the Anglo-Sikh Wars. Amritsar, 1955.

Singhal, D. P. India and Afghanistan: 1876–1907. A Study in Diplomatic Relations. St. Lucia, Australia, 1963.

Sinor, Denis. Orientalism and History. Cambridge, Eng., 1954.

———. "Les relations entre les Mongols et l'Europe jusqu'à la mort d'Arghoun et de Bela IV," *JWH*, III (1954), 1.

"Sir Henry C. Dobbs" (obituary), *JRCAS*, October 1934. Signed P. Z. C. and A. T. W.

Sitaramayya, Pattabhi. History of the Nationalist Movement in India. Bombay, 1950.

Skalov, G. "Khivinskaia revoliutsiia 1920," *Novyi Vostok* (Moscow), 1923, No. 3.

Skrine, F. H. B., and E. D. Ross. The Heart of Asia, a History of Russian Turkestan and the Central Asian Khanates from the Earliest Times. London, 1899.

Slousch, N. "Les Juifs à Boukhara," *RMM*, April 1909.

———. "Les Juifs en Afghanistan," *RMM*, March 1908.

Smirnov, N. A. Istoriia Izucheniia Islama v SSSR. Moscow, 1954.

Smith, R. B. Life of Lord Lawrence. London, 1883. 2 vols.

Smith, Thomas F. A. "German War Literature on the Near and Middle East," *Quarterly Review*, January 1917.

Smith, Vincent A. Akbar, the Great Mogul. Oxford, 1919.

———, ed. Oxford History of India. 1st, 2d, and 3d eds. Oxford, 1919, 1928, 1958.

Smith, Wilfred C. Islam in Modern History. Princeton, N.J., 1957.

———. Modern Islam in India. A Social Analysis. 2d ed. Lahore, 1947.

S.M.R. L'Emir de l'Afghanistan et le Califat. Paris, 1920–21.

Snesarev, A. E. Avganistan. Moscow, 1921.

Sobeleff (Sobolev), Major-General L. N. The Anglo-Afghan Struggle. Translated by Walter E. Gowan. Calcutta, 1885.

"Some Features of the Afghan Problem," *The Asiatic Review*, July 1929.

Spain, James W. "Pakistan's North-West Frontier," *MEJ*, Winter 1954.

———. The Pathan Borderland. The Hague, 1963.

———. "The Pathan Borderland," *MEJ*, Spring 1961.

———. The People of the Khyber, the Pathans of Pakistan. New York, 1963.

Spear, Percival. India, Pakistan and the West. London, 1958.

Spector, Ivar. The First Russian Revolution. Englewood Cliffs, N.J., 1962.

———. The Soviet Union and the Muslim World: 1917–1956. Seattle, 1958.

Spencer, Richard E. The Afghan Educational Picture: An Evaluation. (Institute of Education.) Kabul, 1960. 2 vols. Mimeographed.

Spender, J. A. The Changing East. London, 1926.

Spuler, Bertold. "Ghaznāwids," in Vol. II, *EI*, 2d ed.

———. "Iran: The Persistent Heritage," in G. von Grunebaum, *Unity and Variety*, listed above.

———. The Muslim World. Leiden, 1960. Vol. II: The Mongol Period.

Squires, Sir Giles. "Recent Progress in Afghanistan," *JRCAS*, January 1950.

Stamp, L. Dudley. Asia, an Economic and Regional Geography. London, 1957.

Standish, J. F. "The Persian War of 1856–1857," *MES*, October 1966.

Stebbins, Richard B., ed. The U.S. in World Affairs: 1949. New York, 1950.

Stein, Sir Mark Aurel. Archaeological Reconnaissance in North Western India and South Eastern Iran. London, 1937.

————. Innermost Asia. Oxford, 1928.

————. On Alexander's Track to the Indus. London, 1929.

Stenz, Edward. "Le climat de Kaboul," *Afghanistan*, January-March 1948.

————. The Climate of Afghanistan; Its Aridity, Dryness and Divisions. (Polish Institute of Arts and Sciences in America.) New York, 1946.

Stephens, H.M. Alboquerque. Oxford, 1897.

Stephens, I. "Anglo-Afghan Relations," *Great Britain and the East*, June 6, 1940.

Stewart, Charles E. Through Persia in Disguise, with Reminiscences of Indian Mutiny. London, 1911.

Stewart, Sir D. M. The Second Afghan War, 1878–1880. London, 1903.

Stock, Eugene. The History of the Church Missionary Society: Its Environment, Its Men and Its Work. London, 1899–1916. 4 vols.

Stocqueler, J. H. Life of Sir William Nott. London, 1854. 2 vols.

————. Memorials of Afghanistan, 1838–1842. Calcutta, 1843.

Stoddard, Lothrop. The New World of Islam. New York, 1921.

Stolz, Karl. "Les langues étrangères en Afghanistan," *Afghanistan*, July-September 1955.

————. "Le théâtre afghan," *Afghanistan*, July-September 1954.

Stratil-Sauer, Gustav. From Leipzig to Cabul; An Account of My Motorcycle Ride to Afghanistan and My Nine Months' Imprisonment in That Country. London, 1929.

————. "Prisoner in Afghanistan," *Asia*, August 1929.

Strickland, C. F. "The Economic Development of Afghanistan," *Contemporary Review*, June 1933.

Strizower, Schifra. "The 'Bene Israel' in Israel," *MES*, January 1966.

————. Exotic Jewish Communities. London, 1962.

Strong, John W. "Russian Relations with Khiva, Bukhara and Kokand 1800–1858," Ph.D. Dissertation, Harvard University, 1964. 2 vols.

Stuart, A. "Le chemin de fer central-asiatique projeté par MM. Ferdinand de Lesseps et Cotard," *L'Explorateur*, II (1875).

Stuart, Lt. Col. W. K. Journal of a Residence in Northern Persia and Adjacent Provinces of Turkey. London, 1854.

Sultan Muhammed Khan. Laws and Constitution of Afghanistan. London, 1900.

"Summary of Events," *The Asiatic Quarterly Review*, October 1888.

Sumner, B. H. Peter the Great and the Ottoman Empire. Oxford, 1949.

Sutton, L. P. Elwell. Modern Iran. London, 1942.

Sykes, Christopher. "Some Notes on a Recent Journey in Afghanistan," *Geographical Journal*, October 1934.

————. Wassamus: "The German Lawrence." London, 1936.

Sykes, Sir Percy M. "Afghanistan," in Arberry and Landau, listed above.

————. "Afghanistan: the Present Position," *JRCAS*, April 1940.

————. History of Afghanistan. London, 1940. 2 vols.

————. A History of Persia. London, 1915. 2 vols.

————. "The Rt. Hon. Sir Mortimer Durand," *JRCAS*, October 1939.

Taghiadianz, Mesrovb. Patmutiun Hin Hndkastani. Calcutta, 1841. In Armenian.

Tagore, Saumyendranath. Historical Development of the Communist Movement in India. Calcutta, 1944.

Taillardat, F. "La fin du voyage du Roi Amanullah," *L'Asie Française*, September-October 1928. Signed T.F.

――――. "La politique allemande en Perse," *L'Asie Française*, April 1940.

――――. "La politique anglaise en Afghanistan au XIX siècle," *L'Asie Française*, July-August 1928.

――――. "Nadir Khan: Emir d'Afghanistan," *L'Asie Française*, April 1930. Signed T.F.

――――. "La révolte afghane," *L'Asie Française*, January 1929. Signed T.F.

――――. "Le Roi Amanullah en Angleterre," *L'Asie Française*, May 1928. Signed T.F.

――――. "Le voyage du Roi Amanullah," *L'Asie Française*, February 1928.

Taleb, Muhammad Hussein Khan. "Seyr-e bahar," *MH*, 7th year, No. 1-2.

Tarn, W. W. The Greeks in Bactria and India. Cambridge, Eng., 1951.

Tarzi, Abdul Wahab. "Afghanistan," in Vol. I, Islam Ansiklopedisi. Istanbul, 1945.

Tarzi, Hamidullah H. "Economic Survey of Afghanistan," M.A. Thesis, University of California, Berkeley, 1953.

Tarzi, Mahmud. Az har dahan sokhani va az har chaman samani. Kabul, 1913.

――――. Raudat-i-hikam. Kabul, 1913.

――――. Siahatname-ye seh ghette-ye ruy-e zamin. Kabul, 1915.

――――, trans. Tarikh-e muharebe-ye Rus va Japan. Kabul, 1916–17. 3 vols.

Tate, G. P. The Frontiers of Baluchistan: Travels on the Borders of Persia and Afghanistan. London, 1909.

――――. The Kingdom of Afghanistan. An Historical Sketch. Bombay and Calcutta, 1911.

Tavakulli, Ahmad. Afghanestan: ravabet-e siyassi-ye Iran va Afghanestan. Tehran, 1949.

Tavernier, E. T. Collection of Travels, etc. Being Travels of Monsieur Tavernier, Bernier and Other Great Men. London, 1648. 2 vols.

Tavernier, J. B. Travels in India. Edited by V. Ball. London, 1889.

Taylor, William. Scenes and Adventures in Afghanistan. London, 1842.

Tcharykow, N. V. Glimpses of High Politics. New York, 1931.

Tchokay-Oglu, Moustafa. "Le Turkestan en 1917: pages du souvenirs," *La Revue de Prométhée*, October 1938.

――――. "Le Turkestan et la Russie," *La Revue de Prométhée*, July 1939.

Teer, Edward. Siege of Jellalabad. London, 1904.

Temperley, H. England and the Near East: the Crimea. London, 1953.

Temperley, H. W. V. A History of the Peace Conference of Paris. London, 1924.

Ténèbre, Dr. "The Amir Abroad," *The Modern Review*, May 1928.

Teplinskii, L. B. Sovetsko-afganskie otnosheniia; 1919–1960. Moscow, 1961.

Terentiev (Terent'ev), M. A. Istoriia zavoevaniia Srednei Azii. St. Petersburg, 1906. 3 vols.

――――. Rossiia i Angliia v borbe za rynki. St. Petersburg, 1875–76.

――――. Russia and England in Central Asia. Calcutta, 1876. 2 vols.

Terenzio, Pio-Carlo. La rivalité Anglo-Russe en Perse, et en Afghanistan jusqu'aux accords de 1907. Paris, 1947.

Thackeray, Sir E. T. "Capture of Kabul 1879," *Journal of Royal Engineers,* January 1916.

———. Reminiscences of Afghanistan. London, 1916.

Thackwell, Sir Joseph. The Military Memoirs of Lt. Col. Sir Joseph Thackwell. London, 1908.

Thayer, Philip W., ed. Nationalism and Progress in Free Asia. Baltimore, 1956.

Thesiger, Wilfrid. "The Hazaras in Central Afghanistan," *The Geographical Journal,* September 1957.

———. "A Journey to Nuristan," *The Geographical Journal,* December 1957.

Thomas, Lowell. Beyond Khyber Pass. New York, 1925.

———. "Into Forbidden Afghanistan," *Asia,* March-September 1925.

Thomas P. Christians and Christianity in India and Pakistan. London, 1954.

Thompson, Jack H., and Robert D. Reischauer. Modernization of the Arab World. Princeton, N.J., 1966.

Thomson, Edward. "The Political Prospect in India," *JRCAS,* July 1932.

Thornton, A. P. "Afghanistan in Anglo-Russian Diplomacy: 1869–1873," *Cambridge Historical Journal,* XI (1954), 2.

———. "The Reopening of the Central Asian Question: 1864–9," *History,* n.s. No. 41 (1956).

Thornton, Edward. A Gazetteer of the Countries Adjacent to India on the North-West. London, 1844. 2 vols.

Thornton, Ernest and Annie. Leaves from an Afghan Scrapbook. London, 1910.

Thornton, Thomas H. "Baluchistan and the 'New Indian' Province," *The Asiatic Quarterly Review,* January-April 1888.

Thrupp, Sylvia L. "Tradition and Development: A Choice of Views," *Comparative Studies in Society and History,* October-November 1963.

Tichy, Herbert. Afghanistan, Das Tor nach Indien. Leipzig, 1940.

Tikhomirov, M. N. Prisoedinenie Merva k Rossii. Moscow, 1960.

Tod, J. K. "The Malleson Mission to Transcaspia in 1918," *JRCAS,* January 1940.

Todd, D'Arcy. "Report of a Journey from Herat to Simla via Candahar, Cabool and the Punjaub Undertaken in the Year 1838," *JASB,* May 1844. A slightly altered version appears in Forrest, *Selections from Travels,* listed above.

Tolstov, S. P. Po sledam drevne-khorezmiiskoi tsivilizatsii. Moscow, 1949.

Tompkins, Stuart R. Russia Through the Ages. New York, 1940.

Toynbee, Arnold J. Between Oxus and Jumna. Oxford, 1961.

———. The Islamic World Since the Peace Settlement. London, 1927.

———. A Study of History. Oxford, 1936. Vols. III, VIII.

———. A Survey of International Affairs: 1920–23; 1925; 1929; 1930. Oxford, 1925–31.

———. The World and the West. Oxford, 1953.

"Travels in Kashmir by the Late George Forster," in *The Asiatic Annual Register,* listed above.

"Treaty Between China and Afghanistan," *Amerasia,* March 17, 1944.

Trinkler, Emil. Through the Heart of Afghanistan. Edited and translated by B. K. Featherstone. London, 1928.

Troyanovski, K. M., ed. Siniaiia Kniga. Moscow, 1918.

Tsukamoto, Zenryu. "The Early Stages in the Introduction of Buddhism in China," *JWH*, V (1960), 3.

Tulimsher, Abdul Razak Khan. "Mogham-e shamekh-e askar dar nazar-e Islam," *Al-Falah*, 7th year, No. 7.

Tumanovich, O. Turkmenistan i Turkmen. Ashkabad, 1926.

Turner, T. Hudson. "Unpublished Notices of the Times of Edward I and His Relations with the Mogul Sovereign of Persia," *Archaeological Journal* (London), VIII (1851).

Twiss, W. L. O. "Disarmament, with Special Reference to Asia," *JRCAS*, July 1932.

United Nations. Commission on the Status of Women. Legal Status of Married Women. New York, 1958.

———. Demographic Yearbook: 1958; 1964. New York, 1959, 1965.

———. Economic Commission for Asia and the Far East. Economic Survey. Bangkok, 1955.

———. Educational, Scientific, and Cultural Organization (UNESCO). Basic Facts and Figures. Paris, 1954.

———, ———. Report of the Mission to Afghanistan. Paris, 1952.

———. Statistical Office. National Income and Its Distribution in Underdeveloped Countries. New York, 1951.

———. Statistical Yearbook: 1959; 1965. New York, 1959, 1966.

United States. Department of Commerce. British India, with Special Notes on Ceylon, Afghanistan, and Tibet. Special Consular Reports, Henry D. Baker, American Consul of Bombay and Other Consular Officers. Report No. 72. Washington, D.C., 1915.

———. Department of Health, Education and Welfare. Education in Afghanistan. By Abdul Sassani. (Comparative Studies in Education, OE 14057.) Washington, D.C., 1961.

———. Department of State. Documents on German Foreign Policy, 1918–1945. Series D. Washington, D.C., 1962–64. Vols. XII, XIII.

———, ———. Foreign Relations of the United States: Diplomatic Papers, 1941. Vol. III: The British Commonwealth, the Near East, and Africa. Washington, D.C., 1959.

———, ———. Papers Relating to the Foreign Relations of the United States, 1921–1943. Washington, D.C., 1936–63.

———, ———. Treaties: Friendship and Diplomatic and Consular Representation. Provisional Agreement Between the United States of America and the Kingdom of Afghanistan. (Department of State Publication No. 869. Executive Agreement Series No. 88.) Washington, D.C., 1936.

———. National Archives. State Department Records. Persia: Diplomatic Dispatches, 1883–1906; Teheran: Consular Letters, 1883–1906.

———. Office of Strategic Services, Research and Analysis Branch. Industrial Survey of Afghanistan. (Research and Analysis Report No. 479.) Washington, D.C., 1942.

Upton, Joseph M. The History of Modern Iran. An Interpretation. Cambridge, Mass., 1960.

Urmanova, R. K. "Reformy afganskogo pravitelstva v 1919–1925 gg.," *Izvestia Akademii Nauk Uzbekskoi SSR* (Tashkent), 1958, No. 2.

Urquhart, David. Exposition of Transactions in Central Asia Through Which the Independence of States and the Affection of People, Barriers to the British Possessions in India, Have Been Sacrificed to Russia . . . by Palmerston. London, 1840.

"Usul-e asasi-ye Shura-ye Melli: tashkilat-e majlis," *Kabul*, 1st year, No. 1.

Vakil, S. "Nouristan," *Afghanistan*, July-September 1948.

Vambery, Arminius. "The Anglo-Russian Convention," *The Nineteenth Century and After*, December 1907.

———. The Coming Struggle for India. London, 1885.

———. History of Bokhara. London, 1873.

———. "The Russian Advance in the Pamirs," *New Review*, September 1892.

———. Sketches of Central Asia. Additional Chapters on My Travels, Adventures and on the Ethnology of Central Asia. London, 1868.

———. Travels in Central Asia in 1863. London, 1864.

———. "The Turkomans in Their Political and Social Relations," in Petermann's Geographische Mitteilungen. Gotha, 1864.

Vandal, A. Napoléon et Alexandre I. Paris, 1891–95. 3 vols. Vol. I.

Vansittart, Henry. "On the Descent of the Afghans from the Jews," *Asiatic Researches* (London), II (1799).

Vasifi, Zayd Ad-Din. Tārikh-i-Badakshan (Istoriia Badakshana). Edited and translated into Russian by A. N. Boldyrev. Leningrad, 1959.

Vasiléva, G. P. "Narody Afganistana: Turkmeny," in Narody perednei Azii. Moscow, 1957.

Vatikiotis, P. J. "Muhammad Abduh and the Quest for a Muslim Humanism," *Arabica*, IV (1957), 1.

Vatikiotis, P. J., and G. Makdisi. "Recent Developments in Islam," in P. W. Thayer, ed., Tensions in the Middle East. Baltimore, 1958.

Vaughan, Sir J. L. My Service in the Indian Army, Afghanistan, 1879–80. London, 1904.

Vavilov, N. I., and D. D. Bukinich. Zemledelcheskii Afganistan. Leningrad, 1929.

Véreté, M. "Palmerston and the Levant Crisis, 1832," *Journal of Modern History*, June 1952.

Vernier, Bernard. La politique islamique de l'Allemagne. Paris, 1939.

Vigne, G. T. A Personal Narrative of a Visit to Ghuznee, Kabul and Afghanistan, and of a Residence at the Court of Dost Mohamed, with Notices of Runjit Sing, Khiva, and the Russian Expedition. London, 1840.

Viollis, Andrée. Tourmente sur l'Afghanistan. Paris, 1930.

"The Visit of King Amanullah," *The Modern Review*, January 1928.

Vladimirtsev, B. Ia. Obshchestvennyi stroi mongolov. Leningrad, 1934.

"The Wahabis in India," *Calcutta Review*, Vol. LI, No. cl (1870).

Wala. "We Want Peace and Security," *Afghanistan*, July-September 1948.

Waleh, A. H. "Nooristan," *Afghanistan*, July-September 1951.

"War That's Not in the Papers. Guerilla Warfare on the Russo-Afghan Frontier," *Literary Digest*, August 3, 1929.

Warburton, Sir Robert. Eighteen Years in the Khyber 1879–1898. London, 1900.

Ward, Sir A. W., and G. P. Gooch, eds. The Cambridge History of British Foreign Policy 1783–1919. Cambridge, Eng., 1922–23. 3 vols.

Ward, Robert E., and Dankwart A. Rustow, eds. Political Modernization in Japan and Turkey. Princeton, N.J., 1964.

Watkins, Mary B. Afghanistan: Land in Transition. Princeton, N.J., 1963.

Watt, D. C. "The Sa'dabad Pact of July 8, 1937," *JRCAS*, July-October 1962.

Watt, W. M. Islam and the Integration of Society. London, 1961.

———. Islamic Philosophy and Theology. Edinburgh, 1962.

Webster, Sir Charles. The Foreign Policy of Palmerston 1830–41. London, 1951. 2 vols.

Weintraub, Stanley. Private Shaw and Public Shaw. A Dual Portrait of Lawrence of Arabia and G.B.S. New York, 1963.

Wessels, C. Early Jesuit Travellers in Central Asia. London, 1924.

"Westernization of the East Starts a Revolt," *Literary Digest*, December 15, 1928.

Wheeler, Geoffrey. The Modern History of Soviet Central Asia. New York, 1964.

Wheeler, James T. A Short History of India and of the Frontier States of Afghanistan, Nepal, and Burma. London, 1894.

Wheeler, R. E. M. "Archeology in Afghanistan," *Antiquity* (London), June 1947.

Wheeler, Stephen. The Ameer Abdur Rahman. London, 1895.

Wheeler, W. E. "The Control of Land Routes: Russian Railways in Central Asia," *JRCAS*, October 1934.

Wheeler-Bennett, J. W. The Forgotten Peace. New York, 1939.

Wherry, E. M. "The First American Mission to Afghanistan," *The Moslem World*, April 1918.

White-King, L. "History and Coinage of the Barakzai Dynasty of Afghanistan," *Numismatic Chronicle*, XVI (1896).

Wiet, Gaston. "L'empire néo-byzantin des Omayyades et l'empire néo-Sassanide des Abbassides," *JWH*, I (1953), 1.

Wiet, Gaston, V. Elessief, and P. Wolff. "L'évolution des techniques dans le monde musulman au moyen âge," *JWH*, VI (1960), 1.

Wilber, Donald N. "Afghanistan, Independent and Encircled," *Foreign Affairs*, April 1953.

———, ed. Afghanistan, Its People, Its Society, Its Culture. 1st and 2d eds. New Haven, Conn., 1956, 1962.

———, ed. Annotated Bibliography of Afghanistan. New Haven, Conn., 1956.

———. "The Structure and Position of Islam in Afghanistan," *MEJ*, Winter 1952.

Wilbur, Marguerite E. The East India Company and the British Empire in the Far East. Stanford, Calif., 1945.

Wild, Roland. Amanullah, ex-King of Afghanistan. London, 1932.

Willan, T. S. The Early History of the Russian Company 1553–1603. Manchester, Eng., 1956.

Williams, L. F. Rushbrook, ed. India in 1920. Calcutta, 1921.
———, ed. India in the Years 1924–1925. Calcutta, 1926.
Williams, Maynard O. "Afghanistan Makes Haste Slowly," *National Geographic Magazine*, December 1933.
———. "Back to Afghanistan," *National Geographic Magazine*, October 1946.
Wilson, Sir Arnold T. "Early Spanish and Portuguese Travellers in Persia," *The Asiatic Review*, October 1926.
———. The Persian Gulf. London, 1954.
Wiseman, H. Victor. "The New Constitution of Afghanistan—Some Observations," *Parliamentary Affairs*, August 1965.
Wittfogel, Karl A. Oriental Despotism: A Comparative Study of Total Power. New Haven, Conn., 1957.
Woeikof, Alexandre. Le Turkestan Russe. Paris, 1914.
Wolff, Joseph. Narrative of a Mission to Bokhara. London, 1846. 2 vols.
———. Researches and Missionary Labours. London, 1837.
———. Travels and Adventures of the Reverend Joseph Wolff, D.D., LL.D. 2d ed. London, 1860–61. 2 vols.
Wood, A. C. A History of the Levant Company. Oxford, 1935.
Wood, John. A Journey to the Source of the River Oxus. London, 1872.
Woods, H. C. The Cradle of the War: the Near East and Pan-Germanism. London, 1918.
Woodsmall, Ruth F. Women and the New East. Washington, D.C., 1960.
Wyllie, J. W. G. Essays on the External Policy of India. Edited by W. W. Hunter. London, 1875.
———. "Masterly Inactivity," *Fortnightly Review*, December 1869.
———. "Mischievous Activity," *Fortnightly Review*, March 1870.
Yakubovskii, A. I. "Vosstanie Tarabi v 1238 g.," in *Trudy Instituta Vostokovedenia A.N. SSSR*, XVII (1936).
Yapp, M. E. "Afghanistan," in Dūstūr: A Survey of the Constitutions of the Arab and Muslim States. Leiden, 1966.
———. "Disturbances in Eastern Afghanistan 1839–1842," *BSOAS*, XXVI (1963).
———. "Disturbances in Western Afghanistan 1839–1842," *BSOAS*, XXV (1962).
———. "The Revolution of 1841–1842 in Afghanistan," *BSOAS*, XXVII (1964).
———. "Two British Historians of Persia," in Lewis and Holt, listed above.
Yate, Arthur C. "Afghans at Merv," *The Near East*, December 5, 1919.
———. "Britain's Buffer States in the East: Turkey, Persia and Afghanistan," *JCAS*, V (1918).
———. England and Russia Face to Face in Asia. London, 1887.
———. "The Proposed Trans-Persian Railway," *Proceedings of the Central Asian Society*, February 1911.
———. "The Visit to India of the Amir Habibullah Khan, the Fourth Amir of the Barakzai Dynasty," *The Imperial and Asiatic Quarterly Review*, July 1907.
Yate, C. E. Khurassan and Sistan. London, 1900.
———. Northern Afghanistan, or Letters from the Afghan Boundary Commission. London, 1888.

Yazdī, Sharaf al-Din Ali. Zāfārnāma. Edited by Maulawi Muhammad Ilahdād. Calcutta, 1887–88. 2 vols.

Young, T. Cuyler, ed. Near Eastern Culture and Society: A Symposium on the Meeting of East and West. Princeton, N.J., 1951.

Younghusband, Frank E. The Heart of a Continent. London, 1896.

Younossi, Abdullah. "Economic Development of Afghanistan," M.A. Thesis, University of California, Berkeley, 1955.

Yule, Sir Henry, ed. Cathay and the Way Thither, Being a Collection of Medieval Notices of China. Revised ed. by Henri Cordier. London, 1913–16. 4 vols.

Yunus, Mohammed. Frontier Speaks. Lahore, 1942.

Yunus Khan, S. M. "Shah Wali Khan of Afghanistan," *Asia*, May 1934.

Yusuf, Kaniz F. "Potential Cooperation Between Iran, Pakistan and Afghanistan," Ph.D. Dissertation, Clark University, 1959.

Zadykhina, K. L. "Narody Afganistana: Uzbeki," in Narody perednei Azii. Moscow, 1957.

Zahir, Payanda Muhammad. "Maaref-e Afghanestan," in Anjoman-e Aryana, listed above.

Zahir, Payanda Muhammad, and Sayyid Muhammad Yusuf Elmi. Da Afghanestan da maaref tarikh. (Ministry of Education publication.) Kabul, 1961.

Zeman, Z. A. B. Germany and the Revolution in Russia 1915–1918. Oxford, 1958.

Zenkovsky, Serge A. Pan-Turkism and Islam in Russia. Cambridge, Mass., 1960.

Zhobal, Muhammed Haydar. "Mahmud Tarzi, Pedar-e matba'at," *Irfan,* 1958, No. 2.

———. Negahi be adabiyat-e mo'aser dar Afghanestan. Kabul, 1959.

Ziai, Abdul Hakim. "Challenge of Modern Ideas to Social Values in Afghan Education," in International Islamic Colloquium Papers, December 29, 1957–January 8, 1958. Lahore, 1960.

———. "Fondements du développement intellectuel en Afghanistan d'aujourd'hui," in Vol. II, *TDPMKV.* Moscow, 1963.

———. "General Development of Afghanistan up to 1957," *Afghanistan,* July-September 1961.

Ziemke, Kurt. Als Deutscher Gesandter in Afghanistan. Stuttgart, 1939.

Zinkin, Maurice. Asia and the West. London, 1951.

Zubeyullah Khan. "Favayed-e emumi," *MH,* 2d year, No. 4.

Zumeryali, Aminullah Khan. "Pashto va Pashtologha," *Kaboul Almanach: 1942–43.*

———. "Pashtun," *Kaboul Almanach: 1941–42.*

Zwemer, Samuel M. Islam, a Challenge to Faith. 2d ed. London, 1909.

C. REFERENCE WORKS

Aryana da'iratul ma'aref. Qamus-e jografiya-e Afghanestan. Kabul, 1962. 4 vols.

Atlas of Islamic History. Princeton, N.J., 1954.

Bolshaiia Sovetskaiia Entsiklopedia. 1st and 2d eds. Moscow, 1926–47, 1949–59.

Britannica Book of the Year. 1960–1966.
Collier's Encyclopedia: 1959 Yearbook. New York, 1959.
Dictionary of American Biography. New York, 1932. Vol. VIII.
Dictionary of Indian Biography. Edited by C. E. Buckland. London, 1906.
A Dictionary of Islam. By Thomas P. Hughes. London, 1935.
Dictionary of National Biography. Oxford, 1922.
Enciclopedia Italiana. Milan, 1929. Vol. I.
Encyclopaedia Britannica. 11th, 13th, and 1966 eds.
Encyclopedia of Islam. 1st and 2d eds. Leiden, 1913–36, 1955–   .
Encyclopedia of the Social Sciences. New York, 1951. Vol. XI.
La géographie universelle. Paris, 1929. Vol. VIII: L'Asie occidentale.
La grande encyclopédie. Paris, 1887–1902. Vol. I.
Grande Larousse encyclopédique. Paris, 1960. Vol. I.
Hobson-Jobson. An Anglo-Indian Glossary. Edited by W. Crooke. 2d ed. London, 1903.
The Imperial Gazetteer of India. Oxford, 1907–8. Vols. III, V.
Islam Ansiklopedisi. Istanbul, 1945. Vol. I.
Kaboul Almanach.
The Jewish Encyclopedia. London, 1925. Vol. I.
The Jewish Yearbook. London, 1960.
The Middle East. London, 1948.
The New International Yearbook: 1955. New York, 1955.
An Oriental Biographical Dictionary. Edited by Thomas W. Beale. London, 1894.
The Oxford Economic Atlas of the World. Oxford, 1954.
The Statesman's Yearbook. London, 1879–1948, 1960–67.
UNESCO. Basic Facts and Figures. Paris, 1954.
United Nations. Demographic Yearbook: 1958, 1964. New York, 1959, 1965.
United Nations. Statistical Yearbook: 1959, 1965. New York, 1959, 1966.
The Universal Jewish Encyclopedia. New York, 1939. Vols. I, II.
Yearbook of the UN: 1950. New York, 1950.
The World Almanac. New York, 1960–67.
The World of Learning. 10th and 12th eds. London, 1960, 1963.

D. NEWSPAPERS AND JOURNALS

Afghanistan, Kabul.
Al-Falah, Kabul.
Aman-i-Afghan, Kabul.
Anis, Kabul.
Asia, New York.
The Asiatic Review, London.
Bulletin of the School of Oriental and African Studies, London.
Cahiers du Monde Russe et Soviétique, Paris.
Calcutta Review.
Central Asian Review, London.
Contemporary Review, London.
Daily Mail, London.

Daily Telegraph, London.
Ettelaat, Tehran.
Foreign Affairs, New York.
Fortnightly Review, London.
The Geographical Journal, London.
The Imperial and Asiatic Quarterly Review, Woking.
Iqtisad, Kabul.
Islah, Kabul.
Islamic Culture, Hyderabad.
Islamic Review, London.
Izvestia, Moscow.
Izvestia, Tashkent.
Jewish Social Studies, New York.
Journal Asiatique, Paris.
Journal des Débats, Paris.
The Journal of Asian Studies, Ann Arbor, Mich.; Durham, N.C.
Journal of Modern History, Chicago.
Journal of World History, Paris.
Journal of the American Oriental Society, New Haven, Conn.
Journal of the Asiatic Society of Bengal, Calcutta.
Journal of the Royal Asian Society, London.
Journal of the Royal Central Asian Society, London.
Kabul, a Literary Magazine.
Literary Digest, New York.
Living Age, New York.
Majalle-ye Herat.
The Middle East Journal, Washington, D.C.
Middle Eastern Affairs, Chicago.
Middle Eastern Studies, London.
The Modern Review, Calcutta.
The Moslem World, Hartford, Conn.
The National Geographic Magazine, Washington, D.C.
The Near East, London.
The New York Times.
The Nineteenth Century and *The Nineteenth Century and After*, London.
Orient, Paris.
Oriente Moderno, Rome.
Le Petit Parisien.
Pravda, Moscow.
Proceedings of the Central Asian Society, London.
Revue des Deux Mondes, Paris.
Revue des Etudes Islamiques, Paris.
Revue du Monde Musulman, Paris.
Siraj al-Akhbar Afghaniyeh, Kabul.
Studia Islamica, Paris.
Sunday Express, London.
The Times, London.
United Empire, London.
United Service Magazine, London.

Index

Index

Abbas the Great, Shah, 44
Abbas, Mirza, 73
Abbasid dynasty, 219, 303, 346
Abd al Haq Betab, 179
Abdali, Ahmad Khan, *see* Ahmad Shah Durrani
Abdali tribe, 44ff. *See also* Durrani tribe
'Abduh, Muhammed, 165n, 209n
Abdul Ahad Dawi, 179
Abdul Ali Mostaghni, 179
Abdul Ghaffar Khan, 323–30 *passim*
Abdul Ghias Khan, 87
Abdul Ghiyas, 286
Abdul Hadi, 169
Abdul Kalam Azad, 218, 220
Abdul Kerim Munshi, 55
Abdul Hamid II, Sultan, 163, 431
Abdul Rashid Gelia, 358
Abdul Rashid Ibrahim Efendi, 210
Abdul Samad Khan Hindi, 76
Abdul Subhan Khan, 141
Abdul Wakil, 286
Abdullah Jan, 88
Abdullah Khan Qari, 179
Abdullah, Sheikh Achmed, 216n
Abdur Rahman Khan, 8, 32–37 *passim*, 66, 86n, 117, 183, 194n, 368, 394; and exiles, 66, 163, 181; reign, 129–62; mentioned, 29, 34n, 220, 243, 247f, 281, 300, 319, 382, 394
Abu Ali Ibn Sina, 14, 346
Abu-Sayid al Balkhi, 14
Achaemenid Empire, 13, 347
Achakzai subtribe, 30, 56
adab, 72
Adam subtribe, 31
Adamec, Ludwig, 221n
adat, 137
administrative structure, 88, 134–36, 183, 248, 298–99
Adrianople, Treaty of, 95
Afghan Academy, *see* Pashto Tulana
Afghan Motor Transport Company, 194

Afghan Turkestan, 11, 33, 57, 247, 316; as administrative unit, 134, 139, 183, 248. *See also* northern Afghanistan; Turkestan
Afghan Youth League, 323
Afghana, King Solomon's commander-in-chief, 29n
Afghānī, Seyed Jamal ad-Din al-, 86, 163, 165n, 176f, 214
Afghanistan (periodical), 359
Afridi tribe, 26, 55, 117, 160, 231n, 255; size and structure, 31–32, 43, 417; uprisings of, 323, 330
Afzal Khan, 86n
Aga Ahmed Khan, 267n
Agabekov, George, 278
Ahmad Fakhmi Bey, 188
Ahmad, Fazl, 369
Ahmad Shah Durrani, 24, 30, 46–51 *passim*, 61, 142, 219
Ahmadiya sect, 38
Ahmedzai subtribe, 31, 289, 418
Aimaq Hazaras, 34
Aïne-ye-Irfan, 244f, 311
air force, 297, 337, 371
Aka subtribe, 31
Akbar, Moghul emperor, 414
Akhramovich, R. T., 367
Alamzai subtribe, 32
al-Balagh, 219
al-Bīrūni, Abū Rayhān, 29
Alexander I, Tsar, 91
al-Falah, 311, 344
al-Hilal, 213, 219
Ali Ahmad Khan, 289
Ali Ahmad Naimi, 179
Ali Akbar, 173
Ali Khel (subtribe), 31
Ali, Mohammed (historian), 3, 129n, 158n, 275, 282n
Aligarh Institute, 185, 187, 219–20
Aligarh Institute Gazette, 213
Alikozai subtribe, 30, 47

DATE DUE

MAR 1 '88			
			PRINTED IN U.S.A.